STAND
ON GUARD
FOR WHOM?

STAND ON GUARD FOR WHOM?

A PEOPLE'S HISTORY OF THE CANADIAN MILITARY

YVES ENGLER

Montréal/Chicago/London

Copyright ©2021 Yves Engler

Thank you for purchasing this Black Rose Books publication. No part of this book may be reproduced or transmitted in any form, by any means electronic or mechanical including photocopying and recording, or by any information storage or retrieval system–without written permission from the publisher, or, in the case of photocopying or other reprographic copying, a license from the Canadian Copyright Licensing Agency, Access Copyright, with the exception of brief passages quoted by a reviewer in a newspaper or magazine. If you acquired an illicit electronic copy of this book, please consider making a donation to Black Rose Books.

Black Rose Books No. UU416

A co-publication of RED Publishing
203 32nd Street West, Saskatoon, Saskatchewan, S7L 0S3

Library and Archives Canada Cataloguing in Publication
Title: Stand on guard for whom? : a people's history of the Canadian military / Yves Engler.
Names: Engler, Yves, 1979- author.
Description: Includes bibliographical references.
Identifiers: Canadiana (print) 2021022116X | Canadiana (ebook) 20210221194 | ISBN 9781551647579 (hardcover) | ISBN 9781551647555 (softcover) | ISBN 9781551647593 (PDF)
Subjects: LCSH: Canada—History, Military.
Classification: LCC UA600 .E52 2021 | DDC 355/.033071—dc23

Cover by Frank Myrskog

C.P.35788 Succ. Léo-Pariseau
Montréal, QC, H2X 0A4

Explore our books and subscribe to our newsletter:
blackrosebooks.com

Ordering Information

CANADA	USA/INTERNATIONAL	UK/IRELAND
University of Toronto Press	University of Chicago Press	Central Books
5201 Dufferin Street	Chicago Distribution Center	50 Freshwater Road
Toronto, ON	11030 South Langley Avenue	Chadwell Heath, London
M3H 5T8	Chicago, IL 60628	RM8 1RX
1-800-565-9523	(800) 621-2736 (USA)	+44 (0) 20 8525 8800
utpbooks@utpress.utoronto.ca	(773) 702-7000 (International) orders@press.uchicago.edu	contactus@centralbooks.com

TABLE OF CONTENTS

Introduction 7
1. King and Empire Roots 15
2. Conquering Canada 22
3. Soldiers for the Wealthy and White 29
4. Gunboat Diplomacy 40
5. Special (and Secret) Forces 55
6. On the Battlefield 67
7. Winning Hearts and Minds 109
8. In the Shadows 118
9. Cratering the Environment 135
10. Nuclear Armageddon 147
11. A Culture of Sexism and Racism 154
12. Hierarchy Versus Democracy 171
13. Our Spying Eyes 182
14. Subject to Uncle Sam 196
15. NATO Rules 210
16. Helping Veterans or Promoting War 219
17. Marketing Militarism 229
18. Lies and Propaganda 251
19. A Maple Military-Industrial Complex 279
20. Conclusion 324
Bibliography 333
Endnotes 341

Introduction

"Canada, more than most other countries, can act in its own interest in the sure knowledge that our interest is everyone's interest. We have no other."

Brooke Claxton, Minister of Defence[1]

"Nations maintain armed forces for one purpose, which is to have an instrument to apply coercive and, if necessary, deadly force in the pursuit of the government's objectives. Why otherwise would the force be armed?"

Douglas L. Bland[2]

- In the middle of the night on February 29, 2004, Canadian special forces "secured" the airport from which US Marines forced Haiti's elected president, Jean-Bertrand Aristide, onto a flight to the Central African Republic.
- In the late 1970s Canadian troops trained in Jamaica as part of a plan to secure Montréal-based Alcan's bauxite mines in case of popular unrest or seizure.
- In 1932 two Canadian frigates bolstered a dictatorship in El Salvador that engaged in one of the worst massacres of peasants in the history of the Americas.
- In the late 1800s and early 1900s Royal Military College of Canada trained officer William Heneker led numerous expeditions to conquer different parts of West Africa and published an influential British training manual, which noted how "the great thing is to impress savages with the fact that they are the weaker, and… enforce the will of the white man."

I'VE BEEN INVESTIGATING the question 'Is Canada a force for good in the world?' for many years. Many of my books and articles have touched on the military, but this is my first to focus on what is arguably the most important element of Canadian foreign policy.

Military might has long been considered the critical "pointed stick" of a nation's foreign policy. Prussian general and military theorist Carl von Clausewitz famously proclaimed that "war is merely the continuation of policy by other means." Anyone who studies history understands that recorded memories of entire millennia are primarily records of wars.

Military might is usually central to foreign policy. In Canada's case the military's budget is four times the funds devoted to diplomacy and international aid.

If Canada is a force for good in the world, then Canada's armed forces must also be a force for good. Alternatively, if the Canadian Forces (CF) have acted to advance the interests of the rich and powerful to the detriment of ordinary people then that premise does not hold.

***

Thousands of books detail different aspects of the Canadian military and warfare. This is the first general overview to tackle the subject from the perspective of those harmed or disenfranchised by Canadian wars, repression and military culture.

Like my previous books the goal is to cut through the thick veil of propaganda, spin and mythology that has built up over decades about Canada's role in the world. My objective is to burst the bubble of shallow cheerleading — often paid for and directed by arms of the military — regarding the Canadian armed forces. This book is an attempt to stand on the sidelines and instead of shouting, "sis boom bah, go Canada go," point out when "our team" is causing harm. With that purpose in mind this introduction presents a quick overview of the CF before getting into greater detail in subsequent chapters.

***

The Canadian Forces' roots are in a British force that brutally dispossessed First Nations. After Confederation the Canadian military suppressed the Metis and indigenous peoples on the Prairies and expropriated reserve territory for bases and to compensate white soldiers returning from war.

Initially a central function of the militia was to quell labour unrest. Its early leaders were largely well to do, and the force has remained close to wealth holders.

This book details the history of Canadian gunboat diplomacy and special forces deployments. It also outlines wars in Sudan, South Africa, World War I, World War II, Korea, Iraq, Serbia, Afghanistan, Libya and Iraq/Syria as well as UN deployments that ousted elected governments in Haiti and the Congo.

US, British and other forces have employed Canada's vast terrain and sophisticated facilities to improve their fighting skills and weaponry. Chemical and biological weapons were tested in Canada and the CF contributed to their development. Canada has also aided nuclear weapons testing and proliferation. In the 1950s and 60s the Department of National Defence (DND) funded and supported psychiatric research the CIA used to refine torture techniques employed on many unfortunate individuals across the globe.

Though it receives little attention, the CF's ecological footprint is immense. It ranges from decimating animal life to releasing substantial greenhouse gases into the atmosphere.

Close to their British counterparts during Canada's first eight decades, the CF has been greatly influenced by the US military since. Over the past 70 years Canada and the US have signed hundreds of military accords and founded the belligerent NATO alliance.

The CF is a patriarchal, homophobic social force and has been a hot bed of white supremacy. For decades gender and racial discrimination were explicit and imposed from above.

CF structures and norms contradict pluralistic, democratic values. Loyalty, conformity and obeying orders are important to the CF. There's little room to challenge authority or injustice and voting is nearly nonexistent.

War reveals a schizophrenic Canadian identity. Some believe Canada is the "peaceable kingdom" and Canadians an "unmilitary people." Others claim Canadians are naturally gifted soldiers and gained nation status on the battlefields of incredibly absurd and destructive wars.

The CF zealously protects its image and promotes its worldview. It aggressively shapes coverage of its affairs, benefitting from close ties to the CBC and Canadian Press during its first few decades.

DND operates a history department, postsecondary institution and media outlets, as well as spending lavishly on war commemorations. Not satisfied with the ideological influence of their massive bureaucracy, the CF has initiated various "arms-length" institutions to promote their interests. Through the cadets and other initiatives, the military spends hundreds of millions of dollars a year on outreach to children.

In addition to a cozy relationship with the press, the CF is well connected to the corporate class. The military appoints leading capitalists to honorary positions and does extensive outreach to the corporate sector. Top military and DND officials are often given well paid positions to lobby on behalf of arms makers.

Weapons procurement is a significant source of profit. Canada's aerospace, shipbuilding and space industries are heavily dependent on arms contracts. Other high-tech sectors have benefited from military procurement and research spending. Since WWII DND has spent tens of billions of dollars on scientific research and technological development. The military, for instance, played a central role in stimulating Canadian computer technology and expertise.

International arms sales are big business. A number of government departments and crown corporations help arms companies export. Ottawa has generally been ambivalent towards international arms control measures, facing pressure from arms companies seeking exports and a CF opposed to restrictions on its operations.

***

The CF/DND is far and away the largest federal government department. There are approximately 70,000 active soldiers, 30,000 reservists and 25,000 DND employees. In 2021 DND's budget was $24 billion.

Almost as many individuals work out of "Pentagon North" as any other government ministry. About 8,500 employees are based at the 15-hectare campus that has 11 interconnected buildings on two million square feet of building space.[3] DND has dozens of other worksites in the nation's capital.[4]

Across the country, DND manages the "largest infrastructure portfolio in the federal government" with over 20,000 buildings, 5,500 kilometers of roads and 3,000 kilometers of water works.[5] Its many bases and stations cover over two million hectares, which is half the land of Switzerland.[6] The Royal Canadian Navy operates about 50 frigates, submarines and other vessels.[7] The air force has 400 aircraft and the army tens of thousands of land vehicles.[8]

The machinery, buildings and land the CF manages are worth tens, maybe hundreds, of billions of dollars.

The military is a powerful educational force. DND runs the only federally funded degree granting university, the Royal Military College of Canada, and two dozen other specialized educational facilities such as the Canadian Forces School of Meteorology and Royal Canadian Electrical and Mechanical Engineers School. It also has countless relationships to dozens of universities and colleges, spending tens of millions of dollars a year on university research. One of its major university focused arms is Defence Research and Development Canada, which has 1,400 employees and a $350 million budget.[9]

DND/CF has the largest PR machine in the country, employing hundreds of public affairs officials. It also has massive intelligence gathering capacities, including the Communications Security Establishment's 2,700 employees and $700 million budget.[10]

The CF has its own police and legal system. There are some 1,400 active military police and 600 reserve police.[11] Members are subject to military law and tried in military courts even when the alleged crimes are committed off-duty and aren't related to military affairs. Dozens of judges and lawyers administer the CF's legal system.

A separate ministry, Veterans Affairs has 4,000 employees and over 50 offices across the country.[12] Possessing a budget independent of the CF, Veterans Affairs spent over $5 billion in 2021.[13]

The Canadian Coast Guard and Canada Border Services Agency are also separate departments with thousands of employees. Thousands working in other government departments participate in arms procurement and other projects associated with the CF.

DND's budget is more than ten times Environment and Climate Change Canada's, the principal department supposed to protect our natural environment.[14] Military spending is four times the size of all international affairs and aid expenditures combined.[15] In recent years DND has consumed over 20 per cent of discretionary federal spending (funds not tied to debt servicing or transfer payments).[16]

During WWI the military gobbled up 60 percent of all federal government expenditures.[17] An incredible 80 percent of federal funds were spent on warfare during WWII and that number topped 40 percent during the Korean war.[18]

Canada has long ranked among the world's top military spenders. According to the Stockholm International Peace Research Institute, Ottawa spent more on its military than all but 12 countries in 2020.[19] In the early 1990s Canada was the world's ninth largest military spender.[20]

Among the 29 members of NATO Canada is the sixth highest military spender.[21] It is one of only five members of the alliance, note Royal Military College professors Christian Leuprecht and Joel Sokolsky, with a "full-spectrum military".[22]

Canada far outspends its proportion of the global population. With 0.5 percent of the world's people, Canada is responsible for 1.5% of international military spending.[23]

***

The CF has a predilection for war. In 2012 the chief of the defence staff publicly demanded a new war. "We have some men and women who have had two, three and four tours and what they're telling me is 'Sir, we've got that bumper sticker. Can we go somewhere else now?'" General Walter Natynczyk told Canadian Press. "You also have the young sailors, soldiers, airmen and women who have just finished basic training and they want to go somewhere and in their minds it was going to be Afghanistan. So if not Afghanistan, where's it going to be? They all want to serve."[24]

It is not surprising the head of the military would want to go to war (that's his job after all). But it is remarkable he felt comfortable telling the media as much.

The CF's predilection for war does periodically seep into the press. "We're going to be warfighters", were the words Adam Moore, commander of the 3rd Battalion, Princess Patricia's Infantry, used to dismiss a new crop of soldiers in 2018.[25]

As part of its warfighting enthusiasm, the CF promoted what some euphemistically describe as "forward defence". Drawing a dubious hockey analogy, former commander of the CF Rick Hillier claimed "the best defense for Canada is a good offense. We must play a significant part in the world to prevent that violence and conflict coming home."[26] Echoing this thinking, the government's 2017 "Strong, Secure, Engaged: Canada's Defence Policy" claims the CF has to "actively address threats abroad for stability at home" and that "defending Canada and Canadian interests ... requires active engagement abroad." A logic that can, of course, be used to justify participating in endless US-led military endeavors.

Always on the lookout for ways to expand their fighting capacities, the CF has repeatedly used the political openings offered by warfare to expand and improve their future war-making capabilities. *Ottawa Citizen* military reporter David Pugliese revealed that in the midst of NATO's 2011 bombing of Libya CF leaders pushed the government to spend $600 million on armed drones. A similar effort was pursued towards the end of WWII. The navy leadership sought to acquire new vessels to guarantee a powerful fleet after the war.[27]

A type of "forward defence" logic even got a CF member off murder charges. Former army reservist Peter Khill was charged with second-degree murder for firing two shotgun blasts that killed an unarmed Jon Styres of the Six Nations of the Grand River. Khill's "former military service and training was central to his claim of self-defence", reported the *National Post*.[28] The defence argued that when Khill was woken by an individual who broke into his truck in the middle of the night, his four years as an army reservist kicked in. Rather than stay inside his locked home and call 911, he instinctively ran out of the house with a loaded shotgun. In his closing address, Khill's lawyer said soldiers are trained to "neutralize" threats. "Soldiers react proactively, that's how they are trained," noted Khill's lawyer about a killing that left deep scars in indigenous communities.[29] In 2018, Khill was found not guilty.

1. King and Empire Roots

THE CANADIAN MILITARY'S ROOTS are British. The CF grew out of the force that conquered large parts of Turtle Island and much of the world.

The British fought on and off for a century to dispossess the Mi'kmaq. They conquered today's Nova Scotia by putting the heads of Mi'kmaq soldiers on spikes and offering bounties to kill women and children.[1] Founder of the Halifax fort, Edward Cornwallis paid settlers and soldiers to kill any Mi'kmaq as part of a bid to take their land and end their resistance to British rule. In *We Were Not the Savages: A Mi'kmaq Perspective on the Collision Between European and Native American Civilizations* Daniel N. Paul writes, "how many Mi'kmaq were killed during the carnage following Cornwallis' proclamation is unknown, although some records mention scalps being brought in by the bagful."[2] Hundreds of Mi'kmaq were deported to Newfoundland and thousands died fighting. By the mid-1760s the Mi'kmaq had been largely wiped out in Nova Scotia.[3]

Alongside their war against the Mi'kmaq the British military forcibly removed over 10,000 of 14,000 Acadians from the Maritimes between 1755 and 1764.[4] British forces burned Acadian hamlets. Many civilians perished in this war against France, Acadian militias and the Mi'kmaq. During the expulsion of these descendants of French colonists, who sometimes mixed with the indigenous, thousands died, mostly from disease and drowning.[5]

After British forces conquered Québec during this period General Jeffery Amherst's forces gave indigenous chiefs in the Great Lakes region blankets and a handkerchief from a smallpox hospital. Commander of British forces in North America, Amherst wrote: "Could it not be contrived to Send the Small Pox among those Disaffected Tribes of Indians? We must, on this occasion, Use Every Stratagem in our power to Reduce them." Later in July 1763 the British general wrote an even more explicitly genocidal directive: "You will do well to try to inoculate the Indians by means of blankets as well as to try every other method that can serve to extirpate this execrable race."[6]

Established as a naval base on Mi'kmaq territory in 1749, Halifax was Britain's primary naval base in North America for much of the next century and a half. The force stationed in Halifax aided London's efforts to control the lucrative Caribbean slave plantations. Two years into the 1791-1804 Haitian Revolution much of the Halifax-based squadron supported Britain's effort to quell the great slave revolt.[7] The British wanted to ensure their freedom struggle didn't inspire slaves in Jamaica, Barbados, etc. and also wanted to take control of the incredibly lucrative French colony.

Three decades later British forces crushed the democratic rebellion against the so-called "Family Compact" in today's Québec. In the final major battle, 70 "patriots" were killed by British troops on December 14, 1837, at Saint Eustache (three Brits died).[8] Another 17 of those struggling for an elected legislative council were hung.[9]

Six years after suppressing the "patriots" democratic struggle British forces repressed strikers during the construction of canal stations along the Saint Lawrence River.[10] On June 13, 1843, the military killed between eight and 20 workers protesting for better pay, reduced hours and the right to buy food from local farmers.[11] Dozens of labourers at the Beauharnois Canal near Montréal were "shot, and cut down, and driven into the river and drowned."[12]

Much of the British garrison in Canada left for Crimea during the 1853-56 war.[13] Many Canadians also volunteered for British units fighting Russia.

In response to India's anti-colonial rebellion of 1857 1,000 men were recruited in Canada to create the 100th Regiment. Ultimately, it was posted to Gibraltar and Malta.[14]

One of the officers who helped quash the "patriot"/republican rebellion of 1837 played an important part in violently suppressing resistance in the Punjab region of today's India in 1848-49. Major

General Sir John Eardley Wilmot Inglis was one of dozens of Canadian-born individuals who rose to prominence in the British military from the mid-1700s through the early 1900s. In his 1891 book *Canadians in the Imperial Naval and Military Service Abroad* Hampden Burnham details dozens of Canadian-born individuals who served in today's Afghanistan, Pakistan, Sri Lanka, Crimea, Caribbean and Africa.[15] Nova Scotian William Hall received a Victoria Cross medal for bravery in India in 1857.[16] Many of the individuals who helped the British Empire conquer different parts of the world were commemorated during their lives or had streets, parks and mountains in this country named in their honour.[17]

During the latter half of the 1800s "recourse to the use of British gunboats was a standard response to 'difficulties' with native peoples of the coast," explains Robert Galois in an article on the 1872 burning of Kitsegukla. In *Gunboat Frontier: British Maritime Authority and Northwest Coast Indians, 1846-1890* Barry Gough details numerous examples of 'gunboat diplomacy' to suppress First Nations in what's now British Columbia. Innumerable villages and canoes were destroyed in these raids and dozens of indigenous people killed. Often the navy would demand individuals be handed over under threat of destroying the village.[18]

Generally, the missions were framed as efforts to enforce 'the rule of law', even though it wasn't uncommon for drunk British sailors to enter indigenous villages and "molest Indian girls."[19] Additionally, colonial officials deliberately spread smallpox among First Nations in the area (the extent is hotly contested).[20]

Individuals were sometimes hung after being tried by military jury. In January 1853 naval officers conducted a hearing aboard the *Beaver*, which sentenced two Cowitzen to death.[21] "This summary measure," Captain Augustus Leopold Kuper informed Rear-Admiral John Moresby, "will no doubt have a most beneficial effect for the safety of the colonists against attacks from the Indians in future."[22]

In 1864 the 50-gun frigate *HMS Sutlej* ferried the New Westminster Rifle Corps towards the Tsilhqot'in nation near today's Williams Lake,

BC. The mostly former Royal Engineers helped capture six Tsilhqot'in chiefs who were executed, which Prime Minister Justin Trudeau and Premier Christy Clark apologized for a century and a half later.

That year *Sutlej* also participated in a mission that destroyed nine villages and dozens of canoes in Clayoquot Sound.[23] At least 15 were killed. In one instance, notes Gough, Sutlej launched "heavy fire on the surrounding bush to clear it" and then "burnt Mooyahhat by rocket fire."[24] Lieutenant Hugh Stewart boasted to the London-based Lords of the Admiralty that the mission in Clayoquot Sound "produced profound discouragement" and the Nuu-chah-nulth had "abandoned all ideas of resistance."[25]

In 1865 the 22-gun *HMS Clio* "totally destroyed" the houses and canoes at Ku-Kultz near present-day Port Hardy.[26] First Lieutenant Charles J. Carey reported, "we fired upon the Ranch, and totally destroyed it, with 50 or 60 large canoes."[27]

The next year *HMS Forward* intimidated a number of indigenous communities on the lower Nass River. According to Gough, ship captain Lieutenant D'Arcy Denny "thought that the best way to make recalcitrant Indians into good and obedient subjects of Her Britannic Majesty Queen Victoria was to bring them on board ship and give them a sound flogging."[28] The British vessel fired its guns to warn the Nisga and Tsimshian that they could easily destroy their villages. After attending friendship dances put on by Nisga chiefs, Denny fired a twelve-pounder rocket "to show them how easily their huts could be burnt down by those destructive missiles."[29]

In 1872 *HMS Scout* transported four-dozen men from Esquimalt to Haida Gwaii. BC's first lieutenant-governor, Sir Joseph William Trutch, requested the vessels to deal with the "unruly conduct of Indians at several points along the N.W. Coast and Queen Charlotte's Island."[30]

After Confederation the CF remained British dominated. The War Office in London appointed the General Officer Commanding the Canadian Militia/Chief of the General Staff, which was but a stop in a career enforcing the empire. Before becoming the first General Officer Commanding the Canadian Militia Edward Selby Smyth, was stationed in India, South Africa, Ireland and Mauritius.[31] His successor, Lieutenant-General Richard George Amherst Luard, fought in Crimea and China while Lieutenant General Sir Edward Thomas Henry Hutton served in the Anglo-Zulu War, First Anglo-Boer War, Anglo-Egyptian War, Nile Expedition and in Ireland.[32] After commanding the Canadian Militia until 1900 Hutton led the Australian Military Forces.[33] The first Chief of the General Staff, Sir Percy Henry Noel Lake, previously saw service in Afghanistan, Sudan and Ireland.[34] After his 1904-1908 posting in Canada, Lake served in India and Iraq.[35]

In 1908 Sir William Dillon Otter was the first Canadian appointed Chief of the General Staff.[36] But British officers continued to dominate the CF leadership. Between 1906 and 1912, 70 British officers served an average of three years in Canada and 37 British officers were stationed here at the start of WWI.[37]

Going in the opposite direction, the Royal Military College was created in 1876 largely to train "proper white gentlemen" to be officers of British imperialism, according to Andrew B. Godefroy.[38] "Suffering from its own shortage of officers, especially those with technical educations and military training, the British Army offered over a dozen commissions annually to graduates of RMC during the 1880s."[39] And the annual allotment for the Kingston, Ontario, based school was frequently supplanted with more sizable recruitment drives.

Between 1880 and 1900 RMC-trained soldiers participated in at least 28 imperial campaigns.[40] Usually commissioned to British units, RMC graduates fought in dozens more expeditions over the next 15 years.

In 1884, 385 Canadians were recruited to join British forces in Sudan. At the end of the century 7,000 Canadians joined mostly British units in southern Africa. London covered most of their costs while Ottawa and Lord Strathcona, Canada's wealthy High Commissioner in Britain, also contributed.[41] The British head of the CF, Colonel Edward

Hutton, pressed Prime Minister Wilfred Laurier to support the war effort.⁴² Without informing Laurier, for instance, Hutton published mobilization plans in the *Canadian Military Gazette*.⁴³ As a result of the dispute, Hutton was recalled and Ottawa extended its control over the CF with the 1904 Militia Act.⁴⁴

Established in 1910, the Royal Canadian Navy (RCN) took over Royal Navy bases in Esquimalt and Halifax. Britain donated its first two vessels and almost all the RCN's initial officers were British.⁴⁵ To join one had to be a British subject and the RCN operated under the King's Regulations and Admiralty Instructions. The Naval Service Act of 1910 permitted Ottawa to put the RCN at the disposal of His Majesty.

The British also spurred the creation of the Canadian Air Force. During WWI over 20,000 Canadians joined the nascent British air force and London suggested Canada raise its own air units.⁴⁶ Near the end of the war, Ottawa authorized the creation of an England-based Canadian Air Force, which disbanded after Britain cut its funding just after the war. In 1920 the UK gifted Canada 114 aircraft and nine airstrips to create an Air Force stationed in the UK.⁴⁷

During WWI hundreds of thousands of Canadians fought under British command. Likewise, thousands of Canadians served in British units in WWII. Even in the Korean war, which Ottawa joined at Washington's behest, the army fought in the Commonwealth division.⁴⁸

The CF inherited many of its traits from the British and was for years labeled the "Shock Army of the British Empire."⁴⁹ Its manuals and tactical training came from there and many senior officers were trained in British staff colleges.⁵⁰ In the 1930s, noted prominent diplomat and army officer Maurice Pope stated, the Canadian Army was "British through and through with only minor differences imposed upon us by local conditions."⁵¹ Into the 1960s the CF continued to rely on British Army doctrine.⁵²

To gain a sense of the pro-British sentiment amongst CF leaders, Commander of Military District 5 Colonel JP Landry criticized a 1923 defence scheme because it was developed in Canada and "should actually be prepared and considered by the Imperial Defence Council" in London.[53] Three years later Director of Military Operations and Intelligence James Sutherland Brown said the Canadian militia would generally be "content to leave our [foreign] affairs to the trained personnel furnished by Great Britain at international conferences."[54]

The origins of the CF were colonial. The British army and navy built an empire by stealing others' homes, reshaping their economies to the benefit of Mother England and enforcing London's rule over unwilling subjects. The CF were built on a foundation of colonial exploitation. One might argue this is solely of historical interest, but as we shall see there was never a clear break with the colonial mindset of enforcing imperial rule.

2. Conquering Canada

Right from its beginning the CF crushed indigenous resistance to colonialism. The best-known example came only a few years after Confederation when the military and militia suppressed the Métis and First Nations on the prairies.

Fearing the loss of their land, language and religion after Ottawa purchased the Hudson Bay Company, the Métis ousted federal government authority and established a local provisional government. In response Colonel Garnet Wolseley led 400 British regulars and 800 Ontario and Québec militiamen in the Red River expedition. After an arduous three-month journey to today's Winnipeg, they captured Fort Garry and extinguished Louis Riel's provisional government.

For the next three years the militia garrisoned Manitoba, harassing and killing at least one Métis.[1] "The militia played a significant role in the establishment of government authority in the Northwest", notes John Grodzinski.[2]

The Northwest Mounted Police (NWMP) took charge of pacifying the west in 1873. Organized on military lines, the word "police" was added to the North West Mounted Rifles' name when Washington expressed concern about a military buildup near its border.[3] Like other British colonial police, the NWMP was largely led by former military.[4]

The NWMP participated in the military's response to the Métis, as well as concurrent Cree and Assiniboine rebellions in 1885. Five thousand Canadian/British troops and militiamen were deployed to Saskatchewan and Alberta to subjugate the Métis and plains First Nations. With much of their land taken by treaty and the bison decimated, the Cree, Blackfoot, Blood, Peigan and Saulteaux were under pressure from settlers' farms, towns and railways. Métis fur traders faced similar pressures though they also worried about whether the federal government would respect their river-lot homesteads and farms.

Hundreds of Métis and indigenous were killed in a bid to enforce Ottawa's control of the West. Lieutenant-Colonel William D. Otter led a force that attacked Cree and Assiniboine warriors in 1885 near Battleford, Saskatchewan.[5] Without orders to do so, the 'father' of Canada's army asked permission to "punish [Cree leader] Poundmaker."[6] As such, the *Montreal Daily Star* coined the term "Otterism" as a "synonym for merciless repression."[7]

The infamous pass system — requiring individuals to receive permission to leave their reserve from the local Indian Agent — was initiated to deal with the North-West Rebellion. In May 1885 Major-General Frederick Middleton asked the lieutenant-governor of the North-West Territories, "would it not be advisable to issue proclamation warning breeds [Métis] and Indians to return to their Reserves and that all those found away will be treated as rebels. I suppose such a proclamation would be disseminated without difficulty."[8] Lieutenant-Governor Edgar Dewdney responded, "all good and loyal Indians should remain quietly on their Reserves where they will be perfectly safe and receive the protection of the soldiers and that any Indian being off his Reserve without special permission in writing from some authorized person, is liable to be arrested on suspicion of being a rebel, and punished as such."[9] Completely illegal, the pass system would remain in place for six decades.

Many former soldiers administered the pass system on the prairies as Indian Agents. Describing the late 1880s/early 1890s, former agent George Gooderham noted, "a great many of the Agents at that time were old military men who felt they must run the whole show. They said to the Indians 'You only do what I say you must do or must not do.'"[10]

***

Veteran land grants cost First Nations greatly. From 17th century New France to WWII, white soldiers were compensated with indigenous land, which was sometimes taken specifically for this purpose.[11] Describing the thinking after WWI, Desmond Morton writes, "it was unprecedented and therefore unthinkable that a war could end without some effort being made to settle soldiers on the land. Tradition, mythology, and concern about rural depopulation overruled memories of the waste and failure of military bounty."[12]

French colonial authorities encouraged soldier settlement by granting them land.[13] In the latter half of the 1600s soldiers were discharged, rather than disbanded, to protect New France from First Nations.[14] Morton notes, "veterans from the Carignan-Salières regiment had been settled in the valley of the Richelieu as a bulwark against the Iroquois."[15]

Disbanded soldiers populated Halifax beginning in 1749. Some of those who fought for the British against the Mi'kmaq in the Maritimes received their victims' land.[16]

During the late 1700s individuals who came north after fighting for Britain in the American Revolution received 200 acres per person to "encourage their resettlement" and "to develop the western frontier of Canada."[17] Thousands of British veterans of the War of 1812 were compensated with land in today's Manitoba, New Brunswick and elsewhere.[18]

In the mid-1800s British officers who served in Canada were often given land upon retirement.[19] In a bid to reduce costs, London offered land (and free passage) to veterans in Britain if they relinquished their pensions. Through the initiative hundreds received land in the vicinity of nascent towns such as Toronto and Hamilton.[20] The settlement of retired British soldiers also helped reduce the cost of garrisoning the colony. After hundreds of former British soldiers were settled in southern Ontario, part of the Canadian Rifle Regiment returned to England.[21]

Veterans of the Crimean war were given land in such disparate places as Cornwall, Ontario, and New Westminster, BC.[22] Those who repelled the US based Fenian raids in the 1860s later received 160 acres.[23]

After Confederation veterans continued receiving indigenous land. Those who fought in the 1870 Red River Rebellion received 160 acres while veterans of the 1885 North West Rebellion were granted 320 acres.[24] "In 1870 and again in 1885," notes Morton, "vast tracks of land in the Northwest were given to militiamen sent west to save Confederation."[25]

Soldier settlement on the prairies "offered security from possible American and Métis or Native threats," notes James Murton in *Creating a Modern Countryside: Liberalism and Land Resettlement in British Columbia*. But "the soldiers' contribution to Canadian security was more important as part of the overall plan to resettle the prairies with Euro-Canadians and develop the grasslands into commercial farms."[26]

Under the Volunteer Bounty Act Canadians who served in South Africa were entitled to 320 acres of Dominion land on the western prairies.[27] Over two million acres in Alberta and Saskatchewan were made available to 7,000 men who served in South Africa.[28] Partly to reinforce the militia on the prairies, Ottawa also assisted the settlement of British Boer War veterans.[29]

Over 25,000 took advantage of the WWI Soldier Settlement Act, which offered veterans 160 acres and other farming supports.[30] Despite significant indigenous contribution to the war, 86,000 acres of reserve territory was expropriated for non-indigenous veterans after WWI.[31] Parts of at least eight reserves on the prairies were taken and about a third of the land given to WWI veterans was reserve lands.[32]

With the Soldier Settlement Board permitted to purchase "idle" reserve lands a free-for-all of dispossession ensued. In March 1920 Minister of the Interior Arthur Meighen told Parliament, "scarcely a week passes without a surrender being made in some province of a portion of a reserve." In one instance, the St. Paul, Alberta, branch of the Canadian Legion asked for veterans to be given parts of the Saddle Lake Reserve since it was the finest farming land nearby and 500 Cree did "not make any effort to use the land to its best advantage."[33]

An important aim of the Soldier Settlement Act was to increase "the British element in our population."[34] According to Desmond Morton and Glenn Wright, Meighen had a vision that "soldier settlement could make him a latter-day Clifford Sifton, peopling the west not with foreigners but with patriotic native sons and selected fellow-Britons."[35]

The WWII Veterans Land Act also offered ex-servicemen land. Additional government funds were made available to purchase livestock, receive training and buy farm equipment. Tens of thousands of returned soldiers benefited from the Veterans Land Act. Hundreds of WWII veterans received land in the Peace River District of British Columbia and Alberta, including territory taken from the Fort St. John Beaver Band reserve.[36]

Over the course of decades soldiers were compensated with a great deal of indigenous land. Additionally, the military has repeatedly expropriated reserve territory for bases.[37] Often seized under the War Measures Act, when the CF acceded to pressure to return indigenous land it was usually despoiled. "In Canada, the military acted like a giant, using Indian land like stepping stones across the country", explained Brian Lloyd, a former British Army bomb-disposal expert who cleaned up Canadian sites. "You find an Indian nation, and you find range contamination."[38]

The naval base in Esquimalt was built on land taken from the Songhees. Established in the 1840s, it led to the "first placement of British Columbia Indians on a reserve."[39]

At the start of the 1900s militia units sought pieces of reserves near Kamloops, Salmon Arm and elsewhere in BC's Okanagan for rifle ranges and military camps.[40] CFB Chilliwack was built on land taken from the Three Sto:lo; CFB Petawawa was land from the Algonquins of Golden Lake; CFB Gagetown on Oromocto territory.[41]

In the early 1950s thousands of square kilometres of land was taken from the Cold Lake and Canoe Lake First Nations to create the massive Primrose Lake Air Weapons Range northeast of Edmonton.[42] DND officials were largely indifferent to the devastating impacts on their hunting, trapping and fishing. They rejected an Indian Affairs settlement proposal as "grossly excessive."[43] The sudden loss of the Dene people's northern forest was "catastrophic", resulting in crippling social ills.⁴⁴ An inquiry into their dispossession conducted a half-century later concluded: "We do find that the creation of the Primrose Lake Air Weapons Range had such a profound impact on the community that, within one generation, a self-reliant and productive group of people became largely dependent upon welfare payments. The cumulative impact was to destroy the community as a functioning social and economic unit."⁴⁵

During WWII 1,000 hectares of Chippewa Territory was appropriated for a CF training ground near Sarnia, Ontario. After the Kettle and Stoney Point First Nation rejected their offer, the government expropriated the land under the War Measures Act.⁴⁶ At the time the Crown Canada Company had a similar sized piece of land nearby, but it would have cost the military more.⁴⁷

As part of the expropriation, over a dozen families were forced to relocate to the Kettle Point reserve and the two bands were merged. Promised the return of their land after the war, the CF failed to follow through.⁴⁸ After decades of protest a government committee in 1992 recommended returning the land. The military resisted. The CF's half-century occupation of Stony Point land ultimately led to the 1995 Ipperwash Crisis in which the Ontario Provincial Police killed Ojibway protester Dudley George. The land was finally returned in 2016.⁴⁹ But it was despoiled by the previous military activity.

Ditto for Enoch Cree land near Edmonton. Tens, maybe hundreds, of thousands of bombs were dropped on the Yekau Lake Practice Bombing Range on the Enoch Cree Nation Reserve.⁵⁰ Lied to about the scope of the shelling, a golf course and the Enoch Cree Nation Cultural Grounds had to be shuttered after an independent consultant discovered a 105-millimetre shell and 12,000 munitions sitting in and around a lakebed. The consultant concluded that as many as 200,000 munitions could be at the bottom of the lake, prompting concerns about toxic leaching.⁵¹

Land returned to the Okanagan Indian Band was also contaminated with munitions.⁵² In 2016 the band, near Vernon, sued DND and the attorney general of Canada over unexploded ordnance and used munitions on their territory.[53] A 2011 DND report estimated 20,000 hectares of land in the area may be contaminated and stated there have been "10 confirmed UXO [Unexploded Explosive Ordnance]-related deaths" on the Okanagan practice range since WWII.[54]

At the start of the 1900s 6,630 acres of the Tsuu T'ina Nation Reserve was taken to build CFB Calgary.[55] Over decades it was littered with shrapnel and ammunition. When pushed to return Tsuu T'ina land the CF made a half-hearted attempt to clean up. A former British Army bomb-disposal expert who cleaned up Canadian sites, Brian Lloyd, told the *New York Times*: "In 1981, the military had 1,000 soldiers in here for 16 days. They certified the land free and clear of explosives, and then dumped it back on the nation. Since the military declared the land cleared, we have pulled out one million items of ordnance, expended rounds, live rounds."[56]

Clearly the CF have been no friend to First Nations. Rather it has been an instrument of dispossession and repression. The wealthy and powerful wanted indigenous land, wanted to destroy their way of life and build a capitalist economy. The military was critical for accomplishing these tasks. But indigenous people were not the only target of the Canadian military.

3. Soldiers for the Wealthy and White

INITIALLY A CENTRAL FUNCTION OF THE MILITIA was to quell labour unrest.[1] Between 1867 and 1933 the military aided the civil power at least 133 times and strikes represented half of all deployments.[2] While technically designed to maintain law and order, writes Mike O'Brien, militia "intervention in industrial disputes ... [were] in virtually all cases to the advantage of employers."[3]

In 1877 the 2nd Battalion Queen's Own Rifles of Toronto was dispatched to Belleville to oppose striking locomotive engineers and during a general strike in Québec City the next year troops opened fire, killing one and wounding at least 10 of those seeking better working conditions.[4] When indigenous and white fishery workers struck on the Fraser River in 1900 and 1901 the militia was employed to allow Asian workers, co-opted by the cannery owners, to act as strike breakers.[5] In 1903 the militia was called out in Niagara Falls to "awe the strikers", reported the *Hamilton Spectator*, who were mainly "Italians, Negroes, Poles, Hungarians and Croatians."[6] Companies often paid the cost of deploying the militia. During a strike on Vancouver Island in 1890 Dunsmuir & Sons put up some of the soldiers for six months.[7]

In its longest deployment in aid of the civil power, the militia was called out for over a year during a coal miners' strike near Nanaimo, BC, in 1912-14.[8] Along with members of the permanent force, almost a thousand militia members from Victoria and Vancouver were deployed to weaken those fighting for union recognition and safer conditions at a deadly mine.[9]

In response to their suppression of labour struggles, unions repeatedly passed resolutions calling for an end to the deployment of the militia during strikes. Some unions even sought to prohibit their members from joining the militia.[10] According to David Bercuson and J. L. Granatstein, "workers, angry at the breaking of their strikes, came to detest the militia."[11]

Prime Minister Wilfred Laurier was clear about the political utility of the militia. In 1902 he told Lord Dundonald, newly appointed British commander of the Canadian Militia, "you must not take the militia seriously for though it is useful in suppressing internal disturbances, it will not be required for the defence of the country, as the [US] Monroe Doctrine protects us against aggression."[12] Echoing Laurier's sentiment, seven years later Minister of Militia Frederick Borden noted, "the reason for the existence of the militia in this country is well understood. The principal object is perhaps the upholding of the civil power in the different parts of the Dominion."[13]

During WWI the militia suppressed a number of strikes and military intelligence officers monitored the International Workers of the World (IWW) and other leftist labour groups. In *Scarlet to Green: A History of Intelligence in the Canadian Army 1903-1963* S. R. Elliott reports, "district intelligence officer watched calls for 'one big union' closely and had non-commissioned officers attend meetings in plainclothes."[14] They reported on support for the IWW's attempt to unify industrial and craft unions into a single, combative, working-class organization. In September 1918, 14 working class organizations, including the IWW, Social Labour Party, Russian Social Democratic Party and Chinese Labour Association, were declared unlawful associations.[15]

In the years after WWI the CF helped suppress the Winnipeg General Strike, Vancouver General Strike and a number of other major labour disputes in Québec and the Maritimes. The nascent air force even engaged in reconnaissance during the May-June 1919 Winnipeg General Strike.[16]

Soon after that most politically explosive strike in Canadian history, the Minister of Militia introduced a bill to increase the permanent force from 5,000 to 10,000.[17] Minister Sydney Mewburn argued for the increase because "circumstances have arisen throughout the whole country which seem to indicate an absolute necessity that Canada should have some force available for the preservation of law and order in this country."[18] Similarly, fear of domestic disorder was the primary reason to expand the militia in the early 1880s.[19]

In maybe the most remarkable deployment against those seeking to improve their working conditions, between 1922 and 1925 a total of 5,000 militiamen were dispatched to quell three miners' strikes in Cape Breton.[20] Upper Canada College alumni Major-General Herbert C. Thacker aggressively defended the interests of the British Empire Steel Corporation (Besco), the largest industrial consortium in the country. As part of the deployment against the 1922 coal miners' strike near Glace Bay, Thacker requested Halifax-based destroyers the *Patriot* and *Patrician*. His request was endorsed by the senior naval officer in Halifax but blocked by military headquarters in Ottawa.[21] Thacker also sought air support, even though neither the air nor naval force were included under the terms of the Militia Act.[22]

After the strike concluded the president of the union commented: "The wage schedule was accepted by miners under the muzzle of rifles, machine guns and gleaming bayonets with further threatened invasions of troops and marines, with warships standing to."[23]

The next year steelworkers in Sydney, Nova Scotia, withdrew their labour in a bid to gain union recognition and improve their pay and schedules. At Besco's request the same judge that requisitioned the military the previous year, Duncan Finlayson, called for the militia "in anticipation of disorders that might arise." Thacker complied immediately and the military backed up the provincial police as they prevented public gatherings, including union meetings and picketing.[24]

The heavy-handed military presence sparked sympathy strikes elsewhere.[25] The labour movement's protests spurred changes to the Militia Act. Believing the Cape Breton deployment was an "unfair and indecent attempt to cow the men into submission", Prime Minister Mackenzie King sought to have the Militia Act amended "so as to prevent corporations from taking advantage of the powers which can be exercised, through any Judge to whom appeal may be made, where civil authorities themselves are unwilling to take the initiative required."[26]

The Militia Act was modified to force judges to gain the provincial attorney general's approval before troops could be dispatched. But the changes didn't stop the militia's deployment against Cape Breton strikers the next year. At Besco's invitation Judge Finlayson requested troops, which Nova Scotia Attorney General Walter J. O'Hearn supported. General Thacker again deployed 2,000 troops to Cape Breton.[27] Despite (or perhaps because of) his aggressive response to Cape Breton strikers, Thacker was made chief of the general staff in 1927.[28]

Significant changes were made to the Militia Act in 1933. From 1934 to 1972 the military was called out to suppress five strikes.[29]

Between the two world wars military intelligence "spied on suspected labour agitators."[30]

During the Great Depression the CF was responsible for unemployed "relief camps". Fearing revolution, army commander Andrew G. L. McNaughton sought to get young men without jobs off the streets and out of cities. Over 100,000 unemployed youth were housed in DND administered work camps that paid 20 cents a day to log and build roads.[31]

The CF also oversaw internment camps during WWII.[32] Over 20,000 Japanese-Canadians were held as were tens of thousands of others, including hundreds of Communists and Jewish refugees from the Nazis.[33] The two highest profile political detainees were the Communist president of the Canadian Seamen's Union, J. A. Sullivan, and Montréal Mayor Camillien Houde who condemned national registration as a prelude to conscription.

After WWII the military was involved in a number of labour stoppages. They intervened to pressure strikers at a number of shipyards on Vancouver Island to return to work or face dismissal.[34] The RCN also monitored potential Communist agitators on Vancouver Island. A navy intelligence officer at Esquimalt issued a three-page report on labour unions in 1951 that read: "The main Communist-line unions are the Canadian Seamen's Union, United Electrical Workers, the Union of Mine and Smelter Workers, and the Wood Workers International Union. Although all of these unions were once influential, the Reds are gradually being eliminated by the Union congresses themselves."[35]

After mutinies on three different ships at the start of 1949 the RCN leadership worried about "Communist" influence within its ranks. Fearing they were associated with a Communist-inspired strike in the Canadian merchant marine, the defence minister ordered an inquiry into the state of the RCN.[36] Despite the concern, no evidence of Communist influence was found.[37]

The CF also suppressed nationalist dissent in Québec. After thousands of students protested and rioted, a mechanized infantry battalion was deployed to the outskirts of Montréal in early 1969.[38] A year and a half later 6,000 troops were deployed across the province after the Front de Libération du Québec (FLQ) kidnapped Britain's trade commissioner in Montréal, James Cross, and provincial labour minister Pierre Laporte.[39] During the 1970 "October Crisis" tanks rolled down Saint Catherines Street and troops patrolled residential neighbourhoods.[40] The CF monitored demonstrations in Montréal and assumed hundreds of tasks.[41]

The Pierre Trudeau government invoked the War Measures Act, which gave 85,000 regular servicemen special constables powers and allowed the security forces to detain individuals without charge.[42] More than 450 people were jailed and a handful of media outlets censored.[43] (Some police chiefs in western provinces used the suspension of civil liberties to crack down on hippie-type groups there.[44])

Some believe the War Measures Act was invoked after 3,000 students gathered in support of the FLQ's demands. In other words, the objective of the government overkill was to blunt the nationalist left in Québec. Others argue the employment of the War Measures Act "was a psychological weapon used by Trudeau and his inner circle to bring the intellectual community to heel by discrediting any sympathies for the politics of confrontation."[45] Author of *Winning Back the Intellectuals: Inside Canada's First War on Terror 1968-1970*, McMaster professor Michael Gauvreau argued: "Internally, it aimed to forestall within the Liberal Party itself any collectivist or economically egalitarian deviation from the grand design of reconstructing the Canadian state on a new basis. Trudeau wanted to quash any expectations of an expanded welfare state in order to establish a stable political and social order achieved through managerial competence, ideals that could not be achieved if the Liberal Party was squabbling over the meaning of liberty and the role of the state."

Amidst growing support for the recently formed Parti Québécois, the CF planned to suppress a nationalist, working-class, uprising in Québec. In April 1972, 60 high-ranking military officers, including eight generals, discussed Operation Neat Pitch at a Montréal hotel.[46] The plan to deploy troops in Québec was later leaked to the press. During the get together two high-ranking British servicemen gave a presentation on their experience in Northern Ireland and distributed a document titled Tactical Operations in Northern Ireland.[47] In the lead-up to the 1976 Olympics in Montréal the CF practised occupying the city. During the games over 15,000 troops were deployed as part of OPERATION GAMESCAN.[48]

In another episode of employing the CF against the Québecois, anti-conscription protesters were gunned down in spring 1918. In August 1917 Robert Borden's government passed the Military Service Act, which sparked widespread dissent, particularly in Québec. In late March 1918 anti-conscription protests erupted in Québec City after some French speakers were arrested for not carrying their conscription exemption cards. Martial law was proclaimed and over a thousand English-speaking soldiers were deployed to maintain order and enforce conscription. At least four were killed and dozens injured when soldiers opened fire on protesters.[49]

***

The initial leaders of the militia were largely well to do. They were mostly British and the class lines in that country's military were stark. Between 1683 and 1871 wealthy individuals purchased officerships in the British Army so an overwhelmingly upper-class officer corps led mostly peasant/working-class troops/cadets. (Some pre-Confederation Canadians purchased British officerships. Cornwall-born James McGill Strachan, for instance, paid for a commission in the 68th [Durham] Foot Regiment and would return to Toronto as an officer in the mid-1830s.[50] Ditto for Alexander Roberts Dunn, a Toronto born aristocrat who would later organize the 100th [Prince of Wales' Royal Canadian)] Regiment of Foot, which was raised in Canada to fight against the Indian Mutiny of 1857.[51])

While not as class stratified as Britain, early Canadian officers were rarely of working class, peasant or indigenous background. In "Manhood and the Militia Myth: Masculinity, Class and Militarism in Ontario, 1902-1914" Mike O'Brien writes, "Canada's military leadership was much more middle-class in its orientation than was its British counterpart. As in Britain, however, the 'hoi polloi' [commoners] were excluded from the officer corps. Officers had to be able to afford expensive uniforms and kits, and those who lacked the means to keep up either the appearance or the 'social obligations' of officer status were effectively shut out from higher rank."[52]

Officers were selected for their influence and social standing. Similar to a private club, senior officers exercised a veto over prospective candidates.[53] In "The Montreal Militia as a Social Institution Before World War 1" Carman Miller writes, "led and financed by the city's wealthy and powerful, hierarchically organized, and committed to the support of the civil and social order, the militia was a very middle-class institution."[54]

A number of elite institutions promoted militarism and produced CF leaders. Established in 1876, the Royal Military College of Canada overwhelmingly trained the sons of the middle and upper class.

At a time when few attended universities, a University of Toronto college set up the first volunteer militia regiment. In 1862 the head of University College and previous president of the entire university, John McCaul, pushed students to establish the University and College Rifle

Company of the Queen's Own Rifles of Toronto. Professors were first captain and first lieutenant of the company.[55]

Just before Confederation, Upper Canada College (UCC) formed a Rifle Company attached to the 2nd Battalion Volunteer Militia Rifles of Canada. For years the older boys in this prestigious high school participated in weekly drills that included rifles and bayonets.[56] The introduction to *A History of Upper Canada College: 1829-1892* details some prominent UCC graduates: "In the Army we have the names of General Charles Robinson, commander of the forces in the Mauritius; General Samuel Jarvis; General Sir Francis Colborne; General Ingall, of Chester; Colonels Dunn and Wells, who charged with the Six Hundred at Balaclava; Lieut. Maule, who also distinguished himself in the Crimea, and was killed there; Col. G. T. Denison, who won, against the military experts of the world, the Czar's great prize for the best history of Cavalry Tactics; and many others."[57] The first Canadian awarded Britain's prestigious Victoria Cross, Alexander Roberts Dunn, studied at UCC.[58]

Many of the leaders of the Toronto volunteer militia went to the famed private school. Between 1875 and 1937 six former UCC graduates commanded The Queen's Own Rifles (William D. Otter, Joseph M. Delamere, Henry M. Pellatt, Arthur J. E. Kirkpatrick, Reginald Pellatt and Ralph B. Gibson).[59] So did distinguished generals Henry D. Crerar and James Neil Gordon.[60]

A number of these individuals came from extremely wealthy families. The paternal grandfather of Canada's first general, William Otter, was principal of King's College in London, Ontario, and a bishop. William's father moved to Canada to make his fortune and ended up working for the Canada Company, a British chartered land company colonizing Upper Canada.

Sir Henry Pellatt was the son of a captain who opened the stock brokerage firm Pellatt and Osler.[61] He co-founded Toronto Electric Light, which became international behemoth Brascan, and built the 98-room Casa Loma as his private residence. Son of Henry Pellatt, Reginald Pellatt was president of Pellatt and Pellatt, Stockbrokers. For his part, Kirkpatrick oversaw the Canadian operations of Baltimore-based United States Fidelity and Guaranty while Delamere was a member of the exclusive Toronto Club, which played an important role in shaping a national ruling class.

At the time of Confederation, the Toronto Club was an important point of contact between the wealthy and officer corps. The uber-elite Toronto Club's 1878 bylaws waived the entrance fee for officers: "By the consent of the Committee or quorum thereof, the officers of Her Majesty's Forces stationed in Canada, or on duty in the Dominion, and the officers of the Active Militia Permanent Force of the Dominion of Canada, may be admitted to the privileges of the Club (with the exception of voting) for a period of not less than one year on payment of the annual subscription in advance without entrance fee."[62]

Officer in the 5th Battalion of the Toronto militia, David Breakenridge Read was a member. A secretary-treasurer of the Toronto Club, Colin Harbottle was commander of the 75th (Mississauga) Battalion and commanding officer of the Toronto Scottish Regiment.[63] Another member of the club was Major and Commanding Officer in the Ninth Toronto Light Horse D'Alton Lally McCarthy, who founded the law firm that became McCarthy Tétrault.[64]

Canada's oldest and most prestigious private club still has various ties to the CF. In his 2011 memoir, Trilateral Commission Executive Committee member Roy MacLaren writes, "Tom Bata, Hal and Eric Jackman, and other friends from the Toronto Club also served as honorary colonels."[65]

A number of officers were also members and president of the Toronto based National Club. Founded in 1874, the elite social club was headed by Brigadier-General Charles H. Mitchell, Colonel Noel G. Marshall, Colonel George T. Denison and Colonel William K. McNaught. In 1902 the senior military officer in Canada, Lieutenant General The 12th Earl of Dundonald Douglas Mackinnon Baillie Hamilton, "attended a great Militia banquet given by Colonel [Henry] Pellatt at the National Club."[66]

A century later the president of the National Club was Blake Goldring, one of the most prominent wealthy Canadian militarists. Other honorary colonels were also members of the club.

The National Club and Toronto Club have played an important role in solidifying the corporate class' influence. Support for militarism has been part of these social institutions' worldview. But wealth-holders have also advanced a number of more explicitly militarist social clubs.

Brainchild of UCC graduate William Otter, the Royal Canadian Military Institute (RCMI) was established in 1890 as a social club for military officers and (later) "civilians with like interests". RCMI's initial patron was Governor General Lord Stanley and the Toronto-based institute received early financial support from Eaton's, Bank of Commerce, Toronto Street Railway, Simpson's, Imperial Bank and the Osler and Hammond brokerage firm.[67] A top Canadian banker and Conservative senator, James Mason was a cofounder and subsequent president of RCMI.[68] (Mason also played an important role in creating the Empire Club of Toronto and was chief organizer of the reserve militia.) UCC graduates Joseph Delamere, Ralph B. Gibson and Arthur Kirkpatrick also served as early presidents of RCMI.[69]

Retail store owner John C. Eaton and Bank of Commerce head Sir Edmund Walker financed the RCMI-spawned Canadian Defence League, which agitated for universal military training and service in the lead up to WWI. In "Manhood and the Militia Myth: Masculinity, Class and Militarism in Ontario, 1902-1914" Mike O'Brien writes that this period "saw the rise of a specifically militarist movement in Canada, embodied in such organizations as the Toronto-based [Royal] Canadian Military Institute (CMI) and the pro-conscription Canadian Defence League (CDL)… These organizations counted among their membership many leading figures from the professional and commercial middle classes, but drew little or no support from the working classes."[70]

Suspicion of democracy, free thought and liberty drove the push for military training in the early 1900s. An anonymous contributor to the CDL journal argued that military instruction in school would help Canada escape the socialist wave.[71] O'Brien postulates that an aim of the CDL was to build a quiescent labour force and that militarist conceptions of "manliness" were a stand-in "for the politics of class".[72] Military training was often equated with middle-class ideals of self-control and obedience.[73] Prominent journalist Colonel Charles F. Hamilton argued that military training would encourage "positive mental" and physical "improvement" — especially for those of a "more depressed ... social position" — by promoting "promptness, a sense of duty, the power of working in concert [and] the habit of accepting instructions from authorized persons." A descendant of a United Empire Loyalist, William Hamilton Merritt made a similar point. He claimed that working-class recruits would learn "the discipline of the heart, which is ... natural to the better class of men and carries the coarser natures along with it."[74]

***

To sum up what has been presented so far, the roots of the CF were in the British colonial army. What eventually became the Canadian military was used to directly colonize large areas of what is now Canada, suppressing indigenous people and forcing them into "reserves" that were a fraction of their original lands. Commanders of the militia and later the Canadian armed forces were typically upper class and their attitudes were largely pro-Empire and anti-working class. The militia and CF were frequently used to suppress strikes and clamp down on political activity the wealthy viewed as dangerous.

Next, we will look at CF activities abroad that also helped the rich and powerful.

4. Gunboat Diplomacy

THE ROYAL CANADIAN NAVY (RCN) was officially established in 1910. Prior to the RCN's formal creation, Canada's Fisheries Protection Services had a small fleet.[1] Begun in 1886, it had eight armed cruisers, six icebreakers and 18 other vessels by 1904.[2]

The RCN's creation was spurred by Germany's challenge to Royal Navy supremacy, the centralization of its command and a push for the Dominions (Canada, Australia, New Zealand and South Africa) to finance the RN's expansion. In Canada the debate was also shaped by the declining threat of US invasion.

Creating a navy divided opinion in both British and Canadian ruling circles. The RN wanted dominions to support their centralized command, but switched tack to tap into the "dominions drive for fuller military self-sufficiency, and the opportunity that sentiment afforded for useful assistance to the mother country."[3] At the 1909 Imperial Defence Conference RN leadership supported Canada and Australia establishing small navies that could reinforce the empire. Ambivalent towards fully backing the RN, Prime Minister Wilfrid Laurier leapt at the proposal, which would cost him in the subsequent election as Conservative Party leader Robert Borden deftly (if cynically) used the issue to weaken Laurier in Québec. Fearing entanglement with British imperialism, many in Québec opposed the RCN (or support for the RN). *Le Devoir* labeled the RCN's first ship "Canadian in times of peace, imperial in times of war."[4] Some Québecois took up the slogan: "your sons will be taken from their homes by force to be sent abroad in the Canadian Navy."[5]

The British orientation of the RCN was stark. Its first two vessels were donated by Britain and it took over RN bases in Esquimalt and Halifax. Almost all initial RCN officers were British and to join one had to be a British subject.[6] The RCN operated under the King's Regulations and Admiralty Instructions and the Naval Service Act of

1910 permitted Ottawa to put the RCN at the disposal of His Majesty. In announcing the RCN's creation Minister of Marine and Fisheries Louis Brodeur explained, "it proclaims to the whole British Empire that Canada is willing and proud to provide ... for local naval defence and to safeguard her share in the commerce and trade of the Empire."[7]

During its first three decades the RCN supported two British wars and sent ships to protect that country's interests in Mexico, El Salvador and elsewhere. In 1921 the RN seconded an officer to Naval Services Headquarters in Ottawa to direct North American intelligence for the British Empire.[8]

At the start of WWI the RCN had two cruisers and 400 men.[9] It doubled in size during the war. RCN growth then slowed. At the outbreak of WWII the Navy had 11 combat vessels and 1,500 permanent members as well as 1,700 reservists.[10] During WWII the RCN expanded 50 fold, reaching 500 ships and 90,000 men.[11] By the end of the war it was the fourth largest navy (after the US, UK and Russia) in the world.[12]

After WWII most RCN cadets were released and its vessels decommissioned. Still, it remained sizable and the Korean War gave it a big boost. During most of the quarter century after WWII the RCN had an aircraft carrier and in the late 1950s it considered acquiring nuclear armed submarines. A number of naval engineers were trained on the matter in the UK and a Nuclear Submarine Survey Team was formed in 1958 to examine the cost and feasibility of nuclear subs.[13] In the early 1960s the RCN had 62 ships in service and 20,000 men.[14]

During this period the RCN shifted its focus from the RN to the US Navy (USN). In the late 1940s and 1950s it adopted USN tactical and communications procedures as well as aircraft types.[15] Today, the RCN has close ties with the USN.

Fred Crickard and Gregory Witol contrast the difference in thinking between the leaderships of five navies with historic connections to Britain. While the Indians, Argentinians and South Africans saw themselves "as hegemons or would-be hegemons of regional sea power", write Crickard and Witol, "the Australian and Canadian navies left the mantle of the British Empire and donned that of the US Navy. The leadership in both countries see their navies as part of great armadas led by a major naval power prepared to fight anywhere on the globe."[16]

The RCN has bombed and blockaded countries during wars. It has also participated in international patrols and exercises designed to expand Canadian influence or pressure countries.

Since its creation the RCN has repeatedly flexed its muscles in the western hemisphere. According to military historian Sean Maloney, "on twelve occasions between 1915 and 1993 Canadian naval forces were used for 'Gunboat Diplomacy' in the region [Caribbean and Central America], to 'exert a delicate and discreet threat [short of declared war] to secure national objectives.' Notable operations included Mexico (1915), Costa Rica (1921), El Salvador (1932), St. Lucia (1958), and Haiti on multiple occasions since 1963."[17]

The first recorded instance of Canadian gunboat diplomacy was during the Mexican Revolution. In 1915 *Her Majesty's Canadian Ship (HMCS) Rainbow* was dispatched to protect British interests and the expatriate community in the Pacific port city of Mazatlan.[18] Later that year, Ottawa sent *HMCS Athabasca* further south to Manzanillo.[19]

A more brazen case of gunboat diplomacy occurred in Central America a few years later. In 1917 the Royal Bank loaned $200,000 to unpopular Costa Rican dictator Federico Tinoco just as he was about to flee the country. A new government refused to repay the money, saying the Canadian bank knew the public despised Tinoco and that he was likely to steal it. "In 1921," *Canadian Gunboat Diplomacy* notes, "in Costa Rica, Aurora, Patriot and Patrician helped the Royal Bank of Canada satisfactorily settle an outstanding claim with the government of that country."[20]

In 1932 RCN destroyers *Skeena* and *Vancouver* provided support to a month-old military coup government that brutally suppressed a peasant and indigenous rebellion in El Salvador.[21] With the two vessels in the region, London informed Ottawa that a "communist" uprising was underway and there was "a possibility of danger to British Banks, railways and other British lives and property" as well as a Canadian-owned utility.[22] Bolstered by the RCN's presence, the military regime would commit "one of the worst massacres of civilians in the history of the Americas" with 10,000-40,000 killed in weeks.[23]

Canada's navy has repeatedly been used in the British Caribbean. Some called for establishing a Canadian navy to take possession of the British colonies, which was supported by many in ruling circles at the time. During the debate over the RCN's creation Conservative Québec MP Archibald de Léry Macdonald argued "that if [the Bahamas] were a part of Canada the need [for] the navy would be as evident that no person could properly object."[24]

Prior to the RCN's establishment Canadian vessels began "wintering" in Bermuda. In 1905 Canada's "flagship" vessel conducted manoeuvres with the RN's North America and West Indies Squadron.[25]

At the start of WWI *HMCS Niobe* escorted Canadian soldiers to Bermuda, which they garrisoned for much of the war (as well as St. Lucia).[26] Between the two world wars RCN vessels regularly patrolled and exercised in the Caribbean.[27] Through the 1930s RCN vessels exercised with the RN America and West Indies Squadron in the winter.[28]

Soon after WWII broke out *HMCS Prince Henry* and *Prince David* were dispatched to Bermuda.[29] For part of the war the RCN had a small base — *HMCS Somers Isles* — in that British colony. RCN vessels also transported Canadian troops to replace British forces in Jamaica from 1940-1946, as well as in Bermuda, Guyana and the Bahamas during segments of this period. A Canadian also commanded naval forces in Trinidad during part of WWII.[30]

The RCN continued to operate in the region after WWII. In 1947 a carrier, two cruisers and eight destroyers exercised in the West Indies.[31] Through the 1950s 30 RCN vessels and 5,000 sailors trained in Bermuda.[32] From the early 1960s to the early 1990s the RCN had a small base in Bermuda. According to navy lore, signs still hang in some

Bermuda saloons saying, "No dogs or Canadian sailors allowed." Their rowdy behavior included stealing a city bus in the middle of the night and driving scooters "off jetties and right into the harbour."[33]

In a chapter titled "Maple Leaf Over the Caribbean: Gunboat Diplomacy Canadian Style" Sean Maloney writes: "Since 1960, Canada has used its military forces at least 26 times in the Caribbean to support Canadian foreign policy. In addition, Canada planned three additional operations, including two unilateral interventions into Caribbean states."[34]

The Canadian navy participated in the 1962 US blockade of Cuba.[35] According to Lieutenant Bruce Fenton, the RCN "assumed responsibility for surveillance of Soviet submarines in the North Atlantic while the United States Navy was engaged in operations around Cuba."[36] A Canadian aircraft carrier, two submarines and 22 specialized antisubmarine ships searched for Soviet subs in the Atlantic.[37] Incredibly, the mission didn't have official political support. The commander in Halifax (Flag Officer Atlantic Coast) Kenneth Lloyd Dyer quietly deployed his forces and simply said the operation was part of fleet exercises with the US Navy.[38] In *The Sea Is at Our Gates: the History of the Canadian Navy*, former naval commander Tony German describes a mission tacitly approved by the defence minister but not by the prime minister or external minister who disagreed on Cuba. German writes, "the Navy, with Maritime Air Command, honored Canada's duty to stand by her North American ally, without one scrap of paper, memo, minutes, or message, or one public announcement to give it direction or approval."[39] For his part, Jack Granatstein labeled Dyer's actions during the Cuban Missile Crisis the "the single greatest breach of proper civil-military relations in Canadian history."[40]

Still, German and other militarist authors support the self-deployment. Naval historian Peter Haydon writes, "one cannot find fault with Admiral Dyer's decision to take action without direction from Naval Service Headquarters; he merely did what he believed was in the best interests of the fleet and national defence."[41]

When 23,000 US troops invaded the Dominican Republic in April 1965 a Canadian warship was sent to Santo Domingo, in the words of Defence Minister Paul Hellyer, "to stand by in case it is required."[42] Two Canadian gunboats were deployed to Barbados' independence celebration the next year in a bizarre diplomatic maneuver designed to demonstrate Canada's military prowess. Maloney writes, "we can only speculate at who the 'signal' was directed towards, but given the fact that tensions were running high in the Caribbean over the Dominican Republic Affair [US invasion], it is likely that the targets were any outside force, probably Cuban, which might be tempted to interfere with Barbadian independence."[43] Of course, Canadian naval vessels were considered no threat to Barbadian independence.

At the request of Grenada's government, Ottawa deployed a vessel to the tiny country during its 1974 independence celebration. In *Revolution and Intervention in Grenada* Kai Schoenhals and Richard Melanson write, "the United Kingdom and Canada also sent three armed vessels to St. George's to shore up the [Eric] Gairy government", which faced significant pressure from the left.[44]

During the 1970s and 80s the RCN planned and exercised an invasion of Jamaica. Code-named NIMROD CAPPER "the objective of the operation revolved around securing and protecting the Alcan [bauxite] facilities from mob unrest and outright seizure or sabotage."[45]

In May 1963 two Canadian naval vessels joined US, British and French warships that "conducted landing exercises up to the [Haiti's] territorial limit several times with the express purpose of intimidating the Duvalier government."[46] A year later *HMCS Saskatchewan* went to Haiti again.[47] These missions were largely aimed at guaranteeing that François "Papa Doc" Duvalier did not make any moves towards Cuba and that a Cuban-inspired guerilla movement did not seize power.[48] In 1974 another Canadian warship was deployed to Haiti. This time "Canadian naval vessels carried out humanitarian aid operations to generate goodwill with the Haitian government so that Haiti would support Canadian initiatives in la Francophonie designed to limit

French interference in Canadian affairs."[49] In response to upheaval in the years after Jean Claude "Baby Doc" Duvalier fled, warships were again deployed to Haiti in 1987 and 1988.[50]

The RCN remains active in the Caribbean. After a deadly earthquake rocked Haiti in 2010, the government deployed two vessels and 2,000 troops instead of Canada's Heavy Urban Search and Rescue (HUSAR) Teams, which are trained to "locate trapped persons in collapsed structures."[51] According to internal documents the Canadian Press examined after the disaster, government officials feared that post-earthquake "political fragility has increased the risks of a popular uprising, and has fed the rumour that ex-president Jean-Bertrand Aristide, currently in exile in South Africa, wants to organize a return to power."[52] *HMCS Athabascan* and *Halifax* were part of Canada's deployment to police Haiti's traumatized and suffering population.

Understanding the public wanted Canada to aid earthquake victims, Prime Minister Stephen Harper told the press, "ships of the Atlantic fleet were immediately ordered to Haiti from Halifax, loaded with relief supplies."[53] Not true. "A [Halifax] Chronicle Herald reporter and photographer embedded with the military for the mission observed that they didn't have much food, water, medical equipment or tents to distribute, beyond what they needed for their own crews."[54] Nor did *HMCS Athabaskan* bring much food or water, according to a Canadian Press report.

RCN involvement in the Middle East dates back a half century and since the fall of the Berlin Wall they've regularly patrolled the region. *HMCS Provider* and two destroyers were dispatched to the eastern Mediterranean during the May 1967 Egypt-Israel crisis, which was sparked by repeated Israeli incursions into that country and Egypt's obstruction of Israeli shipping through the Straits of Tiran.[55] With Prime Minister Lester Pearson criticizing Egypt's blockade, President Gamal Abdel Nasser ordered the 800 Canadian troops in the country to leave Egypt within 48 hours. Former Canadian ambassador to Egypt, John Starnes suggested the KGB intercepted a top secret

DND invasion plan code named Exercise Lazarus and passed it on to the Egyptians, which spurred Nasser's hostility to Canada. Exercise Lazarus included a naval landing.⁵⁶

During the First Iraq war Canada dispatched destroyers *HMCS Terra Nova* and *Athabaskan* and supply vessel *Protecteur* to the Persian Gulf. About 1,000 soldiers were aboard the three vessels sent before a UN resolution was passed.⁵⁷

In 1998 *HMCS Toronto* was deployed to support US airstrikes and through the 1990s Canadian warships were part of US carrier battle groups enforcing brutal sanctions on Iraq. In the year before and after the second US-led invasion of Iraq, at least 10 Canadian naval vessels conducted maritime interdictions, force-support and force-projection operations in the Arabian Sea. In a book about "Operation Apollo" Richard Gimblett writes, "there are few places on the surface of the earth farther from either of our coasts than the Arabian sea, yet the Canadian Navy sustained operations of significant forces in that distant theater for the better part of two full years."⁵⁸ Canadian frigates often accompanied US warships used as platforms for bombing raids in Iraq.⁵⁹ A month before the commencement of the March 2003 US invasion, Canada sent a command and control destroyer to the Persian Gulf to take charge of Taskforce 151 — the joint allied naval command. Opinion sought by the Liberal government concluded that taking command of Taskforce 151 could make Canada legally at war with Iraq.⁶⁰ After the US was thought to have control of the country, Gimblett notes, "the bottom had fallen out of the anti-terrorism 'market' in the Gulf of Oman" so the Canadian warships left the region.⁶¹

Alongside US ships Canadian vessels ran a number of provocative manoeuvres off Iran's coast in 2008. In one instance a *National Post* reporter aboard *HMCS Protecteur* explained, "the usual tense games were played this weekend as this Canadian warship responsible for refueling and replenishing a coalition task force in the Indian Ocean passed in a heavy haze through one of the world's most dangerous flashpoints. Iranian radio operators trying to hail the Protecteur were interrupted by Omanis who firmly told their neighbours not speak to the Canadians who were making an 'innocent passage' through Omani territorial waters."⁶²

In January 2012 an RCN vessel departed to the Mediterranean Sea, according to the *Ottawa Citizen*, "for at least one year to provide a persistent Canadian presence near potential flashpoints."⁶³ Six months later *HMCS Regina* was also dispatched to the region to join the growing US military presence off Iran's coast. The *National Post* reported, "having the Charlottetown and other Canadian warships near Iran fits with the Harper government's strong opposition to Iran's suspected plan to acquire nuclear weapons."⁶⁴

RCN vessels regularly deployed to the Asia-Pacific as well. After visiting *HMCS Ottawa* and *Winnipeg* in Singapore in 2017, Chief of Defence Staff Jonathan Vance declared, "if one wants to have any respect or gravitas you have to be in that region."⁶⁵ To contain growing Chinese power Washington sought to stoke longstanding territorial and maritime boundary disputes in the South China Sea between China and the Philippines, Malaysia, Vietnam and other nations. As part of efforts to rally the region against China, the US Navy regularly conducted "freedom of navigation" operations near or through disputed waters.

The RCN supported Washington's aggressive posture. During a six-month tour of Asia in 2017 *HMCS Ottawa* and *Winnipeg* conducted "freedom of navigation" operations near disputed waters alongside US, Japanese, Australian and other countries' warships. When the two Canadian gunboats travelled with allied ships through the South China Sea, Chinese vessels "shadowed" them for 36 hours.⁶⁶ On another occasion a Chinese intelligence vessel monitored *HMCS Winnipeg* and *Ottawa* while they exercised with a South Korean ship.⁶⁷

In addition to participating in patrols, the military sought out a small base or "hub" in Southeast Asia — probably in Singapore — with a port facility.⁶⁸

Exerting naval power in the region is nothing new for the RCN. Canadian vessels have regularly visited Asian ports since *HMCS Grilse*,

Qu'Appelle and *Saskatchewan* were deployed to the region in 1968.[69] Canada has participated in every US-led Rim of the Pacific Exercise training off Hawaii since 1971.[70] Towards the end of the US war in Vietnam, *HMCS Terra Nova* and *Kootenay* were sent to Southeast Asia to support Canadian forces serving on the International Commission of Control and Supervision.[71]

In 1964 *HMCS Mackenzie, Frazier* and *Saint Laurent* joined British, Australian, Indian, Pakistani and New Zealand vessels in an exercise in the Bay of Bengal. According to the commander of the *Mackenzie*, Tony German, the mission was designed to be a "deterrent to Indonesia's President Sukarno ... who was bearing hard on Malaysia."[72] London had recently pushed to merge its colonies of North Borneo, Sarawak and Singapore with Malaya to create Malaysia, which Indonesia viewed as a bid to extend colonial authority on its border.

Immediately after US forces invaded Korea in 1950, Ottawa sent *HMCS Athabascan, Cayuga* and *Sioux* to the region.[73] Ultimately eight RCN destroyers completed 21 tours in Korea between 1950 and 1955.[74] During three years of fighting — July 1950 to July 1953 — 3,500 sailors were aboard the warships (about 1,000 did more than one tour).[75]

Canadian ships transported troops and shelled the enemy ashore.[76] They hurled 130,000 rounds at Korean targets.[77] According to a Canadian War Museum exhibit, "during the war, Canadians became especially good at 'train busting.' This meant running in close to shore, usually at night, and risking damage from Chinese and North Korean artillery in order to destroy trains or tunnels on Korea's coastal railway. Of the 28 trains destroyed by United Nations warships in Korea, Canadian vessels claimed eight."[78]

Canadian Naval Operations in Korean Waters 1950-1955 details a slew of RCN attacks that would have likely killed civilians. In the CF-produced history Thor Thorgrimsson and E. C. Russell write about a vessel's "nightly shelling" of an island, an operation whose "main targets were the road and rail communications system" and another mission that "opened fire with star-shell to illuminate the island and then proceeded to pound the outskirts of each village with high explosive."[79] Thorgrimsson and Russell also describe *HMCS Athabaskan* aiming her "4-inch guns" at "several hundred civilians ... digging trenches and preparing military installations" and subsequently firing forty-five shells into a North Korean military headquarters at Popsong'po "but as it was an indirect, unobserved bombardment the results could not be properly assessed."[80]

The vessels bombing Korea often docked in Hong Kong for repairs or a break.[81] A year before the outbreak of the Korean War the RCN sent a naval vessel to China as Mao's forces were on the verge of victory. *HMCS Crescent* backed up a British ship trapped by the Communists on the Yangtze River in 1949.[82] According to Richard Gimblett, the boat was sent too late to stop the Kuomintang's defeat by Mao's forces and was not needed to evacuate Canadians since British boats could remove them. The objective, it seems, was to demonstrate to the US and UK "that Canada was a willing partner," particularly in light of the emerging north Atlantic alliance.[83]

A previous RCN effort to be a "willing partner" in China led to a military disaster. In November 1941 *HMCS Prince Robert* escorted troopship *Awatea* with nearly 2,000 soldiers on board to secure Hong Kong.[84] Within three weeks they were almost all captured or killed by Japanese forces in a futile bid to maintain British control over the colony.

Three years later *Prince Robert* helped the British reoccupy Hong Kong.[85] *HMCS Uganda* was also part of the massive Pacific Fleet London sent to renew European rule over Burma, Malaya, Indonesia, etc. at the end of WWII.[86] For their part, *HMCS Prince David* and *Prince Henry* were transferred to the RN for its battle in Asia since "the Canadian government didn't want to be identified with restoring colonial regimes."[87] (Ottawa's hesitancy was partly influenced by US ambivalence towards British moves in a region Washington sought to dominate.) Ultimately, the Mackenzie King government agreed to have

Canadian ships participate in the Pacific region, but they were "not to be employed in the Indian Ocean."[88] [89]

Embarrassed in the face of their British allies, the RCN command was unhappy about the restrictions placed on their operations.[90] They were apparently unperturbed by the question of Indian independence.

The RCN command also wanted to send a bigger force to Asia than the government. As WWII wound down in Europe, 70 Canadian vessels and 13,000 men were prepared to deploy to Asia.[91] CF leaders sought a larger force even if it meant extending conscription.[92] (The fighting in Asia ended quickly so most of the force failed to deploy.)

During WWII Canadian vessels also deployed to European-controlled Africa. More than a dozen RCN corvettes escorted convoys from the UK to European-controlled North Africa in 1942. Describing a larger follow-up support mission in 1943 a *Hamilton Spectator* headline noted: "Canada Supplied 29 Ships and 3,000 of Her Sailors for North African Action".[93]

Since the mid-2000s the RCN has played a greater role in Africa. As part of what was dubbed Africa's "encirclement by U.S. and NATO warships", *HMCS Athabaskan* led Operation Steadfast Jaguar 2006 in the Gulf of Guinea.[94] A dozen warships and 7,000 troops participated in the exercise, the first ever carried out by NATO's Rapid Response Force.[95]

The following year *HMCS Toronto* participated in a six-ship task group of the Standing Naval Maritime Group 1 of NATO that traveled 23,000 kilometres around the continent. The trip took five months and was the first NATO fleet to circumnavigate Africa. *Toronto* spent a year preparing for a journey that cost taxpayers $8 million.[96]

Oil largely motivated operations off Nigeria's coast. Nigeria's *Business Day* described NATO's presence as "a show of force and a demonstration that the world powers are closely monitoring the worsening security situation in the [oil-rich] Niger Delta."[97] A Canadian spokesperson gave credence to this interpretation of their activities in a region long dominated by Shell and other Western oil corporations.

When the Standing Naval Maritime Group 1 warships patrolled the area Canadian Lieutenant Commander Angus Topshee told CBC, "it's a critical area of the world because Nigeria produces a large amount of the world's light crude oil, and so when anything happens to that area that interrupts that flow of oil, it can have repercussions for the entire global economy."[98]

More broadly, the objective of circumnavigating the continent was to develop situational knowledge of the various territorial waters, especially of Nigeria and Somalia. How knowledge of countries' coastlines was to be used was not made entirely clear, but it certainly wasn't to strengthen their sovereignty. "During the voyage," according to a story in *Embassy* magazine, "the fleet sailed at a distance of 12 to 15 miles off the African coast, just beyond the limits of sovereign national waters. The NATO fleet did not inform African nations it would soon be on the horizon. This, Lt.-Cmdr. Topshee says, was an intentional move meant to 'keep options open.' 'International law is built on precedent,' he says. 'So if NATO creates a precedent where we're going to inform countries, we're going to operate off their coastline, over time that precedent actually becomes a requirement'."[99] To help with the legal side of the operations a lawyer circumnavigated the continent with *Toronto*.

Reportedly, the Nigerians did not appreciate NATO's aggressive tactics. Topshee described the Nigerians as "downright irate" when the fleet approached. "There was real concern they might take action against us."[100]

For *Toronto's* Captain Stephen Virgin, the circumnavigation was largely about preparing NATO forces for a future invasion. "These are areas that the force might have to go back to some day and we need to operate over there to get an understanding of everything from shipping patterns to how our sensors work in those climates."[101]

On the east coast of Africa Canadian naval vessels deployed regularly as part of missions also focused on the Middle East. At various points during 2008, HMCS *Calgary, Iroquois, Charlottetown, Protecteur,*

Toronto and *Ville de Québec* all patrolled off the coast of Somalia. In the summer of that year Canada took command of NATO's Task Force 150 that worked off the coast of Somalia while the US launched periodic airstrikes and Ethiopian troops occupied Somalia.[102]

In early 2011, 15 days before the UN Security Council authorized a no-fly zone over Libya, *HMCS Charlottetown* left Halifax for the North African country. Two rotations of Canadian warships enforced a naval blockade of Libya for six months with about 250 soldiers aboard each vessel. On May 19, 2011, *HMCS Charlottetown* joined an operation that destroyed eight Libyan naval vessels.[103] The ship also repelled a number of fast, small boats and escaped unscathed after a dozen missiles were fired towards it from the port city of Misrata. After the hostilities the head of Canada's navy, Paul Maddison, told Ottawa defence contractors that *Charlottetown* "played a key role in keeping the Port of Misrata open as a critical enabler of the anti-Gaddafi forces."[104]

On one occasion a Canadian warship, part of a 20-ship NATO flotilla purportedly enforcing the UN arms embargo on Libya, boarded a rebel vessel filled with ammunition. "There are loads of weapons and munitions, more than I thought," a Canadian officer radioed *Charlottetown* commander Craig Skjerpen. "From small ammunition to 105 howitzer rounds and lots of explosives."[105] The commander's response, reported the *Ottawa Citizen*, was to allow the rebel ship to sail through.[106]

***

While some might argue that the examples cited above demonstrate that the Canadian navy has helped enforce the rule of law, the question would then be whose law? Certainly not the law of the African, Asian or Caribbean nations that Canadian ships were sent to intimidate. Not international law, which only allows a nation to use military force with UN approval or to defend itself from attack. And it's certainly not any moral law, the foundation of which is generally some version of: "Do unto others as you would have them do unto you." Would Canadians want warships from countries on the other side of the globe patrolling our coasts to intimidate us?

The truth is navies have long been used by nations wishing to project power, to build empires, to force weaker countries to follow their edicts. This was, and is, the behavior of a rich and powerful bully who tries to get his way through intimidation.

Subsequent chapters offer more examples of this form of behavior.

5. Special (and Secret) Forces

"There may be plausible reasons for maintaining elite military defence forces. But no argument can justify keeping the activities — even the composition — of Canada's Special Operations Forces so tightly concealed from Canadian citizens. All we know is that these covert military battalions are available for the Prime Minister to deploy arbitrarily in dirty wars — and to suppress any efforts by indigenous people in other countries to stop the pillaging of their resources by Canadian oil, gas, and mining companies."

Michael Skinner[1]

THE CANADIAN SPECIAL OPERATIONS FORCES Command (CANSOFCOM) has over 2,500 members.[2] Its annual budget is about $270 million and they are equipped with futuristic submachineguns, Ultra-Light Combat Vehicles, automatic grenade launchers, portable X-ray machines and other state of the art weaponry.[3] As this book went to print, CANSOFCOM was procuring three Beechcraft King Air 350ER spy planes for $300 million.[4] Constantly training, a single special forces soldier can fire 50,000 to 70,000 rounds in a year.[5]

The Canadian Special Operations Training Centre was set up in 2012. It offers CANSOFCOM "an academic engine capable of delivering university level education, research and publications."[6]

Since the mid-2000s Canada's special forces have expanded significantly. In 2006 the CF created CANSOFCOM to oversee the 427 Special Operations Aviation Squadron (SOAS), Joint Incident Response Unit-Chemical, Biological, Radiological and Nuclear (JIRU-CBRN), Special Operations Regiment (CSOR) and Joint Task Force 2 (JTF2).

SOAS is a covert air force dedicated to supporting the other three units. Based at CFB Petawawa in Ontario, SOAS has a squadron of tactical helicopters.

JIRU is an incident response team focused on chemical, biological, radiological and nuclear incidents. It operates in conjunction with the RCMP domestically and with different elements of the CF internationally.[7]

The bulk of CANSOFCOM is CSOR and JTF2. Composed of army, navy and air force personnel, CSOR applicants go through a 16-week selection course.[8] Its 750 members are based at CFB Petawawa, which has heavy artillery ranges and area for large manoeuvre training.

CSOR engages in international reconnaissance, training and kill missions. It also provides back up to JTF2.

JTF2 is the "jewel in the crown" of CANSOFCOM, according to then overall commander Mike Rouleau.[9] The most secretive and skilled unit of the CF, JTF2 engages in rescue operations, deep reconnaissance missions and international assassinations. Patterned after the British SAS (Special Air Service), it's considered among the world's elite special operations units.[10] In 2017, for instance, a JTF2 member in Iraq claimed the longest ever recorded sniper kill.[11]

As part of creating JTF2 in 1993, the RCMP disbanded its Special Emergency Response Team. Initially, there were about a hundred members, primarily drawn from the Princess Patricia's Canadian Light Infantry and Canadian Airborne Regiment, which was responsible for a series of brutal incidents in Somalia in 1993. (One of the two Airborne Regiment soldiers who killed a Somali in a controversial incident on March 4, 1993, Brent Countway, later joined JTF2.[12])

JTF2's size was increased from 130 to 300 between 1997 and 2001.[13] In 2001 JTF2 received a $120 million budget boost over six years to expand its capabilities and size from around 300 to 600 personnel. Exact figures are kept secret, but its commander called JTF2 a "very big unit" in 2016, which is divided into a number of squadrons.[14]

JTF2 represents the cream of the CF's "assaulter" crop. After three years in the armed forces soldiers can inquire if they have what it takes to apply to join JTF2. Those authorized by their unit's chain of command to try out must complete rigorous physical fitness and swim tests, as well as a selection interview and cognitive tests. The select few who pass this stage undergo a demanding week of tests at heights, in water, confined spaces, etc. The high stress tactical settings are designed to assess an applicant's capacity to identify threats, use weapons, work in teams and make decisions under physical and mental duress. Individuals who pass this phase go through a seven-month special operations assaulter course.[15] Only 10 to 20 percent of soldiers' green-lighted to train for JTF2 make the grade.[16]

Described as a Counter-Terrorism Unit, during its first quarter century JTF2 is not known to have fired a shot in any domestic terrorism operation.[17] Rather it has been employed in so-called "black ops" abroad. Canadian Institute of Strategic Studies director David Rudd said JTF2 are trained "to infiltrate into dangerous areas behind enemy lines, look for key targets and take them out. They don't go out to arrest people. They don't go out there to hand out food parcels. They go out to kill targets."[18]

JTF2 and CSOR often train and deploy with the US Delta Force and Navy Seals.[19] "In recent years," noted a 2017 *Washington Examiner* story, "JTF-2 has worked very closely with U.S. forces in operations around the globe."[20] They often operate under US command. In fact, a great deal of the information about JTF2 missions has come to light because the US military is more forthcoming with information on their special forces' operations.

By participating in secretive operations with their US counterparts, CANSOFCOM helps strengthen the bonds between the two countries' militaries. Important to many in the Canadian political establishment, these relations help develop intra-military bonds.

An example of these ties is Nicolas Matern, a special forces operative in Afghanistan and former commander of JTF2 and CSOR.[21] In 2008 Brigadier General Matern became deputy commanding general, coalition and infrastructure for multinational corps-Iraq 1, which reported directly to the US general who led the 170,000-strong foreign force in Iraq.[22]

CANSOFCOM is highly secretive. Its exact size isn't public information.[23] Similarly, its budget is not listed in the federal government's annual financial report.²⁴ It also bypasses standard procurement rules and their purchases are officially secret.²⁵

While the Communications Security Establishment, CSIS and other government agencies face at least nominal oversight, CANSOFCOM does not. During a 2006 Senate Defence Committee meeting CANSOFCOM Commander Colonel David E. Barr responded by saying, "I do not believe there is a requirement for independent evaluation. I believe there is sufficient oversight within the Canadian Forces and to the people of Canada through the Government of Canada — the minister, the cabinet and the Prime Minister."²⁶

The commander of CANSOFCOM simply reports to the defence and prime minister. "Even the U.S. President does not possess such arbitrary power," notes Michael Skinner in a *CCPA Monitor* story titled "Canada's Ongoing Involvement in Dirty Wars."²⁷

Their secrecy is an important part of their utility. "Deniability" is central to the appeal of special forces, noted Major B. J. Brister.²⁸ The government is not required to divulge information about their operations so Ottawa can deploy them on controversial missions and the public is none the wiser. A 2006 Senate Committee on National Security and Defence complained their operations were "shrouded in secrecy". The senate committee report explained, "extraordinary units are called upon to do extraordinary things ... But they must not mandate themselves or be mandated to any role that Canadian citizens would find reprehensible. While the Committee has no evidence that JTF2 personnel have behaved in such a manner, the secrecy that surrounds the unit is so pervasive that the Committee cannot help but wonder whether JTF2's activities are properly scrutinized."²⁹ Employing stronger language, *Toronto Sun* columnist Peter Worthington pointed out that, "a secret army within the army is anathema to democracy."³⁰

***

Canadian special forces have (probably) operated in Haiti, Bosnia, Rwanda, Kosovo, Congo, Peru, Iraq, Libya, Colombia, Afghanistan and elsewhere.³¹ In their most sustained deployment to any country, special forces were probably in Afghanistan continuously between 2001 and 2014. Alongside their US and British counterparts, 40 JTF2 members invaded the Asian nation in late 2001. (In fact, a former JTF2 member, described below, says he was deployed briefly to the Afghanistan/Pakistan border in 1998.[32]) The Canadians fought within the US force structure.[33]

In their first six months of fighting, JTF2 members reportedly killed 115 Taliban or Al Qaeda fighters and captured 107 Taliban leaders.[34] They also handed over prisoners who would be sent to the US prison at Guantanamo Bay.[35]

By early 2002, however, the British were questioning the tactics used by US and Canadian special forces. According to David Pugliese, "the concern among the British was that the ongoing raids [by Canadians and Americans] were giving Afghans the impression that the coalition was just another invading foreign army that had no respect for the country's culture or religion."[36]

On May 24, 2002, JTF2 members were part of a raid on Band Taimore, a village 80 kilometres west of Kandahar. In their search for Taliban and al-Qaeda leaders, the foreign forces killed several innocent civilians, including children, and took many others into custody.[37] Unsurprisingly, those living in the village were angered by the night attack.

According to documents CBC obtained through access to information, a JTF2 member said he felt his commanders "encouraged" them to commit war crimes in Afghanistan.[38] The soldier, whose name was not released, claimed a fellow JTF2 member shot an Afghan with his hands raised in the act of surrender. The allegations of wrongdoing were first made to his superior officers in 2006 yet the military ombudsman didn't begin investigating until approached directly by the soldier two years later. The JTF2 member told the ombudsperson's office "that although he reported what he witnessed to his chain of command, he does not believe they are investigating, and are being 'very nice to him.'"[39] After a three-and-a-half-year investigation, the

CF's National Investigation Service cleared the commanders, but they failed to release details of the allegations, including who was involved or when and where it happened.[40] The public was supposed to simply trust the National Investigation Service.

In 2005 a senior JTF2 commando choked and "almost killed" a subordinate in an unprovoked altercation at a forward operating base in Afghanistan.[41] The perpetrator was never tried in court, even though he admitted the principal facts and five soldiers witnessed the attack (including three who pulled the warrant officer off his victim). According to CBC, the CF decided it couldn't bring charges without exposing the assaulter's name and his membership in the secretive unit.[42]

A report by a closed-door board of inquiry into special forces violence in Afghanistan concluded that they took secrecy too far, leaving their commanders in the dark about missions. The report was released two years after being requested by the *Toronto Star* and CBC under access to information legislation. According to CBC, "access to information officials have spent two years going over the document with a fine-tooth comb to produce a censored version for public consumption."[43]

Canadian special forces participated in highly unpopular night-time assassination raids in the central Asian country. In 2008 the *Globe and Mail* reported, "a top Canadian commander has defended his forces' night raids on Afghan homes after a leading human-rights group and the Kabul government condemned the controversial tactic."[44] After describing an Afghanistan Independent Human Rights Commission report criticizing night-time assassination raids and the CF's reaction to the report, the article noted: "the Globe and Mail is bound by an embedding agreement at Kandahar Air Field that forbids detailing Special Forces operations." Presumably this was the journalist's way of relaying special forces operational information without being thrown off the base.

"At the Kandahar airfield", *Shadow Wars* explains, "Canadian military public affairs officers threatened journalists with expulsion from the installation if they dare to write about special forces operating from the base. Some reporters were even told not to look in the direction of the JTF2 compound as they walked by."[45] On February 12, 2002, *Toronto Star* reporter Mitch Potter was removed from a base after reporting on JTF2 night operations as well as the guard towers around a prisoner detention centre.[46] Potter claimed his expulsion was retaliation for criticizing the restrictions placed on journalists.[47]

Throughout the war special forces were on the ground. "What Canadians don't seem to understand is that … Special Forces have been on the ground continuously since 2001", noted CBC defence reporter Murray Brewster on the last day of 2010. "Even when our battle groups haven't been there, they've been there. It's a huge hole in our understanding of what has gone on in Afghanistan."[48] Even though they were supposedly covered by the 2008 parliamentary vote to cease combat operations by 2011, JTF2 continued to fight in Afghanistan. And when the government subsequently announced a training mission until 2014, they (apparently) remained after the promised withdrawal date.[49]

To the west, CANSOFCOM followed US forces into Iraq. In late 2014, 69 special forces were deployed there, which was tripled a year later. A tactical helicopter detachment, intelligence officers and a combat hospital in Iraq, as well as 200 CF members at a base in Kuwait, supported the 200 special forces.[50] Despite being framed as a "training" mission, the Canadians repeatedly engaged in battle, even killing someone with a record breaking 3.5-kilometre sniper shot.[51]

More than 200 highly skilled soldiers provided training, weaponry and combat support to Kurdish forces accused of ethnically cleansing areas of Iraq they captured. In mid-2017 special forces reportedly oversaw a hurried $10 million arms purchase for Kurdish forces, presumably because they can bypass the CF's customary procurement rules.[52] The Canadians also provided support to Shia government forces, some of which massacred Sunnis in areas of Iraq they captured from Daesh.[53]

After the 2003 US-led invasion of Iraq, JTF2 commandos reportedly worked alongside their British and US counterparts. While Ottawa refused to confirm it, the Pentagon and British Foreign Office told CBC JTF2 was instrumental in the March 2006 rescue of British and Canadian Christian Peace activists held hostage in Iraq.[54]

A number of media outlets reported on CANSOFCOM's presence in Libya in 2011. On February 28, CTV.ca reported "that Canadian special forces are also on the ground in Libya" while *Esprit de Corps* editor Scott Taylor noted CSOR's flag colours in the government's post-war celebration.[55] But, any Canadian "boots on the ground" in Libya violated United Nations Security Council Resolution 1973, which explicitly excluded "a foreign occupation force of any form on any part of Libyan territory."[56]

Few details about Canadian special forces activities in Libya became public, but presumably they engaged alongside allied British, US and French special forces. (Journalists in Libya during the conflict repeatedly spotted armed westerners who appeared to be special forces or former soldiers employed by private companies.) According to a BBC report titled "Inside story of the UK's secret mission to beat Gaddafi", British special forces were "co-ordinating certain NATO air attacks."[57]

On February 29, 2004, JTF2 commandos took control of the airport from which Haitian president Jean-Bertrand Aristide was bundled ("kidnapped" in his words) onto a plane by US Marines and deposited in the Central African Republic.[58] According to AFP, "about 30 Canadian special forces soldiers secured the airport on Sunday [Feb. 29, 2004] and two sharpshooters positioned themselves on the top of the control tower."[59] Reportedly, the elite fighting force entered Port-au-Prince five days earlier ostensibly to protect the embassy. The JTF2 deployment was part of the Canada/France/US campaign to destabilize and overthrow Haiti's elected government.

Amidst a February 2019 general strike that nearly toppled the Ottawa-backed president, heavily-armed Canadian special forces were videoed patrolling the Port-au-Prince airport.⁶⁰ The Haiti Information Project suggested that they helped family members of President Jovenel Moïse's corrupt, repressive and unpopular government flee the country.⁶¹

Through the 1990s JTF2 were deployed to the Balkans. Pugliese explains, "JTF2 operatives were also a fixture on every major peacekeeping mission, acting as advisers to contingent commanders. An assignment such as the one in Bosnia, for instance, had become so part of its routine that JTF2 had regular rotations to the former Yugoslavia just like other Canadian Forces units."⁶² Without the UN knowing, small teams of special forces were inserted into Bosnia and Herzegovina. In *We Were Invincible: Testimony of an Ex-commando*, Denis Morisset (more below) recounts a joint JTF2–British SAS operation to assassinate an alleged war criminal and four of his bodyguards. According to a number of accounts, JTF2 killed Serbian snipers harassing UN soldiers. In *Canadian Spies and Spies in Canada* Peter Boer writes, "on more than one occasion, when regular Canadian troops were under fire, two-man teams from JTF2 slipped into the surrounding countryside to hunt for enemy snipers."⁶³ Morisset describes participating in a number of these assassination missions.⁶⁴ After killing a number of Serbian snipers Morisset realized his victims only sought to frighten — not kill — UN forces.⁶⁵

During NATO's Spring 1999 air war on the former Yugoslavia JTF2 reportedly helped gather information and direct bombers from the ground. Conservative MP David Price said, "they're working with the KLA [Kosovo Liberation Army]. They're gathering intelligence. They're targeting, they're looking where the bombs are falling and the next bombs should go."⁶⁶ Supportive of the JTF2 deployment — but wanting Parliament informed — Price claimed a "very, very solid" military source with "direct involvement" in JTF2 operations told him they helped train the KLA and gather intelligence on bombing targets.⁶⁷ As per usual, the government denied Price's claim.

In *We Were Invincible* Morisset makes numerous explosive claims about his time with JTF2, including the above-mentioned assassinations in the Balkans and deployment to the Afghan/Pakistan border in 1998. On the eve of the book's 2008 French language publication the CF claimed it was a threat to national security and arrested an individual who says he was part of the secretive unit during its first eight years.[68] *We Were Invincible* is the only known insider's account of a force in which each member is forced to sign a confidentiality agreement.

According to Morisset, he was deployed to the Colombian jungle to rescue NGO and church workers "because FARC guerrillas threatened the peace in the region."[69] The Canadian soldiers were unaware that they were transporting the son of a Colombian leader, which prompted the leftist FARC to give chase for a couple days. On two different occasions they came under fire from FARC guerrillas. Two Canadian soldiers were hit in the firefight and immediately after the operation one of the wounded soldiers left the CF with post-traumatic stress disorder.[70] To the south, Morisset was dispatched to Peru in late 1996 after the Túpac Amaru guerrilla group took dozens of foreign diplomats (including Canadians) hostage at the Japanese embassy in Lima. JTF2 participated in the US-led rescue effort, which left all 14 guerrillas dead including many who were reportedly executed.[71]

When Indonesian control over East Timor collapsed in the late 1990s, JTF2 were sent to that country. They paved the way for a larger US military contingent. Morisset writes that Canadian troops oversaw a small village where "the poor villagers were terrorized by our presence."[72]

Special forces commandos have been deployed to Africa on numerous occasions. They were dispatched to Mali in 2013 to "protect Canadian personnel who are already operating in the troubled African country," reported the Canadian Press.[73] In 2009 JTF2 soldiers flew to Chad and/or Burkina Faso in a bid to secure the freedom of kidnapped Canadian diplomats Robert Fowler and Louis Guay.[74]

At the end of 1998 JTF2 descended on the Central African Republic as part of a UN force sent to secure key areas around Bangui, the capital. Pugliese points out that Ottawa announced the deployment of 300 Canadian peacekeepers to the Central African Republic but said nothing about the JTF2 operatives.[75] Earlier in 1998, JTF2 commandos accompanied former general Roméo Dallaire to Arusha, Tanzania, for his testimony at the International Criminal Tribunal for Rwanda.[76]

In Fall 1996 JTF2 escorted UN Secretary General's Special Envoy to the Great Lakes Region of Central Africa Raymond Chrétien to Kinshasa and General Maurice Baril into eastern Congo. Morisset provides a harrowing account of the JTF2 operation to bring Baril to meet Rwandan-backed rebel leader Laurent Kabila. The convoy came under fire upon which US Apache and Blackhawk helicopters launched a counterattack on the Congolese, but one Canadian died.[77]

Two years earlier JTF2 were inserted secretly into another part of Africa's Great Lakes region. In *Tested Mettle: Canada's Peacekeepers at War* Scott Taylor and Brian Nolan write: "A sizable contingent of JTF2 had been deployed into Africa. To provide additional 'security' for the U.N. mission in Rwanda, MacLean and his team had set up an 'advanced operational base' in Uganda. From there they would launch long-range, covert intelligence patrols deep into Rwandan territory."[78]

JTF2's first mission may have been to Somalia in 1993, according to Pugliese. "The Defence Department still declines to discuss, or deny, whether the JTF2 was involved in the Somalia killing. But a review of military records points to intriguing links that suggests the March 4 incident [when Canadian soldiers killed a Somali civilian] could have been the counterterrorism unit's first foray into missions affecting 'the national interest.'"[79]

For two decades the Airborne Regiment was the primary special force. They were trained to destroy critical installations, engage in psychological warfare, counter guerrilla operations, etc.[80]

Harkening back to their origins, a new CANSOFCOM uniform was released in 2017 modeled after the WWII Devils Brigade.[81]

Officially known as the Canadian/American First Special Service Force, the Devils Brigade comprised 900 Canadians and 900 Americans under a single command.[82] Considered hugely successful, they carried out sabotage missions and organized resistance in North Africa, Italy and southern France.[83]

Much of the Devils Brigade was trained at Camp X located between Whitby and Oshawa on the shore of Lake Ontario. The highly secretive facility was run by the British Security Coordination, a Western Hemisphere focused WWII organization, and Canada's federal government. Historian Bruce Forsythe explained: "Trainees at the camp learned sabotage techniques, subversion, intelligence gathering, lock picking, explosives training, radio communications, encode/decode, recruiting techniques for partisans, the art of silent killing and unarmed combat."[84]

Camp X agents were usually sent behind enemy lines, including in former colonies such as Burma. Some were also trained in signals intelligence and Camp-X helped build up what would become the Communication Security Establishment.[85]

***

While the use of "special forces" during war is perhaps understandable, the legitimacy of their actions should be circumscribed by the morality of a particular war. This should be obvious to all but those who believe "our wars" are always moral. So, for example, few Canadians would argue that any of what German special forces did during WWII was moral since they served Hitler's regime.

Special forces operations outside of formal wars, which represents a large part of JTF2's activities, raise other moral questions. Their secrecy and lack of political responsibility threaten democracy and promote authoritarian behavior. Unchecked, unaccountable, military power has rarely been good for ordinary people.

The morality of special forces and CF during wars is the subject of the next chapter.

6. On the Battlefield

"Prolonged peace is always a time of trial for any military"
David Bercuson[1]

AS PREVIOUSLY DISCUSSED, the Canadian military was the British military for many decades after Confederation in 1867. At the time there was no pretence of Canada being a "force for good in the world" or "peacekeeper by nature" or even any sort of neutrality. Canadians fought for "God and Empire" and schoolchildren were taught that British imperialism brought "progress" to "backward, uncivilized, non-Christians". It was the duty of British and other European imperialists to "civilize" the world.

The notion of the "White Man's Burden" was a primary justification for Canadian participation in British wars. While the explicit racism used as Canadians marched off to Africa became less direct, the underlying concept of the "White Man's Burden" can be traced through Canada's military history. Certainly, the idea that Canadians troops would help "build democracy" in Haiti or Afghanistan or the Congo smacks of this racist sentiment.

Sudan

When it occupied Egypt, Britain took control of Sudan, which had been under Egyptian rule for half a century. But indigenous forces increasingly challenged foreign rule. Tens of thousands of Sudanese laid siege to British/Egyptian controlled Khartoum from March 13, 1884, to January 26, 1885. After cutting the 60,000-person city off from its supplies, the indigenous forces wrested control of Khartoum from famed English General Charles Gordon.

Nearly four hundred Canadian boatmen were recruited to transport soldiers and supplies to rescue Gordon and defend Britain's position on the upper Nile. A veteran of the 1870 Red River expedition to defeat Louis Riel in Manitoba, the British general in charge of the mission to save Gordon explicitly requested "Canadian Voyageurs". General Wolseley believed these Canadian watermen, with experience in the fur trade, were best suited to navigate the raging cataracts of the Nile River.

The Voyageurs were deployed to Sudan under the British flag. But Canadian officials helped recruit the men, got some of them leave and organized a farewell for the expedition.[2] They also celebrated the expedition's return and today the names of the Canadians who ventured to Sudan are recorded in the book of remembrance in the memorial chamber of the Peace Tower on Parliament Hill.[3]

While Britain had overwhelming superiority of arms, moving men and supplies up the Nile was incredibly laborious. As such, the Sudanese "Mahdist" forces captured Khartoum before the British reinforcements reached the city. With Gordon dead and the expedition having various logistical difficulties, they put off attempting to recapture Khartoum. Still, British forces left a great many dead. In one battle 300 to 400 Sudanese died with 14 killed on the British/Egyptian side.[4] In another confrontation 1,100 Sudanese lost their lives in contrast to the 74 Egyptian/British fighters who died.[5]

Boer War

Between 1899 and 1902 more than 7,000 Canadians fought in the (second) Boer War. At least 270 of them were killed or died of disease during this effort to strengthen Britain's position in southern Africa.

In the late 1800s the descendants of Dutch settlers increasingly found themselves at odds with British interests in southern Africa. Large quantities of gold were found thirty miles south of the Boer capital, Pretoria, in 1886. The prime minister of the UK's Cape Colony, Cecil Rhodes, and other British mine owners wanted to get their hands on more of the loot.

There was also a geostrategic calculation. The Boer gold and diamond fields were drawing the economic heart of southern Africa away from the main British colonies on the coast. If this continued London feared that the four southern African colonies might unite, but outside of the British orbit, which threatened its control of an important shipping lane.

The war was devastating for the Boers. As part of a scorched-earth campaign the British-led forces burned their crops and homesteads and poisoned their wells. About 200,000 of these descendants of Dutch settlers were rounded up and sent to concentration camps. Twenty-eight thousand (mostly children) died of disease, starvation and exposure in these camps.[6]

"Canadian troops became intimately involved in the nastier aspects of the South African war," notes Chris Madsen.[7] Whole columns of Canadian troops participated in search, expel and burn missions. In the paper "Canadian Troops and Farm Burning in the South African War" Madsen adds that "organized columns of troops descended upon areas still offering resistance and destroyed farms in those vicinities on the slightest pretext."[8]

Canadian forces killed thousands of Boer cattle and looting was commonplace. One Canadian soldier wrote home, "as fast as we come up the country ... we loot the farms."[9] Another wrote, "I tell you there is some fun in it. We ride up to a house and commandeer anything you set your eyes on. We are living pretty well now."[10] There are also numerous documented instances of Canadian troops raping and killing innocent civilians.[11]

About 100,000 Black Africans were also held in concentration camps but the British didn't keep statistics, so we don't know how many died.[12]

To justify the war British officials criticized Boer treatment of Blacks. In *Painting the Map Red: Canada and the South African War, 1899-1902*, Carman Miller notes the self-serving nature of this claim. "Although imperialists had made much of the Boer maltreatment of the Blacks, the British did little after the war to remedy their injustices."[13] In fact, the war reinforced white/British dominance over the region's indigenous population. The peace agreement with the Boer included a guarantee that Black Africans would not be granted the right to vote before the two defeated republics gained independence and they would not gain full civil rights until the end of apartheid nine decades later.

WWI

Nearly 60,000 Canadian soldiers died in World War One and another 150,000 returned home physically wounded. Many more were scarred for life.

Over four days nearly 16,000 Canadian were killed or gravely wounded fighting for a few yards of terrain at Passchendaele.[14] During the battle for Hill 70 there were 9,000 Canadian casualties while militarists boast that Canadians "killed or wounded an estimated 25,000 Germans" fighting for the largely inconsequential hill.[15]

The total number of Germans and others killed by Canadians during the war is unknown. Canadians killed many Germans who surrendered though.[16] In a 1929 book English poet Robert Graves wrote, "the troops that had the worst reputation for acts of violence against prisoners were the Canadians."[17] One Canadian soldier wrote his parents, "after losing half of my company there [Neuville-Vitasse], we rushed them and they had the nerve to throw up their hands and cry, 'Kamerad.' All the 'Kamerad' they got was a foot of cold steel thro' them from my remaining men while I blew their brains out with my revolver without any hesitation."[18] Some Canadian commanders even ordered their soldiers not to take prisoners.[19]

In "The Politics of Surrender: Canadian Soldiers and the Killing of Prisoners in the Great War" official military historian Tim Cook points out that the evidence of these killings came from interviews the CBC conducted with aging veterans for a 1960s radio series. "Dozens of Canadians testified to the execution of German prisoners," Cook said of the 600 WWI interviews. But "none of these grim accounts found their way into the final 17-hour script."[20]

A century after it began, many still believe Canada fought tyranny during WWI. But Germany had universal (male) suffrage and Ottawa was allied with the brutal Russian Czar.

The ruling elites of France, Germany, England and Russia saw war as a way to weaken working class challenges in their countries. The other major force that spurred WWI was inter-imperial rivalry in Europe. It was a struggle for global supremacy between up-and-coming Germany and the imperial powers of the day, Britain and France.

Support for the British Empire was Ottawa's primary motive for joining the war. As Prime Minister Robert Borden saw it, the fight was "to put forth every effort and to make every sacrifice necessary to ensure the integrity and maintain the honour of our empire."[21] He justified conscription as a way to preserve Canada's imperial standing.

Canadian troops supported the colonial system in the Caribbean during the war. Hundreds of them garrisoned Bermuda from 1914-1916 and St. Lucia from 1915-1919.[22]

For Africans, the First World War represented the final chapter in the European conquest of their territory. A handful of Canadian pilots fought in East Africa, including naval air serviceman H. J. Arnold, who helped destroy a major German naval vessel during the British/Belgian/South African conquest of German East Africa.[23] Commandant of Canada's Royal Military College from 1909 to 1913, Colonel J. H. V. Crowe commanded an artillery division for famed South African General Jan Christiaan Smuts and later published *General Smuts' Campaign in East Africa*.

About one million people died as a direct result of the war in East Africa.[24] Fighting raged for four years with many dying from direct violence and others from the widespread disease and misery it caused. Hundreds of thousands of Africans were conscripted by the colonial authorities to fight both in Africa and Europe.

Members of the RCN Volunteer Reserve patrolled the coast of west Africa.[25] The son of a Quebec City MP and grandson of a senator, Sir Charles MacPherson Dobell commanded an 18,000-man Anglo-

French force that captured the Cameroons and Togoland. The Royal Military College graduate's force defeated the Germans in fighting that destroyed many villages and left thousands of west Africans dead. Early in the two-year campaign Dobell's force captured the main centres of Lomé and Douala and he became de facto governor over large parts of today's Togo and Cameroon. A telegram from London said, "General Dobell should assume government with full powers in all matters military and civil."[26]

British officials justified seizing the German colony as a response to the war in Europe, but to a large extent WWI was the outgrowth of intra-imperial competition in Africa and elsewhere. In "The Anglo French 'Condominium' in Cameroon, 1914-1916", Lovett Elango points to "the imperialist motives of the campaign", which saw the two allies clash over their territorial ambition. Elango concludes, "the war merely provided Britain and France a pretext for further colonial conquest and annexation."[27] After the German defeat the colony was partitioned between the two European colonial powers.

Fresh from leading the Anglo-French conquest of German West Africa, Dobell commanded a force that attempted to seize Gaza during the Sinai and Palestine Campaign. As many as 400 Canadians (about half recruited specifically for the task) also fought in British General Edmund Allenby's Jewish Legion that helped conquer modern day Israel/Palestine in 1917.[28]

Canada also played a small part in Britain's acquisition of Iraq from the Ottoman Empire. Between 1916 and 1919 a few dozen Canadian troops fought in Mesopotamia and Persia.[29] Some Canadians also helped "hold the Batum-Tiflis-Baku-Krasnovodsk line to Afghanistan" and flew with the British Royal Air Force when they were "quelling what became known as the Third Afghan War in 1919."[30]

The First World War was horrific for Russians. Hundreds of thousands perished from the fighting and many more died from hunger and disease caused by the conflict. Bolshevism grew in response to the misery brought upon the country by a brutal Czar. The French, English and US responded to the Bolshevik's rise to power by supporting the Russian monarchists (the Whites) in their fight to maintain power. Six thousand Canadian troops invaded Russia to defend the status quo. Canadian gunners, notes Roy MacLaren, won "a vicious reputation amongst the Bolsheviks for the calm skill with which they used shrapnel as a short-range weapon against foot soldiers."[31]

The war against the Bolsheviks was initially justified as a way to reopen WWI's Eastern Front (the Bolsheviks signed a peace treaty with Germany). Canadian troops, however, stayed after WWI ended. In fact, 2,700 Canadian troops arrived in the eastern city of Vladivostok on January 5, 1919, two months after the war's conclusion.[32] A total of 3,800 Canadian troops went to Siberia, which the Whites continued to control long after losing Moscow, St. Petersburg and most of the western part of the country. Ottawa maintained its forces in Russia after the conclusion of WWI partly to persuade the British that Canada merited inclusion in the Paris Peace conference that would divvy up the spoils of the war. Prime Minister Borden wrote, "we shall stand in an unfortunate position unless we proceed with Siberia expedition. We made definite arrangements with the British government on which they have relied ... Canada's present position and prestige would be singularly impaired by deliberate withdrawal."[33]

Ottawa also feared the rise of anti-capitalism and hoped military participation would lead to economic opportunities in Russia after the revolution was defeated. On December 1, 1918, Borden wrote in his diary that he was "struck with the progress of Bolshevism in European countries."[34] Alongside its military force, Ottawa established a Trade Commission in Vladivostok and the Royal Bank opened an office in the city. The Royal Bank convinced Canadian commanders to post eight soldiers around their branch.[35]

WWII

Over one million Canadians fought in WWII.[36] Forty-five thousand died.

Unlike Canada's other wars, WWII was ultimately justifiable. But Nazi expansionism's threat to British interests, not opposition to fascism or anti-Semitism, led Ottawa to battle.

In the lead-up to WWII, Mussolini's Italy invaded Abyssinia (Ethiopia), the only independent African country. (Ethiopians beat back an Italian invasion three decades earlier.) Employing mustard gas and other brutal tactics, the Italians killed tens of thousands of Ethiopians directly with many more dying as a result of dislocation.

The 1935 invasion contravened a series of "friendship treaties" signed by the two countries. It also violated Article X of the League of Nations, which explicitly forbade aggression among the organization's members. Nonetheless, Ottawa's overall position opposed collective League action against Italy and ultimately recognized Italian sovereignty over Ethiopia.[37]

Another significant backdrop to WWII was the struggle between fascism and liberal democracy in Spain. In that country's 1936 elections a left-wing coalition government won office. The Catholic church, landed gentry and big business immediately looked to overthrow the government with the help of General Francisco Franco, commander of Spain's overseas military. In this armed struggle, Franco was assisted by Hitler's Germany, Fascist Portugal and Mussolini's Italy. The Nazis gave Franco's forces hundreds of planes and tanks, as well as artillery, and sent 16,000 German men.[38] "Spain functioned as a testing ground for Hitler's incipient war machine and was also something of a secret playground for the young pilots of Germany's Condor Legion", explains Michael Petrou in *Renegades: Canadians in the Spanish Civil War*.[39] Benito Mussolini's Italy also sent 75,000 soldiers, 90 warships and launched more than 5,000 air raids against democratic Spain.[40]

Canada largely sided with the Fascists during the Spanish civil war. Ottawa refused repeated requests from Spain's elected government to sell it weaponry. When the Spanish government tried to build support for its cause by sending three elected representatives to Québec, Montréal's mayor cancelled the hall rented for the meeting. The RCMP spied on the Spanish Solidarity Committee, which organized Canadians to cross the Atlantic to fight fascism. In April 1937 Ottawa passed the Foreign Enlistment Act in a bid to block Canadians from fighting on behalf of the Republican government. Canadian officials claimed, "these youths are being sent to Spain, largely for the sake of gaining experience in practical revolutionary work and will return to this country to form the nucleus of a trained core."[41] The more than 1,600 men and women who crossed the Atlantic had an alternate version: They sacrificed themselves in defence of an elected government and against the rising tide of fascism.[42]

During this period Canada found no fault in supplying war materials to the fascist Japanese army that occupied Korea and massacred the Chinese in Manchuria. In the years leading up to the start of the European front of WWII, Japan was the third largest importer of Canadian non-ferrous metals.[43] Canada was Japan's chief supplier of nickel, a militarily important commodity. Japan imported 9,000 tons of Canadian nickel in 1937, 10,000 tons in 1938 and 7,000 tons in the first half of 1939 alone.[44]

Throughout the mid-to late-1930s leftist organizations, peace groups and self-styled "friends of China" called for an economic and military boycott of Japan to end Canada's complicity with Japanese expansionism. But corporate Canada "promoted trade with Manchuria and the rest of the Japanese empire."[45]

Ottawa tacitly supported Japan's brutal 1931 invasion of Manchuria that left 20,000 Chinese dead.[46] "Whatever may be thought of the moral or ethical rights of the Japanese to be in and to exercise control over Manchuria their presence there must be recognized as a stabilizing and regulating force," noted the Canadian diplomat who opened the first Canadian mission in Japan, Hugh Llewellyn Keenleyside.[47] Six years later the Canadian ambassador to China, Randolph Bruce, told the *Toronto Star* that Japan's invasion of Nanking, to the west of Manchuria, was "simply an attempt to put her neighbour country into decent shape, as she has already done in Manchuria."[48]

Some 20,000 women were raped and tens of thousands of Chinese killed in the six weeks after Japan entered Nanking.[49] Yet Canadian officials in the region, who received reports regarding the massacres, were more worried about Japan's sinking of the *USS Panay* and *HMS Ladybird* than the human rights situation.[50]

Canadian diplomats viewed China as a weak and divided country subject to Communist influence. On the other hand, they were impressed by Japan's ability to exert itself in East Asia. Through Ottawa's accession to Anglo-Japanese military and commercial treaties Canada and Japan were imperial allies and most-favored trading partners.

Canadian support for fascism in Japan and Spain in the years leading to WWII should bedevil the notion that Canada joined the war to combat this perverse political system/ideology. Prime Minister MacKenzie King, in fact, was sympathetic to European fascism. "The truth", wrote King in 1938, "is Hitler and Mussolini, while dictators, have really sought to give the masses of the people some opportunity for enjoyment, taste of art and the like and, in this way, have won them to their side."[51] In September 1936, King wrote in his diary that Hitler "might come to be thought of as one of the saviors of the world."[52]

There is also a perception that Canada joined the war to defeat anti-Semitism. To the contrary, many Canadian leaders held anti-Jewish views. King said, "I'm coming to feel that the democratic countries have allowed themselves to be too greatly controlled by the Jews and Jewish influence."[53] When the PM visited Germany in June 1937, he failed to mention (publicly or privately) the Nuremberg laws.[54] In existence since mid-1935, these laws codified anti-Semitism in Germany.

Canadian and British officials sympathized with Hitler's antagonism towards the Soviet Union and European left. Moscow sought an alliance with London and Paris against Hitler. From early 1938 until the official outbreak of WWII in September 1939 Moscow proposed sending a major military force to entice Britain and France into an anti-Nazi alliance. Instead of making an alliance that could have halted Hitler, Britain and France pressured Czechoslovakia to surrender its ethnic German Sudetenland region to the Fuhrer (after he annexed Austria).[55] This emboldened Hitler and enabled Germany's push eastwards.

Colonial competition spurred the war. This was particularly clear in Asia. Ottawa began to rearm in 1936-37 not due to Germany but for a war in the Pacific.[56] Until spring of 1939 military planners were more focused on the Pacific than the Atlantic.[57]

Nazi expansionism's threat to British interests led Ottawa to war. As Desmond Morton and Jack Granatstein explain, "Canada went to war in September 1939 for the same reason as in 1914: because Britain went to war."[58] And the war was a huge boost to Canada's depressed economy.

In August 1939 the Canadian Manufacturers Association sent a delegation to Britain to investigate war production.[59] The trade mission went "in the hope of gaining for its members a share in the profits of British rearmament", according to official historian C. P. Stacey. "People so situated were bound to see war as an economic opportunity."[60]

During WWII industrial production was over $9.5 billion ($100 billion in today's money).[61] Another $1.5 billion was spent on defence construction and the expansion of war plants. Between 1939 and 1945 Canada's Gross National Product ballooned from $5.6 billion to $11.8 billion.[62] Canada's steel and aluminum capacity expanded significantly.[63] General Motors, Ford and Chrysler's Canadian auto plants produced over 800,000 military vehicles for Canadian and British Commonwealth armies.[64] The WWII War Supply Board was led by Ford Motor Canada president Wallace Campbell.

The CF committed major humanitarian crimes during the war. Most ominously, Canadian bombers helped destroy German cities and civilian infrastructure. A large number of Canadian pilots participated in an effort to destroy three dams in the Ruhr Valley. In *Dam Busters: Canadian Airmen and the Secret Raid Against Nazi Germany*, Ted Barris details a bid to flood the region and destroy the civilian economy.

The aim of the strategic bomber offensive was to crush civilian morale. According to the British general in charge of bomber command, Arthur Harris, "the destruction of German cities; the killing of German workers and the destruction of civilized life throughout Germany ... the destruction of houses, public utilities, transport and lives; the creation of a refugee problem on an unprecedented scale; and the breakdown of morale ... [These] are expected and intended aims of our bombing policy. They are not byproducts of attempts to hit factories."[65]

The bombing effort left 600,000 Germans dead and more than five million homeless.[66] But the raids had only a minimal impact on German war production until late in the campaign.[67]

During WWII Canada's defence zone included the West Indies and British Guyana. Supporting the colonial system, Canadian troops replaced British forces in Jamaica from 1940-1946, as well as in Bermuda and the Bahamas during segments of this period.[68] Perceptions of race underlay the deployment of Canadian troops. According to Defence Minister Norman Rogers, the governor of Jamaica "had intimated that it will be risky to remove all white troops."[69] The situation in the Bahamas was even more sensitive. In June 1942 rioting broke out over the low wages received by Black labourers. Canadian troops arrived in the Bahamas just after the riots and their main task was to protect a paranoid governor, the Duke of Windsor.[70]

(The CF enjoyed its deployment in the Caribbean. Just after WWII came to a close Canada's chief military planner put forward a scheme to replace the British military in the Caribbean/Atlantic region. "For Canada to assume these responsibilities might be a happy solution to an otherwise confusing situation of overlapping defence interests," wrote Canada's chief military planner in 1946.[71])

Canadians fought by land, sea and air in colonial Africa. Describing a support mission in 1943 a *Hamilton Spectator* headline noted: "Canada Supplied 29 Ships and 3000 of Her Sailors for North African Action".[72] Many Canadian fighter pilots also operated over the continent. "During the Second World War," notes Canadian African studies scholar Douglas Anglin, "considerable numbers of Canadian airmen served in RAF squadrons in various parts of the continent, particularly North Africa."⁷³ More than a half-dozen Canadian pilots defended the important RAF base at Takoradi, Ghana, and others traveled there to follow the West African Reinforcement Route, which delivered thousands of fighter planes to the Middle East and North African theatre of the war. A team of French-speaking Canadians with broadcasting skills grouped in Accra, Ghana, supported the Allied invasion of French North Africa.⁷⁴

Canadian troops fought to protect British rule in Asia. Ottawa sent 1,975 troops to defend Hong Kong in the fall of 1941. "Hong Kong constituted an outpost which the Commonwealth intended to hold," read an External Affairs message to London in response to a request for troops.⁷⁵ But the troops had limited training and the mission was doomed from the outset. Nearly a third of the Canadians deployed to Hong Kong perished in a futile effort to stop Japan's conquest of the British colony.

Partly to help Britain regain Hong Kong, a number of Chinese-Canadians were covertly deployed into China.⁷⁶ According to Roy MacLaren in *Canadians Behind Enemy Lines, 1939-1945*, they were sent because "whenever the Japanese capitulated, it would be useful to have on hand a team to enter Hong Kong promptly to help re-establish the British writ there."⁷⁷

Canadians also helped re-establish the "British writ" in another Asian island city-state. One of Vancouver Lieutenant Colonel Arthur R. Stewart's first tasks in Singapore was to raise the Union Jack over municipal buildings to greet the first Allied troops to return.⁷⁸

A few hundred Canadians fought with British, Australian and US special forces who carried out secretive operations in Malaya, parts of China and some Pacific islands.⁷⁹ The Number One Canadian Special Wireless Group was dispatched to Australia during the war.⁸⁰ Its 330 members mostly monitored Japanese signals throughout the Dutch East Indies (Indonesia).⁸¹ Canadians also participated in psychological warfare efforts in Burma, Siam, Indochina, Malaya and the Dutch East

Indies.⁸² In early 1945 over 3,000 Canadian airmen served with the RAF or RCAF in Southeast Asia.⁸³ Canadian Air Force units attacked Japanese positions in India and Burma and also provided transport support.⁸⁴

Dozens of Canadian army officers aided the re-conquest of Burma, which had been a British colony for a century.⁸⁵ At least one Canadian, Jean Paul Archambault, was killed there.⁸⁶

Canadians also helped Britain re-conquer Malaya (Malaysia).⁸⁷ At least 16 Chinese-Canadians were sent behind enemy lines to carry out sabotage missions, organize local resistance and prepare for the collapse of Japanese control.⁸⁸ After the Japanese defeat they aided the British in suppressing the independence movement there. Canadians helped disarm the Malayan People's Anti-Japanese Army.⁸⁹ Major CD Munro and Sergeant Charlie Chung were sent to the northern part of the state of Kedah "where trouble had developed with the local guerrilla forces."⁹⁰ At the start of 1946 a few dozen Canadian intelligence officers served in the radio station at Kuala Lumpur and aided psychological warfare operations. Lieutenant Bob Elliott continued to operate in Malaya until March 1947.⁹¹

Korea

"I can be a hero over there pulling hand grenades out with my teeth, was my impression. I joined basically for the adventure, not patriotism. I didn't even know where Korea was. I didn't care where Korea was. I just thought: I want to go to war. I want that experience."

Canadian soldier Don Hibbs⁹²

Eight Canadian warships and 26,000 Canadian troops fought in the 1950-53 Korean War.⁹³ The US-led UN force was largely responsible for massively expanding what was essentially a civil war. As many as four million died.

At the end of WWII the Soviets occupied the northern part of Korea, which borders Russia. US troops controlled the southern part of the country. A year into the occupation, a cable from Canadian diplomats in Washington, Ralph Collins and Herbert Norman, reported on the private perceptions of US officials: "[There is] no evidence of the three Russian trained Korean divisions which have been reported on various occasions ... there seems to be a fair amount of popular support for the Russian authorities in northern Korea, and the Russian accusations against the conservative character of the United States occupation in civilian Korea had a certain amount of justification, although the situation was improving somewhat. There had been a fair amount of repression by the Military Government of left-wing groups, and liberal social legislation had been definitely resisted."[94] Noam Chomsky provides a more dramatic description of the situation: "When US forces entered Korea in 1945, they dispersed the local popular government, consisting primarily of antifascists who resisted the Japanese, and inaugurated a brutal repression, using Japanese fascist police and Koreans who had collaborated with them during the Japanese occupation. About 100,000 people were murdered in South Korea prior to what we call the Korean War, including 30-40,000 killed during the suppression of a peasant revolt in one small region, Cheju Island."[95]

In sharp contrast to its position on Japan and Germany, Washington wanted the (Western dominated) UN to take responsibility for Korea in 1947. The Soviets objected, claiming the international organization had no jurisdiction over post-WWII settlement issues (as the US argued for Germany and Japan). Instead, Moscow proposed that all foreign forces withdraw from Korea by January 1948. Washington demurred, convincing member states to create the United Nations Temporary Commission on Korea (UNTCOK) to organize elections in the part of Korea occupied by the US. For its part, the Soviet bloc boycotted UNTCOK. Canada joined UNTCOK.

The UN-sponsored election in South Korea led to the long-term division of that country and Canada's involvement in a conflict that would cause untold suffering. On May 10, 1948, the southern part of Korea held UNTCOK-sponsored elections. In the lead-up to the election left-wing parties were harassed in a campaign to "remove Communism" from the south. As a result, left-wing parties refused to participate in elections "wrought with problems" that "provoked an uprising on the island of Cheju, off Korea's southern coast, which was brutally repressed."[96]

The official story is that the Korean War began when the Soviet-backed North invaded the South on June 25, 1950. The US then came to the South's aid. In *Korea: Division, Reunification, and US Foreign Policy* Martin Hart-Landsberg notes, "the best explanation of what happened on June 25 is that Syngman Rhee deliberately initiated the fighting and then successfully blamed the North. The North, eagerly waiting for provocation, took advantage of the southern attack and, without incitement by the Soviet Union, launched its own strike with the objective of capturing Seoul. Then a massive U.S. intervention followed."[97]

Korea was Canada's first foray into UN peacekeeping/peacemaking and it was done at Washington's behest. US troops intervened in Korea and then Washington moved to have the UN support their action, not the other way around. The UN resolution in support of military action in Korea referred to "a unified command under the United States."[98] Incredibly, UN forces were under US General Douglas MacArthur's control, but he was not subject to the UN. Canadian Defence Minister Brooke Claxton later admitted, "the American command sometimes found it difficult to consider the Commonwealth division and other units coming from other nations as other than American forces."[99]

After US forces invaded, Ottawa immediately sent three gunboats. Once it became clear US forces wouldn't succeed immediately, Canadian ground troops were dispatched.

A couple dozen Canadian pilots served with the US fighter squadron in Korea.[100] Flying 66 combat missions, which mostly bombed ground targets, J. J. McBrien was the first Canadian to win the US Navy's distinguished flying Cross.[101]

Two million North Korean civilians, 500,000 North Korean soldiers, one million Chinese soldiers, one million South Korean civilians, ten thousand South Korean soldiers and 95,000 UN soldiers (516 Canadians) died in the war.[102] The fighting on the ground was ferocious as was the UN air campaign. General MacArthur instructed his bombers "to destroy every means of communication and every installation, factory, city and village" in North Korea except for hydroelectric plants and the city of Rashin, which bordered China and the Soviet Union, respectively.[103] "We went over there and fought the war and eventually burned down every town in North Korea," General Curtis LeMay, head of US air command during the fighting, explained three decades later. "Over a period of three years or so, we killed off ... twenty percent of the population of Korea as direct casualties of war, or from starvation and exposure."[104]

Crimes committed by Canadian troops, even against allied South Koreans, largely went unpunished. Those found guilty of murdering or raping Korean civilians were usually released from prison within a year or two. In one disturbing example, a half dozen Canadian troops who beat South Korean soldiers and then raped and killed two South Korean women barely spent any time in jail.[105]

Canada's intervention in Korea went beyond defending the South Korean regime. After pushing North Korean troops back to the 38th parallel, the artificial line that divided the North and South, the UN force moved to conquer the entire country. Ottawa supported the UN resolution allowing foreign troops to cross the 38th parallel.[106] The US-led force continued north in a bid to undermine China's new Communist government. US officials, particularly UN force commander Douglas MacArthur, repeatedly attacked China's government. Before China entered the war US aircraft bombed that country while carrying out air missions in northern Korea.[107] Even more ominous, both MacArthur and (later) President Truman publicly discussed striking China with nuclear weapons.[108]

UN troops pushed north even after the Chinese made it clear they would intervene to block a hostile force from approaching their border. Beijing was particularly worried about northern China's dependence on energy from the Yalu River power station in northern Korea.

Stand on Guard For Whom? — 83

Six months after the US intervened in the Korean civil war the UN voted to brand China an aggressor in the conflict. Yet Beijing only sent forces into Korea after hundreds of thousands of hostile troops approached its border. From the Chinese perspective the People's Liberation Army defended the country's territorial integrity, which was compromised by US bombings and the control of Formosa by foreign backed forces. Canada voted for the UN motion describing China as an aggressor.[109]

A series of factors led to the war. For starters, North Korean leader Kim Il-sung wanted to reunite the country under his authority, which didn't bother Moscow or Beijing. In *The Hidden History of the Korean War* I.F. Stone argues that the US and two of its main regional allies also wanted war. In an election three weeks before the fighting Syngman Rhee lost control of South Korea's parliament, which wanted to reunify the country. A war Rhee could blame on the North would weaken those calling for peaceful reunification of the country, thereby strengthening his hand. For his part, Chiang Kai-shek, the leader of Formosa (Taiwan), worried that more countries would follow Britain and recognize China's Communist government, undermining his ability to speak on behalf of China at the UN Security Council and elsewhere. Chiang believed the regional tension created by war would deter other countries from recognizing Mao's government, which is what happened with Canada. Washington, particularly the general in charge of the US occupation of Japan, backed Rhee and Chiang's position.

At a broader level the US sought to weaken China after its successful nationalist revolution. Washington pushed to encircle the country by supporting Chiang Kai-shek in Taiwan, building military bases in Japan, backing a right-wing dictator in Thailand and seeking to "establish a pro-Western state" in Vietnam.[110]

***

The modern Canadian military was born on the backs of the Koreans, Chinese and others killed in the Korean war. According to Bertram C. Frandsen, "the outbreak of the Korean War on 25 June

1950 was the catalyst that changed the perspective of the government and DND towards the maintenance of armed forces in peacetime. This new perspective was to affect governments and the armed forces for the next forty years."[111]

After World War II the CF shrunk dramatically.[112] From a high of nearly 500,000 members, the regular army was reduced to 16,000 by 1947.[113] The size of the RCAF and RCN were slashed as well.

Prime Minister Mackenzie King was prepared to whittle the CF down further. A 1947 White Paper called for further demobilization and to focus public spending on social programs.[114] Before WWII the CF had 10,000 members and a relatively small number of ships and aircraft.[115] There wasn't a tradition of a large standing army and no inherent reason to maintain one.

Defence Minister Brooke Claxton and the chiefs of the three branches of the military pushed back against the outgoing PM. Outside of the government the Chamber of Commerce launched an anti-communist campaign that pushed for greater military spending.[116] In 1947 the Canadian Industrial Preparedness Association, which became the Canadian Association of Defence and Security Industries, was established. At the Canadian Club in January 1951 the president of Ford Canada, Rhyn McSale, called for increased arms production, higher taxes and a ban on the Communist Party.[117]

The civil war on the Korean Peninsula came at an opportune moment for the Canadian and US militaries. Endorsed by the Washington-dominated UN, the conflict justified military expansion and a war economy. Prominent External Affairs officer Escott Reid explained that "the creation of the [1949] North Atlantic alliance did not result in rearmament. Rearmament was the result of the Korean War."[118] Echoing Reid, Defence Minister Claxton said, "Korea made our people realize what was involved in Communist aggression and what was needed to stop it. Moreover, it accustomed the people of Canada ... to the idea of having large numbers of men and large amounts of money tied up in our common effort."[119]

Military spending doubled between 1950-51 and 1951–52.[120] It doubled again the next year.[121] Spending on the CF went from $361 million in 1949 to $1.9 billion in 1953.[122] By 1953 40% of the federal government budget was devoted to the military or NATO Mutual Aid.[123] During this three-year period the CF nearly tripled in size, growing from 40,000 to 105,000 members.[124]

Lifeblood of the RCN, Korea spurred the navy's rise "out of the postwar doldrums to become an effective force."[125] At the start of 1950 the RCN faced a reduction in its budget, but the outbreak of war led to increased funding. In a PhD thesis titled "The rise and fall of the Royal Canadian Navy, 1945-1964" Wilfred Gourlay notes, "the Korean conflict inaugurated a rapid expansion of the RCN almost on the scale of the World War II build up."[126]

The Korean war enabled the RCN leadership to fulfill its end of WWII plan for a large permanent navy. Gourlay writes that Vice Admiral Herbert Rayner's proposal was "not [to] be fulfilled until the fear generated by the Korean War created the political will to find the 20,000 personnel navy planned by Captain Rayner in 1945."[127] In "The Rise and Fall of Canada's Cold War Air Force, 1948-1968" Bertram Frandsen makes a similar point regarding the RCAF. He writes that the Korean War "was the catalyst for the creation of the Big Air Force."[128]

The Department of Defence Production was created in response to the Korean war.[129] It was responsible for seven Crown corporations, including the Canadian Commercial Corporation.[130] The Department of Defence Production secured weapons for the war in East Asia and delivered Mutual Aid to NATO allies in Europe.[131]

Rearmament also steered research contracts to corporate Canada.[132] Korean war procurement kick-started Canadian ship building. Orders during the early 1950s, notes Tony German in a history of the RCN, "injected technical advances into industry as never before, not just in building hulls but in a great range of high tech equipment — electronic, electrical, mechanical. This was a real boost to the economy and made thousands of jobs."[133]

By the end of the war 260,000 workers — one out of eight industrial jobs — were directly or indirectly involved in military production.[134] Minister Claxton claimed, "defence had become the biggest single industry in Canada."[135]

Conflict in Korea gave Washington a pretext (outlined two months earlier in infamous National Security Council statement NSC 68) to strengthen its position in the region and to ramp up military spending. Privately, Secretary of State Dean Acheson admitted as much. He said, "Korea came along ... [and] created the stimulus which made [for] action" on NSC 68 and provided "an excellent opportunity ... to disrupt the Soviet peace offensive, which ... is assuming serious proportions and having a certain effect on public opinion."[136] Acheson further admitted that the decision to fight in Korea was "a purely political one" that "had made it politically possible for the United States to secure congressional and public support for a quick and great increase in defense expenditures; for further assistance to those of its friends who are willing to make a similar increased effort; for the imposition of needed controls, higher taxes, the diversion of manpower in the armed forces and defense industries, etc."[137]

In many ways the Korean War marks the beginning of the permanent war economy in the US. It helped the US economy out of a slight recession and put to rest talk of a post-WWII depression (WWII ended the Great Depression).

Military spending was a way for the government to stabilize the cyclical (boom and bust) nature of capitalism. To the titans of industry military Keynesianism — government seeking to stimulate economic demand — was a more acceptable form of social spending. Unlike many other types of public spending — education, health, welfare, pensions, etc. — military spending reinforces elite dominance (see chapter 3). In discussing the turn to military Keynesianism with the Korean War, political economy professors Jonathan Nitzan and Shimshon Bichler write: "The prospect of military demobilization, particularly in the United States, seemed alarming. The U.S. elite remembered vividly how soaring military spending had pulled the world out of the Great Depression, and it feared that falling military budgets would reverse this process. If that were to happen, the expectation was that business would tumble, unemployment would soar, and the legitimacy of free-market capitalism would again be called into question."[138]

The Korean War served similar economic purposes in Canada. It justified a dramatic increase in military spending, which had broad economic benefits. "Wartime [WWII] demand had inspired the first really large-scale manufacturing in Canada", explains historian Desmond Morton.[139] The Korean War helped rekindle manufacturing demand.[140]

The Korean War also strengthened Canada's ties to the US economy. A joint US-Canada industrial mobilization planning committee met two months into the war and, according to a history of Canada's role in Korea, decided "that study should be made of the basic industrial programs of the two countries and of the steps necessary to meet the production and supply requirements involved."[141]

The Korean War spurred Canada-US arms sales. "Bilateral defence economic transactions increased rapidly during the 1950s as a result of the outbreak of the Korean War and the subsequent mobilization efforts", explain Alistair Edgar and David Haglund.[142]

The fighting also increased the ties between the Canadian and American militaries. While the CF mostly fought with their traditional Commonwealth allies, for the first time Canadian troops relied on American support weapons.

Incredibly, fighting in Korea was used to justify stationing Canadian troops in Europe and rearming the colonial powers. According to Claxton, "NATO owes the fact that it was built-up to the Communist aggression in Korea … To meet the challenge of Korea required a buildup of our forces comparable to what was needed to meet our commitments to Europe."[143]

As per the Washington/Ottawa storyline, the North Korean leadership's effort to unite the country under its direction was part of a worldwide communist conspiracy. Who controlled the distant, impoverished, country was of limited import to most North Americans so US/Canadian decision makers claimed Moscow stoked the conflict to divert attention from its plan to invade Western Europe.[144] In response, thousands of Canadian troops were dispatched to France and Germany in 1951.[145] They would remain in Europe for four decades.[146]

Alongside its support for an integrated NATO force stationed throughout Europe, Ottawa armed the colonial powers as they devoted much of their military resources to suppressing independence movements. Between 1950 and 1958 Canada donated a whopping $1,526,956,000 ($8 billion today) in ammunition, fighter jets, military training, etc. to European countries through NATO's Mutual Aid Program.[147] Canadian weaponry was employed to suppress independence movements in Algeria, Kenya, Vietnam, Congo, Angola, etc.[148]

The arms donations helped Canada correct its post-WWII balance of payment deficit with the US (Canada imported more than it exported).[149] To correct the imbalance, Washington paid for Canadian produced weaponry to be delivered to the UK and elsewhere.

The Korean War legitimated a series of draconian measures targeting suspected Communists, Soviet-sympathizers and "subversives". Two months into the war the RCMP established a highly secretive espionage operation and internment plan known as PROFUNC (PROminent FUNCtionaries of the Communist Party). In 2010 CBC's Fifth Estate and Radio-Canada's Enquête aired shows on "this secret contingency plan, called PROFUNC, [which] allowed police to round up and indefinitely detain Canadians believed to be Communist sympathizers."[150] In case of a "national security" threat up to 16,000 suspected Communists and 50,000 sympathizers were to be apprehended and interned in one of eight camps across the country.

Continuing until 1983, the plan was highly detailed. Police stations across the country would receive a signal to open their PROFUNC lists and apprehend said individuals. The "Communists" would then be taken to "reception centres" where they would be restricted from talking and anyone attempting to flee would be shot. Eventually, the "Communists" would be moved to one of the regional internment camps where their contact with the outside world would be limited to a single one-page letter each week. Their children would be sent to live with other family members.[151]

Under the Emergency Powers adopted during the Korean War the government instituted Canada's first warrantless domestic wiretapping program. Code-named "Picnic", it required telephone companies to wiretap anyone deemed "likely" to communicate "for purposes that may be prejudicial to the security or defence of Canada."[152]

The secret order was signed by the PM, defence minister, justice minister and citizenship minister. It called for a five-year prison term and $10,000 ($60,000 today) fine for anyone revealing the program. Claiming extra constitutional authority, the secret order said, "nothing in any Act of the Parliament of Canada or of a legislature or in any enactment made thereunder or in any other law shall be deemed to limit or affect the operation of this Order."[153]

Supposed to expire with fighting in Korea, the wiretapping program continued until at least the 1970s. But, even 65 years later, the government refused Trent University professor Dennis Molinaro access to a key Picnic document, which was hidden in the files of Privy Council clerk Norman Robertson.[154] After Molinaro went to the CBC about the stonewalling, the government relented.

Picnic and PROFUNC were implemented amidst fear mongering over Korea, as well as the creation of NATO and the Five Eyes intelligence sharing arrangement (see below).

Seven decades after the conclusion of the Korean War that country remains divided. The belligerents have yet to sign a peace agreement and a small number of Canadian troops remain in the country. Nearly 30,000 US troops are stationed in Korea's demilitarized zone and the peninsula remains an international flashpoint.

Persian Gulf War

Along with the US, UK, France and Italy, Canada contributed significant military forces to the first Iraq war in 1990-91. Five thousand CF personnel were deployed to the Middle East.[155] Three RCN vessels were dispatched, and for a time, Commander Canadian Naval Task Group Persian Gulf War Duncan Miller oversaw 60 ships from numerous countries.[156]

Most significantly, two dozen CF-18s were deployed.[157] Among few other coalition members, Canadian fighter jets engaged in combat. CF-18 Hornets joined US and British ships in destroying most of Iraq's hundred plus naval vessels in what was dubbed the "Bubiyan Turkey Shoot."[158] Coalition bombing destroyed much of Iraq's civilian infrastructure. The country's electricity production was largely demolished as were major dams, sewage treatment plants, telecommunications equipment, port facilities, oil refineries, etc.[159] Twenty thousand Iraqi troops and thousands of civilians were killed.[160]

Initially part of a UN mandate, Canada's military operations went beyond what the UN authorized. The UN resolution allowed for attacks against Iraqi establishments in Kuwait while the US-led forces bombed across Iraq. The Canadian government was hawkish in the lead-up to the conflict. Foreign minister Joe Clark said, "the United Nations might not work, there might be veto ... if there is a veto, we in Canada are prepared to discard the United Nations and we are prepared to take unilateral action."[161] Ottawa had little time or interest in waiting for sanctions or diplomacy to solve the crisis unleashed by Iraq's invasion of Kuwait.

George H. W. Bush wanted to deepen the US foothold in the region and Ottawa was prepared to contribute. The first Gulf War was largely designed to reverse the Middle East's decolonization process, what Mark Curtis described as the open "rehabilitation of colonialism and imperialism."[162]

In between the 1991 and 2003 US-led wars on Iraq Canada helped enforce a devastating sanctions regime. To enforce sanctions, Ottawa provided a warship for most US carrier battle groups patrolling the Arabian Gulf. To aid a series of US airstrikes in 1998 *HMCS Toronto* was deployed to the Persian Gulf along with two Canadian Hercules air-to-air refueling aircraft.[163]

While Canada officially did not participate, CF leaders pushed to join the second US-led invasion of Iraq in 2003. Defence Minister Bill Graham told Janice Stein and Eugene Lang that the military "would have much preferred to go to Iraq."[164] According to the two authors of *Unexpected War*, the CF leadership sought to force the government to join Operation Iraqi Freedom through various "traps".[165] Canada did ultimately participate in the 2003 invasion.

While the Jean Chrétien government didn't do what the George W. Bush administration wanted above all else — publicly endorse the invasion by joining the "coalition of the willing" — the CF provided various forms of support to the US-led war:

At least 10 Canadian naval vessels conducted maritime interdictions, force-support and force-projection operations in the Arabian Sea between January 2002 and December 2003. These Canadian frigates usually accompanied US warships used as platforms for bombing raids in Iraq. A month before the commencement of the US invasion, Canada sent a command and control destroyer to the Persian Gulf to take charge of Taskforce 151 — the joint allied naval command. Opinion sought by the Liberal government concluded that taking command of Taskforce 151 could make Canada legally at war with Iraq.[166]

At least 30 Canadian soldiers were incorporated into US and British units that invaded Iraq. "At least one of the Canadians ... is with the British 7th Armoured Brigade, a unit now taking part in heavy fighting near Basra," reported the *Ottawa Citizen* a week after the invasion.[167] For his efforts Major Ghislain Sauvé received the Most Excellent Order of the British Empire pinned to his uniform by the Queen at Buckingham Palace. Other countries that chose not to participate in the invasion withdrew their exchange officers assigned to British and US units. No Canadian soldier was pulled from an exchange because of Iraq.

Ottawa provided three CC-130 aircraft to support the US-led war and Canadian pilots flew AWAC surveillance planes that helped guide fighter jets over Iraq.[168] In April 2008 the *Ottawa Citizen* reported, "Canadian Forces Personnel learned to operate Canada's newest military plane, the giant Boeing C-17, by training on American jets, including flying those planes into Iraq in support of the U.S. war."[169]

Much of modern air war takes place from the ground and through NORAD the CF provided logistical support to US air strikes. More generally, Canadian war planners helped mastermind the invasion from US Central Command (CENTCOM) in Tampa, Florida. When the planning centre was moved on February 11, 2003, Ottawa transferred 25 "military planners" from Tampa to the US military's forward command post in Qatar.[170] "Canada has helped to determine the whole strategy for fighting this war," noted Richard Sanders.[171]

Future head of the CF, General Walt Natynczyk helped plan the invasion from US headquarters in Kuwait and then served as deputy commander of US forces in Baghdad. Natynczyk was in charge of 35,000 troops in Iraq and Governor General Michaëlle Jean presented him with the Meritorious Service Cross for his service in the US-led mission.[172]

Canadian Brigadier-General Nicholas Matern took over as deputy commanding general of the 18th Airborne in Iraq. Matern served as deputy to US Lieutenant General Lloyd Austin III, commander of the 170,000-strong Multi National Corps-Iraq. Matern was Canada's third general to serve in the command group of Operation Iraqi Freedom. His predecessor, Major General Peter Devlin, told the *Washington Post* that the multinational element brings "greater legitimacy to the effort here in Iraq."[173]

Yugoslavia

Canada participated in NATO's 78-day war on Serbia in the spring of 1999.[174] Eighteen Canadian fighter jets dropped 530 bombs in 682 sorties — approximately 10 percent of NATO's bombing runs.[175]

Along with British, Dutch and US vessels, Canadian Auroras conducted armed patrols off Yugoslavia.[176] They gathered intelligence, intercepted ships with weaponry and reduced the flow of oil and other goods into the country.[177] Operation Sharp Guard contributed to a 33% per day inflation rate in the Yugoslav economy.[178]

About two thousand died during NATO's bombing.[179] Hundreds of thousands were internally displaced and hundreds of thousands were made refugees. The bombing damaged billions of dollars in infrastructure, including chemical plants, causing an environmental crisis.

Without UN approval, the war contravened international law. According to Osgoode Hall Law Professor Michael Mandel, "the first thing to note about NATO's war against Yugoslavia is that it was flatly illegal both in the fact that it was ever undertaken and in the way it was carried out."[180]

NATO justified its bombing of Serbia as a humanitarian intervention to save Albanian Kosovars. Three weeks into the bombing foreign minister Lloyd Axworthy said, "we cannot stand by while an entire population is displaced, people were killed, villages are burned and looted, and the population is denied its basic rights because it does not belong to the 'right' ethnic group."[181] But, contrary to the government's characterization of the campaign, NATO's bombing of Yugoslavia spurred the ethnic cleansing they claimed to be curbing. The exodus of Albanians from Kosovo began two days after NATO airstrikes commenced.[182] Scott Taylor writes, "the second objective of NATO's air campaign had been the prevention of a humanitarian crisis in Kosovo. In fact, the bombing had triggered a Serbian offensive and a massive exodus of Albanians. In a deft manoeuvre, NATO spin doctors then proclaimed that their air attacks were now necessary to halt a humanitarian crisis."[183]

One of the few scholarly studies that tried to quantify and analyze those killed in Kosovo in the year before the bombing found that Serbs were to blame for 500 of 2,000 killed.[184] Robert Hayden, director of the Center for Russian and East European studies at the University of

Pittsburgh, noted that "the casualties among Serb civilians in the first three weeks of the war were higher than all of the casualties on both sides in Kosovo in the three months that led up to this war, and yet those three months were supposed to be a humanitarian catastrophe."[185]

While NATO leaders claimed humanitarian motives for bombing Serbia, their actions were largely driven by geopolitical and economic considerations. One objective of the war was to expand NATO to the frontiers of the former Soviet Union. Additionally, US and German leaders were frustrated with Yugoslavia's failure to follow foreign imposed economic and political changes. "It was Yugoslavia's resistance to the broader trends of political and economic reform — not the plight of Kosovar Albanians — that best explains NATO's war," wrote John Norris, assistant to Strobe Talbott, the US official responsible for diplomacy during the war and who wrote a glowing introduction to Norris's book.

Afghanistan

"We are going to Afghanistan to actually take down the folks that are trying to blow up men and women ... we're not the public service of Canada, we're not just another department. We are the Canadian Forces, and our job is to be able to kill people."

Rick Hillier, Chief of the Defence Staff[186]

More than 40,000 Canadian troops fought in Afghanistan between 2001 and 2014.[187] Canada spent $20 billion on the military operations and related aid mission in Afghanistan.[188] While the stated rationale of the war was to neutralize al-Qaeda members and topple the Taliban regime, two decades after the US-led invasion the Taliban remained a major actor in the country and Jihadist groups' influence increased. As this book goes to press it appears the Taliban may once again take control of the country.

In 2019 the *Washington Post* published internal documents suggesting top US military and government officials had long considered the war in Afghanistan unwinnable. The "Afghan Papers" also demonstrate their ignorance of Afghanistan and constant lying.

In October 2001 the US unilaterally invaded Afghanistan, launching air strikes in support of Northern Alliance rebels fighting the Taliban government. As mentioned earlier Canada's JTF2 aided these efforts.

Portrayed as a battle against the misogynist Taliban, the foreign intervention benefited an equally unsavory assortment of warlords, who previously imposed the veil and banned education for women as well as destroying schools, museums and cinema halls. Individuals responsible for massive human rights violations during Afghanistan's mid-1990s civil war were appointed to prominent government positions.

Some in the CF sympathized with the Afghan warlords. In March 2006 *Maclean's* reported on General Rick Hillier's "enormous respect for the warlords — even making allowances for those who profit from the poppy business."[189] The magazine quoted the chief of the defence staff saying, "I saw the finest leaders that I have ever had the opportunity to meet. They beat the Russians pretty fairly and squarely, at the end of the day they were responsible for thumping the Taliban and throwing them out, along with a significant number of Al-Qaeda folks."[190] The CF purchased millions of dollars in goods and services from companies run by former warlords.

At the peak over 3,000 Canadians fought a violent counterinsurgency in Kandahar. Between April 2006 and December 2007 Canadian troops fired an astounding 4.7 million bullets, including over 1,650 tank shells and 12,000 artillery rounds.[191] In *A Line in the Sand: Canadians at War in Kandahar* Captain Ray Wiss praised Canadian troops as "the best at killing people … We are killing a lot more of them than they are of us, and we have been extraordinarily successful recently… For the past week, we have managed to kill between 10 and 20 Taliban every day."[192] In September 2006 the CF spearheaded NATO's Operation Medusa aimed at Taliban strongholds in the Panjwaii and Zhari districts of Kandahar. This is how Corporal

Ryan Pagnacco described the airstrikes: "After watching bomb after bomb drop on these targets, I wondered how anything could survive. I figured that when we went in, we'd be walking into a ghost town."[193] The Medusa offensive forced 80,000 civilians to flee their homes, resulted in hundreds of enemy combatant deaths and "at least 50 civilians were killed over several weeks of bombing."[194]

On numerous occasions the western press reported on Canadian troops killing Afghan civilians. "Canadian soldiers have repeatedly killed and wounded civilians while on patrol in civilian areas," noted the *New York Times* in May 2007.[195] In July 2008 Canadian soldiers killed a five-year-old girl and her two-year-old brother after their vehicle got too close to a convoy. The father said afterwards that "if I get a chance, I will kill Canadians."[196] (Because of an agreement between Kabul and Ottawa, Afghans had no legal right for compensation if they were hurt or their property damaged by Canadian soldiers.)

Canadian armoured vehicles regularly fired warning shots at bikes, cars or trucks that got too close, often causing crashes, leaving Afghans injured or worse. In June 2006 France 2 TV showed unedited images of Canadian soldiers searching villages and houses, breaking down doors and interrogating residents. According to a report in *La Presse*, Canadian soldiers were shown telling villagers that it was not smart to join the Taliban because our soldiers are really good, they are well trained and good shots "and you will die". Later, the video shows a Canadian commander saying "too bad for you if you don't want to tell us where the Taliban are hiding. We will come and kill them. We will drop many bombs and fire all over. Is this what you want? Well then continue telling us nothing."[197]

Canadian troops' actions in Afghanistan belie claims of high-minded motives. The CF used white phosphorus as a weapon against "enemy-occupied" vineyards in Afghanistan while Canadian special forces participated in highly unpopular night-time assassination raids.[198]

The most-deadly element of the war was airstrikes. While no Canadian planes dropped bombs in Afghanistan, Canadian troops regularly called in US air strikes.[199] Canadian personnel also operated the NORAD systems that supported US bombing and some heavily-armed Canadian helicopters launched nighttime operations.[200]

Most of the individuals detained by Canadians — and turned over to the Afghan army and prison system — were likely tortured. Under the Geneva Conventions the military force that detains someone is responsible for their treatment and many of those detained by the CF were likely tortured with knives, power cables and open flames. Or raped. The second highest-ranked member of Canada's diplomatic service in Afghanistan from 2006 to 2007, Richard Colvin, reported to a parliamentary committee that "the likelihood is that all the Afghans we handed over were tortured."[201] Additionally, dozens of individuals given to the Afghan army by the CF were unaccounted for, perhaps lost in a prison system that did not keep good records or maybe killed.[202]

Many of those detained by the CF had little to do with the Taliban. According to Colvin, "it was the NDS (Afghan National Directorate of Security) that told us that many or most of our detainees were unconnected to the insurgency ... We detained and handed over for severe torture a lot of innocent people."[203]

The CF regularly handed over children they suspected of Taliban ties to the NDS, which often tortured them. The *Toronto Star* reported that in late 2006 a Canadian soldier heard an Afghan soldier raping a young boy and later saw the boy's "lower intestines falling out of his body."[204] Reportedly, the Canadian military police were told by their commanders not to interfere when Afghan soldiers and police sexually abused children.[205]

Despite attempts to portray the situation otherwise, the invasion of Afghanistan did not have UN approval. After the US invaded, the Security Council was pressured to authorize the use of force to defend the installed Afghan government. Non-American foreign troops in Afghanistan were effectively under US command.

Libya

The CF played an important part in the coalition that waged war on Libya from March to October 2011. Seven CF-18 fighter jets participated, two Canadian naval vessels patrolled the Libyan coast and Canadian special forces were likely on the ground.

Canadian General Charles Bouchard commanded the entire NATO operation. He "personally signed off on every last preselected [bombing] target," according to the *Globe and Mail*.[206]

Bouchard took a belligerent tone. When Italy called for a ceasefire to deliver aid three months into the war, the Canadian commander dismissed it out of hand. "We must continue to stay engaged to prevent that rearming and reinforcement from taking place", Bouchard declared. "Gaddafi is hiding in hospitals, hiding in mosques, he's hiding under various covers everywhere."[207]

The Italians were partly concerned about the growing number of civilian casualties. Two days before foreign minister Franco Frattini called for a cease-fire as many as 19 Libyans, including eight children, were reportedly killed by a coalition strike at the home of a top Gaddafi official 70 km west of Tripoli.[208] A day earlier NATO admitted they hit a house in Tripoli, killing a number of civilians.

The RCAF was responsible for a significant share of coalition bombing. Only the US, France, Britain and Italy contributed more to the air war. Other coalition members frequently "red carded" sorties, declaring they would not contribute. "With a Canadian general in charge," explained the *Globe and Mail*, "Canada couldn't have red-carded missions even if it wanted to, which is why Canadian CF-18 pilots often found themselves in the most dangerous skies", doing the dirtiest work.[209]

CBC reported, "[Major Yves] Leblanc's crew carried out the final mission on the day Gaddafi was captured, and were flying 25,000 feet over when Gaddafi's convoy was attacked."[210] Human Rights Watch found the remains of at least 95 people at the site where Muammar Gaddafi was captured. According to the human rights group, "the vast majority had apparently died in the fighting and NATO strikes prior to Gaddafi's capture" with another six to ten apparently executed by close range gunshot wounds.[211] Some accused NATO forces of helping to murder Gaddafi.

Seven CF-18s dropped at least 700 bombs on Libyan targets.[212] Two months into the bombing United Press International reported that Ottawa "ordered 1,300 replacement laser-guided bombs to use in its NATO mission in Libya" and a month later they ordered another 1,000 bomb kits.[213]

Two Canadian CP-140 Aurora spy planes, with multi-million dollar sensors, participated in the war. They intercepted Libyan communications and waged psychological war, dropping anti-Gaddafi leaflets and broadcasting critical radio transmissions, which the Libyan government tried to jam. According to the Canadian Press, "Canadian CP-140 Aurora surveillance planes recently started broadcasting propaganda messages aimed at forces loyal to Libyan strongman Muammar Gaddafi."[214]

From high in the sky to the country's coastal plains, the CF engaged in combat. Two RCN vessels enforced a naval blockade of Libya. They helped destroy Libyan naval vessels and kept open the port at Misrata for anti-Gaddafi forces.[215]

In contravention of the UN Security Council resolution authorizing a no-fly zone to protect Libyan civilians, Canadian special forces were on the ground. Among a series of similar reports, three weeks after Tripoli fell Canada's state broadcaster reported, "CBC News has learned there are members of the Canadian Forces on the ground in Libya."[216]

Gaddafi's repeated ceasefire offers were rejected or ignored by the rebels' National Transitional Council (NTC). An African Union ceasefire was immediately rejected by the NTC, which demanded Gaddafi resign as a condition for a ceasefire.[217] Briefing notes uncovered by the *Ottawa Citizen* show that foreign minister John Baird pushed the NTC to keep fighting when he visited Benghazi in June 2011. In public he called for an end to the fighting, but in private Baird "impressed upon the National Transitional Council the importance of pushing forward militarily."[218]

The NATO-backed rebels were responsible for significant human rights violations. Amnesty reported, "black Libyans and sub-Saharan Africans are at high risk of abuse by anti-Gaddafi forces."[219] A largely Black town just outside of Misrata was entirely emptied of its 30,000 residents by the rebels.[220]

To justify NATO's intervention, the rebels accused Gaddafi's forces of mass rape, using mercenaries to repress the population and firing on civilians from helicopters and fighter jets. While Gaddafi's forces were responsible for substantial violence early in the uprising, Amnesty International, Human Rights Watch and the International Crisis Group concluded the rape, mercenaries and air fire claims were probably war propaganda.[221]

Begun under the pretext of saving civilians from Gaddafi's terror, the real aim of the war was regime change. The UN "no-fly zone" immediately became a license to bomb Libyan tanks, government installations and other targets in coordination with rebel attacks. NATO also bombed Gaddafi's compound and the houses of those close to him. The military alliance defined "effective protection" of civilians as per UNSCR 1973, noted Hugh Roberts, as "requir[ing] the elimination of the threat, which was Gaddafi himself for as long as he was in power (subsequently revised to 'for as long as he is in Libya' before finally becoming 'for as long as he is alive')."[222]

It's clear from the length of the war, as well as a number of major pro-government demonstrations, that Gaddafi enjoyed substantial support (as did the NTC in parts of the country). Even with NATO's support it took the NTC five months to take Tripoli. Once the capital was lost, Gaddafi's forces hung on for another month in Bani Walid and then a further month in Sirte.

The human toll of NATO's war was significant. The alliance dropped 20,000 bombs on almost 6,000 targets, including more than

400 government buildings or command centres.[223] Dozens, probably hundreds, of civilians were killed in the strikes.[224] NATO erroneously classified some civilian sites they struck as military targets.[225]

Gaddafi's final stronghold, Sirte, was the site of widespread war crimes. Under siege by NATO fighter jets, this city of 100,000 was cut off from outside water, medicine, food and electricity supplies for weeks. After they captured the city the rebels executed hundreds. CBS News reported, "nearly 300 bodies, many of them with their hands tied behind their backs and shot in the head, have been collected from across Sirte and buried in a mass grave. ... There are no names in one graveyard, only numbers: 572 so far and counting."[226]

The outside intervention likely extended fighting between Gaddafi's forces and the rebels. And since Gaddafi's death thousands, probably tens of thousands, have died in fighting. A decade after the foreign-backed war Libya remained divided between two main political factions and hundreds of militias operated in the country of six million.

The instability did not surprise Canadian military and political leaders who orchestrated the war. Eight days before Canadian fighter jets began dropping bombs on Libya, military intelligence officers reported the country would likely descend into a lengthy civil war if foreign countries assisted rebels opposed to Gaddafi. An internal assessment obtained by the *Ottawa Citizen* noted, "there is the increasing possibility that the situation in Libya will transform into a long-term tribal/civil war ... This is particularly probable if opposition forces received military assistance from foreign militaries."[227]

A year and a half before the war a Canadian intelligence report described eastern Libya as an "epicentre of Islamist extremism" and said "extremist cells" operated in the anti-Gaddafi stronghold. In fact, during the bombing, notes *Ottawa Citizen* military reporter David Pugliese, RCAF members privately joked they were part of "al-Qaida's air force".[228] Lo and behold hardline jihadists were the major beneficiaries of the war, taking control of significant portions of the country.

Haiti

On February 29, 2004, JTF2 commandos took control of the airport from which Haitian President Jean-Bertrand Aristide was bundled ("kidnapped" in his words) onto a plane by US Marines in the middle of the night and deposited in the Central African Republic.[229] Members of the elite force reportedly arrived in Port-au-Prince four or five days earlier ostensibly to protect Canada's Embassy and "secure key locations" in the capital.[230] According to the military's account of Operation PRINCIPAL, "more than 100 CF personnel and four CC-130 Hercules aircraft ... assisted with emergency contingency plans and security measures" during the week before the coup.[231]

For the five months after Aristide was ousted 500 Canadian soldiers joined US and French forces in protecting Haiti's foreign installed regime. A resident of Florida during the preceding 15 years, Gérard Latortue was responsible for substantial human rights violations. There is evidence the CF participated directly in repressing the pro-democracy movement. A researcher who published a report on post-coup violence in Haiti with the *Lancet* medical journal recounted an interview with one family in the Delmas district of Port- au-Prince: "Canadian troops came to their house, and they said they were looking for Lavalas [Aristide's party] chimeres, and threatened to kill the head of household, who was the father, if he didn't name names of people in their neighbourhood who were Lavalas chimeres or Lavalas supporters."[232] Haiti and Afghanistan were the only foreign countries cited in the CF's 2007 draft counterinsurgency manual as places where Canadian troops participated in counterinsurgency warfare. According to the manual, the CF had been "conducting COIN [counter-insurgency] operations against the criminally-based insurgency in Haiti since early 2004."[233]

After a deadly earthquake rocked Haiti in 2010 two thousand Canadian troops were deployed while several Heavy Urban Search Rescue Teams were readied but never sent. According to an internal file, Canadian officials worried that "political fragility has increased the risks of a popular uprising, and has fed the rumor that ex-president Jean-Bertrand Aristide, currently in exile in South Africa, wants to organize a return to power."²³⁴ The government documents also explain the importance of strengthening the Haitian authorities' ability "to contain the risks of a popular uprising." To police Haiti's traumatized and suffering population 2,050 Canadian troops were deployed alongside 12,000 US soldiers and 1,500 UN troops (8,000 UN soldiers were already there). Even though there was no war, for a period there were more foreign troops in Haiti per square kilometer than in Afghanistan or Iraq (and about as many per capita).

Congo

The CF played a significant role in the ouster of Congolese independence leader Patrice Lumumba. To undermine the elected prime minister the former colonial power Belgium backed a secessionist movement, a coup and Lumumba's assassination. During this time Canada was a willing partner in Belgian/US policy and actions.

Between 1960 and 1964 nearly 2,000 Canadian troops served in the *Organisation des Nations Unies au Congo* (ONUC) despite Congolese authorities' reservations about their participation. For a time, Canadian Brigadier General Jacques Dextraze was chief of staff for the UN mission and there were nearly always more Canadian officers at ONUC headquarters than those of any other nationality.²³⁵ Canadian troops within the UN force were also concentrated in militarily important logistical positions, including chief operations officer and chief signals officer. Describing the mission, David Bercuson and Jack Granatstein wrote: "At headquarters, which operated in both French and English when sufficient bilingual officers could be found, the Canadians handled everything from telephones ... to dispatch riders. Indeed, to read Canadian messages to Ottawa, it often seemed as if Canadians were running everything."²³⁶

Canada's strategic role wasn't simply by chance. Ottawa pushed to have Canada's intelligence gathering signals detachments oversee

UN intelligence and for Colonel Jean Berthiaume to remain at UN headquarters to "maintain both Canadian and Western influence."[237] (A report from the Canadian Directorate of Military Intelligence noted, "Lumumba's immediate advisers ... have referred to Lt. Col. Berthiaume as an 'imperialist tool'."[238])

Lumumba expressed a desire for "considerations of nationality and race" in the UN force, which was ignored by Canadian officials who were themselves quite race conscious. According to internal files unearthed by Wilfrid Laurier professor Kevin Spooner, military officers were concerned about Canadian troops living with "the native troops serving under United Nations." They did not, however, want to be "accused of refusing to quarter Canadian soldiers with coloured soldiers." Army officials insisted that "it would not be a matter of a colour bar so much as not wishing to quarter our troops with foreign troops who speak a different language whose customs may be widely different from our own."[239]

While Washington and UN officials pressed Lumumba to request a UN force to quell social disturbances in Kinshasa, Lumumba ultimately asked for an international force to halt a rebellion in the east of the country. Twelve days after independence the resource rich eastern province of Katanga declared independence and immediately Belgian company Union Minière began paying tax to the secessionist government rather than the proper legal authority in Kinshasa. That payment totaled 70% of Katanga's entire budget.[240]

While Lumumba never openly argued that Canadian soldiers were undesirable, Soviet officials did. Prior to their deployment the Soviet Union's ambassador to the UN, Vasily Kuznetzov, explained: "Canada is a member of the NATO military block which also includes Belgium which has committed an aggression against the independent Congo. In these conditions the dispatch of Canadian troops, or of troops of any other state belonging to a military bloc of which Belgium is a member, would constitute nothing but assistance to the aggressor from his military ally."[241]

Canadian archives suggest Moscow's criticism wasn't far from the mark. In a private exchange, external minister Howard Green told the Belgian ambassador that Ottawa "would do all [it] could [through its role in ONUC] to avoid making the situation more difficult for the Belgian government."[242] In *A Role for Canada in an African Crisis* Daniel Galvin explains how Ottawa "shaped policy in a manner that offered some support for Belgian actions. They were consistently concerned with the impact of Canadian policy on their [NATO] ally."[243]

Ottawa promoted ONUC and UN Secretary General Dag Hammarskjold's controversial anti-Lumumba position. Ottawa supported Hammarskjold even as he sided with the Belgian-backed secessionists against the central government.[244]

The UN head also worked to undermine Lumumba within the central government. When President Joseph Kasavubu dismissed Lumumba as prime minister — a move of debatable legality and opposed by the vast majority of the country's parliament — Hammarskjold publicly endorsed the dismissal of a politician who months earlier had received the most votes in the country's election.[245]

When Lumumba attempted to respond to his dismissal with a nationwide broadcast, UN forces blocked him from accessing the main radio station. ONUC undermined Lumumba in other ways as well. Through their control of the airport ONUC prevented his forces from flying into the capital from other parts of the country and closed the airport to Soviet weapons and transportation equipment when Lumumba turned to Russia for assistance.

After Lumumba escaped house arrest and fled Leopoldville for his power base in the Eastern Orientale province, Colonel Jean Berthiaume assisted Lumumba's political enemies in capturing him. The UN chief of staff, who was kept in place by Ottawa, tracked the deposed prime minister and informed Joseph Mobutu of Lumumba's whereabouts. Three decades later the Saint-Hyacinthe, Québec, born Berthiaume told an interviewer: "I called Mobutu. I said, 'Colonel, you have a problem, you were trying to retrieve your prisoner, Mr. Lumumba. I know where he is, and I know where he will be tomorrow. He said, what do I do? It's simple, Colonel, with the help of the UN you have just created the core of your para commandos — we have just trained 30 of these guys — highly selected Moroccans trained as paratroopers. They all jumped — no one refused. To be on the safe side, I put our [Canadian] captain, Mario Coté, in the plane, to make sure there was no underhandedness. In any case, it's simple, you take a Dakota [plane], send your paratroopers and arrest Lumumba in that small village — there is a runway and all that is needed. That's all you'll need to do, Colonel. He arrested him, like that, and I never regretted it."[246]

Not long after Mobutu's forces captured Lumumba, he was executed by firing squad and his body was dissolved in acid. Canadian officials celebrated ONUC's role in Lumumba's overthrow.[247]

Dictator for the next three decades, Mobutu developed close ties to Canadian military officials. In the *Eye of the Storm: A History of Canadian Peacekeeping*, Fred Gaffen explains: "Mobutu learned to trust the Canadian officers. This trust was of inestimable value in arranging ceasefires between Congolese and UN forces, negotiating the release of prisoners as well as liaising between UN and Congolese authorities. Mobutu, who became president of the Democratic Republic of Zaire, visited Canada in May of 1964. At that time, he thanked those Canadian officers who had contributed so much to the maintenance of the unity of the country."

UN 'Peacekeeping' Missions

Popularly viewed as a benevolent form of intervention, peacekeeping missions have generally been motivated by broader geopolitical interests. Maintaining the seven-year-old NATO alliance was external minister Lester Pearson's priority when he pushed to intervene in Egypt. After Britain, France and Israel invaded in 1956, Ottawa was primarily concerned with disagreement between the US and the UK over the intervention, not Egyptian sovereignty or the plight of that country's people.

While peacekeeping was generally motivated by larger geopolitical objectives, the large missions in Egypt and Cyprus proved generally positive. But this has often not been the case, as the deployments to Korea (1950), Congo (1960) and Haiti (2004) illustrate.

Most often peacekeeping was Canada's contribution to the Cold War. Sean Maloney explains, "during the Cold War, the United States, the United Kingdom and France, all permanent members of the Security Council, remained aloof in several difficult circumstances as a sort of plausible deniability. Canada was the West's champion in the Cold War U.N. arena."[248]

Contrary to popular understanding, Canadian internationalism has rarely been at odds with US belligerence. Senior security analyst in the Privy Council Office, Peter Jones noted, "we were often involved in peacekeeping missions precisely because we were a charter member of the Western club, rather than in spite of it."[249]

The CF was divided over peacekeeping. From the 1960s until the early 2000s many in the military saw engaging in and promoting peacekeeping as the best way to convince the public to support military expenditures and the CF in general.[250] With Canadians backing the idea of "peacekeeping", some in the CF promoted the idea that a strong force was needed to participate in UN missions.[251]

***

Only one of the wars mentioned above could be described as morally justified. None were fought primarily on behalf of the interests of ordinary people, although the defeat of Hitler's fascism meant that WWII had a good result.

Given that the primary purpose of the military is to fights wars, and that almost every war in human history has been motivated by the interests of the rich and powerful, pacificism seems to make sense for the vast majority. But militarism and war have other negative consequences, even though some of these are presented as beneficial. The next chapters are about some of what accompanies the use of military force.

7. Winning Hearts and Minds

As long as there has been war, the use of force has never been the sole means to conquer people. Once the battles concluded the victors used various strategies to "win the peace". Sometimes severe repression was employed against conquered people; sometimes the victors bought off the old ruling class and they became agents of the conquerors; sometimes a combination of the carrot and stick were used. Many of history's best known "military geniuses" were not only adept at fighting battles, but also at shaping the peace that followed war. Successful armies have long focused on both winning battles and keeping the peace.

The British military, from which the CF came, were experts at maintaining an empire that spanned the globe. The US armed forces, with which the CF is close, employs thousands of experts in "winning the hearts and minds" of people they conquer. Of course the CF does much more than equip, train and direct soldiers to engage in battle.

Aid

Military intervention elicits Canadian aid. Call it the 'intervention-equals-aid' principle or 'wherever Canadian troops kill Ottawa provides aid' principle.

Ottawa delivered $7.25 million to South Korea during the Korean War.[1] During the 1990-91 Iraq war Canada provided $75 million in assistance to people in countries affected by the Gulf crisis.[2] In 1999-2000 the former Yugoslavia was the top recipient of Canadian assistance.[3] Hundreds of millions of dollars flowed into Haiti after Canadian troops helped overthrow the country's elected government in 2004. In the years after the invasions, Afghanistan and Haiti were the top recipients of Canadian "aid". A sizable proportion of the $2 billion in "aid" Canada spent in Afghanistan was a public relations exercise to justify the war.[4]

CF personnel repeatedly linked development work in Afghanistan to the counterinsurgency effort. "It's a useful counterinsurgency tool," is how Lieutenant-Colonel Tom Doucette, commander of Canada's provincial reconstruction team, described the Canadian International Development Agency's work in Afghanistan.[5] Development assistance, for instance, was sometimes given to communities in exchange for information on combatants. After a roadside bomb hit his convoy in September 2009, Canadian General Jonathan Vance spent 50 minutes berating village elders for not preventing the attack. "If we keep blowing up on the roads," he told them "I'm going to stop doing development."[6]

According to the government's 2005 International Policy Statement, "the image that captures today's operational environment for the Canadian Forces" is the "three-block war", which includes a reconstruction role for NGOs.[7] On the third and final block of "three-block warfare" troops work alongside NGOs and civilians to fix what has been destroyed. (The first block consists of combat while the second block involves stabilization operations.)

The CF worked closely with NGOs in Afghanistan. A 2007 parliamentary report explained that some NGOs "work intimately with military support already in the field."[8] Another government report noted that the "Civil-Military Cooperation (CIMIC) platoon made up of Army Reserve soldiers organizes meetings with local decision-makers and international NGOs to determine whether they need help with security."[9]

Some international training and weapon deliveries are labelled "aid". Millions of "aid" dollars are spent on military training missions in other countries such as the Ukraine and Iraq.[10] The CF's Military Training and Cooperation Program had a $15-million budget.[11] In *Security Aid: Canada and the Development Regime of Security* Jeffrey Monaghan lists millions of dollars in different DND projects.[12]

Radio Canada International highlighted an example with a tender notice posted on the government's Buyandsell.gc.ca website in 2017 for 1.2 million cartridges for "AK-47 type weapons".[13] But, the CF doesn't use this gun. The ammunition was for troops in Niger being trained as part of the Counter-Terrorism Capacity Building program, which "provides training, funding, equipment, technical and legal assistance to other states to enable them to prevent and respond to terrorist activity."[14]

Training

Training other countries' militaries is a way to develop and extend influence. Over 1,000 personnel from dozens of southern countries train in Canada every year through the Military Training Assistance Program.[15]

Canadian officials generally tell the media the aim of training other militaries is to help fight terror or the illicit drug trade but a closer look at military doctrine suggests broader strategic and geopolitical motivations. An important objective is to strengthen foreign militaries' capacity to operate in tandem with Canadian and/or NATO forces. According to Canada's Military Training Assistance Program (MTAP), its "language training improves communication between NATO and other armed forces" and its "professional development and staff training enhances other countries compatibility with the CF."[16] At a broader level MTAP states its training "serves to achieve influence in areas of strategic interest to Canada. ... Canadian diplomatic and military representatives find it considerably easier to gain access and exert influence in countries with a core group of Canadian-trained professional military leaders."[17]

When Canada initiated post-independence military training missions in Africa a memo to cabinet ministers described the political value of training foreign military officers. It stated: "Military leaders in many developing countries, if they do not actually form the government, frequently wield much more power and influence domestically than is the case in the majority of western domestic nations ... [It] would seem in Canada's general interest on broad foreign policy grounds to keep open the possibility of exercising a constructive influence on the men who often will form the political elite in developing countries, by continuing to provide training places for officers in our military institutions where they receive not only technical military training but are also exposed to Canadian values and attitudes."[18]

In 1966 Ghana's Canadian-trained army overthrew Kwame Nkrumah, a leading pan Africanist president. After Nkrumah's removal the Canadian high commissioner boasted about the effectiveness of Canada's junior staff officers training program. Writing to the undersecretary of external affairs, C. E. McGaughey noted, "all the chief participants of the coup were graduates of this course."[19] (Canadian major Bob Edwards, who was a training advisor to the commander of a Ghanaian infantry brigade, discovered preparations for the coup the day before its execution, but said nothing.[20])

After Ghana won its independence the CF organized and oversaw a junior staff officers course and took up a number of top positions in the Ghanaian Ministry of Defence. In the words of Canada's military attaché to Ghana, Colonel Desmond Deane-Freeman, the Canadians in these positions imparted "our way of thinking".[21] Celebrating the influence of "our way of thinking", High Commissioner McGaughey wrote the undersecretary of external affairs in 1965 that "since independence, it [Ghana's military] has changed in outlook, perhaps less than any other institution. It is still equipped with Western arms and although essentially non-political, is Western oriented."[22]

Not everyone was happy with the military's attitude or Canada's military, diplomatic and economic support for Nkrumah's ouster. A year after Nkrumah's ouster McGaughey wrote Ottawa, "for some African and Asian diplomats stationed in Accra, I gather that there is a tendency to identify our aid policies particularly where military assistance is concerned with the aims of American and British policies. American and British objectives are unfortunately not regarded by such observers as being above criticism or suspicion."[23] Thomas Howell and Jeffrey Rajasooria echo the high commissioner's assessment in *Ghana and Nkrumah*: "Members of the ruling CPP tended to identify Canadian aid policies, especially in defence areas, with the aims of the U.S. and Britain. Opponents of the Canadian military program went so far as to create a countervailing force in the form of the Soviet equipped, pro-communist President's Own Guard Regiment [POGR]. The coup on 24 February 1966 that ousted Kwame Nkrumah and the CPP was partially rooted in this divergence of military loyalty."[24]

Canadian troops trained a Palestinian security force that served as an arm of Israel's occupation. Part of the US security coordinator office in Jerusalem, dozens of Canadian troops were based in the West Bank as part of Operation Proteus between 2007 and 2021.[25] In a 2010 interview with the *Jerusalem Post*, minister of state for foreign affairs Peter Kent said Operation Proteus was Canada's "second largest deployment after Afghanistan" and it received "most of the money" from a five-year $300 million Canadian aid program to the Palestinian Authority (PA).[26]

In *Security Aid: Canada and the Development Regime of Security* Jeffrey Monaghan details Canada's role in turning Palestinian security forces in the West Bank into an effective arm of Israel's occupation. Monaghan describes a $1.5 million Canadian contribution to Joint Operating Centers whose "main focus ... is to integrate elements of the Palestinian Authority Security Forces into Israeli command."[27]

Like all colonial authorities throughout history Israel looked to compliant locals to take up the occupation's security burden. What is unique about the training and support for the PA security forces is the role of Canadian, British and US trainers. Adam Shatz writes, "it is an extraordinary arrangement: the security forces of a country under occupation are being subcontracted by third parties outside the region to prevent resistance to the occupying power, even as that power continues to grab more land."[28]

A heavily censored 2012 note Postmedia unearthed through an access to information request suggests the goal of Canadian security aid to the PA was designed to protect a corrupt Mahmoud Abbas, whose electoral mandate expired in 2009, from popular backlash. Canadian International Development Agency president Margaret Biggs explained, "the emergence of popular protests on the Palestinian street against the Palestinian Authority is worrying and the Israelis have been imploring the international donor community to continue to support the Palestinian Authority."[29] On numerous occasions the PA security forces, which were vetted by Israel's internal Shin-Bet intelligence agency, disrupted demonstrations in the West Bank against Israel's brutal assaults on Gaza.[30]

After the 2003 invasion Canadian troops trained Iraq's US-led military. High-level Canadian military personnel joined the NATO Training Mission in Iraq to "train the trainers" of Iraq's military. A Canadian colonel, under NATO command, was chief of staff at the Baghdad-based training mission and Ottawa's initial $810,000 was the largest donation to this training centre.[31]

Canadian training in Afghanistan directly enabled the US war effort. A 2012 *Ottawa Citizen* headline explained, "Canadian training mission meant to free up US soldiers for Afghan combat: documents." According to briefing notes prepared for Governor General David Johnston's December 2011 visit to Afghanistan, 950 Canadian soldiers were deployed to Kabul and other Afghan cities to "free up American forces to move to a [more aggressive] combat role."[32]

There are numerous other highly politicized examples of trainings. For example, after the Honduran military overthrew the country's elected president in 2009, a small number of the Central American country's troops continued to train in Canada.[33] During its late 1990s war with anti-monarchist guerrillas JTF2 helped train the Royal Nepalese Army in counterinsurgency techniques. *Ottawa Citizen* journalist Pugliese writes, "the RNA wanted Canadian military advisers to oversee its counterterrorism plans and suggest how best to fight the Communist guerrillas."[34] Eventually, the Maoists forced Nepal's 200-year-old monarchy to be disbanded and won a series of elections. Amidst a decades-long war with the New People's Army, battles with

Muslim groups and hundreds of political assassinations, the CF trained Filipino military personnel. In the early 2000s a small number trained in Canada and CF personnel went to the Philippines in 2008 to train the country's special forces.[35] Since 2014 over 1,000 Canadians troops (a rotation of 200 every six months) deployed to the Ukraine to train a force that included the best-organized neo-Nazis in the world.[36] Far right militia members were part of the force fighting Russian-aligned groups in eastern Ukraine.[37] Canada's military attaché in Kiev, Colonel Brian Irwin, met privately with officers from the Azov battalion, who use the Nazi "Wolfsangel" symbol and praise officials who helped slaughter Poles and Jews during WWII.[38]

Training programs expand Canadian influence by bolstering allies, as well as developing connections and knowledge. For similar reasons, Canadian soldiers regularly participate in international exchanges through OUTCAN ("Outside of Canada"). Hundreds of DND personnel are also based at the NATO, UN and NORAD headquarters as part of the initiative.[39]

Through OUTCAN, defence attachés are based in 30 Canadian diplomatic posts around the world (with cross-accreditation to neighboring countries). These Colonels, supported by sergeants and sometimes a second officer, "help develop a more sophisticated and nuanced understanding of the perspectives and motivations of global actors, and of regional security dynamics."[40]

In addition to the above-mentioned OUTCAN deployments, 2,000 Canadian troops were sprinkled across the globe as part of more than 20 international missions in 2021.[41] This figure didn't count the hundreds of naval personnel patrolling hotspots across the globe.

CF leaders commonly prioritize their international ties over human rights and democracy. In December 2019 Global News revealed that DND intervened with immigration authorities on behalf of retired Egyptian General Khaled Saber Abdelhamed Zahw. A "high-ranking" member of the military that overthrew elected President Mohamed Morsi in 2013, Zahw was deemed "inadmissible" by the

Canada Border Services Agency presumably on human rights grounds. In response, DND Assistant Deputy Minister for Policy Gordon Venner wrote Immigration, Refugees and Citizenship Canada: "It is in our interest to maintain constructive relations with members of the Egyptian military as these relationships enable execution of Canadian Armed Forces operations in the region, most notably Operation CALUMET. ... It is for this reason we would request that [Zahw] and his spouse be issued the appropriate visas."[42] To avoid upsetting Canada–Egyptian military relations Zahw and his wife were issued special visas to enter Canada.

***

Canada's vast terrain and sophisticated facilities have aided US, British and other countries' forces. According to retired RCAF General and Chief of Defence Staff Tom Lawson, "the training that has taken place over the last 40 years at Cold Lake has been excellent in support of wars that took place over Iraq in the 1990s and 2000s, over Serbia during the Kosovo conflict, and even more recently during Libya"[43]

During WWII tens of thousands of British, US, Belgian and French were trained in Canada to pilot and administer aircraft. Tens of thousands of non-Canadians were part of the WWII British Commonwealth Air Training Plan.[44]

Established a few years later, the NATO Air Training Plan trained 5,500 pilots and navigators from ten NATO countries.[45] In the 1950s and 60s RCAF-trained airmen (often armed with Canadian weaponry) likely participated in the murderous suppression of Algerian, Cameroonian, Congolese and Kenyan independence movements.[46]

NATO's Flying Training in Canada (NFTC) trained pilots from Saudi Arabia and UAE in the lead-up and during the war in Yemen that began in 2015.[47] Run by the CF and CAE, the world's largest annual tactical fighter exercise takes place at the Cold Lake Air Weapons Range that straddles the Alberta/Saskatchewan border.[48] US, British and other NATO members participate in the four-week Maple Flag training, which takes place over a heavily forested one million hectare area.[49] Israeli pilots, some of whom likely bombed Gaza and Lebanon, have participated in Maple Flag.[50] Amidst US bombing of Southeast Asia in the 1970s US B-52 bombers practised bombing runs at Cold Lake.[51]

***

While many Canadians might think cooperation and training of friendly countries' military is perfectly acceptable, and that Canada is not responsible for any harm they may do, most would be troubled to learn of this country's involvement in training and research into weapons of mass destruction. That is the subject of the next chapter.

8. In the Shadows

CANADA'S LARGE LANDMASS and many facilities have been used to test various weapons, including chemical and biological weapons. In his 2006 book *Just Dummies: Cruise Missile Testing in Canada* John Clearwater writes, "the United States military tests weapons in Canada and it has done so for fifty years. ... No matter how bizarre the weapon, no matter how dangerous the test, no matter how contrary the weapon to stated foreign policy objectives, Canada has never refused a single testing request from the United States. They have delayed in some cases, but a flat refusal has not been recorded."[1]

Torture Training

In the 1950s the Defence Research Board (DRB) and affiliated researchers helped develop "a scientifically based system for extracting information from 'resistant sources.'"[2] The DRB funded psychiatric research the CIA used to refine torture techniques employed on many unfortunate individuals across the globe.

Framed as a response to Communist/Chinese "brainwashing" during the Korean War, Canadian, British and US officials met to coordinate psychological research a couple months after the CIA initiated a top-secret research program into "all aspects of special interrogation."[3] At the Ritz Carlton Hotel in Montréal on June 1, 1951, DRB Chairman Ormond Solandt, Veterans Affairs psychiatrist Travis E. Dancey, lead British Defence Ministry scientist Sir Henry T. Tizzard as well as CIA researchers Dr. Cyril Haskins and Commander R. J. Williams formalized the research relationship.[4] Chairman of DRB's Human Relations and Research committee, Donald Hebb, suggested the research focus on "confessions", "menticide" and "intervention in the individual mind", which was endorsed by the other attendees.[5]

Three months after the Ritz Carlton meeting Hebb received a secret $10,000 ($50,000 in today's money) grant from the DRB to study sensory deprivation.⁶ Over the next three years the influential McGill University psychology professor received $28,000 more from DRB.⁷

The CIA and US military took interest in his research into the "effects of radical isolation upon intellectual function", which demonstrated the "devastating impact of sensory deprivation" on individuals' psychology.⁸ The majority of student participants described it as "a form of torture."⁹

A disciple of Hebb, John Zubek would become a world leader in sensory deprivation research. The DRB funded his sensory deprivation laboratory at the University of Manitoba from the late 1950s until the early 1970s.¹⁰ At least $275,000 ($1 million in today's money) was spent on a translucent plexiglas dome housed in a soundproofed chamber that could be constantly dark and silent or light with white noise.¹¹

The federal government and CIA put up a half million dollars ($2 million today) for McGill psychologist Ewan Cameron to build on "Hebb's psychological isolation" research in ghastly ways.¹² Cameron's research team forcibly isolated individuals for long periods, gave unsuspecting psychiatric patients electroshocks as well as large doses of LSD and other hallucinogens.¹³ The expressed objective of the research conducted at Montreal's Allan Memorial Institute from the early 1950s until 1965 was to erase existing memories and reprogram individuals' psyches.¹⁴ But, it was effectively a "torture laboratory", notes Naomi Klein.¹⁵ (The federal government and CIA later compensated some of Cameron's victims.¹⁶)

Hebb and Cameron's research significantly influenced the CIA's 1963 Kubark Counterintelligence Interrogation handbook. In *A Question of Torture: CIA Interrogation, from the Cold War to the War on Terror* Alfred McCoy writes, "Dr. Cameron's experiments, building upon Donald O. Hebb's earlier breakthrough, laid the scientific foundation for the CIA's two-stage psychological torture method."¹⁷ First, the torturer creates a state of sensory disorientation and then "self-inflicted" pain in which the disoriented subject can alleviate their discomfort by capitulating. No physical marks need to be left on the victim.¹⁸

In subsequent decades these 'enhanced interrogation' methods would be employed against South Vietnamese, Hondurans, Filipinos, etc. In another book, *Torture and Impunity: The U.S. Doctrine of Coercive Interrogation*, Alfred McCoy writes, "offering visual confirmation of this continuity, the detainees at Guantanamo's Camp X- Ray in 2002 wore prison suits with goggles, gloves, and earmuffs that bear a striking resemblance to equipment Dr. Hebb used to test sensory deprivation on student volunteers at McGill University in 1952."[19]

Through the 1950s and 60s the DRB had a formal research relationship with the CIA. Solandt explained, "if they [CIA] wanted classified research they came to the Board and if we thought it was suitable we paid for it and then passed it along to the U.S."[20] Conversely, the CIA shared some of their research with the DRB.

A CIA liaison officer in Ottawa had formal access to DRB work. According to Solandt, a CIA agent at the US Embassy in Ottawa (introduced to him as such) was free to attend DRB staff and committee meetings.[21]

DRB research into torture and other areas of interest to the CIA facilitated Canadian access to US intelligence. In "Early Years of the Canada-United States Foreign Intelligence Relationship" Kurt F. Jensen and Don Munton write: "Early in 1951, Lt. Gen. Charles Foulkes, the Chairman of the Canadian Chiefs of Staff Committee, visited Lt. Gen. Walter Bedell Smith, the Director of the CIA, to reopen the question of liaison arrangements. Foulkes pointed out to Bedell Smith that no clear link existed between the CIA and Canadian intelligence agencies, which were anxious to review CIA National Intelligence Survey papers. Bedell Smith agreed to provide Canada with Agency studies provided that the material did not circulate beyond National Defence."[22]

Chemical and Biological Weapons

Canada has contributed significantly to the development and use of chemical and biological weapons (CBW). While a number of books discuss the subject, military and government officials have sought to suppress information about chemical weapons (munitions that use chemicals formulated to inflict harm) and biological warfare (employing living organisms, natural poisons or toxins to debilitate).[23]

In maybe the oldest confirmed case of BW use, General Jeffery Amherst's forces gave indigenous chiefs blankets and a handkerchief from a smallpox hospital not long after Britain conquered today's Québec. This act of genocide did little to diminish his reputation until recently. I wrote this book while living on Amherst Street, which the city of Montréal renamed Atateken at the end of 2019.

After German forces employed chlorine gas on Canadians at Ypres in 1915, the Canadian Corps repeatedly used chlorine and phosgene gas.[24] "Canadians gassed everything that moved whenever they could," noted Jack Granatstein.[25] The Canadian Corps was the most enthusiastic user of poison gas on the Western Front.[26]

Chemical warfare contributed significantly to the Allies' victory despite earlier agreements to restrict these weapons.[27] The Hague Convention of 1899 (reaffirmed in 1907) called on governments to "abstain from the use of projectiles, the sole object of which is the diffusion of asphyxiating or deleterious gases."[28]

Québec City-born Lieutenant General Charles Macpherson Dobell commanded a British force that was the first to use poison gas in the Middle East campaign.[29] The Royal Military College of Canada graduate planned the April 1917 Second Battle of Gaza against Ottoman forces, which employed "2,000 gas-shells specially shipped from England."[30]

Later in 1917 hundreds of Canadians fought with British General Edmund Allenby during the Sinai and Palestine Campaign. About 10,000 cans of asphyxiating gas were fired during the Allenby-led Third Battle of Gaza.[31]

To the north, the British air force dropped diphenylchloroarsine against the Bolsheviks in Murmansk and Archangel in the summer of 1919.[32] Red Army soldiers fled in panic of a gas that caused uncontrollable coughing and individuals to vomit blood.³³ About 600 Canadians fought in Murmansk and Archangel.³⁴

Canada was also complicit in the British Empire's employment of chemical warfare elsewhere. In 1919 Secretary of State for War Winston Churchill argued privately, "I do not understand this squeamishness about the use of gas. We have definitely adopted the position at the Peace Conference of arguing in favour of the retention of gas as a permanent method of warfare. ... I am strongly in favour of using poisoned gas against uncivilised tribes."³⁵

Just after WWI the British are thought to have gassed Iraqis and Afghans.³⁶ A small number of Canadians fought with the British in Mesopotamia and Afghanistan.³⁷

Many CBW have been researched, tested and produced in this country. For years the army had a Directorate of Chemical Warfare and Smoke. "Canada's chemical and biological warfare program began in 1937", writes John Bryden in *Deadly Allies: Canada's Secret War 1937-1947*, "when its military leaders decided to undertake secret research into the defensive and offensive aspects of chemical warfare, apparently without consultation with either the government or Parliament."³⁸

In September 1937 Frederick Banting, the co-discoverer of insulin, discussed the "possibilities of BW" with the head of the National Research Council General Andrew McNaughton.³⁹ Even though Canada signed the 1925 Geneva Protocol outlawing CBW, the Nobel Prize winner wrote McNaughton that "undoubtedly the next development in war will be the utilization of epidemic disease as a means of destroying an enemy."⁴⁰

Prior to his February 1941 death, Banting led the National Research Council's Associate Committee on Medical Research, which oversaw CBW efforts. Writing before the worst of Hitler's crimes were committed or known, the WWI veteran's diary is chock-full of wild anti-German outbursts. He scribbled about killing "three or 4 million young Huns — without mercy — without feeling" and "those Huns at home, those Huns of Hitler — it is our job to kill them."⁴¹ Shaping his thinking on biological weapons, Banting believed wars should target the entire population. Banting wrote: "in the past, war was confined for the most part to men in uniform, but with increased mechanization of armies and the introduction of air forces, there is an increased dependence on the home country, and eight to ten people working at home are now required to keep one man in the fighting line. This state of affairs alters the complexion of war. It really amounts to one nation fighting another nation. This being so, it is just as effective to kill or disable ten unarmed workers at home as to put a soldier out of action, and if this can be done with less risk, then it would be advantageous to employ any mode of warfare to accomplish this."[42]

A great deal of research and production of CBW took place in Canada during WWII.[43] The University of Toronto, McGill, Queen's and other educational institutions engaged in military-directed CBW research.[44] Alongside colleagues at Defence Research Establishment Suffield, Defence Research Establishment Ottawa and Grosse Isle Research Station, the university scientists investigated a bevy of initiatives to turn biological organisms into weaponry.[45] According to Bryden, Canada was "first among the Allies to develop munitions to disperse infected insect bait and then infected insects or their pupae – a program which the Americans expanded grandly. Another all-Canadian biological warfare novelty was the tons of refined peat which were to serve as carrier for pathogenic organisms suitable for spreading epidemic diseases. There's nothing of the defensive nature to this weapon."[46]

Canadians developed a fifty-pound mustard gas cluster bomb.[47] The US military discussed employing the weapon in an invasion of Japan, which would have had killed many civilians.[48]

Canadian testing facilities played an important role in advancing CBW. During WWII a super-secret germ warfare research facility operated on the former quarantine station at Grosse Ile, which is 50 km from Québec City. Under Canada-US management, the isolated and uninhabited island in the Saint Lawrence River produced rinderpest (a cattle virus) and anthrax spores.[49] A great deal of anthrax was produced on the island for US and British forces. Bacterial Bacillus anthracis continued to be produced at Grosse Isle a year after Hitler's death.[50]

Among the largest CBW research centres in the world, Defence Research Establishment Suffield (DRES) was funded by Britain during WWII. Suffield was popular with the British and US chemical warfare services partly because 'volunteers' in Canada were exposed to more dangerous scenarios.[51] In fact, a US Chemical Warfare Service expert who studied German research methods after WWII found no equivalent to Canada's casualty causing experiments. He wrote, "the Nazis seem to have been afraid of using human observers directly. The method used was to expose the portion of the uniform to be tested and then to have a man put it on and observe his reactions."[52] (Germany also seems to have banned offensive BW use. In *Pathogens for War: Biological Weapons, Canadian Life Scientists, and North American Biodefence* Donald Avery writes, "any offensive program was barred by Hitler's interdict against BW development."[53])

A few thousand 'volunteer' soldiers were exposed to mustard, blister and tear gas as well as other toxic agents at Suffield.[54] In one test mustard gas was dropped on the soldier 'volunteers' from planes, which caused painful blisters and burns, including on some of their penises.[55] In another study "very small quantities" of the highly toxic chemical VX was applied to the skin of nine "test subjects" for up to 12 hours "to determine the rate of evaporation, decomposition and absorption."[56]

A good number of the 'volunteers' had little education or English and were offered limited information about the risks of the testing.[57] Begun during WWII, 3,700 human guinea pigs would be used over three decades.[58] Some of the 'volunteers' were injured permanently and after decades of campaigning DND and Veterans Affairs offered them each $24,000 in compensation in 2004.[59]

'Volunteer' soldiers were not the only victims of chemical agent testing. In July 1953 US Army planes secretly sprayed 6 kg of zinc cadmium sulfide, a carcinogen, on Winnipeg.[60] Eleven years later they dropped the odourless, colourless and nearly invisible substance on Medicine Hat, Alberta.[61]

Local governments were fed a cover story. "In Winnipeg, they said they were testing what they characterized as a chemical fog to protect Winnipeg in the event of a Russian attack," said Lisa Martino-Taylor, author of *Behind the Fog: How the U.S. Cold War Radiological Weapons Program Exposed Innocent Americans*. "They characterized it as a defensive study when it was actually an offensive study."[62]

The Winnipeg and Medicine Hat experiments were part of the Tripartite Military Agreement on Chemical and Biological Warfare research.[63] In 1946 Canada, Britain and the US set up the CBW research sharing arrangement.

At its founding meeting in Fort Detrick, Maryland, Canadian representatives pushed to continue the WWII CBW research exchange. Director of the Army Operational Research Group, Omond Solandt called "close scientific cooperation ... more important than cooperation at the policy level" and reported that the army chief of staff promised generous financial assistance for "fundamental and basic research at Kingston and field experiments at Suffield ... with BW munitions."[64] Until the collapse of the Tripartite Agreement in 1969 Canadian scientists, notes Avery, played an "important support role ... in facilitating American and British offensive BW programs."[65] During this period DND established a series of CBW initiatives. In 1947 DRB created a Special Weapons Advisory Committee, which worked closely with the US Chemical Weapons Corps.[66] Two years later a CF Nuclear, Biological and Chemical School was established in Borden, Ontario (it was initially named Joint Atomic, Biological and Chemical Warfare School).[67]

As part of the Tripartite Agreement the military committed substantial funds to research efforts in Kingston.[68] In 1946 DND signed an accord with Queen's University to continue its biodefence lab.[69] Through the Korean War the Guilford Reed led Defence Research

Laboratory at Queen's studied mosquito vectors and how to mass produce mosquito colonies.[70] The idea was to disperse infected insect bait over a specific area in a bid to sustain infected insect colonies. Researchers experimented with a 500-pound bomb that could carry 200,000 flies, using canned salmon as infected bait.[71]

Reed also helped turn shellfish toxin into a weapon.[72] In an outgrowth of the Kingston lab's research, the DRB asked the Department of Fisheries for a large-scale harvest of shellfish. A facility in Nova Scotia concentrated their naturally occurring toxins and sent it to Fort Detrick in Maryland. Avery writes, "from the perspective of the US Chemical Corps this arrangement had enormous advantages both in maintaining its own bioweapons arsenal and in assisting the Central Intelligence Agency to develop special assassination weapons for its covert global operations."[73] In the 1970s the CIA attempted to kill Cuban President Fidel Castro with a nearly untraceable pill consisting of shellfish toxin.[74]

Other BW the CIA employed in Cuba were researched in Canada. In the 1970s the CIA employed mosquito-borne viral pathogen Venezuelan equine encephalitis and released African swine fever virus on the island nation.[75] An African swine fever virus outbreak in 1971 forced the Cuban government to slaughter 500,000 pigs, which the UN Food and Agricultural Organization labeled that year's "most alarming event".[76] Weaponizing African swine fever and Venezuelan equine encephalitis was tested at Grosse Isles in the 1950s.[77]

At a 1958 Tripartite Conference on Toxicological Warfare meeting US, British and Canadian officials agreed that "all three countries should concentrate on the search for incapacitating and new lethal agents."[78] They believed "research should be continued on organophosphorus compounds [nerve agents] specifically in areas where there is a possibility of marked enhancement in speed of action and resistance to treatment."[79] In the 1960s Canadian scientists helped their British and US counterparts research the highly toxic V (venomous) nerve agent.[80]

***

Defence Research Establishment Suffield was one of the largest CBW research centres in the world for decades. A 1989 *Peace Magazine* article about DRES explained, "for almost 50 years, scientists from the Department of National Defence have been as busy as beavers expanding their knowledge of, and testing agents for, chemical and biological warfare (CBW) in southern Alberta."[81]

Suffield had the largest landmass of any military training base in the Commonwealth. Many skilled scientists have also been stationed there. According to Avery, DRES had "excellent laboratory equipment, an adequate animal colony and most important, a well-trained staff for carrying out trials with pathological organisms."[82]

During the Korean War 25-pound shells filled with highly toxic Sarin were tested at Suffield.[83] In the mid-1960s US Air Force jets sprayed BW simulants over Suffield to test spraying fatal diseases on a population.[84] DRES was important to US researchers during the war in Vietnam. Famed investigative reporter Seymour Hersh explained, "Suffield has become colossally important to the CBW people here in the last year. Ever since the uproar came out over tests within the United States (the summer of 69) it's a known thing in Washington that Suffield has become the US prime testing area now."[85]

Until 1989 significant quantities of CW agents, including sarin and VX, were stockpiled at the Alberta base.[86] In the 1970s DRES had 260 105-millimetre shells charged with agent GB (Sarin), a potent nerve agent.[87] During this period Canada's Honest John rockets could be loaded with Sarin.[88]

CBW research at DRES declined after the US-instigated collapse of the Tripartite Agreement in 1969. But DRES received a boost from US President Ronald Reagan's support for CBW. A DND booklet about Suffield boasted that "the 1980s will be remembered at DRES as one of renewal in the areas of chemical, biological, and biomedical research." It added that DRES was "no longer a remote testing station, but an establishment with two major integrated laboratory-based programs supported by extensive facilities."[89]

In New Brunswick DND sprayed millions of litres of chemical agents at CFB Gagetown.[90] Between 1956 and 1984 more than one billion grams of agents Orange, Purple and White were sprayed on or near CFB Gagetown.[91]

The US tested these agents at CFB Gagetown for use in its war in Vietnam. A 1968 US Army memorandum titled "defoliation tests in 1966 at base Gagetown, New Brunswick, Canada" explained: "The department of the army, Fort Detrick, Maryland, has been charged with finding effective chemical agents that will cause rapid defoliation of woody and Herbaceous vegetation. To further develop these objectives, large areas similar in density to those of interest in South East Asia were needed. In March 1965, the Canadian ministry of defense offered Crops Division large areas of densely forested land for experimental tests of defoliant chemicals. This land, located at Canadian forces base Gagetown, Oromocto, New Brunswick, was suitable in size and density and was free from hazards and adjacent cropland. The test site selected contained a mixture of conifers and deciduous broad leaf species in a dense undisturbed forest cover that would provide similar vegetation densities to those of temperate and tropical areas such as South East Asia."[92]

Canadian scientists also helped develop the defoliants used to deny food to areas supporting anti-colonial insurgencies in Asia. The McGill labs overseen by CBW director at the DRB, Otto Maass, researched the herbicides sprayed by the British and US in Malaya and Vietnam.[93]

The toll on Vietnam was staggering. Some three million Vietnamese were exposed to the cancerous chemical Agent Orange, which can also cause immune deficiencies and damage one's nervous system.[94] Spread between generations through breast milk, food and the water supply, Agent Orange victims' children and grandchildren are often born with serious disabilities.

Through the 1960s US forces sprayed tens of millions of litres of material containing chemical herbicides and defoliants in Vietnam,

Laos and Cambodia.[95] One aim was to deprive the guerrillas of cover by defoliating forests and rural land. Another goal of these defoliation efforts was to drive peasants from the countryside to the US-dominated cities, which would deprive the national resistance forces of their food supply and rural support.

During the Vietnam War Canadian manufacturers sold the US military significant amounts of "polystyrene, a major component in napalm," according to *Snow Job: Canada, the United States and Vietnam (1954 to 1973)*.[96] Napalm is a flammable liquid agent that can cause burns, asphyxiation, unconsciousness and death. The US employed napalm liberally in Vietnam and for years Canadian planes were equipped to deliver the mainly gasoline based incendiary weapon.[97]

During the Korean War Canadian researchers discovered a thickening agent for flamethrower fuels (napalm).[98] A "team at Suffield worked on a flamethrower", reports Jonathan Turner, "to deliver this new and improved fuel from tanks."[99]

During the fighting in Korea napalm was produced at Defence Research Chemical Laboratories (DRCL). In *A History of the Defence Research Board of Canada* Donald Godspeed explains, "the production of flamethrower fuel became an urgent requirement during the Korean War since the fuel was required by the fighting troops. The pilot plant at DRCL worked 24 hours a day for seven days a week until the order was fulfilled."[100]

Tens of thousands of litres of napalm were employed by UN forces in Korea.[101] A *New York Times* reporter, George Barrett, described the scene in a North Korean village after it was captured by US-led forces in February 1951: "A napalm raid hit the village three or four days ago when the Chinese were holding up the advance, and nowhere in the village have they buried the dead because there is nobody left to do so. This correspondent came across one old woman, the only one who seemed to be left alive, dazedly hanging up some clothes in a blackened courtyard filled with the bodies of four members of her family.

"The inhabitants throughout the village and in the fields were caught and killed and kept the exact postures they had held when the napalm struck — a man about to get on his bicycle, fifty boys and girls playing in an orphanage, a housewife strangely unmarked, holding in her hand a page torn from a Sears Roebuck catalogue crayoned at Mail Order No. 3,811,294 for a $2.98 'bewitching bed jacket — coral.' There must be almost two hundred dead in the tiny hamlet."[102]

This *New York Times* story captured the attention of External Affairs Minister Lester Pearson. In a letter to the Canadian ambassador in Washington, Hume Wrong, he wondered how it might affect public opinion and complained about it passing US media censors. "[Nothing could more clearly indicate] the dangerous possibilities of United States and United Nations action in Korea on Asian opinion than a military episode of this kind, and the way it was reported. Such military action was possibly 'inevitable' but surely we do not have to give publicity to such things all over the world. Wouldn't you think the censorship which is now in force could stop this kind of reporting?"[103]

The Canadian government also sought to suppress information about possible BW use. After the outbreak of a series of diseases at the start of 1952, China and North Korea accused the US of using biological weapons. (The claims have neither been conclusively substantiated nor disproven with a 2017 *Socialism and Democracy Journal* article titled "Biological Warfare in the Korean War: Allegations and Cover-up" noting that at least some of the accusations were correct.[104]) In *Orienting Canada* John Price details Ottawa's highly disingenuous and authoritarian response to the accusations, which were echoed by some Canadian peace groups. While publicly highlighting a report that exonerated the US, Pearson concealed a more informed External Affairs analysis suggesting biological weapons could have been used. Additionally, when the *Ottawa Citizen* revealed that British, Canadian and US military scientists had recently met in Ottawa to discuss biological warfare, the external minister wrote the paper's owner to complain. Invoking national security, External Affairs "had it [the story] killed in the *Ottawa Journal* and over the CP [Canadian Press] wires."[105]

Price summarizes: "Even without full documentation, it is clear that the Canadian government was deeply involved in developing offensive weapons of mass destruction, including biological warfare, and that Parliament was misled by Lester Pearson at the time the accusations of biological warfare in Korea were first raised. We know also that the US military was stepping up preparations for deployment and use of biological weapons in late 1951 and that Canadian officials were well aware of this and actively supported it. To avoid revealing the nature of the biological warfare program and Canadian collaboration, which would have lent credence to the charges levelled by the Chinese and Korean governments, the Canadian government attempted to discredit the peace movement."[106]

There has often been extreme information control regarding CBW. During WWII the head of the Directorate of Chemical Warfare and Smoke, Otto Maass, censored stories about Canada's BW program.[107] Another incident of suppression took place three years after the war. In May 1948 the *Yorkshire Post* Ottawa correspondent went to CF station Churchill in Manitoba and interviewed defence minister Brooke Claxton. Sent to his editor in London, the story explained, "in a secret base near Suffield Alberta, scientists have been working since the war ended on the production of lethal germs, and this research has resulted in the production of such deadly bacteria that enough to kill the bulk of the world's population can be stored in a large bottle." The *Yorkshire Post* London editor Ralph Loveless didn't believe his reporter and sent a copy of the dispatch to the high commissioner at Canada House to ask if he "can confirm or amplify the information". The high commissioner cabled Ottawa, which pushed to have the story killed. It was never published.[108]

After reporting that US forces secretly tested BW stimulants over US cities in 1953, the *Ottawa Citizen* inquired about whether any Canadian cities had been included in these toxic experiments. DND officials denied that anything similar had taken place over Canadian airspace. But three years later they were forced to admit that US planes had sprayed aerosols "over a part of Winnipeg."[109]

As opposition to the US war in Vietnam grew military officials repeatedly denied that the CF stockpiled chemical munitions. That was a lie.[110] So were blanket assurances that DRES scientists didn't engage in offensive BW research.

In a 2005 article former NDP MP Jim Fulton said that when he brought up nerve agent testing during question period he faced "extraordinary push back."[111] "In the 15 years I was in the House of Commons, I never saw the level of unusual security procedures that then surrounded me raising that in question period," he told the *Toronto Star*.[112] A week after raising the issue in 1988 his office on Parliament Hill was broken into and Fulton says his chemical testing paperwork were the only files touched.[113]

While they went to great lengths to keep information about CBW research from the public, the government defended CBW in bilateral and diplomatic forums. For example, after successfully testing an atomic bomb in 1952 the British military downgraded CBW research. Canada's DRB opposed the British move. A memo in response noted, "CBR (chemical, biological and radiological) weapons represent the only known alternative to nuclear weapons for achieving large area affects. In fact, in some respects they are more attractive weapons. For example, they may destroy an enemy's will to resist without destroying the economic features of his countryside and cities. In addition, they may be employed covertly."[114]

At a 1966 UN discussion the Canadian representative "found it unacceptable that the proposal should present as a fact the idea that the Geneva Protocol prohibited the use of chemical weapons without mentioning the qualifications given in the text of that document."[115] Three years later Canada abstained on a widely supported UN resolution affirming the comprehensive character of the Geneva Protocol.[116]

Canada's commissioner at the International Control Commission, which was supposed to enforce the peaceful reunification of Vietnam, defended US defoliant use.[117] In 1962 Gordon E. Cox denied they were a war material, but rather "readily-available, commercially-prepared herbicides which I myself have used in my garden in Canada and which I have never considered to be of the slightest danger to my children or their pets."[118]

(To get a sense of the rationalizations floating in government circles at the time, disarmament division official A. W. Robertson sent a 1968 memo to Canada's primary arms control negotiator, George Ignatieff, claiming that incapacitating chemical gases were "increasingly being advocated on humanitarian grounds … [and] that even the use of nerve gases, though they are lethal, would seem to be an infinitely quicker and less painful way of killing than that provided by … acceptable weapons."[119])

In the mid-1980s the US Congress restricted funding for President Ronald Reagan's bid to "modernize" the US military's CW. They wanted NATO support. At a meeting of the alliance in 1986 many members objected to the US initiative, but Canada's representative spoke in favour and "Canada didn't refuse deployment of binary chemical weapons on our soil even though some of the other countries did so."[120]

The CF developed plans to employ CW. In 1968 External Affairs discovered a secret accord between the Pentagon and DND in which the US could ask the CF "to engage in CW in some unspecified future circumstances."[121] The two militaries sought to make US chemical munitions compatible with CF weapon systems so "USA chemical shells can be fired from Canadian field guns."[122] External Affairs was troubled to learn that these arrangements were not simply abstract policy projections but definite CF operational strategies.[123]

In more recent years, Canadian troops used white phosphorus during the war in Afghanistan. In a 2008 letter to the *Toronto Star* Corporal Paul Demetrick claimed the CF used white phosphorus as a weapon against enemy-occupied vineyards. Former Chief of Defence Staff Rick Hillier confirmed the use of the smoke-producing agent often employed to light up an area. Discussing the difficulties of fighting the Taliban in areas with 10-foot tall marijuana plants, the general said, "we tried burning them with white phosphorous — it didn't work."[124]

In 2009 NATO forces were accused of burning an 8-year-old Afghan girl with white phosphorus munitions.[125] The publicity given to this claim and a US counterclaim that the Taliban used white phosphorus prompted the Afghan government to announce an investigation. It's unclear if it was ever done.

***

The military's research into chemical and biological weapons has been veiled in secrecy. The intended harm was so great and the idea so distasteful to most that the work had to be conducted in secret.

Strangely, many other aspects of what the Canadian Forces do may be a greater threat to life on our planet, but they are not kept secret. Rather, they hide in plain sight.

9. Cratering the Environment

Though it receives relatively little attention, the CF's ecological footprint is immense. It ranges from decimating animal life to releasing substantial greenhouse gases (GHG) into the atmosphere. In fact, DND emits far more carbon than any other institution. According to the government's 2017 defence policy review, DND "represents more than half of the Government of Canada's greenhouse gas emissions."[1] Despite that CF operations were exempted from the government's emission reduction targets.[2]

Military vehicles, planes, warships, etc. consume significant fossil fuels. But even before becoming CF property war tools emit a great deal of carbon and other pollutants. Manufacturing guns, tanks, submarines, naval frigates, fighter jets, etc. consumes significant energy and produces many waste products. Bullet and small arm production generate hazardous wastes such as ozone-depleting substances, volatile organic compounds and heavy metals.

The CF operates a few hundred planes and naval vessels and has 30,000 land vehicles.[3] Once built, planes, vessels and tanks all guzzle petrol even if rarely used outside of drills. A Forbes headline aptly referred to "Fuel-Sucking Military Vehicles". A Humvee consumes around a litre of gas every five kilometers it travels while naval frigates carry 665,000 litres of fuel.[4]

Fighter jets are incredibly fuel intensive. During six months of bombing Libya in 2011 a half dozen RCAF jets consumed 14.5 million pounds (8.5 million litres) of fuel.[5] An hour of flying a CF 18 consumes hundreds of litres of fuel and in a usual year RCAF planes log thousands of training hours. For their part, the Snowbird performance aircraft participate in dozens of airshows in multiple locations each year. Nine CT-114 Tutors usually perform for about 35-minutes at these events.

Since 1992 the RCAF has had five mid-air refuelling aircraft that can each carry 24,000 pounds of jet fuel.[6] According to a 2018 *Skies Mag* article, the CC-130HT aerial refuelling aircraft "has been extensively used since its operational introduction in 1993."[7] Two Canadian air-to-air refuelling tankers supported the bombing of Libya in 2011 and between late 2014 and 2018 they distributed 65 million pounds of fuel for the (mostly US) bombing of Syria and Iraq.[8]

Flying is fuel intensive and its climatic impact is generally about twice the CO_2 emitted alone. The release point of the carbon enhances its warming impact and other flying "outputs" produce additional climatic impacts. Fighter jets burn an especially toxic fuel, which allows them to fly higher and faster than commercial aircraft.[9]

***

A century later the ecological toll of WWI lingers in eastern France. The traces of trench networks and blast holes remain visible while huge amounts of ordnance are collected each year. Near Verdun, France, a 700 square kilometre no-go Red Zone has over 10 million explosives.[10] The soil has elevated concentrations of copper, lead, zinc, mercury and tin. Arsenic levels in parts of the Red Zone continue to rise, meaning the chemicals are acting up.

Seven decades after the war unexploded ordnance and debris litter central Korea.[11] Deforestation in the north is partly due to fires caused by bombings, which destroyed dams and thousands of acres of farmland.[12]

The first Gulf War resulted in a "toxic battlefield." While the Iraqis fouled the air by burning oil wells, coalition forces destroyed pipelines, refineries and sewers, spilling sewage and oil.[13] The US also fired shells with depleted uranium, which probably increased the incidence of cancer and congenital disease for those nearby.[14] During the war the CF disposed of plastics, batteries, medicine, dead animals, unexploded ordnance, etc. in burn pits. A large CF base abroad can burn tens of thousands of kilograms of waste daily.[15]

During the 1999 bombing of Serbia NATO jets dropped bombs containing depleted uranium.[16] NATO's effort, the author of "Environmental impact of the war in Yugoslavia on south-east Europe" notes, "to destroy industrial sites and infrastructure caused dangerous substances to pollute the air, water and soil."[17] The deliberate destruction of chemical plants caused significant environmental damage.[18]

Environmental protection wasn't part of the agreement between the NATO-led International Security Assistance Force and the UN or Afghan government.[19] US bombing in Afghanistan disrupted important migratory passageways for birds. To destroy crops during the 2000s war Canadian and US forces employed incendiary white phosphorus munitions, which are linked to ailments in animals.[20] The CF also littered the landscape with tens of millions of bullets and shells. Leftover Canadian mortars reportedly killed three children in February 2009, prompting a demonstration calling for "death to the Canadians."[21]

The Kandahar airfield, which housed tens of thousands of Canadian troops, was responsible for significant waste. A "poo pond" of human waste fouled the air while large quantities of hazardous waste material accumulated.[22] These included oils, lubricants, solvents, pesticides, detergents, compressed gas cylinders, bulbs and batteries, nickel-cadmium and lithium as well as waste containing asbestos and contaminated soils etc.[23] A leaked US Army memo stated that the burn pit at its largest Afghan base posed "long-term adverse health conditions" to those breathing the air.[24]

NATO severely damaged Libya's Great Manmade River aquifer system.[25] On July 22, 2011, NATO planes bombed and destroyed much of its pipe-making facilities at Brega. Without providing evidence, NATO claimed Gaddafi's forces stored weapons at the facility and fired rockets from the site. Attacking the source of 70% of the population's water may have been a war crime. Human Rights Investigations wrote, "even if rockets were being fired from within the location (for which no evidence has been produced) or this facility was being used for military storage by Gadaffi forces, or housed armoured vehicles, attacking the pipe-making factory in a way that leaves it severely damaged is illegal as this facility is important to the water supplies of Libyan civilians."[26]

Since the 2011 war millions of Libyans have faced a chronic water crisis.[27]

Dogs of War

It's unclear how many dogs or canine units there are in the ranks of the Canadian Forces. But the CF has long employed animals. According to Army Public Affairs officer Jeff Pelletier, "throughout its history, the Canadian Army (CA) has relied on animals to take on various tasks, including communication, transportation and troop morale. No matter what job they did, thousands of dogs, pigeons, horses and other animals have played vital roles in the success of the CA."[28]

From the slaughter of horses during the Boer war to dogs killed in Afghanistan, the CF is responsible for many animal deaths. More than a quarter of the 600 horses that departed with the first Canadian contingent sent to the Boer war in 1899 died on the way there.[29] Upon arrival in South Africa a horse's life expectancy was around six weeks.[30] During the conflict 50,000 horses were sent to South Africa from Canada.[31] Over 300,000 horses and 50,000 mules died on the British side in what eyewitness Frederick Smith labelled a "holocaust".[32]

The animal slaughter was even worse during WWI. An incredible eight million horses were killed transporting soldiers, arms and supplies.[33] Approximately 130,000 horses were sent from Canada to Europe during the conflict.[34] The 1920 book *The Horse in War and Famous Canadian War Horses* includes a photo of a group of horses felled during WWI. A veterinarian who served at Passchendaele recounted trying to calm horses and mules when "their eyes expressed nothing but absolute fear."[35]

Valued for their homing instinct and speed, pigeons were widely used as messengers during WWI. In addition to over one hundred thousand pigeons, the allies employed messenger dogs as well as cats and terriers to kill rats in the trenches.[36] Many of these animals were killed in the conflict.

On the other side, Canadian soldiers killed dogs the Germans used as spies.[37] They also killed horses and pigeons the Germans employed.

During WWII hundreds of thousands of horses, mules, donkeys, pigeons, etc. perished. In the Second World War thousands of dogs died sniffing out anti-personnel mines, including the Royal Rifles of Canada's canine mascot memorialized in *Sergeant Gander: A Canadian Hero*. Awarded the Dickin Medal in 2000, Gander was sent with the Canadian regiment to the British colony of Hong Kong in December 1941. According to Canadian Press, "Gander attacked and chased off Japanese troops on at least two occasions during the battle before being killed while carrying an enemy grenade away from a group of wounded Canadian soldiers."[38]

Many CF scout dogs were also killed during Korean War patrols. For its part, the Canadian military killed an unknown number of Chinese transport mules as well as domestic and farm animals in Korea.[39] Off the coast, an official RCN history of the Korean War describes an incident in which *HMCS Athabaskan*'s sonar team detected contact, mistakenly bombing a school of fish.[40]

Domestic animals and livestock were also killed during the 1999 bombing of Yugoslavia. The *New York Times* described, "a number of pigs and cows ... killed and injured" by NATO bombs in Merdare.[41] In Afghanistan the CF used dozens of dogs to sniff out roadside bombs and other explosives or target enemy combatants.[42] An unknown number were injured or killed. To help carry equipment while on patrol Canadian troops employed a pint-sized Afghan donkey they named Hughes.[43]

Hundreds of camels were killed during fighting in Libya. In one NATO strike hundreds of camels reportedly transporting weapons were bombed.[44]

A memorial at Confederation Park in Ottawa commemorates animals used in conflicts. The Animals in War Dedication "features a life-size war dog and three bas-relief plaques on three boulders; one dedicated to dogs, one to mules and one to horses."⁴⁵ It also refers to the pigeons used by the CF since the Boer War. Canada's military animals are honoured with a special purple poppy and since 1943 the British Dickin Medal has been awarded to animals that demonstrate particular bravery and devotion.

Animals have also been abused in CF training and testing. In 2009 DND used 4,000 live animals, mostly rodents, for research and an undisclosed number of larger animals to train battlefield doctors.⁴⁶ Goats and pigs were employed to simulate blast trauma and amputations.⁴⁷ After years of pressure from animal rights activists, the number of animals used for testing in 2018 was down to 882.⁴⁸

A 2012 report in *Military Medicine* noted that Canada was one of only six NATO countries still using live mice, ferrets and pigs for military purposes. Some claim this violated federal animal welfare guidelines, which require alternatives to be used when possible.⁴⁹

Between 1997 and 2012, 1,500 pigs were used for chemical-warfare experiments at DRDC Suffield.⁵⁰ Exposed to sarin and mustard gas, "the animals suffer seizures, irregular heartbeats, difficulty breathing, bleeding and possibly even death", according to Justin Goodman, author of a 2012 study on military animal testing.⁵¹

The CF has long decimated wildlife in chemical weapons experiments. During WWII "animals were used extensively in chemical warfare trials", notes Christopher Robin Paige in "Canada and Chemical Warfare 1939-1945".⁵² The testing site at Suffield was established partly because of its "adequate animal colony" while the Grosse Ile research station near Québec City produced anti-animal agents probably used by the US to decimate Cuban pigs.⁵³ A large number of crustacean were killed developing a shellfish toxin poison.⁵⁴ Beginning in the late 1940s British, US and Canadian scientists "cooperated in spraying pathogens in the area of the Bahama Islands in the Caribbean", notes Leonard Cole in *Clouds of Secrecy: The Army's Germ Warfare Tests Over Populated Areas*. "Details of the tests are still secret, but they involved highly virulent organisms. Thousands of animals died as a result of the tests. Although [Director of British Chemical Defence Establishment R. G. H.] Watson does not refer to human victims, he mentions the death of 'major animal species' including guinea pigs, mice, rabbits, and monkeys."[55] Agent Orange and Agent Purple were tested on animals at CFB Gagetown from the late 1950s until the 1980s.[56]

The RCN regularly disrupts ocean habitat. Huge blasts make the water shutter, scarring and harming orcas that approach Bentnick Island, an explosive test range 30 kilometres southeast of Victoria. Despite committing not to set off explosions within 1,000 metres of whales or other marine mammals, the RCN repeatedly ignored the Marine Mammal Mitigation Procedure. "They closed down this area to recreational fishing to save the whales, and then the navy sets off phosphorus bombs and 50 caliber guns," said Paul Pudwell, a whale-watching captain in Sooke, BC, in 2018. "They do it 20, 30 times a year. We can't fish there, but you can go shoot it up?"[57]

Deafening noise released by underwater navy sonar is thought to cause hearing loss and the beaching of whales, dolphins and seals. In 2012 the RCN admitted to employing sonar in an area with orcas, which saw "Little Victoria" wash ashore with signs of trauma to her head, neck and right side. Lacking outward signs of broken bones, the whale was believed to be the victim of underwater noise. DND refused to comment on "Little Victoria's" death.[58]

***

Impacting large sea life, naval frigates use the ocean as their trash can. Ships dump food waste in the Arctic sea and navy guidelines permit Canadian submarines to dump oily bilge water into the sea. Anecdotes in various military histories suggest RCN vessels have discharged a great deal of oil during war. More recently, *HMCS Calgary* spilled 10,000-20,000 litres of F-76 fuel into the Georgia Strait in February 2018 while *HMCS Halifax* spilled "an unspecified quantity of oil" into the Halifax harbour in July 2019.[59] *HMCS Athabaskan* dumped 800 litres of fuel into the same waterway in January 2016.[60] Earlier in the decade *HMCS*

St. John's spilled 9,000 litres of diesel fuel into the Halifax harbour and *HMCS Preserver* spilled another 14,000 litres there.[61]

Even after they are no longer operational, naval vessels pollute the seas. Many RCN vessels have been sunk to the ocean floor.[62] In 2007 US and Canadian gunboats, as well as fighter jets, disposed of *HMCS Huron* 100 km off of Vancouver Island. Officially, the method of disposal was listed as "firing by naval sea sparrow missiles, aircraft machine guns, and naval gunnery (including MK48 torpedoes)."[63] *HMCS Huron* was sunk two kilometres down to the ocean floor. In response Jennifer Lash, from the group Living Oceans, complained that the military was "treating the ocean like a garbage dump ... No one even knows what kind of marine life there is down there."[64]

Huge amounts of toxic material have been released at naval testing sites. According to an internal assessment of CF Maritime and Experimental Test Ranges (CFMETR), 93,000 kilometres of copper wire and 2,200 tons of lead, lithium batteries and other toxic materials were dumped at Nanoose Bay between 1965 and 1995.[65] While they refuse to allow independent scientists to investigate the torpedo-testing site, the RCN insists its soft mud bottom can absorb these toxins.

On the east side of Vancouver Island, CFMETR is largely used by US nuclear-powered and nuclear weapons-capable submarines.[66] In the 1990s US submarines fired thousands of torpedoes at the facility. (The soft seabed allows them to retrieve expensive torpedoes.)

DND suspects dozens of lakes or underwater spots are laden with unexploded ordnance.[67] For nearly half a century, the CF pounded Lac Saint-Pierre, near Trois-Rivières, with shells as big as 155 millimeters (the size of a large fire extinguisher).[68] DND admits that more than 300,000 projectiles were tested in Lac Saint-Pierre and they maintain a year round 'caution zone' at a lake that had 8,000 live shells on its bottom five years after shelling ended in 2000.[69] Lead and mercury from the weaponry can harm animal and human health.

There are over one thousand known munitions dumpsites off the east coast.[70] After WWII 180,000 tons of munitions was dumped just offshore of Sydney, Nova Scotia.[71]

In 2010 DND reported that chemical and biological munitions were disposed in over 100 sites across the country.[72] CBC interviewed a former military officer who said in the late spring of 1985 he was ordered to escort a flatbed truck along an empty road to a freshly dug pit at CFB Gagetown. Over 40 full or semi-full barrels — some dented or in various states of decay — were dumped in the spongy soil. Most of them were wrapped with an orange stripe with the words "Agent Orange".[73]

From the end of WWI until the 1970s the CF dumped chemical weapons into the ocean. After the Great War the military disposed some chemical weapons in the Atlantic. On a larger scale the Directorate of Chemical Warfare and Smoke dumped many containers full of mustard and nerve gas munitions into the sea at the end of WWII.[74]

A large quantity of chemical munitions were dumped 8,200 feet below sea level one hundred kilometers from Tofino, on Vancouver Island.[75] In 1946 the RCN sunk 30,000 drums of mustard gas near Sable Island, 160 km east of Halifax.[76] In total 2,800 tons of mustard gas was dumped around the canyons in the eastern Scotian Shelf, a 700 km long and 100+ km wide area.[77] According to the CF, chemical or biological weapons were dumped in at least 28 sites off the east coast.[78]

Exposure to these chemicals causes cancers and depresses immune systems in sea life.[79] They also pose a potential threat to fishers and oil exploration teams. (Oil interests pushed the government to map the chemical weapons dumps in the Atlantic.)

After WWII the Canada-Britain-US tripartite Advisory Committee on the Effectiveness of Gas Warfare Materiel in the Tropics shared data from a number of test sites.[80] Between 1945 and 1947 the US and Canada exploded more than 30,000 chemical arms on the Panamanian island of San Jose.[81] Uninhabited by humans and relatively isolated (though not too far to get supplies from the mainland), the island was used to conduct "chemical warfare tests under existing jungle conditions."[82]

In 2001 Ottawa refused Panama's request for help to clean up 3,000 unexploded Canadian-made mustard-gas shells and at least eight unexploded 500 and 1,000-pound bombs containing phosgene and cyanogen chloride.[83] A large amount of munitions were also dropped into the sea around the island. Across Canada there is unexploded ordnance at "several hundred" sites, according to a government analysis.[84] In 2011 Wellers Bay near Trenton, Ontario, was closed to the public after DND personnel found hundreds of kilograms of weapons fragments. They believed "500-pound bombs" may still be buried underground in a popular beach area where bombers trained during WWII.[85]

Toxins from remnants of explosives and unexploded ordnance seep into local ecosystems and drinking water. "Unexploded or deflagrated RDX [a common explosive] does not degrade in soil and, because of its solubility in water, migrates easily to groundwater and off military property," a 2011 DND report says. "This may trigger a serious environmental problem and becomes a public health concern if the groundwater is used for drinking."[86]

Shooting ranges also pose a threat to local water sources. The lead in bullets can seep into local ecosystems. A potent neurotoxin, lead alters the formation of the brain and is an important cause of intellectual disability and behavioural problems (the steep decline in violent crime over the past four decades has been linked to the elimination of leaded gasoline.[87])

Bases are also full of pesticides and herbicides.[88] An internal report (made public in 1997) described CFB Shearwater and CFB Greenwood as a "cocktail of toxic chemicals." It found 542 CF sites contaminated across the country requiring cleanup.[89] Philip J. Anido points out that since the French constructed Quebec City's Citadel in the late 1600s, colonial military installations have left contaminated waste.[90]

Beyond the toxins at military sites, CF training has damaged robust and rare fauna.[91] To dig trenches soldiers often rip out prairie grasses while trucks drive over flora and ground-bird nesting areas.[92] Destruction in the north was particularly stark. In "The Cold War on Canadian Soil: Militarizing a Northern Environment" Whitney Lackenbauer writes, "military mega-projects radically transformed the human and physical geography of the North. Bulldozers tore permafrost off the ground, disrupting ecosystems and creating impassable quagmires."[93]

The Distant Early Warning (DEW) Line, a network of 63 radar and communication stations in the Arctic Circle, was an ecological calamity. Built in the early 1950s to counter the purported Russian menace, the 4,500-kilometer line from the northwest coast of Alaska to the eastern shore of Baffin Island required 460,000 tons of material to be transported north.[94] Alongside maritime and land transport, 45,000 commercial flights delivered goods as many as 5,000 kms.[95] And 9.6 million cubic yards of gravel was produced on site.[96]

The off-road vehicles brought to the north damaged vegetation and melted permafrost. Activities associated with the DEW line were linked to depleted fish stocks and agitating caribou and other game indigenous peoples subsisted on.

When the DEW line was abandoned a few years after being completed an incredible amount of material was left behind.[97] There were rotted vehicles in lakes, containers full of hazardous materials and dumps leaking arsenic and PCBs. When the cleanup began three decades after the sites were abandoned, over 200,000 cubic metres of soil contaminated by diesel fuel was placed in nearby "land farms" where it was tossed and turned until the hydrocarbon evaporated to more acceptable levels.[98] Additionally, 35,000 cubic metres of waste — mostly soil contaminated with PCBs and lead — was shipped south to be incinerated or buried.

About 1,000 km south of the DEW line, the 98 radar sites of the "Mid Canada Line" spilled PCB's and other toxic substances for decades. For years the Mushkegowuk Council, which represents seven indigenous communities in northern Ontario, campaigned for the government to clean up the heavy metals, DDT, asbestos, PCBs and petroleum hydrocarbon from the abandoned radar sites that contaminated their soils, groundwater, animals and foods. Nearly a half century after the line was abandoned Ontario and Ottawa put up $100 million to clean up Mid-Canada Line contamination.[99]

In the 1980s low level training flights by US, British and German fighter jets in Labrador scared wildlife and damaged the Innu's way of life. As a result of supersonic jets skimming the ground, ducks laid eggs a month early, caribou changed migration patterns and beavers all but vanished.[100]

***

For some reason there has been little political scrutiny of the military's ecological footprint or the fact its GHG emissions are exempted from reductions targets. In 2017 Tamara Lorincz, author of a report titled "Demilitarization for Deep Decarbonization", pointed out that not a single MP publicly questioned the climate impacts of new fighter jets or the CF in general.[101]

Ironically, Googling the topic mainly turns up articles about the CF protecting the environment. Military statements, for example, describe the RCN's role in defending offshore energy platforms from possible attack and resulting ecological damage. The 1971 White Paper on defence called for the RCAF to survey Canadian waters to detect pollution from foreign vessels and arrest ships that breached Canadian environmental regulations.[102] A few years after the DEW and Mid Canada Lines caused extensive ecological damage, the White Paper asserted that the CF would ensure "a harmonious natural environment" in the north.[103]

The military can 'greenwash' its operations partly because the environmental movement largely ignores the CF and warfare. But regardless of this blind spot from many environmentalists militarism is inherently anti-ecological.

10. Nuclear Armageddon

EVEN MORE DANGEROUS than chemical/biological warfare and potentially the most ecologically damaging of all military activity are nuclear weapons. Even though this country is not a formal nuclear power, if one were to rank the world's 200 countries in order of their contribution to the nuclear arms race Canada would fall just behind the nine nuclear armed states. For years CF leaders pushed for Canada to formally acquire nuclear weapons. They also supported the USA's atomic weapons.

Uranium from Great Bear Lake in the Northwest Territories was used in the only two nuclear bombs ever dropped on a human population.[1] In *Northern Approaches: Canada and the Search for Peace* James Eayrs notes, "the maiming of Hiroshima and Nagasaki was a by-product of Canadian uranium."[2] The uranium in the atomic bomb dropped on Hiroshima was refined in Port Hope, Ontario, and some of it was probably extracted from Port Radium in the Northwest Territories.[3]

Canada spent millions of dollars (tens of millions in today's money) to research bomb development.[4] Immediately after successfully developing the technology, the US submitted its proposal to drop an atomic bomb on Japan to the tri-state WWII Combined Policy Committee meeting, which included powerful Canadian minister C. D. Howe and a British official.[5] Though there is no record of his comments at the July 4, 1945, meeting, Howe apparently supported the US proposal. After the Japanese were subjected to this lethal assault Howe declared, "it gives me pleasure to announce that Canadian scientists played an important role, having been intimately connected, in an efficient manner, to this great scientific development."[6] (Reflecting the racism in Canadian governing circles, in his (uncensored) diary Prime Minister McKenzie King wrote, "it is fortunate that the use of the bomb should have been upon the Japanese rather than upon the white races of Europe."[7])

The Combined Policy Committee grew out of the August 1943 Québec Agreement merging US and UK nuclear weapons programs. Signed in Québec City, the accord constrained atomic weapon use and information sharing. While Canada didn't formally sign the secret agreement, the federal government was represented on the Combined Policy Committee because of its significant contribution to atomic weapons research.

Canada supported the British nuclear weapons program. During WWII its atomic project was moved to this country for protection.[8] In the years after the war the Defence Research Board (DRB) offered "expertise, diplomatic capital and Canadian facilities" to the UK's Atomic Weapons Research Establishment (AWRE) as they sought to detonate a bomb.[9] DRB officials asked their American counterparts if the British could test a nuclear weapon in US facilities and a number of DRB scientists were loaned to AWRE.[10] In *The Defence Research Board of Canada, 1947 to 1977* Jonathan Turner writes: "(DRB head Omond) Solandt saw the utility of having Canadians trained in the design and development of atomic weapons. Defence Research Board would send three electronics physicists and two radiochemists. The five scientists were to be paid by the DRB and seconded to the Atomic Weapons Research Establishment; they were to go for a period of two years, which would include some preparation work, the [Atomic bomb] test, and some reporting after the test."[11]

Hundreds of Canadian military personnel participated in postwar US and British nuclear weapons development. Between 1946 and 1963, 700 CF members took part in 29 nuclear weapons trials in the US and South Pacific.[12]

During the past 70 years Canada has often been the world's largest producer of uranium, the building block of atomic weapons.[13] From 1942 to 1954 Saskatchewan and Ontario mines supplied 30% of the uranium for the US nuclear weapons program.[14] "Through the 50s and early 60s most of the uranium refined at" Port Hope, Ontario, notes Carole Giangrande in *The Nuclear North*, "ended up in nuclear weapons."[15] By 1959 Canada had sold $1.5 billion worth of uranium to the US bomb program (uranium was then Canada's fourth biggest export).[16]

Home to Canada's primary uranium and radium refining operations for decades, Port Hope, Ontario, was full of radioactive waste.[17] According to one study, 30 centimetres beneath Port Hope's surface lead levels were 22 times the acceptable limit.[18] At the surface they were nearly five times the limit.[19]

For decades residents of the town of 15,000 were left in the dark about the scope of the toxicity around them. But the CF knew. In *Blind Faith, Port Hope and Public Charity for a Corporate Citizen: The Nuclear History of Port Hope, Ontario* Penny Sanger writes that the military used the city to train for the aftermath of nuclear warfare. Soldiers practiced mapping radiation hot spots and moving through contaminated terrain after a nuclear attack.[20] (A $1.3 billion cleanup of the town finally began in 2012.[21])

Canada has sold dozens of nuclear reactors to a half dozen countries and they have often been financed with aid dollars.[22] Through the Colombo assistance plan, for instance, Atomic Energy Canada Limited helped India set up a nuclear reactor in the 1950s. Canada provided the reactor (called Cyrus) India used to develop the bomb. Ottawa proceeded with its nuclear commitment to India despite signals from New Delhi that it was going to detonate a nuclear device. In *The Politics of CANDU Exports* Duane Bratt writes, "the Indians chose to use Cyrus for their supply of plutonium and not one of their other reactors, because Cyrus was not governed by any nuclear safeguards."[23]

Pakistan then responded to its neighbour by using CANDU reactor technology to produce materials for its own nuclear arsenal.[24] In *Atomic Accomplice: How Canada Deals in Deadly Deceit* Paul McKay notes that Canadian uranium fired the nuclear arsenals of numerous countries, including the apartheid regime in South Africa. As white rule came to an end, it was discovered that Canada had assisted Pretoria in developing its capacity to manufacture nuclear weapons.[25]

As the world's top exporter of uranium, Canada has contributed to Depleted Uranium (DU), which can release minute radioactive particles linked to lung cancer and other health ailments.[26] The CF had DU weaponry for decades, only removing DU munitions from its PHALANX weapon system in 1998 after the US navy replaced the DU in its PHALANX mounted cannons.[27]

Since the late 1990s US warplanes have fired DU munitions in Yugoslavia, Afghanistan and Iraq.[28] Cruise missiles launched at Iraq in the early 1990s also contained DU.[29]

Ottawa has largely failed to enforce its rules on restricting DU exports. Nuclear Safety Commission regulations and the Canada-US Nuclear Cooperation Agreement should prohibit Canadian uranium from being used in DU weapons, but Ottawa has been lax in its enforcement.

Since 2007 Canada has abstained on a series of UN resolutions concerning DU munitions.[30] Backed by the vast majority of General Assembly members, the resolutions don't even call for the abolition of DU. They simply call for transparency in their use to enable clean up.[31]

In disarmament talks and other diplomatic forums Canada has generally supported its allies' nuclear weapons. In August 1948 Canada voted against a UN call to ban nuclear weapons.[32] In *Just Dummies — Cruise Missile Testing in Canada* John Clearwater writes, "the record clearly shows that Canada refuses to support any resolution that specifies immediate action on a comprehensive approach to ridding the world of nuclear weapons."[33] Since that book was published the Stephen Harper/Justin Trudeau regimes have not changed direction.[34]

Canada was one of six countries to oppose a 2012 UN vote asking Israel to place its nuclear weapons program under International Atomic Energy Agency controls.[35] In 2015 Canada helped block an international plan to hold a conference on diminishing the stockpile of nuclear weapons in the Middle East.[36] Canada voted against holding and then refused to attend the 2017 Conference to Negotiate a Legally Binding Instrument to Prohibit Nuclear Weapons, Leading Towards their Total Elimination.³⁷ Two-thirds of all countries were represented at a conference that negotiated the Treaty on the Prohibition of Nuclear Weapons, which entered into force in January 2021.

The US has conducted nuclear weapons tests in Canada. In 1952 Canadian officials permitted the US Strategic Air Command to use Canadian air space for training flights of nuclear-armed aircraft. At the same time, reports Ron Finch in *Exporting Danger: A History of the Canadian Nuclear Energy Export Programme,* the US Atomic Energy Commission conducted military tests in Canada to circumvent oversight by domestic "watchdog committees."³⁸ As part of the agreement, Ottawa committed to prevent any investigation into the military aspects of nuclear research in Canada. In early 1956 Canada ruled out banning nuclear tests in this country because they "improved our nuclear defence potential."³⁹

The CF backed US nuclear testing over External Affairs' objections. In *Avoiding Armageddon: Canadian Military Strategy and Nuclear Weapons, 1950–63* Andrew Richter writes, "opposition of DND to controls on nuclear tests appear to have had some effect — as did the strong opposition of both the United States and Britain."⁴⁰

Since 1965 nuclear-armed US submarines have fired torpedoes at CF Maritime Experimental and Test Ranges (CFMETR), Nanoose Bay. Having endorsed Nuclear Weapons Free legislation, BC's NDP government sought a review of Nanoose Bay's environmental impacts in the late 1990s. In response Ottawa expropriated CFMETR's land in the first hostile expropriation of provincial property since the early 20th century.⁴¹

Pierre Trudeau's government claimed to be suffocating the arms race but allowed the US to test cruise missiles at CFB Cold Lake.⁴² The Mulroney government continued this policy. Cruise missiles were designed for unprovoked "first strike" nuclear attacks.⁴³

Only a few years after the first one was built, Ottawa allowed the US to station nuclear weapons in Canada. According to John Clearwater in *Canadian Nuclear Weapons: The Untold Story of Canada's Cold War Arsenal,* the first "nuclear weapons came to Canada as early as September 1950, when the USAF [US Air Force] temporarily stationed eleven 'Fat Man'-style atomic bombs at Goose Bay Newfoundland."[44] In 1963 Lester Pearson's government brought Bomarc missiles to Canada and gave Washington (effective) control over these nuclear missiles.

Acquiring Bomarcs was highly contentious among the civil service and cabinet (it precipitated the fall of John Diefenbaker's government). But DND "was nearly universally in favour of" procuring these nuclear weapons.[45] In their push for Bomarcs, CF leaders disparaged Diefenbaker to US officials.[46]

The last batch of the US nuclear weapons stored at Canadian airbases — Genie air-to-air missiles — were returned in 1984.[47]

Canadian forces based in Europe were equipped with nukes. At the height of Canadian nuclear deployments in the late 1960s the CF had between 250 and 450 atomic bombs at its disposal.[48] These included nuclear tipped Honest John surface-to-surface missiles and the Germany based CF-104 Starfighter, which operated without a gun and carried nothing but a thermal nuclear weapon (MK 28 bomb).[49]

Canadian airmen placed significant "importance" on acquiring an "offensive nuclear-strike role."[50] The RCAF began secret negotiations with their US counterparts for nuclear weapons. "The clandestine nature of these discussions over the assignment of nuclear targets begs the question as to the RCAF's motivation for secrecy," notes *Swords, Clunks and Widowmakers: The Tumultuous Life of the RCAF's Original One Canadian Air Division*.[51] Airforce leaders didn't want government officials to know their plans.

Beginning in 1950, notes Clearwater, the "Canadian military longed for the weapon which separated the military haves from the have-nots."[52] In 1960 DND developed a position in favour of formally acquiring nuclear weapons.[53] Jonathan Turner notes, "the [Defence Research] Board, and especially the Chiefs of Staff, were keen to acquire Canadian atomic and nuclear weapons."[54] A 1961 Joint Staff paper titled "Nuclear Weapons for Canadian Forces" opened by saying its objective was "to present a rationale in support of nuclear weapons for the Canadian Armed Forces."[55] External Affairs was opposed.[56] General George Pearkes believed Canada should acquire nuclear weapons because it, unlike other countries, would never use them unreasonably.[57]

To this day Canada participates in the NATO Nuclear Planning Group and contributes personnel and financial support to NATO's Nuclear Policy Directorate.[58] In 1954 Canada backed NATO forces' use of nuclear weapons.[59] These ghastly weapons remain "a core component of the Alliance's overall capabilities."[60] Through NATO Canada has effectively committed to fighting a nuclear war if any country breached its boundaries.[61]

***

The nuclear weapons debate and the CF's push to acquire them highlights the negative effects of "military culture" on democracy. CF leaders were willing to keep secrets from elected officials and side with a foreign country's military over other Canadian government departments in order to gain access to the most powerful weapons ever produced. This makes sense to generals whose job is tied to commanding the greatest military might possible, even if it runs counter to democratic oversight.

But this is just one of many examples of the negative effects of military culture.

11. A Culture of Sexism and Racism

AS STATED EARLIER, the military is by far the largest Canadian government department, employing the largest number and purchasing the most equipment. But its influence is far greater than its economic footprint. The CF expends enormous resources on ideological outreach, which greatly influence the Canadian self-image. It promotes the idea that serving in the military is the ultimate act of citizenship, that fighting in wars is worthy of memorials, ovations at sporting events and an annual statutory holiday. With soldiering glamorized in film, TV, books and journalism, it should not be surprising when military culture negatively influences Canadian society.

Patriarchy

"While women are present and have advanced in the CF," wrote Lynne Gouliquer in Soldiering in the Canadian Forces: How and Why Gender Counts!, "it seems equally evident that women's presence is tolerated officially while being rejected and marginalized in reality and culturally."[1] Giving weight to Gouliquer's 2011 PhD thesis, former Supreme Court justice Marie Deschamps found a "culture of misogyny" in the CF "hostile to women and LGTBQ members."[2] Her 2015 investigation concluded, "the overall perception is that a 'boys club' culture still prevails in the armed forces."[3] Four years later Deschamps told the House of Commons defence committee there had been little progress in eliminating sexism within the CF.[4]

Until 1979 women were excluded from the military colleges.[5] Until 1989 women were excluded from combat roles in the CF.[6] In 2000 the submarine service was opened to women.

Women represented 16.3% of military personnel in 2021.[7] The military brass says it hopes to increase that number to 25% by 2027.

In 1990 DND began monitoring gender equity.[8] A 1992 survey found that 26.2% of female CF respondents were sexually harassed in the previous 12 months.⁹ Subsequent investigations showed steady improvements.¹⁰ But in 2016 over a quarter of women still reported having been victims of sexual assault at least once since joining the CF and Deschamps' review found "an undeniable problem of sexual harassment and sexual assault in the CAF."¹¹ Between April 1, 2016, and March 9, 2021, there were 581 sexual assault and 221 sexual harassment complaints implicating CF members.¹²

In 2017 plaintiffs in five separate cities united to sue over sexual assault, harassment and gender-based discrimination in the CF. Four years later the federal government put up another $900 million to settle lawsuits from 4,600 CF members and DND employees who faced gender discrimination and sexual assault.¹³

A 2019 report found little progress in combating sexual assaults. It concluded that nearly 900 CF personnel said they were victims of sexual assault in the past year with 4.3 per cent of women in the regular forces saying they'd been victims.¹⁴ Another study showed that soldiers tried in military courts for sexual abuse were acquitted at far greater rates than defendants in civilian courts.¹⁵ It added that the CF kept the rate of acquittal confidential.

Sexual violence during international deployments has received little attention. When Nichola Goddard became the first female CF member to die in Afghanistan it came to light that she wrote her husband about sexual violence on the base. Goddard wrote about "the tension of living in a fortress where men outnumbered women ten to one" and "there were six rapes in the camp last week, so we have to work out an escort at night."¹⁶ But, the CF only admits to investigating five reports of sexual harassment or assault in Afghanistan between 2004 and 2010.¹⁷ Author of *Sunray: The Death and Life of Captain Nichola Goddard* Valerie Fortney said she "hit a brick wall" when she sought to investigate sexual harassment in Afghanistan.¹⁸

Spousal abuse is a significant concern in military communities. Various aspects of military life make spouses particularly vulnerable to abuse.¹⁹ In *The First Casualty: Violence Against Women in Canadian*

Military Communities Deborah Harrison writes, "the abused military wife has two major strikes against her. First, her husband's occupation is at the high end of the spectrum of occupations that legitimate controlling behaviour and explicitly devalue women. Second, such aspects of her lifestyle as postings [to different locations], the intimidatory culture of the military, and [for some] residency in a PMQ [military housing] exacerbate her vulnerability to her husband's control."[20]

A 2000 study titled "Report on the Canadian Forces' Response to Woman Abuse in Military Families" found a great deal of hostility from victims towards the CF. It noted, "almost every survivor we interviewed felt bitter, not only toward her husband or former husband, but toward the CF as well. Regardless of the positive or negative quality of their interactions with individual supervisors, MPs, padres, social work officers, or FRC staff, survivors had negative things to say, overall, about the CF."[21]

Veterans have repeatedly engaged in shocking gender-based violence. In 2017 Lionel Desmond killed his wife, daughter, mother and himself while Robert Giblin stabbed and threw his pregnant wife off a building before killing himself in 2015.[22]

The perpetrators of the two worst incidents of patriarchal violence in Canadian history were drawn to the CF. Before allegedly carrying out a 2018 van attack in Toronto that left 10 mostly women dead Alek Minassian posted on Facebook about the "Incel Rebellion," a community of "involuntarily celibate" men who hate women. Minassian also cited his (short) military service.

In 1989 Marc Lépine massacred fourteen women at the Université de Montréal while shouting "you're all a bunch of feminists, and I hate feminists!" Lépine previously failed his attempt to join the CF.[23]

After the Montréal massacre members of the elite Airborne Regiment reportedly held a celebratory dinner to honour Lepine.[24]

A patriarchal purveyor of violence, the CF is the institutional embodiment of 'toxic masculinity'.

***

Members suspected of being gay were systematically purged from the CF until 1992.[25] During WWII medical personnel labeled soldiers involved in same gender sex as suffering from "psychiatric disorders".[26] In the two decades after WWII gay and lesbian members were labeled "sex deviants" and discharged. When the three branches of the CF were unified in the late 60s, a new administrative order excluded gays and lesbians.[27]

The Special Investigative Unit spied on soldiers suspected of being queer. They photographed members' cars in "cruisy areas" and conducted surveillance near gay bars.[28] An administrative order stated, "if a person subject to the Code of Discipline [CF member] becomes aware or suspect that a member of the Canadian Forces is a homosexual, or has a sexual abnormality, he shall report the matter to the commanding officer."[29]

A 1960s effort by Carleton University's psychology department to develop a "fruit machine" to detect queers was heavily influenced by academics who worked for the Defence Research Board, DND, army, navy and air force. DRB funded the research into the "fruit machine".[30]

During the 1980s at least 170 individuals were formally released from the CF for homosexuality. The actual number may have been significantly higher.[31] Many individuals outed by the CF were then ostracized by their families and friends.[32]

After decades of resistance from within and outside the CF, Special Investigations Unit officer Michelle Douglas fought her 1989 expulsion under administrative release item 5d: "Not Advantageously Employable Due to Homosexuality". An impending hearing before the Federal Court prompted the government to ban discrimination on the basis of sexual orientation in the CF.

The CF leadership resisted until the end. In response to changes announced in 1991, Chief of Defence Staff John de Chastelain said the policy would not prevent the military from refusing to tolerate "sexual misconduct which can be demonstrated to have a disruptive effect on operational effectiveness."[33]

Today, there are at least a dozen openly gay officers. In 2017 Jonathan Vance was the first chief of defence staff to participate in a Pride parade. But queers in the CF still face substantial stigma.

White Supremacy

Given its roots as an appendage of the British colonial military it should be no surprise that the CF has been a hot bed of white supremacy. For decades institutional racism was explicit and imposed from above.

Few non-whites were part of the militia. Bitter with the appointment of a Black Indian agent BC militia leader Lt.-Col. Charles Flick declared to a superior in 1912, "the Canadian militia is a military organization of white men who represent the Anglo-Saxon race, and men of colour have nothing to do with our deliberations."[34] In the 1930s the Black community in Nova Scotia was largely excluded from the militia. A survey of 14 militia units found that none wanted Black personnel, calling instead for the formation of coloured units or sub-units.[35]

During the First World War recruiting officers in BC generally refused to accept Chinese Canadians. They had to travel to other provinces to enlist. Then in April 1917 the Ottawa-based assistant attorney general wrote, "regulations do not permit of the enlistment of Chinamen in the Canadian Expeditionary Force."[36]

Japanese Canadians were only accepted into the CF after significant lobbying. The BC government discouraged their enlistment partly because it didn't want them to gain the vote.[37] Associate deputy minister of the national war services, Lieutenant-Colonel Léo Richer La Flèche, noted, "if these men are called upon to perform the duties of citizens and bear arms for Canada, it will be impossible to resist the argument that they are entitled to the franchise."[38]

Sikhs in British Columbia were also blocked. Military leaders suggested they could join the war but felt they should enlist in India.[39]

In the east Black Canadians seeking to fight in Europe faced similar prejudice (though the location from which they made their request significantly impacted acceptance rates).[40] Chief of the General Staff General W. G. Gwatkin vehemently opposed African-Canadian enlistment. In April 1916, in the midst of a recruiting crisis, he wrote, "the civilized negro is vain and imitative; in Canada he is not impelled to enlist by a high sense of duty; in the trenches he is not likely to make a good fighter."[41]

After significant pressure the military authorized a Negro Construction Battalion in July 1916. The Nova Scotia raised battalion was under the command of white officers.[42] Not allowed to fight or attend recreational activities with other CF units, they cut lumber, dug trenches and built huts.[43] Some government officials wrote "n…er" on their documents.[44]

People of colour allowed to join the war effort were generally given lower status tasks. In charge of the military district that included BC, Brigadier C. V. Stockwell warned, "it would be very lowering to the prestige of the white race if they were to become the menials of the coloured races."[45]

For years navy and air force racism was codified. Sometimes, however, local recruiters ignored or weren't aware of racist directives, which varied depending upon institutional needs and public pressure.

The 1906 British "Regulations for the Entry of Naval Cadets" said, "candidates must be of pure European descent."[46] In 1938 the RCN initiated exclusionary policies, which the federal cabinet quickly approved. The policy required recruits to be of "Pure European Descent and of the White Race."[47]

Prior to WWII, the RCAF's "colour line" was stricter than the RCN's. Its policy stated, "all candidates must be British subjects and of pure European descent."[48] In 1941 the deputy director of manning in the personnel branch at headquarters, H. P. Crabb, issued a clarification letter to all recruiting offices regarding "Orientals and Negro applicants". It stated, "only those of European descent will be accepted for appointment or enlistment in Aircrew."[49] In other words, Asian and Black applicants could enlist but they were only eligible for less prestigious ground duty positions.[50]

At the start of 1946 the RCAF reinstated a requirement that applications from Black, "Oriental" and "former enemy aliens" be forwarded to headquarters for approval. Denying there were restrictions placed upon the eligibility of "coloured applicants", the chief of the air staff claimed "coloured" applications had to be sent to headquarters to "carefully scrutinize" whether the applicant could "mix" with whites, which was "for the protection and future welfare of the applicant."[51] The policy was still employed by the RCAF in 1956.[52]

The CF has largely failed to recognize its history of racist enlistment policies. There has not been an official apology, let alone affirmative action policies to correct the injustice. Even after the end of racist enlistment policies, sought-after ranks in the RCN and RCAF, as well as the army, were reserved for white men. It wasn't until 2016, for instance, that a Black person captained a sea-going RCN vessel.[53]

Despite making up 20% of the Canadian population, visible minorities represented 9.6 per cent of the CF in 2021.[54]

Racism remains a significant issue in the CF. In 2019 CBC reported on two Black civilian employees at CFB Halifax who faced years of discrimination from CF bosses, which forced them out of their jobs.[55] The previous year it was revealed that a white reservist who repeatedly called Black soldiers "n...ers" would not face any disciplinary measures.[56] The stated reason was that the individual, whose father was a senior reserve soldier, was "under a lot of pressure" during training.[57] Incredibly, during the investigation Defence Minister Harjit Sajjan inquired about the treatment of the accused — not the victims — after the mother of the soldier who made the slurs complained to his office.[58]

In 2016 three former CF members sued over systemic racism. Their suit claimed that "derogatory slurs, racial harassment and violent threats are tolerated or ignored ... Victims of racism within the

Canadian Forces are forced into isolation, subjected to further trauma and, in many cases, catapulted toward early release."[59]

One of those who launched the suit was Wallace Fowler who detailed his experience of racism in a series of articles and a book titled *Checkmate*. In the early 2000s his daughter was spat on in school, a bus driver called his son a "n...er" and his wife had bananas thrown at her at the base in Esquimalt. Fowler filed numerous official complaints, which were effectively ignored.[60] Worse still, he faced retribution and an apparent cover-up, highlighting systemic racism in the force.

In the years before this book went to print there was a stream of stories about right wing extremists in the military:

- In 2020 the CF reinstated reservist Boris Mihajlovic, who was an active member of Blood and Honour, a banned neo-Nazi terrorist organization.
- In 2019 the *Winnipeg Free Press* identified Army Reservist Master Cpl. Patrik Mathews as a neo-Nazi who posted racist posters across that city.[61]
- In 2019 CBC reported on a sailor in Halifax with a tattoo on his arm featuring the word "infidel" in the shape of a rifle.[62]
- In 2018 Ricochet reported that three soldiers in Alberta operated an online white supremacist military surplus store that glorified white-ruled Rhodesia (Zimbabwe).[63]
- A 2018 VICE investigation concluded that former Nova Scotia reservist Brandon Cameron was a prominent member of the neo-Nazi Atomwaffen Division.[64]
- On Canada Day 2017 five CF members disrupted an indigenous rally in front of a statue of violent colonialist Edward Cornwallis in Halifax. The soldiers were members of the Proud Boys, which described itself as "a fraternal organization of Western Chauvinists who will no longer apologize for creating the modern world."[65]
- The three founders of Québec anti-Islam/immigrant "alt right" group La Meute were ex-military.[66] Radio-Canada found that 75 members of La Meute's private Facebook group were

CF members.⁶⁷ After it received media attention the CF banned active members from participating in the organization, but afterwards La Meute co-founder Patrick Beaudry told *La Presse* "I have many friends and relatives still in the Forces."⁶⁸

A CF report leaked to the media found at least 53 military members connected to hate groups or hate activity between 2013 and 2018.⁶⁹

A scholar of Canada's far-right, Ryan Scrivens told VICE there was a history of right-wing extremists in the CF: "Within the Canadian military, there are distinct neo-Nazi and racist skinhead groups operating across the country and training for what they believe is a future race war."⁷⁰

***

Militarism and war stoke xenophobia. They engender an "Us vs. Them" mentality that makes individuals more receptive to racism. There is also a need to dehumanize the enemy.

Revealing their racist sentiment, some of the Voyageurs deployed to Sudan in 1884 told the *Toronto Globe* that Egyptians were "filthy", "detestable" and "dirty".⁷¹ During the war in South Africa Boers were labeled cruel, crafty, "wicked people" while during WWI Canadian soldiers disparaged Germans as "Huns", "Heinies" and "krauts".⁷² During WWI 8,500 Ukrainians and other 'enemy aliens' were interned for no justifiable security reason. At the end of WWI the Great War Veterans Association was openly racist. It supported, sometimes violent, attacks on new Canadians.⁷³ After rumours a disabled veteran was harmed by a Greek waiter, veterans damaged Greek-owned restaurants on the Danforth in Toronto in 1917.⁷⁴ They also smashed up Chinese-owned businesses in Halifax.⁷⁵

During WWII Germans and Japanese were subjected to significant racism. Twenty thousand Japanese-Canadians were interned for no justifiable security reason.

In the early 1950s Canadian troops denigrated the "yellow horde" of North Korean and Chinese "chinks" they fought.⁷⁶

During the 1992-93 Somali mission Corporal Matt Mackay, a self-confessed neo-Nazi who declared he'd quit the white supremacist movement two years before going to Somalia, gleefully reported "we haven't killed enough n...ers yet."[77] Another Canadian soldier was caught on camera saying the Somalia intervention was called, "Operation Snatch Nig-nog." Yet another soldier explained how Somalis were not starving; "they never were, they're lazy, they're slobs, and they stink."[78]

Some Canadian soldiers in Afghanistan described the Taliban and local population as "towel heads" and "camel jockeys".[79] Even Chief of the Defence Staff Rick Hillier publicly referred to the enemy in Afghanistan as a "bowl of snakes."[80]

In a sign of its xenophobia, the CF ordered 650 training targets in 2015 with ethnic descriptions. Soldiers fired at names like "Somali Male AK 47" and "Bosnian Male RPG".[81]

To repeat, warfare engenders an "Us vs. Them" mentality that breeds xenophobia and militarists tend to promote a "scary" worldview amenable to racism. In a bid to pad their budget, they exaggerate self-serving security threats. The danger posed by China, Iran, North Korea, Russia, Taliban, Islamic terror, etc. are exaggerated while the danger posed by pandemics, private automobiles, industrial pollutants or climate disturbances are ignored.

First Nations

As discussed previously, Canadian militarism has disproportionately affected First Nations. But there has also been longstanding indigenous participation in Canadian militarism. Sixty Mohawk and two-dozen Métis boatmen joined the 385 men who navigated the raging cataracts of the Nile River to re-conquer Khartoum in 1884.[82] With enlistment rates above the national average, 4,000 indigenous men volunteered during WWI.[83] Over 3,000 indigenous men enlisted to fight in WWII and several hundred more volunteered for service in the US-led destruction of Korea.[84]

During WWI and WWII indigenous people generally faced fewer restrictions on enlistment than Black, Japanese, Chinese and Indo-Canadians. But education requirements still effectively excluded them from the RCN and RCAF. A 1944 recruitment manual on "Enlistment of Indians and Half Breeds" noted "care should be taken when accepting applications from or approaching Indians as prospective recruits. Here education standards are strictly adhered to. Experience has shown that they cannot stand long periods of confinement, discipline and strenuous physical and nervous demand incidental to modern army routine. On the other hand, some very fine Indians have been enlisted, but these are usually persons who have had their schooling and training in Indian residential school."[85]

During WWI the senior Indian Affairs official in Winnipeg, Lieutenant Colonel Glen Campbell, sought to raise an indigenous battalion by recruiting from the Elkhorn residential school.[86] An unknown number of the 4,000 indigenous people who fought in WWI were in a cadet corps at a residential school, which removed indigenous children from their families to assimilate them into the colonizers' culture.

Cadet Corps existed at many residential schools and were for many years "a core part of the federal government presence in the North and on reserves."[87] The Mohawk Institute in Brantford, Ontario — "the oldest continuously operated Anglican residential school in Canada" — set up the Mohawk Institute Cadet Corps in the 1800s.[88] During the 1930s the Cecilia Jeffery Residential School Cadet band toured Ontario, Manitoba and the US. With the Kenora, Ontario, kids' indigeneity part of the spectacle, the residential school band was invited to play at the King's coronation in England in 1937, 1938 World's Exhibition in Glasgow and a Royal visit to Winnipeg in 1939.[89]

In 1953 military officials deliberated privately over whether they should seek the permission of indigenous parents for their children's participation in the cadets. Reflecting a colonial attitude, the officers concluded it wasn't necessary.[90]

In 1958 the BC Indian commissioner wrote that he was "greatly impressed with the integrating values of [cadet] camps to these lads."[91]

In the mid-1960s DND signed an accord with Indian Affairs and Northern Development to recruit from the Cadet Corp at residential schools. As part of the agreement, a recently shuttered Cadet Corp was reopened at the Churchill Vocational School, which used a former CF base in the Manitoba town.[92]

Other residential schools benefited from CF infrastructure. In the 1940s-50s indigenous students were housed in a former CF training complex near Prince Albert, Saskatchewan.[93] Two decades later Commanding Officer of Thunder Bay District J. A. Mitchell proposed that CFS Armstrong become a "residential vocational training school for the local Indians."[94]

Similar to kids being taken from their families to advance the colonial project, the Inuit were ripped from their homes to establish Canadian/CF dominion over the far north. In 1949 RCAF Station Resolute Bay was established 800 km from the North Pole and the next year Canadian Forces Station Alert was located on the northeastern tip of Ellesmere Island, the northern most point of Canadian territory. As part of solidifying the base and Ottawa's territorial claims, 87 Inuit living in northern Québec were forcibly relocated 2,000 km north to Resolute Bay and Ellesmere Island in 1953.[95]

As discussed earlier, waste from the DEW Line, a network of 63 radar and communications stations in the Arctic Circle connected to Station Resolute Bay, was linked to depleted fish stocks and agitated caribou indigenous peoples subsisted on.[96] A half-century after the DEW line was abandoned in the mid-1960s the Department of Indian Affairs and Northern Development was still cleaning up 21 DEW Line sites.[97] With little consultation, the DEW line pushed northern indigenous peoples into a wage economy and sedentary lifestyle. The massive project left deep social scars.[98]

One thousand kilometres south of the DEW line, 98 "Mid Canada Line" radar sites spilled PCB's and other toxic substances for decades.

Representing seven indigenous communities in northern Ontario, the Mushkegowuk Council campaigned to have the government clean up the heavy metals, DDT, asbestos, PCB's and petroleum seeping out of the abandoned radar sites.[99] In researching the "Mid Canada Line" site at Moosonee, Laurentian University PhD candidate Sue Heffernan wrote that its "social and physical (landscape) impacts ... were irrelevant to the military planners" and that "local people almost seem to have been 'invisible'" during their construction.[100]

In Labrador low-level training flights by NATO fighter jets scared wildlife and damaged the Innu's way of life. As a result of supersonic jets skimming the ground, ducks laid eggs a month early, caribou changed migration patterns and beavers all but vanished.[101] Through the 1980s hundreds of Innu were arrested and forcibly relocated for opposing the military's appropriation of their lands and damage to their way of life.[102]

Incredibly, the 1971 White Paper on Defence claimed the CF needed to deepen its footprint in the far north to maintain the "harmonious natural environment."[103] For their part, indigenous leaders said the CF buildup in the north threatened the landscape and their cultural survival. In 1986 Chief of the Assembly of First Nations George Erasmus saw "no military threat in the Canadian North" outside the CF.[104] Echoing this thinking, President of the Inuit Circumpolar Conference Mary Simon (appointed Canada's governor-general in July, 2021), later decried measures "justified by the government on the basis of defence and military considerations... [that] often serve to promote our insecurity."[105]

Further south, the CF suppressed land struggles. In aid of the civil power, the military was deployed during the standoff with the Mohawks of Kanehsatake and Kahnawake in 1990. The CF played a smaller role at Gustafsen Lake, Ipperwash and Elsipogtog as well as in monitoring indigenous groups.

The military was deployed during the 1990 Oka Crisis, which was spurred by Mohawk opposition to the expansion of a golf course and housing on land that included an indigenous burial ground. About 2,500 regular and reserve troops were put on standby while 800 members of the Royal 22e Regiment relieved Sûreté du Québec police at the Kahnawake and Kanesatake barricades.[106] Two fighter planes, three high-tech Leopard tanks, numerous artillery elements and 20 helicopters were also engaged. Additionally, an "Aurora reconnaissance aircraft gathered photo intelligence at Oka," noted P. Whitney Lackenbauer, "while a special unit collected signals intelligence."[107]

It is widely known that members of the Royal 22e Regiment were on the front line of the conflict for a month. It is less recognized that military personnel and equipment were "moved discreetly from Valcartier to Montreal" at the start of the 78-day standoff.[108]

After the summer 1990 Oka Crisis the military continued to target the Mohawks. The CF police's Special Operations Branch engaged in covert reconnaissance and, in its first scheduled action, JTF2 special forces surveyed the reserve. According to David Pugliese, "JFT2 would play a key role in conducting surveillance on the cigarette and gun smuggling rings, in particular, those operating in Akwasasne and Kanesatake."[109] In 1994 the CF trained for an invasion of Kahnawake, Akwesasne, Kanehsatake and Tyendinaga. Alongside 4,000 federal and provincial police, 1,500 soldiers prepared for "Scorpion Saxon".[110] JTF2 also trained for the operation and to respond to any indigenous solidarity protests elsewhere. "JTF2 would be needed to deal with any attacks by natives on key points such as water treatment plants and highways," Pugliese writes.[111] The invasions were called off after the media reported the plans and CSIS warned the government it risked causing "grave political violence".[112]

The CF supported the 1993 Ontario Provincial Police deployment at Camp Ipperwash. A special military investigation unit surveyed the Ojibway protesters' re-occupation of land the CF took from them during WWII.[113]

Two years later the RCMP employed CF armoured personnel carriers and other equipment, including land mines, against Shuswap traditionalists at Gustafsen Lake.[114] The CF supported the violent police action against individuals who organized a Sun Dance on land they claimed a legal right to.[115] JTF2 are mentioned a couple times in RCMP files about the conflict in the BC interior in which tens of thousands of rounds were fired.[116] Some of the Shuswap traditionalists insist JTF2 — not the RCMP — engaged them in battle after a land mine detonated in their path on September 15, 1995.[117]

In 2013 the CF's National Counter-Intelligence Unit monitored the Mi'kmaq-led anti-fracking camp in Elsipogtog, New Brunswick.[118] While no CF personnel were involved in the eventual police raid, the military provided the RMCP with space for a staging area at CFB Gagetown and CF Moncton Detachment. The military also provided lunches for 60 to 100 personnel, according to a "Request for Canadian Forces Assistance" form submitted by the RCMP.[119]

Despite claiming not to spy on Canadians, the CF monitored indigenous dissent.[120] Between 2010 and mid-2011 the CF's National Counter-Intelligence Unit produced at least eight reports concerning indigenous organizations.[121] *Policing Indigenous Movements* documents CF surveillance of the 2012-13 Idle No More protests. In that book Andrew Crosby and Jeffrey Monaghan note how they "closely monitored Idle No More related events which were construed in DND reporting as an open quote domestic security threat."[122]

A 2012 report shared with the Five Eyes intelligence network mentioned the Mohawks of Akwesasne as a potential threat.[123] Similarly, a draft version of the military's 2007 counter-insurgency manual highlighted "radical Native American Organizations" as potential military targets. "The rise of radical Native American organizations, such as the Mohawk Warrior Society, can be viewed as insurgencies with specific and limited aims," the 250-page manual stated. "Although they do not seek complete control of the federal government, they do seek particular political concessions in their relationship with national governments and control (either overt or covert) of political affairs at a local/reserve ('First Nation') level, through the threat of, or use of, violence."[124] Two years in development, the manual was to guide CF doctrine and fighting practices for years.

Over the past two decades there has been a push to commemorate indigenous contributions to Canadian militarism. A growing number of landmarks and monuments honour or bear the names of indigenous veterans. Established in 2001, the National Aboriginal Veterans Monument in Ottawa is apparently the only official monument in Ottawa commemorating indigenous peoples or history.[125] The third Canadian Ranger patrol group headquarters, a monument at CFB Borden and a Parry Sound statue are dedicated to top WWI indigenous sniper Francis Pegahmagabow.[126] WWII and Korea veteran Tommy Prince has a statue, school, street, base, drill hall, educational scholarship and cadet corps named in his honour.[127] A 2018 navy statement noted, "the Royal Canadian Navy (RCN) has a long history of ties to the Indigenous peoples of Canada. In fact, it paid homage to them by naming two separate classes of ships after them — the wartime Tribal-class and the post-war Iroquois-class destroyers — and several other vessels, including three Oberon-class submarines."[128]

Receiving input from its Defence Aboriginal Advisory Group, the CF operates various programs focused on indigenous youth. CF recruiters participate in National Aboriginal Day events and oversee the Aboriginal Entry Plan, a three-week training program.[129] In 1971 the CF introduced the Northern Native Entry Program and the Cadet Corps has long worked with band councils and schools on reserves.[130] Bold Eagle, Raven and Black Bear are CF training programs for 16-25-year-olds from reserves. Partnering with the Federation of Saskatchewan Indian Nations and the Saskatchewan Indian Veteran's Association, the CF launched Bold Eagle in 1990. It's a "five-day Culture Camp" conducted by First Nations elders "followed by a military recruit training course."[131]

The military's immense resources and cultural clout enables it to attract indigenous youth. Today, the indigenous proportion of the CF is near their share of the general population (three per cent).[132] At least 2,300 indigenous people are part of the CF.[133]

Still, indigenous members of the CF face "systemic racism," according to a 2016 report by the Defence Aboriginal Advisory Group. "We strongly believe there is a systemic issue within the Department of National Defence (DND) and Canadian Armed Forces (CAF) that is rampant throughout all ranks and elements of Land, Air Force and Navy."[134]

***

Given its history of colonizing the lands belonging to indigenous people and its "King and Country" racist past, or the misogyny of warrior culture, it is no surprise the CF has a problem with sexism and racism. In some ways this is simply a reflection of a societal problem. But as the next chapter points out, elements of military command structures reinforce the most undemocratic and ignorant impulses of Canadian society.

12. Hierarchy Versus Democracy

"Military hierarchies sensibly insist upon obedience to orders and upon prompt, total discipline. Ethics, however, demurs, insisting upon conditional and contextual obedience to orders, which ought to be obeyed if lawful. So there is often, but not always, tension between the demands of military authority (or command) and the demands of ethical judgment (or conscience)"

J. H. Toner[1]

CF CULTURE AND STRUCTURES are frequently in opposition to pluralistic, democratic, values. So are the demands of warfare. This is why people with extreme right-wing beliefs are often attracted to the military as it conforms to their views on how society should function.

Loyalty, conformity and obeying orders are considered essential by the CF. There's little room to challenge authority or injustices and voting is nearly nonexistent.[a] Political meetings are not allowed on base and it is prohibited to establish a feminist, environmental or socialist club.[2]

Large sums are spent on uniforms, medals, ribbons, etc. designed to stir loyalty, strengthen discipline and reinforce hierarchy. Restrictions on head and facial hair engender conformity and obedience. So does hazing, polishing boots, pressing uniforms, etc. More obviously, saluting and marching in formation teach individuals to obey commands.

The CF is incredibly hierarchical. Ranging from Private Basic/Ordinary Seaman to General/Admiral, there are nineteen ranks in the CF.[3] In deference to authority, the lower ranks must salute and obey orders from higher ranks. CF uniforms, badges and bars help individuals know who they must salute and obey.

---

[a] *HMCS Uganda* is the only ship in naval history known to have voted to leave a war, according to Tony German in The Sea is at Our Gates: the history of the Canadian Navy. Towards the end of WWII Ottawa announced that only volunteers would be deployed to the Pacific. Already fighting off Okinawa, the crew of Uganda was asked to vote on whether they wished to continue operating there. A mix of inhospitable living conditions, Kamikaze attacks and a demeaning speech by the captain prompted two-thirds of the crew to vote to return home.

There are few ways to legitimately challenge authority in the CF. Military members are not permitted to sign petitions complaining of unjust conditions. Nor are the rank-and-file allowed to unionize. Majority rule or even influence runs counter to CF principles. The rank-and-file collectively refusing an order is considered mutiny and is punishable by life in imprison (formerly by death).[4]

Military personnel are not entitled to jury trials. Unlike a number of European countries, the CF military justice system is not under civilian authority. CF members are subject to military law and tried in military courts even when the alleged crimes are committed off-duty and aren't related to military affairs.

Soldiers have to follow a DND code of values and ethics and Queens Regulations and Orders, which reinforce hierarchy and undercut solidarity. Members are required to reveal secrets about their peers when supervisors ask. Failure do so is severely punished.[5]

CF members are restricted in what they can say publicly or post online. Under the Defence Administrative Orders and Directives and Queens Regulations and Orders, soldiers are not allowed to discredit the CF or discourage other troops from their duties. Any "enunciation, defence or criticism, expressed or implied, of service, departmental or government policy" is forbidden.[6] With the rise of social media the chief of defence staff ordered CF members to obtain authorization before posting information on Facebook or other online outlets. In 2006 Rick Hillier wrote, "members are to consult with their chain of command before publishing [CF]- related information and imagery to the internet, regardless of how innocuous the information may seem."[7]

Through dozens of publications distributed on bases the hierarchy shapes the flow of information within the force and has been prepared to aggressively censor information. During the mid-1990s United Nations Protection Force mission in Yugoslavia, an image-conscious DND failed to gather proper records of casualties.[8] Confused by the lack of accurate records, the editor of the army's *Garrison* newspaper, Captain Bob Kennedy, published a Canadian casualty list. A few days after he gave an interview about Canadian casualties in the Balkans, the head of Public Affairs advised Kennedy "his services were no longer required" and he was dismissed from the military.[9]

The military brass also tried to shutter critical military-focused media. In *Unembedded: Two Decades of Maverick War Reporting*, Scott Taylor describes the military's effort to kneecap *Esprit de Corps*, which aimed "to contribute to the esprit de corps that has made the Canadian military one of the finest professional armed forces in the world."[10] To gain access to Air Canada military charters in the late 1980s, the magazine was to obtain DND "approval for all editorial content prior to publication."[11] But in 1991 *Esprit de Corps* criticized the appointment of Marcel Massé as defence minister and interviewed Vice Admiral Chuck Thomas after he resigned as vice chief of defence. In response DND directed Air Canada to stop carrying *Esprit de Corps*. The airline sent the magazine a note saying, "due to concerns over editorial content, the Department of National Defence has ordered Air Canada to cease distribution of Esprit de Corps aboard military charter flights."[12]

Almost entirely distributed in-flight at the time, DND's move might have crippled the magazine, but the CF backed down after *Esprit de Corps* went public and then privately threatened to reveal a possible conflict of interest between Chief of Defence Staff John de Chastelain and *Canadian Defence Quarterly*.[13]

When *Esprit de Corps* helped expose the military's attempt to cover up the 1993 killings in Somalia, the CF again targeted the magazine. Taylor writes, "memos were sent to the CANEX military retail stores, ordering them to cease the sale of our publication; the copies we had donated through the Royal Canadian Legion were to be burned, according to the official directive from National Defence Headquarters."[14] Even more debilitating for the magazine, DND asked *Esprit de Corps* defence clients to "cancel their advertising contracts."[15]

More than other large bureaucratic institutions, the CF is highly secretive. "In the culture of the Canadian Army," writes Isabel Campbell, "the idea that the public had a right to note, to debate, and to participate in decisions violated principles of military loyalty; loyalty, discretion, and privilege dominated even in matters where security was irrelevant."[16]

To enable democratic oversight of public institutions the Access to Information Act gives individuals the right to government records for a small fee. The Directorate of Information Support of the Strategic Joint Staff can restrict information for numerous reasons, including if deemed "injurious to the conduct of international affairs, the defence of Canada or the detection, prevention or suppression of subversive or hostile activities."[17] While sensitive information is rarely released, censorship is often employed arbitrarily or to avoid embarrassment. In 2006 the *Ottawa Citizen*'s David Pugliese detailed the results of 23 access requests in which 87 pieces of information were censored for "security reasons", which had previously been released or were available on government web sites.[18]

DND has repeatedly broken access laws. In early 2019 Pugliese reported that top military officers denied the existence of an internal report even though they were warned doing so would be illegal under the Access to Information Act.[19] The office of the CF's top legal adviser, Judge Advocate General Commodore Geneviève Bernatchez, denied the existence of an internal report highlighting problems with the court martial system even though there were electronic and paper copies of the document.[20]

This incident came on the heels of a DND official telling the pre-trial hearing of Vice Admiral Mark Norman that his superiors deliberately omitted his name from documents to skirt access rules. After receiving an access request concerning Norman, the official brought it to his superior. According to the late 2018 testimony, "he gives me a smile and says … 'Don't worry, this isn't our first rodeo. We made sure we never used his name [in internal communications]. Send back nil return.'"[21]

In 2015 the Federal Court of Appeal reprimanded DND for responding to an information request concerning the sale of military assets by saying it would take 1,100 days to retrieve the information.²² Under access law public institutions must produce records within 30 days or inform the requester of a reasonable extension.

Informed an officer attended a talk Rideau Institute director Steven Staples delivered about the war in Afghanistan on January 26, 2006, Pugliese requested all CF documents mentioning public speeches in Halifax between January 15 and 30 of that year. Department officials claimed they did "a thorough and complete search" and couldn't find any record of an officer who attended the function and wrote a report. But the officer assigned to Staples' speech inadvertently left a record. When the *Ottawa Citizen* turned it over to the information commissioner, DND acknowledged the record existed.²³

The secrecy is long-standing. In 1996 Information Commissioner John Grace pointed to a "culture within ND[national defense]/CF of secrecy and suspicion of those seeking information."²⁴ As part of its cover-up of murders in Somalia in 1993, CF officials illegally doctored documents concerning the torture and killing of 16-year-old Shidane Arone. As part of an investigation into the March 1993 slayings in Somalia, CBC reporter Michael McAuliffe requested briefing notes for officers dealing with the media. DND was caught hiding documents, wildly inflating the cost of releasing them and altering files. At the 1995-97 inquiry into the killings in Somalia, Chief of Defence Staff Jean Boyle admitted the CF deliberately violated the spirit of Access to Information rules, while a colonel and commander were convicted by a military court of altering documents requested under that legislation. *Dishonoured Legacy: The Lessons of the Somalia Affair: Report of the Commission of Inquiry into the Deployment of Canadian Forces to Somalia* described DND's "unacceptable hostility toward the goals and requirements of access to information legislation."²⁵

Officials even thumbed their nose at the official inquiry set up to look into a cover-up reaching to the upper echelons of the CF/DND. *Dishonoured Legacy* notes: "Document disclosure remained incomplete throughout the life of the Inquiry. It took the form of a slow trickle

or sons in the military were granted the vote.³⁹ So were indigenous men in the military and basically everyone else fighting who ended up voting for the pro-conscription Conservatives by a 12 to 1 margin.⁴⁰)

Similar to WWI, during WWII legislation was used to clamp down on undesirables. The Communist Party of Canada was declared an unlawful association in the spring of 1940, and it stayed that way even after the USSR became a war ally. Empowered to issue their own search warrants, RCMP officers were ordered to arrest members of more than a dozen banned organizations.⁴¹

Hundreds of Communists were sent to internment camps overseen by the CF. The two highest profile political detainees were the Communist president of the Canadian Seamen's Union, Pat Sullivan, and the Mayor of Montréal, Camillien Houde.⁴² Houde was interned (without trial) for four years because he called on Quèbec men to ignore the national registration measure introduced by Ottawa.

Over 20,000 Japanese Canadians were imprisoned during the war.⁴³ Thousands of others, including hundreds of Jewish refugees from the Nazis, were also interned.⁴⁴

There was formal censorship during WWII. A dozen publications were banned and at least three corporate dailies — *Vancouver Sun, Le Droit* and *Le Soleil* — were fined for breaching censorship regulations.⁴⁵ Many books were also banned.⁴⁶ At its high point the DND Directorate of Censorship oversaw nearly 1,000 employees who mostly opened mail.⁴⁷ More than 45 million letters and packages were opened during WWII.⁴⁸

During the Korean War there was censorship in theatre (Korea and Japan). More than 17 reporters were expelled and many stories were suppressed.⁴⁹ In Canada government officials also pressured the media to suppress information. In response to gory radio reports, Defence Minister Brooke Claxton asked CBC Chairman Arnold Davidson Dunton, who had been general manager of the WWII Wartime Information Board, "to advise radio stations to prioritize propriety" (socially proper behaviour).⁵⁰

of information rather than an efficient handing over of material. Key documents were missing, altered, and even destroyed. ... Some key documents were disclosed officially only after their existence was confirmed before the Inquiry by others. ... Finally, faced with altered Somalia-related documents, missing and destroyed field logs, and a missing National Defence Operations Centre computer hard drive, we were compelled to embark on a series of hearings devoted entirely to the issue of disclosure of documents by DND and the Canadian Forces through DND's Directorate General of Public Affairs, as well as to the issue of compliance with our orders for the production of documents."

The military also has a more explicit means of bypassing information requests since access rules don't apply to important elements of the CF. The Communication Security Establishment was renamed and formally transferred to DND in 1975 after a CBC TV program brought it to public attention. It was believed that the secrecy of its operations could be more easily maintained under DND than the National Research Council.[26]

Since the early 2000s DND has massively expanded special forces personnel partly because they are not required to divulge information about their operations. Ottawa can deploy these troops abroad and the public is none the wiser. But, noted right-wing *Toronto Sun* columnist Peter Worthington, "a secret army within the army is anathema to democracy."[27]

If Canada's armed forces exist to protect our democracy, why does its leadership flout laws meant to protect citizens' rights to know what the government is doing?

***

With an "unequivocally" regressive cultural value, warfare "makes for a conservative animus on the part of the populace", explained Thorstein Veblen in 1904. "During war time, and within the military organization at all times, under martial law, civil rights are in abeyance; and the more warfare and armament the more abeyance."[28]

At the beginning of WWI Robert Borden's government passed the War Measures Act. It granted the state sweeping powers to imprison almost anyone considered a security threat.[29] Hundreds of pacifists and antiwar activists were arrested under the act.[30]

The government banned the International Workers of the World (IWW) and a dozen other revolutionary or Bolshevik organizations.[31] Public meetings (except for church) held in Russian, Ukrainian, Finnish and other languages were outlawed.[32] The War Measures Act empowered the state to imprison entire ethnic groups, which led to the internment of 8,500 mostly Ukrainian-Canadians during WWI (as well as hundreds of others who were not in any way affiliated with the enemy).[33]

There were at least 24,000 political trials during WWI of individuals accused of being at odds with some element of the war.[34] In *Polarity, Patriotism, and Dissent in Great War Canada, 1914-1919* Brock Millman writes: "By 1917 it would have been rather hard for a Canadian to express any opinion in any way, in any medium, or to be considered to harbour any thought conceivably prejudicial to the government's war policy and not be in danger of prosecution, apt to lead to rather heavy punishment. It could be dangerous, even, to be acquainted with such a person, particularly if he were a member of one of a number of organizations that, from time to time, found themselves the particular objects of government loathing."[35]

The War Measures Act also allowed "censorship and contro[l] and suppression of publications, writings, maps, plans, photograph[s] communication and means of communication."[36] Over 250 publicatio[ns] were banned by the Press Censor's Office and many books and fi[lms] were censored.[37]

Under the WWI Military Voters Act conscientious objec[tors] including Mennonites and Doukhobors, lost their right to vote [in the] 'conscription election'.[38] Ditto for those from enemy countrie[s who] immigrated to Canada after March 1902 and who did not have [been] serving in the CF. (On the other hand, women with husbands, [

After the outbreak of a series of diseases at the start of 1952, China and North Korea accused the US of using biological weapons. Though the claims have neither been conclusively substantiated or disproven — some internal documents are still restricted — in *Orienting Canada: Race, Empire, and the Transpacific*, John Price details Ottawa's authoritarian response to the accusations, some of which were made at the time by Canadian peace groups. When the *Ottawa Citizen* revealed that British, Canadian, and US military scientists had recently met in Ottawa to discuss biological warfare, Pearson wrote the paper's owner to complain and squash the story elsewhere. Price writes: "In reaction to a 2 May Ottawa Citizen article revealing that tri-national meetings of military scientists to discuss biological warfare were being held in Ottawa and other Canadian cities, [External Affairs Deputy Under-Secretary Escott] Reid noted that Pearson felt that such articles played into the hands of communist propagandists and that he now felt he had to write to Mr. Southam (owner of the Citizen) to complain. Omar Solandt, head of the Defence Research Board, reported Reid, had told Pearson at a meeting to discuss the fallout from the accusation, that 'as soon as he heard of the story he had taken measures to see that it was not carried further and had it killed in the Ottawa Journal and over the CP wires.' On the grounds of national security, the truth about Canadian involvement in biological warfare preparations remained hidden."[51]

During the war Canadian Peace Congress chairman James Endicott was bitterly denounced for, among other things, accusing the US-led forces of employing biological weapons. Pearson called Endicott, who had been a college friend, a "red stooge" and the "bait on the end of a Red hook."[52] Pearson even called for individuals to destroy the Peace Congress from the inside. The external minister publicly applauded 50 engineering students who swamped a membership meeting of the University of Toronto Peace Congress branch. He proclaimed, "if more Canadians were to show something of this high-spirited crusading zeal, we would very soon hear little of the Canadian Peace Congress and its works. We would simply take it over."[53]

Government attacks spurred media and public hostility.⁵⁴ A number of public venues refused to rent their space to the Peace Congress and Endicott's Toronto home was firebombed during a large Peace Congress meeting.⁵⁵

The "conservative animus" unleashed in more recent wars has been less extreme.⁵⁶ In the lead-up to the first Gulf War many media reported a rumor that body bags were thrown on the lawn of a soldier in Victoria. It probably never happened, according to Bob Bergen, but was used to discredit antiwar activists.⁵⁷

During the war in Afghanistan 16 University of Regina professors sent a letter to the school's president saying it should withdraw from an initiative offering free tuition to the children of dead soldiers. Project Hero was created by retired Chief of Defence Staff Rick Hillier who infamously declared "we're not the public service of Canada ... We are the Canadian Forces, and our job is to be able to kill people."⁵⁸ The letter noted that Project Hero is "a glorification of Canadian imperialism in Afghanistan and elsewhere."⁵⁹ The political and media backlash was ferocious. Saskatchewan Premier Brad Wall condemned the letter and Regina-Qu'Appelle MP Andrew Scheer said the professors' actions were "disgusting".⁶⁰

***

War reveals a schizophrenic Canadian identity. Some believe Canada is the "peaceable kingdom" and Canadians are an "unmilitary people."⁶¹ Others claim Canadians are natural soldiers and gained nation status on the battlefields of incredibly absurd and destructive wars. During the Boer war the *Canadian Military Gazette* claimed, "much soldier blood runs in the veins of Canadians" and "the Canadian soldier is born, and that no making is necessary."⁶²

Though less direct today, it's not uncommon to hear that Canadians are the best soldiers in the world. As Prime Minister Stephen Harper noted in 2011, "soldier for soldier, sailor for sailor, airman for airman, the Canadian Armed Forces are the best in the world."⁶³ More importantly, some argue that wars created Canadian assets by saying it would take 1,100 days to retrieve the information.[22] Under access law public institutions must produce records within 30 days or inform the requester of a reasonable extension.

Informed an officer attended a talk Rideau Institute director Steven Staples delivered about the war in Afghanistan on January 26, 2006, Pugliese requested all CF documents mentioning public speeches in Halifax between January 15 and 30 of that year. Department officials claimed they did "a thorough and complete search" and couldn't find any record of an officer who attended the function and wrote a report. But the officer assigned to Staples' speech inadvertently left a record. When the *Ottawa Citizen* turned it over to the information commissioner, DND acknowledged the record existed.[23]

The secrecy is long-standing. In 1996 Information Commissioner John Grace pointed to a "culture within ND[national defense]/CF of secrecy and suspicion of those seeking information."[24] As part of its cover-up of murders in Somalia in 1993, CF officials illegally doctored documents concerning the torture and killing of 16-year-old Shidane Arone. As part of an investigation into the March 1993 slayings in Somalia, CBC reporter Michael McAuliffe requested briefing notes for officers dealing with the media. DND was caught hiding documents, wildly inflating the cost of releasing them and altering files. At the 1995-97 inquiry into the killings in Somalia, Chief of Defence Staff Jean Boyle admitted the CF deliberately violated the spirit of Access to Information rules, while a colonel and commander were convicted by a military court of altering documents requested under that legislation. *Dishonoured Legacy: The Lessons of the Somalia Affair: Report of the Commission of Inquiry into the Deployment of Canadian Forces to Somalia* described DND's "unacceptable hostility toward the goals and requirements of access to information legislation."[25]

Officials even thumbed their nose at the official inquiry set up to look into a cover-up reaching to the upper echelons of the CF/DND. *Dishonoured Legacy* notes: "Document disclosure remained incomplete throughout the life of the Inquiry. It took the form of a slow trickle of information rather than an efficient handing over of material. Key documents were missing, altered, and even destroyed. ... Some key documents were disclosed officially only after their existence was confirmed before the Inquiry by others. ... Finally, faced with altered Somalia-related documents, missing and destroyed field logs, and a missing National Defence Operations Centre computer hard drive, we were compelled to embark on a series of hearings devoted entirely to the issue of disclosure of documents by DND and the Canadian Forces through DND's Directorate General of Public Affairs, as well as to the issue of compliance with our orders for the production of documents."

The military also has a more explicit means of bypassing information requests since access rules don't apply to important elements of the CF. The Communication Security Establishment was renamed and formally transferred to DND in 1975 after a CBC TV program brought it to public attention. It was believed that the secrecy of its operations could be more easily maintained under DND than the National Research Council.[26]

Since the early 2000s DND has massively expanded special forces personnel partly because they are not required to divulge information about their operations. Ottawa can deploy these troops abroad and the public is none the wiser. But, noted right-wing *Toronto Sun* columnist Peter Worthington, "a secret army within the army is anathema to democracy."[27]

If Canada's armed forces exist to protect our democracy, why does its leadership flout laws meant to protect citizens' rights to know what the government is doing?

***

With an "unequivocally" regressive cultural value, warfare "makes for a conservative animus on the part of the populace", explained Thorstein Veblen in 1904. "During war time, and within the military organization at all times, under martial law, civil rights are in abeyance; and the more warfare and armament the more abeyance."[28]

At the beginning of WWI Robert Borden's government passed the War Measures Act. It granted the state sweeping powers to imprison almost anyone considered a security threat.[29] Hundreds of pacifists and antiwar activists were arrested under the act.[30]

The government banned the International Workers of the World (IWW) and a dozen other revolutionary or Bolshevik organizations.[31] Public meetings (except for church) held in Russian, Ukrainian, Finnish and other languages were outlawed.[32] The War Measures Act empowered the state to imprison entire ethnic groups, which led to the internment of 8,500 mostly Ukrainian-Canadians during WWI (as well as hundreds of others who were not in any way affiliated with the enemy).[33]

There were at least 24,000 political trials during WWI of individuals accused of being at odds with some element of the war.[34] In *Polarity, Patriotism, and Dissent in Great War Canada, 1914-1919* Brock Millman writes: "By 1917 it would have been rather hard for a Canadian to express any opinion in any way, in any medium, or to be considered to harbour any thought conceivably prejudicial to the government's war policy and not be in danger of prosecution, apt to lead to rather heavy punishment. It could be dangerous, even, to be acquainted with such a person, particularly if he were a member of one of a number of organizations that, from time to time, found themselves the particular objects of government loathing."[35]

The War Measures Act also allowed "censorship and control and suppression of publications, writings, maps, plans, photographs, communication and means of communication."[36] Over 250 publications were banned by the Press Censor's Office and many books and films were censored.[37]

Under the WWI Military Voters Act conscientious objectors, including Mennonites and Doukhobors, lost their right to vote in the 'conscription election'.[38] Ditto for those from enemy countries who immigrated to Canada after March 1902 and who did not have family serving in the CF. (On the other hand, women with husbands, brothers or sons in the military were granted the vote.[39] So were indigenous men in the military and basically everyone else fighting who ended up voting for the pro-conscription Conservatives by a 12 to 1 margin.[40])

Similar to WWI, during WWII legislation was used to clamp down on undesirables. The Communist Party of Canada was declared an unlawful association in the spring of 1940, and it stayed that way even after the USSR became a war ally. Empowered to issue their own search warrants, RCMP officers were ordered to arrest members of more than a dozen banned organizations.[41]

Hundreds of Communists were sent to internment camps overseen by the CF. The two highest profile political detainees were the Communist president of the Canadian Seamen's Union, Pat Sullivan, and the Mayor of Montréal, Camillien Houde.[42] Houde was interned (without trial) for four years because he called on Quèbec men to ignore the national registration measure introduced by Ottawa.

Over 20,000 Japanese Canadians were imprisoned during the war.[43] Thousands of others, including hundreds of Jewish refugees from the Nazis, were also interned.[44]

There was formal censorship during WWII. A dozen publications were banned and at least three corporate dailies — *Vancouver Sun*, *Le Droit* and *Le Soleil* — were fined for breaching censorship regulations.[45] Many books were also banned.[46] At its high point the DND Directorate of Censorship oversaw nearly 1,000 employees who mostly opened mail.[47] More than 45 million letters and packages were opened during WWII.[48]

During the Korean War there was censorship in theatre (Korea and Japan). More than 17 reporters were expelled and many stories were suppressed.[49] In Canada government officials also pressured the media to suppress information. In response to gory radio reports, Defence Minister Brooke Claxton asked CBC Chairman Arnold Davidson Dunton, who had been general manager of the WWII Wartime Information Board, "to advise radio stations to prioritize propriety" (socially proper behaviour).[50]

Government attacks spurred media and public hostility.[54] A number of public venues refused to rent their space to the Peace Congress and Endicott's Toronto home was firebombed during a large Peace Congress meeting.[55]

The "conservative animus" unleashed in more recent wars has been less extreme.[56] In the lead-up to the first Gulf War many media reported a rumor that body bags were thrown on the lawn of a soldier in Victoria. It probably never happened, according to Bob Bergen, but was used to discredit antiwar activists.[57]

During the war in Afghanistan 16 University of Regina professors sent a letter to the school's president saying it should withdraw from an initiative offering free tuition to the children of dead soldiers. Project Hero was created by retired Chief of Defence Staff Rick Hillier who infamously declared "we're not the public service of Canada … We are the Canadian Forces, and our job is to be able to kill people."[58] The letter noted that Project Hero is "a glorification of Canadian imperialism in Afghanistan and elsewhere."[59] The political and media backlash was ferocious. Saskatchewan Premier Brad Wall condemned the letter and Regina-Qu'Appelle MP Andrew Scheer said the professors' actions were "disgusting".[60]

***

War reveals a schizophrenic Canadian identity. Some believe Canada is the "peaceable kingdom" and Canadians are an "unmilitary people."[61] Others claim Canadians are natural soldiers and gained nation status on the battlefields of incredibly absurd and destructive wars. During the Boer war the *Canadian Military Gazette* claimed, "much soldier blood runs in the veins of Canadians" and "the Canadian soldier is born, and that no making is necessary."[62]

Though less direct today, it's not uncommon to hear that Canadians are the best soldiers in the world. As Prime Minister Stephen Harper noted in 2011, "soldier for soldier, sailor for sailor, airman for airman, the Canadian Armed Forces are the best in the world."[63] More importantly, some argue that wars created Canadian

After the outbreak of a series of diseases at the start of 1952, China and North Korea accused the US of using biological weapons. Though the claims have neither been conclusively substantiated or disproven — some internal documents are still restricted — in *Orienting Canada: Race, Empire, and the Transpacific*, John Price details Ottawa's authoritarian response to the accusations, some of which were made at the time by Canadian peace groups. When the *Ottawa Citizen* revealed that British, Canadian, and US military scientists had recently met in Ottawa to discuss biological warfare, Pearson wrote the paper's owner to complain and squash the story elsewhere. Price writes: "In reaction to a 2 May Ottawa Citizen article revealing that tri-national meetings of military scientists to discuss biological warfare were being held in Ottawa and other Canadian cities, [External Affairs Deputy Under-Secretary Escott] Reid noted that Pearson felt that such articles played into the hands of communist propagandists and that he now felt he had to write to Mr. Southam (owner of the Citizen) to complain. Omar Solandt, head of the Defence Research Board, reported Reid, had told Pearson at a meeting to discuss the fallout from the accusation, that 'as soon as he heard of the story he had taken measures to see that it was not carried further and had it killed in the Ottawa Journal and over the CP wires.' On the grounds of national security, the truth about Canadian involvement in biological warfare preparations remained hidden."[51]

During the war Canadian Peace Congress chairman James Endicott was bitterly denounced for, among other things, accusing the US-led forces of employing biological weapons. Pearson called Endicott, who had been a college friend, a "red stooge" and the "bait on the end of a Red hook."[52] Pearson even called for individuals to destroy the Peace Congress from the inside. The external minister publicly applauded 50 engineering students who swamped a membership meeting of the University of Toronto Peace Congress branch. He proclaimed, "if more Canadians were to show something of this high-spirited crusading zeal, we would very soon hear little of the Canadian Peace Congress and its works. We would simply take it over."[53]

nationhood. In a history of the 1884 Voyageurs' expedition to Sudan, Roy MacLaren notes, "the Canadian boatman had shown in a unique fashion that Canada was indeed becoming a nation."[64] Similar to the Sudanese deployment, militaristic-minded Canadians claimed battles during the Boer war represented nationhood. In 1900 Prime Minister Wilfrid Laurier told the House of Commons he felt "the pride of pure patriotism" seeing Canadians fight in South Africa who "revealed to the world that a new power had arisen in the west."[65]

It's now more commonly claimed that Canada, in Lester Pearson's formulation, "became nationally conscious and proud of our Canadian identity" during WWI.[66] In *Empire to Umpire* Norman Hillmer and Jack Granatstein write, "the view has often been expressed that Canada became a nation on the battlefield, Easter Monday 9 April 1917, when the Canadian Corps broke the German stranglehold on Vimy Ridge."[67]

Taking martial patriotism further, some suggest the CF is responsible for Canadian democracy and human rights standards. Responding sardonically to this thinking, John Conway noted "it seems that our whole democratic system rests on the firm foundation of our military, not only the defenders of our freedoms but also the authors of our freedoms."[68] But, as detailed elsewhere in this book, the military suppressed an electoral democracy movement (the Patriots) and struggles for basic justice (labour, Québécois, indigenous, etc.).

There is a better argument to be made that the democracy we have exists despite the Canadian Forces. Not only does the CF operate in anti-democratic ways, some of its branches operate beyond the rule of effective law. This is the subject of the next chapter.

13. Our Spying Eyes

DND has vast intelligence gathering capacities. Thousands work in intelligence and cyber warfare, but little is known about their operations since there is no external oversight.[1]

The Communications Security Establishment (CSE) is a DND run intelligence-gathering agency. It employs more than 2,700 mathematicians, engineers, linguists, analysts, computer scientists, etc.[2] Its annual budget is over $700 million.[3] The agency has a variety of high-tech gadgets, including surveillance planes.[4] In 2011 CSE moved into a new $1.2 billion home. The seven-building, 110,000 square metre complex is connected to the Canadian Security Intelligence Service's (CSIS) headquarters in Ottawa.[5]

Unlike CSIS, CSE is largely foreign focused. It seeks to "protect the computer networks and information of greatest importance to Canada" from international attack.[6] CSE also gathers international signals intelligence (SIGINT), which it defines as "intelligence acquired through the collection of electromagnetic signals."[7] Historically, CSE largely intercepted electronic communications between embassies in Ottawa and other nations' capitals.[8] Today, CSE monitors phone calls, radio, microwave and satellite, as well as emails, chat rooms and other Internet exchanges. It engages in various forms of data hacking, sifting through millions of videos and online documents daily.[9] Or, as Vice reporter Patrick McGuire put it, CSE "listens in on phone calls and emails to secretly learn about things the Canadian government wants to secretly learn about."[10]

While the military established a signals communications subcommittee in 1921, CSE traces its history to WWII.[11] During WWII CSE's predecessors intercepted and analyzed codes and cipher communications from Vichy France, Germany and Japan.[12] In October 1939 Canada's first army SIGINT station was inaugurated in Ottawa and wireless stations were later established in Grand Prairie,

Alberta, and Victoria, BC.[13] (The first Canadian-based SIGINT facility was established in 1925 by the British navy in Esquimalt, BC.[14])

Canada received substantial US and British backing to establish its SIGINT capacities.[15] London wanted Canada to "assume responsibility for transpacific traffic", notes Kurt Jensen in *Cautious Beginnings: Canadian foreign intelligence 1939-1951*. "It was important to have access to Japanese communications traffic with the Western hemisphere, Malaya, and the East Indies."[16] Alongside a number of European colonies in Asia taken or threatened by Japan, Canada's Examination Unit also monitored ciphers between the WWII Vichy Regime and France's North African colonies.[17]

After WWII the government established the Communications Branch of the National Research Council, which was renamed Communications Security Establishment three decades later. Following a 1946 order-in-council to "continue the wartime effort", the SIGINT unit was authorized to fill 179 staff positions.[18] Jensen explains, "the Gouzenko story [a Soviet diplomat who defected in September 1945, alleging widespread Russian spying in Canada] is almost entirely absent from the debate on Canadian postwar foreign intelligence. While the Soviet Union figured prominently in Canadian foreign intelligence interests, it was not an exclusive focus. The available evidence suggests that Canada had broad foreign intelligence interests that reflected current Canadian foreign policy interests."[19]

Before the conclusion of WWII, military officials pushed to maintain SIGINT efforts after the war. "DND intelligence chiefs fought long and hard to preserve Canada's small autonomous SIGINT capacity", writes Jensen.[20] The CF wanted to maintain its close ties to the US and British intelligence services. A 1945 Canadian Joint Intelligence Committee statement requested: "That approval be given to maintain adequate Canadian post-war intercept facilities on a scale sufficient to ensure a fair Canadian contribution to the general pool of wireless intelligence set up between Canada and other Empire countries and the United States."[21]

The incipient Cold War justified further expanding signals intelligence capacities. During the Korean War there was a sharp increase in SIGINT personnel and by 1954 the Communications Branch had over one hundred employees, which grew more slowly over the subsequent decades.[22] By 1990 CSE had over 800 employees, which did not include another thousand military personnel who operated SIGINT stations across the country and internationally.[23]

SIGINT posts were established on the east and west coasts as well as in the north. According to a table produced by blogger Jerry Proc, there have been more than 50 Canadian SIGINT stations opened during the past century.[24] Major military listening posts were established in Gander Newfoundland, Masset, BC and Ellesmere Island, Nunavut.[25] Near Ottawa, CF Station Leitrim has been a communications interception hub since WWII. Canada also had a listening facility in Germany from 1989 to 1993 and in Bermuda between 1963 and 1993.[26] Just as the conclusion of WWII didn't curtail Canadian SIGINT operations neither did the end of the Cold War. Through the 1990s the number of CSE employees edged up slightly while the September 11, 2001, attacks in the US spurred a major expansion.[27] By 2021 CSE's staff was over 2,700.[28]

During this period CSE took an ever more active role in 'counterterrorism' and foreign intelligence.[29] The agency's sophisticated equipment and analytical and linguistic resources contributed significantly to the 2001-14 occupation of Afghanistan. The agency's website says it played a "vital role" in the central Asian country and CSE head John Adams boasted that they were responsible for more than half the "actionable intelligence" Canadian soldiers used in Afghanistan.[30] That included monitoring Taliban forces and leaders as well as allied Afghan government officials.[31] Information CSE provided protected Canadian troops from attack and helped special forces assassinate Afghans.

CSE contributed intelligence to the March 2006 special forces operation to rescue two Canadians and a British hostage held by insurgents in Iraq.³² CSE aided the deployment to Iraq-Syria that began in 2014.³³ The agency probably hacked ISIL computers and smartphones and CSE officials likely staffed a state-of-the-art intelligence centre in Kuwait.³⁴ (Presumably, CSE supported the 2011 bombing of Libya, 2004 coup in Haiti and other CF deployments, but I couldn't confirm as much.)

Five Eyes

Generally, CF deployments operate within the "Five Eyes" intelligence-sharing framework.³⁵ Since its creation CSE has been part of the Washington-led intelligence-sharing agreement. The main contributors to the accord are the US National Security Agency (NSA), Australian Defence Signals Directorate (DFS), New Zealand's Government Communications Security Bureau (GCSB), British Government Communications Headquarters (GCHQ) and CSE. A series of post-WWII accords, beginning with the 1946 UKUSA intelligence agreement, created the "AUS/CAN/NZ/UK/US EYES ONLY" arrangement.³⁶

Writing prior to the Internet, author of *Target Nation: Canada and the Western Intelligence Network* James Littleton notes, "almost the entire globe is monitored by the SIGINT agencies of the UKUSA countries."³⁷ With major technological advancements in recent decades, the Five Eyes now monitor billions of private communications worldwide.³⁸ Probably the most important intelligence sharing alliance in human history, the head of CSE in the early 2000s Keith Coulter called the Five Eyes "the greatest and most historical partnership that we have had."³⁹

The Five Eyes accord is ultra-secretive and operates with little oversight. NSA whistleblower Edward Snowden labeled it a "supra-national intelligence organisation that doesn't answer to the known laws of its own countries."⁴⁰

In addition to sharing information they've intercepted, collected, analysed and decrypted, the five SIGINT agencies exchange technologies and tactics. They also cooperate on targeting and "standardize their terminology, codewords, intercept-handling procedures, and indoctrination oaths, for efficiency as well as security."[41]

CSE special liaison officers are embedded with Five Eyes counterparts while colleagues from the US, Britain, Australia and New Zealand are inserted in CSE. NSA has had many long-term guest detachments at CSE facilities.[42] An NSA document Snowden released described how the US and Canadian agencies' "co-operative efforts include the exchange of liaison officers and integrees."[43]

NSA has trained CSE cryptanalysts and in the 1960s the US agency paid part of the cost of modernizing Canadian communications interception facilities.[44] With CSE lacking capacity, intelligence collected at interception posts set up in Canadian embassies (more below) was remitted to NSA for deciphering and analysis.[45] In his 1986 book Littleton writes, "much of the SIGINT material collected by Canada is transmitted directly to the U.S. National Security Agency, where it is interpreted, stored, and retained. Much of it is not first processed and analyzed in Canada."[46]

Five Eyes agencies have helped each other skirt restrictions on spying on their own citizenry. Former Solicitor-General Wayne Easter told the *Toronto Star* that it was "common" for NSA "to pass on information about Canadians" to CSE.[47] Conversely, former CSE officer Michael Frost says NSA asked the agency to spy on US citizens.[48] In *Spyworld: Inside the Canadian and American Intelligence Establishments* Frost reveals that on the eve of the 1983 British election Prime Minister Margaret Thatcher asked GCHQ to spy on two cabinet ministers "to find out not what they were saying, but what they were thinking."[49] Reflecting the two agencies close ties, GCHQ requested CSE's help on this highly sensitive matter.[50] Frost notes that CSE wasn't particularly worried about being caught because GCHQ was the agency tasked with protecting Britain from foreign spying.

In the lead-up to the US-British invasion of Iraq NSA asked Canada and the rest of the Five Eyes to spy on UN Security Council members. On January 31, 2003, NSA SIGINT department deputy chief of staff for regional targets wrote alliance counterparts: "As you've likely heard by now, the agency is mounting a surge particularly directed at the UN Security Council (UNSC) members (minus US and GBR [Great Britain] of course) for insights as to how membership is reacting to the ongoing debate RE: Iraq, plans to vote on any related resolutions, what related policies/negotiating positions they may be considering, alliances/dependencies, etc. — the whole gamut of information that could give US policymakers an edge in obtaining results favorable to US goals or to head off surprises."[51]

While CSE reportedly rejected this NSA request, a number of commentators suggest CSE has shown greater allegiance to its Five Eyes partners than Canadians.[52] Littleton writes, "the agreements may not explicitly say that the United States, through its SIGINT organization, the National Security Agency (NSA) dominates and controls the SIGINT organizations of the other member nations, but that is clearly what the agreements mean."[53]

An NSA history of the US–Canada SIGINT relationship released by Snowden labelled Canada a "highly valued second party partner", which offers "resources for advanced collection, processing and analysis, and has opened covert sites at the request of NSA. CSEC shares with NSA their unique geographic access to areas unavailable to the US."[54]

CSE has cited the arrangement to justify secrecy. When the BC Civil Liberties Association launched a legal challenge over CSE's spying on Canadian citizens the SIGINT agency's lawyer argued it couldn't disclose information to the courts because its Five Eyes counterparts might respond by curbing or even halting the flow of intelligence. A CSE note claimed, "damaging trust and respect through disclosure of information against the expressed wishes of one or more of our Five Eyes partners would have a detrimental effect on future collaborative efforts, consequently harming not only the interests of Canada, but also those of our closest partners."[55]

The Five Eyes accord has made Canada complicit in belligerent US-UK foreign policy decisions. It has also pushed Ottawa towards their global strategic outlook.

CSE's secretive nature, limited oversight and (historically at least) undefined mandate gave it significant latitude to determine its own objectives. In 2000, professor Stuart Farson wrote, "in CSE, the policies and procedures are internally derived and have been neither explicitly requested nor approved by the responsible minister."[56] An investigation of its operations two years earlier concluded that a small part of CSE reports were "security related".[57]

A CBC TV program brought Canadian SIGINT operations to public attention in 1974. The government responded by re-naming the organization and bringing it under DND so its anonymity could be better maintained.[58] Ottawa didn't officially acknowledge CSE's existence until 1983. At that time external minister Jean-Luc Pépin told the Special Senate Committee on the Canadian Security Intelligence Service: "The Communications Security Establishment advises on, and provides the means of ensuring the security of federal government communications. It also provides, with the support of the Canadian Forces Supplementary Radio System, a service of signals intelligence in support of Canada's foreign and defence policies. I should explain that 'signals intelligence' is the term given to information gathered about foreign countries by intercepting and studying their radio, radar, and other electronic transmissions."[59]

Ottawa didn't admit its Five Eyes relationship until 1995. A government statement to a House of Commons committee noted that Canada participated in "the collection of foreign signals intelligence" with the US, UK, Australia and New Zealand as per "international agreements, which … date back to the second world war."[60]

As part of reorganizing Canada's intelligence operations, which led to the 1984 creation of CSIS, the Special Senate Committee on the Canadian Security Intelligence Service proposed the government establish oversight of CSE.[61] Similarly, the opposition parties pushed the Liberal government to put CSE under control of the new national security bill.[62] They refused.[63] It wasn't until 1996 that a commissioner was established to monitor the legality of CSE's activities.[64]

For more than half a century CSE (and its predecessor) functioned without official mandate. CSE operated under secret orders in council until 2001. That year's Anti-Terrorism Act (Bill C-36) gave CSE a statutory mandate, which amended the National Defence Act. Among other things, it called on the agency to acquire foreign intelligence from the "global information infrastructure" and detailed the defence minister's role in authorising information collection that might "inadvertently" target Canadians' private communications.[65]

As the Internet came onto the scene CSE was instructed to conduct Computer Network Exploitation. It went from intercepting communications ("data in motion") to seeking information on foreign computer systems ("data at rest"). According to Bill Robinson, who runs SIGINT focused blog Lux Ex Umbra, "it became a hunter as well as a gatherer."[66] CSE could hack into computer systems, implant malware and copy information.[67]

In 2017 CSE was further empowered to carry out offensive operations against foreign actors. The Communications Security Establishment Act authorized CSE "to degrade, disrupt, influence, respond to or interfere with the capabilities, intentions or activities" of international targets.[68] In effect the intelligence agency could seek to take a government offline, shutter a power plant, knock a drone out of the sky or interfere in court proceedings and elections in countries Ottawa doesn't deem "democratic". There is no requirement that the target threaten Canadian security.

The legislation forbids offensive cyber activities that could cause injury or death or "obstruct, pervert or defeat the course of justice or democracy."[69] But, these limitations don't apply if CSE conducts cyberattacks on behalf of a CF operation or receives approval of the foreign minister.[70] Additionally, there is no independent oversight of CSE's new offensive capabilities and CSE is allowed to do "anything that is reasonably necessary to maintain the covert nature of the activity."[71]

Incredibly, CSE's mandate was expanded only two years after Snowden's revelations prompted US decision-makers to rein in the NSA (2015 USA Freedom Act). Instead of facing more stringent rules, CSE brought in a series of measures to avoid what the *Toronto Star* labelled a "Canadian Snowden".[72] According to a document that paper uncovered, the SIGINT agency spent $45 million to upgrade the federal government's Top Secret network to avoid "insider threats".[73]

As part of the Snowden revelations, it came to light that CSE hacked Mexican computers and spied on Brazil's Department of Mines and Energy.[74] CSE also planted sophisticated malware on mobile phones and maintained a network of infected computers to attack targets without being detected. To mask their involvement CSE hacked into random computers outside the Five Eyes alliance to use them to launch cyberattacks.[75]

In what likely violated Canadian law, the SIGINT agency used the free Internet services at Toronto's Pearson airport to track thousands of individuals' wireless devices for days after they left the terminal.[76] CSE also shared the metadata — time, origin and destination of phone calls, electronic messages and other modes of telecommunication — of Canadian citizens with the rest of the Five Eyes.[77]

Snowden revealed that Canadian diplomatic posts house SIGINT equipment as part of US-led spying efforts.[78] One NSA document claimed CSE operated clandestine surveillance activities in "approximately 20 high-priority countries."[79] In his 1994 book Frost describes CSE listening posts at a number of embassies or consular posts while two papers in the early 2000s cite Abidjan, Beijing, New Delhi, Bucharest, Rabat, Kingston (Jamaica), Mexico City, Rome, San Jose (Costa Rica), Warsaw and Tokyo as diplomatic posts where CSE (probably) collected information.[80]

At NSA's behest CSE opened interception posts at a number of Canadian diplomatic outposts in the 1970s and 1980s.[81] They sought to open a communications site in Algeria to help NSA spy on Muammar Gaddafi's Libya.[82]

Since the start of the 1960s CSE has listened to Cuban leaders' conversations from an interception post inside the embassy in Havana. (Ottawa maintained diplomatic and economic relations with Cuba after its 1959 revolution, reports *Three Nights in Havana*, partly because "the United States secretly urged [Prime Minister] Diefenbaker to maintain normal relations because it was thought that Canada would be well positioned to gather intelligence on the island."[83]) A senior Canadian official, reports *Inside Canadian Intelligence: Exposing the New Realities of Espionage and International Terrorism*, "admitted that the U.S. made 'far greater use' of our intelligence during the [October 1962] Cuban Missile Crisis than has been revealed."[84] Pentagon and State Department sources cited Canada and the UK as the only countries that "supply any real military information on Cuba" with Canada providing "the best" military intelligence.[85]

Canada also spied on Cuba from a diplomatic post outside that country. In the early 1980s CSE wanted to establish a communications post in Jamaica, notes Frost, to intercept "communications from Fidel Castro's Cuba, which would please NSA to no end."[86]

CSE also gathered intelligence on Palestinians for Israel. Frost notes, "[former Palestinian Liberation Organization chairman] Yasser Arafat's name, for instance, was on every [CSE] key word list. NSA was happy about that."[87] According to files released by Snowden, CSE spied on Israel's enemies and shared the intelligence with that country's SIGINT National Unit. "Palestinians" was a "specific intelligence topic" of an NSA-GCHQ-CSE project shared with their Israeli counterpart.[88]

In the late 1980s the Soviets jammed US and British listening operations in Moscow. In response, they asked CSE to take up the slack. "From summer 1987 to summer 1989", notes Frost, "it was Canada that was providing the most powerful Western nations with the intelligence that had been so crucial to them and, in fact, to the whole Western Alliance."[89]

In the late 1970s and early 80s CSE apparently spied on Parti Québecois communications with France.[90] While he wasn't familiar with its operations, Frost said CSE had a "French Problem" section focused on Québec's sovereignty movement.[91]

Economic espionage is a significant and growing component of CSE's focus. In the *CCPA Monitor* Asad Ismi labelled it the "espionage arm of corporate Canada".[92] In 1995 the agency began hiring more individuals with economics, commerce and international business qualifications "to build up its own analytical capacity in economic intelligence."[93]

In 1985 the government asked CSE to gather intelligence that could help a Canadian firm bidding for a major pipeline contract in India.[94] A few years earlier the CSE overheard the US ambassador in Ottawa detailing his country's negotiating position on a US$5 billion wheat sale to China, which helped Canada win the contract.[95] CSE is also thought to have secured information useful to negotiating the mid-1990s North American Free Trade Agreement and World Trade Organization rules.[96]

As part of the Snowden revelations the *Guardian* reported: "[CSE] has participated in secret meetings in Ottawa where Canadian security agencies briefed energy corporations. Claims of spying on the [Brazilian mining and energy] ministry by CSEC come amid the Canadian government's increasingly aggressive promotion of resource corporations at home and abroad, including unprecedented surveillance and intelligence sharing with companies. According to freedom of information documents obtained by the *Guardian*, the meetings — conducted twice a year since 2005 — involved federal ministries, spy and police agencies, and representatives from scores of companies who obtained high-level security clearance."[97]

CSE is but one component of DND's intelligence juggernaut. Not counting the CSE, the CF has greater intelligence gathering capacities than any organization in the country.⁹⁸ But their budget and size are not public information. Additionally, there is no external oversight, only internal military directives.⁹⁹

Over the years the CF has operated various intelligence units, including the Canadian Intelligence Corps and Intelligence Branch. A 2002 audit of CF Intelligence found that 2,000 personnel engaged in "intelligence" gathering, but only 400 of them wore an Intelligence Branch cap badge.¹⁰⁰

Intelligence has an entire school. The Canadian Forces School of Military Intelligence was established at Camp Petawawa in 1947.¹⁰¹ Now based in Kingston, it offers a variety of intelligence and cyber focused courses.

The Kingston based 21st Electronic Warfare Regiment (21 EWR) provides trained army electronic warfare operators and support personnel. With about 350 members, 21 EWR intercepts and deciphers enemy communications.¹⁰² According to former army commander Lt.-Gen. Andrew Leslie, the unit employs "sophisticated equipment that does strange things."¹⁰³ 21 EWR can block remote controlled explosives, provide electromagnetic bubbles around Canadian troops and initiate accidents in bomb-making factories.¹⁰⁴ 21 EWR operations are classified and the unit refuses to discuss its capabilities, but the media reported on their participation in Afghanistan and Iraq (after 2014).¹⁰⁵

Created in 2013, the Canadian Forces Intelligence Command (CFINTCOM) carries out a wide range of intelligence activities. According to the government's 2017 Defence Policy review, "CFINTCOM is the only entity within the Government of Canada that employs the full spectrum of intelligence collection capabilities while providing multi-source analysis."¹⁰⁶ Comprised of five units, CFINTCOM includes the Canadian Forces Joint Imagery Centre (providing imagery intelligence), Joint Meteorological Centre (providing weather related information to support CF operations), Mapping and Charting Establishment (providing geospatial information and geomatics), Canadian Forces National Counter-Intelligence Unit (which identifies and investigates threats by foreign intelligence services) and Joint Task Force X.

Headquartered in Kingston, Ontario, JTFX spies conduct human intelligence operations worldwide in support of CF programs. During overseas missions they sometimes recruit and oversee local intelligence agents and engage in psychological operations (PSYOPS). They participated in the war in Afghanistan.[107]

In 2018 JTFX opened a $52 million state-of-the-art facility at CFB Kingston that includes an indoor live-fire training range.[108] The facility was named after Sir William Samuel Stephenson who led the WWII western hemisphere focused British Security Coordination, inspired the James Bond character and played an important role in creating the CIA.

About 1,000 soldiers are part of CFINTCOM and its budget was more than $80 million.[109] Annually CF intelligence produces over 5,000 reports, which are shared with the top brass and other government departments as well as international allies.[110]

The 2017 Defence Policy Paper called for adding 300 military intelligence positions and expanding CFINTCOM's scope. It described the need to "build CFINTCOM's capacity to provide more advanced intelligence support to operations, including through an enhanced ability to forecast flashpoints and emerging threats, better support next generation platforms and understand rapid developments in space, cyber and other emerging domains."[111] The policy paper also called for offensive cyber capabilities. "A purely defensive cyber posture is no longer sufficient", it noted. "Accordingly, we will develop the capability to conduct active cyber operations focused on external threats to Canada in the context of government-authorized military missions."[112]

Unlike CSE or CSIS, no legislation spells out when and how CFINTCOM operations can take place. Nor is there civilian oversight.[113] The chief of defence staff and military leaders are responsible for monitoring CF intelligence activities.

In 2019 the National Security and Intelligence Committee of Parliamentarians (NSICOP) suggested establishing an oversight body and legislation to guide CF intelligence.[114] DND was "solidly opposed to the idea of civilian legislative oversight."[115] In its first annual report NSICOP concluded that the scope and authority of CF intelligence is "unknown to Canadians".[116] At the start of 2020 NSICOP said it was concerned DND was violating the law with regards to the collection and use of information about Canadians in its operations outside the country. The parliamentary committee asked the attorney general to look into DND's practices.[117]

Obviously spending taxpayers' dollars on organizations with little political oversight runs contrary to democratic norms. The idea that Canadians should simply trust intelligence agencies to do what's best for them smacks of dictatorship. The practice of Canadian intelligence agencies spying on behalf of foreign countries or asking foreign intelligence agencies to spy on Canadians is totalitarian.

Unfortunately, intelligence is not the only area where the CF works on behalf of a foreign government. NORAD, the subject of the next chapter, makes Canada a junior partner to US militarism.

14. Subject to Uncle Sam

CANADA HAS HUNDREDS OF MILITARY ACCORDS with the US. According to DND, there are "80 treaty-level agreements, more than 250 memoranda of understanding, and 145 bilateral forums on defence" between the two countries' militaries.[1] Given the size and resources of the two militaries, it is clear which is the senior and which is the junior partner in any such agreement.

The 2008 Canada-US Civil Assistance Plan provides "a framework for the military of one nation to provide support to the military of the other nation while in the performance of civil support operations to the primary agency (e.g., floods, forest fires, hurricanes, earthquakes, and effect of a terrorist attack)."[2] A 2002 Bi-National Planning Group accord allows US troops to enter Canada in response to a "threat, attack or civil emergency" concerning critical infrastructure or to protect "potential targets" such as nuclear power plants or oil and gas pipelines.[3]

Set up in 1940, the Permanent Joint Board on Defence (PJBD) is the highest-level Canada-US defence forum. It coordinates continental defence and standardizes arms and equipment.

NORAD

The most important bi-national military accord is the North American Aerospace Defence Command (NORAD) ("Air" was changed to "Aerospace" in 1981). Renewed indefinitely in 2006, the Cold War accord was supposed to defend the two countries from an invasion by Soviet bombers coming from the north.[4] Initially NORAD focused on radar and fighter jets. As technologies advanced, it took up intercontinental ballistic missiles, cruise missiles and space-based satellites.

About 1,000 Canadian military personnel directly supported NORAD's operations in 2021.[5] At its high point 15,000 CF members were associated with the command.[6] Hundreds of Canadians oversee elements of NORAD. NORAD's commander-in-chief is a US Air Force general and an RCAF general is deputy commander, which is among the most prestigious appointments in the RCAF.

NORAD's central collection and coordination facility is based at the Peterson Air Force Base near Colorado Springs, Colorado. In 2021, 150 Canadians were stationed at the bi-national headquarters.[7] NORAD also has three subordinate regional headquarters located at Elmendorf Air Force Base in Alaska, Tyndall Air Force Base in Florida and Canadian Forces Base Winnipeg.

Established in 1957 — though signed the next year — newly elected Prime Minister John Diefenbaker faced "heavy pressure from the military" to back the agreement.[8] Then Chairman of the Chiefs of Defence Staff Charles Foulkes later admitted to a House of Commons defence committee that "we stampeded the incoming Conservative government with the NORAD agreement."[9]

Before NORAD's creation the RCAF had been expanding ties to the US command in Colorado Springs. In 1951 RCAF attached a number of liaison officers to Colorado Springs.[10] The air force misled the politicians about the scope of these efforts.[11] In *Dilemmas in Defence Decision-Making: Constructing Canada's role in NORAD, 1958-96* Ann Crosby points out that the CF pursued NORAD discussions secretly "in order to address the politically sensitive issues without the involvement of Canadian political representatives."[12]

While the CF frame the alliance as an exclusively military matter, NORAD's political implications are vast.[13] The accord impinges on Canadian sovereignty, influences weapons procurement and ties Canada to US belligerence.

External Affairs officials immediately understood that NORAD would curtail sovereignty. An internal memo explained, "the establishment of NORAD is a decision for which there is no precedent in Canadian history in that it grants in peace time to a foreign representative operational control of an element of Canadian Forces in Canada."[14] Under the accord the Colorado-based commander of NORAD could deploy Canadian fighter jets based in this country without any express Canadian endorsement.

For over a decade the US commander of NORAD effectively controlled nuclear tipped Bomarc missiles based near North Bay, Ontario, and La Macaza, Québec. According to the agreement, the Canadian battle staff officer on duty in North Bay would receive authorization from the Colorado Springs commander, "allow[ing] for the release and firing of nuclear armed Bomarc missiles without specific Canadian government authorization."[15]

NORAD also deepened the US military footprint in Canada. As part of the accord, the US set up the Distant Early Warning (DEW) line across the Arctic in the late 1950s.[16] NORAD also drove Ottawa to formally accept US Bomarc missiles in 1963. According to Crosby, the agreement that laid the basis for NORAD effectively — unbeknownst to Prime Minister Diefenbaker — committed Canada to acquiring US nuclear weapons for air defence.[17]

NORAD pushed the CF towards US arms systems. It has also heightened pressure to add and upgrade radar, satellite, jets, vessels, etc.[18] In the late 1950s the RCAF pushed for interceptor jets so Canada could be "a full partner in NORAD". Air Marshal Hugh Campbell explained that "if Canada was not providing any effective weapons in the air defence system … Canada could no longer be a full partner in NORAD."[19] More recently, CBC reported that Canada may be "compelled to invest in technology that can shoot down cruise missiles as part of the upcoming overhaul of the North American Aerospace Defence Command."[20]

NORAD is presented as a defensive arrangement, but that can't be taken seriously when its lead actor has 1,000 international bases and special forces deployed in 149 countries.[21] Rather than protect Canada and the US, NORAD supports violent missions led by other US commands.[22] In 1965 NORAD's mandate was expanded to include surveillance and assessment sharing for US commands stationed worldwide (United States European Command, United States Pacific Command, United States Africa Command, etc.).[23]

NORAD has clearly drawn Canada into US belligerence.[24] During the July 1958 US invasion of Lebanon NORAD was placed on "increased readiness" while US troops checked secular Arab nationalism after Iraqis toppled a Western-backed king (at the same time British troops invaded Jordan to prop up the monarchy there).[25]

In a higher profile incident, Canadian NORAD personnel were put on high alert when the US illegally blockaded Cuba in October 1962.[26] This transpired even though Prime Minister Diefenbaker hesitated in fully supporting US actions during the Cuban Missile Crisis.[27]

During the 1973 Ramadan/Yom Kippur/Arab–Israeli War Canadian equipment and personnel at NORAD headquarters were put on heightened alert.[28] Washington wanted to deter the USSR from intervening on Egypt's behalf.[29] Canadian politicians weren't consulted or notified about the heightened alert for around ten hours, which spurred Pierre Trudeau's government to request changes to the agreement.[30]

Simultaneously, however, they added a provision allowing either country "to take unilateral action using facilities or forces normally assigned to NORAD."[31] The move to have Canadian NORAD personnel automatically participate in unilateral US initiatives was prompted, according to the commander-in-chief of NORAD, to make it easier to "justify this action politically and to the news media."[32]

NORAD systems offered surveillance and communications support for the 1991 war on Iraq.[33] They monitored the region and provided information to launch US Patriot surface-to-air missiles. NORAD ballistic missile warnings were also sent to Ottawa and Canadian units in Bahrain.[34]

NORAD also supported the 2003 invasion of Iraq.[35] The same can be said for US bombing in Afghanistan, Libya, Somalia, etc.

In the 1980s NORAD was given a 'war on drugs' mandate. Regional NORAD headquarters, including North Bay, installed new computers to track suspected aerial drug trafficking. The computers enabled instant communication with law enforcement agencies.[36] In 1993 NORAD's responsibilities were formally extended to "monitoring of aircraft suspected of smuggling illegal drugs into North America."[37]

Through NORAD Canada supported various initiatives to weaponize space.[38] United States Space Command (USSPACECOM), which is now part of US Strategic Command, shares NORAD surveillance and warning facilities in Cheyenne Mountain.[39] Canadians posted to NORAD have helped research space weaponry and the CF accessed space-based early warning systems through NORAD.[40] Additionally, Canadian personnel have been posted to USSPACECOM and its subcomponent US Air Force Space Command.[41]

One reason CF personnel were posted to USSPACECOM in the 1980s was to access planning related to space-based ballistic missiles.[42]

Between 1968 and 1981 NORAD included an "ABM Clause" restricting Canada's participation in ballistic missile programs (cabinet only learned of its deletion in 1985).[43] Opposed by the military, the clause read, "this Agreement will not involve in any way a Canadian commitment to participate in an active ballistic missile defence."[44]

Even before the George W. Bush administration officially ripped up the Anti-Ballistic Missile Treaty with Russia in 2001, Defence Minister David Pratt wrote US Secretary of State Colin Powell committing "to amend the NORAD agreement to take into account NORAD's contribution to the missile defence mission."[45]

While Paul Martin's Liberals claimed to oppose ballistic missile defence (BMD), they granted "full cooperation by NORAD in missile-defence work," explained Richard Sanders in a *Press for Conversion* report on the subject.[46] In 2004 Ottawa formally permitted the US BMD system to use data from NORAD's "Integrated Tactical Warning/Attack Assessment".[47]

The CF has enabled BMD through the NORAD Space Surveillance Network.[48] While Canada officially dropped out of the missile defence partnership, Ottawa initiated an amendment to NORAD's treaty to further enable space research in 2004. In a letter to US Secretary of Defense Donald Rumsfeld that year, defence minister David Pratt laid out that NORAD would provide a "mutually beneficial framework to ensure the closest possible involvement and insight for Canada, both government and industry, in the U.S. missile defence program."[49]

Canadian officials endorsed BMD within NATO, which the alliance labelled a "core element of ... collective defence."[50] A 2016 DND policy guide suggested Canada formally participate in BMD.[51]

It's called "missile defence" because it's designed to defend US missiles sites after they launch offensive operations. US-installed missile defence systems in Romania and Korea, for instance, are designed primarily to stop opponents' missiles following a US first strike.[52]

Space-based missiles run counter to the Outer Space Treaty and United Nations General Assembly resolution on Prevention of an Arms Race in Outer Space.[53] The Outer Space Treaty bars participating states from putting weapons of mass destruction in orbit, on the moon or in space or testing weapons or establishing bases in space. It states, "the Moon and other celestial bodies shall be used exclusively for peaceful purposes."[54]

Beyond wasting resources on an antisocial endeavour, weaponizing space increases the likelihood of nuclear war. US space-based missile defence interceptors able to eliminate Russia's early warning satellites without warning puts that country on edge, ratcheting up the arms race.

Interoperability

NORAD is in some ways just the tip of the Canada-as-junior-partner-to-US-military iceberg. As Janice Gross Stein and Eugene Lang wrote: "Canada's generals and admirals tend to be more concerned about their relationships with their American counterparts than they are with their own political masters in Ottawa."[55]

This is confirmed by the Canadian Forces' own documents. "Maintaining interoperability [with the US] is the key to the future relevance of the CF," noted the chief of defence staff in his 2002 annual report.⁵⁶ The government's 2017 Defence Policy cited the importance of being "interoperable"/"interoperability" with US and NATO forces at least 19 times.

At its most basic "interoperability" means the ability for military forces to act together seamlessly because their doctrines, processes and equipment are compatible. NATO defines interoperability as "the ability for Allies to act together coherently, effectively and efficiently to achieve tactical, operational and strategic objectives."⁵⁷

But the political implications of this fairly elastic military buzzword are significant. The search for interoperability has been used to justify participating in belligerent US-led missions. In explaining the RCN's role in enforcing brutal sanctions on Iraq during the late 1990s and early 2000s Minister of National Defence Art Eggleton said, "this operation is extremely beneficial in ensuring our interoperability with our allies and particularly the United States. It will further strengthen our navy's relationship with the U.S. Navy."⁵⁸ A decade and a half later militarists justified warfare in Iraq on similar grounds. In a story titled "A military perspective of Canada's [2014-21] mission in Iraq" former Brigadier-General Jim Cox wrote, "the Canadian Armed Forces reap enormous professional, doctrinal and industrial benefits from remaining interoperable with US forces in all five domains of modern warfare: land, sea, air, space and cyberspace."⁵⁹

A bid for "interoperability" shapes weapons acquisitions. At the 2017 Dubai Air Show RCAF Commander Michael Hood said interoperability was "the most important thing" in determining the purchase of a new fighter jet. "Every step less of interoperability is one step less of effectiveness, so interoperability is right at the top of the list beside operational advantage", Hood told *Defense News*.⁶⁰

The quest to stay interoperable with advanced US military technology isn't cheap. Naval historian Richard Gimblett writes about how "the stringent requirements to be interchangeable one-for-one with American warships demanded continuous upgrades of advanced communications and other technical modifications."⁶¹ A similar dynamic took place with the airforce. After some interoperability hiccups during the bombing of the former Yugoslavia in 1999, notes Desmond Morton, "Canada is spending $1.3 billion on an Incremental Modernization Program to update as many of our aging fighters as the government thinks it can afford."⁶²

Interoperability with NORAD and NATO partners was a critical consideration in purchasing fighter jets.⁶³ Proponents of spending huge sums on F-35 fighter jets argued it "will sustain Canadian air force interoperability with allied states such as the United States and the United Kingdom."⁶⁴

The more emphasis placed on interoperability by Canada and other NATO members the better for US arms manufacturers. Not only does the US have by far the most advanced military, the US Congress restricts foreign weapons purchases, so NATO standardization overwhelmingly takes place on US terms.⁶⁵ A high-profile example is Lockheed Martin's F-35 Joint Strike Fighter, which tied most NATO members to the US company's $1.5 trillion program. Governments purchased the incredibly expensive planes and Lockheed directed business to companies in participating countries.

The search for interoperability may even influence who runs the CF. "Over the last 15 years or more, there has not been one Chief of Staff who has not been vetted or trained by the U.S. Armed Forces", wrote Tony Seed in a 2017 article titled "'Interoperability' — Euphemism for integration and annexation of Canadian Forces in the service of empire-building."⁶⁶

Chief of defence staff from 2005-08, Rick Hillier graduated from the US Army War College and was the first Canadian deputy commander of General III Corps, which is based in Texas. He also commanded NATO's International Security Assistance Force in Afghanistan in 2004.⁶⁷

Chief of defence staff from 2008-12, Walter Natynczyk attended US Army War College and became deputy commander of General III

Corps. Through this role he helped plan the 2003 US/British invasion of Iraq from Kuwait and then served as deputy commanding general of the Multi-National Corps in Baghdad.[68] Natynczyk was in charge of 35,000 troops in Iraq.

Chief of defence staff from 2012-15, Tom Lawson was deputy commander of NORAD in Colorado Springs in 2011–2012 and previously attended the United States Air Force Air Command and Staff College and United States Air Force Air War College.[69]

A March 2017 dispatch from the US embassy in Ottawa to the State Department in Washington titled "Canada Adopts 'America First' Foreign Policy" highlighted Parliamentary Secretary to the Minister of Foreign Affairs (Canada-US Relations) Andrew Leslie's close ties to the US military. The former chief of transformation and chief of the land staff, reports the memo, "has extensive ties to U.S. military leaders from his tours in Afghanistan."[70] (Chrystia Freeland was appointed foreign minister, according to the memo uncovered through a freedom of information request, "in large part because of her strong U.S. contacts" and that her "number one priority" was working closely with Washington."[71])

Pushing the concept of interoperability further, secret discussions were held to "fully integrate" the US and Canadian militaries. According to the CBC, in 2013 meetings for a "Canada-U.S. Integrated forces program" were "led at the highest levels, with then Chief of the Defence Staff Gen. Tom Lawson and the Chairman of the U.S. Joint Chiefs of Staff Gen. Martin Dempsey meeting on 'several occasions' to hash out a plan that included an option for 'fully integrated forces.'"[72] Not shared with Canadian political leaders, the plan was to set up integrated air, sea, land and special forces to operate under a unified command when deployed internationally. The public broadcaster noted, "efforts were ultimately shut down and refocused on improving interoperability between the forces."

The push for closer military ties often takes place without politicians present. In discussing the post-WWII Canada–US Basic

Security Plan, Richard Goette and Howard Coombs write: "While Canadian and American military officers were amicable towards a more intimate relationship between their services, Canadian diplomats practiced increased caution in their approach, as they were suspicious of American intentions and wary about implications for Canadian sovereignty. As a consequence of these differences, military officers from Canada and United States often undertook informal discussions with each other in an effort to avoid the involvement of the diplomats and the political baggage that came along with them."[73] Over the years politicians have repeatedly restrained the CF leadership's integrationist tendencies.[74]

Through NORAD the US commander of the alliance has de facto control over a number of military installations in Canada. In some circumstances US forces are authorized to enter Canada under that country's command. During the 2010 Vancouver Olympics, for instance, US troops were quietly deployed.[75]

The depth of the Canada-US military alliance is such that if US forces attacked this country it would be extremely difficult for the CF to defend our soil. In fact, given its entanglements with their southern counterparts the CF would likely enable a US invasion. As with the 2003 invasion of Iraq — which Ottawa officially opposed — some Canadian troops on exchange in the US might march north and, as is the norm when the US invades another country, Canadian officers would likely operate NORAD systems aiding the aggression.

This level of cooperation and integration is a major historical reversal. Decades into the 20th century the CF actively organized to combat US expansionism. In *Cautious Beginnings: Canadian Foreign Intelligence 1939 – 1951* Kurt Jensen notes, "the primary preoccupation of military intelligence and planning was response to an attack by the United States."[76]

Canadian Defence Scheme One was an elaborate plan to defend against US invasion. The 1921 initiative included a plan to seize some northern US cities to buy time for British reinforcements. According to the plan, London's Caribbean colonies could be used against the US: "The West Indies are admirably situated as bases for naval operations against the Southern States and particularly against the Panama Canal."[77]

Canadian military planners were right to be concerned. In the decades after the War of 1812 border disputes led to the 1846 Oregon Treaty and Irish Fenians attacked Canada from the US in the 1860s. In 1898 a 200-man Yukon Field Force was created out of fear the US might seek to seize the region in the wake of the Klondike Gold Rush. During that decade Canadian officials feared war between the US and Britain because they were in conflict over a Venezuela/Guyana territorial dispute. Through the 1920s and 30s US military planners crafted detailed invasion plans. Ostensibly for a war with Britain, Canada War Plan Red included abolishing the Canadian government and holding territory "in perpetuity".[78] A 1928 draft of the plan added, "it should be made quite clear to Canada that in a war she would suffer grievously."[79] The invasion plans, which were approved by the secretary of war and secretary of navy, remained current until WWII.[80]

Unpalatable as it may be to some, the USA is the only nation that could realistically invade Canada.[81] But, notes Marc Milner, Canada is largely "indefensible from the only country in a position to attack her."[82]

The "defence" sector ignores US threats because it is not oriented towards protecting Canada from aggression. Rather, Canada's "defence" community is aligned with the US empire's quest for global domination.

Instead of simply labeling CF leaders US lackeys, it's important to understand the history and professional interest driving relations. As detailed in Chapter 1, the CF was set up to serve the most powerful military of the day. For decades everything was done to be "interoperable" with British military equipment, training and tactics.[83] CF leaders gloried in empire and Britain's quest for global domination.

As the US replaced Britain as global hegemon, CF leadership shifted its orientation from the chief conquering power to its successor.

This shift was relatively seamless for economic, geographical, linguistic, cultural and racial reasons. It was but one part of a broader Canadian transition from privileged position within the British empire to the US empire.

Then, as now, the CF's relationship to the lead military power enabled its growth. In the early 1900s London pushed Ottawa to spend more on the military while Paul Cellucci revealed that when he was appointed US Ambassador to Canada in 2002 his only instruction was to press for increased military spending.[84] During a 2016 speech to the Canadian Parliament US President Barack Obama called on the federal government to increase its military spending.[85] In 2018 President Donald Trump sent Prime Minister Justin Trudeau a letter calling on Canada to improve its military preparedness and the next year top national security adviser Robert O'Brien said it was an "urgent priority" for Washington to get Canada and other NATO members to spend 2% of GDP on the military.[86]

One way to look at the CF's desire for close relations with their US counterparts is through the lens of professional hockey. Most players would prefer to be on the fourth line of an NHL club than the top unit of an AHL team. You may get less ice time but there's better training opportunities and travel conditions as well as better pay and bigger crowds. In the military world, US forces have the best equipment and greater prospects of seeing action around the world.

Partnering with the US military offers CF members exciting opportunities and authority. After attending the Air Force's Accelerated Aircraft Maintenance Officer Course in Texas and working at an air base in Qatar, RCAF Major Marcelo Plada told a US military website in 2019: "The Exchange Program has allowed me to grow my Aircraft Maintenance Management skills. I never would have had the opportunity to work at such a high warfighting level if I had stayed in Canada."[87] Similarly, General, and future chief of the defence staff, Walter Natynczyk, likely found it exhilarating to lead 35,000 international troops as part of the US occupation of Iraq.

In the lead-up to the 2003 invasion of Iraq CF and foreign affairs officials were granted access to daily briefs at US Central Command in Tampa, Florida, where reports were fed via video teleconference from all the US commands in the Gulf and the CIA.[88] Despite not (officially) participating in the war, Canada was alone with the UK in gaining this intelligence access.

Through their US counterparts the CF access "a sophistication of defence technology unavailable in Canada", notes Crosby in her book on NORAD.[89] A Canadian general is the vice commander of NORAD's advanced (mostly US) capabilities and runs the entire command when the US commander is absent.

Alongside better gear and opportunities, the CF/Canada is generally well treated. In 1996 Washington and Ottawa agreed "to share clean-up costs related to some former military installations in Canada," notes P. Whitney Lackenbauer. "But the process was delayed by U.S. congressional concerns that this pact could be construed as a precedent for critics of American military activities around the world."[90] Similarly, in the 1960s Washington didn't want Ottawa to share its nuclear weapons accord with the allied West German government because they weren't given "the same level of control afforded Canada in the Canada-US agreement."[91]

More than any other country, US forces trust their Canadian counterparts. In discussing the two countries' most significant bilateral military accord, Ann Griffiths explains, "NORAD brings the Canadian military more deeply within the US defense establishment than any other ally. The United States quite simply, would not entrust such responsibilities to the military of any other close ally, not even Britain."[92]

The critical discussion of Canada-US military relations focuses on CF subservience to their US counterparts. But, according to another interpretation of the relationship, the CF takes advantage of their US counterparts. The CSE, for instance, has received far more US intelligence through its partnership with the NSA than the other way around.⁹³ In NORAD, notes Gordon Wilson, the Canadians are "equal partners in spite of the difference of operational contribution."⁹⁴

The benefits of this close relationship for the Canadian military seem clear. What is less discussed is the political price that is paid in terms of independence and sovereignty. Do Canadians want to be so closely tied to the US military and its policies around the world? Is it possible to be a force for good in the world while being, in effect, a junior partner to the US Empire?

This is not just a question for the CF. As the next chapter illustrates, every country that belongs to NATO must make a similar calculation.

15. NATO Rules

"NATO has been the foundation of the foreign policy of Canadian governments ever since it was formed in 1949, and it will continue to be so."

Lester Pearson, 1963[1]

"NATO in reality had determined all of our defence policy. We had no defence policy, so to speak, except that of NATO. And our defence policy had determined all of our foreign policy. And we had no foreign policy of any importance except that which flowed from NATO."

Pierre Trudeau, 1969[2]

"[NATO is] the alliance to which Canada had devoted perhaps 90 percent of its military effort since 1949."

Jack Granatstein, 2007[3]

"[Canada has] participated and contributed to every NATO mission, operation and activity since NATO's founding."

Canada's Ambassador to the North Atlantic Council Kerry Buck, 2018[4]

ESTABLISHED IN 1949, NATO IS A MILITARY ALLIANCE operating under the stated principle that an "attack against one Ally is considered as an attack against all Allies." In 2021 it had 30 member states.

NATO is headquartered in Brussels at a $2 billion (€1.3 billion) building. The organization has a $3.3 billion annual operating budget with Canada providing $165 million a year.[5] Some 650 Canadians work at NATO headquarters and its satellite locations.[6]

NATO doesn't have its own army; rather member states devote their forces to its missions. Countries contribute a ship to a NATO patrol, aircraft to a bombing campaign or soldiers to an invasion.

NATO has various committees and bodies, including a Military Intelligence Committee, Defence Policy and Planning Committee, Conference of National Armaments Directors Committee, Air and

Missile Defence Committee, Aviation Committee and Committee on Public Diplomacy.

Its industrial advisory group is a "body of senior industrialists of NATO member countries, acting under the Conference of National Armaments Directors providing a forum for free exchange of views on industrial, technical, economic, management and other relevant aspects of research, development and production of armament equipment within the Alliance."[7]

NATO's Standardization Organization seeks to integrate everything from common terminology to complex technical standards to logistic and industrial interoperability. Over 1,300 NATO Standardization Agreements bind members to minimum interoperability standards from safe drinking water to air-to-air refuelling to satellite-based tactical data systems.[8]

NATO supports various militarist organizations in this country and operates a public diplomacy division. Founded in 1966 the NATO Association of Canada, formerly Atlantic Council of Canada, promotes the alliance. With an office in Toronto its staff and interns organize public events and publish different materials.

A number of Canadian organizations receive NATO's largesse. The Conference of Defence Associations' conferences have received support from NATO while the Canadian Global Affairs Institute has held numerous joint symposiums with NATO.[9] In the late 1980s the Canadian Institute for Strategic Studies had "agreements with NATO's Information Service to conduct a national/regional speakers tour."[10]

Some believe NATO was a Canadian idea. At the UN General Assembly in September 1947 External Affairs Minister Louis St. Laurent warned the floor that if the Security Council's veto crisis were not resolved countries would establish a NATO-type organization. His speech was the "first public proposal by a cabinet minister in the Atlantic area for an alliance for that region."[11] In March 1948 Canada, Britain and the US held top-secret talks about the possibility of creating a North Atlantic alliance.[12]

Officially, NATO was the West's response to an aggressive Soviet Union. But the Cold War can be traced to Canada and its allies' 1917 invasion of Russia, attempts to isolate that country throughout the 1920s and support for the Nazis' anti-Bolshevik posture. The idea that the US, or even Western Europe, was threatened by the Soviet Union after World War II is laughable. *NSC 68 and the Political Economy of the Early Cold War* notes, "at the end of the war, the Soviet Union lay in ruins virtually unimaginable to anyone who did not live through it. An estimated twenty-five million Soviet citizens and soldiers lost their lives fighting the invading Germans."[13] The US, on the other hand, came out of WWII much stronger than when they entered it. The continental US was untouched by fighting while the US economy benefited greatly from war production and exports.

After the destruction of WWII, the Soviets were not interested in fighting the US and its allies. In April 1945 Canada's ambassador to Russia, Dana Wilgress, concluded that "the interests of the Soviet privileged class are bound up with the maintenance of a long period of peace."[14] The Soviet elite, the ambassador continued in an internal memo, was "fearful of the possibility of attack from abroad" and "obsessed with problems of security."[15] Wilgress believed the Soviets wanted a post-war alliance with the UK to guarantee peace in Europe (with a Soviet sphere in the East and a UK-led West.) Internally, US officials came to similar conclusions. Noam Chomsky notes the first supreme commander of NATO, Dwight Eisenhower's "consistent view that the Russians intended no military conquest of Western Europe."[16] A May 1949 US Department of Eastern European Affairs memo explained, "the Soviet Union will not resort to direct military action against the West in the near future and expects and counts on a period of several years of peace."[17]

Rather than a defence against possible Russian attack, NATO was largely conceived as a reaction to growing socialist sentiment in Western Europe. During WWII self-described communists opposed Mussolini in Italy, fought the fascists in Greece and resisted the Nazi occupation of France. As a result, they had a great deal of prestige after the war, unlike the wealth-holders and church officials who backed the fascists. If not for US/British interference, communists, without Moscow's support, would probably have taken power in Greece and won the 1948 election in Italy. In France the Communist Party won 30 percent of the first post-war vote, filling a number of ministries in a coalition government.

At the time of Italy's first post-war election External Affairs Deputy Under-Secretary Escott Reid explained, "the whole game of the Russians is obviously to conquer without armed attack."[18] For his part, Lester Pearson decried an "attempt at a complete Russian conquest of Italy by constitutional or extra-constitutional means" and described class struggle by workers as a "new and sinister kind of danger, indirect aggression."[19]

US officials were equally concerned. George Kennan, the top US government policy planner at the time of NATO's formation, considered "the communist danger in its most threatening form as an internal problem that is of western society."[20] For his part NATO commander Eisenhower explained: "One of the great and immediate uses of the [NATO] military forces we are developing is to convey a feeling of confidence to exposed populations, a confidence which will make them sturdier, politically, in their opposition to Communist inroads."[21]

Pearson expressed similar sentiments. In March 1949 he told the House of Commons: "The power of the communists, wherever that power flourishes, depends upon their ability to suppress and destroy the free institutions that stand against them. They pick them off one by one: the political parties, the trade unions, the churches, the schools, the universities, the trade associations, even the sporting clubs and the kindergartens. The North Atlantic Treaty Organization is meant to be a declaration to the world that this kind of conquest from within will not in the future take place amongst us."[22]

NATO planners feared a weakening of self-confidence among Western Europe's elite and the widely held belief that communism was the wave of the future. NATO strengthened the Western European elite's confidence to face growing left-wing parties and movements. Additionally, "Secret anti-Communist NATO protocols" committed alliance countries' intelligence agencies to preventing communist parties from gaining power. After the fall of the Berlin Wall, information surfaced regarding groups the CIA and MI6 organized to "stay-behind" in case of a Soviet invasion of Western Europe. No invasion took place, of course. Instead, *NATO's Secret Armies* notes: "The real and present danger in the eyes of the secret war strategists in Washington and London were the at-times numerically strong Communist parties in the democracies of Western Europe. Hence the network in the total absence of a Soviet invasion took up arms in numerous countries and fought a secret war against the political forces of the left. The secret armies ... were involved in a whole series of terrorist operations and human rights violations that they wrongly blamed on the Communists in order to discredit the left at the polls."[23]

In one sense the popular portrayal of NATO as a defensive arrangement was apt. After Europe's second Great War the colonial powers were economically weak while anti-colonial movements could increasingly garner outside support. The Soviets and Mao's China, for instance, aided the Vietnamese. Similarly, Egypt supported Algerian nationalists and Angola benefited from highly altruistic Cuban backing. The international balance of forces had swung away from the colonial powers.

To maintain their colonies European powers increasingly depended on North American diplomatic and financial assistance. NATO was created partly to avoid a fracturing among the leading capitalist countries. In 1953 Pearson described "the unity and strength that have been so patiently and effectively built up, especially since the establishment of NATO."[24] In effect, the north Atlantic alliance was designed to maintain unity among the historic colonial powers — and the US — in the midst of a de-colonizing world.

NATO passed numerous resolutions supporting European colonial authority. Ottawa recognized the colonies of Vietnam,

Cambodia and Laos as "associated states" of France, according to an internal report, "to assist a NATO colleague, sorely tried by foreign and domestic problems."[25] More significantly, Canada gave France tens of millions of dollars in military equipment through NATO's Mutual Aid Program. These weapons were used to suppress the Vietnamese, Cameroonian and Algerian independence movements. Similarly, Canadian and US aid was used by the Dutch to maintain their dominance over Indonesia and West Papa New Guinea, by the Belgians in the Congo, Rwanda and Burundi and by the British in numerous places. Through NATO's Mutual Aid Program Canada donated a whopping $1,526,956,000 ($8 billion today) in ammunition, fighter jets, military training, etc. to European NATO countries between 1950 and 1958.[26]

Canadian officials had an incredibly expansive definition of NATO's defensive character. For Lester Pearson the north Atlantic pact justified European/North American dominance across the globe. As part of the parliamentary debate over NATO Pearson said: "There is no better way of ensuring the security of the Pacific Ocean at this particular moment than by working out, between the great democratic powers, a security arrangement the effects of which will be felt all over the world, including the Pacific area."[27] Two years later he said, "defence of the Middle East is vital to the successful defence of Europe and north Atlantic area."[28] In 1953 Pearson went even further, "there is now only a relatively small [5,000 kilometre] geographical gap between southeast Asia and the area covered by the north Atlantic treaty, which goes to the eastern boundaries of Turkey."[29]

How little NATO had to do with the Cold War is demonstrated by it becoming more aggressive after the demise of the Soviet Union. In 1999 Canadian fighter jets dropped 530 bombs in NATO's illegal 78-day bombing of Serbia. During the 2000s tens of thousands of Canadian troops fought in a NATO war in Afghanistan. In 2011 a Canadian general led NATO's attack on Libya in which seven CF-18 fighter jets and two Canadian naval vessels participated.

Designed to bring Western Europe under the US geopolitical umbrella, NATO has become more belligerent as its Cold War pretext fades further from view. In a dangerous game of brinksmanship with Moscow, NATO massed troops and fighter jets on that country's border in 2017. Alongside 200 soldiers in both Poland and Ukraine, 500 Canadian troops led a mission to Latvia while the US, Britain and Germany headed NATO missions in Poland, Lithuania and Estonia.

In the late 1990s Canada strongly supported NATO enlargement to the Czech Republic, Poland and Hungary.[30] Subsequently, Lithuania, Latvia, Bulgaria, Romania, Slovakia, Slovenia, Albania, Croatia and Montenegro were added to the alliance, which put NATO on Russia's doorstep. NATO expansion broke US, German and French promises to Soviet/Russian leader Mikhail Gorbachev regarding the reunification of Germany, an important Cold War divide. In 1990 Gorbachev agreed not to obstruct German reunification and for the new Germany to be part of NATO in return for assurances that the alliance wouldn't expand "one inch eastward".[31]

NATO is a nuclear weapons club. These monstrous bombs are "a fundamental component" of the alliance's military planning.[32] Through NATO Canada has effectively committed to fighting a nuclear war if any country breached its boundaries.[33] Additionally, the alliance does not restrict its members from using nuclear weapons first.[34]

In 1954 Canada voted to allow NATO forces to accept tactical nuclear weapons through the alliance's policy called MC 48, The Most Effective Pattern of NATO Military Strength for the Next Few Years. According to *Canada and UN Peacekeeping*, external minister Pearson "was integral to the process by which MC 48 was accepted by NATO."[35] Stationed in France and Germany as part of Ottawa's NATO commitment the CF-104 Starfighter operated without a gun and carried nothing but a thermonuclear weapon (MK 28 bomb).[36] More than 150 RCAF aircraft in Europe carried warheads in the 60s.[37] Today Canada participates in the NATO Nuclear Planning Group and contributes personnel and financial support to NATO's Nuclear Policy Directorate.

In 2017 the Justin Trudeau government "hid behind Canada's NATO membership", according to NDP foreign affairs critic Hélène Laverdière, when it opposed international efforts to ban nuclear weapons.[38] Similarly, when Ottawa abstained on a 2007 UN resolution calling for nuclear armed countries to remove their weapons from high alert status Canada's ambassador to the UN disarmament conference, Marius Grinius, explained that the resolution was incompatible with NATO policy.

At a time when he made a big display about "suffocating" the (nuclear) arms race Pierre Trudeau justified nuclear tipped cruise missiles testing in Canada. In 1983 the PM said, "having declared our support for the two track strategy, Canada should bear its fair share of the burden which that policy imposes on the NATO alliance."[39] In the late 1950s external minister Howard Green and diplomat Norman Robertson pushed for Canada to participate on a number of UN disarmament and arms control committees and study groups. Army head Charles Foulkes contacted Robertson, notes Sean Maloney, to "question whether this was in Canada's best interests since Canada was part of NATO."[40]

Unhappy with John Diefenbaker's attitude during the Cuban Missile Crisis and refusal to accept nuclear tipped Bomarc missiles, John F. Kennedy's administration used NATO's political authority to precipitate the downfall of his minority government. On January 3, 1963, the outgoing commander of NATO, US General Lauris Norstad, made a surprise visit to Ottawa where he publicly claimed Canada would not be fulfilling her commitments to the north Atlantic alliance if she did not acquire nuclear warheads. Diefenbaker believed the US general came to Canada "at the behest of President Kennedy" to set the table "for Pearson's conversion to the United States nuclear policy."[41] Norstad's visit deepened the split within cabinet over the deployment of Bomarc missiles and precipitated the Diefenbaker's government's fall a month later.

The north Atlantic alliance has been used to justify various other forms of militarism. In 2011 defence minister Peter MacKay cited

NATO when explaining a plan to build Canadian bases in a half dozen countries spanning the globe. He said, "the focus of the planning, let's be clear, is our capability for expeditionary participation in international missions … We are big players in NATO."[42]

NATO is used to justify budget outlays. In one of a string of similar commentaries, a 2017 *National Post* editorial bemoaned "Canada's continuing failure to honour our pledge to NATO allies to spend 2 per cent of GDP on defence."[43] In 2006 NATO countries adopted a pledge to put 2% of economic output into their military, which most alliance member states failed to attain.

Calling for expanding the fighter fleet, senior military officials told the *Globe and Mail* in 2017 that Canada didn't have sufficient fighter jets to simultaneously meet its NATO and NORAD obligations.[44]

In a history of the first century of the navy Marc Milner describes a series of reports in the mid-1960s concluding that the RCN was "too small to meet Canada's NATO obligations" and should be expanded "to meet NATO and North American commitments."[45]

NATO has even been invoked to justify arming the US war machine. In 1967 the prime minister responded to calls by opponents of the war in Vietnam to end the Defence Production Sharing Agreement, the arrangement under which Canada sold the US weapons, with the claim that to do so would imperil NATO. Lester Pearson claimed this "would be interpreted as a notice of withdrawal on our part from continental defence and even from the collective defence arrangements of the Atlantic alliance."[46]

While not requiring the level of integration into the US military of NORAD, NATO still primarily enforces the will of the US empire. It also promotes military spending and a militarist outlook.

A similar logic prevails in the subject of the next chapter. An organization that is supposed to serve the interests of veterans, also promotes militarism.

16. Helping Veterans or Promoting War

VETERANS AFFAIRS CANADA IS A BEHEMOTH. Its more than $5 billion budget is two and a half times the size of Environment and Climate Change Canada.[1] There are over 50 Veterans Affairs offices across the country and the ministry has about 4,000 employees.[2]

VA is responsible for veterans' pensions, benefits and services (as well as for the RCMP and a small number of civilians). Over 600,000 former soldiers receive benefits through VA.[3]

Established at the end of WWII, VA ballooned to 22,000 staff by 1947.[4] It helped former soldiers with health insurance, pensions and education. In the three decades after the war the Veterans Land Act assisted 140,000 ex-servicemen in buying a house or farm.[5] WWII veterans who weren't resettled under the Veterans Land Act or did not receive subsidized vocational retraining or education were entitled to a credit for a home, furniture or business.[6]

Veterans' benefits and the post-war Veterans Charter were "an important building block" of the welfare state.[7] By the end of 1943 the government had decided that a social welfare state was necessary to avert a postwar depression.[8] The government-produced *Origins and Evolution of Veterans Benefits in Canada 1914-2004* explained: "Veterans benefits have been a building block of the Canadian social welfare state. They have provided a social laboratory for Canadians and made them aware of what is possible when government acts decisively to meet a demonstrated social economic need (and, in the case of the Second World War, to anticipate it). By serving the particular good, veterans benefits have also served the common good. Many of the social benefits we take for granted today originated or were pioneered in the context of Canadian veterans benefits, including free hospital coverage, vocational retraining for the disabled, federal support to post-secondary educational institutions, business development loans, publicly funded legal aid, income support for the needy, and homecare."⁹ᵃ Over the years VA has administered or funded innumerable initiatives. Its Vetcraft Shops employed disabled veterans and their dependants who also made the Legion's poppies. VA funds the Queen's University based Canadian Institute for Military and Veteran Health Research. The institute "serves as a focal point for 43 Canadian universities who have agreed to work together in addressing the health research requirements of the Canadian military, Veterans and their families. The institute … acts as a conduit between the academic community, government organizations (e.g. National Defence and Veterans Affairs Canada and Health Canada), industry and similar international organizations."[10]

The ministry has also adopted various proclamations concerning veterans' rights. The government has adopted Veterans Charters, Veterans Bill of Rights and Veterans Ombudsman. The ombudsperson is supposed "to review and address complaints by [VA] clients and their representatives arising from the application of the provisions of the Veterans Bill of Rights; to identify and review emerging and systemic issues related to programs and services provided or administered by the Department or by third parties on the Department's behalf that impact negatively on clients."[11]

Despite the ombudsperson, Charter and Bill of Rights, veterans continue to face numerous problems. According to government data, at least 2,250 veterans were homeless in 2015.[12] Veterans have above average rates of suicide and mental illnesses such as depression and post-traumatic stress disorder (PTSD).[13]

Public Relations

Veterans Affairs operates a substantial public relations department. To disseminate its perspective, it employs dozens of communications

---

[a] War has enabled other important social gains. Income tax was introduced in 1917 to help pay for WWI. Canada's first direct tax on personal and business income was partly a response to criticism from farmers and others that men were conscripted but not wealth. During WWII more than two dozen crown corporations were established and the government ordered employers to bargain with labour unions notes David J Bercuson and Jack Granatstein in Dictionary of Canadian Military History. Additionally, women gained opportunities to pursue formal work.

officials. The ministry spends tens of millions of dollars annually articulating a one-sided version of Canadian military policy. "Veterans of the Korean War are everyday Canadians who became heroes by standing up for what we as a nation believe in: peace, freedom, and justice", notes its description of a war that left as many as four million dead.[14] The site's description of "Canada and the South African War, 1899-1902" claims the resource-fueled conflict "pitted British freedom, justice, and civilization against Boer backwardness."[15] The CF's purported "defence of freedom" and "pursuit of world peace" are favoured themes on the VA website.

VA has published many books and pamphlets. Two of its titles are *Valour Remembered: Canadians in Korea* and *Canada and the First World War: Valour Remembered.*

VA's public relations department worked closely with the CBC and National Film Board (NFB) to produce films promoting its perspective. With the NFB it co-produced *Home to the Land*, a 1945 documentary about the Veteran's Land Act.[16] In 1955, VA, the Legion and Crawley Films Canada produced a tribute to veterans titled *The Long Silence*, which aired on CBC.[17] In 1963 the ministry and NFB sponsored *Fields of Sacrifice* about the cemeteries and memorials where Canada laid its war dead in Europe.[18] Two years later VA and DND supported a 38-minute war commemoration CBC TV broadcast on Remembrance Day.[19]

The ministry continues to finance media production and pours millions of dollars into TV and other advertising. During the 2014 NHL playoffs VA ran 33 30-second spots.[20]

As part of its cultural outreach, VA funds partnerships with the world of sport. In 2016 it paid $7,000 for a "Play Hard Fight Hard: Sports and the Canadian Military" exhibit at Canada's Sports Hall of Fame in Calgary.[21] That year it also put up $150,000 for a Canadian Football League (CFL) veterans' tribute and presentation of the Jake Gaudaur Veterans' Award, which is given to the player "who best demonstrates the attributes of Canadian Veterans in times of war, military conflict, and peace."²² A press release announcing the 2017 trophy recipient noted, "Canadians take pride in the nation's rich history and military heritage, and a large measure of that is owed to the selfless service and contributions of Canada's Veterans, still-serving members, and those who have made the ultimate sacrifice."²³ The $150,000 in public money financed a number of CFL/VA collaborations, including a Grey Cup Meet and Greet and Remembrance Tribute. The 2017 tribute claimed, "to be Canadian means to stand on guard for peace, freedom and democracy. This has been bravely demonstrated countless times by Canadian women and men in uniform."²⁴

The ministry spends millions of dollars on war monuments, including the Ottawa-based National War Memorial, Korean War Monument, National Victoria Cross Memorial, Veterans Memorial Highway, National Aboriginal Veterans Monument, Boer War Memorial, etc. There are more than 7,500 memorials registered with VA's National Inventory of Military Memorials.²⁵

VA spends heavily on other "awareness" activities. Between 2006 and 2014 the department's Community Engagement Partnership Fund dished out $13 million for hundreds of small projects recognizing veterans such as $5,000 for a Remembrance Day service at the University of British Columbia.²⁶ Millions of dollars are spent every year on Canada Remembers, which included "awareness and participation of Canadians in remembrance activities."²⁷

Through project grants and some core funding VA backs various groups. These include the Royal Canadian Legion, Canadian Peacekeeping Veterans Association, Canadian Association of Veterans in United Nations Peacekeeping, Canadian Veterans Advocacy, Veterans UN-NATO Canada, National Council of Veterans Associations, Aboriginal Veterans Autochtones, War Amps, Gulf War Veterans Association of Canada, Hong Kong Veterans' Association, NATO Veterans Organization of Canada, Saskatchewan Indian Veterans Association and Army, Navy and Air Force Veterans. These groups have produced/commissioned numerous reports and books. The Korea

Veterans Association of Canada published *The Korea Veterans Association of Canada Memorial Book: Korean War, 1950-53* and *Peacekeeping, 1953-56* and greatly aided *Deadlock in Korea: Canadians at War, 1950-1953.*[28] The Saskatchewan Indian Veterans Association published *We Were There* "to let Indian children know that their fathers and grandfathers fought for the freedom we now cherish."[29]

***

With dozens of organizations, representing hundreds of thousands of individuals, veterans are a well-organized political force. Drawing on a mix of martial nationalism and popular support for social services, veterans can spur political backlash. They contributed to Stephen Harper's defeat in the 2015 election. In a sign of (over-the-top) progressive support of their campaign, a 2015 Tyee story titled "seven ways the Harper government has waged war on its own veterans", reported that the "Conservatives closed offices, cut 900 jobs, clawed back benefits, killed lifetime pensions for Afghanistan veterans, and failed to spend $1.13 billion of the Veterans Affairs budget."[30]

In addition to weakening the reactionary Harper government, veterans' groups have won important progressive victories. After two decades of campaigning, the War Amps and other veterans' groups won "seriously disabled veteran" legislation in 1995.[31] After multiple decades of struggle, veterans of the 1941 disaster in Hong Kong received up to $24,000 in compensation in 1998. Sent to reinforce British defenders of the colony, 2,000 poorly trained Canadians were soon overwhelmed by Japanese forces. Most of those who survived spent 44 months in brutal Japanese prison camps. After being denied benefits, indigenous veterans of WWI and WWII won $20,000 each in 2002.[32] Two years later veterans groups won $24,000 for former soldiers exposed to toxic agents (mustard gas, tear gas, etc.).[33] About 3,700 CF members were employed as human guinea pigs from WWII until the 1970s.[34] Some of the 'volunteers' — many of whom had little education or English and were offered limited information about the risks of the testing — were injured permanently.[35]

Chairman of the National Council of Veterans Associations, Cliff Chadderton, claimed the government only offered compensation after his group sought a ruling from the Human Rights Commission in Geneva on whether Canada violated the Geneva Conventions' prohibition on using soldiers in experiments.[36] Veterans' groups also helped win $20,000 in compensation for individuals harmed by toxic defoliants (Agent Orange) tested at CFB Gagetown in New Brunswick.[37] The decade-long campaign drew attention to Canada's role in testing these cancerous chemicals, which US forces unleashed on the Vietnamese.

Soldiers or civilians who've been harmed by CF chemical testing certainly deserve compensation. Similarly, those who suffered physical or mental ailments at war must be looked after by the government that deployed them. The burden of caring for soldiers harmed abroad should be "costed in" to any mission.

But, more often than not, veterans' organizations have used their cultural standing to uphold militarism and reactionary politics. At the end of WWI veterans attacked leftist union officials in Vancouver opposed to conscription. Angry about their criticism of Canada's invasion of Russia, veterans also sacked the Socialist Party headquarters in Winnipeg, destroying a piano and educational materials.[38]

At the end of WWI, the Great War Veterans Association called for businesses to fire foreign workers. They also wanted those deemed disloyal by the Alien Investigation Board to be deported and all but $75 ($800 today) of their property to be confiscated and given to soldiers or their widows.[39]

At the end of WWII the Legion pushed for returning soldiers to be granted seniority rights for time spent in the military. Much to the chagrin of organized labour, the Legion pushed the federal government to breach seniority clauses in collective agreements.[40] Seeing an opportunity to break the union, Ford Motors in Windsor pushed to replace union employees with returning soldiers, which led to a bitter strike.[41] (Labour called on the government to expand employment opportunities for veterans.)

Veterans have sought to suppress criticism of Canadian militarism. In the early 1980s the NFB and CBC co-produced *The Kid Who Couldn't Miss* about Canada's top WWI flying ace Billy Bishop. The program questioned "what part of his legend is myth and what part truth. But one thing is clear, heroism — like war itself — is neither as simple nor as glorious as we would like."[42] This was too much for the chairman of the National Council of Veterans Associations and CEO of the War Amps, Cliff Chadderton, and some other veterans whose campaign against the film led to a Senate Subcommittee on Veterans Affairs hearing. The subcommittee questioned spending public funds on the film and the NFB acquiesced to adding a disclaimer at the start of the film. Chadderton was not satisfied. He wanted the film withdrawn, claiming "anything less is an unforgiveable attempt to destroy the well-deserved legend of Billy Bishop and an insult to all war veterans."[43]

After CBC showed *The Valour and the Horror* in 1992 Chadderton launched a campaign to block the three-part series from being rebroadcast or distributed to schools. The series claimed Canadian soldiers committed unprosecuted war crimes during WWII and that the British-led bomber command killed 600,000 German civilians as part of a top-secret campaign to weaken public morale (even the bombers, flying at night, were largely unaware of their true mission). The veterans' campaign led to a Senate inquiry, a CRTC hearing and a lawsuit.[44] Stoking the upheaval Deputy Minister of Defence Robert Fowler complained to CBC President Gérard Veilleux that by broadcasting the series, "a medium as powerful as television has been used to denigrate the efforts of those who surely deserve better treatment from a grateful nation."[45] Ultimately, CBC said it would not rebroadcast *The Valour and the Horror* without amendments.[46]

In the mid-2000s the Legion, Air Force Association of Canada and other veteran groups battled Canadian War Museum historians over an exhibition about the WWII allied bomber offensive. After shaping its development, the Legion objected to a small part of a multifaceted exhibit, which questioned "the efficacy and the morality of the …

massive bombing of Germany's industrial and civilian targets."⁴⁷ With the museum refusing to give the veterans an effective veto over its exhibit, *Legion Magazine* called for a boycott.⁴⁸ The Legion's campaign led to hearings by the Senate Subcommittee on Veterans Affairs and prompted the Canadian War Museum to ask senior DND historian Serge Bernier to write a report on the matter. Bernier concluded the exhibit was hurtful to the veterans.⁴⁹ The controversy led to the director of the museum, Joe Guerts, resigning and a new display glossed over a bombing campaign explicitly designed to destroy German cities.⁵⁰

Formed in 1926, the Royal Canadian Legion is the biggest veterans' organization. It claimed 300,000 members and 1,400 Branches.⁵¹ While its core political mandate is improving veterans' services, the Legion has long advocated militarism and a reactionary worldview. In the early 1930s it pushed for military build-up and its 1950 convention called for "total preparedness".⁵² In 1983 its president, Dave Capperauld, supported US cruise missiles tests in Alberta and into the early 1990s the Legion took "an uncompromising stand on the importance of maintaining a strong Canadian military presence in Europe through NATO, and by supporting the United States build-up of advanced nuclear weapons."⁵³

The Legion has also espoused a racist, paranoid and pro-empire worldview. In the years after WWII it called for the expulsion of Canadians of Japanese origin and ideological screening for German immigrants.⁵⁴ A decade before WWII, reports *Branching Out: The Story of the Royal Canadian Legion*, "Manitoba Command unanimously endorsed a resolution to ban communist activities, and provincial president Ralph Webb ... warned that children were being taught to spit on the Union Jack in Manitoba schools."⁵⁵

Long after the end of the Cold War the organization remained concerned about "subversives". Legion members must sign a statement that begins: "I hereby solemnly declare that I am not a member of, nor affiliated with, any group, party or sect whose interests conflict with the avowed purposes of the Legion, and I do not, and will not, support any organization advocating the overthrow of our government by force or which advocates, encourages or participates in subversive action or propaganda."⁵⁶

***

A slew of initiatives that help former soldiers access civilian work double as militarist propaganda. Modeled after an American program of the same name, the Helmets to Hard Hats initiative gives veterans, reservists and current soldiers priority access to jobs and training opportunities in the trades. The Canada Company Military Employment Transition Program assists CF members, reservists and veterans in obtaining non-military employment. It offers participating companies/institutions, including Via Rail, Irving Shipbuilding and University of New Brunswick, the status of Designated Military Friendly Employer and National Employer Support Awards. Taking this a step further, Barrick Gold hired a Director of Veteran Sourcing and Placement to oversee a Veterans Recruitment Program. According to program Director Joel Watson, "veterans self-select to put service before self, which says much about their individual character, drive and willingness to work together in teams."⁵⁷

While job training and placement efforts have a social value, these initiatives generally promote the idea that soldiers have a unique social value.

Innumerable public and private initiatives reinforce veterans' cultural standing. VIA Rail partnered with the Royal Canadian Legion to pay tribute to veterans.⁵⁸ A number of public transit authorities allow veterans to ride free on Remembrance Day and during some other days while their buses carry signs reading, "Lest We Forget".

In the mid-2000s every province adopted a special licence plate to signify the driver is a veteran.⁵⁹ Special license plates are only one of the many auto-centred initiatives that reinforce militarism. Many cities offer free parking to veterans and exempt Legions from property taxes. In 2018 a Ford dealership in Kingston, Ontario, offered a special discount package to former or current soldiers.⁶⁰ Its release stated, "whether you're a local weather presenter, a plumber or play drums in a weekend cover band, your way of life is possible, in part, due to the brave sacrifice of the men and women of the Canadian Armed Forces."[61]

Are soldiers more valuable to society than teachers? Are they more essential than the people who drive buses or clean our waste? Is what they do more honourable than caring for elders, reporting the news or providing essential social services?

Or, if danger is the primary criteria, how about those who build houses or feed us? Over the past half-century tens of times more Canadian construction workers have been killed on the job than soldiers. While 158 Canadian soldiers died in Afghanistan between 2002 and 2014, there were 843 agriculture-related fatalities in Canada between 2003 and 2012.[62]

The truth is soldiers are "venerated" not because of the danger they face or their heroism, but because fighting wars must be made to appear heroic to motivate anybody to do it. Fighting wars driven by rivalries between rich and powerful people is particularly difficult to sell. Patriotism, nationalism and other forms of "herding the masses" are used to sell militarism and wars that are in the interests of the small few who profit from them.

But veterans associations are only a small part of those pushing militarism. The next chapter explores other ways the CF and its backers promote the interests of the military, to gather recruits and shape discussion of war, military preparedness and the CF.

17. Marketing Militarism

THE INSTITUTIONS AND THE METHODS used to promote the Canadian Forces are similar to those marketing Coke. Convincing people to buy something so very unhealthy requires a massive sales pitch, which includes getting at customers young.

Cadets

The cadets are a powerful tool for drawing teens into militarism. To familiarize young people with the CF the military spends more than $300 million a year on the Royal Canadian Sea Cadets, Royal Canadian Army Cadets and Royal Canadian Air Cadets.[1] The largest and oldest government-funded youth program, over 50,000 kids were part of the free afterschool initiative in 2020.[2] Participants may receive school credits and the government offers up hundreds of thousands of dollars a year in post-secondary scholarships to cadets.[3] They sometimes also receive cash bonuses for attending.[4]

According to the CF's description, "it is a national program for young Canadians aged 12 to 18 who are interested in participating in a variety of fun, challenging and rewarding activities while learning about the Sea, Army and Air activities of the Canadian Armed Forces."[5] Nine to 12 year-olds are also eligible for the Navy League Cadets.

The National Defence Act authorizes the minister to establish cadet chapters.[6] In 1969 the Directorate of Cadets was established after the three branches of the military were consolidated.[7] The directorate sets policy and coordinates the activities of the Sea, Army and Air Cadets.

Established in 1971, the Army Cadet League of Canada is a private charity that supports cadets. With branch offices in every province and territory, the league's $20+ million budget is funded through a mix of private donations and DND grants.

Military manufacturers often support the cadets. In 2018 Irving Shipbuilding invested $100,000 in the Royal Canadian Sea

Cadet Education Foundation.[8] For most of a half-century Canadair (Bombardier) sponsored a number of air cadet squadrons.[9]

Serving personnel, reservists and individuals given a military commission train the cadets. Part of the CF Reserve, the Cadet Instructors Cadre is the largest officer branch in the CF.[10] Military officials say the program is designed to teach teens how to become good citizens, but cadets learn about the CF's procedures and traditions and are taught to appreciate its emblems and symbols. According to an official description, one aim of the cadets is "to stimulate the interest of youth in the sea, land, and air activities of the Canadian Forces."[11]

The program instils reverence for warfare. Cadets often attend Remembrance Day celebrations and other military commemorations. "Growing up as a Canadian cadet," explains Kelly Jarman in "The Cost of Canada's Militarist Culture: Perspectives From a Former Cadet", "I was taught that the military is the most important aspect of society and that it deserves unquestioned respect. Trips to museums, Remembrance Day parades and even school assignments were all designed to instill in us the idea that soldiers are noble and that wars are fought for democracy and freedom. The very idea of citizenship is linked to military culture, something that became evident when we toured the HMCS Fredericton naval war ship during a so-called 'Citizenship Trip.'"[12]

The cadet program develops obedient soldiers rather than politically active citizens. Participants are subject to the military's hierarchal rank system. The CF boasts that cadets "develop a great sense of pride and discipline through their involvement in a hierarchical system that allows them to hone their leadership skills as they grow older and they learn to care for younger cadets."[13]

Along with socializing members into its rank system, cadets can learn marksmanship, parachuting and other military skills. Much of the training takes place at summer camps on bases. Historically, the base training simulated warlike scenarios. In a horrific training mishap, six teens died and dozens were injured when a live grenade exploded at a cadet camp in Valcartier, QC, in 1974.[14]

The cadets began as a paramilitary group explicitly designed to prepare youth for war. The first "drill association" was set up to train boys to fight in 1861.[15] Expanding its support to schools providing military training, Ottawa issued a Militia General Order that authorized the formation of 74 "Associations for Drill in Educational Institutions" in 1879. Two decades later Ontario granted $50 ($1,500 today) to schools with more than 25 boys in the cadets.[16] In 1908 the Department of Militia and Defence provided instructors, arms, books and exams to school-age males in an effort to standardize the different cadet training programs in Ontario and Québec secondary schools.[17]

Conflict spurred drill activity. The 1860-65 US Civil War, 1866–67 Fenian Raids, 1869–70 Red River Rebellion and 1885 Northwest Rebellion sparked interest in "drill associations". During WWI 64,000 children were in the Cadet Corps.[18] Some 40,000 former cadets fought in the First World War.[19]

Girls weren't officially admitted to the cadets until the 1970s. In 1975 Parliament changed the word "boys" to "persons" in the cadet legislation. But patriarchy dies hard. Controversy erupted in 2016 over a code-of-conduct pamphlet given to cadets that referred to the four Bs — "boobs, belly, bums, boxers". In what some viewed as shaming female cadets, the pamphlet said girls should not wear shirts that "reveal their developing bits" (breasts).[20]

A series of reports suggest that sexual abuse is a problem in the organization.[21] In 2016 VICE News "obtained documents that prove that the Canadian Forces' cadet program has grappled with hundreds of cases of sexual assault, harassment, discrimination, and abuse" over the decades.[22]

In 2006 Ottawa agreed to pay $8 million to 35 former sea cadets who were sexually assaulted.[23] As this book went to print, a number of other sexual abuse lawsuits were pending. A suit launched in 2016 from former cadets in the Atlantic provinces alleged the organization created an environment "which encouraged or fostered silence and obedience" when abuse took place.[24] Some suggest that abusers are attracted to cadet training positions since it puts them in contact with children and the hierarchical structure — having to obey commanding officers — enables abuse.[25]

Schools

The cadets and militia have operated in schools for more than a century. Before WWI Minister of Militia Sam Hughes promoted the militia partly as a source of instructors to train cadets and Boy Scouts.[26] In 1909 Honorary Colonel Sir Donald Gordon Smith put up a half million dollars ($10 million in today's money) "for the encouragement of physical and military training in public schools."[27]

Since WWII the CF has initiated innumerable public relations and recruitment efforts targeting children. In partnership with the Kiwanis Club the RCAF began an annual Kids' Day in 1957. Modeled after an initiative set up by the US Air Force, a RCAF memo described it as "highly worthwhile" for those "concerned with community relations, long-range recruiting, and education of the public."[28]

In 1961 the air force distributed posters and individual folders of the poem "High Flight" by former RCAF pilot John Magee to schools in Ontario. Every student who took the Ontario Departmental English Literature Examination was "required to make an intensive study of this poem."[29]

From the late 1950s through the early 1960s the RCAF advertised on high school book covers. In 1960 a Windsor recruiter wrote air force headquarters that "the school book covers are an excellent media of advertising" and a "way of keeping the RCAF in front of students during their complete term."[30] A North Bay unit reported that the covers "make school authorities more amenable and cooperative to the officer's request for a period [to make their pitch] later in the school term."[31] A recruiter in St. John's added that it "serves as a very satisfactory investment of public relations between the RCAF and high schools, particularly in those one and two room schools in remote communities in this province where liaison visits are not made."[32]

Begun in 1955, NORAD Tracks Santa is a massive outreach program organized by the joint US/Canada command. It receives over 100,000 phone calls in the 23 hours before Christmas and tens of millions of visits to its website in December as well as a million downloads of its Track Santa app.[33] The 150 CF members stationed at the NORAD headquarters in Colorado Springs participate in the call centre on Christmas Eve.[34]

For four decades the 38 Canadian Brigade Group's Signal Regiment has visited hundreds of elementary school children each December as part of Operation RADIO SANTA.[35] The soldiers set up a military command post where the children dictate their Christmas lists to the North Pole. Along with speaking directly to Santa, the students tour the mobile command post, view different military equipment and ask soldiers questions.[36]

The CF often showcases its equipment at schools. In 2007 the army brought a tank to schoolyards in St. John's, Newfoundland. CBC reported that a Grade 4 "class at Holy Cross Elementary school were given a first-hand show-and-tell session with a tank and related gear."[37]

Military recruiters often participate in career and education fairs at schools. In April 2019 the CF set up a virtual reality shooting range at a school in Kingston to recruit students from across the Catholic District School Board of Eastern Ontario.[38]

An army co-op program gives students four high school credits and pays them to join the reserves where they train to shoot machine guns and throw grenades.[39] The RCN operated a similar high school co-op program. Students in the Victoria area can serve in the reserves after school, receive up to four high school credits and are paid to do basic training in the summer.[40]

Veterans Affairs produces "learning resources" designed for different school grades. In 2012 an education officer with VA explained: "At the beginning of the school year, we send a promotional kit to all schools, containing an example of each of the learning resources available for that year. ... There is also a Veterans' Week Speakers

Program and DND co-ordinates visits by Canadian Forces members to schools."[41]

At the height of the war in Afghanistan, the CF launched Operation Connection which called on soldiers to make "visits to schools ... Telephone your children's schools or your grandmother's seniors' residence and ask if you and/or your unit could be of help planning a Canadian Forces Day event or setting up a Remembrance Day program."[42]

Militarist organizations also run school initiatives. The Canadian War Museum lent schools free learning kits, which contain artefacts related to WWI and other materials to support in-class lessons. In the late 1980s, according to professor Peter Langille, the DND-backed Canadian Institute for Strategic Studies developed a "high school curriculum program to counterbalance the peace movement."[43]

Historica Canada's Canadian Forces Memory Project reached hundreds of thousands of students.[44] The initiative brings veterans and CF members to schools and its digital archive offers educators more than 3,000 firsthand stories and 1,500 original artefacts chronicling Canadian military history.[45] In *Warrior Nation*, Ian McKay and Jamie Swift describe the Memory Project message to students: "In essence, the story goes, warriors, made us what we are today. Warriors led us in the past and should govern in the future; and, if you are lucky, you too might grow up to be a warrior."[46]

Since the early 2000s DND, Canadian Heritage and VA have ploughed millions of dollars into the Memory Project.[47]

In southern Ontario there is a private military boarding school. The Robert Land Academy is for boys in grades 6 through 12.

Across the country more than a dozen public schools are named after famous battles (Vimy Ridge, Juno Beach, Passchendaele, etc.) or soldiers (Jeffry Amherst, Roméo Dallaire, Arthur Currie, etc.). In higher education Brock University is named after Major-General Sir Isaac Brock; Dalhousie University is named after General George Ramsay, 9th Earl of Dalhousie; McGill University is named after Colonel James

McGill and Simon Fraser University is named after Captain Simon Fraser.[48]

Post-Secondary Educational Institutions

The CF has numerous post-secondary educational institutions and is well entrenched within academia. Responsible for professional development of CF members, the Canadian Defence Academy (CDA) is comprised of Canadian Forces College, Royal Military College Saint-Jean and Royal Military College of Canada.

Created in 1943, the Toronto-based Canadian Forces College is a military school for senior and general officers. For its part, Royal Military College Saint-Jean offers a two-year, general military college diploma for Quebeckers, filling in the gap between high school and university usually taken by CEGEPs. The Royal Military College in Kingston is the only federally run university. DND provides about $70 million annually to RMC and the defence minister is chancellor of an institution established in 1876.[49]

For 50 years DND ran Royal Roads Military College on Vancouver Island. In 1995 it became a public university, but it "maintains strong ties with the Canadian Forces."[50]

DND operates two dozen other specialized educational facilities ranging from Canadian Forces School of Meteorology to Canadian Forces Language Schools. The 75-year-old Royal Canadian Electrical and Mechanical Engineers School is housed in a 140,000 square foot building at CFB Borden.[51] Nearby is the Canadian Forces Medical Services School, which is the CF Health Services primary training centre. With a 25 person staff and substantial media facilities, the Defence Public Affairs Learning Centre in Gatineau seeks "to develop a cadre of professional Public Affairs Officers in the Canadian Armed Forces, and to give defence personnel, especially Canadian Armed Forces members, the training and expertise they need to connect effectively with Canadians and provide communications advice to senior leaders of the Canadian Armed Forces."[52]

DND also employs the expertise of various other post-secondary institutions. In 2006 the CDA helped a number of colleges add military diplomas and programs formerly provided at military institutions. The Canadian Armed Forces College Opportunities Program offers diplomas in Military Arts and Sciences. In 2012 the Association of Canadian Community Colleges provided input to the House of Commons Standing Committee on National Defence on "Maintaining the Readiness of the Canadian Forces."[53] A number of colleges, such as the Northern Alberta Institute of Technology, offer special services to help CF personnel.[54]

The Canadian Officers Training Corps was launched at McGill, Queens and the University of Toronto in 1912.[55] The University Naval Training Division and Royal Canadian Air Force University Reserve Training Program were added subsequently. According to Lee Windsor, deputy director of University of New Brunswick's Gregg Centre for the Study of War and Society, the Canadian Officers Training Corps "introduced university undergraduates to a form of military service on campus, providing them with leadership and other military training and preparing them to join the reserve or the regular force if they wished to do so."[56]

In 2011 the Senate standing committee on national security and defence recommended re-establishing the Canadian Officers Training Corps. The University of Alberta hosted a trial of a program that "allow[ed] people to simultaneously obtain a university degree while also gaining leadership experience in the Canadian Armed Forces (CAF) Reserves."[57] It may be expanded to other universities.

Defence procurement contracts often require companies to sponsor university research. The government's Industrial and Technological Benefits Policy boasts that between 2014 and 2017 it directed $82 million into universities, colleges and public research labs.[58] As part of its contract under the National Shipbuilding Strategy, Seaspan donated $2 million to the University of British Columbia to establish a Research Chair in Naval Architecture and Marine Engineering.[59] Irving Shipbuilding contributed $500,000 to establish the Irving Shipbuilding Chair in Marine Engineering and Autonomous Systems at Dalhousie, which was headed up by a long-time Defence Research and Development Canada (DRDC) scientist.[60] Boeing helped Memorial University set up a Mechatronic Development and Prototyping Facility while Lockheed Martin gave Dalhousie $2-million for research into "quantum computing, physics and material sciences."[61] (Dalhousie is a member of the Aerospace and Defence Industries Association of Nova Scotia while the University of New Brunswick is a member of that province's branch.[62])

Canadian universities have received tens of millions of dollars from the US Navy, US Air Force, US Strategic Defense Initiative or US Defense Threat Reduction Agency.[63] In a study published by the Canadian University Press Service during the US war in Vietnam, Ian Wiseman wrote that "every university in Canada received money from the US Defense complex."[64] A Ploughshares Monitor investigation in the 1980s concluded that Canadian universities received $825,000 per year on average from the US military.[65]

Among the most controversial US Department of Defense funded projects at a Canadian university, McGill researchers studied the use of ballistics/cannons — instead of rockets — to explore the earth's upper atmosphere and launch satellites. The High Altitude Research Project (HARP) used a very large gun to fire the models to high speeds and altitudes. Based in Barbados, HARP operated in conjunction with the United States Ballistic Research Laboratory.[66]

More recently, Demilitarize McGill criticized a number of contracts between the university's researchers and Canadian military. In 2015 McGill's Aerospace Mechatronics Lab received $380,000 from DND to develop "unmanned ground, air, and marine vehicles" and build "3D world representation models of the urban battle space to improve soldier situational awareness."[67] The Aerospace Mechatronics Lab garnered another $245,000 to research unmanned ground vehicles (UGVs) to support "military missions in complex operating environments."[68] For its part, the DRDC put up $230,000 for a collaboration between McGill's Department of Electrical and Computer Engineering, Israel's Technion and Lockheed Martin on missile guidance systems technology.[69]

The McGill Shockwave Physics Group (SWPG) conducted DND funded research on thermobaric explosives, which use oxygen from the surrounding air to generate high-temperature explosions that are generally of a longer duration than those produced by a conventional condensed explosive. Projects SWPG worked on were titled: "Interaction of a blast wave with a metalized explosive fireball"; "Measurement of the Limit of Shock Precompression and Induction Delay Time of Liquid Explosives"; "Near-Field Impulse Effects from Detonation of Heterogeneous Explosives".

***

DND also influences academic debate about the CF and Canadian military affairs. They occasionally partner with academic institutions on workshops and hold scholarly conferences such as the RCN's "Submarines in Canada: Past, Present and Future."[70] In 2015 DND gave the University of New Brunswick Milton F. Gregg Centre for the Study of War and Society half a million dollars to produce educational material about Canada's Victoria Cross recipients who demonstrated "conspicuous bravery" fighting on behalf of the British Empire between 1856 and 1945.[71]

The Canadian Defence Academy Press and the Canadian Special Operations Forces Command Professional Development Centre publish scholarly books while the DND backed/operated *Canadian Military Journal*, *Canadian Naval Review* and *Canadian Army Journal* publish peer-reviewed articles.[72]

Many university programs have been funded by DND's Security and Defence Forum (SDF). It was established in 1967 to "develop a domestic competence and national interest in defence issues of relevance to Canada's security."[73]

Previously named the Military and Strategic Studies Program, SDF included a Scholarship and Internship program, Special Projects, a Chair of Defence Management Studies and funding for "centres of expertise". SDF's scholarship and internship initiative ploughed $300,000 a year into academic awards that "support graduate and post-graduate studies in Canadian defence and security issues."[74] SDF also funded a handful of 12-month internships each year "for students with Master's degrees who are interested in working in security and defence-related organizations."[75]

SDF channeled hundreds of thousands of dollars annually into special projects. This included funding conferences and other efforts to facilitate collaboration among "security" scholars. It also includes funds to give "members of the SDF community an opportunity to visit Canadian Forces operations or bases" and to "bring students from SDF centres and SDF award recipients to National Defence Headquarters."[76]

SDF funded a dozen "centres of expertise", including Queen's Chair of Defence Management Studies and Centre for International Relations, Carleton's Centre for Security and Defence Studies, Wilfrid Laurier's Centre for Military, Strategic & Disarmament Studies, University of Manitoba's Centre for Defence and Security Studies, University of Calgary's Centre for Military and Strategic Studies. To receive SDF funding departments generally committed to offering a minimum number of courses with "significant security and defence content."[77]

In some instances, military money made up a significant share of a department's budget. In 2008-09, for instance, Dalhousie's Centre for Foreign Policy Studies received more than half its budget from SDF and the navy, which paid the salary of a Dalhousie Defence Fellow affiliated with the centre.[78]

Alongside its support for "centres of expertise", SDF funded a Chair of Defence Management Studies. DND gave Queen's University's Defence Management Studies more than $200,000 annually.[79] As chair of the Queen's program through the 2000s Douglas Bland received $825,000 to "conduct outreach activities with the Canadian public …

and Parliament about security and defence issues."[80] Bland called the mid-2000s counterinsurgency war in Afghanistan "the right mission for Canada and the right mission for the Afghan people" and criticized "years of Liberal [party] neglect of ... defence policy and the Canadian Forces."[81]

Dozens of academics writing on military, security and foreign policy issues received SDF funds. They generally articulated pro-military positions, which caused a minor controversy during the war in Afghanistan. In a 2008 article University of Ottawa professor Amir Attaran wrote, "when DND needs a kind word in Parliament or the media — presto! — an SDF sponsored scholar often appears, without disclosing his or her financial link."[82] Even SDF proponent and ardent militarist Jack Granatstein admitted in a 2011 op-ed "what the government seems to want from SDF academics is uncritical support for its partisan policies."[83]

SDF and its predecessor Military and Strategic Studies Program (MSSP) launched a number of university departments. Université du Québec à Montréal's Centre d'études des politiques étrangères et de sécurité was created with funds from MSSP in 1991 while Queen's Defence Management Studies "was established in 1996 with financial support from the Canadian Department of National Defence."[84] MSSP and the militarist Donner Canadian Foundation funded the establishment of Dalhousie's Centre for Foreign Policy Studies (CFPS) in 1971.[85] In a 1992 article on the history of CFPS, professor Danford W. Middlemiss wrote, "the principal source of continuing financial support for the CFPS since its founding has been the Department of National Defence's MSSP."[86] Middlemiss also pointed to CFPS' "liaison activities with National Defence Headquarters" and says the department "continues to cooperate closely with Maritime command."[87]

York's chair in strategic studies was also established with MSSP funds. With former Brigadier General George Bell taking a senior administrative position at the university, York attracted military funds in the early 1970s. Ken Bell and Desmond Morton write, "his influence helped ensure that York's 'chair' gradually developed into a lively centre for strategic studies, even at a time when universities were being forced to retrench."[88]

The SDF budget ranged from $2–2.5 million annually. But that didn't include the cost of administering the program or hundreds of thousands of dollars in bursaries SDF distributed each year through the Association of Universities and Colleges of Canada.[89]

After nearly a half-century SDF was replaced with the Defence Engagement Program. Initially DEP scaled down support for university departments but the 2017 defence policy review "increased investment in academic outreach to $4.5 million per year in a revamped and expanded Defence Engagement Program." As part of this push to support academic projects, DND established the Mobilizing Insights in Defence and Security (MINDS) program in 2019.

SDF gave the military influence in the social sciences. So does the DND-funded and overseen Royal Military College of Canada (RMC). Its 150+ faculty have schooled a number of prominent CF commentators. They also publish many articles and books on military themes.

Adding to the military's influence within academia is DND's directorate of history. Official military historians have been highly influential. They have published at least 40 official volumes and dozens of other works and dominated academic discussion of war into the 1960s.[90]

At the end of WWI the Department of Militia and Defence established a historical section.[91] Wanting its historians to write the "foundational studies" of Canadian wars, WWI and II records were tightly controlled. Only "accredited regimental historians" and military researchers could access the documents.[92] In *Clio's Warriors: Canadian Historians and the Writing of the World Wars* Tim Cook writes, "it has been the official historians of the Department of National Defence who, for much of the 20th century, have controlled the academic writing on the two world wars."[93]

Official CF historians developed the notion that Canada was "born" during the battle at Vimy Ridge. In 1935 Colonel Archer Duguid claimed Vimy was "almost exclusively" a Canadian show that forged the Canadian Corps into "one homogeneous entity" even though most of those fighting were first-generation British immigrants.[94] In the 1969 book *The Road Past Vimy: the Canadian Corps 1914-1918* Lieutenant Colonel D. J. Goodspeed wrote, "no matter what the constitutional historians may say, it was on Easter Monday, April 9, 1917, and not on any other date, that Canada became a nation."[95] This is absurd. As Jamie Swift and Ian McKay demonstrate in *The Vimy Trap: Or How We Learned to Stop Worrying and Love the Great War*, it was a relatively inconsequential battle fought in a pointless and horrific war.

But official historians' influence has extended far beyond the "Great Wars". In 1919 the historical section published the first in a three-volume series titled "A history of the organization, development and services of the military and naval forces of Canada from the peace of Paris in 1763, to the present time." Immediately after the Korean War official historians wrote two books on the subject and published another in 1966.[96] (Academics all but failed to revisit Canada's role in Korea until the late 1990s.)[97]

During its first four decades the historical section greatly influenced the discussion of military matters. "From 1915 to 1960," Cook writes, "it was the official historians, augmented by only a few others — memoirists, regimental historians, and a handful of journalists — who controlled this burgeoning field [military history]."[98]

The historical sections had both direct and indirect influence. Official historians published a large share of the early books on Canadian militarism. Additionally, they greatly influenced academia. The historical section was the "graduate school in military history", notes DND historian William A. Douglas, until "university departments started producing postgraduates."[99] Roger Sarty echoes this opinion in "The Origins of Academic Military History in Canada, 1940-1967". The article traces the roots of the most important publications in establishing Canadian academic military history. "The main impetus [of the seven publications]", Sarty writes, "came from the Canadian Army's official history programme in the Second World War, and the Army's decision to establish a history department at the Royal Military College of Canada. These initiatives opened opportunities for gifted young and mid-career scholars, whose interest in military subjects originated or was sharpened by their military service during the Second World War. These scholars became some of the most prominent historians in the country."[100]

In the two decades after WWII individuals who worked in the military's historical sections filled many academic posts in military history and associated fields.[101] And they were often influential in their field.[102] Head of the War Artist Program and deputy-director of the Historical Section at Canadian Army Headquarters in London, George Stanley led the history department at the Royal Military College after WWII.[103] During his career Stanley was president of the Canadian Historical Association and Kingston Historical Society, as well as a member of the Massey Commission Committee on Historic Sites and Monuments and the Archaeological and Historic Sites Board of Ontario.[104] He was also chairman of the federal government's Centennial Publications Committee.

At the military-run Royal Military College Stanley taught Jack Granatstein and Desmond Morton. These two individuals, who both worked in DND's historical section, published hundreds of books and articles on Canadian military history and foreign policy.[105]

A military historian for two decades, Colonel Charles Stacey has had "more influence on how Canadians view their nation's military history" than any other individual.[106] He published a dozen books and in 2000 Granatstein wrote that Stacey's "books continue to be read and to have great influence on military and foreign policy historians."[107]

During WWII Stacey took charge of the historical section at Canadian military headquarters in London and directed the army's historical section for 14 years after the war.[108] (Stacey returned to

DND between 1965 and 1966 to consolidate the army, air force and navy historical sections into a Directorate of History.) Stacey operated under strict conditions. Superiors often interceded in his work and the minister approved publication of his books.[109] On a number of occasions cabinet discussed and recommended changes to Stacey's work.[110] After reading an early draft of a Royal Canadian Army Medical Corp history, Stacey told a new member of the historical section to tone down his criticism: "You cannot conceive the sensitiveness of official people concerning records for publication. … Even the most apparently harmless comments can arouse a surprising amount of suspicion and resentment."[111] During his time at DND Stacey led the Canadian Historical Association.

DND's Directorate of History and Heritage is significant. A dozen historians are part of the directorate's 50-person staff "mandated to preserve and communicate Canada's military history and foster pride in a Canadian military heritage."[112] They answer "1,000 questions of an historical nature" annually, helping high school students with assignments and academics navigate archival inquiries.[113] The directorate also works with the media. In the early 1990s, for instance, senior military historian Brereton Greenhous was a special advisor during production of the CBC film *Dieppe 1942*.[114] Similarly, director of the historical section Stacey vetted *Canada At War*, the first television miniseries to document Canada's part in WWII, before the National Film Board produced program played on CBC.[115]

The directorate also helped veterans exert political pressure. After the backlash to a Canadian War Museum exhibit (see above) that mentioned the WWII Allied Bomber Command targeting civilians, senior DND historian Serge Bernier was asked to write a report. Bernier concluded the exhibit was hurtful to the veterans.[116]

DND's Directorate of History and Heritage also supports the Organization of Military Museums of Canada. The 50-year-old organization seeks "to preserve the military heritage of Canada by encouraging the establishment and operation of military museums."[117]

Accredited CF museums receive space in a DND establishment and financial assistance. According to CF Administrative Order 27-5, "the role of CF Museums is to preserve and interpret Canadian military heritage in order to increase the sense of identity and esprit de corps within the CF and to support the goals of the Department of National Defence."[118]

The more than 60 CF museums regularly partner with the Canadian War Museum, which has a 100-person staff and $65 million a year budget.[119] The 55,000 square foot Heritage Canada run museum near Parliament Hill was re-opened in 2005 at the cost of $136 million.[120] Part veteran commemoration and part war memorial, the Canadian War Museum houses a large collection of CF Artists Program works and showcases obsolete military equipment.

**

Other CF-created content directly shapes the public discussion. The military produces dozens of publications. Among the more significant, *The Maple Leaf* is distributed weekly to bases across Canada while *Trident* and *Lookout* cover the naval bases in Halifax and Esquimalt respectively.[121]

The military's many websites make articles, speeches, reports and other types of information easily accessible to the public. DND/CF websites generally give one-sided, nationalistic, accounts of military actions.

As part of its online strategy, the CF has a number of YouTube channels.[122] It also employs Facebook, Twitter, Pinterest, Flickr and other social media platforms to promote its positions and recruit new members.

DND spends $10-$20 million annually on recruitment.[123] The CF advertises on Xbox video games and Twitter, as well as bus shelters and Stanley Cup playoff broadcasts.[124] Describing it as "one of the primary windows through which Canadians view their military", Lieutenant-Colonel Michael Goodspeed calls "recruiting advertising ... the most powerful form of PR available to the CF."[125] Its "Fight Distress,

Fight Fear, Fight Chaos—Fight with the Canadian Forces" recruiting campaign won a series of marketing awards in the late 2000s.[126]

Recruitment and community outreach are closely intertwined. With millions of Canadians watching Snowbird airshows every year, DND calls them an "important public relations and recruiting tool."[127] The RCAF does flyovers at hundreds of special events every year.[128] Jets flew by the opening game of the 2019 NBA finals and the Toronto Raptors' victory celebration.

The CF's military parachute demonstration team performs across the country. In the half century since their founding the SkyHawks have performed for more than 75 million spectators worldwide.[129] The SkyHawks do significant media outreach, regularly inviting journalists to skydive with them. Offering media workers the opportunity to jump out of a plane at 12,000 feet facilitates close and trusting relations.[130]

The CF are regularly showcased at professional sports games. CF personnel attend military appreciation events organized by most Canadian NHL teams. Described as "memorials to the brave deeds and sacrifices" of the Air Force, retired RCAF Colours are on permanent display where the Toronto Maple Leafs and Raptors play.[131]

About three dozen professional full-time musicians are part of the RCN's Naden Band. Operating since 1940, the band performs at dozens of public events every year and collaborates with the Canadian College of Performing Arts, University of Victoria Faculty of Music and Victoria Symphony.[132]

For 15 years DND financed the Québec City International Festival of Military Bands. It included concerts and parades all over the city and a military tattoo at the Québec Coliseum. Traditionally a military performance of music, tattoos have evolved into elaborate displays of armed forces. The CF supports the annual Fort Henry Tattoo in Kingston, Ontario, which combines military drill, musical acts and fireworks. The Royal Nova Scotia International Tattoo is the largest annual indoor tattoo in the world. The week-long event in Halifax includes over 2,000 performers and is a full theatrical production.

The founder of the Royal Nova Scotia International Tattoo, Colonel Ian Fraser, produced the 1967 Canadian Armed Forces Tattoo, which included 1,700 CF personnel. Performed over 150 times in nearly 50 cities, it was the largest mobile tattoo in history.[133]

The CF spends tens of millions of dollars every year on medals, ribbons, badges, flags, banners, squadron colours, performance uniforms and regimental insignia, as well as parades, change-of-command ceremonies and other formal events. While mostly designed to stir loyalty, strengthen discipline and reinforce hierarchy, CF pomp is often designed to improve perceptions of the force and stoke nationalist sentiment.

Military parades or ceremonies can be a way to ramp up nationalist sentiment or support for the CF. With the war unpopular among Quebeckers, the military organized a large send-off parade when the Valcartier based Royal 22nd Regiment was dispatched to Afghanistan in 2007. Two thousand uniformed soldiers marched through Québec City in a 'support-the-troops' public-relations offensive.

After waging war in Libya in 2011 the Conservatives organized an $850,000 nationally televised celebration for Canada's "military heroes", which included flyovers from a dozen military aircraft. Prime Minister Stephen Harper told the 300 military personnel brought in from four bases: "We are celebrating a great military success ... Soldier for soldier, sailor for sailor, airman for airman, the Canadian Armed Forces are the best in the world.[134]"

The military and Canadian Heritage spend tens of millions of dollars to commemorate wars.[135] Commemorating "glorious" wars can boost the CF's standing. Bruised by the long and unpopular war in Afghanistan, the CF sought "several positive, proactive communication opportunities" to shore up its image.[136] According to an internal file Canadian Press uncovered, the military had "plans for commemorative activities, including a series of World War I events", which were to receive millions of dollars of CF money through 2020.[137]

Other government departments also promote militarism. Militarist associations are overrepresented among the background images of Canadian passports.[138] Similarly, the Citizenship Guide for new Canadians sings the praises of militarists. Prioritizing soldiers above reporters, poets, janitors, etc., the government set up a program in 2014 to allow foreign nationals who join the CF to get their citizenship fast tracked.[139]

Military 'valour' is even granted unique protection in the Criminal Code. A section dealing with the "Unlawful Use of Military Uniforms or Certificates" bars anyone other than the recipient from wearing a CF uniform or service insignia (medals, ribbons, badges, etc.) or any imitation of the above likely to be mistaken for said uniform or insignia. Some militarists campaign against the scourge of so-called "Stolen Valour".

CF Public Affairs

In addition to the means described above, the CF operates the largest PR machine in the country. To protect its image and promote its worldview the CF spends hundreds of millions of dollars annually on public relations and related military commemorations.[140] Over six hundred staff members work on public relations and related military commemorations.[141] A 2013 document *Embassy* magazine uncovered through an access to information request said DND had "over 13 independent public affairs organizations."[142]

Hundreds of Public Affairs Officers (PAOs) work from Public Affairs Headquarters in Ottawa and a-half-dozen regional offices.[143] Additionally, every CF base, army division and naval headquarters employs PAOs.[144] DND's website lists contact information for 50 different media relations offices.[145]

PAOs write press releases, organize press conferences, monitor the news, brief journalists, befriend reporters and editors, or perform various other media-related activities. A large proportion of the news stories about the military are based on CF statements and events.

As a large bureaucracy, DND is considered a "credible" source of information, meaning their claims demand less scrutiny/investigative expense than those of dissidents or antiwar groups.

The CF closely follows the coverage of military affairs. "DND's sprawling media relations machine keeps tabs on tens of thousands of newspaper articles a year," reported *Embassy*.[146] During 2012-13 DND monitored 29,519 newspaper articles.[147] Journalists' questions, who contacts the department most frequently, the information released to each reporter, etc. is compiled and made available to relevant officials.[148] Building reporter profiles helps Public Affairs respond to the thousands of media requests DND receives annually. Depending on Public Affairs' assessment of the reporter and question/request they may fulfill it, stall, release partial information, etc.

As part of a plan to induce positive coverage and deter critical reporting, David Pugliese revealed that a new chief of defence staff in 2015 called for the "weaponization of public affairs."[149] On the positive side, Jonathan Vance proposed leaking "good news" stories to "friendly" journalists hoping they would portray the military positively. Reporters were expected to participate in the scheme because a leak can lead to a high-profile story (with little effort) and "friendly" journalists would gain access to the chief of defence staff and other top officials.

While leaking official documents is run-of-the-mill in government PR, the repressive element of Vance's "weaponization of public affairs" was more controversial. Journalists producing unflattering stories about the military were to be the target of phone calls to their boss, letters to the editor and other 'flack' designed to undercut their credibility in the eyes of readers and their employers.[150]

The CF didn't stop at complaining to journalists' bosses. The top brass repeatedly asked the military's National Investigative Service (NIS) to investigate reporters' sources. In 2011 NIS investigated prominent CTV journalist Robert Fife after he uncovered documents about Chief of Defence Staff Walt Natynczyk spending over $1 million in public funds flying to hockey games and a Caribbean vacation.[151] Pugliese described this as a blatant "intimidation tactic by the NIS against a journalist who was clearly not playing military cheerleader."[152]

In a similar incident, NIS spent more than a month investigating how Pugliese obtained information about a major Pacific Ocean military exercise in spring 2012. While the *Ottawa Citizen* defence reporter said the information came from a US Navy release, which the NSI investigation ultimately supported, DND officials believed Pugliese was tipped off by a friendly PAO. *Esprit de Corps* editor Scott Taylor pointed out that the investigation had nothing to do with operational security. "No classified information was divulged. No operational security jeopardized. No Canadian sailors' lives were put in peril as a result of Pugliese's rather innocuous story, but [defence minister Peter] MacKay's timetable for release [of the information] had not been strictly adhered to."[153]

According to Taylor, NIS was employed on at least four occasions to investigate the source of information for stories.[154] Yet, in none of these instances was classified material reported.

Buying into the notion the CF is a benevolent force requires accepting the idea that it is reasonable for it to expend significant resources "selling itself". A way to judge whether this is true is by treating military ads like other consumer advertising: The more they spend, the more likely what they are selling is bad for you.

And that's before considering the outright lies the CF has disseminated or their impact on the media and academia, which is the subject of the next chapter.

18. Lies and Propaganda

THE JUSTIFICATIONS GIVEN for deploying Canadian troops abroad have often been transparently false. Government officials generally claim some humanitarian rationale to mask wars motivated by geostrategic and corporate interests. Blatant manipulation of public opinion becomes the order of the day.

As discussed previously, the CF employs a massive public relations/propaganda machine. The military understands that information is power so shaping what people learn is designed as if it's an essential part of a battle plan. Recognizing this helps make sense of past propaganda efforts, which have been about more than just disseminating CF spin, but also influencing media.

Information Control

While the tactics have varied based on technologies, balance of power and type of conflict, the CF has pursued extensive information control during wars. There was formal censorship during WWI, WWII and the Korean War. In recent air wars, the military largely shut the media out while in Afghanistan they brought reporters close.[1]

At the height of the fighting in Kandahar, Afghanistan, DND spent considerable resources "spinning" the war. The CF produced books, articles and movies about the conflict. More significantly, they trained and embedded reporters in their operations.

While CF produced/vetted content influenced discussion of the war, the military focused its efforts on influencing coverage in major media outlets. PR personnel fed journalists the government's line at "operational briefings", explained James Laxer after perusing documents uncovered through access to information. "At what are called 'message events' where journalists are updated on developments in Afghanistan, officials from Foreign Affairs, National Defence and the Canadian International Development Agency are to present the government line following 'dry runs' to make sure the briefing motivates journalists to adopt what is called the 'desired sound bite'."[2]

Significant energy was devoted to training/influencing the reporters deployed to Afghanistan. The Journalist Familiarization Course prepared reporters to accompany military patrols all the while deepening their affinity with the military. "The purpose of the course is to make you in the media familiar with us and what we do," PAO Major Jean Morissette told the *National Post*. "The better you understand us, the better it is for us."[3]

In a 2007 *Walrus* article about the Journalist Familiarization Course, Semi Chellas wrote: "At Meadford [training grounds] I also learned this: it's hard to be objective when you're hurtling backward through the air. We'd entrusted the soldiers with our safety and in return we'd hoped to impress them with our courage. There was an exhilarating sense that we were all in this together — and it was only nine in the morning on our first day. As we stood around afterwards with our Dixie cups full of watery green refreshment, one reporter remarked that we were quite literally 'drinking the Kool-Aid.' I can only imagine how difficult it would be to stay objective if your life actually depended on the soldiers around you."[4]

As it prepared journalists for military life, the CF trained its members to manage reporters in the field. At the Canadian Manoeuvre Training Centre (CMTC) in Wainwright, Alberta, the CF established a "media cell" and hired journalism students to play act as "embedded", "unilateral" and Afghan journalists. According to University of Calgary Centre for Military & Strategic Studies professor Bob Bergen, "the primary purpose of the media cell: training soldiers to become comfortable working with and managing the news media."[5] After the "media cell" exercises garnered attention, the CF barred reporters from observing CMTC.[6]

The CF embedding (or in-bedding) program brought reporters into the military's orbit by allowing them to accompany soldiers on patrol and stay on base. "The military does not embed journalists out of a conviction that the public has a right to know what is going on in Afghanistan," noted Carleton journalism professor Allan Thompson. "The military's mandate is to build support for the Afghanistan mission by using the media to show the troops in action, to 'push information.'"[7]

When they arrived on base senior officers were often on hand to meet journalists. Top officers also built a rapport with reporters during meals and other informal settings. Throughout their stay on base PAOs were in constant contact, helping reporters with their work. After a six-month tour in Afghanistan PAO Major Jay Janzen wrote: "By pushing information to the media, the Battalion was also able to exercise some influence over what journalists decided to cover. When an opportunity to cover a mission or event was proactively presented to a reporter, it almost always received coverage."[8]

Alarmed about a growing casualty list and other negative news, in fall 2006, the Prime Minister's Office directed the military to "push" reconstruction stories on embedded journalists. Through an access request the *Globe and Mail* obtained an email from Major Norbert Cyr saying, "the major concern [at Privy Council Office] is whether we are pushing development and [Foreign Affairs] issues with embeds."[9] In an interview with *Jane's Defence Weekly*'s Canadian correspondent, the embedded journalist described what this meant on the ground: "We've been invited on countless village medical outreach visits, ribbon-cutting ceremonies, and similar events."[10]

In addition to covering stories put forward by the military, 'embeds' tended to frame the conflict from the perspective of the troops they accompanied.[11] By eating and sleeping with Canadian soldiers, reporters often developed a psychological attachment, writes Carleton professor Sherry Wasilow, in *Hidden Ties that Bind: The Psychological Bonds of Embedding Have Changed the Very Nature of War Reporting.*[12]

Embedded journalists' sympathy towards Canadian soldiers was reinforced by the Afghans they interviewed. Afghans critical of Canadian policy were unlikely to express themselves openly with soldiers nearby. Scott Taylor asked, "what would you say if the Romanian military occupied your town and a Romanian tank and journalist showed up at your door? You love the government they have installed and want these guys to stay! Of course the locals are smiling when a reporter shows up with an armoured vehicle and an armed patrol."[13]

Public Affairs officials believed the embedding program "improved" coverage. Major Janzen wrote, "the development of rapport and shared experience resulted in better media relations existing between the military and their embedded media than the military and nonembedded journalists."[14] Another PAO told Bob Bergen that embedding led to sympathetic stories as well as longer-term bonds. "Measuring embedding on the basis of press clippings is an error. The real success is the growth of understanding [of the military] in the media."[15]

Although the embedding program gave journalists access to the military, it deterred (or excluded) other forms of reporting. In *The Savage War: The Untold Battles of Afghanistan*, Murray Brewster writes, "early in the war the Army had a deep, vested interest in keeping the spotlight squarely and tightly focused on itself. The embedding program was weighted toward telling individual soldier stories, not exploring the bigger picture."[16]

The CF determined who could stay at their base and often they refused independent journalists. In the Fédération professionnelle des journalistes du Québec magazine *Trente*, Louise Bourbonnais described being denied access to the base for a film/book project with a CF media official "subtly making me understand that it is difficult to control an independent journalist."[17] Additionally, reporters outside the wire were blocked from accessing military sites or personnel. When reporting from Afghanistan as a "unilateral" Scott Taylor was refused access to the military on a number of occasions. At one point he was told by a soldier "since you're not embedded, you get no access" to film a medical incident at a Canadian camp.[18]

The embedding program restricted journalists to six-week stays at the Kandahar base. The reason, according to Taylor, is "the less time you spend there, the easier it is to get fooled."[19]

Most Canadian journalists who gathered news in Afghanistan did so under the CF Media Embedding Program Ground Rules. As part of the agreement, reporters had to focus primarily on CF and Canadian government activities. A reporter could be expelled for spending "an inordinate amount of time covering non-military activities", which was an attempt to discourage journalists from covering Afghans.[20]

Under the embed agreement the military could also restrict the release of information and images. It allowed the CF to control "any other information the task force commander orders restricted for operational reasons."[21]

"The censorship," noted *Globe and Mail* reporter Geoffrey York, was "tougher and more arbitrary than I had expected."[22] After several extended stays in Afghanistan, Canadian Press reporter Murray Brewster said, "I can't emphasize enough how political this thing [embedding rules] was. It's all about protecting the brand."[23] Another Canadian Press reporter concurred. Bill Graveland noted, "they are really, seriously trying to manage the media."[24]

(Some reporters, of course, embraced the embedding program. Erstwhile Postmedia militarist, Matthew Fisher, boasted he was "embedded more in Afghanistan than any other reporter" while the *Globe and Mail*'s Christie Blatchford said it was "fascinating" spending time with the troops.[25])

The military/government closely monitored embedded reporters. In an email the *Globe and Mail* acquired through an access request, PAO Norbert Cyr reported that the Privy Council requested "to know which embeds are in theatre and what they are doing." Information about journalists' stories, questions and the information divulged to them was compiled and circulated to the Ottawa headquarters of Joint Task Force Afghanistan, Foreign Affairs, Canadian International Development Agency, CF Psychological Operations and the Privy Council Office.[26] The Canadian Press's Graveland complained about PAOs monitoring his interviews. He described "giant satellite dishes" through which the military "check emails and eavesdrop on telephone calls. They watch everything we do. They know immediately what we've written or what we're saying."[27]

A number of journalists who broke the embedding agreement were subject to "immediate removal" from military facilities.[28] On a number of occasions, the CF reprimanded embeds or suddenly removed them from a base. After reporting on a Chinook helicopter crash he survived, Canadian Press journalist Colin Perkel said he faced "excommunication", which meant the CF refused to take him on patrol or provide him with information.[29] In another instance of the military asserting its power over 'embeds', Christie Blatchford, *Toronto Star* reporter Rosie DiManno and two other journalists were suddenly removed from a forward operating base by helicopter after a Canadian and US soldier were killed by friendly fire.[30] The military told them it was for their safety, but a *Globe and Mail* access to information requested document suggested an ally, probably US special forces, asked for their removal.[31]

While in Afghanistan the CF brought reporters close, the military largely shut the media out during recent air wars.[32] In the former Yugoslavia, Libya and Iraq/Syria they tightly controlled access to pilots and other information on the ground.

To justify restricting photos and interviews of deployed CF members DND claimed concern for soldiers and their families' safety.[33] Since the first Gulf War they've repeatedly invoked this rationale to restrict information during air wars. Deputy chief of Defence Staff Ray Henault said the media couldn't interview pilots bombing Serbia because "we don't want any risk of family harassment or something of that nature, which, again, is part of that domestic risk we face."[34]

But, as Bob Bergen reveals in *Balkan Rats and Balkan Bats: The Art of Managing Canada's News Media during the Kosovo Air War*, it was based on a rumour that antiwar protesters put body bags on the lawn of a Canadian pilot during the 1991 Gulf War.[35] It likely never happened and, revealingly, the military didn't invoke fear of domestic retribution to curtail interviews during the more contentious ground war in Afghanistan.

During the bombing of Serbia military officials claimed they conducted an assessment into risks for pilots and their families, but Bergen points out that a postwar search of DND records failed to uncover any risk assessment.[36] According to Bergen, Chief of Staff for Joint Operations Brigadier-General David "Jurkowski even considered it [domestic risk] hearsay, but used the myth nonetheless as a reason for restricting the information the Canadian Forces provided to Canadians about the Kosovo air war."[37]

Bergen points out how air wars lend themselves to censorship since journalists cannot accompany pilots during their missions or easily see what's happening from afar. "As a result," Bergen writes, "crews can only be interviewed before or after their missions, and journalists' reports can be supplemented by cockpit footage of bombings."[38]

While the CF has pursued extensive information control during recent wars, there was formal censorship during WWI, WWII and the Korean War. During WWI the government aggressively repressed information about a war with no clear and compelling purpose other than rivalry between up-and-coming Germany and the imperial powers of the day, Britain and France. In *The Fog of War: Censorship of Canada's Media in World War Two* Mark Bourrie writes, "no one could publicly criticize the Army or Navy. People were not allowed to advocate a negotiated peace and, eventually could not even discuss the reasons for the war or suggest the Allies were partially to blame for it. The government, along with most newspaper and magazine owners, flooded propaganda into the marketplace of ideas. Censorship created the illusion that these official ideas were the only version of reality."[39]

Many artists, cinematographers and photographers were hired to depict Canadians fighting. Canada's official war art program created almost 1,000 works of art.[40] On the home front the government produced war posters to recruit soldiers and rally public opinion. They also organized a speakers bureau of "'five minute men' who inspired patriotic support for Canada's war effort."[41]

In World War I, only a small number of Canadian reporters were allowed access to a trench line that barely moved for three years.[42] British and French allies controlled the fighting zone and threatened to shoot journalists who approached without permission.[43] Author of *Propaganda and Censorship during Canada's Great War*, Jeffrey Keshen writes, "to obtain access to battle zones, some publishers wrote authorities that patriotism, not the desire for sensationalism and newspaper sales, would guide their reporters."[44]

First World War coverage was largely produced or overseen by Canadian-raised British newspaper baron William Maxwell Aitken (later Lord Beaverbrook). Given the rank of lieutenant-colonel, Aitken ran Canada's War Records Office in London. His office wrote inspiring tales of a war that left millions, including 60,000 Canadians, of young men dead. With 60 researchers, cameramen and support staff, the War Records Office mostly based their stories on military press releases and statements by generals.[45] Bourrie writes, "Aitken was eyewitness to very little. He rarely went near the front, and simply wrote press releases based on memos from military intelligence agents."[46]

Aitken even glorified a disastrous battle in St. Eloi, Belgium where 1,400 Canadians were accidentally killed by allied fire.[47] According to army newspaper *The Maple Leaf*, Aitken is "considered the father of today's Public Affairs Branch."[48]

Canadian Press

CP was established during the First World War. A predecessor newswire disseminated Associated Press stories in Canada but the war spurred criticism of the US news agency, which did not cheerlead British/Canadian policy loud enough for some (Washington had yet to join the fighting). "In effect, an arm of the British Foreign Ministry", Reuters offered Canadian newspapers free wire copy during the war.[49] But the British press agency would only deliver the service to Ottawa. If the federal government "wanted to ensure that this pro-war imperial news service was distributed effectively across the country", it had to subsidize a telegraph connection to the West Coast.[50] To support CP the federal government put up $50,000 ($800,000 in today's dollars) a year, which lasted for six years.[51]

During WWII the Canadian Press' ties with the military were particularly close. CP "cemented" itself as Canada's national news service during the war. "To accomplish this," Gene Allen writes in a history of the organization, "CP cultivated unprecedentedly close relations with Canada's military authorities — who had reasons of their own for wanting extensive coverage of the national war effort — and thereby moved some distance away from traditional notions of journalistic independence."[52] In an extreme example, CP recruited a CF public relations officer who led reporters into battle zones. Bill Boss remained with the same unit but began reporting for the news service.[53]

Canadian Press was the main source of news copy during the war. It "acquiesced to all censorship requirements", notes Kate Barker, "providing the country with a diet of soft features rather than hard war news stories."[54]

CBC

During its first few decades the CBC had close ties to the military. The public broadcaster's initial nine-person board included General Victor Odlum and Colonel Wilfred Bovey.[55] During WWII the military, other government agencies and the Canadian Legion produced a significant amount of CBC programming.[56] In a long history of the public broadcaster Knowlton Nash describes how the recently created "CBC also went to war. More than ever before or since, during the war years the CBC became almost an arm of government."[57] According to the "CBC War Effort" pamphlet, the public broadcaster's aim was "to inspire the nation as a whole and every individual to greater effort. To put everyone in the proper frame of mind to accept willingly the inevitable sacrifices involved in the war effort."[58]

For the 13 years after WWII CBC was led by Arnold Davidson Dunton, general manager of the Wartime Information Board.[59]

Throughout the 1950s CBC participated in civil defence tests and its representatives attended National Defence College courses in Kingston.[60] During the 1950–53 Korean War CBC provided radio recordings to destroyers, Station Radio Maple Leaf and other outlets accessed by Canadian soldiers.[61] In 1956 DND opened Radio Canadian Army Europe in Germany. It was managed by CBC staff on loan to the military and lasted for a decade and a half.[62]

CBC worked closely with military PR and showed military-produced content. A director of Naval Information proposed the 1958 CBC program *Challenge From the Sea* while CBC-TV broadcast a 38-minute DND and Veterans Affairs supported war commemoration on Remembrance Day 1965.[63] In *A Christmas Letter*, a CF/NFB produced film aired on CBC Christmas Day 1960, Defence Minister Douglas Harkness notes: "As party to the North Atlantic Treaty Organization, we are strongly committed to protecting the rights and freedoms of ourselves and our allies. ... Canada, through the United Nations, has also accepted the role of peacemaker in the Middle East along the troubled zone between Israel and Egypt; in Asia, where Canada is a member of the Truce Commission in Laos; and now in the Congo, where a new African state struggles to find its way to nationhood. ... I am sure we can all agree that the splendid efforts being made by these men and women will help lead to a world at peace with itself."[64]

The CF transported CBC correspondents abroad. During the early 1960s UN mission in the Congo three CBC reporters traveled to the newly independent central African nation aboard RCAF aircraft. After receiving military administered inoculations, Mallory Schwartz reported "they were closely tied to [Canadian] Army Signals, which was their only means of communicating with the CBC."[65] On air CBC TV's Norman DePoe lauded the Canadian peacekeeper's work as "something to be proud of."[66] Schwartz described the Congo correspondents' "reports" as "wholly positive about the role Canada was playing in the Congo", even though Canadian soldiers undermined elected independence leader Patrice Lumumba.[67]

Leading CBC TV correspondent for decades, David Halton, reported close ties to the military. "I deployed to Vietnam with" the Canadian International Commission of Control and Supervision force, he wrote in a story in which he also noted: "I found it easier (and generally safer) covering a war with regular army units, as opposed to reporting independently."[68]

The public broadcaster's close ties to the military made it highly deferential, according to Mallory Schwartz in *War on the Air: CBC-TV and Canada's Military, 1952-1992*. "When CBC-TV produced programs that raised controversial questions about defence policy, the forces or military history, it did so with considerable care. Caution was partly a result of the special relationship between the CBC and those bodies charged with the defence of Canada."[69]

CBC's ties to DND sometimes translated into formal censorship. After broadcasting *The Homeless Ones* in 1958 Deputy Federal Civil Defence Co-ordinator Major-General George S. Hatton requested the film's withdrawal from the NFB Library and the public broadcaster cancelled its planned rebroadcast.[70] Hatton insisted the CBC clear all content on civil defence with his staff.[71]

The public broadcaster's independence from DND has increased over the years. But, since its inception the government has appointed CBC's board and provided most of its funds.

Conference of Defence Associations

Established in 1932, the Conference of Defence Associations (CDA) describes itself as a "non-partisan, independent, non-profit organization [that] expresses its ideas and opinions with a view to influencing government security and defence policy."[72]

Minister of Defence Donald Matheson Sutherland backed CDA's creation.[73] Since its inception CDA has been directly or indirectly financed by DND.[74] Initially, member associations paid a small part of the funds they received from DND to CDA. But, three decades later the role was reversed. CDA received a block grant from DND and parcelled out the money to its various member associations.[75]

Since its creation, defence ministers and governor generals (as commander in chief) have regularly appeared at CDA's annual conference.[76] The governor general, prime minister, defence minister and chief of the defence staff are honorary patrons or vice patrons of the organization.[77]

At the height of Canada's war in Afghanistan CDA received a highly politicized five-year $500,000 contract from DND. University of Ottawa professor Amir Attaran wrote, "that money comes not with strings, but with an entire leash."[78] To receive the money CDA committed to producing 15 opinion pieces or letters to the editor in major Canadian newspapers, generating 29 media references to the organization and eliciting 100 requests for radio/television interviews. The media work was part of a requirement to "support activities that give evidence of contributing to Canada's national policies."[79] CDA didn't initially disclose its 2007-12 DND sponsorship agreement, which was reviewed by cabinet.[80]

CDA also receives funding from arms manufacturers and military service providers. CDA's annual conference in Ottawa has been sponsored by General Dynamics, Lockheed Martin, Boeing Canada, ATCO Structures & Logistics, Irving Shipbuilding, etc.[81]

CDA represents 50 military associations ranging from the Naval Association of Canada to the Canadian Infantry Association, Royal Canadian Legion to the Military Intelligence Association. It is run by high-ranking former officers.

CDA publishes *Security and Defence Briefings*, *Vimy Papers* and *Presentations and Position Papers*. The organization's quarterly journal *ON TRACK* "promotes informed public debate on security and defence issues and the vital role played by the Canadian Armed forces in society."[82] CDA has also published influential books such as Queens professor Douglas Bland's *A Nation at Risk: The Decline of the Canadian Forces*.

To encourage militarist research, CDA awards a number of prizes. It puts on an annual graduate student symposium where $3,000 goes to the winning paper, $2,000 to second place and $1,000 to third place. CDA co-sponsors the Ross Munro Media Award to a "journalist who has made a significant contribution to understanding defence and security issues" and gives the Vimy Award to a "Canadian who has made a significant and outstanding contribution to the defence and security of Canada and the preservation of (its) democratic values."[83]

CDA advocates militarism. Its first official resolution noted "the urgent need for an increased appropriation for national defence."[84] At almost every CDA convention between 1946 and 1959 a resolution passed in favour of compulsory military training.[85] A 1968 resolution called for universal military training, expressing concern that a generation of Canadians had become "unused to the idea of military service."[86]

In the 1980s CDA developed the idea of the "Total Defence of Canada". In 1985 Colonel H. A. J. Hutchinson told a CDA meeting: "I would say that the Total Defence of Canada requires much more than just the support of the Canadian Armed Forces, it involves the organization of our total economy, our industrial base, towards a single objective — the defence of this country."[87] Hinting at the need to talk up US President Ronald Reagan's revival of Cold War rhetoric, Hutchison said this "can only be made [possible] if the Canadian people perceive that it is necessary and that, in fact, it is the only course of action open to them."[88]

A 2000 CDA report funded by the Business Council on National Issues, the Molson Foundation and DND advocated increased military spending to defend free trade. It claimed "the defence establishment, including the Canadian Forces, plays a key role in an international policy which provides the insurance and the means which allow the national interest to flourish. It contributes to stability at home and abroad, thus supporting the development of an environment congenial to trade."[89]

Royal Canadian Military Institute

For more than a century the Royal Canadian Military Institute (RCMI) has operated as a social club for military officers and (later) "civilians with like interests". In 1890 the RCMI was set up "to provide in an Institute for the defence forces of Canada a Library, museum and club for the purposes of the promotion of military art, science and literature, to gather and preserve the records of the defence forces, and develop its specialized field in Canadian history."[90] Today, it claims to be "the pre-eminent Canadian forum for discussion, research and education on defence, security and foreign affairs."[91]

The Toronto-based institution publishes a journal, policy papers and books. It also operates a library and museum and holds Military History Nights, a lecture series and annual concert at Roy Thomson Hall (the 25th anniversary show was titled "Sacrifice & Glory: Commemorating a Legacy"). Its officials contribute regularly to major media outlets.[92]

The institute has been dominated by ardent imperialists. In *The Sense of Power: Studies in the Ideas of Canadian Imperialism* Carl Berger described RCMI as the "centre of martial imperialists" in the early 1900s while the institute boasted that most of its 500 members in 1910 were descendants of United Empire loyalists.[93] As Canada moved away from its British imperial roots, the organization added the "Royal" prefix to Canadian Military Institute in 1948.[94] RCMI executive member Major George Drew proclaimed, "let us who know what the love of Empire really means keep before us the vision of a great United Empire of from two or three hundred million white Britons to cooperate in peace as well as in war."[95]

In 1892 the Ontario and federal governments began giving the institute a $100 ($1,500 today) annual subsidy.[96] During a mid-1970s controversy over its exclusion of women, Chief of Defence Staff General Jacques Dextraze, "warned he could no longer be vice patron of an organization that barred women. Nor was it likely that the Institute could continue to receive its [federal government] grant if it continued to discriminate."[97]

Canadian International Council

For many years the Canadian Institute of International Affairs (now Canadian International Council) received an annual grant from DND.[98] The Canadian Institute for Strategic Studies (CISS), which was folded into the Canadian International Council in 2008, had greater ties to the CF. An associate member of the DND-funded Conference of Defence Associations (see above), former military officers largely ran CISS and its initial sponsors were DND, Royal Canadian Legion and CDA.[99] The idea for creating CISS emanated from a CDA meeting.[100]

A 37-year veteran of the air force, Brigadier-General Don W. Macnamara played a central role in creating the institute in 1976.[101] After 35 years with the RCAF, Major General Fraser Holman became director and chairman of CISS' board in the late 1990s.[102] He would be joined by former Chief of the Defence Staff General Ramsey Withers.[103]

Individuals also moved in the other direction. CISS' last president, David Rudd, was hired as an analyst by the Canadian Forces' Operational Support Command.[104]

CISS' mandate was to "provide a forum for, and be the vehicle to stimulate the research, study, analysis, and discussion of the strategic implications of the major national and international security issues, events, and trends as they affect Canada."[105]

Heavily reliant on government funds, CISS operated a number of joint initiatives with DND "to promote the White Paper [on bolstering the military] and explain the Soviet threat."[106] As part of this effort, CISS trained more than 300 officers for a DND Speakers Bureau in the first quarter of 1988.[107] CISS also worked with DND and Foreign Affairs to set up the Pearson Peacekeeping Centre in 1994.[108]

CISS promoted militaristic positions. CISS officials often expressed an aggressive strain of militarist thought. In 2007 CISS head Alex Morrison criticized Ottawa for emphasizing the military's role in peacekeeping, telling the *Toronto Star*, Canadian soldiers were viewed as "simply a bunch of do-gooders … The government (convinced) a heck of a lot of Canadians that our military weren't real military when, of course, they are and they're proving it in Afghanistan."[109]

Canadian Global Affairs Institute

The military identified the Canadian Defence and Foreign Affairs Institute (CDFAI), now Canadian Global Affairs Institute (CGAI), under the rubric of "defence-related organization and defence and foreign policy think tanks."[110]

Since 2002 the institute has operated an annual military journalism course run with the University of Calgary's Centre for Military and Strategic Studies. A dozen Canadian journalism students receive scholarships to the 10-day program, which includes a media-military theory component and visits to armed forces units.[111] The stated objective of the course is "to enhance the military education of future Canadian journalists who will report on Canadian military activities."[112] But that description obscures the political objective. In an article titled "A student's look inside the military journalism course" Lola Fakinlede writes: "Between the excitement of shooting guns, driving in tanks, eating pre-packed lunches, investigating the insides of coyotes and leopards — armoured vehicles not animals — and visiting the messes, we were learning how the military operates. ... Being able to see the human faces behind the uniform, being able to talk to them like regular people, being able to see them start losing the suspicion in their eyes and really start talking candidly to me — that was incredible."[113]

Captain David Williams was forthright concerning the broader political objective of the program. In 2010 he wrote, "the intent of this annual visit has always been to foster a familiarity and mutual understanding between the CF and the future media, two entities which require a symbiotic relationship in order to function."[114]

Along with the CDA, the institute gives out the annual Ross Munro Media Award recognizing a "journalist who has made a significant contribution to understanding defence and security issues."[115] The winner receives a handsome statuette, a gala dinner attended by Ottawa

VIPs and a $2,500 prize.[116] The political objective of the award is to reinforce the militarist culture among reporters who cover the subject.

While not forthcoming on its finances, the institute received some military backing. DND's Security and Defence Forum provided funding to individuals who pursued a year-long internship with the institute.[117] CGAI also held numerous joint symposiums with DND, NATO and NORAD.[118]

The institute also received financial support from large arms contractors such as General Dynamics and Lockheed Martin Canada, as well as Com Dev, ENMAX, SMART Technologies and the Defense News Media Group.[119] A January 2020 CGAI conference on Modernizing North American Defence, which painted Russia and China as apocalyptic threats, was sponsored by Lockheed Martin, General Dynamics, MDA, ADGA, BAE Systems, L3 Harris Technologies Raytheon and Boeing.[120]

"Initial funding" for CDFAI, notes Howard D. Fremeth in a PhD thesis on "Canada's military-cultural memory network", "came mostly from a single patron, Robert J. S. Gibson."[121] Honorary colonel of the 10th Battalion Calgary Highlanders, the wealthy Calgary businessman "had a deep personal connection to the military." After helping secure funding for the Centre for Military and Strategic Studies at the University of Calgary, Gibson supported the creation of a think tank that wouldn't have to deal with "the impediments resident in academia."[122] Gibson was chair of the CGAI Board.

Multibillionaire militarist Frederick Mannix also helped the registered charity. The honorary colonel was honorary director of CGAI.

Canadian Association of Defence and Security Industries

The Canadian Association of Defence and Security Industries (CADSI) represents arms manufacturers. In 2014 CADSI president Tim Page told the press that arms control measures should be relaxed and celebrated a $15 billion Light Armoured Vehicle sale to Saudi

Arabia as a "good day for Canada."[123] While they backed controversial arms deals and loosened restrictions on weapons sales, CADSI also promoted a "scary" worldview and forward foreign policy. "Social media powerful tool for terrorists, expert warns panel discussion on counter-terrorism at CADSI conference," noted a 2015 *Ottawa Citizen* headline.[124] The article quoted former director of counterterrorism for the Canadian Security Intelligence Service, Ray Boisvert, predicting decades of politically motivated religious violence empowered by technology.

In a 2019 CADSI social media campaign titled "My North, My Home — Our Canada, It's All our Duty" an earnest-looking narrator declares: "They say when the going gets tough, send in the Canadians." The video shows white soldiers showing Black children how to read as we are told, "they say the world needs more Canada."[125]

Influencing Parliament

The CF draws members of Parliament into their orbit through various means. Set up by DND's Director of External Communications and Public Relations in 2000, the Canadian Forces Parliamentary Program was labeled a "valuable public-relations tool" by the *Globe and Mail*.[126] Different programs embed MPs in the army, navy and air force.[127] According to the *Canadian Parliamentary Review*, the MPs "learn how the equipment works, they train with the troops, and they deploy with their units on operations. Parliamentarians are integrated into the unit by wearing the same uniform, living on bases, eating in messes, using CF facilities and equipment."[128] As part of the program, the military even flew MPs to the Persian Gulf to join a naval vessel on patrol.[129]

The Canadian Leaders at Sea Program takes influential individuals on "action-packed" multi-day navy operations.[130] Conducted on both coasts numerous times annually, nine parliamentarians from all parties participated in a Spring 2017 excursion and a handful took part in 2018.[131] After participating Liberal MP Anju Dhillon told the House of Commons, "I saw first-hand the sacrifices that our men and women in the navy have made to protect our country."[132]

Commander of the Atlantic Fleet Commodore Craig Baines, described the initiative's political objective: "By exposing them to the work of our men and women at sea, they gain a newfound appreciation for how the RCN protects and defends Canada at home and abroad. They can then help us spread that message to Canadians when they return home."[133] And vote for more military spending.

The CF coordinates an annual Air Force Day on Parliament Hill. During the event MPs and senators demonstrate their appreciation for the RCAF's "dedication" to Canada.[134]

To celebrate the RCN the Navy League of Canada hosts Navy and Coast Guard Day. The DND-backed group organizes a gala "to showcase the Royal Canadian Navy and the Canadian Coast Guard to Canada's elected officials."[135] It includes senior RCN leaders, arms industry executives and representatives of veterans' organizations and the Coast Guard.

Sponsored by the CF, the annual Army Run in Ottawa is partly designed to draw politicians and political staffers. "From the cannon used as a 'starter's pistol' to the 'dog-tag' medals placed around all participants necks at the finish line, this unique event is 'military' from start to finish", notes the official site.[136]

Since 1959 the CF has organized a ceremonial guard. During the warm months mostly army personnel perform a daily Changing of the Guard ceremony on Parliament, are posted at the Governor General's residence, provide Guards of Honour for visiting dignitaries and offer a number of other services to promote the CF in the capital.

The NATO Parliamentary Association is another group that brings MPs into the military's orbit. Established in 1955, the association seeks "to increase knowledge of the concerns of the NATO Parliamentary Assembly among parliamentarians."[137] In *The Blaikie Report: An Insider's Look at Faith and Politics* long-time NDP external and defence critic Bill Blaikie describes how a presentation at a NATO meeting convinced him to support the organization's bombing of the former Yugoslavia.[138]

CF and DND officials regularly brief MPs and senators at defence committees. So do Royal Military College and other DND financed professors as well as CF (and arms companies) backed groups such as the Canadian Global Affairs Institute, Conference of Defence Associations and Royal Canadian Military Institute (see above).

Corporate Class

Not only does the Canadian Forces lobby members of Parliament, it makes serious efforts to build relations with "captains" of industry. Beyond the arms sector's ties to current and former CF leaders, corporate Canada has extensive ties to the CF. The military has long sought to draw the wealthy close and the titans of industry have reciprocated.

As mentioned above the Canadian Leaders at Sea Program takes influential individuals, including corporate executives, on "action-packed" multi-day navy operations.[139] Describing a November 2019 mission that took seven "upper echelon business leaders" aboard *HMCS Regina*, Maritime Forces Pacific Public Affairs officer Janice Lee noted: "As the days at sea progressed, they got an up-close look at a sailor's experience, which they could bring back and share in their corporate environment."[140]

CF leaders sometimes join the boards of non-arms elements of corporate Canada. In 2008 TD Bank hired former Chief of Defence Staff Rick Hillier and he was appointed chair of a Telus Community Board (as well as the Advisory Board of Provincial Aerospace).[141] After a long government and military career General Andrew McNaughton became president of the Canadian Pulp and Paper Association, which was pleased with his effort to direct unemployed youth into forestry work during depression era relief camps.[142] Following WWII, notes Lawrence Aronsen, "many Canadian officers retiring from the service found that they could obtain relatively important positions in the rapidly expanding private business sector."[143] Eleven of 18 board members of the Canadian Industrial Preparedness Association, which later became more arms focused, were former senior military officers.[144] It was led by Colonel Victor Sifton.[145]

As noted in an earlier chapter, wealth-holders promote the military in various ways and in return the military looks after them. Eaton's, Bank of Commerce, Toronto Street Railway, Simpson's and Imperial Bank provided early financial support to the Royal Canadian Military Institute.[146] The militarist lobby group's initial patron was Governor General Lord Stanley.

The Canadian Forces Liaison Council (CFLC) is a group of mostly business leaders who promote the benefits of Reserve Force training and experience to companies. Established in 1978, CFLC's main objective is to secure reservists with leaves of absence from work. But its ExecuTrek Program also exposed civilian employers to the CF. They take businesspeople on to ships or aircraft as well as into the field to watch reserve "infantry soldiers crawl through barbed wire at night while live bullets whiz over their heads."[147]

"Directly responsible to the Minister of National Defence", CFLC national chair Scott M. Shepherd, as this book went to press, is founder and CEO of Northstar Trade Finance, a global trade finance solutions firm.[148] CFLC national vice-chair is *St. John's Telegram* Publisher (Emeritus) Miller H. Ayre.[149] Its Ontario chair is Nautical Lands Group vice chair and principal, Paul Hindo.[150] The Alberta chair is Gary R. Agnew, a partner with human resource firm Cenera, and the Saskatchewan chair is Vaughn Solomon, CEO of the real estate focused firm Western Group of Companies.[151] Alongside these mid-level capitalists, the previous CFLC national chair was John Craig Eaton, scion of the department store dynasty, and billionaire Fred Mannix was Alberta chair.[152]

Founded by Mannix, Reserves 2000 is another militarist initiative promoted by wealth-holders and encouraged by the CF. Led by

"Honorary Colonels", the organization was created to halt a planned reduction of the reserves.[153]

The ideological institutions of corporate Canada also promote the CF in various other ways. In 2017 the Smith School of Business at Queen's developed a program in which former special forces soldiers train students.[154] Led by security firm Reticle Ventures Canada, the initiative was modeled after US university programs in which former Navy SEALs run obstacle courses for hedge fund and financial service managers.

Ivey School offers University of Western Ontario business students an opportunity to train at CFB Meaford. Combat veterans run a weeklong Leadership Under Fire boot camp for Ivey students.[155]

The Canadian Manufacturers & Exporters, Aerospace Industries Association of Canada, Canadian Chamber of Commerce and Council of Chief Executives promote militarism, though rarely do they speak in favour of military retrenchment or withdrawing from military alliances. Canadian Manufacturers and Exporters spokesperson, Derek Lothian, responded to criticism of a $15 billion Light Armoured Vehicle sale to Saudi Arabia by saying the monarchy was "a long-time ally of both Canada and the United States."[156] For its part, the Aerospace Industries Association of Canada called on Ottawa to purchase Lockheed Martin's controversial F-35 jet in the 2010s and publicly campaigned in favour of Ronald Reagan's so-called "Star Wars" or Strategic Defense Initiative, which ramped up Cold War tensions.[157] The Chamber of Commerce also promoted a militarist, pro-US, foreign policy. Long headed by former defence minister Perrin Beatty, a 2010 chamber report titled Strengthening Our Ties: Four Steps Toward a More Successful Canada-U.S. Partnership explained, "modern security challenges necessitate pushing back the border by identifying threats long before they arrive. Such a perimeter approach to security allows for the identification of threats long before they reach North American shores."[158] In other words, the government should deploy the CF to deal with "threats" abroad before they impact Canadian trade.

Representing 150 top CEOs, the Canadian Business Council (formerly Canadian Council of Chief Executives) promoted militarism. During the organization's 40th anniversary celebration in 2016 former head Thomas D'Aquino said the Canadian Business Council was "pressing for more muscle" in foreign policy.[159] They supported the George W. Bush Administration's 2003 invasion of Iraq and "Star Wars" missile defence while organizing a "TRIBUTE TO THE CANADIAN FORCES."[160]

At the annual general meeting of the CCCE in 2003 CEO Thomas D'Aquino presented a paper titled "Security and Prosperity: The Dynamics of a New Canada-United States Partnership in North America." It noted: "The imperative that must drive Canada forward is based on three core assumptions: first we must be capable of making a vastly more effective contribution to the defence and security of our homeland — on land, along our coastlines and in our airspace. The choice is clear: either we affirm our sovereignty effectively, or we run the risk of losing it. The second assumption is that we must move to a new phase of co-operation with the United States in enhancing the defence and security of the continent. The third assumption is that Canada must be an effective player in the collective effort to combat terrorism globally."[161]

In 1981 CCCE/Canadian Business Council predecessor, the Business Council on National Issues, launched a Task Force on Foreign Policy and Defence, which Peter Langille claimed was motivated by "growing recognition of the financial opportunities arising from heightened Cold War tensions and the American arms buildup."[162] Six of the executives represented major defence contractors and the three-year task force visited the CF stationed in Europe, NATO headquarters, NORAD, the Joint Chiefs of Staff and other DND officials.[163] A member of the Conference of Defence Associations and director of the Canadian Institute for Strategic Studies, former Brigadier-General George Bell oversaw and drafted the Business Council's pro-military position paper entitled "Canada's Defence Policy: Capability Versus Commitments."[164]

The 60-page report bemoaned the "benign neglect and inadequacy of resources for nearly 20 years" that made the CF "incapable of meeting the international military commitments which Canada has assumed."[165]

The Business Council worked with the Canadian Global Affairs Institute and leading militarist ideologues Jack Granatstein and David Bercuson. After the September 11, 2001, attacks in the US, the Business Council and Canadian Global Affairs Institute published a report by Bercuson, Granatstein, John Ferris, Rob Huebert and Jim Keeley titled "National Defence, National Interest: Sovereignty, Security and Canadian Military Capability in the Post 9/11 World". The paper said it was "incumbent on Canadian governments to ensure that Canada's military forces are well-funded, equipped to the highest standards, and recruited and trained to fight alongside the best, against the best."[166]

There are various formal and informal channels through which corporate Canada transmitted ideas to the CF leadership. The Aerospace Industries Association of Canada contributed significantly to DND's defence industrial preparedness task force at the end of the 1980s.[167] Eight of the 17 original members of DND's industrial preparedness committee represented major defence contractors.[168]

In 2021 the advisory board of the DND-backed Conference of Defence Associations Institute included the founder of the $50 billion investment management firm AGF Management Blake C. Goldring, president of Belgian military firm RHEA André Sincennes and former head of Bombardier, Provigo and the Montréal Stock Exchange Pierre Lortie.[169] It also included less influential businesspeople such as the president of Pioneer Group Tim Hogarth, CEO of A.U.G. Signals George A. Lampropoulos, head of Sakto Corporation Sean Murray and senior director of strategy and government relations at General Dynamics Canada Kelly Williams (a former commodore in the RCN).[170]

A similar dynamic is at play with the DND-backed Canadian Global Affairs Institute. A half dozen Calgary business figures sit on the board of an organization honorary colonels Frederick Mannix and Robert J. S. Gibson founded.[171]

The board of governors of the Royal Military College included a number of businesspeople. Bank of Montreal vice-president Barbara Dirks, Four Seasons Hotels & Resorts Vice President Jane Burnell-Fraser, Bennett Jones Vice Chairman Lawrence E. Smith and other corporate executives were on the RMC board when this book went to print.[172]

Awards are another of the ways the military woos influential individuals. The DND-instigated and financed Conference of Defence Associations gives out an annual Vimy Award to a "prominent Canadian who has made outstanding contributions towards the security and defence of Canada and the preservation of our democratic values."[173] The Vimy prize has been awarded to billionaire Frederick Mannix and hedge fund founder Blake C Goldring.[174] Similarly, DND-backed Valour Canada (formerly Calgary Military Museums Society) gives out the General Sir Arthur Currie Award to those who "work to connect Canadians with their proud military heritage."[175] Mannix and former head of Bow Valley Industries and part-owner of the Calgary Flames, Daryl Kenneth Seaman, received the Currie prize.[176] So did Stanley Albert Milner who was dubbed "one of the most successful Canadian business leaders in the petroleum industry."[177]

In recognition of "exceptional deeds that bring honour to our country", the Meritorious Service Medal (Military Division) was given to Blake Goldring, William J. Coyle and other wealthy individuals.[178] While granted by the governor general, the CF approves candidates for the military version of the prize.

Mostly focused on soldiers, the Canadian Forces Decoration, Chief of Defence Staff Commendation and Canadian Forces Medallion for Distinguished Service have been given to business leaders who hold an honorary rank. These include multimillionaires Hal Jackman, Vaughn Solomon Schofield and Philip Thomas Jenkins.[179]

In a more substantial and longer standing effort to generate elite backing, the military offers honorary ranks to influential non-soldiers. According to the CF's website, the rank of honorary colonel, honorary lieutenant-colonel, honorary captain, etc. are "bestowed upon prominent members of the community for their influence."[180]

Dozens of well-to-do and ultra-wealthy individuals have received honorary ranks. In 2011 Blake Goldring was appointed first-ever honorary colonel of the Canadian Army.[181] The ultra-wealthy hedge fund manager was previously honorary colonel of the Royal Regiment of Canada.[182] Frederick Mannix was honorary lieutenant-colonel or honorary colonel of the Calgary Highlanders between 1980 and 1994.[183] In charge of the $10 billion Empire Life group of companies, Hal Jackman was a former honorary colonel of the Toronto based Governor General's Horse Guards while the former CEO of Chapters, Chairman of the Board of SNC-Lavalin and Managing Director of Callisto Capital, Lawrence N. Stevenson, was honorary colonel of the Queen's Own Rifles of Canada Regiment.[184] Beer scion and owner of the Montréal Canadiens, Geoff Molson was honorary colonel of Royal Military College Saint-Jean.[185] His brother Andrew Molson was honorary colonel of the Royal Montréal Regiment.[186]

At the time of her 2018 death Sonja Bata was the longest serving honorary captain of the Navy.[187] Her husband, founder of global shoe empire Bata Shoes, was honorary colonel in the Hastings and Prince Edward Regiment from 1999 to 2007.[188] At the time of writing Stanley Albert Milner was honorary lieutenant colonel in the South Alberta Light Horse and honorary member of the Loyal Edmonton Regiment while another wealthy oilman, Bob Brawn, was honorary colonel of the 746 Calgary Communications Squadron.[189] Board member and advisor at British Petroleum, Bank of Nova Scotia, Brookfield Asset Management, Deutsche Bank, etc., Roy MacLaren was honorary colonel of the 7th Toronto Regiment, Royal Canadian Artillery.[190]

Billionaire Power Corporation President André Desmarais was president of the honorary members of Les Voltigeurs de Québec, the army's oldest French-speaking regiment.[191] The Grand ami international de Les Voltigeurs has included American David

Rockefeller, Venezuelan Gustavo Cisneros, German Riprand Arco-Zinneberg and a number of other ultra-wealthy individuals.[192]

Alongside these leading global capitalists, many prominent local businesspeople have been granted honorary ranks. Kingston Furniture and Funeral Home magnate James Reid was honorary colonel CFB Kingston 21 Electronic Warfare Regiment while "well-respected member of the Victoria business community", Mandy Farmer, was honorary captain CFB Esquimalt.[193] In 2012 the CEO of Pioneer Group Tim Hogarth was appointed honorary colonel of the Royal Hamilton Light Infantry Regiment and vice-chair and principal of Nautical Lands Group, Paul Hindo was honorary colonel of the Cameron Highlanders of Ottawa.[194]

Honorary colonels are supposed to advocate for their regiment, advise on relevant policy matters and promote broader military interests. An early 2000s initiative "led by Honorary Colonels from across the nation" was launched called Reserves 2000. It successfully pushed back against a planned reduction in the reserves.[195] a

The first honorary colonel dates to 1895. Hamilton real-estate owner John Morison Gibson was made honorary lieutenant-colonel 13th Battalion Volunteer Militia Light Infantry.[196] Gibson was the first of numerous wealthy patrons of the militia. Principal shareholder of the Hudson's Bay Company, president of the Bank of Montreal and co-founder of Canadian Pacific Railway, Lord Strathcona Donald Smith was honorary colonel of Montréal's Victoria Rifles and Winnipeg Highland Regiment.[197] The first honorary colonel of the Royal Montréal Regiment was Lord Mount George Stephen, Canada's richest individual.[198] President of Herald Publishing Company and vice-president of the Bell Telephone Company of Canada, as well as board member of Canadian Pacific Railway, Royal Trust Company and Bank of Montreal, Robert MacKay was honorary colonel of the 5th

---

a When head of the Canadian Bar Association John Hoyles became honorary colonel to the Office of the Judge Advocate General in 2013 it sparked criticism from some lawyers. A retired colonel and University of Ottawa law professor, Michel Drapeau argued that Hoyles faced "at the very least an appearance" of a conflict of interest since his position would undermine his ability to criticize the military's legal system.

Royal Scots.[199] Numerous other leading Montréal businessmen were honorary colonels in the early 1900s.[200]

According to the honorary lieutenant-colonel of the 37 Signal Regiment Cheryl Robertson, "early appointments were captains, quote-unquote, of industry — people with deep pockets."[201] This was not by chance. Honorary colonels, notes Carman Miller, were "carefully chosen for their long purses."[202] At the start of the 20th century Prime Minister Robert Borden pointed out how it was "of greatest advantage to the Militia to be able to enlist the interest and sympathy of gentlemen of position and wealth by connecting them to Regiments."[203]

During its first years the navy was on fragile political footing. In a bid to widen its support base, the Royal Canadian Naval Volunteer Reserve was established in 1923.[204] Reserve units of between 50 and 100 men were set up in communities across the country "officered by local men of standing within the community who served without pay."[205] The early leaders of the Vancouver and Toronto Naval Reserve were ultra-wealthy individuals.[206]

In my research I did not uncover a single representative of Canada's four million unionized workers who received a militarist award or sat on the board of one of these institutions. While some individuals from academia, media and public institutions were recognized by militarist institutions, representatives of working-class organizations were not.

***

It is difficult to square the idea that the Canadian military is a force for good in the world with the scope of CF propaganda targeted at those who fund it. It is equally unsettling that they shape how the media portrays it. Even worse are attempts to undermine the independence of academic institutions that are supposed to provide Canadians with unbiased research. And what other government department spends so much on influencing the people supposed to oversee it?

But CF efforts to "get its way" extend beyond these activities. The next chapter discusses how Canada's "military-industrial complex" operates.

19. A Maple Military-Industrial Complex

IN HIS FAREWELL ADDRESS Republican President Dwight Eisenhower warned of the "military-industrial complex's" influence over US politics. A similar military-industrial complex exists in Canada and is partly a "branch plant" to the one south of the border. Canadian promoters of the military mimic their US counterparts and many arms manufacturers are active in both countries.

Arms Industry

More politically dependent than almost all other industries, arms manufacturers play for keeps in the nation's capital. They target ads and event sponsorships at decision makers while hiring insiders and military stars to lobby on their behalf.

Arms sellers' foremost concern in Ottawa is winning government contracts. But they also push to increase CF funding, its ties to the US military and government support for arms exports, as well as resisting arms control measures.

The Canadian Association of Defence and Security Industries (CADSI) is the primary industry lobby group. Representing over 900 corporations, CADSI has 20 staff in Ottawa.[1] With an office near Parliament Hill, CADSI lobbyists focus on industry-wide political concerns. The association's 2016 report described: "An intense engagement plan that included hundreds of engagements with targeted decision makers, half of which were with Members of Parliament, key ministers and their staffs, including the Prime Minister's Office. From one-on-one meetings, to roundtables, to parliamentary committee appearances, to our first ever reception on Parliament Hill, we took every opportunity to ensure the government understood our industries and heard our message."[2]

CADSI's events in Ottawa often include government agencies.[3] Defence Research and Development Canada and Public Safety Canada participate in CADSI's annual SecureTech Conference and Trade Show. The minister of public safety or a deputy minister usually speaks at the 200-booth "public safety and security showcase."[4]

The CANSEC arms bazar is the largest event CADSI organizes in the nation's capital. For more than two decades the annual conference has brought together representatives of arms companies, DND, CF, as well as the Canadian Commercial Corporation, Defence Research and Development Canada, Innovation, Science and Economic Development Canada, Public Services and Procurement Canada, Trade Commissioner Service and dozens of foreign governments.[5] In 2019 more than 11,000 people attended the two-day conference, including 14 MPs, senators and cabinet ministers, and many generals and admirals.[6] The minister of defence usually speaks at the 600-booth exhibit.

In a sign of its influence, CADSI's international arms delegations often include diplomats, military officials and representatives of crown corporations. Additionally, a federal trade commissioner was embedded into CADSI in 2010 to facilitate international arms sales.[7]

Many of CADSI's members are also part of the Canadian Manufacturers & Exporters, Business Council of Canada, Canadian Chamber of Commerce or Aerospace Industries Association of Canada. Through their lobbyists on Parliament Hill and public statements, these groups also promote militarism and a pro-US foreign policy, though rarely do they speak in favour of withdrawing from military alliances or bucking Washington on an international issue.

The 30-year-old Canadian Sporting Arms and Ammunition Association, 60-year-old Canadian Shooting Sports Association and 150-year-old Dominion of Canada Rifle Association, which represents a dozen provincial and territorial rifle associations, also advocate on behalf of arms interests on Parliament Hill.

Companies devote significant energy and resources to winning CF contracts, which have represented as much as half of federal government procurement spending.[8] To gain a share of the public funds on offer they target ads at DND and CF leaders, promoting their products in washrooms and bus shelters where DND and CF officials congregate. Rideau Institute founder Steven Staples pointed out that "you can't walk around in Ottawa without tripping over some arms dealer on Spark Street."[9]

Arms sellers also sponsor talks and exhibits attended by Ottawa insiders. They promote their brand at the Canadian War Museum, Gatineau-Ottawa airshow, Ottawa Chamber of Commerce, Conference of Defence Associations, etc.

Beyond promoting their wares in the nation's capital, companies advertise aggressively in publications read by Ottawa insiders such as iPolitics, *Ottawa Business Journal* and *Hill Times*. ("Today's Morning Brief is brought to you by Canada's Combat Ship Team," noted a regular iPolitics ad. "Lockheed Martin Canada is leading a team of BAE Systems, CAE, L3 Technologies, MDA and Ultra Electronics to deliver the Royal Canadian Navy's future fleet of surface combatants."[10]) Their ads also foot much of the bill for journals read by military officials such as the *Canadian Defence Review*, *Canadian Naval Review* and *Esprit de Corps*.

Arms companies' constantly lobby MPs and DND officials. In a "12-Month Lobbying Activity Search" of the Office of the Commissioner of Lobbying of Canada in early 2020, the names CAE, Bombardier, General Dynamics, Raytheon, BAE, Boeing and Airbus Defence were listed dozens of times. Lockheed Martin's name alone appeared 40 times.[11]

To facilitate access to government officials, international arms makers maintain offices in Ottawa. Lockheed Martin, Boeing, Northrop Grumman, BAE, General Dynamics, L-3 Communications, Airbus, United Technologies, Rayethon, etc. all have offices in Canada's capital and most of them are a few blocks from Parliament.

A sales pitch carries more weight when it comes from a friend, CF "star" or experienced veteran. As a result, arms companies contract former CF and DND leaders to lobby on their behalf. Long-time Project Ploughshares campaigner Kenneth Epps explains: "there are many cases of government officials who, very early after retiring, become lobbyists or advocates of certain types of equipment or representatives of particular companies. They come from government and know the ins and outs of how government decisions are made, who in government to contact and what arguments might be useful to advocate for certain types of equipment."[12]

In 2017 Lockheed Martin contracted retired air force commander André Deschamps to lobby for military contracts while Irving Shipbuilding hired former vice-admiral James King to push for Arctic and offshore patrol ship contracts.[13] After former deputy commander of NORAD Donald McNaughton retired in 1989, the consulting firm ADLOG appointed him vice-president and marketed his military expertise.[14] Many other former CF officials have taken up top positions at consultancy and lobbying firms. After retiring as chief of the defence staff in 1983 and deputy minister of the Department of Transport five years later, Ramsey Withers presided over Government Consultants International.[15] In 1983 three leading DND bureaucrats set up CFN Consultants.[16] A late 1980s CFN brochure highlighted its "in-depth knowledge of Canadian government and military requirements, military specifications, contracting procedures and associated budgetary considerations."[17] Headquartered two blocks from Parliament, CFN Consultants remains dominated by retired military leaders.[18] In 2018 all four of CFN Consultants' "senior partners" or "partners" had long careers in the military and six of the lobbying firm's eight "associates" and "consultants" were former CF or government procurement officials (the other two previously worked in government relations for arms firms).[19]

But contracting former CF/DND as lobbyists is a half measure. Some arms firms offer executive positions to retired CF leaders. In 2013 former deputy commander at NORAD and commander of NATO forces in Libya Charles Bouchard was appointed "country lead for Lockheed Martin Canada" in a bid to convince Ottawa to purchase its F-35 jets.[20] Four years later L3 Technologies appointed

Major General Richard Foster to oversee its Canadian business. The press release announcing its hiring of the former commander of the RCAF and deputy commander of the Joint Operations Command highlighted "his extensive military experience and work with foreign governments."[21] In 2012 former navy commodore Kelly Williams became General Dynamics Canada's senior director of strategy and government relations, while three weeks after Lieutenant-General Andrew Leslie retired as chief of transformation for the CF, CGI Group appointed him to lead an Ottawa-based business unit seeking to "serve the Canadian Forces around the globe."[22] After serving in the CF for 30 years Major General David Fraser became COO of INKAS Armored Vehicle Manufacturing.[23] Former Commander of Air Command and Chief of the Air Staff Allan DeQuetteville was made vice-president of Boeing Canada in 1998, while three months after resigning in 1996 former Chief of Defence Staff Jean Boyle went to work for Boeing.[24] In the early 1990s former Brigadier General Walter Niemy led Bombardier's military division.[25] He was succeeded in 1994 by David Huddleston who previously led the RCAF.[26] Similarly, General Paul Manson became head of strategic planning in the defence systems unit of Unisys Canada soon after retiring in 1989.[27]

In the 1989 book *Ottawa Inside Out: Power, Prestige, and Scandal in the Nation's Capital* Stevie Cameron details the case of Admiral James Wood, former head of Maritime Command, who became vice president of Saint John's Shipbuilding and president of Saint John Naval Systems. Cameron writes, "before he assumed the Maritime Command in 1983, Wood worked at Defence Headquarters in Ottawa — where he headed the committee that chose Saint John's Shipbuilding to build the original six frigates. And Saint John Naval Systems is a new subsidiary of Saint John's Shipbuilding with program support responsibilities for the new frigates. In other words, Wood headed the committee that chose the company to build new frigates, moved to the Maritimes as the senior naval officer, and then moved to work for the company that was buying the ships — and which got the contract to build six more."[28]

The CF-leader-to-arms-executive pipeline is important to the upper echelon of the military. In 2008 columnist Don Martin pointed out that "dozens of retired officers pocket salaries they could never have dreamed of as soldiers."[29]

The prospect of a lucrative post-retirement industry position increases the likelihood that CF leaders identify the military's interests with arms makers. The 'rent a general' pipeline strengthens interest in expensive new weaponry and opposition to arms control measures. Since many Canadian weapons companies are branch plants of US firms, lucrative post-retirement positions also increase CF leaders' support of the US military-industrial complex.

It's not only CF leaders who use their public sector careers as a springboard to lucrative arms industry positions. Weapons makers often hire top bureaucrats who were formerly responsible for arms procurement.

Two weeks after stepping down as deputy minister of defence in 2017 — after years of procurement work — John Turner was appointed vice president of operations at arms contractor PAL Aerospace.[30] In 2011 CGI Group hired 12-year DND veteran Ken Taylor as vice-president of cyber security in Canada. A CGI Group press release noted: "In his new role, Ken will work closely with both government and commercial clients as part of the newly formed Canadian Defence, Public Safety and Intelligence business unit under the leadership of Lieutenant-General (retired) Andrew Leslie."[31] After three decades "as a federal public servant in the defence and procurement fields", Janet Thorsteinson was named vice-president government relations of CADSI in 2010.[32]

DND and procurement officials also take up positions as lobbyists and on company boards. To help sell its secure telecommunications system, Gryphon Secure contracted John Turnbull, who formerly worked with DND military intelligence and was a Communications Security Establishment employee.[33] In 1989 Pratt and Whitney Canada appointed William Teschke, former deputy minister of the procurement-focused Department of Regional Industrial Expansion, to its board.[34]

Representatives of the arms industry also find their way into government positions. In 2014 CADSI president Tim Page was appointed to the board of directors of the Defence Analytics Institute. So was CAE director Christyn Cianfarani, Aerospace Industries Association of Canada vice-president Iain Christie and L-3 Communications vice-president Peter Gartenburg.[35] Appointed to the board of directors of MacDonald, Dettwiler and Associates (MDA) in 2000, David Emerson was made industry minister in 2004 and then appointed international trade minister.[36] At that time MDA was owned by the USA's Orbital Sciences, a major ballistic missile defence rocket-maker.[37] Emerson spoke glowingly of BMD's corporate benefits.[38] A former lobbyist for BAE systems, United Defense and Airbus Military, retired general Gordon O'Connor was appointed minister of defence in 2006.[39] That year, former head of CAE, Derek Burney, oversaw the transfer of power from Paul Martin's Liberals to Stephen Harper's Conservatives. A subsequent chief of staff for Harper, Nigel Wright, previously directed Hawker Beechcraft, a partner of US military giant Lockheed Martin. Wright was a top executive at Onex, which controlled CMC Electronics of Montreal (formerly Canadian Marconi Company) between 1988 and 2004.[40]

Shipbuilding

Since its creation prior to WWI an important objective of the navy has been to sustain Canadian shipbuilding.[41] Describing initial RCN purchases, Marc Milner writes, "the government insisted that the ships be built in Canada, at extra cost and with some delay, in part to foster the development of a modern shipbuilding industry."[42]

WWII was a eureka moment for Canadian shipbuilding. Benefiting from Royal Navy expertise and technology, hundreds of vessels were built at Canadian shipyards during the war.[43] The size of both Canada's navy and merchant marine exploded.[44]

In the decades after WWII defence expenditures continued to represent at least a fifth of spending on ships.[45] During this period naval contracts "stimulated Canadian shipbuilding, electronic and other high-technology industries."[46] As discussed further below, RCN contracts helped create a domestic computer industry. In the late 1950s and 1960s the ship industry received a major boost from the hydrofoil warship program. According to Tony German, the initiative "paid for pulling Canadian shipbuilding right into the computer age, brought in sophisticated quality assurance, developed the Marine use of exotic steels and aluminum structures, and introduced gas turbine marine propulsion."[47]

In 2011 Ottawa announced a $33 billion 30-year naval contract with Irving and Seaspan shipyards (subsequent estimates put the cost of acquiring 15 combat vessels at $77 billion and $286 billion over their lifecycle).[48] A CBC.ca headline noted: "Shipbuilding deals will stabilize industry, [Prime Minister Stephen] Harper says."[49] An assistant deputy minister at Public Works and Government Services Canada, Tom Ring wrote, "Canada's shipbuilding industry is now on the cusp of resurgence thanks to the federal government's National Shipbuilding Procurement Strategy."[50]

The National Shipbuilding Procurement Strategy required companies to make "value proposition" commitments to spur the marine industry. As part of its commitment to invest 0.5% of its contract revenues in marine innovation, Irving Shipbuilding invested $4.5 million in the Centre for Ocean Ventures and Entrepreneurship (COVE) in Dartmouth, Nova Scotia, in 2017.[51] COVE brings together ocean science researchers, post-secondary institutions, R&D-intensive companies, start-up companies and the Nova Scotia government to develop a cluster of marine innovation and commercialization.[52]

National Shipbuilding Procurement Strategy contracts are largely "cost-plus", which "provides perverse incentives for industry to increase costs," according to a 2015 PricewaterhouseCoopers report on the strategy. "If the profit percentage is fixed, increased costs result in increased profits."[53] Over the years RCN shipbuilding procurements have often been organized on a cost-plus basis.[54]

Of course shipbuilding has many industrial spinoffs.[55] Most of the value of a vessel is usually produced away from the shipyard. A cruiser or destroyer generally includes missiles, guns, helicopters, etc. as well as a multitude of high-tech gadgets (sonar, radar, weather, communications, tactical display, etc.).[56]

RCN upkeep is big business. In 2017 Thales Canada received a $5.2-billion contract to maintain new ships.[57] The next year Raytheon Canada was awarded a $700 million two decade-long contract to upgrade and maintain rapid-fire "R2-D2" guns on war ships.[58]

Even getting rid of vessels creates spinoffs. In 2017 DND paid $13 million to Marine Recycling to dispose of *HMCS Preserver* and *Auxiliary Vessel Quest*.[59] The next year Marine Recycling was awarded a $5.7 million contract to dispose of *HMCS Athabaskan*.[60]

Aerospace

Since WWII Canada has had one of the largest aerospace industries in the world. In 2020 it was the fifth largest.[61] A dynamic high-tech sector, aerospace companies conduct a fifth of all research and development work in Canada.[62]

The aerospace industry has greatly benefited from war and military spending. As Barney Danson, former minister of defence, said in 1982: "Defence procurement in the aircraft and aerospace field, with which I am most familiar, has been critical in making companies like De Havilland [Bombardier], Canadair, Pratt and Whitney, CAE, Fleet, SPAR, and others world leaders in the civil high technology marketplace."[63]

Flying largely began as a military endeavor. The Canadian Air Force was born in Britain during WWI. In 1922 the Canadian Air Force sought new aircraft. "Believing the time was ripe to establish an aircraft industry," write Ron Pickler and Larry Milberry, "Ottawa specified that the aircraft be built in Canada."[64] By the eve of WWII, nearly 300 aircraft had been manufactured in Canada.[65]

To create popular support for the air force the military promoted flying. In 1927 defence minister J. L. Ralston announced assistance to airplane clubs.⁶⁶ According to W. A. March, "by the late 1920s, these clubs and the RCAF had come together in an informal alliance to spread air-mindedness to the Canadian public, with the airshow becoming their most potent weapon."⁶⁷

WWII was an incredible boon to Canada's aircraft industry. Over one hundred thousand pilots, air gunners, wireless operators, etc. were trained through the British Commonwealth Air Training Plan at 150 sites across Canada.⁶⁸ About 3,500 aircraft were used to train airmen from Britain, Australia, New Zealand and Canada.⁶⁹ More than ten thousand more aircraft were manufactured in Canada and mostly shipped across the pond.⁷⁰

After WWII the civil air transport sector couldn't generate enough demand for manufacturers to succeed.⁷¹ This concerned air force leaders who believed aircraft manufacturing capability was vital.⁷² The RCAF's 1949 procurement policy noted that "a sound aircraft industry must be maintained in Canada."⁷³

The air force had surplus equipment after WWII so the industry was sustained through maintenance work and a myriad of international initiatives.⁷⁴ The industry benefited from large aircraft donations to European countries through NATO's Mutual Assistance Program. After that initiative ended Ottawa offered aircraft to Tanzania, Ghana and others. DND argued that training newly independent African countries' militaries would strengthen the "Canadian aircraft industry which has been adversely affected by the reduction in our [NATO] Mutual Aid Programme."⁷⁵ They hoped that building military relations with those countries would spur future aircraft purchases.

After WWII government-run aircraft manufacturers were offered to capitalists at a cut rate. Victory Aircraft and Canadair, reported Robert Bothwell, "were to be disposed of to private interests, on favorable terms, on condition that they become the nucleus of an active Canadian aircraft industry."⁷⁶ Victory was sold to the UK's Hawker Siddeley and Canadair to the USA's Electric Boat Company.

After running into difficulties Canadair was re-nationalized in 1976 and then privatized again a decade later.[77]

In the early 1960s the military was the source of 80% of aircraft expenditures.[78] As late as the mid-1970s, the CF represented almost all of leading aircraft firm Canadair's contracts.[79] Military spending remains important to CAE, Bombardier, Pratt and Whitney Canada, Héroux-Devtek, etc.

The Aerospace Industries Association of Canada (AIAC) Vision 2025 repeatedly discusses the importance of defence procurement. One of "six priorities" listed in the 2019 report is to "maximize defence procurement and government partnerships to drive new industrial growth."[80] In October 2020 president of the industry lobby group Aéro Montréal Suzanne Benoît called on the federal government to use "projects related to the defence of our country" to "help the aerospace supply chain". She added, "countries such as the United States have demonstrated that they will continue to provide unwavering support to the defence sector, enabling the development of advanced technologies transferable to commercial aircraft."[81]

AIAC lobbied Ottawa to purchase 65 F-35 fighter jets. In 2012 the *Toronto Star* reported, "the F-35 jet has been the whipping boy for auditors and politicians all week, but it remains the darling of Canada's aerospace industry."[82] At the time over 70 Canadian companies already built parts on contracts expected to be worth billions over the course of the plane's production run.[83]

Aircraft firms have been leading beneficiaries of military subsidy programs. The Defence Industry Productivity Program (DIPP) doled out some $2 billion in the 1980s and 1990s.[84] Most DIPP funds went to aerospace companies. In *Silent Partners: Taxpayers and the Bankrolling of Bombardier* Peter Hadekel describes DIPP as "a thinly disguised giveaway to Canadian aerospace companies."[85] Less than 7% of the money loaned through DIPP had been repaid by 1995.[86]

An important RCAF supplier, Pratt and Whitney Canada received $723 million in loans through DIPP (and more in other subsidies).[87]

For its part, Bombardier received $245 million in DIPP funds.[88] Bombardier also received hundreds of millions of dollars through the Strategic Aerospace and Defence Initiative set up in 2007.[89] Ditto for CAE and Pratt and Whitney.[90]

Subsidies

All military manufacturers are heavily subsidized. According to a Coalition to Oppose the Arms Trade estimate, Canadian arms suppliers received $5 billion in grants and unpaid loans from 1976 to 2006.[91]

The Defence Industrial Research (DIR) program offered grants that covered up to 50 per cent of the cost of applied research projects relevant to the military.[92] Established in 1961, DIR shelled out hundreds of millions of dollars. Administered and funded by DND and the National Sciences and Engineering Council, DIR provided funding and partnership support to industries developing military-related projects and technologies. It also facilitated partnerships between DND, universities and companies.[93]

Partly to stimulate arms exports to the US the Defence Industry Productivity Program doled out $2 billion to Canadian corporations.[94] According to an internal description, "the Program provides added opportunities for Canada's industry to compete in foreign defence markets by partially offsetting the financial assistance granted to foreign companies by their governments."[95]

From the early 1980s to the mid 2000s Technology Partnerships Canada handed out hundreds of millions of dollars in unrepaid loans to arms companies. In 2007 it was replaced with the Strategic Aerospace and Defence Initiative, which "supported strategic industrial research and pre-competitive development (R&D) projects in the aerospace, defence, space and security industries."[96] The initiative dished out tens of millions of dollars a year.[97]

In 2018 the Liberal government launched the Innovation for Defence Excellence and Security (IDEaS) program. Framed as a new way to "solve specific defence and security challenges", IDEaS supported the development of solutions from their conceptual stage, through prototype testing and capability development.[98] IDEaS was to pump $1.6 billion into military research initiatives over 20 years.[99]

Arms companies also benefit from various other general subsidy programs. In one example, General Dynamics Land Systems-Canada received millions of dollars in grants through the southern Ontario-based Next Generation Manufacturing Canada Advanced Manufacturing Supercluster.[100]

One reason most of the world's biggest arms manufactures have a Canadian subsidiary is to access government subsidies. The 1989 book *Le Québec militaire: les dessous de l'industrie militaire québécoise* claims the province oriented its industrial policy towards the arms sector because that's what the federal government supported.[101]

Technological Effects

Since WWII DND has spent tens of billions of dollars on scientific research and technological development. The money has spurred some socially useful innovations as well as our capacity to harm each other and the environment. It has also subsidized corporations. According to Andrew Godefroy, "DND research laboratories designed and built Canada's first computer, rocket and satellites."[102]

Since WWII the military has taken an interest in national technological development. In the hopes of accessing the most advanced weapons and building broader backing for the CF, military leaders expressed interest in shaping scientific and industrial policy.[103] In 1947 the head of the chiefs of staff Charles Foulkes argued that Canada had to be ready to "subsidize industry [in peacetime] in the interests of national security."[104] The next year Defence Research Board (DRB) chairman Omond Solandt told the Canadian Manufacturing Association that "industrial preparedness in peace time is just as important to victory as is military preparedness. ... if the full potential of Canadian victory is to be reached quickly in the event of war, we must start now to form plans for the use of industry to strengthen the research and development side of industry and foster the partnership of science, industry, and the Armed Forces that is so essential to victory."[105] Solandt added that the government should invest in areas "where the civilian interest is not great", but that would benefit "the normal expansion of industry."[106]

To stimulate scientific advancement the Defence Research Board was established in 1947. Within a decade it had grown to 2,600 staff, including 630 scientists.[107]

DRB worked closely with corporate Canada.[108] Top representatives of Northern Electric, Canadian Marconi and RCA Victor were part of DRB's electronic advisory committee. They sought research contracts for their firms.[109]

DRB awarded its first industrial contract to Consolidated Mining (COMINCO) in 1949. Corporations received many subsequent contracts. Alongside contracts, industry representatives benefited from courses put on by DRB's Electronics Laboratory, which advanced early computer development (see below).[110]

Reflecting its role as a conduit for channeling public funds to the corporate sector, DRB financed fundamental research. Andrew Godefroy notes that DRB "was allowed to adopt and promote an agenda of 'science for the sake of science' at the expense of science in support of military application."[111] In 1950, for instance, it opened the Institute for Theoretical Astrophysics at the University of Toronto.[112]

DRB advanced development of communications, batteries, metallurgy, respirators, radiac instruments and many other domains.[113] DRB's laboratory at Fort Churchill, Manitoba made advances on fuels and lubricants in cold weather, winter clothing, snow characteristics, etc.[114]

DRB morphed into the Defence Research and Development Branch and then Defence Research and Development Canada (DRDC).[115] In 2019 DRDC had 1,400 employees and a $350 million budget.[116]

DRDC operates seven different programs that channel money into various research initiatives and eight leading facilities that test technologies and weapons. In recent years DRDC laboratories worked on unmanned ground vehicles, unmanned aerial vehicles, unmanned maritime systems and autonomous intelligence. DRDC's predecessor, the DRB, produced chemical and biological weapons (see Chapter 8) and built a highly accurate Heller anti-tank weapon.[117]

DRDC works with other government departments and agencies. It manages a "Canadian Safety and Security Program" that includes representatives of the CF, Public Safety Canada, universities and information and communications technologies companies.

DRDC collaborates with a multitude of academics and educational institutions.[118] It has a Research Partnership Program with Natural Sciences and Engineering Research Council and Social Sciences and Humanities Research Council.[119] DRDC scientists have postings at universities and participate in various co-op programs.[120]

Internationally, DRDC scientists work closely with the US Defense Advanced Research Projects Agency (DARPA). They also work with NATO and Israeli partners.[121]

"Industry" is "an important partner", according to DRDC's website.[122] DRDC collaborates with the corporate sector on many initiatives. They have employee exchanges and licensing agreements with companies to commercialize technologies as well as material transfer and collaborative research agreements.[123]

The Canadian Association of Defence and Security Industries does regular events with DRDC.[124] They publicly promote DRDC and tout its benefits. So does the Aerospace Industries Association of Canada.

Digital Research

According to John Vardalas, in *The Computer Revolution in Canada — Building National Technological Competence*, "It was the 'invisible hand' of Canadian military enterprise that incited companies such as Ferranti Canada, Computing Devices of Canada, Canadian Aviation Electronics, RCA Victor, and Canadian Marconi to increase their competence in digital electronics."[125]

DRB and the military played a central role in stimulating computer technology and expertise. Vardalas writes, "without a doubt, military enterprise was the primary force behind Canada's early participation in the digital electronics revolution."[126] As late as the 1970s DND was responsible for nearly half of all electronics research spending in the country.[127]

Canada's first computer was sponsored by DRB. Begun just after WWII, the "University of Toronto Electronic Computer" (UTEC) project was a training ground for expertise in computer technology. The CF supported university computation centres to ensure there were Canadian mathematicians, scientists and engineers trained in the use of computers and Canada was self-reliant in the emerging domain.[128] The UTEC initiative led directly to the world's first computerized urban traffic control system in Toronto.[129]

RCN contracts helped create a domestic computer industry. The navy birthed and nurtured Ferranti Electric Canada (later Ferranti Packard Computer), which became Canada's leading computer research company.[130] Ferranti UK established an electronics R&D group at its Canadian subsidiary to develop an automated system for ships to relay tactical data from radar and sonar. The decidedly un-stereotypical branch plant developed a PCM-based radio system for passing digital data between ships.[131] Known as DATAR, the US Navy would later adopt the extremely expensive technology. As it developed expertise in digital electronics from its military work, Ferranti-Canada sought to convert it into civilian products.[132]

In the latter half of the 1950s Defence Research Telecommunications Establishment (DRTE) designed and built the first transitory general-purpose computer in Canada.[133] Fully developed by 1960, the DRTE computer stimulated Canadian expertise in miniaturization of digital electronics.[134]

In 1955 DRTE's transistor section set up a training program for engineers from military firms to work at their Ottawa laboratory for six months. They hoped the engineers would return to their companies and share what they'd learned about transistor circuit design. Major firms such as Canadian Westinghouse, Northern Electric, Canadian Marconi, Computing Devices of Canada and Canadian Aviation Electronics sent one or more engineers to DRTE.[135] Through military procurement contracts these and other firms also gained access to a sophisticated R&D environment.[136]

DND funded electronics research because firms were unwilling or unable to do so. The military sought to distribute the benefits of computer research regionally. Far from the centre of Canadian digital electronics activity, the military financed early software research at the University of British Columbia. UBC's computer department nourished the growth of software companies such as MDA, Sydney Development Corporation and Basic Software Group.[137]

Space

The nexus where the military, technological advancement and corporations have met is in space. Until the late 1960s DND led Canada's push into space and even after most space capabilities were transferred to civilian control a military component remained.[138]

Canada was the third country after the US and Soviet Union to have a satellite in orbit. Alouette I was launched into space in 1962 and Alouette II was sent up three years later. Defence Research Telecommunications Establishment (DRTE) designed and built the Alouettes.[139] DRTE operated world class radio physics and electronics laboratories and led the way in ionospheric research.[140] Additionally, space-focused rocket experiments took place at Churchill Research Range in northern Manitoba.[141]

The CF sought to turn space into a potential battleground.[142] The zenith of its push to militarize space was the RCAF's mid-1960s Space Defence Program.[143] "Canada vigorously investigated and pursued defence roles that contributed to active missile defence, space control, and the potential deployment of space-based weapons," noted Andrew Godefroy in a chapter about the quarter-century after WWII.[144]

During this period opposition to the militarization of space grew, finding expression in the 1967 UN Outer Space Treaty, which barred participating states from putting weapons of mass destruction in orbit, on the moon, or in space, or testing weapons and establishing bases in space.[145] Partly in response to growing international concern, the federal government transferred space capabilities to civilian control. Telesat Canada, the Department of Communications and (later) the Canadian Space Agency (CSA) were established to oversee communication satellites and space work.

But a military dimension remained. DND cooperated with these agencies and some pushed for "an autonomous CSA that embodies DND objectives."[146] More directly, DND operates various space initiatives. The air force has a Director General Space, Directorate of Space Development and Canadian Space Operations Cell. In 2012 the CF put $337 million into the ninth Wideband Global Satellite Communications System (WGS-9), which is a high-capacity satellite communications system set up by the US and Australian militaries.[147] (General Dynamics Canada won two contracts worth $70 million as part of the initiative.[148])

DND put over $250 million into the Medium Earth Orbit Search and Rescue (MEOSAR) satellite project that supports the US Air Force's GPS III satellites.[149] When fully operational it is expected to significantly reduce the time required to locate a distress signal.[150]

Alongside British and Dutch forces, the CF is part of the US Air Force Space Command Advanced Extremely High Frequency communications system.[151] It's a series of communications satellites used for secure communications.

DND's Project Sapphire detects and tracks debris in medium earth orbit and geostationary satellites.[152] To help protect their space assets and to gather data on objects re-entering the earth's atmosphere, Sapphire feeds the US Air Force's Space Surveillance Network.[153] After 2021 Surveillance of Space 2 will replace Sapphire to continue delivering information to the US Space Surveillance Network.

DND also works with their US counterparts on various other space initiatives. The Canada-US Defence Space Cooperation Working Group and Space Cooperation ad hoc Working Group are forums for space cooperation activities.[154] Most importantly, the Canadian and US militaries deal with space issues through NORAD.[155]

Canada's civilian space policy has been closely integrated with US policy. The Canadian space program has relied on US support to access outer space. The US National Aeronautics and Space Administration (NASA) helped launch the Alouettes and Canada's RADARSAT-2. A civilian agency, NASA has had close ties to the US Department of Defense as James E. David details in *Spies and Shuttles: NASA's Secret Relationships with the DoD and CIA*.

The US has aggressively militarized space. The Pentagon has put satellites into space to enable first strike ballistic missile defence. A number of Canadian initiatives support US BMD. Through the 2000s Canadian military and National Research Council scientists worked with their US counterparts on BMD projects.[156] The space-based Quantum Well Infrared Photodetectors is a Canadian backed project that enables BMD weapons to distinguish between missiles and decoys.[157] Canada has also supported the US push to weaponize space through NORAD.[158]

Alongside military initiatives, Canada's broader space policy aids BMD. The highly advanced RADARSAT-2 imaging satellite helped US war fighters determine targets for BMD.[159] RADARSAT-2 was developed through a partnership between CSA and MDA. (MDA grew out of DND's support for computer research at UBC.[160]) Canadian taxpayers put up $445 million for the initiative or about 85 per cent of the total cost.[161] For its investment, the federal government, mainly the CF, was promised large amounts of imagery as well as "priority access" to RADARSAT-2 in emergencies.[162]

DND's project Polar Epsilon used RADARSAT-2 data for "Space-Based Wide Area Surveillance and Support Capability." The $60 million project utilizes RADARSAT-2 imagery as part of the Radarsat

Constellation Mission, which is a follow-up to the RADARSAT-2 spacecraft.[163] In 2013 MDA received a $700-million contract to build, launch and operate the RADARSAT Constellation Mission.[164] It will also enable BMD.

Besides MDA, other Canadian companies have run radars and satellites that comprise the BMD network. ATCO Frontec maintained and operated BMD SSPARS radar bases in the US, Greenland and UK; AUG Signals did radar image/data processing for BMD target detection and tracking; CAE produced simulation products for designing and developing Boeing's BMD weapons.[165]

Amidst widespread opposition to the BMD forerunner, Strategic Defense Initiative (or "star wars"), industry representatives told a joint 1985 Senate and House of Commons committee dealing with Canadian participation in SDI research that the benefits were too great to walk away from.[166]

Government space contracts have been important to some firms. De Havilland (now part of MDA) parlayed its success with the Alouette in the 1960s to win contracts on Canadarm1 and 2, which played a significant role in NASA's subsequent space shuttle fleet and International Space Station.[167]

In 2018 MDA, Honeywell, IMP Aerospace, Magellan, Aerospace Industries Association of Canada and others launched a public relations/lobbying initiative to force the government to fund Canadarm3. Combined with pressure from NASA, the DontLetGoCanada campaign succeeded. In 2019 Ottawa put up $2 billion for a new space program, which will be part of the Lunar Gateway space station NASA wants to orbit the moon and land on a lunar outpost.[168]

A $2.3-billion industry, Canadian space research has led to profitable spinoffs.[169] In 1981 the *Globe and Mail* used Anik A3 satellite technology to relay news in computerized form across the country for the first time while beginning in 1999 a Nimiq satellite provided its initial television services.[170] (Telesat contracted arms behemoth Lockheed Martin to build Nimiq.) The McGill university blog "Moments That

Matter: Canadian History Since 1867" explains, "listening to the radio, watching television, and using our GPS navigation systems are all forms of technology that … would not have been possible without Canada's initiative to study the Earth's atmosphere and launch its satellite, the Alouette 1, in 1962."[171]

Nationalism and the Economy

Most successful capitalist nations have nurtured sizeable arms industries. One reason is that the weapons sector is research and development focused. While it has varied over time, military companies were responsible for 20-25% of Canadian R&D in the late 1980s.[172] In 2018, Innovation, Science and Economic Development Minister Navdeep Bains credited the military sector for over $400 million in R&D spending, which he said was four and a half times the rate of Canadian manufacturing in general.[173]

Arms production is generally capital-intensive. Its large investments in equipment — rather than workers — is conducive to high profit margins.

When a country has its own weapons industry, military spending can boost the economy.[174] Conversely, if a country purchases most of its arms from abroad it is a drain on the economy. Industry-funded studies suggest military spending in Canada boosts GDP.[175] There's no doubt that military spending has long sustained important segments of Canadian industry. Shipyards, aerospace firms and many high-tech companies have depended on military contracts.

Military and government officials have long highlighted the broader economic benefits of supporting arms manufacturing. A 1964 Defence Production Department paper titled "Defence Expenditure and its Influence on the Canadian Economy" noted, "the resulting technological advances in the complex production operations of highly sophisticated weapons systems spread readily into other areas of Canadian production. The economy as a whole is made stronger and better able to make its way in world markets."[176] An early 1960s

Royal Commission on Government Organization made the same point: "Defence research, development and production now constitute collectively one of the major stimuli to technological progress, and thereby to the competitive strength and growth potential of a nation's industrial economy."[177]

In 2017 the government's "Strong, Secure, Engaged: Canada's Defence Policy" promoted the arms industry as a driver of growth. The defence policy paper repeatedly references the value of military spending on the economy, arguing "this vital sector also helps keep Canada's economy vibrant and innovative with over 30 percent of defence occupations in innovation-relevant science and technology-related fields."

In 2018 the chair of Finance Minister Bill Morneau's growth council, Dominic Barton ("one of the most connected people in the world", according to the *Financial Post*) noted, "if we want to grow ... the defence sector is going to play an essential part in doing that. [Military spending] is how we're going to get some of the leading-edge innovation that we can then commercialize and transform the broader economy."[178]

Military procurement policies serve nationalist economic aims. A bevy of different policies are designed to spur domestic employment, technology and profits.

Military procurement is exempt from "free trade" agreements that generally prohibit "buy local" initiatives. Under World Trade Organization and Canada-Europe Comprehensive Economic Trade Agreement (CETA) rules, governments are allowed to pursue nationalistic military procurement policies.[179]

"Buy Canada" military procurement "offset" policies require a contractor to invest a dollar into the Canadian economy for every dollar the government spends on defence purchases. Canadian content offsets can be obtained in various ways. The contractor can set up shop here or purchase products from Canadian suppliers or subcontract work to Canadian companies. Or they can make co-production arrangements or licensed production agreements or even transfer technology.[180]

Combined with the Defence Production Sharing Agreement (more below), offset requirements have integrated Canadian companies into the value chains of larger, mostly US-based, firms. As a result, Canadian firms largely produce components for weapons system sold in the US and internationally. At one-point Massachusetts based Raytheon contracted with 800 Canadian firms to fulfil offset requirements.

Offset rules have led international firms to set up Canadian subsidiaries. In 1960 Canada purchased the CF-104 starfighter from Litton. With no components of the aircraft made in Canada, the Los Angeles based firm established Litton Systems Canada to produce the airplane's guidance system to fulfill "Canadian content" requirements.[181]

Procurement policy isn't simply nationalistic. Arms purchases are often designed to spread economic benefits to different regions and politically important ridings. In 2005 Fisheries and Oceans Minister Geoff Regan outlined the regional offsets from a massive helicopter contract to Sikorsky Aircraft. The minister promised the contract would bring "$1 billion of work to aerospace companies in Atlantic Canada, with Ontario gaining $2-billion worth of industrial activity, Québec $995 million, and Western Canada $390 million."[182]

The government helps companies outside the major centres bid on arms contracts. In 2019 Ottawa put up $800,000 for a three-year project to assist companies in five northern Ontario cities to access defence contracts.[183]

Short term political calculations are often part of spreading military contracts to different regions. In 2020 *National Post* columnist Matt Gurney claimed military procurement "was doing a bang-up job" at "regional vote buying" while the *Globe and Mail*'s Jeffrey Simpson described offsets as "a fancy word for jobs scattered in sensitive political locations across Canada."[184]

The National Shipbuilding Procurement Strategy offers a high-profile example of the regional politics at play. On the day the strategy was signed, Stephen Harper presided over ceremonial events on both the west and east coasts. To maximize media attention the prime minister signed the accord with Irving Shipbuilding in Halifax in the morning and then flew across the country to do the same with Seaspan in BC.

After being bypassed, the Davie shipyard near Québec City launched a campaign to gain some of the work. A new Liberal government conceded.

Defence Production Sharing Agreement

Signed in 1956 the Defence Production Sharing Agreement (DPSA) is designed to avoid trade imbalances in military sales between Canada and the US.[185] The bilateral trade accord allowed Canadian companies to bid on US military contracts and the associated Defence Development Sharing Program facilitates research sharing. In effect, the DPSA makes Canadian companies part of the US defence industrial base. "As a result [of the DPSA], most military items shipped between Canada and the United States do not require permits," noted a 2016 Global Affairs Canada report on foreign defence and security exports.[186]

The DPSA improved Canadian firms' access to the world's most lucrative arms market. Additionally, it offered them access to advanced military technology and facilitated participation in US firms' global value chains.[187] For every dollar Canadian firms exported to the US military under the DPSA they sold another 50 cents worth of that product to another country.[188]

The DPSA appealed to the Pentagon because Canadian firms were relatively sophisticated suppliers. But there was also a political element to the DPSA. The Pentagon wanted to tie Canadian firms to the US military industrial complex in the hope that would spur them to advocate a pro-US military policy.[189] A 1958 US national security document described the importance of maintaining a "healthy" "Canadian defense industry" for the US to "receive the same excellent cooperation in the joint defense effort that has prevailed in the past."[190]

In a sign of the DPSA's success, president of Canadian Marconi John H. Simmons highlighted the importance of Ottawa aligning with US military policy at a defence committee review of NORAD. In a 1987 speech labeled "a summation of the general feeling among industry representatives", Simmons testified, "it is vital to Canada that the defence industrial base survives and grows, and it is vital to the defence industry that it retains its access to the US defence market and continues to be considered as part of the US defence industrial base. To achieve both of these goals, it is therefore vital that Canada continue to co-operate with the US in defence areas generally, and in NORAD in particular."[191]

Canada's Weapons Industry

"Defence" is a $10 billion a year industry that employs 60,000 Canadians.[192] Hundreds of companies produce bullets, rifles and armoured vehicles. Other firms construct naval vessels and offer flight simulation services. An important part of Canada's weapons industry makes components for larger weapons systems produced by US giants.

Arms manufacturing reached its high point during WWII when a quarter of economic output was focused on military production. At the start of the 1950s, defence minister Brooke Claxton claimed the sector was still "the biggest single industry in Canada."[193]

To access lucrative military contracts and generous subsidies, US and British weapons makers' have long set up Canadian subsidiaries. In 1911 Ottawa invited Britain's Vickers Sons and Maxim to establish a Canadian division to produce vessels for the nascent RCN.[194] Canadian Vickers was given "an extended lease on the land [for a shipyard] and deferred taxes."[195]

Four decades later the British-based Sperry Corporation established a Canadian subsidiary "to exploit the commercial opportunities of the new wave of defence spending."[196]

Most of the biggest US, French and British weapons companies have Canadian subsidiaries. Lockheed, Raytheon, General Dynamics, Boeing, Thales, BAE, Pratt & Whitney, etc. all have sizeable Canadian divisions, which conduct research and employ thousands.

General Dynamics Mission Systems-Canada is a prime example. The subsidiary of the US-based behemoth has over 2,000 employees and does research and development work.[197] Tracing its Canadian history to 1948, General Dynamics has ties to Canadian educational institutions, politicians and the CF. In the journal *Canadian Military History*, Frank Maas wrote, "the CF has continued to purchase LAVs because they have been successful in the field, and they support a domestic producer, General Dynamics Land Systems Canada (GDLS-C), that cooperates closely with the military."[198] A major international exporter, GDLS' London, Ontario, operations exist largely because of interventionist military industrial policy. A 2013 federal government report on "Leveraging Defence Procurement Through Key Industrial Capabilities" lists GDLS as one of three "Canadian Defence Industry Success Stories."[199] While it's a division of a US firm, General Dynamics Canada is deeply rooted in this country.

L-3 Wescam is another subsidiary of a US firm that is a multinational arms dealer. Based at a 330,000-square-foot facility in Hamilton, L-3 Wescam has offices in the UK, Jordan, Australia, Japan, Italy, Saudi Arabia, France, Spain, Germany, Ecuador, UAE and the US.[200] Its military history dates to the late 1950s when Westinghouse Canada developed a stabilized camera mount for the Canadian Defence Research Establishment.[201] In recent years the leader in electro-optic and infrared imaging has produced guidance systems for missiles and unmanned drones, as well as components for the Cobra Attack Helicopter.[202] It provided surveillance technology for Blackhawk helicopters the Saudis used in Yemen.[203]

Formally part of a larger US conglomerate, Pratt & Whitney Canada is a multinational in its own right. With 4,000 of its 10,000 employees outside Canada, the Montréal firm does its own research, development and marketing.[204] Founded in 1928, the firm has provided engines for Chinese, Israeli, Saudi, UAE and Colombian military helicopters and aircraft.[205] Pratt & Whitney Canada operates airplane and helicopter maintenance centres in Europe, Asia, Africa and the Middle East.[206]

There are also a number of important Canadian-headquartered military suppliers. Canada's largest military firm is CAE. With 90% of its revenue derived internationally, the Montréal based flight simulator company has won billions of dollars in military contracts. CAE trains thousands of Canadian, US, British, UAE, Saudi, etc. fighter pilots each year in dozens of locations around the world.[207] CAE has created synthetic training environments for many major US Air Force weapons systems. It trained the operators of Predator and Reaper drones, for instance.[208] CAE has an important US subsidiary in Tampa Bay, Florida, and the company openly talked about profiting from increased US military spending. "Le patron de CAE veut profiter de la hausse des budgets de l'armée américaine" (CAE boss wants to take advantage of rising US military spending), read a 2018 *La Presse* headline.[209]

CAE trained Israeli military personnel and worked with Israel's Aeronautics Defense Systems and Israel Aerospace Industries.[210] At a facility in the UAE, CAE trained Saudi and UAE pilots that began bombing Yemen in 2015. It also operated the only freefall centre in Europe entirely dedicated to military parachuting and ran (with the CF) the NATO Flying Training in Canada, which trains pilots from many countries.

Southern Ontario-based armoured vehicle maker Streit Group produced vehicles in a half dozen countries. Its UAE based plant delivered hundreds of armoured vehicles to the Saudi/UAE war on Yemen.[211] It also exported vehicles to Sudan, South Sudan, Libya, Afghanistan, Iraq, Nigeria, the Philippines, Singapore, Ukraine and a number of other countries.[212]

Winnipeg-based PGW Defence Technology produces "one of the most accurate sniper rifles in the world", explained then Chief of the Defence Staff Rick Hillier in 2005.[213] Alongside its weapons deliveries, the company offers training support and coordinates with military agencies on ammunition research. PGW sold rifles to the Canadian, British, US, South Korean, Ukrainian, Saudi and UAE militaries and boasted they "customize for special forces". PGW rifles were repeatedly discovered with Saudi backed forces fighting in Yemen from 2018 to 2021.[214]

Héroux-Devtek was established to produce weapons during WWII. The world's third-largest manufacturer of aircraft landing gear, the Montréal based firm has 2,000 employees spread out in Canada, the US, UK and Spain.[215] It's a major contractor to the US Air Force and for many years it supplied automatic firearms to Canadian and NATO forces.[216]

Military Privatization

Military procurement has long been big business. But the CF didn't turn to private contractors in a meaningful way for services, training and maintenance work until the 1990s. The privatization of "non-core military jobs" has grown substantially since, as has contracting private security companies. DND has spent billions of dollars on various service contractors.

Calgary-based ATCO-Frontec garnered hundreds of millions of dollars in contracts to support CF personnel and installations. They managed CFS Alert in Nunavut and the Saskatchewan-based NATO Flying Training in Canada.[217] The firm also oversaw bases in Bosnia and Afghanistan.[218] At the Kandahar airfield in Afghanistan ATCO provided "waste management services, fire crash and rescue, utilities and maintenance."[219] The firm was hired by the US Air Force and NATO to construct and manage military installations.[220]

Montréal based SNC Lavalin won billions of dollars in military service contracts.[221] In partnership with US firm PAE, SNC oversaw a series of contracts to construct and manage CF bases in Kandahar, Bosnia and Kabul worth hundreds of millions of dollars.[222] From 2011 to 2019 SNC received $500 million to help service minor warships.[223]

Private contractors also make large sums training the RCAF. CAE became a global leader in flight simulation by training Canadian and US air force pilots. Founded in 2000 by three former RCAF pilots, Discovery Air Defence signed a long-term contract in 2017 worth between $480 million and $1.4 billion to train RCAF as well as army and RCN members.[224]

More controversially, the CF contracts private security companies to train members and provide security. In 2016 Reticle Ventures, which was set up by former JTF2 commander Steve Day, announced a plan to invest $50 million to build Canada's most advanced private military training facility.[225] The CF was a client of Reticle Ventures.[226]

Between 2005 and 2011 Academi (formerly Blackwater) was paid over $10 million to train JTF2 personnel and CF police.[227] In 2008 CF personnel participated in courses put on at Academi's Terrorism Research Center to learn what drives people to support an insurgency or become insurgents. The CF contract said, "it is vital that soldiers have the training to understand the people whom they will assist and those that will pose a grave and present danger."[228] The CF continued to train with Blackwater's successor through at least 2017.[229]

The CF also taps private military companies' (PMC) expertise in other ways. In 2013 Toronto-based Globe Risk founder Alan Bell "shared his experiences working in the PMC industry" at a Canadian Special Operations Forces Command and US Joint Special Operations University symposium on "The Role of the Global SOF [Special Operations Forces] Network in a Resource Constrained Environment".[230]

The federal government also hired PMCs to protect diplomats and embassies overseas. During the war in Afghanistan DND spent tens of millions of dollars on PMCs.[231] They paid $10 million for private security to guard Canada's "signature" $50 million aid project to repair the Dahla dam in Kandahar province.[232]

The federal government contracted Saladin to protect its embassy in Kabul.[233] Saladin also helped secure Prime Minister Stephen Harper during a visit there in 2007 and protected forward operating bases in Kandahar province.[234] Saladin has a troubling history. Its predecessor, KMS, trained and possibly equipped Islamic insurgents battling Russian forces in Afghanistan in the 1980s and it sent mercenaries into Nicaragua as part of the Iran Contra Affair.[235]

During the war in Afghanistan Saladin, DynCorp and other PMCs had larger numbers of armed men than most of the NATO countries occupying Afghanistan. In 2008 Canadian Brigadier General Denis Thompson explained: "Without private security firms it would be impossible to achieve what we are achieving here. There are many aspects of the mission here in Afghanistan, many security aspects that are performed by private security firms that which, if they were turned over to the military, would make our task impossible. We just don't have the numbers to do everything."[236]

Private security firms in Afghanistan operated under guidelines that practically guaranteed significant civilian casualties. After a Canadian officer was killed by a PMC employee in August 2008, Canadian Major Corey Frederickson explained that the "normal contact drill [for PMCs] is that as soon as they get hit with something then it's 360 [degrees], open up on anything that moves."[237]

Private Security Companies

Canada has a thriving private security industry that is largely an offshoot of the military. Many former CF personnel own or work for private security companies (PSC).

With large sums of public resources put into their training, Canadian special forces are sought after by PSCs. According to the CF, "[t]he world-renowned reputation of JTF2 as a SOF ... unit has drawn attention from many of these security firms."[238] Numerous JTF2 soldiers quit to work for private companies operating in Iraq after the 2003 US invasion. In 2006 the *Ottawa Citizen* reported, "records previously released under the access to information law have shown that Joint Task Force Two officers are concerned the unit is losing personnel to private military firms. Former JTF2 have found work as guns-for-hire with companies in Africa and Iraq."[239]

GardaWorld, Blackpanda and Academi employed former Canadian special forces.[240] Former CF members worked for Muskoka-based Executive Security Services International as bodyguards in

Africa.²⁴¹ "Founded in the mid-2000s by Canadian military veterans", Tundra Group protected forward operating bases in Afghanistan.²⁴² For their part, Toronto-based ICEN Group hired "elite trained, former special forces personnel [to] provide close security protection for executives travelling to dangerous operating environments."²⁴³

Run by retired Canadian Brigadier General Ian Douglas, Black Bear Consulting operated in numerous African countries. In his 2000 book *Fortune's Warriors* former Canadian Airborne Regiment commando Jim Davis writes that Douglas offered to introduce him to officials of the notorious mercenary outfit Executive Outcomes if he sought employment.²⁴⁴ Davis instead went to work for Globe Risk Holdings. The Toronto company supplied security support in many African countries and had offices in Kabul and Kandahar as well as Iraq.²⁴⁵ Set up by Alan Bell, a 12-year veteran of the British Special Forces who moved to Canada, Globe Risk tried to open a branch in Sierra Leone in 1999. At the time the *National Post* reported: "Next month, Alan Bell and Jim Davis, two former soldiers, are travelling to Sierra Leone, a country few would dare visit, to open a branch of their private security company. For the two enterprising Canadians, the explosive mix of diamonds, road blocks, feuding rebel groups and child soldiers represents an irresistible business opportunity."²⁴⁶ Globe Risk planned to train the president's bodyguards and build a local security force capable of guarding airports and seaways.²⁴⁷ Driving the initiative forward was a plan to open a large bauxite mine in the country.

With 90,000 employees worldwide, Montréal based GardaWorld is the world's largest privately held PSC. A 2014 Canadian Business profile described Garda's business as "renting out bands of armed men to protect clients working in some of the Earth's most dangerous outposts."²⁴⁸ Garda operated in 35 countries including Iraq, Afghanistan, Colombia, Pakistan, Nigeria, Algeria, Yemen, Somalia and Libya. Established in 1995, the invasions of Afghanistan and Iraq in the early 2000s propelled Garda's international growth. Iraq represented nearly a quarter of its $683 million in revenue in 2006.

"We are an employer of choice for Veterans and Reservists," said Christian Paradis, senior vice president of Garda.[249] The former cabinet minister in the Stephen Harper government added, "we recognize the value of their skills and abilities developed within the Canadian Armed Forces."[250] The Montréal company regularly advertises in *Esprit de Corps* calling on the magazine's CF readership to "translate your military skills into a Gardaworld career."[251] The company also runs a Veteran and Reservist Employment Program.

A number of CF officers were in the upper echelons of Garda. The head of its Libya operations was former CF Lieutenant-Colonel Andrew Zdunich and the head of Garda's Afghan operations, Daniel Ménard, previously commanded CF operations in Afghanistan. (Ménard had been court-martialled for having sexual relations with a subordinate in Afghanistan and recklessly discharging his weapon.[252]) Garda's board also included prominent former US and British military and security officials.

In 2007 four Garda employees were kidnapped in Iraq. They were later killed. Garda was engulfed in controversy in Afghanistan as well. In 2012 two of its employees were caught with dozens of unlicensed AK-47 rifles and jailed for three months.[253]

Garda's most controversial foray abroad was in Libya. Sometime in the "summer of 2011", according to its website, Garda began operating in the country.[254] After Libya's National Transition Council captured Tripoli (six weeks before Muammar Gaddafi was killed in Sirte on October 20, 2011) the rebels requested Garda's assistance in bringing their forces "besieging the pro-Qaddafi stronghold of Sirte to hospitals in Misrata", reported Bloomberg.[255] Garda's involvement in Libya may have contravened that country's laws as well as UN resolutions 1970 and 1973, which the Security Council passed amidst the uprising against Gaddafi's four-decade rule. Resolution 1970 mandated all UN member states "to prevent the provision of armed mercenary personnel" into Libya while Resolution 1973 mentioned "armed mercenary personnel" in three different contexts.[256] In an article titled "Mercenaries in Libya: Ramifications of the Treatment of

'Armed Mercenary Personnel' under the Arms Embargo for Private Military Company Contractors," Hin-Yan Liu pointed out that the Security Council's "explicit use of the broader term 'armed mercenary personnel' is likely to include a significant category of contractors working for Private Military Companies."[257]

Contravening international law can be good for business. As the first Western security company officially operating in the country, Garda's website described it as the "market leader in Libya" with "over 3,500 staff providing protection, training and crisis response."[258] Garda's small army won a slew of lucrative contracts in Libya.

The Montréal company protected European Union Border Assistance Mission (EUBAM) personnel who trained and equipped Libyan border and coast guards in a bid to curtail African migrants from crossing the Mediterranean. Garda's four-year EUBAM contract garnered attention in early 2014 when 19 cases of arms and ammunition destined for the company disappeared at the Tripoli airport. But the company didn't let this loss of weapons deter it from performing its duties. According to Intelligence Online, company officials asked, "to borrow British weapons to ensure the safety of EU personnel."[259] The request found favour since Garda already protected British interests in Libya, including Ambassador Dominic Asquith. In *Under Fire: The Untold Story of the Attack in Benghazi*, Fred Burton and Samuel M. Katz describe the ambassador's protection detail: "Some members of Sir Dominic Asquith's security detail were undoubtedly veterans of 22 Special Air Service, or SAS, Great Britain's legendary commandos, whose motto is 'Who Dares Wins.' Others were members of the Royal Marines Special Boat Service, or SBS."[260]

In June 2012 a rebel group attacked Asquith's convoy in Benghazi with a rocket-propelled grenade. "The RPG-7 warhead fell short of the ambassador's vehicle", notes *Under Fire*. Two Garda operatives "were seriously hurt by fragmentation when the blast and rocket punched out the windshield of the lead vehicle; their blood splattered throughout the vehicle's interior and then onto the street."[261]

There are few regulations constraining Canadian PSCs' international operations. Unlike the US and South Africa, "Canada does not have legislation designed to regulate either the services provided by Canadian PMSCs [private military security companies] operating outside of Canada or the conduct of Canadian citizens working for foreign PMSCs."[262] Furthermore, Ottawa has not signed the international convention against the recruitment, use, financing and training of mercenaries and has been little involved with the Human Rights Council's Working Group on the use of mercenaries.[263]

Arms Control Measures

Pushed by arms companies seeking exports and a CF opposed to restrictions on its operations, Ottawa has generally been ambivalent towards international arms control measures.

Official data on arms exports is largely worthless since the government doesn't compile it on far and away Canada's largest customer, which happens to be "the most warlike nation in the history of the world", in the words of former US President Jimmy Carter.[264] Most arms exports to the US are excluded from official arms export statistics. The scope of the omission is immense with as much as 70% of Canadian arms exports going to that country.[265]

Forty nations on the federal government's Automatic Firearms Country Control List (AFCCL) can purchase or receive Canadian automatic weapons without a special permit.[266] Prior to the introduction of the AFCCL in 1991, the Criminal Code effectively prohibited the private export of Canadian-made automatic weapons. Saudi Arabia was one of 13 countries on the initial list. In fact, the AFCCL was created partly because a GM Diesel factory in London, Ontario, wanted to export a thousand light armoured vehicles fitted with machine guns to the Saudi monarchy.[267]

As discussed previously, Canada has voted against many UN moves to ban nuclear weapons. The Harper government opposed various initiatives to curtail nuclear weapons and the Justin Trudeau government boycotted a UN treaty to rid the world of nuclear weapons supported by two thirds of member states.²⁶⁸

Since 2007 Canada has abstained on a series of UN resolutions concerning Depleted Uranium munitions.²⁶⁹ Backed by the vast majority of General Assembly members, the resolutions don't even call for the abolition of DU, but only for transparency in their use to enable clean up.²⁷⁰

Canada took seven years to heed the Convention on Cluster Munitions, which often leave unexploded bomblets that later wreak havoc on unintended targets. Eighty-nine states pledged to eliminate the deadly weapons before Ottawa got on board.²⁷¹ More troubling, Canada's appropriating legislation allows the CF to participate in joint military operations with countries that refused to sign the convention (notably the US). Director of the Cluster Munition Coalition, Laura Cheeseman said, "Canada cannot claim to have banned cluster bombs when it proposes to allow its military to help others use the weapons."²⁷²

In another form of assistance, Canadian-based Royal Bank, Manulife, Sun Life Financial and CI Financial invested $565 million in companies that manufactured cluster bombs.²⁷³ According to a 2016 report by Dutch peace group PAX, about half of this sum was invested in Textron, which sold cluster bombs to Saudi Arabia despite it killing Yemeni children with these bombs.²⁷⁴

Canadian diplomats recommended a minimalist United Nation's Arms Trade Treaty (ATT), which was designed to limit weapons from getting into conflict zones and the hands of human rights violators. Taking a position that put Canada offside with the bulk of the international community, Ottawa's representative to the ATT negotiations in 2012, Habib Massoud, called for the proposed arms tracking secretariat to be "minimal, small, and flexible" and financed entirely through existing UN budgets. "In Canada's view," noted Massoud, "detailed reporting about each and every [arms] transaction can, in certain circumstances, be both impractical and unrealistic. The sheer volume of such transactions would overwhelm virtually any administrative system now in existence."[275]

In an age of instant communication, Canadian officials argued it was too complicated to keep track of weapons sales. At the time Amnesty International launched a campaign claiming the global banana trade was better regulated than the arms market.[276]

Canada was slow to join the ATT. One hundred and four countries, including most NATO-members and major arms producers, acceded to the ATT before Ottawa.[277] Canada's appropriating legislation to "accede" to the treaty was also highly flawed. Flouting the ATT, Canadian military exports to the US are exempt from licensing and reporting requirements. Project Ploughshares published a report titled "Canada's ATT legislation: A loophole you could drive a tank through".[278]

Ottawa has allowed Canadian companies to flout UN arms embargos. Southern Ontario-based Streit Group exported armoured vehicles to Sudan, South Sudan and Libya in violation of UN sanctions.[279] Two separate UN reports investigating sanctions enforcement concluded that Streit Group violated arms embargoes.[280] Canadian officials claimed they were unable to pursue Streit Group since the vehicles were exported from a plant in the UAE and thus fell outside Canada's arms export regime. But human rights lawyer Paul Champ claimed there was ample evidence to investigate and possibly prosecute the company for violating the Special Economic Measures Act.[281]

In fact Streit Group received Canadian financial and political support. The armoured vehicle maker received export aid from Canada's Global Markets Action Plan and international trade minister Ed Fast and Conservative MP Ted Opitz visited Streit Group's plant in London, Ontario in 2015.[282]

In contravention of UN resolution 1970 and 1973, Waterloo-based Aeryon Labs supplied Libyan rebels fighting Gaddafi's government with a three-pound, backpack-sized Unmanned Aerial Vehicle.[283] In

June 2011 the president of Ottawa-based Zariba Security Corporation, Charles Barlow, traveled 36 hours on a rebel operated fishing boat from Malta to the rebels training facility in Misrata.[284] ("A former military officer", Barlow told a parliamentary committee meeting in 2014, "I ran the Afghanistan intelligence response team, the national level team for Afghanistan at the Department of National Defence. They've sent me to pretty much every place that Canada sent people for the last 20 years."[285]) In Misrata Barlow taught the rebels how to operate this Canadian-developed drone, which was used to gather intelligence on the front lines. Not only did Ottawa not pursue Barlow or Aeryon officials, the company said it was approached by Canadian officials and the drone was reportedly paid for out of Libyan government assets frozen in Canada.[286]

This disregard for an international rules based order was nothing new. After the UN passed an arms embargo against South Africa in 1977, Ottawa ignored the export of dual use technologies. Crown company Canadair sold the apartheid regime amphibious water bombers, which according to the manufacturer, were useful "particularly in internal troop-lift operations."[287] (The official buyer was the South African forestry department.)

Subsidizing Arms Exports

Not only is Canada's military-industrial complex allowed to flout international law, various government departments and crown corporations help arms companies export. As discussed previously, Defence Research and Development Canada, Innovation, Science and Economic Development Canada, Public Services and Government Services Canada have aided arms companies over the years. Ditto for Atlantic Canada Opportunities Agency, Federal Economic Development Agency for Southern Ontario, Industry Canada, Economic Development Agency of Canada for the Regions of Québec and Western Economic Diversification Canada. Since the 1970s the Defence Industry Productivity Program, Technology Partnerships

Canada and Strategic Aerospace and Defence Initiative have given weapons companies billions of dollars.

More specific to international sales, partnerships between Canadian and other countries' arms firms have been underwritten with public funds. The Canada-Israel Industrial Research and Development Fund, for instance, pumped tens of millions of dollars into joint research ventures on military specific projects.[288]

The Department of Industry, Trade and Commerce promoted international arms sales. In the early 1970s it spent about $40 million annually "to develop and sustain the technological capability of Canadian defence industry for the purpose of defence export sales or civil export sales arising from that capability."[289]

The Defence Programs Bureau (DPB) marketed military products internationally for decades. DPB was established in 1963 "in recognition of the need for a highly specialized industrial and trade-oriented branch within the Canadian government to promote the export of Canadian Defence products."[290]

During the last years of Shah Mohammad Reza's rule DPB had a representative in Tehran. Canada sold about $60 million ($300 million today) worth of arms to Iran in the 1970s at a time when Amnesty International reported, "no country in the world has a worse record in human rights than Iran."[291]

DND has long promoted arms exports. Its website highlights different forms of support to arms exporters. "Learn how the Department of National Defence can assist in connecting Canadian industry to foreign markets", explained one section.[292] Another noted: "Learn how the Department of National Defence keeps Canadian companies informed of business opportunities at the North Atlantic Treaty Organization (NATO)."

Based in 30 diplomatic posts around the world (with cross-accreditation to many neighbouring countries), Canadian Defence Attachés promote military exports. According to DND's website, these colonels who are supported by sergeants and sometimes a second officer, assist "Canadian defence manufacturers in understanding and accessing foreign defence markets ... facilitate Canadian industry access to relevant officials within the Ministries of Defence of accredited countries ... support Canadian industry at key defence industry events in accredited countries ... raise awareness in accredited countries of Canadian defence industrial capabilities ... provide reports on accredited country defence budget information, items of interest, and trade issues to Canadian industry."[293]

Arms manufacturers have participated in trade missions with the minister of trade or prime minister. Diplomats in the field have also helped weapons companies connect with foreign governments. During Indonesia's occupation of East Timor, the federal government supported Canadian weapons makers' participation in trade fairs and trade missions to Indonesia and Ottawa even sponsored a military trade fair in Jakarta.[294]

The Trade Commissioner Service also supports the weapons industry. In 2010 a Trade Commissioner was embedded within the Canadian Association of Defence and Security Industries.[295] CADSI missions receive financial support from the Global Opportunities for Associations program and Western Economic Diversification Canada awarded CADSI funds to enable Western Canadian companies to participate in international arms events and delegations.[296] Officials from DND, Global Affairs and Trade Commissioner Service participated in CADSI trade missions to Kuwait, Saudi Arabia, Israel, UAE, etc.[297] Representatives of DND often talk up Canadian military equipment as part of delegations to international arms fairs such as the UK's Defence Security and Equipment International Exhibition.[298]

An objective of RCN visits to international ports has been to spur commercial relations, especially arms sales. Lieutenant Bruce Fenton writes, "Canadian warships can serve as venues for trade initiatives, as examples of Canadian technology, and as visible symbols of Canadian interest in a country or region. In countries where relationships are built over time, as is the case with many Asian and Middle Eastern countries, a visit by a Canadian warship can be an important part of a dialogue that can lead to commercial opportunities for Canadian industry."299

When ships were sent to enforce sanctions on Iraq in the 1990s, they also showcased Canadian vessels to the Kuwaiti navy. According to a 1995 DND report, *HMCS Calgary* was employed "as a platform for SJSL [Saint John's Shipbuilding Limited] Kuwait Offshore Missile Vessel proposals and for Ambassador [to Kuwait J. Christopher] Pool to promote Canadian industry and technology."300 In the mid 1990s RCN visits to the Middle East were credited with generating tens of millions of dollars in contracts for CAE Electronics and Computing Devices Canada.301

Naval frigates have been sent to the UAE during the Abu Dhabi-based International Defence Exhibition and Conference (IDEX), the largest arms fair in the Middle East and North Africa. In 2013, noted Lieutenant Jonathan Douglas, "[HMCS] Toronto played host to Emirati dignitaries and representatives of the roughly 30 Canadian defence firms attending IDEX, providing a forum for networking against the backdrop of a floating symbol of Canadian naval power."302 Six years later, researcher Anthony Fenton tweeted, "Canadian Commander of Bahrain-based naval task force visits UAE arms bazaar where over 50 CDN companies are flogging their wares."303

To help the arms companies, commander of the Bahrain-based Combined Task Force 150 Commodore Darren Garnier led a Canadian military delegation to IDEX 2019.304 The arms companies also received support from "15 trade commissioners and representatives from the Government of Ontario, National Defence, Global Affairs Canada, and the Canadian Commercial Corporation."305

Export Development Canada has provided export credit for arms sales.306 Another Crown Corporation facilitates weapons sales. Initially called War Supplies Limited, the Canadian Commercial Corporation (CCC) draws Canadian arms suppliers and foreign buyers together and is the middleperson on sales, meaning the contracts are secured by the government of Canada.

With a government appointed board, the CCC has 140 full-time employees. The crown corporation signs upwards of 2,000 contracts with the US Department of Defense annually.[307] In total CCC signs over $1 billion a year in contracts and enables $3 billion worth of exports.[308]

During WWII War Supplies Limited was established to negotiate US munitions orders. At the end of the conflict CCC replaced War Supplies Limited. The crown corporation sold Canadian weaponry to the US Department of Defense under the 1956 Defence Production Sharing Agreement (see above). For years CCC's president was also director of the DPSA.[309]

CCC openly capitalizes on warfare. During the war in Afghanistan CCC president Marc Whittingham wrote in the *Hill Times*, "there is no better trade show for defence equipment than a military mission."[310] During the 1991 Gulf war CCC set up a 24-hour telephone hotline to ensure that weapons "requests from allies wouldn't get snarled in red tape."[311] When the US was at war in Vietnam the CCC shared an office in Ottawa with the US Defense Contract Administration Services.[312]

Expanding beyond its historical emphasis on the Pentagon and NASA, CCC increasingly acted as a middleperson between Canadian arms manufacturers and other governments. In 2009 the crown corporation established the Global Defence and Security Sales to build its international customer base. In 2020 CCC claimed to have operations in 81 countries.[313] According to a 2011 *Embassy* article, "the Canadian Commercial Corporation has been transformed from a low-profile Canadian intermediary agency to a major player in promoting Canadian global arms sales."[314] It began emulating aspects of the US Defense Department's Foreign Military Sales program, which facilitates that country's global arms sales.

Describing the Canadian Association of Defence and Securities Industries (CADSI) as one of four "key industry association partners", CCC participated in CADSI trade missions to Kuwait, England, UAE and elsewhere.[315] In his 2017 book *Security Aid: Canada and the Development*

Regime of Security Jeffrey Monaghan writes, "CCC representatives have accompanied the Minister of International Trade to Libya, Peru, Russia, Ghana, Nigeria, and other locations to export Canadian security and military materials."[316]

The CCC brokered a highly controversial light armoured vehicle sale to Saudi Arabia. The $10-15 billion General Dynamics Canada deal for 1,000 combat vehicles included training Saudi troops and years of maintenance work.[317] CCC continued to facilitate arms sales to the Saudi monarchy even after it came to light that they were used in Yemen.

The CCC stays mum about the social consequence of the arms sales they broker.[318]

A Leading Arms Exporter

On a per capita basis Canada is a leading arms exporter. At 0.5% of the world's population Canadian companies represent around 2% of global arms exports.[319]

In absolute numbers Canada usually ranks somewhere between eighth and fifteenth largest arms exporter.[320] The Geneva-based Small Arms Survey consistently ranks Canada among the top 15 exporters of pistols, rifles and light machine guns.[321] Over half of Canadian "defence" sector sales are exports.[322]

Canadian weapons makers have repeatedly fueled controversial wars. Weapons sales swelled alongside the US military buildup in Vietnam. According to David J. Bercuson and Jack Granatstein, "Canadian industry sold some $12.5 billion in ammunition, aircraft parts, napalm, and other war materials to South Vietnam and the US."[323] *Snow Job: Canada, the United States and Vietnam (1954 to 1973)* notes: "American planes [that dropped bombs and napalm] were often guided by Canadian made Marconi-Doppler navigation systems and used bombing computers built in Rexdale, Ontario. The bombs could have been armed with dynamite shipped from Valleyfield, Québec; polystyrene, a major component in napalm, was supplied by Dow

Chemical. Defoliants came from Naugatuck Chemicals in Elmira, Ontario, and air-to-ground rockets were furnished by the Ingersoll Machine and Tool Company. On the ground, American infantry and artillery units were supplied by De Havilland Caribou built at Milton, Ontario. Less lethal Canadian products included Bata boots for the troops and the famous green berets of the Special Forces which came from Dorothea Knitting Mills in Toronto ... Canadian Arsenals Ltd, a Crown corporation, sold small arms, fill for artillery shells, mines, bombs, grenades, torpedo warheads, depth charges and rockets."[324]

Three weeks after elected President Salvador Allende was overthrown by General Augusto Pinochet, EDC announced a $5 million credit for Chile to purchase six Twin Otter aircraft from De Havilland. At the time the *Canadian Defence Quarterly* lauded the Twin Otter's capabilities in carrying troops to and from short makeshift strips.

During the 1947-8 Palestinian Nakba (catastrophe) Canadian Zionists bought weapons for the war and ethnic cleansing effort. Between 1950 and 1956 Canadian companies sold Israel significant amounts of weapons. "By the summer of 1950," notes a 150-page thesis detailing Canadian weapons sales to Israel from the state's founding until its 1956 invasion of Egypt, "Israeli arms requests were being placed in Canada with an almost regular frequency, and from this point until the 1956 Suez war, there was never a time when a substantial Israeli arms request was not under consideration by the Canadian government."[325]

Canada continued to arm the Israel Defense Forces (IDF) after it launched a number of murderous raids into Gaza and Egypt that left dozens of soldiers and civilians dead in 1954 and 1955. These weapon sales did not go unnoticed. "In the Strategic Interests of Canada: Canadian Arms Sales to Israel and Other Middle East States, 1949-1956" Barry Bristman notes, "Canada and a few other nations were named by [Egyptian President Abdul] Nasser as being Israel's military suppliers, guilty of strengthening Egypt's great enemy."[326]

Despite IDF human rights violations in Gaza, Lebanon, Syria and the West Bank, Canadian companies continue to sell weapons directly to Israel. Over 100 Canadian weapons makers exported products to Israel, according to a 2009 Coalition to Oppose the Arms Trade (COAT) report. It noted, "Canadian companies like Nortel and Bombardier, and smaller military companies like Frontline Robotics and MDA, are all working directly with the Israeli military. ... Mawashi Corp. in Quebec helps develop body armor used by the Israeli Border Police and Army in suppressing Palestinian demonstrations."[327]

Canadian arms manufacturers also fueled Colombia's dirty war. In the late 1990s DND sold 33 Huey helicopters to the US State Department, which added machine guns and sent them to the Colombian police and military.[328] The Huey sale followed Bell Helicopter Textron Canada's export of 12 helicopters directly to the Colombian air force and police. The helicopter was a type "widely used by the U.S. military in the 1970s in counter-insurgency operations in Vietnam."

Throughout Indonesia's brutal 1975-2000 occupation of East Timor Canadian weapons makers sold their wares to the Indonesian army. In 1998 *Vancouver Sun* columnist Stephen Hume wrote: "Since the invasion of East Timor and the deaths of up to 200,000 ethnic East Timorese, Canada has pumped more than a third of a billion dollars in military exports into Indonesia, an outlaw state repeatedly condemned by the United Nations."[329]

A year into the 2003 US invasion of Iraq Montréal-based SNC Technologies Inc. joined a multinational consortium of ammunition producers providing occupation forces with 300 to 500 million bullets per year for five years. Defence industry analyst Eric Hugel told the *Financial Times*, "we're using so much ammunition in Iraq there isn't enough [US manufacturing] capacity around. ... They have to go internationally."[330]

After the US, Saudi Arabia has been the largest market for Canadian arms exporters for many of the past 30 years. "Canada has been a consistent and significant supplier of armoured vehicles to Saudi Arabia since the 1990s," explained Project Ploughshares in 2008.

Canadian weaponry was frequently used in the devastating Saudi-led war in Yemen. As PhD researcher Anthony Fenton documented in detail, hundreds of armoured vehicles made by Canadian company Streit Group in the UAE were videoed in Yemen.[331] Equipment from three other Canadian armoured vehicle makers — Terradyne, IAG Guardian and General Dynamics Land Systems Canada — was found with Saudi-backed forces in Yemen.[332]

The Saudi coalition used Canadian-made rifles as well. "Canada helped fuel the war in Yemen by exporting more rifles to Saudi Arabia than it did to the U.S. ($7.15 million vs. $4.98 million)", tweeted Fenton regarding export figures from July and August 2018.[333] Despite the war in Yemen and assassination of exiled journalist Jamal Khashoggi, 2018 was a record year for rifle sales to the Saudis.[334]

***

The military-industrial complex is a significant economic force with a great deal of influence over government. Few politicians criticize weapons manufacturing, the harm caused to people elsewhere or the corruption often associated with arms sales. As in the United States the jobs associated with military manufacturing and research are spread across the country, giving the arms industry a veneer of social utility.

But how can making the weapons of war be good for Canadians or ordinary people elsewhere? Giving outsized power to arms manufacturers and the military corrupts us all.

More discussion of the negative effects of the military follow in the conclusion.

Conclusion

"The peace movement is in bad shape in Canada and that's the way it should be"

Robert Coates, defence minister[1]

IS THE CANADIAN MILITARY A FORCE FOR GOOD in the world? Readers can decide for themselves but if you believe in the golden rule, if you prefer improved social services to buying weapons, if you believe democracy means an equal voice for all, if you oppose corruption in government, if you believe negotiating is preferable to fighting, you should have doubts. At a minimum you should support serious reforms of CF practices, policies and alliances.

When polled most Canadians express a mix of anti-militarist opinions together with affection for the CF. The affection is not surprising given the sums spent promoting the military. It should not surprise us that the majority of people prefer spending taxes on education and social services over weapons. Most people prefer peace over war and consider the profit-seeking arms industry self-serving. Most people, when given a choice, want an economy that prioritizes human and environmental welfare over military might. Most Canadians don't want to be a junior partner with the US military.

But how do we get from where we are today, as outlined in this book, to a more peaceful place, one where the golden rule is practised in foreign affairs and Canada is a force for good in the world? While the systemic changes required are beyond the scope of this book, some thoughts on (re)building the peace movement are not.

***

The CF and militarism have always been contested. Anti-militarist activists have generally been on the political fringe, but their activism often constrained policymakers and occasionally determined policy.Significant antiwar sentiment existed among Francophone

Quebeckers during the 1899–1902 Boer war and many Quebeckers opposed establishing a navy in the early 1900s. Most Quebeckers opposed WWI and the introduction of conscription in August 1917 led to a political crisis. In English Canada an assortment of radical leftists and religious pacifists, such as the Doukhobors, Hutterites and Mennonites, opposed the war. Opposition to WWI grew dramatically after Ottawa introduced conscription. Significant segments of organized labour criticized the war, arguing that if labour was to be conscripted so should wealth.

Some within the CCF (the NDP's predecessor) and organized labour opposed the Korean War. Established in 1949, the Canadian Peace Congress led the charge against the deployment to Korea. In response, External Affairs Minister Lester Pearson called for individuals to destroy the Peace Congress from the inside.[2]

During this period the Peace Congress, which was close to the Communist Party, led the battle against nuclear weapons. They promoted the global Stockholm Appeal, which called for "the outlawing of atomic weapons ... We believe that any government which first uses atomic weapons against any other country whatsoever will be committing a crime against humanity and should be dealt with as a war criminal."[3]

In the early 1960s stationing nuclear tipped BOMARC missiles in Canada was highly contentious. Worried about "possible pacifist demonstrations", the RCAF "ordered that the route and time of shipments be kept secret because it feared that some Canadians opposed to BOMARCs might attempt to stir up demonstrations at communities along the trucks route."[4]

Antiwar activism exploded during the US war in Southeast Asia. Many took to the streets against Ottawa's open support for the war in Vietnam and Canadian arms sales to the US. This activism greatly weakened the post-WWII NATO/Cold War consensus.

Through the 1970s and 80s many cities hosted large annual peace marches. About 100,000 (including the author, aged seven, with family and friends) marched in Vancouver on April 27, 1986.[5]

Responding to the peace movement, Vice-Chief of the Defence Staff Ramsey Withers called those opposed to nuclear tipped cruise missiles "dupes of Soviet disinformation."[6] In a more sophisticated response to mid-1980s antiwar activism, the DND-sponsored Canadian Institute for Strategic Studies developed a "high school curriculum program to counterbalance the peace movement," notes Peter Langille.[7]

To appease anti-nuclear activists the Pierre Trudeau government established an Ambassador for Disarmament in 1982.[8] Since the early 1980s over 100 Canadian cities have endorsed the global Mayors for Peace call to abolish nuclear weapons.[9] A number of city councils also acceded to activists' push to become nuclear weapons free zones, including Vancouver and Victoria, which forced some US Navy ships to dock outside the city limits.[10] In Ottawa the Coalition to Oppose the Arms Trade, which campaigned against Canada's largest arms trade show (now called CANSEC), convinced the city in 1989 to stop hosting weapons bazaars on city property.[11]

Tens of thousands marched against Canadian participation in the First Gulf War. In a bid to discredit antiwar activism the CF promoted a rumour that body bags were thrown on the lawn of a soldier in Victoria.[12]

In 1997 Canadian and international groups that pushed for the elimination of anti-personnel landmines won a partial victory with the adoption of the Ottawa anti-landmine treaty (Convention on the Prohibition of the Use, Stockpiling, Production and Transfer of Anti-Personnel Mines and on their Destruction). In 2003 antiwar activists stopped Jean Chrétien from publicly endorsing the US-led invasion of Iraq. With as many as 200,000 at the largest march in Montréal and Quebecers overwhelmingly opposed to the war, the federal government feared that joining George W. Bush's "coalition of the willing" would cost them and boost Québec's independence movement. (While they didn't do what Bush wanted above all else, the Liberals quietly offered numerous other forms of support to a US-led war the CF leadership wanted to join.[13])

After protesters targeted SNC-Lavalin for selling bullets to the US for use in Iraq the Montréal company sold its bullet production arm in 2005.[14] In another partial victory that year, the Canadian Peace Alliance, Échec à la guerre, Ceasefire.ca and others forced the Liberal government to shelve its plan to formally join the US ballistic missile defense.

Demilitarization work is overwhelmingly voluntary. Unlike labour and ecological campaigning, few antiwar activists are paid.

DND's PR capacities are hundreds (maybe a thousand) of times those of all antiwar and disarmament groups combined. The cost of a single 2018 DND report on the public's attitude towards the CF ($145,000) probably equaled the combined budgets of the Canadian Peace Congress, Hamilton Coalition to Stop the War, Regina Peace Council and Coalition to Oppose the Arms Trade![15]

Below is a brief description of some of the more important peace and disarmament groups.

- At its height after the 2003 invasion of Iraq the Canadian Peace Alliance claimed 140 member groups. Founded in 1985, the umbrella organization had one paid employee and became inactive in 2017.
- An influential antiwar force in the 1950s and 60s, the Canadian Peace Congress steadily declined thereafter. Largely dormant from 1990 to the latter part of the 2000s, it began re-establishing chapters across the country in the 2010s.
- Project Ploughshares is the peace research institute of the Canadian Council of Churches. Founded in 1976, it focuses on the arms trade, nuclear disarmament and other military matters.
- An Ottawa based think tank, the Rideau Institute is an outgrowth of Ceasefire.ca, which played an important role in convincing the government not to formally join the US-led BMD program.
- Canadian Voice of Women for Peace, World Beyond War Canada, Canadian Network to Abolish Nuclear Weapons, Canadian

Pugwash Group, Canadians for a Nuclear Weapons Convention, Peace Quest and Science for Peace are other anti-militarist organizations.
- During the last decade the Hamilton Coalition to Stop the War has been the most active city based antiwar group. The Regina Peace Council also remained active.

While generally small, volunteer-based organizations, the CF and police/intelligence agencies take peace activists seriously. They have repeatedly spied on them. The National Archives are filled with RCMP files on anti-nuclear protests and protesters.[16] As outlined in Chapter 6, from 1950 to 1983 the RCMP ran a highly secretive espionage operation and internment plan known as PROFUNC (PROminent FUNCtionaries of the Communist Party).[17] Radio-Canada's Enquête uncovered the name of a thirteen-year girl who was on the list because she attended an antinuclear protest in 1964.[18] In 2006 the CF was caught spying on a talk about the war in Afghanistan by Rideau Institute director Steven Staples.[19] Five years later the military monitored Occupy Edmonton activists after the group briefly hung a banner on a Royal Canadian Air Force monument that read: "Why make war when we can make art?"[20]

Those who campaigned against wars in Korea, Iraq, Afghanistan, etc., as well as nuclear arms and the weapons industry, have civilized the Canadian military. Alongside South Africa, Central America, Palestine, Haiti, etc. solidarity activists, they boosted internationalism and constrained how the CF fights. Compared to what took place in Korea in the early 1950s, for instance, the wars in Afghanistan and Libya were more humane. The Canadian general who oversaw the 2011 NATO bombing of Libya, Charles Bouchard, indirectly alluded to the greater constraints when he declared: "Let's not lose the hearts and minds ... I'll be damned if I have to stand up and apologize for shooting a bus load of people going to a wedding! If you're not sure, don't shoot."[21] While obviously self-serving, the statement also reflects the greater humanist pressure military commanders face.

A vast and evolving institution, the CF's operations, size and existence are determined by various social forces. Canada's military-industrial complex — armed forces, weapons manufacturers, associated thinks tanks, etc. — has a self-interest in expanding militarism. Soldiers invariably want more and better equipment as well as initiatives that enhance their cultural standing. They often seek live action. Those who profit from manufacturing weapons rarely oppose war and almost always seek increased military spending. Think tanks funded by arms companies and the CF rarely oppose militarism.

Corporate Canada backs the CF because it is a source of significant profit, reinforces hierarchy and is important to Canada's largest trading partner. The CF and military industry have tied their ship to our southern neighbour's massive military industrial complex and decision makers consider the CF a tool to garner influence with allies.[22]

Nationalism also drives support for the CF. Most believe states are supposed to have a military to protect their territorial integrity. But the US is the only nation that could realistically invade Canada and the scope of the CF's alliance with its counterparts in that country means it would be difficult for it to defend Canadian soil if US forces attacked.

Despite the commonly held view that states should have militaries, about 20 countries don't have an active military force.[23] They are mostly small Caribbean or South Pacific island nations, but the list also includes Costa Rica, Iceland and Panama. If the CF were abolished, Canada would still have a coast guard, border services agency, municipal police forces and the quasi paramilitary RCMP.

For those who would like to see the size of the CF drastically reduced or even eliminated, it won't be easy or straightforward. It will require significant political mobilization.

Polls generally find significant support for the CF and most Canadians consider the institution a source of pride. Conversely, most Canadians rank the military low among their list of political concerns. Depending on the question and moment, health care, climate change, inequality, jobs, deficit reduction and the economy generally rank higher.

Furthermore, Canadians don't support the leadership's priorities for the CF, which is supporting NATO and joining US-led wars.[24] Most Canadians want the CF to prioritize disaster relief, search and rescue, patrolling Canada's air space, land and maritime areas as well as enforcing Arctic sovereignty.[25] When it comes to international deployments, the public prefers UN peacekeeping missions to NATO wars.[26]

To build political power it's important to highlight the potential benefits of demilitarization to different constituencies. While unions with members who produce arms will seek to preserve those jobs, the broader labour movement needs to hear that public spending on schooling and day care creates far more jobs than arms purchases.[27] For those concerned with housing affordability, the $70 billion spent on naval vessels during the 2020s would cover the cost of building hundreds of thousands of public/coop housing units.

Environmental organizations must be pressured to push demilitarization. CF training damages ecosystems and spews significant GHG emissions into the atmosphere. Wars are even more ecologically damaging. Additionally, militarism is intimately tied to nation state competition, which undercuts the international cooperation needed to overcome the climate crisis. The shift away from nation-state militarism ought to be led by the states that are most powerful and that face the fewest genuine military threats. Canada is a secure and powerful country.

A multitude of small, to large scale, reforms are necessary to demilitarize. While it is essential to reduce the size of the CF, those in the CF require alternative employment and ways to contribute socially. It's important to separate the soldier/DND employee from the military. Individuals enter the force for various reasons. First of all, people need work and educational opportunities. Many young people also seek fulfillment in a team environment while others are comforted by order or believe the PR. Rejecting CF operations and culture is useful, but the same cannot be said for individuals within the institution.

About 100,000 Canadians are in the force and another 25,000 work for DND. These individuals' skills and energies are required to build a more just and sustainable world.

Deep demilitarization requires an alternative political, economic and social vision. How about training some soldiers to clean ordnance, chemicals and other waste from bases as part of advancing reconciliation with first peoples? Once properly cleared, some of the land could be returned to First Nations. The CF could return 500 or 1000 square kilometres a year of its land over a decade or two, which would still leave the CF with about half the landmass of Switzerland.

To weaken militarism, it is imperative to reduce the financial benefits sloshing around the system. Senior CF and DND officials should be restricted from lobbying for at least five years after leaving the public service and other measures ought to be adopted to weaken the link between the military hierarchy and arms firms. Restrictions on international weapons sales should be steadily expanded and an effort made to reduce Canadian companies' involvement in the US military industrial base by abrogating the Defence Production Sharing Agreement.

It is imperative to convert weapons production. Those producing arms require more socially and ecologically sustainable employment. In some instances, this may be relatively straightforward. A light armoured vehicle production line might be rejigged to assemble electric or hydrogen powered buses, for instance. But new plants and significant retraining may be required in other instances.

Ottawa should re-evaluate its military arrangements with Washington, including NORAD. Canada should pull out of NATO. If there ever was any justification for this alliance, it no longer exists. Withdrawing from NATO would dampen pressure to spend on the military and to commit acts of aggression in service of the US-led world order.

***

One part of making the world a better place is to seek out nonmilitary means to solve international and national problems. To do so we need to question and dismantle the military-industrial complex. That means ending the glorification of all things military and understanding where blind nationalism leads.

A peaceful world is possible if we want and work for it.

Bibliography

Aid, Matthew M, Cees Wiebes and Christopher Andrew, Secrets of Signals Intelligence During the Cold War and Beyond (2001)

Balawyder, Aloysius, Canadian-Soviet Relations during the World Wars (1972)

Bamford, James, The Shadow Factory: The Ultra-secret NSA from 9/11 to the Eavesdropping on America (2009)

Barri, Ted, Deadlock in Korea: Canadians at War, 1950-1953 (2010)

Beal, John Robinson, The Pearson Phenomenon (1964)

Beeching, William, Canadian Volunteers: Spain 1936-1939 (1990)

Belanger, Stephanie A H and Daniel Legace Roy, Military operations and the mind: war ethics and soldiers well-being (2016)

Bell, Ken and Desmond Morton, Royal Canadian Military Institute: 100 Years 1890-1990 (1990)

Benn, Carl, Mohawks on the Nile: Natives Among the Canadian Voyageurs in Egypt, 1884-1885 (2009)

Bercuson, David, Canada and the Soviet Experiment: Essays on Canadian Encounters with Russia and the Soviet Union, 1900-1991 (1991)

Bercuson, David and J L Granatstein, War and Peacekeeping: From South Africa to the Gulf- Canada's Limited Wars (1991)

Bercuson, David J and Jack Granatstein, Dictionary of Canadian Military History (1994)

Blum, William, Killing Hope: U.S. Military and CIA Interventions since World War II (2008)

Boer, Peter, Canadian spies and spies in Canada (2005)

Bothwell, Robert, Alliance and Illusion: Canada and the World, 1945-1984 (2008)

Boutilier, James A, The RCN in Retrospect, 1910 – 1968 (1982)

Bratt, Duane, The Politics of CANDU Exports (2006)

Bright, David & Stephen J. Randall and Graeme S. Mount, The Caribbean Basin: An International History (1998)

Bristman, Barry, In the Strategic Interests of Canada: Canadian Arms Sales to Israel and Other Middle East States, 1949-1956 (1991)

Brown, Stephen, Molly Den Heyer and David R Black, Rethinking Canadian Aid (2016)

Bryden, John, Deadly Allies: Canada's Secret War 1937 – 1947 (1989)

Burnham, Hampden, Canadians in the Imperial Naval and Military Service Abroad (2015)

Byron, Brent, Far Eastern Tour: The Canadian Infantry in Korea, 1950-1953 (2007)

Cameron, Stevie, Ottawa Inside Out: power, prestige and scandal in the nation's capital (1989)

Campbell, Isabel, Unlikely Diplomats: the Canadian brigade in Germany, 1951 – 64 (2014)

Cardwell, Curt, NSC 68 and the Political Economy of the Early Cold War (2011)

Chomsky, Noam, What Uncle Sam really wants (1992)

Chomsky, Noam, Necessary Illusions: Thought Control in Democratic Societies (1995)
Clearwater, John, Canadian Nuclear Weapons: The Untold Story of Canada's Cold War Arsenal (1998)
Clearwater, John, Just Dummies: Cruise Missile Testing in Canada (2006)
Collins, Anne, In the Sleep Room: the story of the CIA brainwashing experiments in Canada (2002)
Cook, Tim, No Place to Run: The Canadian Corps and Gas Warfare in the First World War (2000)
Cook, Tim, Clio's Warriors: Canadian Historians and the Writing of the World Wars (2007)
Cowen, Deborah, Military Workfare: The Soldier and Social Citizenship in Canada (2008)
Crosby, Ann Denholm, Dilemmas in Defence Decision-Making: constructing Canada's role in NORAD, 1958-96 (1998)
Davis, Jerome D, To the NATO Review: constancy and change in Canadian NATO policy, 1949 – 1969 (1981)
Dixon, George and G Mercer Adam, A History of Upper Canada College: 1829-1892 (1893)
Dundonald, Earl of, The Earl of Dundonald: My Army Life (1926)
Dutil, Patrice and David MacKenzie, Embattled Nation: Canada's Wartime Election of 1917 (2017)
Eayrs, James, Northern Approaches: Canada and the Search for Peace (1961)
Edgar, Alistair D and David G Haglund, The Canadian Defence Industry in the New Global Environment (1995)
Elliott, S R, Scarlet to Green: a history of intelligence in the Canadian Army 1903 – 1963 (2018)
Endicott, Stephen, and Edward Hagerman, the United States and Biological Warfare: secrets from the early Cold War and Korea (1998)
Engler, Yves, Canada in Africa: 300 Years of Aid and Exploitation (2015)
Engler, Yves, Lester Pearson's Peacekeeping: The Truth May Hurt (2012)
Fairlie, Herbert, Strange Battleground: The Operations in Korea and Their Effects on the Defence Policy of Canada (1966)
Finch, Ron, Exporting Danger: A History of the Canadian Nuclear Energy Export Programme (1996)
Forte, Maximilian C, The New Imperialism, Vol II: Interventionism, Information Warfare, and the Military-Academic Complex (2011)
Fostaty, Gerry, As you were: the tragedy at Valcartier (2011)
Frandsen, Bertram C, The Rise and Fall of Canada's Cold War Air Force, 1948-1968 (2015)
Freeman, Linda, The Ambiguous Champion: Canada and South Africa in the Trudeau and Mulroney Years (1997)
Fromow, D L, Canada's Flying Gunners: A History of the Air Observation Post of the Royal Regiment of Canadian Artillery (2004)
Frost, Mike and Michael Gratton, Spyworld: Inside the Canadian and American intelligence establishments (1994)

Gaffen, Fred, In the eye of the storm: A history of Canadian peacekeeping (1987)
Gaffen, Fred, Forgotten Soldiers (1985)
Gellner, John, Canada in NATO (2015)
Gendron, Robin S, Towards a Francophone Community: Canada's Relations with France and French Africa, 1945-1968 (2006)
German, Tony, The Sea is at Our Gates: the history of the Canadian Navy (1990)
Giangrande, Carole, The Nuclear North: the people, the regions and arms race (1983)
Gilmore, Don, I Swear by Apollo: Dr. Ewen Cameron and the CIA-brainwashing experiments (1987)
Gimblett, Richard, Operation Apollo (2004)
Gimblett, Richard H, William G P Rawling, and William Johnston, The Sea Bound Coast: The official history of The Royal Canadian Navy, 1867 – 1939, Vol 1 (2011)
Gimblett, Richard Howard, Peter T Haydon and Ann L Griffiths, Canadian Gunboat Diplomacy: the Canadian Navy and foreign-policy (2000)
Godefroy, Andrew B, In Peace Prepared: innovation and adaptation in Canada's Cold War Army (2014)
Godspeed, D J, A History of the Defence Research Board of Canada (2012)
Gonick, Cy, Inflation Or Depression: The Continuing Crisis of the Canadian Economy (1975)
Gough, Barry M, Gunboat Frontier: Britain Maritime Authority and Northwest Coast Indians, 1846-90 (1984)
Gouliquer, Lynne, Soldiering in the Canadian Forces: How and Why Gender Counts (2011)
Granatstein, J L and J M Hitsman, Broken promises: a history of conscription in Canada (1977)
Granatstein J L, Canada's Army: Waging War and Keeping the Peace (2002)
Grenier, John, The far reaches of empire: war in Nova Scotia, 1710 – 1760 (2008)
Grey, Jeffrey, The Last Word? Essays on Official History in the United States and British Commonwealth (2003)
Griffiths, Ann, The Canadian Forces and Interoperability: panacea or perdition? (2002)
Guillemin, Jeanne, Biological Weapons: from the invention of state-sponsored programs to contemporary bioterrorism (2006)
Hadekel, Peter, Silent Partners: Taxpayers and the Bankrolling of Bombardier (2004)
Hart-Landsberg, Martin, Korea: Division, Reunification, and U.S. Foreign Policy (1998)
Harrison, Deborah and Lucie Laliberté, No Life Like It: military wives in Canada (1994)
Harrison, Deborah, The First Casualty: Violence Against Women in Canadian Military Communities (2002)
Hastings, Paula Pears, Dreams of a Tropical Canada: Race, Nation, and Canadian Aspirations in the Caribbean Basin, 1883-1919 (2010)
Haydon, Peter T and Ann L Griffiths, Canada's Pacific naval presence: Purposeful or Peripheral (1999)
Hilliker, John and Mary Halloran, Diplomatic Documents and Their Users: Proceedings of the Third Conference of Editors of Diplomatic Documents, Ottawa, 11-13 (1994)

Hillmer, Norman and Jack Granatstein, Empire to Umpire: Canada and the World to the 1990s (2007)

Holt, Richard, Filling the Ranks: Manpower in the Canadian Expeditionary Force, 1914-1918 (2017)

Horn, Bern, No Ordinary Men: Special Operations Forces Missions in Afghanistan (2016)

Horn, Bern, Shadow Warriors: the Canadian Special Operations Forces Command (2016)

Horn, Bern, The Canadian Way of War: serving the national interest (2006)

Isitt, Benjamin, From Victoria to Vladivostok: Canada's Siberian expedition, 1917-1919 (2010)

James, Lawrence, The Savage Wars: British Campaigns in Africa, 1870-1920 (1986)

Jensen, Kurt, Cautious Beginnings: Canadian Foreign Intelligence, 1939-51 (2008)

Jervis, Robert and Adlai E Stevenson, The Meaning of the Nuclear Revolution: Statecraft and the Prospect of Armageddon (1990)

Jockel, Joseph T, Canada in NORAD: 1957 – 2007: a history (2007)

Jokic, Aleksandar, Lessons of Kosovo: The Dangers of Humanitarian Intervention (2003)

Kasurak, Peter, A National Force: the evolution of Canada's army, 1950 – 2000 (2014)

Kaul, Maharaj K, Amnesty International and its neo-colonial mission (2001)

Kealey, Gregory S, Spying on Canadians: The Royal Canadian Mounted Police Security Service and the Origins of the Long Cold War (2017)

Kilford, Christopher R, The Other Cold War: Canada's Military Assistance to the Developing World 1945-1975 (2010)

Kinsman, Gary and Patrizia Gentile, The Canadian War on Queers: national security as sexual regulation (2010)

Klassen, Jerome, Joining Empire: The Political Economy of the New Canadian Foreign Policy (2014)

Krieger, Heike, The Kosovo Conflict and International Law: An Analytical Documentation 1974-1999 (2014)

Lackenbauer, P Whitney, Battle Grounds: the Canadian military and aboriginal lands (2007)

Langille, Peter, Changing the guard: Canada's defence in a world in transition (1990)

Larsen, Mike and Kevin Walby, Brokering Access: Power, Politics, and Freedom of Information Process in Canada (2013)

Levant, Victor, Quiet Complicity: Canadian involvement in the Vietnam War (1986)

Levitt, Joseph Pearson and Canada's Role in Nuclear Disarmament and Arms Control Negotiations 1945-1957 (1993)

Littleton, James, Target Nation: Canada and the Western Intelligence Network (1986)

Lukacs, Martin, The Trudeau Formula: seduction and betrayal in an age of discontent (2019)

Lyon, Peyton V and Tareq Y Ismael, Canada and the Third World (1976)

MacLaren, Roy, Canadians on the Nile (1978)

MacLaren, Roy, Canadians in Russia, 1918-1919 (1976)

MacLaren, Roy, The Fundamental Things Apply: A Memoir (2011)

Madsen, Chris, Another Kind of Justice: Canadian Military Law from Confederation to Somalia (2000)

Maloney, Sean M, Canada and UN Peacekeeping: Cold War by other means, 1945-1970 (2004)

Maloney, Sean M, War with Iraq: Canada's Strategy in the Persian Gulf, 1990-2002 (2002)

McCoy, Alfred A, Question of Torture: CIA Interrogation, from the Cold War to the War on Terror (2006)

McFarlane, Peter, Northern Shadows: Canadians and Central America (1989)

McKay, Ian and Jamie Swift, Warrior Nation: rebranding Canada in an age of anxiety (2012)

McKay, Ian and Jamie Swift, The Vimy Trap: Or, How We Learned to Stop Worrying and Love the Great War (2016)

McQuaig, Linda, Holding the Bully's Coat: Canada and the U.S. Empire (2007)

Mentan, Tatah, The New World Order Ideology and Africa: Understanding and Appreciating Ambiguity, Deceit and Recapture of Decolonized Spaces (2010)

Miller, Judith, Stephen Engelberg and William J Broad, Germs: Biological Weapons and America's secret war (2002)

Miller, Carman, Painting the Map Red: Canada and the South African War, 1899-1902 (1998)

Miller, Duncan and Sharon Hobson, The Persian Excursion: the Canadian Navy and the Gulf War (1995)

Millman, Brock, Polarity, Patriotism, and Dissent in Great War Canada, 1914-1919 (2016)

Milner, Marc, Canada's Navy: the first century (2010)

Monaghan, Jeffrey, Security Aid: Canada and the Development Regime of Security (2017)

Morisset Denis, We were invincible: Testimony of an Ex-Commando (2008)

Morton, Desmond and Glenn Wright, Winning the Second Battle: Canadian Veterans and the Return to Civilian Life (1987)

Morton, Desmond, The Canadian General: Sir William Otter (1974)

Morton, Desmond, Ministers and Generals: Politics and the Canadian militia 1868 – 1904 (1970)

Nadler, John, A Perfect Hell: the forgotten story of the Canadian commandos of the second world war (2006)

Nash, Eve Mills and Kenneth J Harvey, Little White Squaw: A White Woman's Story of Abuse, Addiction, and Reconciliation (2002)

Nash, Knowlton, The Microphone Wars: A History of Triumph and Betrayal at the CBC (1995)

Neary, Peter and J L Granatstein, The Veterans Charter and post-World War II Canada (1997)

Nicholson, G W L, Canadian Expeditionary Force, 1914-1919: Official History of the Canadian Army in the First World War (2015)

Norris, John, Collision Course: NATO, Russia, and Kosovo (2005)

Paul, Daniel N, We Were Not the Savages: A Mi'kmaq Perspective on the Collision Between European and Native American Civilizations (2007)

Paxman, Jeremy and Robert Harris, A Higher Form of Killing: The Secret History of Chemical and Biological Warfare (2002)

Pearson, Lester B, Mike: The Memoirs of the Rt. Hon. Lester B. Pearson, Vol 2: 1948-1957 (1972)

Petrou, Michael, Renegades: Canadians in the Spanish Civil War (2008)

Pickler, Ron and Larry Milberry, Canadair: the first 50 years (1995)

Pile, Tyrone, Beyond the Workable Little Fleet: post-war planning and policy in the RCN 1945 – 1948 (1998)

Pigott, Peter, Canada in Sudan: War Without Borders (2009)

Podmore, Will, British Foreign Policy since 1870 (2008)

Preston, Richard A, Canada and Imperial Defense: a study of the origins of the British Commonwealth's defense organization, 1867 – 1919 (1967)

Preston, Richard Arthur, Canada's RMC: A history of the Royal Military College (1970)

Price, John, Orienting Canada: Race, Empire, and the Transpacific (2011)

Pugliese, David, Canada's Secret Commandos: the unauthorized story of joint task force two (2002)

Pugliese David, Shadow Wars: Special Forces in the New Battle Against Terrorism (2003)

Razack, Sherene, Dark Threats and White Knights: The Somalia Affair, Peacekeeping, and the New Imperialism (2004)

Regehr, Ernie, Arms Canada: The Deadly Business of Military Exports (1987)

Regehr, Ernie and Simon Rosenblum, The Road to Peace (1988)

Regehr, Ernie, Making a Killing: Canada's arms industry (1975)

Reid, Escott, Radical Mandarin: The Memoirs of Escott Reid (1989)

Richelson, Jeffrey T and Desmond Ball, The Ties That Bind: intelligence cooperation between the UKUSA countries – United Kingdom, the United States of America, Canada, Australia and New Zealand (1990)

Richter, Andrew, Avoiding Armageddon: Canadian military strategy and nuclear weapons, 1950–63 (2003)

Ridler, Jason S, Maestro of Science: Omond McKillop Solandt and Government Science in War and Hostile Peace, 1939-1956 (2015)

Roche, Douglas, A Bargain for Humanity: global security by 2000 (1993)

Roger, Sarty, The Maritime Defence of Canada (1996)

Roussopoulos, Dimitrios, Our Generation Against Nuclear War (1983)

Russell, Peter A, How agriculture made Canada: Farming in the Nineteenth Century (2012)

Scharfe, Sharon, Complicity: Human Rights and Canadian Foreign Policy (1996)

Schlegel, John P, The Deceptive Ash: Bilingualism and Canadian Policy in Africa—1957-1971 (1978)

Schoenhals, Kai and Richard Melanson, Revolution and intervention in Grenada: The New Jewel Movement, the United States, and the Caribbean (1986)

Schwartz, Mallory, War on the Air: CBC-TV and Canada's Military, 1952-1992 (2014)

Simpson, Erika, NATO and the Bomb: Canadian defenders confront critics (2002)

Skaarup, Harold A, An Intelligence Advantage: Collective Security Benefits gained by Canada through the sharing of Military Intelligence with the United States of America (1997)

Skaarup, Harold A, Out of Darkness - Light, A History of Canadian Military Intelligence (2005)

Smith, Keith Douglas, Liberalism, Surveillance, and Resistance: Indigenous Communities in Western (2009)

Souare, Issaka K, Africa in the United Nations System: 1945-2005 (2006)

Smith, Susan L, Toxic Exposures: Mustard Gas and the Health Consequences of World War II in the United States (2017)

Spence, Daniel Owen, A History of the Royal Navy: Empire and Imperialism (2016)

Spooner, Kevin A, Canada, the Congo Crisis, and UN Peacekeeping (2010)

Stairs, Denis The Diplomacy of Constraint: Canada, the Korean War, and the United States (1974)

Starnes, John, Closely Guarded: A Life in Canadian Security and Intelligence (2001)

Stein, Janice Gross and Eugene Lang, The Unexpected War: Canada in Kandahar (2008)

Stone, Craig, The Public Management of Defence in Canada (2009)

Stone, I F, The Hidden History of the Korean War (1988)

Stouffer, Ray, Swords, Clunks and Windowmakers: the tumultuous life of the RCAF's original one Canadian air division (2015)

Stursberg, Peter, Lester Person and the American Dilemma (1980)

Sullivan, H and Larry Milberry, Power: The Pratt and Whitney Canada Story (1989)

Tabe, Nancy, Gendered Militarism in Canada: Learning Conformity and Resistance (2015)

Tamblyn, D S, The Horse in War: Horses & Mules in the Allied Armies During the First World War, 1914-18 (2011)

Taylor, Alastair MacDonald, David Cox and J L Granatstein, Peacekeeping: international challenge and Canadian response (1968)

Taylor, Charles, Snow Job: Canada, the United States and Vietnam (1954 to 1973) (1974)

Taylor, Scott, Unembedded: Two Decades of Maverick War Reporting (2009)

Taylor, Scott and Brian Nolan, Tested Mettle: Canada's Peacekeepers at War (1998)

Taylor, Scott, Diary of an Uncivil War: The Violent Aftermath of the Kosovo Conflict (2002)

Taylor, Scott, Inat: Images of Serbia & the Kosovo Conflict (2000)

Tennyson, Brian Douglas, Canada and the Commonwealth Caribbean (1988)

Thorgrimsson, Thor and E C Russell, Canadian Naval Operations in Korean Waters 1950-1955 (1965)

Tracy, Nicholas, Two-Edged Sword: The Navy as an Instrument of Canadian Foreign Policy (2012)

Tucker, Jonathan B, War of Nerves: chemical warfare from World War I to Al Qaeda (2007)

Tucker, Michael, Canadian Foreign Policy: Contemporary Issues and Themes (1980)

Tulchinsky, Gerald J J, Taking Root: The Origins of the Canadian Jewish Community (1993)

Vance, Jonathan F, Death so Noble: Memory, Meaning, and the First World War (1999)

Villafana, Frank R, Cold War in the Congo: The Confrontation of Cuban Military Forces, 1960-1967 (2012)

Wakelam, Randall, Cold War Fighters: Canadian aircraft procurement, 1945 – 54 (2012)

Walton, Richard J, Canada and the U.S.A.: A Background Book about Internal Conflict and the New Nationalism (1972)

Wheelis, Mark and Lajos Rózs, Deadly Cultures: Biological Weapons since 1945 (2006)

Whitaker, Reg and Steve Hewitt, Cold War Canada: The Making of a National Insecurity State, 1945-1957 (2003)

Williams, Susan A, Who killed Hammarskjold: The UN, the Cold War and White Supremacy in Africa (2011)

Wilson, Gordon A, NORAD and the Soviet Nuclear Threat: Canada's Secret Electronic Air War (2012)

Winegard, Timothy C, For King and Kanata: Canadian Indians and the First World War (2012)

Winter, James, Media Think (2005)

Winter, James, Common Cents: Media Portrayal of the Gulf War and Other Events (1992)

Wise, Sydney F, Canadian airmen and the first world war: The Official History of the Royal Canadian Volume I Air F (1980)

Wiss, Ray, A Line in the Sand: Canadians at War in Kandahar (2011)

Zimmerman, David, Maritime Command Pacific: The Royal Canadian Navy's West Coast fleet in the early Cold War (2016)

Notes

Introduction
1. Isabel Campbell, Unlikely Diplomats: the Canadian brigade in Germany, 1951-64, 21
2. Craig Stone, The Public Management of Defence in Canada, 11
3. James Bagnall, Pentagon North vs. The Pentagon: A tale of the military tape, Ottawa Citizen, Sep 30 2016
4. Ibid
5. Strong, Secure, Engaged. Canada's Defence Policy (http://dgpaapp.forces.gc.ca/en/canada-defence-policy/docs/canada-defence-policy-report.pdf)
6. P Whitney Lackenbauer, Battle Grounds: the Canadian military and aboriginal lands, 3
7. List of current ships of the Royal Canadian Navy (https://en.wikipedia.org/wiki/List_of_current_ships_of_the_Royal_Canadian_Navy)
8. List of active Canadian military aircraft (https://en.wikipedia.org/wiki/List_of_active_Canadian_military_aircraft) ; Philip J Anido, Environmental Stewardship on Canadian Military Training Areas, A thesis submitted to the Faculty of Graduate Studies and Research in Partial fulfillment of the requirements for the degree of Master of Arts, Department of Geography Carleton University, Sept 1998 (http://www.collectionscanada.gc.ca/obj/s4/f2/dsk2/tape17/PQDD_0017/MQ36808.pdf)
9. CSPC 2017, Dr. Marc Fortin (https://cspc2017.sched.com/speaker/dr.marcfortin) ; Defence Research and Development Canada (https://en.wikipedia.org/wiki/Defence_Research_and_Development_Canada)
10. Bruce Campion Smith, Politicians urge greater oversight of military intelligence operations, Toronto Star, Apr 9 2019 ; Jim Bronskill, Communications Security Establishment Canada: Super-Secretive $400M Eavesdropping Agency Gets A Little Quieter, Sept 24 2012 (http://www.huffingtonpost.ca/2012/07/25/communications-security-establishment-canada_n_1703703.html)
11. Overview of the Military Police (https://www.mpcc-cppm.gc.ca/01/100/140-eng.aspx)
12. Gloria Galloway, Veterans Affairs shed staff despite increased mental-health risks, Dec 2 2014 (https://www.theglobeandmail.com/news/politics/veterans-affairs-shed-staff-despite-increased-mental-health-risks/article21897819/)
13. 2.0 Departmental Spending (https://www.veterans.gc.ca/eng/about-vac/news-media/facts-figures/2-0)
14. Departmental Plan 2018 to 2019 report, Environment and Climate Change Canada, chapter 4 (https://www.canada.ca/en/environment-climate-change/corporate/transparency/priorities-management/departmental-plans/2018-2019/spending-human-resources.html#c4-1)
15. Paul Heinbecker, Canada's forward defence in the world: Why Ottawa should learn to love the Department of Foreign Affairs, Globe and Mail, Sept 3 2007 (https://www.cigionline.org/articles/canadas-forward-defence-world-why-ottawa-should-learn-love-department-foreign-affairs)
16. Matthew Behrens, Bombs away! How Canada is here to help, Sept 23 2016 (https://rabble.ca/columnists/2016/09/bombs-away-how-canada-here-to-help) ; Thomas Juneau, Canadian Defence Policy in Theory and Practice, 141 ; Alistair D Edgar and David G Haglund, the Canadian Defence Industry in the New Global Environment, preface
17. 150 Years of Canadian National Defence Spending (https://worthwhile.typepad.com/worthwhile_canadian_initi/2017/06/150-years-of-canadian-national-defence-spending.html)
18. Ibid
19. SIPRI Fact Sheet, Trends in World Military Expenditure, 2020, April 2021 (https://sipri.org/sites/default/files/2021-04/fs_2104_milex_0.pdf)
20. Douglas Roche, A Bargain for Humanity: global security by 2000, 62
21. Tamara Lorincz, NATO is the enemy when it comes to fighting climate change, Dec 6 2019 (https://www.saltwire.com/nova-scotia/opinion/local-perspectives/tamara-lorincz-nato-is-the-enemy-when-it-comes-to-fighting-climate-change-385022/)
22. Christian Leuprecht and Joel Sokolsky, Canada's Enhance Forward Presence in the Baltics: An Enduring Commitment to Transatlantic Security, 2016 (http://post.queensu.ca/~leuprech/docs/chapters/Leuprecht_Sokolsky_2016_Canada%20Enhance%20Forward_NATO%20From%20Warsaw.pdf)
23. World military spending rises to almost $2 trillion in 2020, SIPRI, Apr 26 2021 (https://www.sipri.org/media/press-release/2021/world-military-spending-rises-almost-2-trillion-2020#:~:text=(Stockholm%2C%2026%20April%202021),Peace%20Research%20Institute%20(SIPRI).)
24. Troops ready, eager for new overseas missions: Natynczyk, Canadian Press, July 7 2012 (https://www.ctvnews.ca/canada/troops-ready-eager-for-new-overseas-missions-natynczyk-1.869823)
25. Stephen Cook, 'We're going to be warfighters': New commander takes over 3rd Battalion, Princess Patricia's Canadian Light Infantry, Jun 13 2018 (https://edmontonjournal.com/news/local-news/were-going-to-be-warfighters-new-commander-takes-over-3rd-battalion-princess-patricias-canadian-light-infantry)
26. Bern Horn, The Canadian Way of War: serving the national interest, 15
27. Richard H Gimblett, Gunboat diplomacy, mutiny and national identity in the postwar Royal Canadian Navy: the cruise of HMCS Crescent to China, 1949, Thèse présentée à la Faculté des études supérieures de l'université Laval pour l'obtention du grade de Philosophiae Doctor, 2000 (https://www.collectionscanada.gc.ca/obj/s4/f2/dsk2/ftp03/NQ48979.pdf)
28. Christie Blatchford, Jury acquits Hamilton homeowner Peter Khill of murder in shooting of Indigenous man, Jun 27 2018 (https://nationalpost.com/news/canada/hamilton-area-homeowner-peter-khill-found-not-guilty-of-second-degree-murder)
29. Ibid

Chapter 1
1. John Grenier, The far reaches of empire: war in Nova Scotia, 1710-1760, 60 ; Daniel N Paul, We Were Not the Savages: A Mi'kmaq Perspective on the Collision Between European and Native American Civilizations, 158
2. Ibid, 122
3. John Grenier, The Far Reaches of Empire: war in Nova Scotia, 1710-1760, 211
4. Expulsion of the Acadians (https://en.wikipedia.org/wiki/Expulsion_of_the_Acadians)
5. Ibid
6. Jordan Gill, 'Extirpate this execrable race': The dark history of Jeffery Amherst, Apr 29 2017 (https://www.cbc.ca/news/canada/prince-edward-island/jeffery-amherst-

history-complex-1.4089019)
7. Dan Conlin, A Private War in the Caribbean: Nova Scotia Privateering, 1793-1805 (www.cnrsscrn.org/northern_mariner/vol06/tnm_6_4_29-46.pdf) ; Julian Gwyn, Frigates and Foremasts: The North American Squadron in Nova Scotia Waters 1745-1815, 102
8. Bern Horn, The Canadian Way of War: serving the national interest, 112
9. Mitch Abidor, The Patriotes Rebellion (https://www.marxists.org/history/canada/quebec/patriotes-rebellion/introduction.htm)
10. Ruth Bleasdale, Class Conflict on the Canals of Upper Canada in the 1840s, Labour/Le Travailleur, Vol 7, 1981
11. John Kalbfleisch, From the archives: Labourers' struggle ended in bloodshed Montreal Gazette, June 14 2017
12. Ruth Bleasdale, Class Conflict on the Canals of Upper Canada in the 1840s, Labour/Le Travailleur, Vol 7, 1981
13. C P Champion: How the Crimean War of 1853 helped shaped the Canada of today, Oct 28 2014 (https://nationalpost.com/opinion/c-p-champion-how-the-crimean-war-of-1853-helped-shaped-the-canada-of-today)
14. Hampden Burnham, Canadians in the Imperial Naval and Military Service Abroad, 14
15. Ibid, 44– 45
16. William Hall (VC) (https://en.wikipedia.org/wiki/William_Hall_(VC)#:~:text=William%20Nelson%20Edward%20Hall%20VC,Lucknow%20during%20the%20Indian%20Rebellion.)
17. Hampden Burnham, Canadians in the Imperial Naval and Military Service Abroad, 36
18. Barry M Gough, Gunboat Frontier: Britain Maritime Authority and Northwest Coast Indians, 1846-90, 83
19. Ibid, 76
20. 1862 Pacific Northwest smallpox epidemic (https://en.wikipedia.org/wiki/1862_Pacific_Northwest_smallpox_epidemic) ; Greg Lange, Smallpox Epidemic of 1862 among Northwest Coast and Puget Sound Indians, 2003 (https://www.historylink.org/File/5171)
21. Barry M Gough, Gunboat Frontier: British Maritime Authority and Northwest Coast Indians, 1846-1890, 66
22. Ibid, 55
23. Daniel Owen Spence, A History of the Royal Navy: Empire and Imperialism, 58
24. Barry M Gough, Gunboat Frontier, 119
25. Ibid, 121
26. Ibid, 83
27. Ibid
28. Ibid, 194
29. Ibid, 195
30. R M Galois The Burning of Kitsegukla, 1872 (http://www.gitsegukla.net/wp-content/uploads/2019/05/1428-Article-Text-5896-1-10-20100513-2.pdf)
31. Desmond Morton, Ministers and Generals: Politics and the Canadian militia 1868-1904, 31
32. Richard Luard (https://en.wikipedia.org/wiki/Richard_Luard) ; Edward Hutton (British Army officer) (https://en.wikipedia.org/wiki/Edward_Hutton_(British_Army_officer))
33. HUTTON, Sir EDWARD THOMAS HENRY (www.biographi.ca/en/bio/hutton_edward_thomas_henry_15E.html)
34. David J Bercuson and Jack Granatstein, Dictionary of Canadian Military History, 112
35. Major-General Sir Percy Henry Noel Lake, KCB, KCMG Chief of the General Staff — Canadian Army 1904 to 1908 (https://www.blatherwick.net/documents/Commanders%20Canadian%20Army/1904%20to%201908%20MGen%20Sir%20Percy%20Lake.pdf)
36. William D. Otter (https://www.britannica.com/biography/William-D-Otter)
37. Richard A Preston, Canada and Imperial Defense: a study of the origins of the British Commonwealth's defense organization, 1867-1919, 410
38. Andrew B Godefroy, Canadian Soldiers in West African Conflicts 1885-1905 (https://rmcmuseum.ca/wp-content/uploads/CMH-Article-Canadian-Soldiers-in-West-Africa.pdf)
39. Ibid
40. Richard Arthur Preston, Canada's RMC: A history of the Royal Military College, 170
41. Canada & The South African War, 1899-1902 (https://www.warmuseum.ca/cwm/exhibitions/boer/strathconahorse_e.html)
42. Desmond Morton, Ministers and Generals: Politics and the Canadian militia 1868-1904, 154
43. Canadians in South Africa (www.cmhg.gc.ca/cmh-pmc/page-577-eng.aspx)
44. Bern Horn, The Canadian Way of War: serving the national interest, 106-109
45. James A Boutilier, The RCN in Retrospect, 1910-1968, 64
46. Glenn B Foulds and Jonathan Scotland, Royal Flying Corps (https://www.thecanadianencyclopedia.ca/en/article/royal-flying-corps)
47. Jerome D Davis, To the NATO Review: constancy and change in Canadian NATO policy, 1949-1969, 7
48. Peter Kasurak, A National Force: the evolution of Canada's army, 1950-2000, 3
49. Andrew B Godefroy, In Peace Prepared: innovation and adaptation in Canada's Cold War Army, 20
50. Peter Kasurak, A National Force: the evolution of Canada's army, 1950-2000, 3/14 ; Richard A Preston, Canada and Imperial Defense: a study of the origins of the British Commonwealth's defense organization, 1867-1919, 378
51. Peter Charles Kasurak, A National Force: The Evolution of Canada's Army, 1950-2000, 14
52. Ibid, 3
53. Bern Horn, The Canadian Way of War: serving the national interest, 208
54. Ibid, 208

Chapter 2

1. Bern Horn, The Canadian Way of War: serving the national interest, 119; Bob Beal, Red River Expedition (https://www.thecanadianencyclopedia.ca/en/article/red-river-expedition)
2. Bernd Horn, the Canadian Way of War, 118
3. North-West Mounted Police (https://www.thecanadianencyclopedia.ca/en/article/north-west-mounted-police)
4. Gregory S Kealey, Spying on Canadians: The Royal Canadian Mounted Police Security Service and the Origins of the Long Cold War, 224 ; Fadi Saleem Ennab, Rupturing the Myth of the Peaceful Western Canadian Frontier: A Socio-Historical Study of Colonization, Violence, and the North West Mounted Police, 1873-1905, A Thesis submitted to the Faculty of Graduate Studies of The University of Manitoba in partial fulfilment of the requirements of the degree of (https://mspace.lib.umanitoba.ca/xmlui/bitstream/handle/1993/4109/Ennab_Fadi.pdf?sequence=1&isAllowed=y)

5. Bern Horn, The Canadian Way of War: serving the national interest, 128
6. Richard Sanders, From Sir William Otter, to the NDP and the Waffle, Coalition to Oppose the Arms Trade (https://rabble.ca/babble/news-rest-us/captive-canada-empire-and-sons-sir-william-otter-to-ndp-and-waffle) ; Canadian Plains Research Center, 1885 and After: Native Society in Transition, 163
7. Otter, Sir William Dillon (www.biographi.ca/en/bio.php?BioId=41981)
8. Keith Douglas Smith, Liberalism, Surveillance, and Resistance: Indigenous Communities in Western, 63
9. Ibid
10. Ibid, 104
11. Glenn T Wright, Veterans' Land Act (https://www.thecanadianencyclopedia.ca/en/article/veterans-land-act)
12. Desmond Morton and Glenn Wright, Winning the Second Battle: Canadian Veterans and the Return to Civilian Life, 100
13. Robert England, Disbanded and Discharged Soldiers in Canada Prior to 1914, Canadian Historical Review, Vol 27 N 1, March 1946
14. Ibid
15. Desmond Morton and Glenn Wright, Winning the Second Battle: Canadian Veterans and the Return to Civilian Life, 10
16. John Grenier, The Far Reaches of Empire: war in Nova Scotia, 1710-1760, 173
17. lfeesey, The United Empire Loyalists Come to Upper Canada, June 10 2018 (https://torontopubliclibrary.typepad.com/local-history-genealogy/2018/06/the-united-empire-loyalists-settle-in-upper-canada-.html)
18. Desmond Morton and Glenn Wright, Winning the Second Battle: Canadian Veterans and the Return to Civilian Life, 10 ; Robert England, Disbanded and Discharged Soldiers in Canada Prior to 1914, Canadian Historical Review, Vol 27, N 1, March 1946
19. George Raudzens, A Successful Military Settlement: Earl Grey's Enrolled Pensioners of 1846 in Canada, Canadian Historical Review, Vol LIT, N 4, 1971 ; Durie, William Smith (http://www.biographi.ca/en/bio/durie_william_smith_11E.html)
20. George K Raudzens, A Successful Military Settlement: Earl Grey's Enrolled Pensioners of 1846 in Canada, Canadian Historical Review, Vol 52, No 4, Dec 1971
21. Ibid
22. C P Champion, How the Crimean War of 1853 helped shaped the Canada of today, Oct 28 2014 (https://nationalpost.com/opinion/c-p-champion-how-the-crimean-war-of-1853-helped-shaped-the-canada-of-today)
23. James H Marsh, The Canadian Encyclopedia, 1999, 2476 ; Robert England, Disbanded and Discharged Soldiers in Canada Prior to 1914, Canadian Historical Review, Vol 27, No 1, March 1946
24. History and Background: The Administration of Land in Saskatchewan (https://www.saskarchives.com/collections/land-records/history-and-background-administration-land-saskatchewan)
25. Desmond Morton and Glenn Wright, Winning the Second Battle, 100
26. James Murton in Creating a Modern Countryside: Liberalism and Land Resettlement in British Columbia, 61
27. Kent Fedorowich, The Migration of British Ex-Servicemen to Canada and the Role of the Naval and Military Emigration League, 1899-1914 (https://hssh.journals.yorku.ca/index.php/hssh/article/viewFile/16700/15558)
28. Desmond Morton and Glenn Wright, Winning the Second Battle, 100
29. Kent Fedorowich, The Migration of British Ex-Servicemen to Canada and the Role of the Naval and Military Emigration League, 1899-1914 (https://hssh.journals.yorku.ca/index.php/hssh/article/viewFile/16700/15558)
30. Glenn T Wright, Veterans' Land Act (https://www.thecanadianencyclopedia.ca/en/article/veterans-land-act)
31. Timothy Charles Winegard, For King and Kanata: Canadian Indians and the First World War, 155
32. E C Morgan, Soldier Settlement in the Prairie Provinces, Saskatchewan History 11, No 2, 1968 ; Tim Cook, A Many-Layered Legacy, Canada's History, Oct 2018
33. Sarah Carter, Prairie Indian Reserve Land and Soldier Settlement after World War I, Manitoba History Journal, No 37, Spring 1999 (http://www.mhs.mb.ca/docs/mb_history/37/infamousproposal.shtml#029)
34. Ibid
35. Ibid
36. Peter a Russell, How agriculture made Canada, 364 ; Laura Kane, First Nations in Peace River region win battle over 65-year-old error, Canadian Press, Nov 12 2015 (https://globalnews.ca/news/2333958/first-nations-in-peace-river-region-win-battle-over-65-year-old-error/)
37. P Whitney Lackenbauer, Battle Grounds: The Canadian Military and Aboriginal Lands
38. James Brooke, Tsuu T'ina Journal; Indians Stalk a Silent, Deadly Enemy in the Prairie, New York Times, June 19 2000
39. Barry M Gough, Gunboat Frontier British Maritime Authority and Northwest Coast Indians, 1846-1890, 24
40. Keith D Smith, Liberalism, Surveillance, and Resistance Indigenous Communities in Western Canada, 1877-1927, 223
41. P Whitney Lackenbauer, Battle Grounds: the Canadian military and aboriginal lands, 242 ; Eve Mills Nash and Kenneth J Harvey, Little White Squaw: A White Woman's Story of Abuse, Addiction, and Reconciliation, 118
42. Carole Giangrande, The Nuclear North: the people, the regions and arms race, 47-49 ; Primrose Lake Air Weapons Range Report. Cold Lake First Nations Rejected Claim Inquiry. Canoe Lake Cree Nation Rejected Claim Inquiry, Aug 17 1993 (publications.gc.ca/collections/collection_2009/indianclaims/RC31-82-1-1993E.pdf)
43. Ibid
44. P Whitney Lackenbauer, Battle Grounds: the Canadian military and aboriginal lands, 166/171 ; Primrose Lake Air Weapons Range Report. Cold Lake First Nations Rejected Claim Inquiry. Canoe Lake Cree Nation Rejected Claim Inquiry. Aug 17 1993 (publications.gc.ca/collections/collection_2009/indianclaims/RC31-82-1-1993E.pdf)
45. Ibid
46. P Whitney Lackenbauer, Battle Grounds: the Canadian military and aboriginal lands, 78
47. Helen Roos, It Happened as if Overnight: The Expropriation and Relocation of Stoney Point Reserve #43, 1942, Submitted in partial fulfillment of the requirements for the degree of Master of Arts, Faculty of Graduate Studies The University of Western Ontario, May 1998, 52 (https://www.collectionscanada.gc.ca/obj/s4/f2/dsk2/tape17/PQDD_0006/MQ39904.pdf)
48. Ibid
49. Terry Bridge, Feds' 1942 land expropriation dispute resolved with land's return and $95-million payment to Chippewas of Kettle and Stony Point First Nation, April 14 2016 (https://lfpress.com/2016/04/14/feds-1942-land-expropriation-dispute-resolved-with-lands-return-

and-95-million-payment-to-chippewas-of-kettle-and-stony-point-first-nation/wcm/e1e2586b-02d8-42cf-90f7-0b456001a09b)
50. Catherine Griwkowsky, Live bombs found under Enoch golf course, Apr 15 2014 (https://edmontonsun.com/2014/04/15/live-bombs-found-under-enoch-golf-course-feds-had-denied-they-were-there/wcm/0ec7cc41-418a-42c3-8656-e8b18b3e6a76)
51. Ibid
52. Ken MacQueen, Why unexploded bombs are an expensive—and dangerous—problem, Jan 4 2016 (https://www.macleans.ca/news/canada/why-unexploded-bombs-are-an-expensive-and-dangerous-problem/)
53. John Colebourn, Okanagan band files lawsuit against Feds for failing to remove live munitions from reserve land, Oct 5 2016 (https://vancouversun.com/news/local-news/okanagan-band-files-lawsuit-against-feds-for-failing-to-remove-live-munitions-from-reserve-land)
54. Ken MacQueen, Why unexploded bombs are an expensive—and dangerous—problem, Jan 4 2016 (https://www.macleans.ca/news/canada/why-unexploded-bombs-are-an-expensive-and-dangerous-problem/)
55. Keith D Smith, Liberalism, Surveillance, and Resistance: Indigenous Communities in Western, 203
56. James Brooke, Tsuu T'ina Journal; Indians Stalk a Silent, Deadly Enemy in the Prairie, June 19 2000 (https://www.nytimes.com/2000/06/19/world/tsuu-t-ina-journal-indians-stalk-a-silent-deadly-enemy-in-the-prairie.html)

Chapter 3

1. Bern Horn, The Canadian Way of War: serving the national interest, 118
2. Don Macgillivray, Military Aid to the Civil Power: The Cape Breton Experience in the 1920's, Acadiensis Spring 1974
3. Mike O'Brien, Manhood and the Militia Myth, Labour/Le Travail, Vol 42, Fall 1998
4. J J B Pariseau, Disorders, Strikes and Disasters: military aid to civil power in Canada, 1867-1933, 54-6 (http://www.biographi.ca/en/bio/durie_william_smith_11E.html) ; Desmond Morton, French Canada and the Canadian Militia,1868-1914 ; Richard A Preston, Canada and Imperial Defense: a study of the origins of the British Commonwealth's defense organization, 1867-1919, 126
5. Harry Keith Ralston, 1900 strike of Fraser River sockeye salmon fishermen, University of British Columbia Masters Thesis, 1965 (https://open.library.ubc.ca/cIRcle/collections/ubctheses/831/items/1.0105476)
6. Mike O'Brien, Manhood and the Militia Myth, Labour/Le Travail, Vol 42, Fall 1998
7. Desmond Morton, Aid to the civil power: the Canadian militia in support of social order, 1867-1914, Canadian Historical Review, Dec 1970
8. Ibid
9. Peter Silverman, The militia and the coal miners' strike, July 25 2016 (https://legionmagazine.com/en/2016/07/the-militia-and-the-coal-miners-strike/) ; Esther Sharp, The Great War and the Homefront, British Columbia History, Fall 2008
10. Mike O'Brien, Manhood and the Militia Myth: Masculinity, Class and Militarism in Ontario, 1902-1914, Labour/Le Travail, Vol 42, Fall 1998
11. David Bercuson and J L Granatstein, Dictionary of Canadian Military History, 2
12. Desmond Morton, Ministers and Generals: Politics and the Canadian Militia, 1868-1904, 176
13. Don Macgillivray, Military Aid to the Civil Power: The Cape Breton Experience in the 1920's, Acadiensis, Spring 1974
14. S R Elliott, Scarlet to Green: a history of intelligence in the Canadian Army 1903-1963, 54
15. Benjamin Isitt, From Victoria to Vladivostok: Canada's Siberian expedition, 1917-1919, 69
16. J J B Pariseau, Disorders, Strikes and Disasters: military aid to civil power in Canada, 1867-1933, 28
17. J L Granatstein, Canada's Army: Waging War and Keeping the Peace, 156
18. Don Macgillivray, Military Aid to the Civil Power: The Cape Breton Experience in the 1920's, Acadiensis, Spring 1974
19. Ibid
20. Ibid
21. Ibid
22. Ibid
23. Ibid
24. Ibid
25. Ibid
26. Ibid
27. Ibid
28. Ibid
29. J J B Pariseau, Disorders, Strikes and Disasters: military aid to civil power in Canada, 1867-1933, 121
30. David J Bercuson and Jack Granatstein, Dictionary of Canadian Military History, 130
31. Unemployment Relief Camps (https://www.thecanadianencyclopedia.ca/en/article/unemployment-relief-camps)
32. S R Elliott, Scarlet to Green: a history of intelligence in the Canadian Army 1903-1963, 484
33. Patricia E Roy, Internment in Canada Article (https://www.thecanadianencyclopedia.ca/en/article/internment)
34. David Zimmerman, Maritime Command Pacific: the Royal Canadian Navy's West Coast fleet in the early Cold War, 69
35. Ibid, 51/68
36. Richard H Gimblett, What The Mainguy Report Never Told Us: The Tradition of "Mutiny" in the Royal Canadian Navy Before 1949, Canadian Military Journal, Summer 2000
37. James A Boutilier, The RCN in Retrospect, 1910-1968, 238
38. Sean M Maloney, Domestic Operations: The Canadian Approach, Parameters, Autumn 1997 (www.seanmmaloney.com/wp-content/uploads/2016/02/Parameters-US-Army-War-College-Quarterly-Autumn-1997.pdf); Desmond Morton, Aid to the civil power: the Canadian militia in support of social order, 1867-1914, Canadian Historical Review
39. Jacques Castonguay, Les opérations de l'armée et la crise d'Octobre, 110
40. Ibid, 73/81
41. Ibid, 91/94
42. J J B Pariseau, Disorders, Strikes and Disasters: military aid to civil power in Canada, 1867-1933, 123
43. Dominique Clément, The October Crisis of 1970: Human Rights Abuses Under the War Measures Act (https://historyofrights.ca/wp-content/uploads/pubs/article_JCS.pdf) ; Claude Bélanger, Chronology of the October Crisis, 1970, and its Aftermath (faculty.marianopolis.edu/c.belanger/quebechistory/chronos/october.htm)
44. Sean M Maloney, Domestic Operations: The Canadian

Approach, Parameters 27, 1997
45. The October Crisis: Canada's new Liberalism has a baptism by fire, Hamilton Spectator, Oct 4 2010 (https://www.flamboroughreview.com/opinion-story/2172515-the-october-crisis-canada-s-new-liberalism-has-a-baptism-by-fire-/)
46. Quebec invasion plans leaked to PQ in 1972, Apr 6 2002 (https://www.theglobeandmail.com/news/national/quebec-invasion-plans-leaked-to-pq-in-1972/article25294409/)
47. Pierre Dubuc, L'armée dépoussière ses plans d'intervention au Québec, Sept 11 2012 (https://lautjournal.info/20120911/l'armée-dépoussière-ses-plans-d'intervention-au-québec)
48. Michael Brun, Operation Gamescan 76 (https://www.nfb.ca/film/operation_gamescan_76/)
49. Tim Cook, A Many-Layered Legacy, Canada's History, Oct 2018
50. Kevin Plummer, Sleighing Soldiers: The Toronto Tandem Club, The Newsletter of The Friends of Fort York and Garrison Common, V 16, N 5, Dec 2012 (https://www.fortyork.ca/images/newsletters/fife-and-drum-2012/fife-and-drum-dec-2012.pdf) ; James McGill Strachan (https://en.wikipedia.org/wiki/James_McGill_Strachan)
51. Bob Gordon, Canada's First VC Recipient, Vol 25-1, May 18 2018 (espritdecorps.ca/in-the-news/canadas-first-vc-recipient-alexander-dunn-at-the-charge-of-the-light-brigade-balaclava-1854)
52. Mike O'Brien, Manhood and the Militia Myth: Masculinity, Class and Militarism in Ontario, 1902-1914, Labour/Le Travail Vol 42 Fall 1998
53. Carman Miller, The Montreal Militia as a Social Institution Before World War Urban History Review, Vol 19, Issue 1, June 1990
54. Ibid
55. The Queen's Own Rifles of Canada (https://en.wikipedia.org/wiki/The_Queen%27s_Own_Rifles_of_Canada)
56. George Dixon and G Mercer Adam, A History of Upper Canada College: 1829-1892, 105
57. Ibid, 4
58. Bob Gordon, Canada's First VC Recipient, Vol 25-1, May 18 2018 (espritdecorps.ca/in-the-news/canadas-first-vc-recipient-alexander-dunn-at-the-charge-of-the-light-brigade-balaclava-1854)
59. 17 Upper Canada College Cadets (https://qormuseum.org/history/cadets/upper-canada-college-cadet-corps/)
60. Crerar, Henry Duncan Graham (http://www.biographi.ca/en/bio/crerar_henry_duncan_graham_19E.html) ; List of Upper Canada College alumni (https://en.wikipedia.org/wiki/List_of_Upper_Canada_College_alumni#Military_service)
61. Pellatt, Sir Henry Mill (www.biographi.ca/en/bio/pellatt_henry_mill_16E.html)
62. Rules and regulations of the Toronto Club: incorporated by 27 Vic. ch. 92, Can., 1864, and 41 Vic. ch. 67, Ont., 1878 (https://archive.org/stream/cihm_45897/cihm_45897_djvu.txt)
63. Timothy J Stewart, Toronto's Fighting 75th in the Great War 1915-1919: A Prehistory of The Toronto Scottish Regiment ; Patriots, Crooks and Safety-Firsters: Colonels of the Canadian Expeditionary Force (https://matthewkbarrett.com/2015/12/30/the-redeemed/)
64. D'Alton Lally McCarthy fonds 1880-[1959?] 26.5 cm of textual records 4 photographs : b&w ; 20.2 x 15.3 cm or smaller (https://lso.ca/about-lso/osgoode-hall-and-ontario-legal-heritage/collections-and-research/archival-finding-aids/d-alton-lally-mccarthy-pf3)
65. Roy MacLaren, The Fundamental Things Apply: A Memoir, 268
66. The Earl of Dundonald, My Army Life
67. Ken Bell and Desmond Morton, Royal Canadian Military Institute, 33
68. James Mason (Canadian politician) (https://en.wikipedia.org/wiki/James_Mason_(Canadian_politician))
69. Upper Canada College Old Boys Who Served in the Queen's Own Rifles of Canada (https://qormuseum.org/history/cadets/upper-canada-college-cadet-corps/qor-ucc-old-boys/)
70. Mike O'Brien, Manhood and the Militia Myth, Labour/Le Travail, Vol 42, Fall 1998
71. Desmond Morton, The Cadet Movement in the Moment of Canadian Militarism, Journal of Canadian Studies, Vol 13, Summer 1978
72. Mike O'Brien, Manhood and the Militia Myth, Labour/Le Travail, Vol 42, Fall 1998
73. Ibid
74. Ibid

Chapter 4

1. Peter T Haydon and Ann L Griffiths, Canada's Pacific naval presence: Purposeful or Peripheral, 23
2. Tony German, The Sea is at Our Gates: the history of the Canadian Navy, 23
3. Roger Sarty, the Maritime Defence of Canada, 18/59
4. Tony German, The Sea is at Our Gates: the history of the Canadian Navy, 27
5. Marc Milner, Canada's Navy: the first century, 65
6. James A Boutilier, The RCN in Retrospect, 1910-1968, 64
7. Richard Howard Gimblett, Peter T Haydon and Ann L Griffiths, Canadian Gunboat Diplomacy: the Canadian Navy and foreign-policy, 287
8. Marc Milner, Canada's Navy: the first century, 59
9. H H Dodwell, The Cambridge History of the British Empire, Vol 4, 598
10. Tony German, The Sea is at Our Gates: the history of the Canadian Navy, 71
11. Ibid ; Richard Howard Gimblett, Peter T Haydon and Ann L Griffiths, Canadian Gunboat Diplomacy, 67
12. Rob Stuart, Was the RCN ever the world's third largest navy?, Canadian Naval Review, 2009 (https://www.drpaulwcollins.com/wp-content/uploads/2019/06/Was-the-RCN-ever-the-Third-Largest-Navy-Rob-Stuart.pdf)
13. James A Boutilier, The RCN in Retrospect, 1910-1968, 326
14. Peter T Haydon and Ann L Griffiths, Canada's Pacific naval presence: Purposeful or Peripheral, 136
15. Richard Howard Gimblett, Peter T Haydon and Ann L Griffiths, Canadian Gunboat Diplomacy: the Canadian Navy and foreign-policy, 103 ; Marc Milner, Canada's Navy: The First Century, 178
16. Richard Howard Gimblett, Peter T Haydon and Ann L Griffiths, Canadian Gunboat Diplomacy: the Canadian Navy and foreign-policy, 274
17. Ibid,
18. Ibid, 30
19. Ibid, 84
20. Ibid, 30
21. Ibid, 27 ; The Sea Bound Coast: The official history of The Royal Canadian Navy, 1867-1939 vol 1, 913

22. Richard Howard Gimblett, Peter T Haydon and Ann L Griffiths, Canadian Gunboat Diplomacy: the Canadian Navy and foreign-policy, 31
23. Peter McFarlane, Northern Shadows: Canadians and Central America, 48
24. Paula Pears Hastings, Dreams of a Tropical Canada: Race, Nation, and Canadian Aspirations in the Caribbean Basin, 1883-1919, 130
25. Richard H Gimblett, Gunboat diplomacy, mutiny and national identity in the postwar Royal Canadian Navy: The cruise of HMCS Crescent to China, 1949. Thèse présentée à la Faculté des études supérieures de l'université Laval pour l'obtention du grade de Philosophiae Doctor (https://www.collectionscanada.gc.ca/obj/s4/f2/dsk2/ftp03/NQ48979.pdf)
26. Brian Douglas Tennyson, Canada and the Commonwealth Caribbean, 280
27. Richard Howard Gimblett, Peter T Haydon and Ann L Griffiths, Canadian Gunboat Diplomacy, 40 ; Richard H Gimblett, Gunboat diplomacy, mutiny and national identity in the postwar Royal Canadian Navy: The cruise of HMCS Crescent to China, 1949. Thèse présentée à la Faculté des études supérieures de l'université Laval pour l'obtention du grade de Philosophiae Doctor (https://www.collectionscanada.gc.ca/obj/s4/f2/dsk2/ftp03/NQ48979.pdf)
28. Tony German, The Sea is at Our Gates: the history of the Canadian Navy, 68
29. James A Boutilier, The RCN in Retrospect, 1910-1968, 121
30. Daniel Owen Spence, A History of the Royal Navy: Empire and Imperialism, 151
31. Tyrone Pile, Beyond the Workable Little Fleet: postwar planning and policy in the RCN 1945-1948, 61
32. CFS Bermuda (https://en.wikipedia.org/wiki/CFS_Bermuda)
33. Matt Kwong, HMCS Whitehorse: Navy misconduct report may target booze, Jul 16 2014 (https://www.cbc.ca/news/politics/hmcs-whitehorse-navy-misconduct-report-may-target-booze-1.2708083)
34. Richard Howard Gimblett, Peter T Haydon and Ann L Griffiths, Canadian Gunboat Diplomacy: the Canadian Navy and foreign-policy, 147
35. David Zimmerman, Maritime Command Pacific: the Royal Canadian Navy's West Coast fleet in the early Cold War, 153
36. Richard Howard Gimblett, Peter T Haydon and Ann L Griffiths, Canadian Gunboat Diplomacy: the Canadian Navy and foreign-policy, 137
37. Tony German, The Sea Is at Our Gates: the History of the Canadian Navy, 272
38. Marc Milner, Canada's Navy: the first century, 234
39. Tony German, The Sea Is at Our Gates, 272
40. Eric Lerhe, Canada-US Military Interoperability in the War on Terror: At What Cost Sovereignty? (https://dalspace.library.dal.ca/bitstream/handle/10222/15306/Lerhe_Eric_PhD_POLSCI_Oct_2012_D.pdf?sequence=5&isAllowed=y)
41. Marc Milner, Canada's Navy: the first century, 235
42. May 4 1965 (https://www.lipad.ca/full/1965/05/04/2/)
43. Richard Howard Gimblett, Peter T Haydon and Ann L Griffiths, Canadian Gunboat Diplomacy: the Canadian Navy and foreign-policy, 153
44. Kai Schoenhals and Richard Melanson, Revolution and intervention in Grenada: the New Jewel Movement, the United States, and the Caribbean, 29
45. Richard Howard Gimblett, Peter T Haydon and Ann L Griffiths, Canadian Gunboat Diplomacy: the Canadian Navy and foreign-policy, 162
46. Ibid, 151
47. Ibid
48. Ibid
49. Sean M Maloney, Helpful fixer or hired gun? Why Canada goes overseas, Jan 1 2001 (https://policyoptions.irpp.org/fr/magazines/2001-odyssee-espace/helpful-fixer-or-hired-gun-why-canada-goes-overseas/)
50. Richard Howard Gimblett, Peter T Haydon and Ann L Griffiths, Canadian Gunboat Diplomacy, 138
51. Urban Search and Rescue (USAR) (https://www.publicsafety.gc.ca/cnt/mrgnc-mngmnt/rspndng-mrgnc-vnts/rbn-srch-rsc-en.aspx)
52. Canada feared popular uprising in Haiti after quake, Canadian Press, Mar 31 2011 (https://www.ctvnews.ca/canada-feared-popular-uprising-in-haiti-after-quake-1.625850)
53. Aaron Wherry, 'Go Canada Go', Mar 11 2010 (https://www.macleans.ca/uncategorized/go-canada-go/)
54. Roger Annis, Exagerated Claims: Assessing the Canadian Military's Haiti Earthquake Response, Haiti Liberte, Oct 6 2010 (https://canada-haiti.ca/content/exagerated-claims-assessing-canadian-militarys-haiti-earthquake-response)
55. Richard Howard Gimblett, Peter T Haydon and Ann L Griffiths, Canadian gunboat diplomacy: the Canadian Navy and foreign-policy, 137
56. John Starnes, Closely Guarded: A Life in Canadian Security and Intelligence, 198
57. Duncan Miller and Sharon Hobson, The Persian Excursion: the Canadian Navy and the Gulf War, 1
58. Richard Gimblett, Operation Apollo, 156
59. Ibid, 118
60. Janice Gross Stein and Eugene Lang, The Unexpected War: Canada in Kandahar, 82
61. Richard Gimblett, Operation Apollo, 122
62. Yves Engler, Is Canada at war with Iran? The evidence is growing, Aug 30, 2012 (https://ipolitics.ca/2012/08/30/yves-engler-is-canada-at-war-with-iran-the-evidence-is-growing/)
63. Ibid
64. Ibid
65. Matthew Fisher, Canadian warships shadowed by Chinese navy in South China Sea, Jul 14 2017 (https://nationalpost.com/news/canada/matthew-fisher-canadian-warships-shadowed-by-chinese-navy-in-south-china-sea)
66. Ibid
67. Ibid
68. Tina Park, As the North Korean crisis escalates, Canada must step up, Aug 14 2017 (https://www.macleans.ca/opinion/as-the-north-korean-crisis-escalates-canada-must-step-up/) ; Campbell Clark, Canada seeks Asian military hub, June 4 2012 (https://www.theglobeandmail.com/news/politics/canada-seeks-asian-military-hub/article4231097/?ref=http://www.theglobeandmail.com&)
69. Fen Hampson, Canada Among Nations, 1997: Asia Pacific Face-Off, 275 ; Peter T Haydon and Ann L Griffiths, Canada's Pacific naval presence: Purposeful or Peripheral, 137
70. Adam P MacDonald, A Canadian naval turn to East Asia in the making?, Canadian Foreign Policy Journal, Vol 20, Is 3, 2014
71. Richard Howard Gimblett, Peter T Haydon and Ann L Griffiths, Canadian Gunboat Diplomacy: The Canadian Navy and Foreign Policy, 173
72. Tony German, The Sea is at Our Gates: the history of the Canadian Navy, 9

73. Richard Howard Gimblett, Peter T Haydon and Ann L Griffiths, Canadian Gunboat Diplomacy: The Canadian Navy and Foreign Policy, 70
74. Tony German, The Sea is at Our Gates, 231
75. Thor Thorgrimsson and E C Russell, Canadian Naval Operations in Korean Waters 1950-1955, 133
76. James A Boutilier, The RCN in Retrospect, 1910-1968, 267
77. Tony German, The Sea is at Our Gates, 218
78. The Early Cold War, The Korean War (https://www.warmuseum.ca/cwm/exhibitions/navy/galery-e.aspx@section=2-F-3&id=8&page=0.html)
79. Thor Thorgrimsson and E C Russell, Canadian Naval Operations in Korean Waters 1950-1955, 16
80. Ibid, 53
81. Tony German, The Sea is at Our Gates: the history of the Canadian Navy, 220
82. David Zimmerman, Maritime Command Pacific: the Royal Canadian Navy's West Coast fleet in the early Cold War, 43
83. Richard Howard Gimblett, Peter T Haydon and Ann L Griffiths, Canadian Gunboat Diplomacy: The Canadian Navy and Foreign Policy
84. Peter T Haydon and Ann L Griffiths, Canada's Pacific naval presence: Purposeful or Peripheral, 41
85. Ibid, 43
86. Ibid, 45 ; Richard Howard Gimblett, Peter T Haydon and Ann L Griffiths, Canadian Gunboat Diplomacy, 63
87. Tony German, The Sea is at Our Gates: the history of the Canadian Navy, 175
88. Marc Milner, Canada's Navy: the first century, 159
89. Tyrone Pile, Beyond the Workable Little Fleet: post-war planning and policy in the RCN 1945-1948, 32
90. Ibid ; Richard Howard Gimblett, Peter T Haydon and Ann L Griffiths, Canadian Gunboat Diplomacy, 63
91. Peter T Haydon and Ann L Griffiths, Canada's Pacific naval presence: Purposeful or Peripheral, 44
92. Ibid, 59
93. The Hamilton Spectator, June 7 1943 (https://www.warmuseum.ca/cwm/exhibitions/newspapers/operations/northafrican_e.html)
94. Standing NATO Maritime Group 1 under Canadian command (http://www.forces.gc.ca/en/ news/article.page?doc=standing-nato-maritimegroup-1-under-canadian-command/hnocfof9)
95. Tatah Mentan, The New World Order Ideology and Africa, 192
96. Tony Seed, Canada sends warship to Africa, part of NATO Rapid Response Fleet, Aug 1 2007 (https://tonyseed.wordpress.com/2007/08/01/canada-sends-warship-to-africa-as-part-of-nato-rapid-response-fleet/)
97. Ibid
98. We'll hear about a Canadian frigate on a voyage around Africa, CBC Radio — World Report, Sept 3 2007
99. Jeff Davis, Modern Pirates are High Tech and Dangerous, Embassy, Feb 6 2008 (http://www.maritimeterrorism.com/2008/02/06/modernpirates-are-high-tech-and-dangerous/)
100. Ibid
101. HMCS Toronto will be part of a mission of firsts, The Daily News, July 21 2007
102. Patrick Lennox, Canada's presence in the 'arc of instability', Nov 2008 (diplomatonline.com/pdf_files/Diplomatnov08.pdf)
103. Kris Sims, NATO air strikes pound key Tripoli port, May 19 2011 (http://www.nugget.ca/2011/05/19/nato-air-strikes-pound-keytripoli-port-7)
104. Kathleen Harris, Canada's sailors set for more conflict zone, Arctic missions than time on high seas, Oct 26 2011 (https://ipolitics.ca/2011/10/26/canadas-sailors-set-for-more-conflict-zone-arctic-missions-than-time-on-high-seas-rcn-commander/)
105. David Pugliese, The Libya Mission One Year Later: The rules of engagement, Ottawa Citizen Feb 19 2012
106. Ibid

Chapter 5

1. CCPA Monitor July 2013
2. Canadian Special Operations Forces Command - Major-General Pete Dawe Biography (https://www.canada.ca/en/department-national-defence/corporate/reports-publications/transition-materials/defence-101/2020/03/defence-101/cansofcom.html)
3. Ibid ; Sandrine Murray, Canada's Top Commando An Interview With MGen Michael Rouleau, Vol 24, Jan 3 2018 (http://espritdecorps.ca/interview/canadas-top-commando-an-interview-with-mgen-michael-rouleau) ; David Pugliese, Special Ops: wish list of new gear Esprit de Corps, Nov 26 2014
4. Chris Thatcher, Canada gets green light to buy King Air surveillance aircraft Avatar, Oct 12 2018 (https://skiesmag.com/news/canada-gets-green-light-to-buy-king-air-surveillance-aircraft/)
5. Levon Sevunts, Ammunition procurement tender sheds light on secretive Canadian operation in Africa, Aug 3 2017 (http://www.rcinet.ca/en/2017/08/03/ammunition-procurement-tender-sheds-light-on-secretive-canadian-operation-in-africa/)
6. Bernd Horn, Shadow Warriors: the Canadian Special Operations Forces Command, 42
7. Canadian Joint Incident Response Unit, About the unit (https://www.canada.ca/en/special-operations-forces-command/corporate/organizational-structure/joint-incident-response.html)
8. Creating Canada's new Commandos, Ottawa Citizen, Aug 5 2006
9. Bruce Campion-Smith, JTF2 is "jewel in the crown" of Canada's special forces, June 26 2016 (https://www.thestar.com/news/canada/2016/06/26/jtf2-is-jewel-in-the-crown-of-canadas-special-forces.html)
10. Christian Leuprecht and H Christian Breede, Beyond the Movies: The Value Proposition of Canada's Special Operations Forces, Dec 2016 (https://www.macdonaldlaurier.ca/files/pdf/Leuprecht_Breede_Analysis_December2016.pdf) ; David Pugliese, Canada's Secret Commandos: the unauthorized story of joint task force two, 29 ; Denis Morisset, We were invincible, 36
11. Robert Fife, Canadian elite special forces sniper makes record-breaking kill shot in Iraq, June 21 2017 (https://www.theglobeandmail.com/news/politics/canadian-elite-special-forces-sniper-sets-record-breaking-kill-shot-in-iraq/article35415651/)
12. David Pugliese, Canada's Secret Commandos, 91
13. Peter Boer, Canadian spies and spies in Canada, 135 ; David Pugliese, Canada's Secret Commandos, 73
14. Bruce Campion-Smith, JTF2 is "jewel in the crown" of Canada's special forces, June 26 2016 (https://www.thestar.com/news/canada/2016/06/26/jtf2-is-jewel-in-the-crown-of-canadas-special-forces.html)
15. P J Carter, The Proposed Canadian Model for Special Operations Forces Aviation, Part 2 (airforceapp.forces.gc.ca/cfawc/eLibrary/Journal/Vol3-2010/Iss1-Winter/

Sections/05-The_Proposed_Canadian_Model_for_Special_Operations_Forces_Aviation-Part_2_e.pdf)

16. Denis Morisset, We were invincible, 33 ; Colin Freeze, Silent killers: Secrecy, security and JTF2, Dec 7 2010 (https://www.theglobeandmail.com/news/national/silent-killers-secrecy-security-and-jtf2/article1319588/?ref=https://www.theglobeandmail.com&); Peter Boer, Canadian spies and spies in Canada, 129

17. Colin Freeze, Silent killers: Secrecy, security and JTF2, Dec 7 2010 (https://www.theglobeandmail.com/news/national/silent-killers-secrecy-security-and-jtf2/article1319588/?ref=https://www.theglobeandmail.com&)

18. We Were Invincible, Résumé du livre (http://www.jcl.qc.ca/detail_livre/we-were-invincible/)

19. Peter Boer, Canadian spies and spies in Canada, 134 ; Denis Morisset, We were invincible, 37/23

20. Tom Rogan, Why the Canadian sniper story is important, June 22 2017 (https://www.washingtonexaminer.com/why-the-canadian-sniper-story-is-important)

21. Richard Sanders, Canada's Former JTF2 Commando leader was a Deputy Commander in the Iraq War, throughout 2008 (https://coat.ncf.ca/P4C/65/20-21.pdf)

22. Ibid

23. David Pugliese, Getting the Drop on Special Ops, Ottawa Citizen, July 17 2010

24. Ibid ; David Pugliese, Canada's Secret Commandos: the unauthorized story of joint task force two, 28

25. David Pugliese, JTF2 buys new guns; regular troops make do, Ottawa Citizen, Oct 8 2005

26. Standing Senate Committee on National Security and Defence, Nov 20 2006 (https://sencanada.ca/en/Content/Sen/committee/391/defe/44294-e)

27. Michael Skinner, Canada's Ongoing Involvement in Dirty Wars, July 1 2013 (https://www.policyalternatives.ca/publications/monitor/canadas-ongoing-involvement-dirty-wars)

28. David Pugliese, Shadow Wars: Special Forces in the New Battle Against Terrorism, 175

29. Standing Senate Committee on National Security and Defence, Nov 20 2006 (https://sencanada.ca/en/Content/Sen/committee/391/defe/44294-e)

30. Peter Worthington, JTF2 - Canada's secret weapon or a place where trouble hides?, Sept 14 2010 (http://www.torontosun.com/comment/columnists/peter_worthington/2010/09/14/15351521.htm)

31. Christian Leuprecht and H Christian Breede, Beyond the Movies: The Value Proposition of Canada's Special Operations Forces, Dec 2016 (https://www.macdonaldlaurier.ca/files/pdf/Leuprecht_Breede_Analysis_December2016.pdf)

32. Denis Morisset, We were invincible

33. David Pugliese, Canada's Secret Commandos, 117

34. JTF2: Canada's super-secret commandos, July 15 2005 (https://www.cbc.ca/news2/background/cdnmilitary/jtf2.html)

35. Allison Dunfield, Eggleton admits he left PM in dark about JTF2 action, Jan 29 2002 (https://www.theglobeandmail.com/report-on-business/eggleton-admits-he-left-pm-in-dark-about-jtf2-action/article1171820/)

36. David Pugliese, Shadow Wars: Special Forces in the New Battle Against Terrorism, 112

37. David Pugliese, Canada's JTF2 captives vanish at Guantanamo, Ottawa Citizen, Feb 14 2005

38. JTF2 command 'encouraged' war crimes, soldier alleges, Jan 18 2011 (https://www.cbc.ca/news/canada/jtf2-command-encouraged-war-crimes-soldier-alleges-1.992008)

39. Ibid
40. Ibid
41. Ibid
42. Ibid

43. Murray Brewster, Canada's special forces kept too many secrets about Afghan missions, says report, Sep 5 2018 (https://www.cbc.ca/news/politics/special-forces-afghanistan-report-1.4812154)

44. Graeme Smith, Report slams tactic of night raids on homes, Dec 24 2008 (https://www.theglobeandmail.com/news/world/report-slams-tactic-of-night-raids-on-homes/article956873/)

45. David Pugliese, Shadow Wars: Special Forces in the New Battle Against Terrorism, 109

46. Benjamin W Hadaway, Lampreys under a shark: embedded news reporters and the military in the 21st century, Carleton University Thesis 2006, 109

47. Ibid

48. Sharon Hobson, Operations Security and the Public's Need to Know, Canadian Defence and Foreign Affairs Institute, Mar 2011

49. Matthew Fisher, Afghan drawdown has some feeling doomed, Feb 17 2012 (https://theprovince.com/opinion/matthew-fisher-afghan-drawdown-has-some-feeling-doomed)

50. Operation IMPACT (https://www.canada.ca/en/department-national-defence/services/operations/military-operations/current-operations/operation-impact.html)

51. Robert Fife, Canadian elite special forces sniper makes record-breaking kill shot in Iraq, June 21 2017 (https://www.theglobeandmail.com/news/politics/canadian-elite-special-forces-sniper-sets-record-breaking-kill-shot-in-iraq/article35415651/)

52. David Pugliese, Special forces take over 'urgent' weapons purchase for Kurds, but there's no timeline, Ottawa Citizen, Jul 18 2017 (https://nationalpost.com/news/canada/special-forces-take-over-urgent-weapons-purchase-for-kurds-but-theres-still-no-timeline-for-delivering-them/wcm/c37dd92d-7311-450b-8aff-0d6fad615d7f)

53. Tonda MacCharles, Canadian groups report allegations of Yazidi 'massacre' in Iraq, Feb 12 2016 (https://www.thestar.com/news/canada/2016/02/12/canadian-groups-report-allegations-of-yazidi-massacre-in-iraq.html) ; Patrick Cockburn, Mosul's Sunni residents face mass persecution as Isis 'collaborators', July 13 2017 (https://www.independent.co.uk/news/world/middle-east/mosul-sunni-residents-isis-collaboration-persecution-city-liberation-iraq-fighters-killed-massacres-a7839716.html)

54. RCMP confirms its involvement in freeing three Western hostages, Mar 23 2006 (https://www.cbc.ca/news/canada/rcmp-confirms-its-involvement-in-freeing-three-western-hostages-1.609696)

55. Scott Taylor, No gold stars for pulling troops from places they shouldn't have been, Apr 24 2019 (https://www.hilltimes.com/2019/04/24/no-gold-stars-for-pulling-troops-from-places-they-shouldnt-have-been/197325)

56. SC/10200 17, Security Council Approves 'No-Fly Zone' over Libya, Authorizing 'All Necessary Measures' to Protect Civilians, by Vote of 10 in Favour with 5 Abstentions, Mar 17 2011 (https://www.un.org/press/en/2011/sc10200.doc.htm)

57. Mark Urban, Inside story of the UK's secret mission to beat Gaddafi, Jan 19 2012 (https://www.bbc.com/news/magazine-16573516)

58. Joint Task Force 2: Canada's elite fighters, Sep 15 2010 (https://www.cbc.ca/news/canada/joint-task-force-

2-canada-s-elite-fighters-1.873657)
59. Richard Sanders, A Very Canadian Coup: The top 10 ways that Canada aided the 2004 coup in Haiti and helped subject Haitians to a brutal reign of terror, Apr 1 2010 (https://www.policyalternatives.ca/publications/monitor/very-canadian-coup)
60. Haiti Info Project Feb 15 2019 (https://twitter.com/HaitiInfoProj/status/1096629898762829824?fbclid=IwAR37AzmbxaJX_1b0v5p2d-FDWhN2DE2MnGGqRKSTP0Co9phPD88zZW9fGo)
61. Ibid
62. David Pugliese, Canada's Secret Commandos, 83
63. Peter Boer, Canadian spies and spies in Canada, 132
64. Denis Morisset, We were invincible, 94/97
65. Ibid, 100
66. Chretien denies Canadian commandos in Kosovo, Apr 20 1999 (https://www.cbc.ca/news/canada/chretien-denies-canadian-commandos-in-kosovo-1.176746)
67. David Pugliese, Canada's Secret Commandos, 84
68. Jonathan Montpetit, Ex-commando arrested day before book published, April 30 2008 (https://www.thestar.com/news/canada/2008/04/30/excommando_arrested_day_before_book_published.html)
69. Denis Morisset, We were invincible, 137
70. Ibid
71. Ibid,
72. Ibid, 147
73. Canadian special forces offering protection in Mali; but there will be "no mission", Canadian Press, Jan 28 2013 (http://www.macleans.ca/general/canadian-special-forces-offering-protection-in-mali-but-there-will-be-no-mission/)
74. Colin Freeze, Silent killers: Secrecy, security and JTF2, Globe and Mail, Dec 7 2010
75. David Pugliese, Canada's Secret Commandos: The unauthorized story of Joint Task Force Two, 81
76. Ibid, 80
77. Denis Morisset, We were invincible, 160
78. Scott Taylor and Brian Nolan, Tested Mettle: Canada's Peacekeepers at War, 196
79. David Pugliese, Canada's secret commandos, 100
80. Bernd Horn, No Ordinary Men: Special Operations Forces Missions in Afghanistan, 55
81. David Pugliese, New special forces uniform a throwback to Second World War Devil's Brigade, Oct 15 2017 (https://nationalpost.com/news/canada/new-special-forces-uniform-a-throwback-to-second-world-war-devils-brigade)
82. John Nadler, A Perfect Hell: the forgotten story of the Canadian commandos of the second world war, 2
83. Ibid
84. Bruce Forsyth, Camp X — Canada's secret spy school, The Maple Leaf, June 2007 (https://militarybruce.com/camp-x-canadas-secret-spy-school/)
85. Steven Freeland, Carl Freeland: The spy who loved his family and his country, July 5 2018 (https://www.theglobeandmail.com/life/article-carl-freeland-the-spy-who-loved-his-family-and-his-country/)

Chapter 6

1. Ian McKay and Jamie Swift, Warrior Nation: rebranding Canada in an age of anxiety, 177
2. Carl Benn, Mohawks on the Nile: Natives Among the Canadian Voyageurs in Egypt, 1884-1885, 24
3. Richard Preston, Canada's RMC: A History of the Royal Military College, 100 ; Peter Pigott, Canada in Sudan: War Without Borders, 75/61
4. Roy MacLaren, Canadians on the Nile, 107, 107
5. Ibid
6. Robert Page, The Boer War and Canadian Imperialism, Canadian Historical Association Booklets Vol 44, 15
7. Chris Madsen, Another Kind of Justice: Canadian Military Law from Confederation to Somalia, 31
8. Chris Madsen, Canadian Troops and Farm Burning in the South African War, 2005 (www.journal.forces.gc.ca/vo6/no2/history-histoire-eng.asp)
9. Carman Miller, Painting the Map Red, 232
10. Ibid, 232
11. Ibid, 448
12. Lawrence James, The Savage Wars: British Campaigns in Africa, 1870-1920, 69
13. Carman Miller, In Painting the Map Red: Canada and the South African War, 1899-1902,
14. R H Roy, Canada and the Battle of Passchendaele, May 31 2006 (https://www.thecanadianencyclopedia.ca/en/article/battle-of-passchendaele)
15. Hill 70 (https://www.warmuseum.ca/firstworldwar/history/battles-and-fighting/land-battles/hill-70/)
16. Stephanie A H Belanger and Daniel Legace Roy, military operations and the mind: war ethics and soldiers well-being, 100
17. Tristin Hopper, The forgotten ruthlessness of Canada's Great War soldiers, Nov 12 2018 (https://nationalpost.com/news/canada/the-forgotten-ferocity-of-canadas-soldiers-in-the-great-war)
18. Ibid
19. Ibid
20. Ibid
21. Christopher Sharpe, Recruitment and Conscription (Canada) (https://encyclopedia.1914-1918-online.net/article/recruitment_and_conscription_canada)
22. Richard Holt, Filling the Ranks: Manpower in the Canadian Expeditionary Force, 1914-1918, 53
23. Sydney F Wise, Canadian airmen and the first world war, 139
24. Africa and World War I (https://www.dw.com/en/africa-and-world-war-i/a-17573462)
25. The Sea Bound Coast: The official history of The Royal Canadian Navy, 1867-1939, Vol 1, 379-382 ; Stephen Rybak, Rear–Admiral Walter Hose 1875–1965, 2012 (http://www.nauticapedia.ca/Articles/Rybak4_Walter_Hose.php)
26. Lovett Elango, The Anglo-French "Condominium" in Cameroon, 1914-1916: The Myth and the Reality, The International Journal of African Historical Studies Vol 18, N 4, 1985
27. Ibid
28. Gerald J J Tulchinsky, Taking Root: The Origins of the Canadian Jewish Community, 194 ; Marylanders in the Jewish Legion 1918-1919 (https://jewishmuseummd.org/events/marylanders-in-the-jewish-legion-1918-1919/)
29. John Swettenham, Canadians in Mesopotamia, 1918-1919 AHQ report 84, Oct 20 1959 (https://www.canada.ca/en/department-national-defence/services/military-history/history-heritage/official-military-history-lineages/reports/army-headquarters-1948-1959/canadians-mesopotamia-1918-1919.html)
30. John Swettenham, Allied Intervention in Russia 1918-1919: And the Part Played By Canada ; D L Fromow, Canada's Flying Gunners: A History of the Air Observation Post of the Royal Regiment of Canadian Artillery, 25

31. Roy MacLaren, Canadians in Russia, 1918-1919, 79
32. Aloysius Balawyder, Canadian-Soviet Relations during the World Wars, 16
33. David Bercuson, Canada and the Soviet Experiment: Essays on Canadian Encounters with Russia and the Soviet Union, 1900-1991, 31
34. Ibid, 29
35. Roy MacLaren, Canadians in Russia, 229/242
36. Second World War (1939-1945) (http://www.veterans.gc.ca/eng/remembrance/history/second-world-war)
37. Nicholas Tracy, Two-Edged Sword: The Navy as an Instrument of Canadian Foreign Policy, 57 ; Peyton V Lyon and Tareq Y Ismael, Canada and the Third World, 63
38. Michael Petrou, Renegades: Canadians in the Spanish Civil War, xiv
39. Ibid
40. Ibid, xv
41. William Beeching, Canadian Volunteers: Spain 1936-1939, 12
42. Michael Petrou, 'You are history. You are legend.' Canada's last Spanish Civil War vet dies, Sept 11 2013 (https://www.macleans.ca/news/you-are-history-you-are-legend-canadas-last-spanish-civil-war-vet-dies/)
43. John D Meehan, Dominion and the Rising Sun: Canada Encounters Japan, 1929-1941: 181
44. Ibid 158
45. Ibid
46. Ibid
47. Ibid
48. Ibid
49. Ibid
50. Ibid, 167
51. Irving Abella and Harold Martin Troper, None is Too Many: Canada and the Jews of Europe, 1933-1948, 37
52. Ibid
53. William Beeching, Canadian Volunteers: Spain 1936-1939, 11
54. Mark Zuehlke, The Gallant Cause: Canadians in the Spanish Civil War 1936, 128
55. Stalin 'planned to send a million troops to stop Hitler if Britain and France agreed pact' Papers, Oct 20 2008 (http://www.telegraph.co.uk/news/worldnews/europe/russia/3223834/Stalin-planned-to-send-a-million-troops-to-stop-Hitler-if-Britain-and-France-agreed-pact.html)
56. Roger Sarty, The Maritime Defence of Canada, 79/83
57. George Stanley, Canada's soldiers: the military history of an unmilitary people, 353
58. J L Granatstein and Desmond Morton, A Nation Forged in Fire: Canadians and the Second World War, 1939-1945, 11
59. James A Boutilier, The RCN in Retrospect, 1910-1968, 103
60. Ernie Regehr, Making a Killing: Canada's arms industry, 12
61. Arming the Nation: Canada's Industrial War Effort, 1939-1945, A paper prepared for the Canadian Council of Chief Executives and presented at its roundtable on foreign policy and defence, Canadian War Museum, May 27 2005
62. Ibid
63. Robert Bothwell, War, business and world military-industrial complexes, 116
64. Arming the Nation: Canada's Industrial War Effort, 1939-1945, A paper prepared for the Canadian Council of Chief Executives and presented at its roundtable on foreign policy and defence, Canadian War Museum, May 27 2005
65. Combined Bomber Offensive (https://en.wikipedia.org/wiki/Combined_Bomber_Offensive)
66. Canadian War Museum changes controversial wording on WWII bombing, Oct 11 2007 (https://www.cbc.ca/news/entertainment/canadian-war-museum-changes-controversial-wording-on-wwii-bombing-1.635963)
67. Ibid
68. David Bright, Stephen J Randall and Graeme S Mount, The Caribbean Basin: An International History, 71
69. Brian Douglas Tennyson, Canada and the Commonwealth Caribbean, 285
70. Ibid, 291
71. Ibid, 296
72. The North African Campaigns, 1940-1943 (https://www.warmuseum.ca/cwm/exhibitions/newspapers/operations/northafrican_e.html)
73. Douglas G Anglin, Towards a Canadian Policy on Africa, International Journal, Vol 15, No 4, Autumn 1960
74. S R Elliott, Scarlet to Green: a history of intelligence in the Canadian Army 1903-1963, 407
75. Carl Vincent, No Reason why: The Canadian Hong Kong Tragedy, an Examination, 100
76. Gil Murray, The Invisible War: the untold secret story of Number One Canadian Special Wireless Group, Royal Canadian Signal Corps, 1944-1946, 22
77. Roy MacLaren, Canadians Behind Enemy Lines, 1939-1945, 186
78. S R Elliott, Scarlet to Green: a history of intelligence in the Canadian Army 1903-1963, 397
79. Gil Murray, The Invisible War: the untold secret story of Number One Canadian Special Wireless Group, Royal Canadian Signal Corps, 1944-1946, 14
80. Ibid, prologue
81. Ibid, 15
82. S R Elliott, Scarlet to Green: a history of intelligence in the Canadian Army 1903-1963, 395
83. A Sutherland Brown, Forgotten Squared: Canadian Aircrews in Southeast Asia, 1942–1945, Canadian Military History, Vol 8, Is 2, 1999
84. Gil Murray, The Invisible War: the untold secret story of Number One Canadian Special Wireless Group, Royal Canadian Signal Corps, 1944-1946, 14 ; Swords, Clunks and Windowmakers: the tumultuous life of the RCAF's original one Canadian air division, 9
85. Canadians in South-east Asia (https://www.veterans.gc.ca/eng/remembrance/history/second-world-war/southeast-asia)
86. Peter Boer, Canadian spies and spies in Canada, 50
87. Gil Murray, The Invisible War: the untold secret story of Number One Canadian Special Wireless Group, Royal Canadian Signal Corps, 1944-1946, 22
88. Roy MacLaren, Derrière les lignes ennemies: Les agents secrets canadiens durant la Seconde Guerre mondiale ; S R Elliott, Scarlet to Green: a history of intelligence in the Canadian Army 1903-1963, 397 ; Sean M Maloney, Who has Seen the Wind? An Historical Overview of Canadian Special Operations, Canadian Military Journal, Vol 5, No 3, Autumn 2004
89. S R Elliott, Scarlet to Green: a history of intelligence in the Canadian Army 1903-1963, 397
90. Ibid, 398
91. Ibid, 408-409
92. Dan Bjarnason, Triumph at Kapyong: Canada's Pivotal Battle in Korea, 42
93. 10 Quick Facts on... The Korean War (https://www.veterans.gc.ca/eng/remembrance/information-for/educators/quick-facts/korean-war)
94. John Price, Orienting Canada, 180
95. Noam Chomsky, What Uncle Sam really wants, 111

96. John Price, Orienting Canada, 183
97. Martin Hart-Landsberg, Korea: Division, Reunification, and U.S. Foreign Policy, 121
98. William Blum, Killing Hope, 49
99. Denis Stairs, Diplomacy of Constraint, 205
100. Gordon A Wilson, NORAD and the Soviet nuclear threat: Canada's secret electronic air war, 19
101. Tony German, The Sea is at Our Gates: the history of the Canadian Navy, 225
102. Martin Hart-Landsberg, Korea: Division, Reunification, and U. S. Foreign Policy, 133
103. John Price, Orienting Canada, 270
104. Blaine Harden, The U.S. war crime North Korea won't forget, Mar 24 2015 (https://www.washingtonpost.com/opinions/the-us-war-crime-north-korea-wont-forget/2015/03/20/fb525694-ce80-11e4-8c54-ffb5ba6f2f69_story.html?utm_term=.f58bfeb687ab)
105. Chris Madsen, Another Kind of Justice, 110
106. John Hilliker and Mary Halloran, Diplomatic Documents and Their Users, 201
107. I F Stone, The Hidden History of the Korean War, 171
108. Relief of Douglas MacArthur (https://en.wikipedia.org/wiki/Relief_of_Douglas_MacArthur)
109. Peter Stursberg, Lester Person and the American Dilemma, 89
110. Robin S Gendron, Towards a Francophone Community: Canada's Relations with France and French Africa, 1945-1968, 24
111. Bertram C Frandsen, The Rise and Fall of Canada's Cold War Air Force, 1948-1968 (https://scholars.wlu.ca/cgi/viewcontent.cgi?article=2857&context=etd)
112. Andrew B Godefroy, In Peace Prepared: innovation and adaptation in Canada's Cold War Army, 48
113. Ibid, 49
114. Aaron Plamondon, The Politics of Procurement: military acquisition in Canada and the Sea King helicopter, 32
115. Andrew B Godefroy, In Peace Prepared: innovation and adaptation in Canada's Cold War Army, 59
116. Lawrence R Aronsen, Canada's postwar rearmament: another look at American theories of the military-industrial complex" Canadian historical Association Historical Papers, 1981
117. Ibid
118. Bertram C Frandsen, The Rise and Fall of Canada's Cold War Air Force, 1948-1968
119. Jerome D Davis, To the NATO Review: constancy and change in Canadian NATO policy, 1949-1969, 39
120. Fred Bodsworth, How Serious is the Defense Scandal?, Feb 1 1953 (https://archive.macleans.ca/article/1953/2/1/how-serious-is-the-defense-scandal)
121. Marc Milner, Canada's Navy: the first century, 204
122. W A March, Sic Itur Ad Astra: Canadian Aerospace Power Studies. Volume 3 Combat If Necessary, But Not Necessarily Combat, 25
123. Randall Wakelam, Cold War Fighters: Canadian aircraft procurement, 1945-54, 140
124. Tyrone Pile, Beyond the Workable Little Fleet: postwar planning and policy in the RCN 1945-1948, 115
125. Peter T Haydon and Ann L Griffiths, Canada's Pacific naval presence: Purposeful or Peripheral, 111
126. Wilfred Gourlay Dolphin Lund, The rise and fall of the Royal Canadian Navy, 1945-1964: a critical study of the senior leadership, policy and manpower management (https://www.nlc-bnc.ca/obj/s4/f2/dsk1/tape9/PQDD_0001/NQ41360.pdf)
127. Ibid
128. Bertram C Frandsen, The Rise and Fall of Canada's Cold War Air Force, 1948-1968
129. Martin Auger, The Evolution of Defence Procurement in Canada: A Hundred-Year History, Background Paper Publication No. 2020-54-E (https://lop.parl.ca/sites/PublicWebsite/default/en_CA/ResearchPublications/202054E#a6)
130. Ibid
131. Ibid
132. D J Godspeed, A History of the Defence Research Board of Canada, 101
133. Tony German, The Sea is at Our Gates: the history of the Canadian Navy, 234
134. Lawrence R Aronsen, Canada's postwar rearmament: another look at American theories of the military-industrial complex" Canadian historical Association Historical Papers, 1981
135. Ibid
136. Curt Cardwell, NSC 68 and the Political Economy of the Early Cold War Book, 210 ; Noam Chomsky, Necessary Illusions: Thought Control in Democratic Societies, 29
137. Reg Whitaker, Cold War Canada, 392
138. Jonathan Nitzan and Shimshon Bichler, Military Keynesianism and the Military-Industrial Complex, Dec 27 2016 (https://rwer.wordpress.com/2016/12/27/military-keynesianism-and-the-military-industrial-complex/)
139. Peter Langille, Changing the guard: Canada's defense in a world in transition, 25
140. Ibid
141. Denis Stairs, The Diplomacy of Constraint: Canada, the Korean War, and the United States, 104
142. Alistair D Edgar and David G Haglund, The Canadian Defence Industry in the New Global Environment, 63
143. Jerome D Davis, To the NATO Review: constancy and change in Canadian NATO policy, 1949-1969, 39
144. Bernd Horn, the Canadian Way of War: serving the national interest, 244
145. Peter Langille, Changing the Guard, 59
146. Bertram C Frandsen, The Rise and Fall of Canada's Cold War Air Force, 1948-1968
147. John Gellner, Canada in NATO, 21
148. Randall Wakelam, Cold War Fighters: Canadian aircraft procurement, 1945-54, 90
149. Ibid, 137
150. Yves Engler, Repression of the Canadian left, Jan 22 2011 (https://yvesengler.com/2011/01/22/repression-of-the-canadian-left/)
151. Ibid
152. Dave Seglins, 'Secret order' authorizing RCMP's covert Cold War wiretapping program released after 65 years, Jan 16 2017 (https://www.cbc.ca/news/politics/cold-war-wiretapping-secret-order-1.3933589)
153. Ibid
154. Ibid
155. Richard Gimblett, Persian Gulf War, 1990-91, Jan 11 2016 (https://www.thecanadianencyclopedia.ca/en/article/persian-gulf-war-1990-91)
156. Duncan Miller and Sharon Hobson, The Persian Excursion: the Canadian Navy and the Gulf War, 155 ; Ann Griffiths, The Canadian Forces and Interoperability: panacea or perdition, 215 ; Marc Milner, Canada's Navy: the first century, 298
157. Richard Gimblett, Persian Gulf War, 1990-91, Jan 11 2016 (https://www.thecanadianencyclopedia.ca/en/article/persian-gulf-war-1990-91)
158. Blake Stilwell, That time the US and its allies destroyed the entire Iraqi Navy, Apr 29 2020 (https://www.

wearethemighty.com/history/us-navy-gulf-war)
159. Gulf War (ttps://en.wikipedia.org/wiki/Gulf_ War#Coalition_bombing_of_Iraq's_civilian_infrastructure)
160. Gulf War (https://en.wikipedia.org/wiki/Gulf_ War#Casualties)
161. Tareq Y Ismael, Canada and the Middle East: The Foreign Policy of a Client State, 90
162. Mark Curtis, The Great Deception: Anglo-American Power and World Order, 205
163. Andrew Phillips, Bound for the Gulf, Feb 23 1998 (https://archive.macleans.ca/article/1998/2/23/bound-for-the-gulf)
164. Janice Stein and Eugene Lang, Unexpected War, 60
165. Eric Lerhe, Canada-US Military Interoperability in the War on Terror: At What Cost Sovereignty?, Doctor of Philosophy Dalhousie, Aug 2012
166. Janice Gross Stein and Eugene Lang, The Unexpected War: Canada in Kandahar, 82
167. Richard Sanders, Canada's "Secret" Contribution to the War in Iraq, Mar 27 2003 (https://archives.globalresearch.ca/articles/SAN303B.html)
168. Richard Sanders, The Role of Canadian CC-130 aircraft in the Iraq War, Press for Conversion!, 2010
169. David Akin, Canadians flew U.S. jets in Iraq during training, Ottawa Citizen, Apr 22 2008
170. Richard Sanders, Canada's "Secret" Contribution to the War in Iraq, Mar 27 2003 (https://archives.globalresearch.ca/articles/SAN303B.html)
171. Ibid
172. Governor General announces awarding of Meritorious Service Decorations, Jan 24 2006 (https://www.gg.ca/en/media/news/2006/governor-general-announces-awarding-meritorious-service-decorations)
173. Jon Elmer and Anthony Fenton, Canadian General Takes Senior Command Role in Iraq (www.ipsnews.net/2008/01/politics-canadian-general-takes-senior-command-role-in-iraq/)
174. Scott Taylor, INAT: Images of Serbia & the Kosovo conflict, 38
175. Chris Wattie, Forces refused U.S. Request out of Iraq fears, National Post, Sept 10 2004
176. Sean Maloney, The Hindrance of Military Operations Ashore: Canadian Participation in Operation Sharp Guard, 1993-1996, 34
177. Ibid, 30/31
178. Ibid, 53
179. Maja Zivanovic and Serbeze Haxhiaj, 78 Days of Fear: Remembering NATO's Bombing of Yugoslavia, BIRN, Mar 22 2019 (https://balkaninsight.com/2019/03/22/78-days-of-fear-remembering-natos-bombing-of-yugoslavia/)
180. Will Podmore, British Foreign Policy since 1870, 356
181. James Winter, Media Think, 77
182. Scott Taylor, Diary of an Uncivil War: The Violent Aftermath of the Kosovo Conflict, 12
183. Scott Taylor, INAT, 144
184. Aleksandar Jokic, Lessons of Kosovo: The Dangers of Humanitarian Intervention, 141
185. Ibid
186. John Norris, Collision Course: NATO, Russia, and Kosovo, xxiii
187. The Canadian Armed Forces in Afghanistan, Introduction (http://www.veterans.gc.ca/eng/remembrance/history/canadian-armed-forces/afghanistan)
188. Nipa Banerjee, Canada Must Learn Its Own Lessons from Afghanistan, Dec 20 2019 (https://www.cips-cepi.ca/2019/12/20/canada-must-learn-its-own-lessons-from-afghanistan/)

189. John Geddes, Canada in Combat, Mar 20 2006 (https://archive.macleans.ca/article/2006/3/20/canada-in-combat)
190. Ibid
191. David Pugliese, Canadians fired almost five million bullets in Afghanistan in two years, Canwest News Service, Feb 6 2008
192. Ray Wiss, A Line in the Sand: Canadians at War in Kandahar, 188
193. Matthew Brett, Canadians' tall tale, June 29 2008 (https://canadiandimension.com/blog/view/canadians-tall-tale)
194. Dave Markland, Media blind to Afghan civilian deaths, Jan 1 2007 (https://www.army.ca/forums/threads.the-sandbox-and-areas-reports-thread-january-2007.55306/)
195. Carlotta Gall and David E Sanger, Civilian deaths undermine war on Taliban May 12 2007 (https://www.nytimes.com/2007/05/12/news/12iht-13afghan.5681936.html)
196. Graham Thomson, Dead kid's dad vows revenge, Winnipeg Free Press, Aug 1 2008
197. Matthew Brett, Canada in Afghanistan, Jan 9 2009 (https://canadiandimension.com/blog/view/canada-in-afghanistan)
198. Lester Haines, Taliban monster dope plants defy Canadian military, Oct 13 2006 (https://www.theregister.com/2006/10/13/fireproof_forests/) ; Steve Rennie, Army defends Afghanistan night raids, Dec 24 2008 (https://www.thestar.com/news/world/2008/12/24/army_defends_afghanistan_night_raids.html)
199. David S Cloud, U.S. Airstrikes Climb Sharply in Afghanistan, Nov 17 2006 (https://www.nytimes.com/2006/11/17/world/asia/17bomber.html)
200. Gary Lewchuk, Piloting a heavily-armed Griffon helicopter over Afghanistan, May 4 2012 (https://www.forfreedom.ca/?page_id=1371)
201. All Afghan detainees likely tortured: diplomat, Nov 18 2009 (https://www.cbc.ca/news/canada/all-afghan-detainees-likely-tortured-diplomat-1.798059)
202. Canadian Afghan detainee issue (https://en.wikipedia.org/wiki/Canadian_Afghan_detainee_issue)
203. Elusive Pursuits: Lessons from Canada's Interventions Abroad, Canada among Nations 2015, 95
204. Rick Westhead, Don't look, don't tell, troops told, June 16 2008 (https://www.thestar.com/news/2008/06/16/dont_look_dont_tell_troops_told.html)
205. Ibid
206. Paul Koring, Canadian directing war in Libya calls it 'a knife-fight in a phone booth', June 13 2011 (https://www.theglobeandmail.com/news/politics/canadian-directing-war-in-libya-calls-it-a-knife-fight-in-a-phone-booth/article583250/)
207. Campbell Clark, Cracks showing in NATO's Libya strategy, June 22 2011 (https://www.theglobeandmail.com/news/politics/cracks-showing-in-natos-libya-strategy/article625520/)
208. Libya says NATO strike kills 19 civilians, Jun 21 2011 (https://www.aljazeera.com/news/2011/6/21/libya-says-nato-strike-kills-19-civilians) ; France rejects Italian Libya ceasefire call, June 22 2011 (https://www.rfi.fr/en/africa/20110622-france-rejects-italian-libya-ceasefire-call)
209. Daniel Leblanc and John Ibbitson, Canada turns commitment into clout in Libya, Oct 21 2011 (https://www.theglobeandmail.com/news/politics/canada-turns-commitment-into-clout-in-libya/article558644/)
210. Nova Scotia welcomes home Canadian troops, Nov 5 2011 (https://www.cbc.ca/news/canada/nova-scotia/

nova-scotia-welcomes-home-canadian-troops-1.994580)
211. Mary Beth Sheridan and William Branigin, Libyan government orders probe into Gaddafi's death, Oct 25 2011 (https://www.washingtonpost.com/world/middle_east/libya-to-investigate-gaddafis-death/2011/10/24/gIQAjuQtCM_story.html)
212. David Pugliese, The Libya Mission One Year Later: A victory, but at what price?, Feb 18 2012 (https://ottawacitizen.com/news/the-libya-mission-one-year-later-a-victory-but-at-what-price)
213. Canada buying more bombs for Libya, May 18 2011 (https://www.upi.com/Top_News/World-News/2011/05/18/Report-Canada-buying-more-bombs-for-Libya/17851305722508/)
214. Murray Brewster, Canadian surveillance planes join propaganda war; urge Gaddafi forces to go home, Jul 29 2011 (https://ipolitics.ca/2011/07/29/canadian-surveillance-planes-join-propaganda-war-urge-gadhafi-forces-to-go-home/)
215. Eva Hoare, Canadian ship fends off attack by Libyan boats, Winnipeg Free Press, May 13 2011
216. Laura Payton, Canadian diplomats back in Libya, Sep 12 2011 (https://www.cbc.ca/news/politics/canadian-diplomats-back-in-libya-1.1008960)
217. Yves Engler, Canada in Africa 300 Years of Aid and Exploitation, 242
218. Lee Berthiaume, Hawkish Baird urged Libyan rebels to keep up fight, Ottawa Citizen, April 28 2012
219. Libya: Fears for detainees held by anti-Gaddafi forces Aug 30 2011 (https://www.amnesty.org/en/press-releases/2011/08/libya-fears-detainees-held-anti-gaddafi-forces/)
220. Tarik Kafala, 'Cleansed' Libyan town spills its terrible secrets, BBC News, Dec 12 2011 (https://www.bbc.com/news/magazine-16051349)
221. Patrick Cockburn, Amnesty questions claim that Gaddafi ordered rape as weapon of war, 22 Oct 2011 (https://www.independent.co.uk/news/world/africa/amnesty-questions-claim-gaddafi-ordered-rape-weapon-war-2302037.html)
222. Hugh Roberts, Who said Gaddafi had to go?, Vol 33, No 22 Nov 17 2011 (https://www.lrb.co.uk/the-paper/v33/n22/hugh-roberts/who-said-gaddafi-had-to-go)
223. David Pugliese, The Libya Mission One Year Later: A victory, but at what price?, Feb 18 2012 (https://ottawacitizen.com/news/the-libya-mission-one-year-later-a-victory-but-at-what-price)
224. Casualties of the 2011 Libyan Civil War (https://en.wikipedia.org/wiki/Casualties_of_the_2011_Libyan_Civil_War#cite_note-hosted1-22)
225. Unacknowledged Deaths, May 13, 2012 (https://www.hrw.org/report/2012/05/13/unacknowledged-deaths/civilian-casualties-natos-air-campaign-libya)
226. Allen Pizzey, Signs of ex-rebel atrocities in Libya grow, Oct 25 2011 (https://www.cbsnews.com/news/signs-of-ex-rebel-atrocities-in-libya-grow/)
227. David Pugliese, Canadian military predicted chaos in Libya if NATO helped overthrow Gadhafi, Mar 1 2015 (https://ottawacitizen.com/news/national/canadian-military-predicted-chaos-in-libya-if-nato-helped-overthrow-gadhafi)
228. Ibid
229. Joint Task Force 2: Canada's elite fighters, Sep 15 2010 (https://www.cbc.ca/news/canada/joint-task-force-2-canada-s-elite-fighters-1.873657) ; Eric Vandenberg, When will the Dust Settle? Haiti, Canada and the Legacy of Jean-Bertrand Aristide (https://www.cfc.forces.gc.ca/259/290/295/286/vandenberg.pdf)
230. Ibid
231. Richard Sanders, A Very Canadian Coup, Apr 1 2010 (https://www.policyalternatives.ca/publications/monitor/very-canadian-coup)
232. Jeff Heinrich, Canadians threatened us: Haitians, Montreal Gazette Sept 2 2006
233. Jon Elmer, Canada: Counterinsurgency Manual Shows Military's New Face, Mar 22 2007 (www.ipsnews.net/2007/03/canada-counterinsurgency-manual-shows-militarys-new-face/)
234. Canada feared popular uprising in Haiti after quake, Canadian Press, Mar 31 2011 (https://www.ctvnews.ca/canada-feared-popular-uprising-in-haiti-after-quake-1.625850)
235. Kevin A Spooner, Canada, the Congo Crisis, and UN Peacekeeping, 75
236. David Bercuson and J L Granatstein, War and Peacekeeping: From South Africa to the Gulf- Canada's Limited Wars, 219
237. Fred Gaffen, In the eye of the storm, 227; Sean Maloney, Canada and UN Peacekeeping, 122
238. Daniel Galvin, A role for Canada in an African crisis: perceptions of the Congo crisis and motivations for Canadian participation, University of Guelph Dissertation, 2004, 86
239. Kevin A Spooner, Canada, the Congo Crisis, and UN Peacekeeping: 1960-64, 73
240. Jacana Media, Who killed Hammarskjold, 33
241. Alastair MacDonald Taylor, David Cox and J L Granatstein, Peacekeeping: international challenge and Canadian response, 158
242. Daniel Galvin, A role for Canada in an African crisis: perceptions of the Congo crisis and motivations for Canadian participation, University of Guelph Dissertation, 2004, 91
243. Ibid, 88
244. Issaka K Souare, Africa in the United Nations System: 1945-2005, 97
245. Frank R Villafana, Cold War in the Congo: The Confrontation of Cuban Military Forces, 1960-1967, 25
246. Kevin Spooner, Canada, the Congo Crisis, and UN Peacekeeping, 116
247. Ibid, 89
248. Sean Maloney, Canada and UN peacekeeping: Cold War by other means, 1945-197, xii
249. Richard Howard Gimblett, Peter T Haydon and Ann L Griffiths, Canadian Gunboat Diplomacy: the Canadian Navy and foreign-policy, 347
250. Steven Staples, Breaking Rank: A citizens' review of Canada's military spending (https://d3n8a8pro7vhmx.cloudfront.net/polarisinstitute/pages/31/attachments/original/1411065431/breaking_rank.pdf?1411065431)
251. Ibid

Chapter 7

1. Micheal Tucker, Canadian Foreign Policy: Contemporary Issues and Themes, 319
2. House of Commons Debates, Vol 13, 1990)
3. Stephen Brown, Molly den Heyer and David R Black, Rethinking Canadian Aid, Second Edition, 160/162
4. Kim Mackrael, Canada's role in Iraq could mirror Afghanistan, foreign minister says, Globe and Mail, Mar 5 2015 (http://www.theglobeandmail.com/news/politics/foreign-affairs-minister-nicholson-to-speak-about-secret-

trip-to-iraq/article23305564/)
5. June 8, 2006 (https://www.ourcommons.ca/DocumentViewer/en/39-1/NDDN/meeting-5/evidence)
6. David Pugliese, Will Gen. Vance's Threat of Cutting off Afghan Aid Work to Stop Attacks? Sep 29 2009 (https://ottawacitizen.com/news/national/defence-watch/will-gen-vances-threat-of-cutting-off-afghan-aid-work-to-stop-attacks)
7. Walter Dorn and Michael Varey, The Rise and the Demise of the Three Block War, 2009 (www.journal.forces.gc.ca/vol10/no1/07-dornvarey-eng.asp)
8. Yves Engler, Occupation by NGO, Aug 13 2010 (https://www.counterpunch.org/2010/08/13/occupation-by-ngo/)
9. Ibid
10. Canada's engagement in Ukraine (https://www.international.gc.ca/world-monde/country-pays/ukraine/relations.aspx?lang=eng)
11. Evaluation of the Military Training and Cooperation Program May 2019 1258-3-023 (https://www.canada.ca/en/department-national-defence/corporate/reports-publications/audit-evaluation/evaluation-military-training-cooperation-program.html)
12. Jeffrey Monaghan, Security Aid: Canada and the Development Regime of Security, 59
13. Levon Sevunts, Ammunition procurement tender sheds light on secretive Canadian operation in Africa, Aug 3 2017 (https://www.rcinet.ca/en/2017/08/03/ammunition-procurement-tender-sheds-light-on-secretive-canadian-operation-in-africa/)
14. Ibid
15. Detailed Narrative on Transfer Payment Programs Over $5 Million for the Department of National Defence for the period ending Mar 31 2007 (https://www.tbs-sct.gc.ca/dpr-rmr/2006-2007/inst/dnd/dnd08-eng.asp)
16. Peter Langille, Canada in Peacekeeping and Peacekeeping Training in Africa, Briefing N 16, June 2010 (www.ai.org.za/wp-content/uploads/downloads/2011/11/No-16.-Canada-in-Peacekeeping-and-Peacekeeping-Training-in-Africa.pdf)
17. Mark Raymond, Renovating the procedural architecture of international law, Canadian Foreign Policy Journal, Dec 2013
18. Christopher R Kilford, The Other Cold War: Canada's Military Assistance to the Developing World 1945-1975, 219
19. Ibid, 155
20. Gary Hunt, Recollections of the Canadian Armed Forces Training Team in Ghana, 1961-1968, Canadian Defence Quarterly 18, Spring 1989
21. Christopher R Kilford, The Other Cold War, 142
22. Ibid, 143
23. Ibid, 160
24. John P Schlegel, The Deceptive Ash: Bilingualism and Canadian Policy in Africa—1957-1971, 63
25. Operation PROTEUS (https://www.canada.ca/en/department-national-defence/services/operations/military-operations/current-operations/operation-proteus.html)
26. Ilan Evyatar, Canada's continuous commitment, Sept 15 2010 (https://www.jpost.com/Opinion/Op-Ed-Contributors/Canadas-continuous-commitment)
27. Jeffrey Monaghan, Security Aid: Canada and the Development Regime of Security, 141
28. Adam Shatz, Is Palestine Next? The No-State Solution, Jul 14 2011 (https://www.lrb.co.uk/the-paper/v33/n14/adam-shatz/is-palestine-next)
29. Israel urged Canadian government not to cut aid to Palestinians over UN vote: documents, Jul 9 2013 (https://nationalpost.com/news/politics/israel-urged-canadian-government-not-to-cut-aid-to-palestinians-over-un-vote-documents)
30. Yves Engler, Canada's effort to suppress 'popular protests' against Israeli occupation, May 10 2017 (https://canadiandimension.com/articles/view/canadas-effort-to-suppress-popular-protests-against-israeli-occupation)
31. Richard Sanders, Canada's "Open Secret": Deep Complicity in the Iraq War, Press for Conversion! (https://coat.ncf.ca/articles/Canada_in_Iraq.htm)
32. Canada's real new mission in Afghanistan, Ottawa Citizen, Mar 15 2012
33. Jennifer Ditchburn, Military aid flows to Honduras despite coup, July 30 2009 (https://www.theglobeandmail.com/news/politics/military-aid-flows-to-honduras-despite-coup/article1200733/)
34. David Pugliese, Canada's Secret Commandos, 66
35. Stefan Christoff, Is Canadian Military Aid Funding Assassinations in the Philippines?, Nov 8 2007 (www.dominionpaper.ca/articles/1526)
36. Operation UNIFIER (https://www.canada.ca/en/department-national-defence/services/operations/military-operations/current-operations/operation-unifier.html) ; Ukraine: On patrol with the far-right National Militia, BBC, Apr 2018 (https://www.youtube.com/watch?v=hE6b4ao8gAQ)
37. Christopher Miller, In Ukraine, Ultranationalist Militia Strikes Fear in Some Quarters, Jan 30 2018 (https://www.rferl.org/a/ukraine-azov-right-wing-militia-to-patrol-kyiv/29008036.html)
38. Asa Winstanley, Israel is arming neo-Nazis in Ukraine, Electronic Intifada, July 4 2018 (https://electronicintifada.net/content/israel-arming-neo-nazis-ukraine/24876)
39. Strong, Secure, Engaged. Canada's Defence Policy, 2017 (dgpaapp.forces.gc.ca/en/canada-defence-policy/docs/canada-defence-policy-report.pdf)
40. Ibid
41. Nick Westoll, Thousands of cards arrive for Canadian Armed Forces troops after social media appeal, Nov 28 2019 (https://globalnews.ca/news/6227418/canadian-armed-forces-holiday-cards-letters-cfb-trenton/)
42. Brian Hill, Canada has a secret program that grants visas to war criminals, terrorists, security threats, Dec 16 2019 (https://globalnews.ca/news/6289240/canada-secret-program-grants-visas-to-war-criminals-terrorists-security-threats/)
43. Levon Sevunts, Canada postpones major international air force exercise, Dec 13 2018 (https://www.rcinet.ca/en/2018/12/13/canada-postpones-major-international-air-force-exercise/)
44. Norman Hillmer, Fred J Hatch and Patricia Myers, British Commonwealth Air Training Plan, Feb 6 2006 (https://www.thecanadianencyclopedia.ca/en/article/british-commonwealth-air-training-plan)
45. Christopher R Kilford, The Other Cold War: Canada's Military Assistance to the Developing World 1945–1975, 70
46. Yves Engler, Canada in Africa 300 Years of Aid and Exploitation, 91
47. CAE to acquire Bombardier's Military Aviation Training unit to expand training systems integration offering Unit includes NATO Flying Training in Canada (NFTC) program, Jan 26 2015 (https://www.cae.com/news-events/press-releases/cae-to-acquire-bombardiers-military-aviation-training-unit-to-expand-traini/)
48. Dan Black, Combat at Cold Lake, Legion Magazine, Sept 1 2002 (https://legionmagazine.com/en/2002/09/combat-at-cold-lake/)
49. Peter Lozinski, Hundreds of international troops

fill the skies at Cold Lake Air Weapons Range, Jun 12 2016 (https://edmontonjournal.com/news/local-news/hundreds-of-international-troops-fill-the-skies-at-cold-lake-air-weapons-range)
50. Jon Elmer, Good night Battle of Britain, Good morning, Gaza, Dec 1 2005 (https://briarpatchmagazine.com/articles/view/good-night-battle-of-britain-good-morning-gaza)
51. Victor Levant, Quiet Complicity, 204-205

Chapter 8

1. John Clearwater Just Dummies: Cruise Missile Testing in Canada, 199
2. Project MKUltra (https://en.wikipedia.org/wiki/Project_MKUltra)
3. Regan Boychuk, A History of Hypocrisy Canadian complicity links U.S. Cold War torture with cases like Maher Arar's, May 2008 (https://reviewcanada.ca/magazine/2008/05/a-history-of-hypocrisy/)
4. Alfred McCoy, A Question of Torture: CIA Interrogation, from the Cold War to the War on Terror, 35 ; Don Gilmore, I Swear by Apollo: Dr. Ewen Cameron and the CIA-brainwashing experiments, 62
5. In the Sleep Room: the story of the CIA brainwashing experiments in Canada, 47/56 ; Alfred McCoy, A Question of Torture: CIA Interrogation, from the Cold War to the War on Terror, 235 ; Armen Victorian, United States, Canada, Britain: Partners in Mind Control Operations, MindNet, Vol 1, No 81, July 1996 (http://www.elfis.net/elfol0/mkconsp/mkuscan.txt)
6. Richard E Brown, Alfred McCoy, Hebb, the CIA and torture (https://www.uio.no/studier/emner/jus/ikrs/KRIM2950/h11/undervisningsmateriale/Brown.pdf)
7. Don Gilmore, I Swear by Apollo, 64
8. Alford W McCoy, A Question of Torture: CIA Interrogation, from the Cold War to the War on Terror, 35
9. Ibid
10. Cecil Rosner, Isolation: A Canadian professor's research into sensory deprivation and its connection to disturbing new methods of interrogation, Jan 21 2016 (https://www.canadashistory.ca/explore/science-technology/isolation)
11. Ibid
12. Lisa Ellenwood, Group affected by CIA brainwashing experiments wants public apology, compensation from government, May 21 2018 (https://www.cbc.ca/news/canada/project-mkultra-families-meet-1.4662321)
13. A Ojedda, Legacy of a Dark Decade: CIA Mind Control, Classified Behavioral Research and the Origins of Modern Medical Ethics" in 'The Trauma of Psychological Torture' ; Regan Boychuk, A History of Hypocrisy Canadian complicity links U.S. Cold War torture with cases like Maher Arar's, May 2008 (https://reviewcanada.ca/magazine/2008/05/a-history-of-hypocrisy/) ; Bob McKeown, Harvey Cashore and Lisa Ellenwood, Trudeau government gag order in CIA brainwashing case silences victims, lawyer says, Dec 15 2017 (https://www.cbc.ca/news/canada/canadian-government-gag-order-mk-ultra-1.4448933)
14. Ashifa Kassam, The toxic legacy of Canada's CIA brainwashing experiments, May 3 2018 (https://www.theguardian.com/world/2018/may/03/montreal-brainwashing-allan-memorial-institute)
15. Ibid
16. Elizabeth Thompson, Federal government quietly compensates daughter of brainwashing experiments victim, Oct 26 2017 (https://www.cbc.ca/news/politics/cia-brainwashing-allanmemorial-mentalhealth-1.4373590)
17. Alford W McCoy, A Question of Torture: CIA Interrogation, from the Cold War to the War on Terror, 55
18. Regan Boychuk, A History of Hypocrisy Canadian complicity links U.S. Cold War torture with cases like Maher Arar's, May 2008 (https://reviewcanada.ca/magazine/2008/05/a-history-of-hypocrisy/)
19. Alfred W McCoy, Torture and Impunity: The U.S. Doctrine of Coercive Interrogation, 29
20. Regan Boychuk, A History of Hypocrisy Canadian complicity links U.S. Cold War torture with cases like Maher Arar's, May 2008 (https://reviewcanada.ca/magazine/2008/05/a-history-of-hypocrisy/)
21. In the Sleep Room: the story of the CIA brainwashing experiments in Canada, 47
22. Wladyslaw Bulhak and Thomas Wegener Friis Need to Know: Eastern and Western Perspectives
23. D J Godspeed, A History of the Defence Research Board of Canada, 151
24. Tim Cook, No Place to Run: The Canadian Corps and Gas Warfare in the First World War, 95
25. Tristin Hopper, The forgotten ruthlessness of Canada's Great War soldiers, Nov 12 2018 (https://nationalpost.com/news/canada/the-forgotten-ferocity-of-canadas-soldiers-in-the-great-war)
26. Tim Cook, No Place to Run: The Canadian Corps and Gas Warfare in the First World War, 8
27. Ibid, 15
28. History Looking back helps us look forward (https://www.opcw.org/about/history)
29. April 17-19, 1917: The Second Battle of Gaza, First Use of Tanks and Poison Gas in Middle East, Apr 19 2017 (mideasti.blogspot.com/2017/04/april-17-19-1917-second-battle-of-gaza.html)
30. The 2nd Battle of Gaza (https://stevesmith1944.wordpress.com/2017/04/18/the-2nd-battle-of-gaza/)
31. Giles Milton, Winston Churchill's shocking use of chemical weapons, Sept 1 2013 (https://www.theguardian.com/world/shortcuts/2013/sep/01/winston-churchill-shocking-use-chemical-weapons)
32. Maharaj K Kaul, Amnesty International and its neo-colonial mission, 23
33. Giles Milton, Winston Churchill's shocking use of chemical weapons, Sep 1 2013 (https://www.theguardian.com/world/shortcuts/2013/sep/01/winston-churchill-shocking-use-chemical-weapons)
34. G W L Nicholson, Canadian Expeditionary Force, 1914-1919: Official History of the Canadian Army in the First World War, 513
35. Churchill's 1919 War Office Memorandum, May 12 1919 (https://www.nationalchurchillmuseum.org/churchills-1919-war-office-memorandum.html)
36. Tom Heyden, The 10 greatest controversies of Winston Churchill's career, BBC News Magazine, Jan 26 2015 (https://www.bbc.com/news/magazine-29701767) ; Giles Milton, Winston Churchill's shocking use of chemical weapons, Sep 1 2013 (https://www.theguardian.com/world/shortcuts/2013/sep/01/winston-churchill-shocking-use-chemical-weapons)
37. Canadians in Mesopotamia, 1918-1919 (https://www.canada.ca/en/department-national-defence/services/military-history/history-heritage/official-military-history-lineages/reports/army-headquarters-1948-1959/canadians-mesopotamia-1918-1919.html)
38. John Bryden, Deadly Allies: Canada's Secret War

1937-1947, 13
39. Ibid, 22
40. University Toronto Great Past (www.greatpast.utoronto.ca/bios/history27.asp)
41. John Bryden, Deadly Allies: Canada's Secret War 1937-1947, 50
42. Jeanne Guillemin, Biological Weapons: from the invention of state-sponsored programs to contemporary bioterrorism, 47
43. Doug Saunders, Let's not forget Canada's legacy of gas warfare, July 22 2017 (https://www.theglobeandmail.com/opinion/lets-not-forget-canadas-legacy-of-gas-warfare/article35759816/)
44. Stephen Endicott and Edward Hagerman, the United States and Biological Warfare: secrets from the early Cold War and Korea, 214
45. Ibid, 193
46. John Bryden, Deadly Allies: Canada's Secret War 1937-1947, 251
47. Christopher Robin Paige, Canada and Chemical Warfare 1939-1945, A Thesis Submitted to the College of Graduate Studies and Research In Partial Fulfilment of the Requirements For the Degree of Master of Arts In the Department of History University of Saskatchewan Saskatoon, 92 (https://ecommons.usask.ca/bitstream/handle/10388/etd-02252009-160109/CanadaandChemicalWarfare.pdf?sequence=1)
48. Ibid
49. Stephen Endicott and Edward Hagerman, The United States and Biological Warfare, 213
50. John Bryden, Deadly Allies: Canada's Secret War 1937-1947, vii/241
51. Bruce Livesey, Canada's chemical warfare dependency, Toronto Star, Feb 26 1991 ; John Bryden, Deadly Allies: Canada's Secret War 1937-1947, 171
52. Ibid, 175
53. Donald Avery, Pathogens for War: Biological Weapons, Canadian Life Scientists, and North American Biodefence, 45
54. Susan L Smith, Toxic Exposures: Mustard Gas and the Health Consequences of World, 2
55. Rob Evans, Canadian soldiers in mustard gas tests honoured, May 6 2000 (https://www.theguardian.com/world/2000/may/06/freedomofinformation.politics)
56. Bruce Campion-Smith, Nerve Gas Tests Revealed, Toronto Star, July 18 2005
57. Graham Chandler, Chemistry experiments, May 26 2016 (https://legionmagazine.com/en/2016/05/chemistry-experiments/)
58. Bruce Campion-Smith, Nerve Gas Tests Revealed, Toronto Star, July 18 2005
59. Ibid
60. We were Cold War guinea pigs, Oct 13 2017 (https://www.winnipegfreepress.com/opinion/editorials/we-were-cold-war-guinea-pigs-450717813.html)
61. Victor Ferreira, U.S. secretly tested carcinogen in Western Canada during the Cold War, researcher finds, Oct 6 2017 (https://nationalpost.com/news/canada/u-s-secretly-tested-carcinogen-in-western-canada-during-the-cold-war-researcher-discovers#:~:text=Between%20July%209%2C%201953%20and,according%20to%20Lisa%20Martino-Taylor.)
62. Ibid
63. Donald Avery, Pathogens for War, 65/97
64. Ibid
65. Donald Avery, Deadly Cultures: biological weapons since 1945, 85
66. Donald Avery, Pathogens for War, 88
67. Ibid, 66 ; Bernd Horn, Shadow Warriors: the Canadian Special Operations Forces Command, 32
68. Donald Avery, Pathogens for War, 65
69. Ibid, 71
70. Stephen Endicott and Edward Hagerman, the United States and Biological Warfare: secrets from the early Cold War and Korea, 75
71. Ibid
72. Donald Avery, Pathogens for War, 161
73. Ibid, 73
74. Volker Skierka, Fidel Castro: A Biography
75. Judith Miller, Stephen Engelberg and William J Broad, Germs: Biological Weapons and America's secret war, 73 ; Mark Wheelis and Lajos Rózs, Deadly Cultures: Biological Weapons since 1945
76. CIA Link to Cuban Pig Virus Reported, San Francisco Chronicle, Jan 10 1977 (https://www.uky.edu/~rmfarl2/cubabio1.htm)
77. Mark Wheelis and Lajos Rózs, Deadly Cultures: Biological Weapons since 1945, 93
78. Jeremy Paxman and Robert Harris, A Higher Form of Killing: The Secret History of Chemical and Biological Warfare, 183
79. Ibid
80. Jonathan B Tucker, War of Nerves: chemical warfare from World War I to Al Qaeda, 186
81. Diana Chown, Suffield, Chemical Warfare, and Canadian/US Relations, Peace Magazine, Feb 1989 (http://peacemagazine.org/archive/v05n1p12.htm)
82. Donald Avery, Pathogens for War, 62/88
83. John Bryden, Deadly Allies: Canada's Secret War 1937-1947, 252
84. Donald Avery, Pathogens for War, 62/88
85. Ernie Regehr, Making a Killing: Canada's arms industry, 78
86. Thomas Walkom, Canada's legacy of lies on biological weapons, June 27 2013 (https://www.therecord.com/opinion-story/3857983-canada-s-legacy-of-lies-on-biological-weapons/)
87. Donald Avery, Pathogens for War, 154
88. Jonathan Turner, The Defence Research Board of Canada, 1947 to 1977, 205 (https://tspace.library.utoronto.ca/bitstream/1807/71816/1/turner_jonathan_r_201211_PhD_thesis.pdf)
89. Diana Chown, Suffield, Chemical Warfare, and Canadian/US Relations, Peace Magazine, Feb 1989 (http://peacemagazine.org/archive/v05n1p12.htm)
90. Welcome to the official website of the Agent Orange Association of Canada Inc (htps://www.agentorangecanada.com/)
91. Ibid
92. Victor Levant, Quiet Complicity: Canadian Involvement in the Vietnam War, 205
93. John Bryden, Deadly Allies: Canada's Secret War 1937-1947, 92
94. Agent Orange (https://en.wikipedia.org/wiki/Agent_Orange)
95. Activists back French Vietnamese woman's Agent Orange case, Jan 30 2021 (https://toronto.citynews.ca/2021/01/30/activists-back-french-vietnamese-womans-agent-orange-case-2/)
96. David J Bercuson and Jack Granatstein, Dictionary of Canadian Military History, 218
97. Ray Stouffer, Swords, Clunks and Windowmakers: the tumultuous life of the RCAF's original one Canadian air division, 136
98. Jason S Ridler, Maestro of Science: Omond McKillop Solandt and Government Science in War and Hostile

Peace, 1939-1956, 183
99. Jonathan Turner, The Defence Research Board of Canada, 1947 to 1977 (https://tspace.library.utoronto.ca/bitstream/1807/71816/1/turner_jonathan_r_201211_PhD_thesis.pdf)
100. Ibid, 143
101. Napalm (https://en.wikipedia.org/wiki/Napalm)
102. I F Stone, The Hidden History of the Korean War, 258
103. John Price, Orienting Canada, 271
104. Thomas Powell, Biological Warfare in the Korean War: Allegations and Cover-up, Socialism and Democracy, Vol 31, Iss 1, 2017
105. John Price, Orienting Canada, 275
106. Ibid
107. D J Godspeed, A History of the Defence Research Board of Canada, 138 ; Donald Avery, Pathogens for War: Biological Weapons, Canadian Life Scientists, and North American Biodefence, 63
108. John Bryden, Deadly Allies: Canada's Secret War 1937-1947, 247
109. Donald Avery, Pathogens for War, 162
110. Ibid, 155
111. Bruce Campion-Smith, Nerve Gas Tests Revealed, Toronto Star, July 18 2005
112. Ibid
113. Ibid
114. Donald Avery, Pathogens for War, 100
115. The Problem of Chemical and Biological Warfare: CBW and the law of war, Stockholm International Peace Research Institute, 1973
116. The Problem of Chemical and Biological Warfare: a study of the historical, technical, military, legal and political aspects of CBW, and possible disarmament measures, Vol III, CBW and the Law of War, Stockholm International Peace Research Institute (https://www.sipri.org/publications/2000/problem-chemical-and-biological-warfare)
117. Victor Levant, Quiet Complicity, 177
118. Ibid, 176
119. Donald Avery, Pathogens for War, 123
120. Diana Chown, Suffield, Chemical Warfare, and Canadian/US Relations, Feb 1989 (http://peacemagazine.org/archive/v05n1p12.htm)
121. Donald Avery, Pathogens for War, 130
122. Ibid
123. Ibid
124. Lester Haines, Taliban monster dope plants defy Canadian military, Oct 13 2006 (https://www.theregister.com/2006/10/13/fireproof_forests/)
125. Afghanistan: NATO Should 'Come Clean' on White Phosphorus, May 8 2009 (https://www.hrw.org/news/2009/05/08/afghanistan-nato-should-come-clean-white-phosphorus)

Chapter 9

1. A new Canadian approach to defence: Anticipate. Adapt. Act. (https://www.canada.ca/en/department-national-defence/corporate/reports-publications/canada-defence-policy/new-approach-defence.html)
2. Defence Energy and Environment Strategy (https://www.canada.ca/content/dam/dnd-mdn/documents/reports/2017/20171004-dees-en.pdf)
3. P Whitney Lackenbauer, Battle Grounds: the Canadian military and aboriginal lands, 3
4. Michael Graham Richard, 7 Gas Guzzling Military Combat Vehicles, Oct 11 2018 (https://www.treehugger.com/cars/7-gas-guzzling-military-combat-vehicles.html) ; Beth Brown, Access to fuel essential for Royal Canadian Navy's Arctic work, Sept 5 2018 (https://nunatsiaq.com/stories/article/65674fuel_access_key_to_canadian_navys_arctic_work/)
5. Daniel Leblanc and John Ibbitson, Canada turns commitment into clout in Libya, Oct 21 2011 (https://www.theglobeandmail.com/news/politics/canada-turns-commitment-into-clout-in-libya/article558644/)
6. Mike Wolter, 435 Squadron delivers air-to-air refuelling for a quarter century Avatar, June 13 2018 (https://www.skiesmag.com/news/435-squadron-delivers-air-to-air-refuelling-for-a-quarter-century/)
7. Ibid
8. News release, Contract awarded for in-service support of CC-150 Polaris fleet, National Defence, Dec 6 2018 (https://www.canada.ca/en/department-national-defence/news/2018/12/contract-awarded-for-in-service-support-of-cc-150-polaris-fleet.html)
9. Tamara Lorincz, Spending $19 billion on fighter jets won't fight COVID-19 or climate change, May 12 2020 (https://ricochet.media/en/3108/spending-19-billion-on-fighter-jets-wont-fight-covid-19-or-climate-change)
10. Tim Cook, No Place to Run: The Canadian Corps and Gas Warfare in the First World War, 3
11. Eric Talmadge, 64 years after Korean War, North still digging up bombs, July 24 2017 (https://apnews.com/article/dd6256bad51e458cb2e8a1bf64b5c2b6)
12. Charles K Armstrong, The Destruction and Reconstruction of North Korea, 1950-1960 (ttps://apjjf.org/-Charles-K.-Armstrong/3460/article.html)
13. Karl Mathiesen, What's the environmental impact of modern war?, Nov 6 2014 (https://www.theguardian.com/environment/2014/nov/06/whats-the-environmental-impact-of-modern-war)
14. Suadad al-Salhy, Iraq sees alarming rise in cancers, deformed babies, Dec 1 2009 (https://uk.reuters.com/article/uk-iraq-health-war/iraq-sees-alarming-rise-in-cancers-deformed-babies-idUKTRE5B01132009120) ; Serhiy Kurykin, Environmental impact of the war in Yugoslavia on southeast Europe, Report Committee on the Environment, Regional Planning and Local Authorities, Jan 10 2001 (http://www.assembly.coe.int/nw/xml/XRef/X2H-Xref-ViewHTML.asp?FileID=9143&lang=EN)
15. Sharon Adams, Military looks at respiratory illness, Sept 13 2016 (https://legionmagazine.com/en/2016/09/military-looks-at-respiratory-illness/)
16. Serhiy Kurykin, Environmental impact of the war in Yugoslavia on southeast Europe, Report Committee on the Environment, Regional Planning and Local Authorities, Jan 10 2001 (http://www.assembly.coe.int/nw/xml/XRef/X2H-Xref-ViewHTML.asp?FileID=9143&lang=EN)
17. Ibid
18. Chris Hedges, Serbian Town Bombed by NATO Fears Effects of Toxic Chemicals, New York Times, July 14 1999
19. ISAF's environmental legacy in Afghanistan requires greater scrutiny, Sept 1 2014 (https://ceobs.org/isafs-environmental-legacy-in-afghanistan-requires-greater-scrutiny/)
20. Gary E Machlis and Thor Hanson, Warfare Ecology, BioScience, Vol 58, Sept 2008 (https://academic.oup.com/bioscience/article/58/8/729/380940)
21. Angry villagers blame Canadians for explosion that killed two Afghan children, Canadian Press, Feb 23 2009 (https://www.cp24.com/angry-villagers-blame-canadians-

for-explosion-that-killed-two-afghan-children-1.372978?cache=ifpvdgct%3FclipId%3D89563)
22. Derek Stoffel, Burgers and massages in the middle of the desert, CBC, Sep 2 2008 (https://www.cbc.ca/news/world/burgers-and-massages-in-the-middle-of-the-desert-1.698662) ; Emma Graham-Harrison, Kandahar's 'poo pond' gets a stay of execution, Dec 12 2012 (https://www.theguardian.com/world/2012/dec/12/kandahar-airfield-poo-pond-mission)
23. Aisha Abdelhamid, Cleaning NATO's Eco Waste in Afghanistan (http://inspiredeconomist.com/2015/01/07/cleaning-natos-ecowaste-afghanistan/)
24. Spencer Ackerman, Leaked Memo: Afghan 'Burn Pit' Could Wreck Troops' Hearts, Lungs, June 22 2012 (https://www.wired.com/2012/05/bagram-health-risk/)
25. Nafeez Ahmed, War crime: NATO deliberately destroyed Libya's water infrastructure, May 14 2015 (https://theecologist.org/2015/may/14/war-crime-nato-deliberately-destroyed-libyas-water-infrastructure)
26. NATO bombs the Great Man-Made River, July 27 2011 (https://humanrightsinvestigations.org/2011/07/27/great-man-made-river-nato-bombs/)
27. Kieran Cooke, Trouble ahead for Gaddafi's Great Man-Made River, Feb 9 2017 (https://www.middleeasteye.net/columns/trouble-great-man-made-river-1331047422)
28. Jeff Pelletier, The Victoria Cross for animals: The Dickin Medal, Nov 16 2018 (http://espritdecorps.ca/army-articles/the-victoria-cross-for-animals-the-dickin-medal)
29. Mark Zuehlke, Canada's first foreign war, May 15 2017 (https://legionmagazine.com/en/2017/05/canadas-first-foreign-war/)
30. War Horses: the role of horses in the anglo-boer war (1899-1902) (https://somethingovertea.wordpress.com/2016/04/21/war-horses-the-role-of-horses-in-the-anglo-boer-war-1899-1902/)
31. Animals in War Dedication (https://www.canada.ca/en/canadian-heritage/services/art-monuments/monuments/animals-war-dedication.html)
32. Sandra Swart, Horses in the South African War, c. 1899-1902 (http://www.animalsandsociety.org/wp-content/uploads/2016/04/swart.pdf)
33. Christine Tam, From horses to carrier pigeons, millions of war animals saved lives, Global News, Nov 5 2013 (https://globalnews.ca/news/948446/from-horses-to-carrier-pigeons-millions-of-war-animals-saved-lives/)
34. Fred Langan, Morning Glory: Canada's own WWI, Nov 9 2012 (https://www.cbc.ca/news/canada/morning-glory-canada-s-own-wwi-war-horse-1.1259736)
35. Veteran wins Ottawa memorial for animals in war, Oct 22 2012 (https://ottawasun.com/2012/10/22/veteran-wins-ottawa-memorial-for-animals-in-war/wcm/525ecc4a-46be-4345-976f-960c9d12222d)
36. Canada's Great War Album (http://greatwaralbum.ca/Great-War-Album/About-the-Great-War/Animals-in-war)
37. D S Tamblyn, The Horse in War: Horses & Mules in the Allied Armies During the First World War, 1914-18, 109
38. From Gander to Winnie: Remembering those animals who served Canada, Canadian Press, Nov 7 2019 (https://www.princegeorgematters.com/highlights/from-gander-to-winnie-remembering-those-animals-who-served-canada-1832194)
39. Paul Edwards, Unusual Footnotes to the Korean War
40. Thor Thorgrimsson and E C Russell, Canadian Naval Operations in Korean Waters 1950-1955
41. Heike Krieger, The Kosovo Conflict and International Law: An Analytical Documentation 1974-1999
42. Matthew Fisher, Dogs of war: canines key to saving lives in Afghan war, Canwest News, Mar 28 2009 ; Alan Taylor, Afghanistan: Dogs of War, June 3 2014 (https://www.theatlantic.com/photo/2014/06/afghanistan-dogs-of-war/100750/)
43. James McCarten, Afghan donkey named Hughes eases burden for Canadian soldiers, Canadian Press, Apr 2 2008 (https://www.metro.us/afghan-donkey-named-hughes-eases-burden-for-canadian-soldiers/)
44. Rami Al-Shaheibi, Hundreds of armed camels in Libya allegedly burned in NATO airstrike, Associated Press, Aug 5 2011 (https://www.thestar.com/news/world/2011/08/05/hundreds_of_armed_camels_in_libya_allegedly_burned_in_nato_airstrike.html)
45. War Horses, Nov 10 2014 (https://cowboycountrymagazine.com/2014/11/war-horses/)
46. David Pugliese, Animal experiments on the Wane, DND says, National Post, Jan 8 2019
47. Lee Berthiaume, Military uses thousands of live animals every year for training, testing, Calgary Herald, July 23 2013 (https://o.canada.com/news/military-uses-thousands-of-live-animals-every-year-for-training-testing)
48. David Pugliese, Animal experiments on the Wane, DND says, National Post, Jan 8 2019
49. Randy Boswell, Canadian military 'actively' seeking to end animal use in medical training, Ottawa Citizen, Aug 16 2012
50. Brunella Cautela, Use of Animals in Canadian Military, Dec 3 2012 (https://prezi.com/h5rbmxknkz8-/use-of-animals-in-canadian-military/)
51. Randy Boswell, Canadian military 'actively' seeking to end animal use in medical training, Ottawa Citizen, Aug 16 2012
52. Christopher Robin Paige, Canada and Chemical Warfare 1939-1945, A Thesis Submitted to the College of Graduate Studies and Research In Partial Fulfilment of the Requirements For the Degree of Master of Arts In the Department of History University of Saskatchewan Saskatoon (https://ecommons.usask.ca/bitstream/handle/10388/etd-02252009-160109/CanadaandChemicalWarfare.pdf?sequence=1)
53. Stephen Endicott and Edward Hagerman, The United States and Biological Warfare: secrets from the early Cold War and Korea, 213
54. Donald Avery, Pathogens for War, 161
55. Leonard a Cole, Clouds of Secrecy: the Army's germ warfare tests overpopulated areas, 18
56. Then and Now: Community Connections, Mar 2014 (https://www.cheminst.ca/magazine/columns/then-and-now-5)
57. Leyland Cecco, Canada: locals angry after navy holds live fire exercises in orca habitat, Nov 22 2018 (https://www.theguardian.com/world/2018/nov/22/canada-navy-live-fire-exercise-killer-whale-protected-habitat)
58. Michael Mountain, Did a Canadian Navy Sonar Bomb Kill a Beloved Young Orca?, Apr 9 2012 (http://www.earthintransition.org/2012/04/did-a-canadian-navy-sonar-bomb-kill-a-beloved-young-orca/)
59. Frigate forced back to port in Halifax due to oil leak in ship's engine room, Canadian Press, July 10 2019 (https://atlantic.ctvnews.ca/frigate-forced-back-to-port-in-halifax-due-to-oil-leak-in-ship-s-engine-room-1.4502619)
60. Natalie Dobbin, Halifax Harbour fuel spill from HMCS Athabaskan leads to probe by navy, CBC, Jan 28 2016 (https://www.cbc.ca/news/canada/nova-scotia/navy-investigates-hfx-fuel-spill-1.3422826)
61. Department of National Defence ordered to pay

$100,000 for contravening Fisheries Act following fuel spill in Halifax Harbour, News Release, Environment and Climate Change Canada, Apr 20 2016 –(https://www.canada.ca/en/environment-climate-change/news/2016/04/department-of-national-defence-ordered-to-pay-100-000-for-contravening-fisheries-act-following-fuel-spill-in-halifax-harbour.html)

62. Brett Ruskin, How the navy's 'grim reaper' scraps Canada's old military ships, Mar 18 2019 (https://www.cbc.ca/news/canada/nova-scotia/navy-s-grim-reaper-scraps-canada-s-old-ships-1.5039248)

63. Tim Naumetz, Proud Huron going under friendly fire, CanWest News, Ap 4 2007

64. Ibid

65. Robert Matas, B.C. regains torpedo range, Mar 7 2002 (https://www.theglobeandmail.com/news/national/bc-regains-torpedo-range/article4132321/)

66. Sarah O'Donnell, BC'ers want US "city killers" out of Georgia Strait, Ubyssey News, Nov 10 1995

67. Steve Rennie, Canadian waters awash in sunken explosives, U.S. navy expert warns, Feb 25 2008 (https://www.theglobeandmail.com/news/national/canadian-waters-awash-in-sunken-explosives-us-navy-expert-warns/article668340/)

68. Ingrid Peritz, Bombs lie on bed of serene Quebec lake, Aug 19 2005 (https://www.theglobeandmail.com/news/national/bombs-lie-on-bed-of-serene-quebec-lake/article20425191/)

69. Ibid

70. Zoe McKnight and Kelly Sinoski, Over 200 sites across B.C. could hide live munitions, Vancouver Sun, June 17 2013 (https://vancouversun.com/News/Metro/over-200-sites-across-bc-could-hide-live-munitions?r)

71. Joshua McNeely, Military munitions dumped in coastal waters around the Maritimes, Vol 3, Is 3, Dec 2007 (http://mapcmaars.ca/theblog/2007/12/military-munitions-dumped-in-coastal-waters-around-the-maritimes/

72. Susan L Smith, Toxic Exposures: Mustard Gas and the Health Consequences of World War II in the United States, 77

73. Murray Brewster, Ex-soldier says he watched barrels of Agent Orange being buried at Gagetown base, May 23 2018 (https://www.cbc.ca/news/politics/agent-orange-gagetown-eyewitness-1.4673641)

74. Natalie Salat, Searching for Chemical Warfare Dump, Legion Magazine, Nov 1 2004 (https://legionmagazine.com/en/2004/11/searching-for-chemical-warfare-dump/)

75. Susan L Smith, Toxic Exposures: Mustard Gas and the Health Consequences of World War II in the United States, 77

76. Military doesn't know where undersea weapons dumps are, May 1 2002 (http://www.cbc.ca/news/canada/military-doesn-t-know-where-undersea-weapons-dumps-are-1.326214)

77. Joshua McNeely, Military munitions dumped in coastal waters around the Maritimes, Vol 3, Dec 2007 (http://mapcmaars.ca/theblog/2007/12/military-munitions-dumped-in-coastal-waters-around-the-maritimes/) ; Christopher Robin Paige, Canada and Chemical Warfare 1939-1945, A Thesis Submitted to the College of Graduate Studies and Research In Partial Fulfilment of the Requirements For the Degree of Master of Arts In the Department of History University of Saskatchewan Saskatoon (https://ecommons.usask.ca/bitstream/handle/10388/etd-02252009-160109/CanadaandChemicalWarfare.pdf?sequence=1)

78. Kevin Cox, Military dumps a danger, panel told, Jan 22 2002 (https://www.theglobeandmail.com/news/national/military-dumps-a-danger-panel-told/article1020890/)

79. Joshua McNeely, Military munitions dumped in coastal waters around the Maritimes, Vol 3, Dec 2007 (http://mapcmaars.ca/theblog/2007/12/military-munitions-dumped-in-coastal-waters-around-the-maritimes)

80. Christopher Robin Paige, Canada and Chemical Warfare 1939-1945, A Thesis Submitted to the College of Graduate Studies and Research In Partial Fulfilment of the Requirements For the Degree of Master of Arts In the Department of History University of Saskatchewan Saskatoon (https://ecommons.usask.ca/bitstream/handle/10388/etd-02252009-160109/CanadaandChemicalWarfare.pdf?sequence=1)

81. David Pugliese, Chemical weapons from secret Canadian-U.S. mustard gas program in Panama to be destroyed, Ottawa Citizen, July 17 2017

82. Christopher Robin Paige, Canada and Chemical Warfare 1939-1945, A Thesis Submitted to the College of Graduate Studies and Research In Partial Fulfilment of the Requirements For the Degree of Master of Arts In the Department of History University of Saskatchewan Saskatoon (https://ecommons.usask.ca/bitstream/handle/10388/etd-02252009-160109/CanadaandChemicalWarfare.pdf?sequence=1)

83. Doug Saunders, Let's not forget Canada's legacy of gas warfare, July 22 2017 (https://www.theglobeandmail.com/opinion/lets-not-forget-canadas-legacy-of-gas-warfare/article35759816/)

84. Jeff Lewis, Unexploded Ordnance and the Environment — a Legacy of Past Practices (www.journal.forces.gc.ca/vol10/no4/08-lewis-eng.asp)

85. Julian Sher, Jennifer Quinn and Robert Cribb, Unexploded bombs, ammo in 150 possible Ontario locations: DND report, Aug 12 2013 (https://www.thestar.com/news/world/2013/08/12/bombs_in_your_backyard_ontario_home_to_150_possible_locations_of_unexploded_bombs.html)

86. Justin Ling, The Canadian Military Has Finally Developed Green Ammo, Feb 17 2016 (https://news.vice.com/article/the-canadian-military-has-finally-developed-green-ammo-that-wont-poison-drinking-water)

87. Dominic Casciani, Did removing lead from petrol spark a decline in crime?, April 21 2014 (https://www.bbc.com/news/magazine-27067615)

88. Philip J Anido, Environmental Stewardship on Canadian Military Training Areas; rhetoric or reality, A thesis submitted to the Faculty of Graduate Studies and Research in Partial fulfillment of the requirements for the degree of - Master of Arts Department of Geography, Carleton University, Sept 1998 (https://www.collectionscanada.gc.ca/obj/s4/f2/dsk2/tape17/PQDD_0017/MQ36808.pdf)

89. Ibid

90. Ibid

91. Ibid

92. Ibid

93. Whitney P Lackenbauer, The Cold War on Canadian Soil: Militarizing a Northern Environment, American Society for Environmental History, Vol 12, No 4, Special Issue on Canada, Oct 2007

94. Sandro Contenta, DEW Line: Canada is cleaning up pollution caused by Cold War radar stations in the Arctic, Aug 4 2012 (https://www.thestar.com/news/insight/2012/08/04/dew_line_canada_is_cleaning_up_pollution_caused_by_cold_war_radar_stations_in_the_

arctic.html)
95. P Whitney Lackenbauer, Matthew J Farish and Jennifer Arthur-Lackenbauer, The Distant Early Warning (DEW) Line: A Bibliography and Documentary Resource List, Oct 2005 (pubs.aina.ucalgary.ca/aina/dewlinebib.pdf)
96. Sandro Contenta, DEW Line: Canada is cleaning up pollution caused by Cold War radar stations in the Arctic, Aug 4 2012 (https://www.thestar.com/news/insight/2012/08/04/dew_line_canada_is_cleaning_up_pollution_caused_by_cold_war_radar_stations_in_the_arctic.html)
97. Ibid
98. Ibid
99. $103 million pledged to clean up abandoned radar sites in northern Ontario, Jun 22 2009 (https://www.cbc.ca/news/canada/toronto/103-million-pledged-to-clean-up-abandoned-radar-sites-in-northern-ontario-1.778032)
100. Canada's Tibet: The Killing of the Innu, 31
101. James Wilt, Canada Still Doesn't Know How Much Pollution Its Military Emits, Mar 13 2017 (https://www.vice.com/en/article/ypknzj/canada-still-doesnt-know-how-much-pollution-its-military-emits)
102. Whitney P Lackenbauer and Matthew Farish, The Cold War on Canadian Soil: Militarizing a Northern Environment, American Society for Environmental History, Vol 12, No 4, Special Issue on Canada, Oct 2007
103. Ibid

Chapter 10

1. Gordon Edwards, How Uranium from Great Bear Lake Ended Up in A-Bombs ~ A Chronology (http://www.ccnr.org/uranium_events.html)
2. James Eayrs, Northern Approaches: Canada and the Search for Peace, 36
3. Asad Ismi and Kristin Schwartz, We're the Major Supplier of Uranium for Nuclear Weapons, Oct 1 2008 (https://www.policyalternatives.ca/publications/monitor/october-2008-were-major-supplier-uranium-nuclear-weapons)
4. John Price, Orienting Canada: Race, Empire, and the Transpacific, 103
5. Ibid
6. Bianca Mugyenyi, Ottawa must acknowledge its role in atomic bombings of Japan and sign ban, Aug 5 2020 (https://www.thestar.com/opinion/contributors/2020/08/05/ottawa-must-acknowledge-its-role-in-atomic-bombings-of-japan-and-sign-ban.html)
7. Kim Petersen, Canada, Racism, Genocide, and the Bomb: The Legacy of C.D. Howe, Apr 5 2005 (http://www.dominionpaper.ca/original_peoples/2005/04/05/canada_rac.html)
8. Jonathan Turner, The Defence Research Board of Canada, 1947 to 1977, A thesis submitted in conformity with the requirements for the degree of Doctor of Philosophy Institute for the History and Philosophy of Science and Technology University of Toronto, 2012 (https://tspace.library.utoronto.ca/bitstream/1807/71816/1/turner_jonathan_r_201211_PhD_thesis.pdf)
9. Ibid
10. Ibid
11. Ibid
12. Bill Graveland, Nuke-test veterans to get $24,000, Canadian Press, Sept 3 2008 (https://www.thestar.com/news/canada/2008/09/03/nuketest_veterans_to_get_24000.html)
13. Uranium in Canada, Jan 2021 (http://www.world-nuclear.org/information-library/country-profiles/countries-a-f/canada-uranium.aspx)
14. Carole Giangrande, The Nuclear North: the people, the regions and arms race, 99
15. Ibid, 128
16. Ron Finch, Exporting Danger: A History of the Canadian Nuclear Energy Export Programme, 77
17. Carole Giangrande, The Nuclear North, 128
18. Caroja12, Port Hope homeowners worried by toxic soil Global News, Nov 29 2017 (https://globalnews.ca/news/3888326/port-hope-lead-high-levels-homes-2/)
19. Ibid
20. Dennis Riches, Blind Faith: The Nuclear History of Port Hope, Ontario Jan 15 2015 (https://www.mintpressnews.com/MyMPN/blind-faith-nuclear-history-port-hope-ontario/)
21. $1.28B for Port Hope radioactive cleanup, Canadian Press, Jan 14 2012 (https://www.cbc.ca/news/canada/toronto/1-28b-for-port-hope-radioactive-cleanup-1.1275969)
22. Uranium and nuclear power facts (https://www.nrcan.gc.ca/science-and-data/data-and-analysis/energy-data-and-analysis/energy-facts/uranium-and-nuclear-power-facts/20070)
23. Duane Bratt, The Politics of CANDU Exports, 118
24. Nomi Morris, Is Canada to blame? June 8 1998 (https://archive.macleans.ca/article/1998/6/8/is-canada-to-blame)
25. Linda Freeman, The Ambiguous Champion: Canada and South Africa in the Trudeau and Mulroney Years, 104
26. Susan L Smith, Toxic Exposures: Mustard Gas and the Health Consequences of World, 6
27. Edward A Ough, Canadian Forces Uranium Testing Program (in Depleted Uranium: Properties, Uses, and Health Consequences)
28. Depleted uranium (https://en.wikipedia.org/wiki/Depleted_uranium)
29. Marilyn Vogt-Downey, Depleted Uranium Used in Gulf War Produces Health Disaster, Feb 5 1999 (https://socialistaction.org/1999/02/05/depleted-uranium-used-in-gulf-war-produces-health-disaster/)
30. Greg Kerr, Depleted Uranium and Canadian Veterans, Report of the Standing Committee on Veterans Affairs Chair June 2013 41st Parliament, First Session (https://www.ourcommons.ca/Content/Committee/411/ACVA/Reports/RP6197009/acvarp11/acvarp11-e.pdf)
31. UN General Assembly votes on uranium weapons with a large majority in favour of the resolution, Jan 18 2021 (https://www.icbuw.eu/un-general-assembly-votes-on-uranium-weapons-with-a-large-majority-in-favour-of-the-resolution/)
32. Sean Maloney, Canada and UN Peacekeeping, 123 ; Joseph Levitt, Pearson and Canada's Role in Nuclear Disarmament, 69
33. John Clearwater, Just Dummies — Cruise Missile Testing in Canada, 206
34. Socialist Project Steering Committee, A More Dangerous World: The Nuclear Arms Race, the INF Treaty and Canada, March 7 2019 (https://socialistproject.ca/2019/03/more-dangerous-world-nuclear-arms-race-inf-treaty-and-canada/)
35. Canada votes against UN call to open Israel nuclear facilities, Dec 4 2012 (https://www.cbc.ca/news/world/canada-votes-against-un-call-to-open-israel-nuclear-facilities-1.1143943)

36. Mike Blanchfield, Canada cites defence for Israel in blocking UN plan to curb nuclear weapons, May 25 2015 (http://www.cbc.ca/news/politics/canada-cites-defence-for-israel-in-blocking-un-plan-to-curb-nuclear-weapons-1.3087073)
37. 122 countries adopt 'historic' UN treaty to ban nuclear weapons, Jul 7 2017 (https://www.cbc.ca/news/world/un-treaty-ban-nuclear-weapons-1.4192761)
38. Ron Finch, Exporting Danger: A History of the Canadian Nuclear Energy Export Programme, 34
39. Joseph Levitt, Pearson and Canada's Role in Nuclear Disarmament and Arms Control Negotiations 1945-1957, 230
40. Avoiding Armageddon: Canadian military strategy and nuclear weapons, 1950–63, 111
41. Robert Matas, B.C. regains torpedo range, Mar 7 2002 (https://www.theglobeandmail.com/news/national/bc-regains-torpedo-range/article4132321/)
42. Canada's cruise missile testing controversy of 1983, July 15 2018 (https://www.cbc.ca/archives/canada-s-cruise-missile-testing-controversy-of-1983-1.4744435)
43. Carole Giangrande, The Nuclear North: the people, the regions and arms race, 19
44. John Clearwater, Canadian Nuclear Weapons: The Untold Story of Canada's Cold War Arsenal, 18
45. Jonathan Turner, The Defence Research Board of Canada, 1947 to 1977, A thesis submitted in conformity with the requirements for the degree of Doctor of Philosophy Institute for the History and Philosophy of Science and Technology University of Toronto, 206 (https://tspace.library.utoronto.ca/bitstream/1807/71816/1/turner_jonathan_r_201211_PhD_thesis.pdf)
46. Ibid, 209
47. Canada's Connections to Nuclear Weapons, Peace Research, Vol 36, No 2, Nov 2004
48. John Clearwater, Canadian Nuclear Weapons: The Untold Story of Canada's Cold War Arsenal, 23
49. Ibid, 93 ; Jonathan Turner, The Defence Research Board of Canada, 1947 to 1977, A thesis submitted in conformity with the requirements for the degree of Doctor of Philosophy Institute for the History and Philosophy of Science and Technology University of Toronto, 204 (https://tspace.library.utoronto.ca/bitstream/1807/71816/1/turner_jonathan_r_201211_PhD_thesis.pdf)
50. Swords, Clunks and Windowmakers: the tumultuous life of the RCAF's original one Canadian air division, 139
51. Ibid, 125
52. John Clearwater, Canadian Nuclear Weapons: The Untold Story of Canada's Cold War Arsenal, 18
53. Peter Kasurak, A National Force: the evolution of Canada's army, 1950-2000, 69
54. Jonathan Turner, The Defence Research Board of Canada, 1947 to 1977, A thesis submitted in conformity with the requirements for the degree of Doctor of Philosophy Institute for the History and Philosophy of Science and Technology University of Toronto (https://tspace.library.utoronto.ca/bitstream/1807/71816/1/turner_jonathan_r_201211_PhD_thesis.pdf)
55. Andrew Richter, Avoiding Armageddon: Canadian military strategy and nuclear weapons, 1950–63, 90
56. W A March, Sic Itur Ad Astra: Canadian Aerospace Power Studies, Vol 3 Combat If Necessary, But Not Necessarily Combat, 36
57. Erika Simpson, NATO and the Bomb: Canadian defenders confront critics, 149
58. Ernie Regehr, The Canadian Defence Policy Review Briefing papers by O.C., Senior Fellow in Defence Policy and Arctic Security, Aug 23 2016 (http://www.thesimonsfoundation.ca/sites/default/files/Canadian%20Defence%20Policy%20and%20NATO%E2%80%99s%20Nuclear%20Weapons%2C%20Defence%20Policy%20Review%20briefing%20paper%20-%20Aug%20 23%2C%202016.pdf)
59. Matthew Trudgen, Do We Want "Buckets of Instant Sunshine"?: Canada and Nuclear Weapons 1945-1984 (http://www.journal.forces.gc.ca/vol10/no1/08-trudgen-eng.asp)
60. NATO's nuclear deterrence policy and forces, Apr 16 2020 (https://www.nato.int/cps/en/natohq/topics_50068.htm)
61. Ankit Panda, 'No First Use' and Nuclear Weapons, July 17 2018 (https://www.cfr.org/backgrounder/no-first-use-and-nuclear-weapons)

Chapter 11

1. Lynne Gouliquer, Soldiering in the Canadian Forces: How and Why Gender Counts, 283
2. Stephanie Levitz, Military's sexualized culture hostile to women, inquiry says, Canadian Press, Apr 30 2015 (https://globalnews.ca/news/1971501/militarys-sexualized-culture-hostile-to-women-inquiry-says/)
3. Ibid
4. Military slow to fix sexualized culture, Canadian Press, Feb 8 2019 (https://www.theglobeandmail.com/canada/article-canadian-military-slow-to-fix-sexual-assault-problem-former-judge/)
5. Tony German, The Sea Is at Our Gates: the History of the Canadian Navy, 304
6. History of Women in Combat: Canada (https://sistersinarms.ca/history/history-of-women-in-combat/#:~:text=However%2C%20it%20wasn't%20until,finally%20be%20opened%20to%20women.)
7. Lee Berthiaume, Military reports minimal progress in drive to add more women to the ranks, May 12 2021 (https://www.squamishchief.com/national-news/military-reports-minimal-progress-in-drive-to-add-more-women-to-the-ranks-3772237)
8. Elusive Pursuits: Lessons from Canada's Interventions Abroad, Canada among Nations 2015, 163
9. Stephanie A H Belanger and Daniel Legace Roy, Military Operations and the Mind: War Ethics and Soldiers' Well-being, 211
10. Ibid
11. Koskie Minsky, Plaintiffs in Five National Class Actions Team Up to Take Canada to Court in Canadian Armed Forces Systemic Sexual Assault and Harassment Class Actions, Sep 7 2017 (http://www.newswire.ca/news-releases/plaintiffs-in-five-national-class-actions-team-up-to-take-canada-to-court-in-canadian-armed-forces-systemic-sexual-assault-and-harassment-class-actions-643102223.html)
12. Sarah Turnbull, Feds face growing questions over misconduct in the military, as documents show hundreds of cases since 2016, Apr 28 2021 (https://www.ctvnews.ca/politics/feds-face-growing-questions-over-misconduct-in-the-military-as-documents-show-hundreds-of-cases-since-2016-1.5405792)
13. David Pugliese, Approximately 4,600 file claims of sexual misconduct or discrimination against Canadian military, Ottawa Citizen, Apr 14 2021

14. Sexual misconduct persists in military despite efforts to curb assault, May 22 2019 (https://www.cbc.ca/news/politics/sexual-misconduct-military-operation-honour-1.5144601)
15. Gloria Galloway, Military sexual-assault trials have high acquittal rate despite zero-tolerance policy, study finds, June 10 2019 (https://www.theglobeandmail.com/politics/article-conviction-rate-in-military-sexual-assault-trials-lower-than-in/)
16. Janet Bagnall, What the military won't talk about, Montreal Gazette, Oct 12 2010
17. Tamara Lorincz, Canada's Invisible War: Violence Against Women in the Canadian Armed Forces, Canadian Voice of Women for Peace, Mar 2013 (http://vowpeace.org/wp-content/uploads/2013/03/Canadas-Invisible-War-Fact-Sheet.pdf)
18. Janet Bagnall, What the military won't talk about, Montreal Gazette, Oct 12 2010
19. Report on the Canadian Forces' response to woman abuse in military families, May 2000 (https://www.unb.ca/fredericton/arts/centres/mmfc/_resources/pdfs/familyviolmilitaryreport.pdf)
20. Deborah Harrison, The First Casualty: Violence Against Women in Canadian Military Communities, 50
21. Report on the Canadian Forces' response to woman abuse in military families, May 2000 (https://www.unb.ca/fredericton/arts/centres/mmfc/_resources/pdfs/familyviolmilitaryreport.pdf)
22. Laura Fraser, Lionel Desmond killed their daughter and granddaughter, but in-laws say they won't 'demonize' him, Feb 19 2021 (https://www.cbc.ca/news/canada/nova-scotia/desmond-inquiry-s2-d4-1.5919891) ; Robert Giblin, Soldier in Toronto murder-suicide, had PTSD, obituary says, Dec 24 2015 (https://www.cbc.ca/news/canada/toronto/murder-suicide-toronto-1.3380514)
23. Marc Lépine (https://en.wikipedia.org/wiki/Marc_L%C3%A9pine)
24. Sandra Whitworth, Militarized Masculinities & the Politics of Peacekeeping: The Canadian Case
25. Gary Kinsman and Patrizia Gentile, The Canadian War on Queers: national security as sexual regulation
26. Ibid, 69/71
27. Ibid, 72
28. Ibid, 228/366
29. Ibid, 371
30. Ibid, 173/176
31. Ibid, 348
32. Ibid, 229
33. Ibid, 412
34. P Whitney Lackenbauer, Battle Grounds: the Canadian military and aboriginal lands, 28
35. Mathias Joost, Racism and Enlistment: The Second World War Policies of the Royal Canadian Air Force, Canadian Military History, Vol 21 Issue 1
36. Richard Holt, Filling the Ranks, 71
37. Ibid
38. Patricia Roy, The Soldiers Canada Didn't Want: Her Chinese and Japanese Citizens, Canadian Historical Review, Sept 1978
39. Richard Holt, Filling the Ranks, 72
40. Ibid, 73
41. No. 2 Construction Battalion: Breaking New Ground, June 1 2018 (http://espritdecorps.ca/history-feature/no-2-construction-company-breaking-new-ground)
42. David J Bercuson and Jack Granatstein, Dictionary of Canadian Military History, 152
43. Marcelline Selman, Canada's first and only all-black battalion of World War I, Feb 16 2016 (http://theconcordian.com/2016/02/canadas-first-and-only-all-black-battalion-of-world-war-i/) ; Simon Theobald, A False Sense of Equality: The Black Canadian Experiences of the Second World War, Master's thesis University of Ottawa, 2008 (https://www.ruor.uottawa.ca/bitstream/10393/27791/1/MR48629.PDF)
44. Marcelline Selman, Canada's first and only all-black battalion of World War I, Feb 16 2016 (http://theconcordian.com/2016/02/canadas-first-and-only-all-black-battalion-of-world-war-i/)
45. Patricia Roy, The Soldiers Canada Didn't Want: Her Chinese and Japanese Citizens, Canadian Historical Review, Sept 1978
46. Mathias Joost, Racism and Enlistment: The Second World War Policies of the Royal Canadian Air Force, Canadian Military History, Vol 21, Is 1, 2015
47. Ibid
48. R Scott Sheffield, "Of Pure European Descent and of the White Race": Recruitment Policy and Aboriginal Canadians, 1939–1945, Canadian Military History, Vol 5, N 1, Spring 1996
49. Ibid
50. Simon Theobald, Not So Black and White: Black Canadians and the RCAF's recruiting policy during the Second World War, Canadian Military History, Vol 21, Issue 1, 2015
51. Ibid
52. Ibid
53. Donovan Vincent, First black naval commander to have his own ship sails into Canadian History, Feb 21 2016 (https://www.thestar.com/news/insight/2016/02/21/first-black-naval-commander-sails-into-canadian-history.html)
54. Lee Berthiaume, Military reports minimal progress in drive to add more women to the ranks, May 12 2021 (https://www.squamishchief.com/national-news/military-reports-minimal-progress-in-drive-to-add-more-women-to-the-ranks-3772337)
55. Sherri Borden Colley, Another former DND employee comes forward with allegations of racism, Jul 29 2019 (https://www.cbc.ca/news/canada/nova-scotia/racism-dnd-halifax-shearwater-black-civilian-employees-1.5226303?fbclid=IwAR1vgWu1bwWIkb4iumk0XNdAxckA-jv89cJVIV1ilui0NkuEW1m7t628ym8) ; Sherri Borden Colley, DND ordered to pay $25K for 'pure and simple racial prejudice', Jul 14 2019 (https://www.cbc.ca/news/canada/nova-scotia/racial-discrimination-department-of-national-defence-halifax-workplace-apprentice-1.5207193)
56. David Pugliese, White reservist who hurled racial abuse at black soldiers won't be disciplined, Canadian Forces says, Dec 2 2018 (https://nationalpost.com/news/white-reservist-who-hurled-racial-abuse-at-black-soldiers-wont-be-disciplined-army-decides)
57. Ibid
58. Ibid
59. Three former military members launch suit alleging systemic racism in Forces, Canadian Press, Dec 23 2016 (http://www.ctvnews.ca/canada/three-former-military-members-launch-suit-alleging-systemic-racism-in-forces-1.3215528)
60. Miles Howe, The Case of Wally Fowler, Mar 12 2012 (http://www.dominionpaper.ca/articles/4385)
61. Ryan Thorpe, White supremacist in army reserve, Aug 19 2019 (https://www.winnipegfreepress.com/local/white-supremacist-in-army-reserve-553050082.html)
62. Canadian Press, Navy says sailor with 'infidel' tattoo will cover up design after complaint, Jul 10 2019 (https://www.cbc.ca/news/canada/nova-scotia/navy-infidel-tattoo-

halifax-tweet-sailor-1.5206521)
63. Erin Seatter and Jon Milton, Meet the Canadian soldiers behind a white supremacist military surplus store, Oct 29 2018 (https://ricochet.media/en/2394/meet-the-canadian-soldiers-behind-a-white-supremacist-military-surplus-store)
64. Mack Lamoureux and Ben Makuch, Member of a Neo-Nazi Terror Group Appears To Be Former Canadian Soldier, Aug 2 2018 (https://www.vice.com/en_ca/article/7xqe8z/member-of-a-neo-nazi-terror-group-appears-to-be-former-canadian-soldier)
65. Who are the Proud Boys who disrupted an Indigenous event on Canada Day?, Jul 4 2017 (https://www.cbc.ca/radio/asithappens/as-it-happens-tuesday-edition-1.4189447/who-are-the-proud-boys-who-disrupted-an-indigenous-event-on-canada-day-1.4189450)
66. 'We have to be neutral': Canadian Forces warn members affiliated with radical groups, Oct 4 2017 (https://www.cbc.ca/news/canada/montreal/quebec-military-warns-members-joining-groups-la-meute-1.4327085)
67. Ibid
68. Gabriel Béland, Les militaires tenus à l'écart de La Meute, Sep 21 2017 (https://www.lapresse.ca/actualites/national/201709/20/01-5135250-les-militaires-tenus-a-lecart-de-la-meute.php)
69. Stewart Bell and Mercedes Stephenson, Canadian Armed Forces members linked to six hate groups: internal report, May 27 2019 (https://globalnews.ca/news/5322011/canadian-armed-forces-members-linked-to-six-hate-groups-internal-report/)
70. Mack Lamoureux and Ben Makuch, Neo-Nazis Want Canadian Military Training, Oct 22 2018 (https://www.vice.com/en_ca/article/a3pppz/neo-nazis-want-canadian-military-training?utm_source=vicetwitterca)
71. Carl Benn, Mohawks on the Nile: Natives Among the Canadian Voyageurs in Egypt, 1884- 1885, 125
72. David Homsher, Squareheads, Blockheads and Other Epithets As Applied to German Soldiers of World War I, Apr 27 2007 (http://ezinearticles.com/?Squareheads,-Blockheads-and-Other-Epithets-As-Applied-to-German-Soldiers-of-World-War-I&id=544143) ; Tim Cook, No Place to Run: The Canadian Corps and Gas Warfare in the First World War, 12
73. Brock Millman, Polarity, Patriotism, and Dissent in Great War Canada, 1914-1919, 203 ; Desmond Morton and Glenn Wright, Winning the Second Battle: Canadian Veterans and the Return to Civilian Life, 121
74. Ibid, 82
75. Joel Zemel, Halifax Yesterday: The 1919 Anti-Chinese Riots, Oct 26 2020 (https://www.halifaxtoday.ca/halifaxyesterday/halifaxyesterday-the-1919-anti-chinese-riots-2822141)
76. Brent Byron, Far Eastern Tour: The Canadian Infantry in Korea, 1950-1953, 82
77. Sherene Razack, Dark Threats and White Knights: The Somalia Affair, Peacekeeping, and the New Imperialism, 6
78. Ibid
79.
80. Transcript: Rick Hillier on the New Role of Canada's Military, Nov 19 2005 (https://www.tvo.org/transcript/795866/rick-hillier-on-the-new-role-of-canadas-military)
81. Canada helping Brits buy 'Bosnian' and 'Somali' targets for shooting practice, Mar 2 2015 (https://globalnews.ca/news/1855099/canada-helping-brits-buy-bosnian-and-somali-targets-for-shooting-practice/amp/)

82. Lawrence Barkwell, The Nile Voyageurs 1884-1885: Manitoba Metis and Indians of the Nile Expedition (http://www.metismuseum.ca/media/db/07194) ; Carl Benn, Mohawks on the Nile: Natives Among the Canadian Voyageurs in Egypt, 1884-1885, 33
83. Jonathan F Vance, Death so Noble: Memory, Meaning, and the First World War, 246 ; Amelia Reimer, Lest We Forget Aboriginal Peoples' sacrifices for Canada, Nov 11 2015 (http://theindependent.ca/2015/11/11/lest-we-forget-aboriginal-peoples-sacrifices-for-canada/)
84. Indigenous People in the Second World War (http://www.veterans.gc.ca/eng/remembrance/history/historical-sheets/aborigin) ; Aboriginal Veterans (http://www.veterans.gc.ca/public/pages/publications/system-pdfs/Aboriginal-pi-e.pdf)
85. R Scott Sheffield, "Of Pure European Descent and of the White Race": Recruitment Policy and Aboriginal Canadians, 1939–1945 Canadian Military History, Vol 5, N 1, Spring 1996
86. Looking Forward Looking Back, Part Two, False Assumptions and a Failed Relationship, Vol 1 (http://caid.ca/RRCAP1.12.pdf)
87. Deborah Cowen, Military Workfare: The Soldier and Social Citizenship in Canada, 107/108 ; Evan J Habkirk and Janice Forsyth, Truth, Reconciliation, and the Politics of the Body in Indian Residential School History (activehistory.ca/papers/truth-reconciliation-and-the-politics-of-the-body-in-indian-residential-school-history/) ; Canada's Residential Schools: The History, Part 2, 1939 to 2000, Vol 1, 486
88. The Mohawk Institute — Brantford, ON, General Synod Archives, Sept 23 2008 (https://www.anglican.ca/tr/histories/mohawk-institute/) ; The Cadet Movement (https://doingourbit.ca/cadets)
89. Ibid
90. Deborah Cowen, Military Workfare: The Soldier and Social Citizenship in Canada, 107/108
91. Ibid
92. Canada's Residential Schools: The History, Part 2, 1939 to 2000, Vol 1, 487
93. Canada's Residential Schools: Missing Children and Unmarked Burials, Vol 4, Truth and Reconciliation Commission of Canada, 127
94. J A Mitchell, Disposal of Property, National Archives of Canada, CFS Armstrong, May 74 (http://www.c-and-e-museum.org/Pinetreeline/other/other2/other2d.html)
95. High Arctic relocation (https://en.wikipedia.org/wiki/High_Arctic_relocation)
96. Philip Anido, Environmental Stewardship on Canadian Military Training Areas: Rhetoric or Reality, A thesis submitted to the Faculty of Graduate Studies and Research in Partial fulfillment of the requirements for the degree of - Master of Arts Department of Geography Carleton University 1998 (https://www.collectionscanada.gc.ca/obj/s4/f2/dsk2/tape17/PQDD_0017/MQ36808.pdf)
97. Ibid
98. David Neufeld, The Distant Early Warning (DEW) Line: A Preliminary Assessment of its Role and Effects upon Northern Canada, Arctic Institute of North America, May 2002 (http://stankievech.net/projects/DEW/BAR-1/bin/Neufeld_DEWLinehistory.pdf)
99. Cheryl Petten, First Nations still waiting for environmental clean-up, Birchbark, Timmins Vol 4, Is 8, 2005 (https://ammsa.com/publications/ontario-birchbark/first-nations-still-waiting-environmental-clean)
100. Sue Heffernan, The Cold War in the Near North: Moosonee and the Pinetree Radar Line, Nov 3 2013

(http://niche-canada.org/2013/11/03/the-cold-war-in-the-near-north-moosonee-and-the-pinetree-radar-line/)
101. Canada's Tibet: the killing of the Innu, 31
102. Ibid
103. Whitney P Lackenbauer, The Cold War on Canadian Soil: Militarizing a Northern Environment, American Society for Environmental History, Vol 12, No 4 Oct 2007
104. Ibid
105. Whitney P Lackenbauer, The Cold War on Canadian Soil: Militarizing a Northern Environment, American Society for Environmental History, Vol 12, No 4 Oct 2007
106. Ballingall Alex, Oka, Ipperwash, Caledonia — Canada's tense history with Indigenous blockades, Feb 14 2020 (https://www.thestar.com/politics/federal/2020/02/14/oka-ipperwash-caledonia-canadas-tense-history-with-indigenous-blockades.html)
107. P Whitney Lackenbauer, Carrying the Burden of Peace: The Mohawks, the Canadian forces, and the Oka Crisis
108. Ibid
109. David Pugliese, Canada's Secret Commandos: the unauthorized story of joint task force two, 36
110. Ibid
111. Les Habitants Heroes, Apr 11 2015 (https://mohawknationnews.com/blog/tag/jtf2/)
112. Ibid
113. Zig Zag, Ipperwash, 1995 (https://warriorpublications.wordpress.com/2011/02/12/ipperwash-1995/)
114. Ben David Mahony, "Disinformation and smear": the use of state propaganda and military force to suppress aboriginal title at the 1995 Gustafsen Lake standoff, University of Lethbridge (https://www.uleth.ca/dspace/bitstream/handle/10133/189/MQ83763.pdf?sequence=3&isAllowed=y)
115. Jorge Barrera, Gustafsen Lake warrior granted political asylum in US wants return home to Canada, Jan 15 2016 (http://aptnnews.ca/2016/01/15/gustafsen-lake-warrior-granted-political-asylum-in-us-wants-return-home-to-canada/)
116. Settlers In Support of Indigenous Sovereignty, JTF2: From Lima to Oka and Gustafsen Lake, Nov 15 1998 (sisis.nativeweb.org/gustlake/nov1598.html)
117. David Pugliese, Canada's Secret Commandos, 55
118. Lex Gill and Cara Zwibel, Why does Canada spy on its own indigenous communities?, Dec 6 2017 (https://www.opendemocracy.net/en/surveillance-indigenous-groups-canada/)
119. Jorge Barrera, Military's counter-intelligence unit monitored Elsipogtog anti-fracking protests: documents, May 30, 2014 (https://www.aptnnews.ca/national-news/militarys-counter-intelligence-unit-monitored-elsipogtog-anti-fracking-protests-documents/)
120. Steven Chase, Military intelligence unit keeps watch on native groups, Oct 12 2011 (https://www.theglobeandmail.com/news/politics/military-intelligence-unit-keeps-watch-on-native-groups/article557423/)
121. Ibid
122. Policing Indigenous Movements, 105
123. Ibid, 105
124. Bill Curry, Forces' terror manual lists natives with Hezbollah, Mar 31 2007 (https://www.theglobeandmail.com/news/national/forces-terror-manual-lists-natives-with-hezbollah/article17994390/)
125. Amira Hass, Redundant Monuments and the Contest of Victimhood, Oct 31 2017 (https://www.haaretz.com/opinion/.premium-redundant-monuments-and-the-contest-of-victimhood-1.5461315)
126. Francis Pegahmagabow Monument (https://www.veterans.gc.ca/eng/remembrance/memorials/national-inventory-canadian-memorials/details/9344)
127. Tommy Prince (https://en.wikipedia.org/wiki/Tommy_Prince)
128. The RCN and its ties to the Indigenous peoples of Canada, Navy News, May 25 2018 (www.navy-marine.forces.gc.ca/en/news-operations/news-view.page?doc=the-rcn-and-its-ties-to-the-indigenous-peoples-of-canada/jhf5kere)
129. Gord Hill, Canadian Forces Target Aboriginal Youth, Feb 11 2011 (https://warriorpublications.wordpress.com/2011/02/11/canadian-forces-target-aboriginal-youth/)
130. Ibid ; Fred Gaffen, Forgotten Soldiers, 30
131. Canadian Armed Forces Aboriginal Entry Plans, Aug 23 2017 (http://www.nndfn.com/wp-content/uploads/2017/09/CF-Aboriginal-Enrolment-Plans-2017.pdf)
132. Kathleen Harris, Military looks at foreign recruits to boost ranks, May 25 2018 (http://www.cbc.ca/news/politics/caf-military-foreign-recruits-1.4675889)
133. ARCHIVED - Aboriginal Peoples in the Canadian Armed Forces, Project number: BG - 13.016, May 19 2016 (http://www.forces.gc.ca/en/news/article.page?doc=aboriginal-peoples-in-the-canadian-armed-forces/hie8w98n)
134. Indigenous military members endure 'systemic' racism, report claims, Dec 13 2016 (https://www.cbc.ca/news/canada/ottawa/canada-military-indigenous-racism-report-1.3891862)

Chapter 12

1. Stephanie A H Belanger and Daniel Legace Roy, Military operations and the mind: war ethics and soldiers well-being, 37
2. Liberals move Trudeau fundraiser off forces base, Dec 11 2018 (https://www.theglobeandmail.com/politics/article-liberals-move-trudeau-fundraiser-off-canadian-forces-base/)
3. Canadian Forces Identity System (http://www.forces.gc.ca/en/honours-history-badges-insignia/rank.page)
4. Part III Code of Service Discipline (https://laws-lois.justice.gc.ca/eng/acts/n-5/page-11.html)
5. Deborah Harrison and Lucie Laliberté, No Life Like It: military wives in Canada, 25
6. Meaghan Hobman, Loose lips: Free speech and the Canadian Forces, Jun 20 2014 (https://ipolitics.ca/2014/06/20/loose-lips-free-speech-and-the-canadian-forces/)
7. Chris Lambie, Military clamps down on soldier bloggers, Sept 28 2006 (https://www.theglobeandmail.com/technology/military-clamps-down-on-soldier-bloggers/article1104240/)
8. Scott Taylor, Tested mettle: Canada's peacekeepers at war, 207
9. Ibid
10. We weren't always "the one that's read", History (http://espritdecorps.ca/about/)
11. Scott Taylor, Unembedded, 39
12. Ibid, 62
13. Ibid, 63
14. Scott Taylor, Unembedded, 145
15. Ibid
16. Isabel Campbell, Unlikely Diplomats: the Canadian brigade in Germany, 1951-64, 113

17. David Pugliese, Fade to Black, Ottawa Citizen, Sept 30 2006
18. Ibid ; Sharon Hobson, Operations Security and the Public's Need to Know, Canadian Defence and Foreign Affairs Institute, Mar 2011
19. David Pugliese, Canadian military claimed a report didn't exist — even though it 'clearly' did, Jan 16 2019 (https://nationalpost.com/news/canadian-military-claimed-a-report-didnt-exist-even-though-it-did)
20. Ibid
21. Tom Parry, Vice-Admiral Norman's pre-trial hearing hears of possible efforts to withhold records, CBC, Dec 18 2018 (https://www.cbc.ca/news/politics/mark-norman-davie-irving-dnd-1.4951709)
22. Appeal court slams DND's 3-year response to information request, Mar 5 2015 (https://www.thestar.com/news/canada/2015/03/05/appeal-court-slams-governments-3-year-access-to-information-request.html)
23. David Pugliese, DND critic wants answers on defence surveillance, CanWest News Service, July 26 2007 (https://www.ceasefire.ca/dnd-critic-wants-answers-on-defence-surveillance/)
24. Mike Larsen and Kevin Walby, Brokering Access: Power, Politics, and Freedom of Information Process in Canada, 59
25. Dishonoured Legacy: The Lessons of the Somalia Affair: Report of the Commission of Inquiry into the Deployment of Canadian Forces to Somalia (https://publications.gc.ca/site/eng/479844/publication.html)
26. Wesley Wark, Electronic Communications Interception and Privacy: Can the Imperatives of Privacy and National Security be Reconciled?, Office of the Privacy Commissioner of Canada, March 2012 (https://www.cips-cepi.ca/wp-content/uploads/2012/04/WARK_WorkingPaper_April2012.pdf)
27. Peter Worthington, JTF2: Canada's secret weapon or a place where trouble hides?, Toronto Sun, Sept 16 2010
28. Thorstein Veblen, The Theory of Business Enterprise, Chapter 10: The Natural Decay of Business Enterprise (https://brocku.ca/MeadProject/Veblen/Veblen_1904/Veblen_1904_10.html)
29. Herbert Marx, The Emergency Power and Civil Liberties in Canada, McGill Law Review, 1970 (https://lawjournal.mcgill.ca/article/emergency-power-and-civil-liberties-in-canada-the/)
30. War Measures Act (http://www.canadahistoryproject.ca/1914/1914-04-war-measures-act.html)
31. S R Elliott, Scarlet to Green: a history of intelligence in the Canadian Army 1903-1963, 54
32. Benjamin Isitt, From Victoria to Vladivostok: Canada's Siberian expedition, 1917-1919, 70
33. Ukrainian Internment in Canada (https://www.thecanadianencyclopedia.ca/en/article/ukrainian-internment-in-canada#:~:text=Canada's%20first%20national%20internment%20operations,of%20the%20War%20Measures%20Act.)
34. Brock Millman, Polarity, Patriotism, and Dissent in Great War Canada, 1914-1919, 18
35. Ibid, 17
36. Ira Basen, Why Canadian media embraced censorship during WWI, Aug 1 2014 (https://www.cbc.ca/news/why-canadian-media-embraced-censorship-during-wwi-ira-basen-1.2722786)
37. Pearce J Carefoote, Censorship in Canada (http://hpcanpub.mcmaster.ca/case-study/censorship-canada) ; Jeffrey A Keshen, The War on Truth, Canada's History, Vol 95 Aug 2015 ; Mark Bourrie, The Fog of War, 23
38. Patrice Dutil and David MacKenzie, Embattled Nation: Canada's Wartime Election of 1917, 128
39. David J Bercuson and Jack Granatstein, Dictionary of Canadian Military History, 225
40. Tim Cook, A Many-Layered Legacy, Canada's History, Oct 2018 ; Patrice Dutil and David MacKenzie, Embattled Nation: Canada's Wartime Election of 1917, 36
41. 1939-45 Second World War (https://historyofrights.ca/encyclopaedia/main-events/1939-world-war-two/)
42. Patricia E Roy, Internment in Canada, June 11 2020 (https://www.thecanadianencyclopedia.ca/en/article/internment)
43. Ibid
44. Eric Koch, Deemed Suspect: A Wartime Blunder ; Patricia E Roy, Internment in Canada, June 11 2020 (https://www.thecanadianencyclopedia.ca/en/article/internment/)
45. Mark Bourrie, Between Friends: Censorship of Canada's Media in World War II University of Ottawa PHD thesis, 153/434
46. Ibid ; James Naylor, Pacifism or anti-imperialism? The CCF response to the outbreak of World War II, Journal of the Canadian historical Association, Vol 8, No 1, 1997
47. Robert Bergen, Censorship; the Canadian News Media and Afghanistan: A Historical Comparison with Case Studies, Calgary Papers in Military and Strategic Studies, 2009 ; Mark Bourrie, The Fog of War, 45
48. Paul-André Comeau, Claude Beauregard and Edwige Munn, La démocratie en veilleuse: rapport sur la censure: récit de l'organisation, des activités et de la démobilisation de la censure pendant la guerre de 1939-45, 21
49. Stanley Sandler, The Korean War: An Encyclopedia, 271
50. Arnold Davidson Dunton (http://www.thecanadianencyclopedia.ca/en/article/arnold-davidson-dunton) ; Mallory Schwartz, War on the Air, 34
51. John Price, Orienting Canada, 275
52. James Gareth Endicott (https://en.wikipedia.org/wiki/James_Gareth_Endicott)
53. Gary Marcuse and Reginald Whitaker, Cold War Canada, 375
54. Ibid, 369
55. Ibid, 375-377
56. Pearce J Carefoote, Censorship in Canada (http://hpcanpub.mcmaster.ca/case-study/censorship-canada)
57. David Taras and Christopher Waddell, How Canadians Communicate IV: Media and Politics (http://www.aupress.ca/books/120205/ebook/99Z_Taras_Waddell_2012-How_Canadians_Communicate_IV.pdf/), 217 ; Robert W Bergen, Balkan Rats and Balkan Bats: The art of managing Canada's news media during the Kosovo air war, University of Calgary PhD dissertation, 2005, 93/369
58. Daniel Leblanc, General's talk of terrorist 'scumbags' praised, July 16 2005 (https://www.theglobeandmail.com/news/national/generals-talk-of-terrorist-scumbags-praised/article18241070/)
59. Hillier defends scholarship for kids of fallen soldiers, Mar 26 2010 (https://www.ctvnews.ca/hillier-defends-scholarship-for-kids-of-fallen-soldiers-1.496079)
60. Ibid
61. Robert Bothwell, War, business and world military — industrial complexes, 106
62. Bernd Horn, the Canadian Way of War: serving the national interest, 157
63. Statement by the Prime Minister of Canada while in Trapani, Italy, 1 Sept 2011 (https://www.canada.ca/en/news/archive/2011/09/statement-prime-minister-canada-

while-trapani-italy.html)
64. Roy MacLaren, Canadians on the Nile, 91
65. Speech before the House of Commons, Mar 13 1900 (https://www.collectionscanada.gc.ca/primeministers/h4-4060-e.html)
66. Mike: The Memoirs of the Rt. Hon. Lester B. Pearson, Vol 2: 1948-1957, 30
67. Norman Hillmer and Jack Granatstein, Empire Umpire: Canada and the World to the 1990s, 62
68. Ian McKay and Jamie Swift, Warrior Nation: rebranding Canada in an age of anxiety, 257

Chapter 13

1. Bruce Campion Smith, Politicians urge greater oversight of military intelligence operations, Toronto Star, Apr 9 2019
2. Infographic for Communications Security Establishment Canada (https://www.tbs-sct.gc.ca/ems-sgd/edb-bdd/index-eng.html#orgs/dept/110/infograph/people)
3. Infographic for Communications Security Establishment Canada (https://www.tbs-sct.gc.ca/ems-sgd/edb-bdd/index-eng.html#orgs/dept/110/infograph/financial)
4. Murray Brewster, Canada's electronic spy service to take more prominent role in ISIS fight, Canadian Press, Feb 18 2016 (http://www.cbc.ca/news/politics/canada-spy-agency-isis-fight-1.3454617)
5. Colin Freeze, Canada's little-known spy agency comes out into the open, Globe and Mail, Dec 22 2010
6. About CSE (https://cyber.gc.ca/en/guidance/about-cse)
7. Colin Freeze, Canadian spy manual reveals how new recruits are supposed to conceal their identities, Dec 22 2013 (https://www.theglobeandmail.com/news/politics/csec-sends-strong-message-of-privacy-to-new-recruits/article16087626/)
8. H A Skaarup, An Intelligence Advantage: Collective Security Benefits gained by Canada through the sharing of Military Intelligence with the United States of America, 90 (http://www.nlc-bnc.ca/obj/s4/f2/dsk2/ftp04/mq22780.pdf)
9. Dave Seglins, CSE tracks millions of downloads daily: Snowden documents, CBC, Jan 27 2015 (http://www.cbc.ca/news/canada/cse-tracks-millions-of-downloads-daily-snowden-documents-1.2930120)
10. Patrick McGuire, Is CSEC, the Canadian Version of the NSA, Trustworthy?, Sept 4 2013 (https://www.vice.com/en/article/jmkbjd/is-csec-the-canadian-version-of-the-nsa-trustworthy)
11. Kurt Jensen, Cautious Beginnings: Canadian foreign intelligence 1939-1951, 25
12. Our story, Communications Security Establishment (https://cse-cst.gc.ca/en/culture-and-community/history/our-story)
13. Kurt Jensen, Cautious Beginnings: Canadian foreign intelligence 1939-1951, 32/54
14. James Littleton, Target Nation: Canada and the Western Intelligence Network, 92
15. Kurt Jensen, Cautious Beginnings: Canadian foreign intelligence 1939-1951, 49
16. Ibid, 48
17. Ibid, 112
18. Ibid, 160
19. Ibid, 159
20. Ibid, 124
21. Ibid, 134
22. Philip Rosen, The Communications Security Establishment — Canada's Most Secret Intelligence Agency, Library of Parliament, 1993 (http://publications.gc.ca/collections/Collection-R/LoPBdP/BP-e/bp343-e.pdf)
23. Ibid
24. Summary of Canadian Sigint Stations (http://www.jproc.ca/rrp/cdn_sigint_stations.html)
25. James Littleton, Target Nation: Canada and the Western intelligence network, 98
26. Summary of Canadian Sigint Stations (http://www.jproc.ca/rrp/cdn_sigint_stations.html) ; Jeffrey T Richelson and Desmond Ball, The Ties That Bind: intelligence cooperation between the UKUSA countries, 190
27. Bill Robinson, Marking 70 years of eavesdropping in Canada, Sept 1 2016 (https://www.opencanada.org/features/marking-70-years-eavesdropping-canada/)
28. Infographic for Communications Security Establishment Canada (https://www.tbs-sct.gc.ca/ems-sgd/edb-bdd/index-eng.html#orgs/dept/110/infograph/people)
29. Martin Rudner, Canada's Communications Security Establishment, Signals Intelligence and Counter-Terrorism, Intelligence and National Security, 2007
30. Colin Freeze, Canada's little-known spy agency comes out into the open, Globe and Mail, Dec 22 2010
31. Murray Brewster, Canada's electronic spy service to take more prominent role in ISIS fight, Canadian Press, Feb 18 2016 (http://www.cbc.ca/news/politics/canada-spy-agency-isis-fight-1.3454617) ; David Pugliese, Ottawa's electronic spy agency helping military track someone in Canada, censored documents reveal, Ottawa Citizen, Dec 11 2016 (http://nationalpost.com/news/canada/ottawas-electronic-spy-agency-helping-military-track-someone-in-canada-censored-documents-reveal)
32. Martin Rudner, Canada's Communications Security Establishment, Signals Intelligence and Counter-Terrorism, Intelligence and National Security, 2007
33. David Pugliese, Ottawa's electronic spy agency helping military track someone in Canada, censored documents reveal, Ottawa Citizen, Dec 11 2016
34. Murray Brewster, Canada's electronic spies at the centre of beefed-up ISIL intelligence effort, Canadian Press, Feb 18 2016 (https://www.thespec.com/news/canada/2016/02/18/canada-s-electronic-spies-at-the-centre-of-beefed-up-isil-intelligence-effort.html
35. James Cox, Canada and the Five Eyes Intelligence Community, Dec 18 2012 (https://opencanada.org/canada-and-the-five-eyes-intelligence-community/)
36. Kurt Jensen, Cautious Beginnings, 62 ; Paul Farrell, History of 5-Eyes, Dec 2 2013 (https://www.theguardian.com/world/2013/dec/02/history-of-5-eyes-explainer)
37. James Littleton, Target Nation: Canada and the Western Intelligence Network, 94
38. Zheng Weiyu and Meng Tao, A closer look at the Five Eyes intelligence partnership, Nov 6 2018 (https://news.cgtn.com/news/3d3d514e32457a4d30457a6333566d54/index.html)
39. James Bamford, The Shadow Factory: the Ultra-secret NSA from 9/11 to the Eavesdropping on America, 222
40. David Canton, James Bond, Spectre, and the Surveillance Society, Nov 11 2015 (www.slaw.ca/2015/11/11/james-bond-spectre-and-the-surveillance-society/)

41. Jeffrey T Richelson and Desmond Ball, The Ties That Bind: intelligence cooperation between the UKUSA countries — United Kingdom, the United States of America, Canada, Australia and New Zealand, 143
42. James Littleton, Target Nation: Canada and the Western intelligence network, 98
43. Greg Weston, Snowden document shows Canada set up spy posts for NSA, Dec 9 2013 (https://www.cbc.ca/news/politics/snowden-document-shows-canada-set-up-spy-posts-for-nsa-1.2456886)
44. Martin Rudner, Canada's Communications Security Establishment from Cold War to Globalization, Issue 22 of Occasional paper, Norman Paterson School of International Affairs, 2000
45. Ibid
46. James Littleton, Target Nation: Canada and the Western Intelligence Network, 47
47. Tonda MacCharles, Tories deny Canadian spy agencies are targeting Canadians, June 10 2013 (https://www.thestar.com/news/canada/2013/06/10/tories_deny_canadian_spy_agencies_are_targeting_canadians.html)
48. Mike Frost and Michael Gratton, Spyworld, inside the Canadian and American intelligence establishments, 229
49. Ibid, 234
50. Martin Rudner, Canada's Communications Security Establishment from Cold War to Globalization, Issue 22 of Occasional paper, Norman Paterson School of International Affairs, 2000
51. James Bamford, The Shadow Factory: the Ultra-secret NSA from 9/11 to the Eavesdropping on America, 142
52. David Stafford and Rhodri Jeffries–Jones, American – British – Canadian Intelligence Relations 1939-2000, 234
53. James Littleton, Target Nation: Canada and the Western intelligence network, 95
54. Dylan Lubao and Keith Jones, Canadian spy agency set up covert sites worldwide at NSA's request, Dec 14 2013 (https://www.wsws.org/en/articles/2013/12/14/cses-d14.html) ; Greg Weston, Snowden document shows Canada set up spy posts for NSA, Dec 9 2013 (https://www.cbc.ca/news/politics/snowden-document-shows-canada-set-up-spy-posts-for-nsa-1.2456886)
55. Disclosure could prompt Five Eyes cutoff: CSE, Canadian Press, June 3 2016 (https://www.northumberlandnews.com/news-story/6705235-disclosure-could-prompt-five-eyes-cutoff-cse/)
56. David Stafford and Rhodri Jeffries–Jones, American – British – Canadian Intelligence Relations 1939-2000, 235
57. Ibid
58. Wesley Wark, Electronic Communications Interception and Privacy: Can the Imperatives of Privacy and National Security be Reconciled?, March 2012 (https://www.cips-cepi.ca/wp-content/uploads/2012/04/WARK_WorkingPaper_April2012.pdf)
59. Philip Rosen, The Communications Security Establishment: Canada's most secret intelligence agency, Library of Parliament, 1993 (https://publications.gc.ca/site/eng/44110/publication.html?wbdisable=true)
60. Kurt F Jensen, Cautious Beginnings, 171
61. James Littleton, Target Nation: Canada and the Western intelligence network, 159
62. Stevie Cameron, Ottawa Inside Out: power, prestige and scandal in the nation's capital, 195
63. Philip Rosen, The Communications Security Establishment: Canada's most secret intelligence agency, Library of Parliament, 1993 (https://publications.gc.ca/site/eng/44110/publication.html?wbdisable=true)
64. Bill Robinson, Marking 70 years of eavesdropping in Canada, Sep 1 2016 (https://www.opencanada.org/features/marking-70-years-eavesdropping-canada/)
65. Mandate (https://www.cse-cst.gc.ca/en/corporate-information/mandate)
66. Bill Robinson, CSE to get foreign cyber operations mandate, June 24 2017 (https://luxexumbra.blogspot.ca/2017/06/cse-to-get-foreign-cyber-operations.html)
67. Bill Robinson, Marking 70 years of eavesdropping in Canada, Sep 1 2016 (https://www.opencanada.org/features/marking-70-years-eavesdropping-canada/)
68. Mandate, Communications Security Establishment (https://cse-cst.gc.ca/en/corporate-information/mandate)
69. Communications Security Establishment Act (S.C. 2019, c. 13, s. 76) (https://laws-lois.justice.gc.ca/eng/acts/C-35.3/page-3.html?txthl=criminal%20code+section)
70. Justin Ling, Canada's cyber spy agency is about to get a major upgrade, June 21 2017 (https://news.vice.com/story/cse-is-getting-a-major-upgrade)
71. House of Commons of Canada, BILL C-59 An Act respecting national security matters (https://www.parl.ca/DocumentViewer/en/42-1/bill/C-59/first-reading)
72. Alex Boutilier, A Canadian Snowden? CSE warns of "insider threats", July 26 2015 (https://www.thestar.com/news/canada/2015/07/26/a-canadian-snowden-cse-warns-of-insider-threats.html)
73. Ibid
74. Amber Hildebrandt, CSE spying in Mexico: Espionage aimed at friends 'never looks good', Mar 25 2015 (https://www.cbc.ca/news/canada/cse-spying-in-mexico-espionage-aimed-at-friends-never-looks-good-1.3005887)
75. Patrick McGuire, Canada's Cyberspy Agency, CSEC, Hijacks Computers Worldwide to Build Their Spynet, Aug 26 2014 (https://www.vice.com/en_ca/article/7bmdeb/canadas-cyberspy-agency-csec-hijacks-computers-worldwide-to-build-their-spynet)
76. Greg Weston, CSEC used airport Wi-Fi to track Canadian travellers: Edward Snowden documents, Jan 30 2014 (https://www.cbc.ca/news/politics/csec-used-airport-wi-fi-to-track-canadian-travellers-edward-snowden-documents-1.2517881)
77. Colin Freeze, Spy agency accidentally shared Canadians' data with allies for years, June 1 2016 (https://www.theglobeandmail.com/news/national/spy-agency-accidentally-shared-canadians-data-with-allies-for-years/article30243491/)
78. Bill Robinson, CSE still operating embassy collection sites, Oct 28 2013 (https://luxexumbra.blogspot.com/2013/10/cse-still-operating-embassy-collection.html)
79. Greg Weston, Snowden document shows Canada set up spy posts for NSA, Dec 9 2013 (http://www.cbc.ca/news/politics/snowden-document-shows-canada-set-up-spy-posts-for-nsa-1.2456886)
80. Matthew M Aid, Cees Wiebes and Christopher Andrew, Secrets of Signals Intelligence During the Cold War and Beyond, 107 ; Mike Frost and Michael Gratton, Spyworld: Inside the Canadian and American intelligence establishments, 242 ; Martin Rudner, Canada's Communications Security Establishment from Cold War to Globalization, Intelligence & National Security, March 2001
81. Ibid
82. Mike Frost and Michael Gratton, Spyworld: inside the Canadian and American intelligence establishments, 141
83. Robert A Wright, Three Nights in Havana, 101
84. Dwight Hamilton, Inside Canadian Intelligence: Exposing the New Realities of Espionage and International Terrorism, 118
85. Rhodri Jeffreys-Jones and David Stafford, American-British-Canadian Intelligence Relations, 1939-2000, 146

86. Mike Frost and Michel Gratton, Spyworld: inside the Canadian and American intelligence establishments, 118
87. Ibid, 154
88. Glenn Greenwald, Cash, Weapons & Surveillance: the U.S. is a Key Party to Every Israeli Attack, Aug 4 2014 (https://theintercept.com/2014/08/04/cash-weapons-surveillance/)
89. Mike Frost and Michael Gratton, Spyworld, inside the Canadian and American intelligence establishments, 251
90. Ibid, 240
91. Ibid, 242
92. Asad Ismi, Massive Secret Surveillance in Canada, Nov 1 2013 (https://www.policyalternatives.ca/publications/monitor/massive-secret-surveillance-canada)
93. Martin Rudner, Canada's Communications Security Establishment from Cold War to Globalization, Norman Paterson School of International Affairs, Carleton University, occasional paper, N 22, 2000
94. Mike Frost and Michael Gratton, Spyworld, inside the Canadian and American intelligence establishments, 193
95. Martin Rudner, Canada's Communications Security Establishment from Cold War to Globalization, Norman Paterson School of International Affairs, Carleton University, occasional paper, N 22, 2000
96. Ibid
97. Martin Lukacs and Tim Groves, Canadian spies met with energy firms, documents reveal, Oct 9 2013 (https://www.theguardian.com/environment/2013/oct/09/canadian-spies-met-energy-firms-documents)
98. Bruce Campion Smith, Politicians urge greater oversight of military intelligence operations, Toronto Star, Apr 9 2019
99. Ibid
100. Harold A. Skaarup, Out of Darkness - Light, A History of Canadian Military Intelligence, Vol 4, 2006-present (http://silverhawkauthor.com/out-of-darkness-light-a-history-of-canadian-military-intelligence-volume-4-20062011-book-pending_278.html)
101. Harold A Skaarup, An Intelligence Advantage: Collective Security Benefits gained by Canada through the sharing of Military Intelligence with the United States of America, A thesis submitted in partial fulfilment of the requirements for the degree of Master of Arts in War Studies from The Royal Military College of Canada, 70 (http://www.nlc-bnc.ca/obj/s4/f2/dsk2/ftp04/mq22780.pdf)
102. Ian Elliot, It's a great day to be a signaller, Kingston Whig-Standard, Apr 19 2010
103. Ibid
104. Ibid
105. Murray Brewster, Canada's electronic spy service to take more prominent role in ISIS fight, Canadian Press, Feb 18 2016 (https://www.cbc.ca/news/politics/canada-spy-agency-isis-fight-1.3454617)
106. A new Canadian approach to defence: Anticipate. Adapt. Act (https://www.canada.ca/en/department-national-defence/corporate/reports-publications/canada-defence-policy/new-approach-defence.html)
107. Murray Brewster, A parliamentary committee is set to shine a light on the shadowy business of military intelligence, Apr 8 2019 (https://www.cbc.ca/news/politics/military-intelligence-canada-parliamentary-committee-1.5087547)
108. National Defence, Department of National, Defence invests in new facility for Joint Task Force X at CFB Kingston, News release, Oct 5 2018 (https://www.canada.ca/en/department-national-defence/news/2018/10/department-of-national-defence-invests-in-new-facility-for-joint-task-force-x-at-cfb-kingston.html)
109. Micaal Ahmed, Gaining intelligence: an interview with CFINTCOM's rear-admiral Scott bishop, Vol 24, Aug 1 2017 (http://espritdecorps.ca/feature/gaining-intelligence-an-interview-with-cfintcoms-rear-admiral-scott-bishop)
110. Section II - Analysis of Programs by Strategic Outcome - Outcome 1 - DPR - 2014-15 (https://www.canada.ca/en/department-national-defence/corporate/reports-publications/departmental-performance/2014-15/section-ii-strategic-outcome-1.html)
111. Strong, Secure, Engaged: Canada's Defence Policy (http://www.ieee.es/Galerias/fichero/OtrasPublicaciones/Internacional/2017/Canada-Defense-Policy_Jun2017.pdf)
112. 6. A new Canadian approach to defence: Anticipate. Adapt. Act. (https://www.canada.ca/en/department-national-defence/corporate/reports-publications/canada-defence-policy/new-approach-defence.html)
113. More stringent oversight of military intelligence at DND in limbo, Canadian Press, Jan 18 2015 (https://www.thespec.com/news-story/5263606-more-stringent-oversight-of-military-intelligence-at-dnd-in-limbo/)
114. National Security and Intelligence Committee of Parliamentarians, Annual Report 2018 Submitted to the Prime Minister on December 21, 2018 (http://www.nsicop-cpsnr.ca/reports/rp-2019-04-09/2019-04-09_annual_report_2018_public_en.pdf)
115. Murray Brewster, Military intelligence chief insists his people operate within the law, Apr 11 2019 (https://www.cbc.ca/news/politics/military-intelligence-officer-parliament-report-1.5092891)
116. National Security and Intelligence Committee of Parliamentarians, Annual Report 2018 Submitted to the Prime Minister on December 21, 2018 (http://www.nsicop-cpsnr.ca/reports/rp-2019-04-09/2019-04-09_annual_report_2018_public_en.pdf)
117. Charlie Pinkerton, NSICOP asks AG to review how military handles information about Canadians overseas, Mar 12 2020 (https://ipolitics.ca/2020/03/12/nsicop-asks-ag-to-review-how-military-handles-information-about-canadians-overseas/)

Chapter 14

1. The Standing Senate Committee on National Security and Defence, May 26 2014 (https://sencanada.ca/en/Content/Sen/committee/412/secd/51441-e)
2. Message from the Co-Chairs of the Federal-to-Federal Assistance and Information Exchange Working Group On Oct 20 2009 (https://www.publicsafety.gc.ca/cnt/rsrcs/pblctns/cmpndm-ntdstts-cnd-archvd/index-en.aspx?wbdisable=true)
3. Philippe Lagassé, Northern Command and the Evolution of Canada–U.S. Defence Relations, 2003 (http://www.journal.forces.gc.ca/vo4/no1/policy-police-01-eng.asp)
4. Ann Griffiths, The Canadian Forces and Interoperability: panacea or perdition?, 129
5. North American Aerospace Defense Command (NORAD) (https://www.canada.ca/en/department-national-defence/corporate/reports-publications/transition-materials/caf-operations-activities/2020/03/caf-ops-activities/norad.html)
6. Canadian Forces Sentinel, 1967, 16
7. NORAD's Canadian troops plan for a different holiday season, Associated Press, Nov 15 2020 (https://www.stripes.com/news/us/norad-s-canadian-troops-plan-

for-a-different-holiday-season-1.652210)
8. Joseph T Jockel, Canada in NORAD: 1957-2007: a history, 3
9. Ann Denholm Crosby, Dilemmas in Defence Decision-Making: constructing Canada's role in NORAD, 1958-96, 34
10. Bern Horn, The Canadian Way of War: serving the national interest, 250
11. Joseph Jockel, Canada in NORAD: 1957-2007: a history, 22
12. Ann Denholm Crosby, Dilemmas in Defense Decision-Making, 1958-96, 25
13. Joseph Jockel, Canada in NORAD: 1957-2007: a history, 4
14. Ibid
15. John Clearwater, Canadian Nuclear Weapons: The Untold Story of Canada's Cold War Arsenal, 64
16. Gordon A Wilson, NORAD and the Soviet Threat: Canada's Secret Electronic Air War, 43
17. Ann Denholm Crosby, Dilemmas in Defence Decision-Making, 39
18. Richard Howard Gimblett, Peter T Haydon and Ann L Griffiths, Canadian gunboat diplomacy: the Canadian Navy and foreign-policy, 118
19. Joseph Jockel, Canada in NORAD: 1957-2007: a history, 46
20. Murray Brewster, Cruise missile threat biggest priority in upcoming Norad makeover, CBC, Jul 26 2017 (https://www.cbc.ca/news/politics/norad-cruise-missiles-1.4221039)
21. Alice Slater, The US Has Military Bases in 80 Countries, Jan 24 2018 (https://www.thenation.com/article/archive/the-us-has-military-bases-in-172-countries-all-of-them-must-close/) ; Nick Turse, U.S. Special Operations Forces Deployed to 149 Countries in 2017 (https://warisboring.com/u-s-special-operations-forces-deployed-to-149-countries-in-2017/)
22. Ann L Griffiths, The Canadian Forces and Interoperability: panacea or perdition, 99
23. Ann Denholm Crosby, Dilemmas in Defence Decision-Making: constructing Canada's role in NORAD, 1958-96, 69
24. Ibid, 27
25. Joseph T Jockel, Canada in NORAD: 1957-2007: a history, 57
26. Erika Simpson, NATO and the Bomb: Canadian defenders confront critics, 119
27. Ann Denholm Crosby, Dilemmas in Defence Decision-Making, 31
28. David J Angell, Norad and binational nuclear alert: consultation and decision making in the integrated command, Defense Analysis, Vol 4, No 2, 1988
29. Joseph T Jockel, Canada in NORAD: 1957-2007: a history, 91
30. Ibid, 92
31. Ann Denholm Crosby, Dilemmas in Defence Decision-Making: constructing Canada's role in NORAD, 1958-96, 70
32. Ibid
33. Sean M Maloney, War with Iraq: Canada's strategy in the Persian Gulf, 1990-2002, 9 (http://www.queensu.ca/cidp/sites/webpublish.queensu.ca.cidpwww/files/files/publications/Martellos/Martello24.pdf)
34. Ibid
35. Ernie Regehr, BMD, NORAD, and Canada-US Security Relations, Project Ploughshares, Mar 2004)
36. Ann Denholm Crosby, Dilemmas in Defence Decision-Making: constructing Canada's role in NORAD, 1958-96, 95
37. Ibid, 98
38. Ibid, 84
39. Ibid, 87
40. James Fergusson, Shall we dance? The missile defence decision, norad renewal, and the future of Canada-US defence relations, Canadian Military Journal, Summer 2005 (http://www.journal.forces.gc.ca/vo6/no2/inter-01-eng.asp)
41. Ann Denholm Crosby, Dilemmas in Defence Decision-Making: constructing Canada's role in NORAD, 1958-96, 87
42. Ibid
43. Ibid, 8
44. Ibid, 72 ; Bill Robinson, Rethinking NORAD, Feb 1986 (peacemagazine.org/archive/v02n1p19.htm)
45. Richard Sanders, Canada Requested "Missile Defense" Role, Press for Conversion! (https://coat.ncf.ca/our_magazine/links/56/Articles/56_10-21.pdf)
46. Ibid
47. James Fergusson, Shall we dance? The missile defence decision, norad renewal, and the future of Canada-US defence relations, Canadian Military Journal, Summer 2005 (http://www.journal.forces.gc.ca/vo6/no2/inter-01-eng.asp)
48. Ibid
49. Konrad Yakabuski, Think LAVs are thorny? Wait for the missile debate, Apr 21 2016 (https://www.theglobeandmail.com/opinion/think-lavs-are-thorny-wait-for-the-missile-debate/article29700278/)
50. Jeffrey F Collins, Should Canada Participate in Ballistic Missile Defence?, July 2018 (https://macdonaldlaurier.ca/files/pdf/MLI_BMD_FinalWeb.pdf)
51. Ibid
52. Paul H Johnstone, Diana Johnstone and Paul Craig Roberts, From MAD to Madness: Inside Pentagon Nuclear War Planning
53. Mel Hurtig, Rushing to Armageddon, 97
54. Treaty on Principles Governing the Activities of States in the Exploration and Use of Outer Space, including the Moon and Other Celestial Bodies (https://www.unoosa.org/oosa/en/ourwork/spacelaw/treaties/introouterspacetreaty.html)
55. Eric Lerhe, Canada-US Military Interoperability in the War on Terror: At What Cost Sovereignty? (https://dalspace.library.dal.ca/bitstream/handle/10222/15306/Lerhe_Eric_PhD_POLSCI_Oct_2012_D.pdf?sequence=5&isAllowed=y)
56. Andrew C Richter, "ALONGSIDE THE BEST"?: The Future of the Canadian Forces, Naval War College Review, Vol 56, Winter 2003
57. Interoperability: Connecting NATO Forces (https://www.nato.int/cps/en/natohq/topics_84112.htm)
58. Sean M Maloney, War with Iraq: Canada's Strategy in the Persian Gulf, 1990-2002, 36
59. Jim Cox, A military perspective of Canada's mission in Iraq, Mar 30 2015 (http://thevimyreport.com/2015/03/a-military-perspective-of-canadas-mission-in-iraq/)
60. Valerie Insinna, Canadian air chief looks to speed up fighter buy, Nov 11 2017 (https://www.defensenews.com/digital-show-dailies/dubai-air-show/2017/11/11/canadian-air-chief-the-sooner-the-better-on-fighter-acquisition/)
61. Ann L Griffiths, The Canadian Forces and Interoperability: panacea or perdition, 104
62. Ibid, 159
63. Chris Thatcher, RCAF hints at capabilities that

may guide future fighter acquisition Avatar, Apr 24 2018 (https://skiesmag.com/news/rcaf-hints-capabilities-may-guide-future-fighter-acquisition/)
64. Alessandro Gagliardi, Canada's F-35: Too Costly Not To Purchase, Jan 21 2014 (https://natoassociation.ca/canadas-f-35-too-costly-not-to-purchase-2/)
65. Ann Griffiths, The Canadian Forces and Interoperability: panacea or perdition, 184
66. Tony Seed, 'Interoperability' — Euphemism for integration and annexation of Canadian Forces in the service of empire-building, June 12 2017 (https://tonyseed.wordpress.com/2017/06/12/interoperability-euphemism-for-integration-and-annexation-of-canadian-forces-in-the-service-of-empire-building/)
67. A very Canadian coup d'état, Aug 26 2011 (https://www.youtube.com/watch?v=I1mFGxvCK3E)
68. Deputy Minister General (retired) Walt Natynczyk CMM MSC CD (https://www.veterans.gc.ca/eng/about-vac/who-we-are/department-officials/deputy-minister) ; Walter Natynczyk (https://en.wikipedia.org/wiki/Walter_Natynczyk)
69. Thomas J. Lawson (https://en.wikipedia.org/wiki/Thomas_J._Lawson)
70. Ben Norton, Canada Adopts 'America First' Foreign Policy, Global Research, July 5 2019 (https://www.globalresearch.ca/canada-adopts-america-first-foreign-policy-us-state-dept-boasted-2017-appointment-fm-chrystia-freeland/5682794)
71. Ibid
72. James Cudmore, Canadian military explored plan to fully integrate forces with U.S., Sep 30 2015 (https://www.cbc.ca/news/politics/canada-election-2015-military-integration-canada-us-1.3248594)
73. Bernd Horn, The Canadian Way of War: serving the national interest, 280
74. David Zimmerman, Maritime Command Pacific: the Royal Canadian Navy's West Coast fleet in the early Cold War, 48
75. Murray Brewster, Canada, U.S. held joint exercises simulating nuclear attack on both sides of border, Nov 30 2017 (https://www.cbc.ca/news/politics/joint-military-exercises-nuclear-threat-1.4424556)
76. Kurt Jensen, Cautious Beginnings: Canadian foreign intelligence 1939-1951, 22
77. Kevin Lippert, War Plan Red, Appendix B, 132
78. H A Skaarup, An Intelligence Advantage: Collective Security Benefits gained by Canada through the sharing of Military Intelligence with the United States of America, 22 (http://www.nlc-bnc.ca/obj/s4/f2/dsk2/ftp04/mq22780.pdf)
79. Floyd Rudmin, Secret War Plans and the Malady of American Militarism, Feb 17 2006 (https://www.counterpunch.org/2006/02/17/secret-war-plans-and-the-malady-of-american-militarism/)
80. H A Skaarup, An Intelligence Advantage: Collective Security Benefits gained by Canada through the sharing of Military Intelligence with the United States of America (http://www.nlc-bnc.ca/obj/s4/f2/dsk2/ftp04/mq22780.pdf)
81. Marc Milner, Canada's Navy: the first century, 9
82. Ibid, 31
83. Ann Griffiths, The Canadian Forces and Interoperability: panacea or perdition, 160
84. Murray Dobbin, Harper's Taste for War: PM's pride tied to military muscle, U.S. approval, Sep 25 2006 (https://thetyee.ca/Views/2006/09/25/Afghanistan/)
85. Josh Dehaas, 'NATO needs more Canada,' President Obama says in Ottawa, June 29 2016 (https://www.ctvnews.ca/politics/nato-needs-more-canada-president-obama-says-in-ottawa-1.2967595)
86. Teresa Wright, Trump sends letter to Trudeau calling for increase in NATO defence spending, Canadian Press, Jun 22 2018 (https://www.cbc.ca/news/politics/trump-letter-trudeau-nato-1.4719198) ; Murray Brewster, Canada facing renewed pressure from U.S. to meet NATO defence spending benchmark, Nov 23 2019 (https://www.cbc.ca/news/politics/canada-pressure-us-defence-spending-1.5371352)
87. Matthew Wunderlich, Joint, Coalition and Total Force Airmen expediting Rapid Global Mobility at Al Udeid Air Base, Qatar, 8th Expeditionary Air Mobility, Jan 2 2019 (https://www.mcchord.af.mil/News/Article-Display/Article/1723552/joint-coalition-and-total-force-airmen-expediting-rapid-global-mobility-at-al-u/)
88. Eric Lerhe, Canada-US Military Interoperability in the War on Terror: At What Cost Sovereignty?
89. Ann Denholm Crosby, Dilemmas in Defence Decision-Making: constructing Canada's role in NORAD, 1958-96, 36
90. Whitney P Lackenbauer, The Cold War on Canadian Soil: Militarizing a Northern Environment, American Society for Environmental History, Vol 12, N 4, Oct 2007
91. John Clearwater, Canadian Nuclear Weapons: The Untold Story of Canada's Cold War Arsenal, 33
92. Ann Griffiths, the Canadian forces and interoperability: panacea or perdition?, 128
93. Martin Rudner, Canada's Communications Security Establishment, Signals Intelligence and Counter-Terrorism, Intelligence and National Security, 2007
94. Gordon A Wilson, NORAD and the Soviet Threat: Canada's Secret Electronic Air War, 45

Chapter 15

1. Hansard May 20 1963, 62
2. John Gellner, Canada in NATO, 103
3. Jack Granatstein, National Post, Jan 1 2007
4. Stephen Fuhr, Canada and NATO: an alliance forged in strength and reliability, Report of the Standing Committee on National Defence (https://www.ourcommons.ca/Content/Committee/421/NDDN/Reports/RP9972815/nddnrp10/nddnrp10-e.pdf)
5. Le Nouveau "bunker" de L'OTAN, L'Actualite, Oct 2017
6. Ibid ; Erika Simpson, NATO and the Bomb: Canadian defenders confront critics, 11
7. NATO Business Portal, Apr 17 2020 (https://www.nato.int/cps/en/natohq/62249.htm#:~:text=The%20NATO%20Industrial%20Advisory%20Group%20(NIAG)%20is%20a%20high-,and%20production%20of%20defence%20and)
8. Eric Lerhe, Canada-US Military Interoperability in the War on Terror: At What Cost Sovereignty?
9. Ibid
10. Peter Langille, Changing the Guard, 116
11. John Robinson Beal, The Pearson Phenomenon, 95
12. Escott Reid, Radical Mandarin: The Memoirs of Escott Reid, 252
13. Cardwell Curt, NSC 68 and the Political Economy of the Early Cold War, 38
14. Robert Bothwell, Bothwell, Alliance and Illusion, 46
15. Ibid
16. Chomsky, What Uncle Sam really wants, 78

17. Cardwell, NSC 68, 51
18. Wayne Roberts, Canadian Dimension June 1981
19. March 28 1949 (https://www.lipad.ca/full/1949/03/28/8/#1559110)
20. Cy Gonick, Inflation Or Depression: The Continuing Crisis of the Canadian Economy, 231
21. Robert Jervis and Adlai E Stevenson, The Meaning of the Nuclear Revolution: Statecraft and the Prospect of Armageddon, 207
22. Hansard, Mar 28 1949, 2095
23. Daniele Ganser, NATO's Secret Armies, 2
24. Hansard, Jan 29 1954, 1587
25. John Price, Orienting Canada, 282
26. John Gellner, Canada in NATO, 21
27. Hansard, Feb 4 1949, 237
28. Hansard, Oct 19 1951, 196
29. Hansard, Feb 11 1953, 1855
30. Dean F Oliver, Canada and NATO Dispatches: Backgrounders in Canadian Military History (https://www.warmuseum.ca/learn/dispatches/canada-and-nato/#tabs)
31. Dave Majumdar, Newly Declassified Documents: Gorbachev Told NATO Wouldn't Move Past East German Border, Dec 12 2017 (https://nationalinterest.org/blog/the-buzz/newly-declassified-documents-gorbachev-told-nato-wouldnt-23629)
32. Ernie Regehr and Simon Rosenblum, The Road to Peace, 30
33. Ibid, 34
34. Ibid, 33
35. Sean Maloney, Canada and UN Peacekeeping, 53
36. John Clearwater, Canadian Nuclear Weapons, 93/94
37. Ibid, 214
38. Hélène Laverdière, I Am Ashamed Of The Liberals› Position On Nuclear Disarmament Mar 27 2017 (http://www.huffingtonpost.ca/helene-laverdiere/trudeau-nuclear-disarmament_b_15625872.html) ; Erin Hunt, By sitting out nuclear weapons meeting, Canada backtracks on its commitment to peace, Mar 21 2017 (https://www.opencanada.org/features/sitting-out-nuclear-weapons-meeting-canada-backtracks-its-commitment-peace/)
39. Ernie Regehr and Simon Rosenblum, The Road to Peace, 85
40. Sean Maloney, Canada and UN Peacekeeping: Cold War by other means, 1945-1970, 99
41. Peter Stursberg, Lester Pearson and the American Dilemma, 183
42. Laura Payton, Canada considering international bases: MacKay, Jun 2 2011 (https://www.cbc.ca/news/politics/canada-considering-international-bases-mackay-1.1125698)
43. Which branch of the military, exactly, do the Liberals plan to gut this time?, National Post, Mar 24 2017 (https://nationalpost.com/opinion/national-post-view-which-branch-of-the-military-exactly-do-the-liberals-plan-to-gut-this-time)
44. Elinor Sloan, New plan for fighter jet purchase is sensible — but risky, Globe and Mail, Dec 13 2017
45. Marc Milner, Canada's Navy: the first century, 239/244
46. Ernie Regehr, Arms Canada: The Deadly Business of Military Exports, 48

Chapter 16

1. 2.0 Departmental Spending (https://www.veterans.gc.ca/eng/about-vac/news-media/facts-figures/2-0#:~:text=Veterans%20Affairs%20Canada%20ended%20the,families%20and%20other%20program%20recipients.) ; Financial overview — Estimates of Environment and Climate Change Canada: appearance before the Standing Committee (https://www.canada.ca/en/environment-climate-change/corporate/transparency/briefing-materials/appearance-before-standing-committee-environment-sustainable-development/financial-overview-estimates-environment-climate-change.html)
2. Gloria Galloway, Veterans Affairs shed staff despite increased mental-health risks, Dec 2 2014 (https://www.theglobeandmail.com/news/politics/veterans-affairs-shed-staff-despite-increased-mental-health-risks/article21897819/)
3. Facts and Figures Summary (https://www.veterans.gc.ca/eng/about-vac/news-media/facts-figures/summary)
4. Peter Neary and J L Granatstein, The Veterans Charter and post-World War II Canada, 9
5. David J Bercuson and Jack Granatstein, Dictionary of Canadian Military History, 217 ; Peter Neary and J L Granatstein, The Veterans Charter and post-World War II Canada, 9
6. David J Bercuson and Jack Granatstein, Dictionary of Canadian Military History, 173
7. Peter Neary and J L Granatstein, The Veterans Charter and post-World War II Canada, 12
8. David J Bercuson and Jack Granatstein, Dictionary of Canadian Military History, 96
9. The Origins and Evolution of Veterans Benefits in Canada 1914-2004, Reference Paper, Mar 15 2004 (https://www.veterans.gc.ca/public/pages/forces/nvc/reference.pdf)
10. The Canadian Institute for Military and Veteran Health Research (CIMVHR) (https://www.rehab.queensu.ca/research/our-centres/cimvhr)
11. Pierre Jasmin, Ce que les débats taisent, au profit du complexe militaro-industriel, Oct 15 2019 (http://lautjournal.info/20191015/ce-que-les-debats-taisent-au-profit-du-complexe-militaro-industriel)
12. Murray Brewster, At least 2,250 veterans are homeless, according to groundbreaking analysis, Canadian Press, Jan 5 2016 (https://www.cbc.ca/news/politics/2250-canadian-veterans-homeless-1.3390674)
13. Well-supported, diverse, resilient people and families (https://www.canada.ca/en/department-national-defence/corporate/reports-publications/canada-defence-policy/well-supported-diverse-resilient-people-families.html) ; Lee Berthiaume, More than 6,700 Canadian veterans from Afghan war receiving federal assistance for PTSD, Canadian Press, Apr 22 2019 (https://nationalpost.com/news/canada/more-than-6700-veterans-from-afghan-war-receiving-federal-assistance-for-ptsd)
14. Korean War (1950-1953) (http://www.veterans.gc.ca/eng/remembrance/history/korean-war)
15. The South African War (https://www.veterans.gc.ca/eng/remembrance/history/south-african-war) ; Canada & The South African War, 1899-1902 (http://www.warmuseum.ca/cwm/exhibitions/boer/boerwarhistory_e.shtml)
16. Stanley Jackson, Home to the Land, 1944 (https://www.nfb.ca/film/home_to_the_land/)
17. The Long Silence (http://screenculture.org/cesif/node/9720)
18. Donald Brittain, Fields of Sacrifice, 1964 (https://www.nfb.ca/film/fields_of_sacrifice/)
19. Ian McKay and Jamie Swift, The Vimy Trap, 177
20. Jason Fekete, Conservative government spent millions on ads during NHL playoffs, Ottawa Citizen, Sept 18 2014
21. Commemorative Partnership Program - List of

Approved Projects (https://www.veterans.gc.ca/eng/remembrance/commemorative-events/commemorative-partnership/approved-funding)
22. The Canadian Football League and Veterans Affairs Canada present the 2017 Jake Gaudaur Veterans' Award to Luc Brodeur-Jourdain, Veterans Affairs, Nov 23 2017 (https://www.newswire.ca/news-releases/the-canadian-football-league-and-veterans-affairs-canada-present-the-2017-jake-gaudaur-veterans-award-to-luc-brodeur-jourdain-659637233.html)
23. Ibid
24. News Release, Annual tribute to Veterans and Canadian Armed Forces personnel at CFL Western Semi-final playoff game, Veterans Affairs, Nov 12 2017
25. National Inventory of Canadian Military Memorials (http://www.veterans.gc.ca/eng/remembrance/memorials/national-inventory-canadian-memorials)
26. Archived - Community members pay tribute to Veterans in Barrie, Nov 4 2014 (http://news.gc.ca/web/article-en.do?nid=899979)
27. The Disturbing Growth of Militarism in Canada, Collectif Échec à la guerre, May 2014 (http://echecalaguerre.org/wp-content/uploads/Disturbing-growth-of-militarism-in-Canada-May-2014-EAG.pdf)
28. Ted Barri, Deadlock in Korea: Canadians at War, 1950-1953, Acknowledgements
29. Conclusion (https://www.veterans.gc.ca/eng/remembrance/those-who-served/indigenous-veterans/native-soldiers/conclusion)
30. Tom Beaver and Ron Clarke, 'You Have Forgotten': Seven Conservative Attacks on Canada's Veterans, Aug 19 2015 (https://thetyee.ca/Opinion/2015/08/19/Conservative-Attacks-Canadian-Veterans/)
31. Richard Lawrence, War Amps 100th Anniversary Commemorative Envelope Unveiling, Feb 9 2018 (http://espritdecorps.ca/richard-lawrence/war-amps-100th-anniversary-commemorative-envelope-unveiling)
32. Ibid
33. Canadian war vets exposed to mustard gas receive compensation, May 11 2004 (https://www.cbc.ca/news/canada/canadian-war-vets-exposed-to-mustard-gas-receive-compensation-1.515527)
34. Bruce Campion-Smith, Nerve Gas Tests Revealed, Toronto Star, July 18 2005
35. Graham Chandler, Chemistry experiments, May 26 2016 (https://legionmagazine.com/en/2016/05/chemistry-experiments/)
36. Doug Alexander, A fight not finished for vets, Mar 3 2004 (https://www.csmonitor.com/2004/0303/p14s01-woam.html)
37. People harmed by Agent Orange at Gagetown offered $20K, Sep 12 2007 (https://www.cbc.ca/news/canada/new-brunswick/people-harmed-by-agent-orange-at-gagetown-offered-20k-1.663724)
38. Uduak Idiong, Manitoba History: The Third Force: Returned Soldiers in the Winnipeg General Strike of 1919, Manitoba Historical Society, N 34, Autumn 1997 (www.mhs.mb.ca/docs/mb_history/34/thirdforce.shtml)
39. Ibid
40. Peter Neary and J L Granatstein, The Veterans Charter and post-World War II Canada, 105
41. Ibid, 104

42. Mallory Schwartz, War on the Air: CBC-TV and Canada's Military, 1952-1992, 289
43. Ibid, 291
44. Ibid, 307/337
45. Ibid, 308
46. E J Dick, The Valour and the Horror Continued: Do We Still Want Our History on Television?, Journal of the Association of Canadian Archivists, Spring 1993 (journals.sfu.ca/archivar/index.php/archivaria/article/viewFile/.../12854)
47. David Dean, Museums as conflict zones: The Canadian War Museum and Bomber Command, Museum and Society, Mar 2009 (https://www2.le.ac.uk/.../museumstudies/museumsociety/.../dean.pdf)
48. Ibid
49. Robert Bothwell, Randall Hansen and Margaret MacMillan, Controversy, commemoration, and capitulation: the Canadian War Museum and Bomber Command, Queen's Quarterly, Vol 115, Sept 2008
50. David Dean, Museums as conflict zones: the Canadian War Museum and Bomber Command, Museum and Society, Mar 2009 (https://www2.le.ac.uk/.../museumstudies/museumsociety/.../dean.pdf) ; Norman Hillmer, The Canadian War Museum and the Military Identity of an Unmilitary People, Canadian Military History, Vol 19 Is 3, 2010
51. About Us (http://www.legion.ca/who-we-are/)
52. James Hale, Branching Out, 269/98
53. Ibid 218
54. Ibid, 114
55. Ibid, 33
56. The Royal Canadian Legion application for membership (https://portal.legion.ca/membership-eligibility)
57. Barrick Company recruitment program targets veterans, Nov 11 2016 (https://www.jamiiforums.com/threads/waziri-kabudi-mpinzani-wako-katika-majadiliano-na-barrick-ni-komandoo-wa-jeshi.1294178/page-8)
58. The Royal Canadian Legion partners with VIA Rail Canada in unique Poppy Campaign initiative, Oct 31 2018 (https://www.legion.ca/news/2018/10/31/the-royal-canadian-legion-partners-with-via-rail-canada-in-unique-poppy-campaign-initiative)
59. Canadian veteran vehicle registration plates (https://en.wikipedia.org/wiki/Canadian_veteran_vehicle_registration_plates)
60. Stationnement gratuit pour les personnes handicapées et les vétérans à Sherbrooke, Dec 19 2017 (https://ici.radio-canada.ca/nouvelle/1073988/stationnement-gratuit-pour-les-personnes-handicapees-et-les-veterans-a-sherbrooke)
61. James Braden, Ford gives back to military with new vehicle specials, Jan 31 2018 (https://finance.yahoo.com/news/james-braden-ford-gives-back-200000251.html)
62. Canadian death toll in Afghan mission: 158 soldiers, four civilians, Canadian Press, May 9 2014 (https://www.ctvnews.ca/canada/canadian-death-toll-in-afghan-mission-158-soldiers-four-civilians-1.1814248) ; Canadian Agricultural Injury Reporting: Agriculture-Related Fatalities in Canada (https://www.cair-sbac.ca/wp-content/uploads/2017/02/CASA-CAIR-Report-English-FINAL-Web.pdf)

Chapter 17

1. David Pugliese, Sex assaults, high costs, bureaucracy plague Cadet program - reform needed, says group, Jun 16 2016 (https://ottawacitizen.com/news/national/defence-watch/sex-assaults-high-costs-bureaucracy-plague-cadet-program-reform-needed-says-group)
2. Gerry Fostaty, As you were: the tragedy at Valcartier, 14
3. Maria Granados, Paving the Way for Higher Education, May 22 2018 (espritdecorps.ca/cadet-corner/

paving-the-way-for-higher-education-scholarships-help-cadets-reach-their-goals) ; Maxime Corneau, Winner of the 2019 Young Citizens Foundation, July 24 2019 (https://www.armycadetleague.ca/news/winner-of-the-2019-young-citizens-foundation/)
4. Gerry Fostaty, As you were: the tragedy at Valcartier, 44
5. What is Air Cadets? (https://www.111air.ca/what-is-air-cadets.html)
6. The Canadian Forces (continued) (https://laws-lois.justice.gc.ca/eng/acts/n-5/page-8.html?wbdisable=false)
7. HISTORY (https://aircadetleague.com/about-us/history/)
8. Building Ships, hiring veterans, and investing in youth, May 31 2018 (http://shipsforcanada.ca/our-stories/building-ships-hiring-veterans-and-investing-in-youth)
9. Ron Pickler and Larry Milberry, Canadair: the first 50 years, 300
10. Gerry Pash, Largest officer occupation marks centennial, The Maple Leaf, Vol 12, No 2 Jan 2009 (https://web.archive.org/web/20110609140311/http://www.forces.gc.ca/site/commun/ml-fe/article-eng.asp?id=5000)
11. Cadet Program (http://www.204armycadets.com/uploads/7/9/2/9/7929973/cadetfactsheets.pdf)
12. Kelly Jarman, The Cost of Canada's Militarist Culture: Perspectives From a Former Cadet (http://www.mediacoop.ca/story/cost-canada's-militarist-culture-perspectives-form/36973)
13. What is Cadets (https://72armycadets.com/what-is-cadets/)
14. Government settles with cadets in deadly 1974 grenade blast in Valcartier, Canadian Press, Mar 9 2017 (https://www.cbc.ca/news/canada/montreal/valcartier-grenade-cadets-1.4017327)
15. Upper Canada College, A History of The Rifle Company, College Times, 1924, Mar 23 2016 (https://canadaatwarblog.wordpress.com/2016/03/23/upper-canada-college-a-history-of-the-rifle-company-college-times-1924/)
16. Desmond Morton, The Cadet Movement in the Moment of Canadian Militarism, Journal of Canadian Studies, Vol 13, Summer 1978
17. David J Bercuson and Jack Granatstein, Dictionary of Canadian Military History, 183
18. Royal Canadian Army Cadets (https://en.wikipedia.org/wiki/Royal_Canadian_Army_Cadets)
19. Demyan Plakhov, Cadets: Vital To Canada's Society And Military, July 14, 2016 (https://natoassociation.ca/cadets-vital-to-canadas-society-and-military/)
20. Military destroys pamphlets that advised female cadets not to wear shirts that 'reveal their developing bits', Oct 4 2016 (https://nationalpost.com/news/canada/inappropriate-leaflets-from-n-l-squadron-removed-destroyed-military)
21. David Pugliese, Sex assaults, high costs, bureaucracy plague Cadet program - reform needed, says group, Jun 16 2016 (https://ottawacitizen.com/news/national/defence-watch/sex-assaults-high-costs-bureaucracy-plague-cadet-program-reform-needed-says-group)
22. Justin Ling, Documents Show the Canadian Army Cadets Program Is Plagued With Sexual Abuse Allegations, Nov 26 2014 (https://www.vice.com/en/article/xdm7kn/canadian-military-cadet-program-has-a-sexual-assault-problem-documents-show-674
23. Peter Kennedy, Cadet abuse settlement in millions, Apr 8 2006 (https://www.theglobeandmail.com/news/national/cadet-abuse-settlement-in-millions/article4300545/)
24. Douglas Quan, Predators and prey: Canada's military cadets and the sex misconduct problem few talk about, May 24 2016 (https://nationalpost.com/news/canada/cadets)
25. Ibid
26. J L Granatstein and J M Hitsman, Broken promises: a history of conscription in Canada, 16
27. Lara Campbell, Michael Dawson and Catherine Gidney, Worth Fighting For: Canada's Tradition of War Resistance from 1812 to the War on Terror
28. Deborah Cowen, Military Workfare: The Soldier and Social Citizenship in Canada, 81
29. Ibid, 77/78
30. Ibid, 75
31. Ibid
32. Ibid
33. North American Aerospace Defense Command (https://www.norad.mil/Francais/Article/578534/norad-tracks-santa-program-has-record-breaking-success-in-2012/)
34. Holly Lake, Santa's on his way: How NORAD's Christmas tradition got started, Dec 24 2017 (https://ipolitics.ca/2017/12/24/santas-way-norads-christmas-tradition-got-started/)
35. Natasha Tersigni, Communication established with North Pole thanks to 37th Operation RADIO SANTA, Project number: 18-0443, Dec 6 2018 (www.army-armee.forces.gc.ca/en/news-publications/national-news-details-no-menu.page?doc=communication-established-with-north-pole-thanks-to-37th-operation-radio-santa/jpa6f6lx)
36. Brett Purdy, Manitoba soldiers reveal 'top secret' mission to connect Winnipeg kids to Santa, Dec 7 2015 (https://www.cbc.ca/news/canada/manitoba/manitoba-soldiers-reveal-top-secret-mission-to-connect-winnipeg-kids-to-santa-1.3354530)
37. Military might not right for schoolyard, father says, Jun 15, 2007 (https://www.cbc.ca/news/canada/newfoundland-labrador/military-might-not-right-for-schoolyard-father-says-1.675873)
38. Alan S Hale, Catholic school board holds its first job fair in a long time, Apr 2 2019 (https://www.thewhig.com/news/local-news/catholic-school-board-holds-its-first-job-fair-in-a-long-time/wcm/70c3a11b-5620-44da-9cd6-5b82d39b6438)
39. Cooperative Education Military Co-op (schools.yrdsb.ca/markville.ss/teacher/coop/Army.html)
40. Sharon Hill, In the navy: new Windsor co-op program attracting teens to naval reserves, Jan 21 2018 (https://windsorstar.com/news/local-news/in-the-navy-new-windsor-co-op-program-attracting-teens-to-naval-reserves)
41. The disturbing growth of militarism in Canada, May 2014 (https://echecalaguerre.org/wp-content/uploads/Disturbing-growth-of-militarism-in-Canada-May-2014-EAG.pdf)
42. Ibid
43. Ibid
44. Memory Project Newsletter, Winter 2016 (www.thememoryproject.com/newsletter/33:download)
45. Historica Canada (https://en.wikipedia.org/wiki/Historica_Canada)
46. Ian McKay and Jamie Swift, Warrior Nation, 280
47. Howard D Fremeth, Memory, Militarism and Citizenship: tracking the Dominion Institute in Canada's military-cultural memory network, Carleton University PHD Thesis, 2010, 151/178/184
48. Nancy Taber, Generals, colonels, and captains:

Discourses of militarism, education, and learning in the Canadian university context, Canadian Journal of Higher Education, Vol 44, No 2, 2014

49. Audit of Financial Stewardship of Royal Military College of Canada, 7045-80, Nov 2012 (CRS) (http://www.crs-csex.forces.gc.ca/reports-rapports/2012/192p0909-eng.aspx)

50. Royal Roads University (https://ospreyeducation.ca/royal-roads-university/)

51. Royal Canadian Electrical and Mechanical Engineers Corps celebrates 75 years of innovation, integrity and tenacity at their Blue Beret Parade, News Release, May 15 2019, Project number: 19-0132 (www.army-armee.forces.gc.ca/en/news-publications/national-news-details-no-menu.page?doc=royal-canadian-electrical-and-mechanical-engineers-corps-celebrates-75-years-of-innovation-integrity-and-tenacity-at-their-blue-beret-parade/jvmqm199)

52. Defence Public Affairs Learning Centre (https://www.canada.ca/en/department-national-defence/services/benefits-military/education-training/establishments/defence-public-affairs-learning-centre.html)

53. Association of Canadian Community Colleges, Maintaining the Readiness of the Canadian Forces Through Training and Recruitment (https://www.collegesinstitutes.ca/wp-content/uploads/2014/05/20120301_DNDCommittee.pdf)

54. Canadian Forces (https://www.nait.ca/nait/admissions/transfer-and-credit-options/pathways/canadian-forces-testimonials)

55. Paul Axelrod and John G Reid, Youth, University and Canadian society: Essays in the Social History of Higher Education, 85 ; Kathryn M Bindon, Queens men, Canada's men: the military history of Queen's University, 18

56. A call to revive university military training program, Universities News, Jan 25 2012 (http://www.universitiesnews.com/2012/01/25/a-call-to-revive-university-military-training-program/)

57. Civil Military Leadership Pilot Initiative Launched, July 8 2013, Project number: NR 13.220 (http://www.forces.gc.ca/en/news/article.page?doc=civil-military-leadership-pilot-initiative-launched/hjiq6l6c)

58. CANSEC, Innovation, Science and Economic Development Canada Speech, Honourable Navdeep Bains, PC, MP Minister of Innovation, Science and Economic Development Ottawa, Ontario May 31 2017 (https://www.canada.ca/en/innovation-science-economic-development/news/2017/06/cansec.html?=undefined&wbdisable=true)

59. Generating economic benefits—National Shipbuilding Strategy: 2016 annual report (https://www.tpsgc-pwgsc.gc.ca/app-acq/amd-dp/mer-sea/sncn-nss/rapport-report-2016-4-eng.html)

60. Michele Charlton, New Irving Shipbuilding Research Chair at Dalhousie creates Foundation for Leadership in Marine Engineering Leadership May 29 2018 (https://www.dal.ca/news/2018/05/29/new-irving-shipbuilding-research-chair-at-dalhousie-creates-foun.html)

61. Ryan McNutt, Minister of Industry welcomes investment, May 16 2008 (http://www.dal.ca/news/2008/05/16/physics.html)

62. Ibid

63. Maximilian C Forte, The New Imperialism, Vol II: Interventionism, Information Warfare, and the Military-Academic Complex, 35

64. Noam Chomsky, Foreword, Lester Pearson's Peacekeeping, 11

65. Diana Chown, Suffield, Chemical Warfare, and Canadian/US Relations, Feb 1989 (peacemagazine.org/archive/v05n1p12.htm)

66. Project HARP (https://en.wikipedia.org/wiki/Project_HARP)

67. Students' Society of McGill University, Motion Regarding Support of a Campus Free from Harmful Military Technology Development, Oct 22 2014 (https://ssmu.ca/wp-content/uploads/2009/10/General-Assembly-Motion-Support-of-a-Campus-Free-from-Harmful-Military-Technology-Development-2014-10-221.pdf)

68. Ibid

69. Ibid

70. The 100th Anniversary of Canadian Submarines (www.navy-marine.forces.gc.ca/en/navy-life/sub-centennial/sub-centennial.page) ; Toronto International Film Festival Presents Contemporary World Speakers, (http://munkschool.utoronto.ca/feature/toronto-international-film-festival-presents-contemporary-world-speakers-series/)

71. UNB's Toll of War project is 'propaganda,' historian says, Feb 2 2015 (http://www.cbc.ca/news/canada/new-brunswick/unb-s-toll-of-war-project-is-propaganda-historian-says-1.2940076)

72. Scott Taylor, Unembedded: Two Decades of Maverick War Reporting, 63

73. The Security and Defence Forum Backgrounder, Project number: BG-01.009, Apr 4 2001 (http://www.forces.gc.ca/en/news/article.page?doc=the-security-and-defence-forum/hnmx19or)

74. Ibid

75. Security and Defence Forum Year in Review, 2002–2003 (http://publications.gc.ca/collections/collection_2015/mdn-dnd/D3-18-2003-eng.pdf)

76. Security and Defence Forum Year in Review, 2005–2006 (http://publications.gc.ca/collections/collection_2015/mdn-dnd/D3-18-2006-eng.pdf)

77. Jane Kirby, Military Ties at Dalhousie's Centre for Foreign Policy Studies, Sept 7 2009 (http://halifax.mediacoop.ca/story/1874)

78. Ibid

79. Security and Defence Forum Year in Review, 2002–2003 (http://publications.gc.ca/collections/collection_2015/mdn-dnd/D3-18-2003-eng.pdf)

80. Amir Attaran, When think tanks produce propaganda, Globe and Mail, Feb 21 2008

81. Ibid

82. Ibid

83. Jack Granatstein, Fort Fumble on the Rideau: Just say no to military academics, Globe and Mail, Aug 22 2011

84. Onnig Beylerian and Jacques Lévesque, Inauspicious Beginnings: Principal Powers and International Security, viii ; Defence Management Studies (http://www.queensu.ca/dms/)

85. Danford W Middlemiss, Dalhousie University's Centre for Foreign Policy Studies: a brief history, The Canadian political science Association Bulletin, Vol XXI, May 1992

86. Ibid

87. Ibid

88. Ken Bell and Desmond Morton, Royal Canadian Military Institute: 100 years, 77

89. Militarism and Canadian Universities June 15 2011 (http://anthrojustpeace.blogspot.ca/2011/06/militarism-and-canadian-universities.html)

90. Jeffrey Grey, The last word: essays on official history in the United States and British Commonwealth, 17

91. Tim Cook, Clio's Warriors: Canadian Historians and the Writing of the World Wars, 42

92. Ibid, 171
93. Ibid, 3
94. Ian McKay and Jamie Swift, The Vimy Trap, 201
95. Ibid, 190
96. Official Histories (http://www.cmp-cpm.forces.gc.ca/dhh-dhp/his/oh-ho/index-eng.asp) Canada's Army in Korea: The United Nations Operations, 1950–53, and Their Aftermath: a Short Official Account ; Canadian Naval Operations in Korean Waters, 1950-1955 ; Strange Battleground: The Operations in Korea and Their Effects on Canada
97. Tim Cook, Clio's Warriors, 201
98. Ibid, 200
99. Jeffrey Grey, The Last Word? Essays on Official History in the United States and British Commonwealth, 17
100. Roger Sarty, The Origins of Academic Military History in Canada, 1940-1967, Canadian Military History, Vol 23 Is. 2
101. Tim Cook, Clio's Warriors, 210/221
102. Ibid, 6
103. George Stanley (https://en.wikipedia.org/wiki/George_Stanley)
104. Ibid
105. Somalia Cover Up, 248 ; Tim Cook, Clio's Warriors, 210
106. Ibid
107. J L Granatstein, Making history: The late historian Charles P. Stacey was a stickler for the truth, but his objectivity gave way to passion when it came to Mackenzie King, Globe and Mail, Sept 30 2000
108. Wesley C Gustavson, Missing the Boat? Colonel A F Duguid and the Canadian Official History of World War I, University of Calgary Master's Thesis, 1999, 89 ; Colonel Charles Perry Stacey (http://www.cmp-cpm.forces.gc.ca/dhh-dhp/adh-sdh/bio/index-eng.asp)
109. Tim Cook, Clio's Warriors, 137/154
110. Ibid, 183
111. Ibid, 173
112. About DHH: Who we are (http://www.cmp-cpm.forces.gc.ca/dhh-dhp/adh-sdh/index-eng.asp)
113. Military history brought to life, Western Sentinel, Apr 11 2013
114. Mallory Schwartz, War on the Air: CBC-TV and Canada's Military, 1952-1992, 269
115. Ibid, 126
116. Robert Bothwell, Randall Hansen and Margaret MacMillan, Controversy, commemoration, and capitulation: the Canadian War Museum and Bomber Command, Queen's Quarterly, Vol 115, Sept 2008
117. Organization of Military Museums of Canada (http://www.ommcinc.ca/#!home/mainPage)
118. Frequently Asked Questions (http://www.cmp-cpm.forces.gc.ca/dhh-dhp/faq/index-eng.asp?cat=museums&FaqID=56)
119. Quarterly Financial Report for the nine month period ended Dec 31 2015 (http://www.warmuseum.ca/wp-content/uploads/2016/02/quarterly-financial-statements-december-31-2015_e.pdf) ; Museum Reference Guide NPP Standard Operating Procedures (https://www.cfmws.com/en/AboutUs/Library/PoliciesandRegulations/Finance/Documents/MuseumReference%20Guide_e.pdf) ; Serge Bernier, A Brief History of Canadian Forces Military Museums: 1919 to 2004 — Part 2 (http://www.journal.forces.gc.ca/vo6/no2/history-histoire-02-eng.asp)
120. $30-million cost overrun on war museum, May 21 2003 (https://www.cbc.ca/news/canada/ottawa/30-million-cost-overrun-on-war-museum-1.373966)
121. Alan Ng, The Media Analysis of the Canadian Navy Centennial How Military Publications and Civilian Publications Portray News Differently, CMNS 498 Simon Fraser University Honours Thesis, Spring 2011
122. T Mirrlees, The Canadian armed forces "YouTube war": A cross-border military-social media complex, Global Media Journal - Canadian Edition, Vol 8 (http://www.gmj.uottawa.ca/1501/v8i1_mirrlees.pdf)
123. Christian Cotroneo, DND revs recruitment ads, Toronto Star, Nov 5 2006 ; The Disturbing Growth of Militarism in Canada, Collectif Échec à la guerre, May 2014 (http://echecalaguerre.org/wp-content/uploads/Disturbing-growth-of-militarism-in-Canada-May-2014-EAG.pdf)
124. David Pugliese, Xbox Live being used as a billboard for Canadian Forces recruiting ads, Ottawa Citizen, Sept 21 2014
125. Michael Goodspeed, Identifying Ourselves in the Information Age, Canadian Military Journal, Winter 2002 (http://www.journal.forces.gc.ca/vo3/no4/doc/47-48-eng.pdf)
126. Janis L Goldie, Fighting Change: Representing the Canadian Forces in the 2006–2008 Fight Recruitment Campaign, Canadian Journal of Communication, Vol 39, 2014 (http://www.cjc-online.ca/index.php/journal/article/view/2768)
127. Luke F Kowalski, The Public Face of the Royal Canadian Air Force: The Importance of Air Shows and Demonstration Teams to the R.C.A.F., For History 394 A02 Dr. Timothy Balzer, Apr 1 2013 (http://rusiviccda.org/wp-content/uploads/2013/05/The_Public_Face_of_the_Royal_Canadian_Air_Force.pdf)
128. Kamila Hinkson, 'It scared the heck out of me': CF-18 flyby spooks Montrealers, Jun 23 2017 (https://www.cbc.ca/news/canada/montreal/montreal-jets-flyby-alouettes-1.4174578)
129. Canada's Skyhawks Parachute team begins 45th jumping season, May 18 2016 (https://www.theglobeandmail.com/multimedia/canadas-skyhawks-parachute-team-begins-45th-jumping-season/article30080447/)
130. Nicole Munro, The addictive feeling of free-falling: A skydiving first with Canada's SkyHawks (https://www.saltwire.com/nova-scotia/news/the-addictive-feeling-of-free-falling-a-skydiving-first-with-canadas-skyhawks-329467/) ; Skyhawks Take Reporter For Ride Of His Life Category:, July 13 2018 (https://discovermoosejaw.com/local/skyhawks-take-reporter-of-ride-of-his-life)
131. Joanna Calder, Retired Air Force Colours Entrusted to Toronto Maple Leafs, Feb 20 2018 (espritdecorps.ca/army-articles/retired-air-force-colours-entrusted-to-toronto-maple-leafs)
132. The Naden Band of the Royal Canadian Navy (www.navy-marine.forces.gc.ca/en/about/structure-marpac-naden-home.page)
133. Canadian Armed Forces Tattoo 1967 le carrousel militaire des forces canadiennes (tattoo67.com)
134. Globe and Mail, Nov. 24, 2011
135. Brett Clarkson, Celebrating the War of 1812 with a $28-million bang, QMI Agency, Oct 11 2011 (http://www.stcatharinesstandard.ca/2011/10/11/celebrating-the-war-of-1812-with-a-28-million-bang)
136. Carl Meyer, DND points to 'challenges' with former soldiers talking to media, Embassy, July 30 2014
137. Cost of 'Canada 150' commemorations comes out of military operations budget, Mar 14 2014 (http://www.cbc.ca/news/politics/cost-of-canada-150-commemorations-

comes-out-of-military-operations-budget-1.2572425)
138. Nancy Tabe, Gendered Militarism in Canada: Learning Conformity and Resistance, 64
139. Kathleen Harris, Military looks at foreign recruits to boost ranks, May 25 2018 (https://www.cbc.ca/news/politics/caf-military-foreign-recruits-1.4675889)
140. Carl Meyer, DND: Military's 'values' shape 'Canada's identity', Embassy, Nov 23 2011
141. Ibid
142. Carl Meyer, DND points to 'challenges' with former soldiers talking to media, Embassy, July 30 2014
143. David Pugliese, Fed up media officers desert DND, Ottawa Citizen, Sep 25 2011
144. Media Contacts (http://www.forces.gc.ca/en/contact-us/media-contacts.page)
145. Ibid
146. Carl Meyer, DND points to 'challenges' with former soldiers talking to media, Embassy, July 30 2014
147. Ibid
148. Marie-Danielle Smith, DND gave minister more info on public opinion research than on ISIS operation, NATO, Embassy, Oct 28 2015
149. David Pugliese, Gen. Jon Vance responds to concerns over the "weaponization of public affairs" at DND, Sept 21 2015 (http://ottawacitizen.com/storyline/chief-of-the-defence-staff-gen-jon-vance-and-the-weaponization-of-public-affairs)
150. Ibid
151. Ibid
152. Ibid
153. Scott Taylor, DND hits panic button over non-story, Halifax Chronicle Herald, June 9 201
154. Ibid

Chapter 18

1. Patrick Cain, In the line of fire, Ryerson Review of Journalism, Aug 1 1996 (http://rrj.ca/in-the-line-of-fire/)
2. James Laxer, It's time to recalibrate Canada's mission, Globe and Mail, July 22 2008
3. Chris Wattie, Embedded in Ontario as military hones media skills, National Post, July 12 2003
4. Semi Chellas, Good to Go, Walrus, Feb 2007 (http://thewalrus.ca/2007-02-media/)
5. Bob Bergen, Disarming the Media, Alberta Views, Apr 2007 (https://albertaviews.ab.ca/wp-content/uploads/2014/08/Disarming-the-Media-Bob-Bergen.pdf)
6. Ibid
7. Allan Thompson, Outside the wire, Canadian Association of Journalists, Vol 12 Winter 2007 (http://caj.ca/wp-content/uploads/2010/mediamag/winter2007/mediawinter2007.pdf)
8. Jay Janzen, Op ATHENA ROTO 0 Embedded Media, Canadian Army Journal Fall/Winter 2004 (http://publications.gc.ca/collections/Collection/D12-11-7-3-4E.pdf)
9. Robert Bergen, Censorship; the Canadian News Media and Afghanistan: A Historical Comparison with Case Studies, Calgary Papers in Military and Strategic Studies, 2009 ; Steven Chase, PM's office sought 'a positive spin' from reporters, June 4 2008 (http://www.theglobeandmail.com/news/national/pms-office-sought-a-positive-spin-from-reporters/article959572/)
10. Sharon Hobson, The Information Gap: Why the Canadian Public Doesn't Know More About its Military, Prepared for the Canadian Defence and Foreign Affairs Institute, June 2007 (http://dspace.africaportal.org/jspui/bitstream/123456789/10386/1/The%20Information%20Gap%20%20Why%20the%20Canadian%20Public%20Doesnt%20Know%20More%20About%20its%20Military%202007.pdf?1)
11. Sherry Wasilow, Hidden Ties that Bind: The Psychological Bonds of Embedding Have Changed the Very Nature of War Reporting, Stream, Vol 4, No 1, 2011
12. Ibid
13. Vern Huffman, As Generals Send the Nation to War, Canadian Dimension, Nov 2006 (https://canadiandimension.com/articles/view/as-generals-send-the-nation-to-war-vern-huffman)
14. Jay Janzen, Op ATHENA ROTO 0 Embedded Media, Canadian Army Journal Fall/Winter 2004 (http://publications.gc.ca/collections/Collection/D12-11-7-3-4E.pdf)
15. Sharon Hobson, The Information Gap: Why the Canadian Public Doesn't Know More About its Military, Prepared for the Canadian Defence and Foreign Affairs Institute, June 2007 (http://dspace.africaportal.org/jspui/bitstream/123456789/10386/1/The%20Information%20Gap%20%20Why%20the%20Canadian%20Public%20Doesnt%20Know%20More%20About%20its%20Military%202007.pdf?1)
16. Murray Brewster, The Savage War: The Untold Battles of Afghanistan, 263
17. Louise Bourbonnais, Pas d'indépendants en Afghanistan, Trente, Dec 2007 (http://www.fpjq.org/opinion-pas-dindependants-en-afghanistan/)
18. Scott Taylor, Military passes on touching photo op, Halifax Chronicle-Herald, Jan 29 2007
19. Lyndsie Bourgon, Reporting from the front lines, King's Journalism Review, Feb 19 2008
20. Ulrich Mans, Christa Meindersma and Lars Burema, Eyes Wide Shut? The Impact of Embedded Journalism on Dutch Newspaper Coverage of Afghanistan, The Hague Centre for Strategic Studies, Apr 2008
21. Rebecca Lamarche, The challenges of embedded war reporting, King's Journalism Review, Jan 24 2013
22. J Sheppard, Globe columnist, reporters on 'embedded' journalists, June 8 2006 (http://www.theglobeandmail.com/opinion/globe-columnist-reporters-on-embedded-journalists/article1100382/?page=all)
23. Rebecca Lamarche, The challenges of embedded war reporting, King's Journalism Review, Jan 24 2013
24. Ashley Walters, All Disquiet on the Western Front, This Magazine, Jan 2009
25. CDA and Matthew Fisher rush to military's defence, May 5 2009 (http://www.ceasefire.ca/?p=1302#sthash.NScPlpWh.dpuf)
26. Authorities watching embedded reporters closely, Canadian Press, Sept 13 2009 (http://www.ctvnews.ca/authorities-watching-embedded-reporters-closely-1.433999)
27. Ashley Walters, All Disquiet on the Western Front, This Magazine, Jan 2009
28. Ulrich Mans, Christa Meindersma and Lars Burema, Eyes Wide Shut? The Impact of Embedded Journalism on Dutch Newspaper Coverage of Afghanistan, Apr 2008 (https://www.svdj.nl/wp-content/uploads/2015/12/417.pdf)
29. Rebecca Lamarche, The challenges of embedded war reporting, King's Journalism Review, Jan 24 2013
30. Christopher Waddell, Inside the Wire, Literary Review of Canada, Apr 2009 (http://reviewcanada.ca/magazine/2009/04/inside-the-wire/)
31. Robert Bergen, Censorship; the Canadian News Media and Afghanistan: A Historical Comparison with

Case Studies, Calgary Papers in Military and Strategic Studies, 2009
32. Patrick Cain, In the line of fire, Ryerson Review of Journalism, Aug 1 1996 (http://rrj.ca/in-the-line-of-fire/)
33. Lee Berthiaume, Military intelligence warns of terrorists harassing Canadian Forces personnel, families online, Ottawa Citizen, Mar 24 2015
34. Robert W Bergen, Balkan Rats and Balkan Bats: The art of managing Canada's news media during the Kosovo air war, University of Calgary PhD dissertation, 2005, 276
35. David Taras and Christopher Waddell, How Canadians Communicate IV, 217 (http://www.aupress.ca/books/120205/ebook/99Z_Taras_Waddell_2012-How_Canadians_Communicate_IV.pdf/)
36. Robert W Bergen, Balkan Rats and Balkan Bats: The art of managing Canada's news media during the Kosovo air war, University of Calgary PhD dissertation, 2005, 276
37. Ibid, 369
38. Ibid, 216
39. Mark Bourrie, The Fog of War, 23
40. Lord Beaverbrook (http://www.warmuseum.ca/firstworldwar/history/after-the-war/history/lord-beaverbrook/)
41. Donald Page, 'Canadians and the League of Nations before the Manchurian Crisis,' a discussion of Canadian public opinion and pressure groups during the 1920s, University of Toronto PhD thesis 1972, 66
42. Ibid, 179
43. Mark Bourrie, Canada's evolving military censorship, Apr 30 2010 (http://ottawawatch.blogspot.ca/2010/04/canadas-evolving-military-censorship.html)
44. Jeffrey A Keshen, The War on Truth, Canada's History, Vol 95, Aug 2015
45. Kate Barker, Breaking the News by Following the Rules: Canadian War Correspondents in World War Two Continued a Tradition of Bending to Authority, Submitted to Prof. Horn, Aug 1 2013 (www.katebarker.com/pdfs/MRPfinal.pdf)
46. Mark Bourrie, The Fog of War: Censorship of Canada's Media in World War Two, 22
47. Robert Bergen, Censorship; the Canadian News Media and Afghanistan: A Historical Comparison with Case Studies Calgary Papers: In Military and Strategic Studies
48. Word warriors and camera combatants unite, The Maple Leaf, Vol 16, No 5, May 2013 (http://publications.gc.ca/site/archivee-archived.html?url=http://publications.gc.ca/collections/collection_2013/dn-nd/D12-7-16-5-eng.pdf)
49. Gene Allen, News across the Border: Associated Press in Canada, 1894-1917, Journalism History, Vol 31, Winter 2006
50. Ibid
51. The Canadian Press history (http://www.thecanadianpress.com/about_cp.aspx?id=77)
52. Gene Allen, Making National News, 133
53. Charles Enman, Legendary war correspondent always 'got the goods', Ottawa Citizen, Oct 19 2007
54. Ibid
55. A E Powley, Broadcast from the front: Canadian radio overseas in the second world war, 13 ; Leonard Walter Brockington, Behind the Diary: A King's Who's Who Biographies (1888-1966) (https://www.collectionscanada.gc.ca/king/023011-1050.47-e.html)
56. Timothy John Balzer, The Information Front: The Canadian Army, Public Relations, and War News during the Second World War, 2 ; Knowlton Nash, The Microphone Wars, 187
57. Ibid, 178
58. Ibid, 186
59. Arnold Davidson Dunton (http://www.thecanadianencyclopedia.ca/en/article/arnold-davidson-dunton) ; Mallory Schwartz, War on the Air: CBC-TV and Canada's Military, 1952-1992
60. Ibid
61. Ibid
62. Canadian Broadcasting Corporation: a brief history, 31
63. Ibid, 71 ; Ian McKay and Jamie Swift, The Vimy Trap, 177
64. Mallory Schwartz, War on the Air: CBC-TV and Canada's Military, 1952-1992, 112
65. Ibid, 119
66. Ibid
67. Ibid
68. Ibid, 18
69. Ibid, 98
70. Ibid, 81
71. Ibid, 81
72. CDA Institute Annual Conference on Security and Defence, Feb 18 2016 (http://www.veterans.gc.ca/eng/about-us/department-officials/minister/photos/gallery/786)
73. Alexander W Morrison, The Voice of Defence, 8
74. John Geddes, The CDA gets $100,000 a year from the Department of Defence, Macleans, Nov 15 2007 (http://www.ceasefire.ca/?p=187)
75. Alexander W Morrison, The Voice of Defence, 191
76. Ibid, 59
77. Harold A Skararup, Out Of Darkness — Light, Vol 1, 225
78. Amir Attaran, When think tanks produce propaganda, Feb 21 2008 (http://www.theglobeandmail.com/opinion/when-think-tanks-produce-propaganda/article1051916/)
79. Ibid
80. Ibid
81. 2015 Ottawa Conference on Security and Defence, Mar 2015 (http://www.cdainstitute.ca/images/SD/March_2015_-_SD.pdf) ; On Track, Vol 8 No 4 Dec 2003 (http://www.cdainstitute.ca/images/ontrack8n4.pdf)
82. ON TRACK (http://www.cdainstitute.ca/en/research-and-publications/on-track)
83. Vimy Award (http://www.cdainstitute.ca/en/awards/vimy-award)
84. Alexander W Morrison, The Voice of Defence, 8
85. Ibid, 192–194
86. Ibid
87. Linda McQuaig, Holding the Bully's Coat: Canada and the U.S. Empire, 179
88. Ibid
89. Steven Staples, Breaking Rank: A citizens' review of Canada's military spending, The Polaris Institute, 2002
90. Royal Canadian Military Institute (https://en.wikipedia.org/wiki/Royal_Canadian_Military_Institute#cite_note-1)
91. About the RCMI (http://www.rcmi.org/About-Us-(1).aspx)
92. Eric Morse, The deadly chaos behind Putin's mysterious acts, Mar 24 2015 (http://www.theglobeandmail.com/opinion/the-deadly-chaos-behind-putins-mysterious-acts/article23595418/)
93. Ibid, 34
94. Our History: More than a Century of Tradition (http://www.rcmi.org/About-Us-(1)/History.aspx)
95. Ken Bell and Desmond Morton, Royal Canadian Military Institute, 48

96. Desmond Morton, The Canadian General, 136
97. Ken Bell and Desmond Morton, Royal Canadian Military Institute, 79
98. Canadian Institute of International Affairs Annual Report, 1988
99. Alexander W Morrison, The Voice of Defence, 231 ; Peter Langille, Changing the Guard: Canada's Defence in a World in Transition, 109
100. Adam Chapnick, Canada's Voice: The Public Life of John Wendell Holmes, 206
101. Anita Jansman, Retired general and Queen's professor wins Vimy Award, Sep 17 2013 (https://www.queensu.ca/gazette/content/retired-general-and-queens-professor-wins-vimy-award)
102. Major-General D.F. Holman, CD (Ret'd) (http://www.cfc.forces.gc.ca/136/385-eng.html)
103. David Pugliese, Former chief of defence staff Gen. Ramsey Withers dies, Dec 30 2014 (http://ottawacitizen.com/news/politics/former-chief-of-defence-staff-gen-ramsey-withers-dies)
104. Europe's Arctic Defence Agenda (http://www3.carleton.ca/csds/eventdetails/1011rudd.htm)
105. Canadian Institute of Strategic Studies (http://www.policy.ca/policy-directory/Detailed/Canadian-Institute-of-Strategic-Studies-270.html)
106. Peter Langille, Changing the Guard, 116
107. Ibid
108. Evaluation of the Pearson Peacekeeping Centre, Apr 2007 (http://publications.gc.ca/collections/collection_2016/mdn-dnd/D58-168-2007-eng.pdf)
109. Allan Woods, Support for Afghan mission can grow: Polls, Aug 1 2007 (http://www.thestar.com/news/canada/2007/08/01/support_for_afghan_mission_can_grow_polls.html)
110. Evaluation of Security and Defence Forum (SDF) Class Grant Program, May 2010 (http://www.crs.forces.gc.ca/reports-rapports/pdf/2010/150P0921-eng.pdf)
111. Lola Fakinlede, Inside the Canadian military journalism course, July 3 2013 (http://www.j-source.ca/article/inside-canadian-military-journalism-course)
112. Military Journalism Course (http://www.cgai.ca/military_journalism_course)
113. Lola Fakinlede, Inside the Canadian military journalism course, July 3 2013 (http://www.j-source.ca/article/inside-canadian-military-journalism-course)
114. David Williams, Canadian Journalism Students Visit the Regiment, June 9 2010 (http://www.strathconas.ca/canadian-journalism-students-visit-the-regiment)
115. Ross Munro Award 2010 (http://www.cgai.ca/ross_munro_award_2010)
116. Steven Staples, CDA says media give new depth to word 'shallow', Hill Times, Aug 5 2008 (http://www.ceasefire.ca/?p=232#sthash.WBdkpKDY.dpuf)
117. Security and Defence Forum — year in review, 2009-2010 (publications.gc.ca/collections/collection_2011/dn.../D3-18-2010-eng.pdf)
118. Ibid
119. Ian McKay and Jamie Swift, Warrior Nation, 230 ; 2005 Canadian Defence & Foreign Affairs Institute (CDFAI) Annual Report (https://d3n8a8pro7vhmx.cloudfront.net/cdfai/pages/38/attachments/original/1411797745/CDFAI_Annual_Report_2005.pdf?1411797745)
120. Modernizing North American Defence (https://www.cgai.ca/modernization_of_north_american_defence)
121. Howard D Fremeth, Memory, Militarism, and Citizenship: Tracking the Dominion Institute, A thesis submitted to the Faculty of Graduate and Postdoctoral Affairs in partial fulfilment of the requirement for the degree of Doctor of Philosophy, Carleton, 2010, 203
122. Ibid
123. Canada planning to sell guns and military equipment to developing countries to maintain domestic arms industry, Postmedia, Jan 5 2014 (https://nationalpost.com/news/canada/canada-planning-to-sell-guns-and-military-equipment-to-developing-countries-to-maintain-domestic-arms-industry)
124. Ian MacLeod, Social media powerful tool for terrorists, expert warns, Nov 26 2015 (http://ottawacitizen.com/news/politics/social-media-powerful-tool-for-terrorists-expert-warns)
125. Matthew Behrens, Canada's Saudi weapons sales a moral race to the bottom, Nov 29 2018 (https://rabble.ca/columnists/2018/11/canadas-saudi-weapons-sales-moral-race-bottom)
126. Jane Taber, When parliamentarians go to war, Oct 22 2010 (https://www.theglobeandmail.com/news/politics/ottawa-notebook/when-parliamentarians-go-to-war/article1381081/) ; Department of National Defence and Canadian Armed Forces Parliamentary Program (https://www.canada.ca/en/department-national-defence/programs/parliamentary-program.html)
127. Ibid
128. Louise Rousseau, Parliamentarians in Uniform, Vol 26, No 3, 2003 (http://revparl.ca/english/issue.asp?param=59&art=23)
129. Ibid
130. Kylee Mackay, Canadian Leaders at Sea: civilians get an unforgettable experience, Crowsnest, Oct 24 2016 (www.navy-marine.forces.gc.ca/en/news-operations/news-view.page?doc=canadian-leaders-at-sea-civilians-get-an-unforgettable-experience/iumuuidb) ; Sue Ellen MacGowan, Canadian Leaders at Sea program engages women, Nov 1 2017 (www.navy-marine.forces.gc.ca/en/news-operations/news-view.page?doc=canadian-leaders-at-sea-program-engages-women/j92z99r8)
131. Darrell Samson, Canadian Leaders at Sea, May 25 2017 (https://www.facebook.com/notes/darrell-samson/canadian-leaders-at-sea/1445483335508978/) ; Ryan Melanson, Parliamentarians become sailors for a day, Lookout, Jan 27 2018 (http://www.lookoutnewspaper.com/parliamentarians-become-sailors-day/)
132. Statements By Members, Canadian Leaders at Sea Program, Oct 3 2018 (https://openparliament.ca/debates/2018/10/3/anju-dhillon-1/)
133. Kylee Mackay, Canadian Leaders at Sea: civilians get an unforgettable experience, Crowsnest, Oct 24 2016 (http://www.navy-marine.forces.gc.ca/en/news-operations/news-view.page?doc=canadian-leaders-at-sea-civilians-get-an-unforgettable-experience/iumuuidb)
134. Sue Cocek, Air Force Day on Parliament Hill celebrates RCAF members, past and present, July 4 2019 (https://skiesmag.com/news/air-force-day-on-parliament-hill-celebrates-rcaf-members-past-and-present/#:~:text=On%20June%204%2C%20 2019%2C%20Senator,Hill%2C%20in%20Ottawa%2C%20Ont.)
135. Scott Taylor, Navy Day on Parliament Hill, Nov 23 2017 (http://espritdecorps.ca/navy-day-on-parliament-hill)
136. About (https://armyrun.ca/about-army-run/#:~:text=From%20the%20cannon%20used%20 as,military%E2%80%9D%20from%20start%20to%20 finish.&text=It's%20a%20chance%20for%20the,thank%-20them%20for%20their%20support.)
137. Canadian NATO Parliamentary Association (CANA) (http://www.parl.ca/diplomacy/en/associations/cana)

138. Bill Blaikie, The Blaikie Report: An Insider's Look at Faith and Politics, 152

139. Kylee Mackay, Canadian Leaders at Sea: civilians get an unforgettable experience Image Gallery Participants in the Canadian Leaders at Sea program Crowsnest, Oct 24 2016 (http://www.navy-marine.forces.gc.ca/en/news-operations/news-view.page?doc=canadian-leaders-at-sea-civilians-get-an-unforgettable-experience/iumuuidb) ; Sue Ellen MacGowan, Canadian Leaders at Sea program engages women, Navy News, Nov 1 2017 (http://www.navy-marine.forces.gc.ca/en/news-operations/news-view.page?doc=canadian-leaders-at-sea-program-engages-women/j92z99r8)

140. Janice Lee, Corporate leaders experience navy life in HMCS Regina, Lookout, Dec 13 2019 (https://www.lookoutnewspaper.com/corporate-leaders-experience-navy-life-hmcs-regina/)

141. TD hires former general Hillier to wow clients, Sep 3 2008 (https://www.cbc.ca/news/business/td-hires-former-general-hillier-to-wow-clients-1.706544)

142. Melissa Clark Jones, A Staple State: Canadian industrial resources in Cold War, 84 ; Wallace Clement, Challenge of Class Analysis, 53

143. Lawrence R Aronsen, Canada's Postwar Re-armament: Another Look at American Theories of the Military-Industrial Complex, Canadian Historical Association Historical Papers, 1981

144. Ibid

145. Ibid

146. Ibid, 33

147. ExecuTrek (http://www.forces.gc.ca/en/business-reservist-support/events-executrek.page)

148. Canadian Forces Liaison Council biographies, National Defence, Scott Sheperd (https://www.canada.ca/en/department-national-defence/services/benefits-military/supporting-reservists-employers/about-canadian-forces-lisison-council/biographies.html)

149. Ibid

150. Steven Fouchard, Honorary Colonel of the Canadian Army aims to be 'a good ambassador', May 7 2018 (http://www.army-armee.forces.gc.ca/en/news-publications/national-news-details-no-menu.page?doc=honorary-colonel-of-the-canadian-army-aims-to-be-a-good-ambassador%2Fjgb8gn0d)

151. Supporting reservists and employers (http://www.forces.gc.ca/en/business-reservist-support/council-member.page)

152. Canadian Forces Liaison Council biographies, National Defence (https://www.canada.ca/en/department-national-defence/services/benefits-military/supporting-reservists-employers/about-canadian-forces-lisison-council/biographies.html)

153. Mathew Preston, Saving the Canadian Army Reserve: A review of Relentless Struggle, Jan 18 2020 (https://reserves2000.ca/saving-the-canadian-army-reserve-a-review-of-relentless-struggle/)

154. David Common, Soldiers of fortune: MBA students get leadership lessons from ex-commandos, Mar 10 2017 (https://www.cbc.ca/news/canada/reticle-commando-training-business-students-1.4017870)

155. Organizational Behaviour (https://www.ivey.uwo.ca/hba/courses/leadership-under-fire-developing-character/)

156. Kyle Duggan, Canada arms exports continue to rise, explosives sales double in 2013, Mar 10 2014 (http://www.davidmckie.com/canada-arms-exports-continue-to-rise-explosives-sales-double-in-2013/)

157. The Aerospace Industries Association of Canada (AIAC) Submission to the Standing Committee on Finance's Pre-budget Consultations Immediate Measures to Maintain and Increase our Global Aerospace Market Share, Aug 2011 (http://www.parl.gc.ca/Content/HOC/Committee/411/FINA/WebDoc/WD5138047/411_FINA_PBC2011_Briefs%5CAerospace%20Industries%20Association%20of%20Canada%20E.pdf) ; Stephanie Findlay, F-35 jet still popular with aerospace industry, Toronto Star, Apr 6 2012 (http://www.thestar.com/news/canada/2012/04/06/f35_jet_still_popular_with_aerospace_industry.html) ; James G Fergusson, Canada and ballistic missile defense, 1954-2009, 93

158. Canadian Chamber of Commerce, Strengthening Our Ties: Four Steps Toward a More Successful Canada-U.S. Partnership, Dec 7 2010

159. Martin Lukacs, The Trudeau Formula: seduction and betrayal in an age of discontent, 240

160. Steven Staples, Canada's Military Lobby, July 9 2006 (https://canadiandimension.com/articles/view/canadas-military-lobby-steven-staples) ; Tribute to the Canadian Forces, Remarks By Thomas D'Aquino, 2009

161. Thomas d'Aquino, Security and Prosperity: The Dynamics of a New Canada-United States Partnership in North America, Jan 14 2003 (http://thomasdaquino.ca/assets/presentations_2003_01_14.pdf)

162. Peter Langille, Changing the Guard: Canada's Defence in a World in Transition, 108

163. Ann Denholm Crosby, Dilemmas in Defence Decision-Making, 131 ; Linda McQuaig, Holding the Bully's Coat: Canada and the U.S. Empire

164. Changing the Guard, 108/112

165. Ibid

166. Canadian Defence and Foreign Affairs Institute, National Defence, National Interest: Sovereignty, Security and Canadian Military Capability in the Post 9/11 World, 2003 (https://d3n8a8pro7vhmx.cloudfront.net/cdfai/pages/41/attachments/original/1413661056/National_Defence_National_Interest.pdf?1413661056)

167. Ann Denholm Crosby, Dilemmas in Defence Decision-Making, 129

168. Ibid, 132

169. Officers of the CDA Institute (https://cdainstitute.ca/about-us/board-of-directors/)

170. Ibid

171. HCol (Ret'd) Frederick P. Mannix (https://www.alberta.ca/aoe-fred-mannix.aspx)

172. Hugh d. Segal, cm — Conference of Defence Associations 2015 Vimy Award Winner, Sep 1 2015, Announcements and Press Releases (https://cdainstitute.ca/hugh-d-segal-c-m-conference-of-defence-associations-institute-2015-vimy-award-winner/)

173. Vimy Award 2019 Laureate: Former National Security Advisor to the Prime Minister and CSIS Director, Richard B. Fadden, Sep 25 2019 (https://cdainstitute.ca/vimy-award-2019-laureate-former-national-security-advisor-to-the-prime-minister-and-csis-director-richard-b-fadden-o-c/)

174. Previous recipients of the prestigious Vimy Award include: (https://cdainstitute.ca/awards/vimy-award-previous-winners/)

175. Welcome to Valour Canada's ARface (https://arface.info/build/a85U09jkaxJ8g2wjwTgDYQ)

176. General Sir Arthur Currie Award Dinner 2019 (https://valourcanada.ca/events/general-sir-arthur-currie-award-dinner-2019/)

177. The Alberta Order of Excellence (https://www.lieutenantgovernor.ab.ca/aoe/business/stanley-milner/index.html)

178. Levels and Insignia (https://www.gg.ca/en/honours/

canadian-honours/meritorious-service-decorations-civil-division/levels-and-insignia)

179. Hal Jackman (https://en.wikipedia.org/wiki/Hal_Jackman) ; Canadian Forces Liaison Council biographies (https://www.canada.ca/en/department-national-defence/services/benefits-military/supporting-reservists-employers/about-canadian-forces-lisison-council/biographies.html)

180. Honorary Colonels (http://www.rcaf-arc.forces.gc.ca/en/honorary-colonels/index.page)

181. Blake Goldring, C.F.A, M.S.M., LL.D (https://www.ivey.uwo.ca/lawrencecentre/about-us/advisory-council/blake-goldring/#:~:text=In%202011%2C%20Blake%20was%20appointed,service%20on%20November%2024%2C%202017.)

182. Blake Goldring (https://en.wikipedia.org/wiki/Blake_Goldring)

183. HCol (Ret'd) Frederick P. Mannix (https://www.alberta.ca/aoe-fred-mannix.aspx)

184. Henry Newton Rowell Jackman (https://www.thecanadianencyclopedia.ca/en/article/henry-newton-rowell-jackman) ; Stevenson, Lawrence. (https://qormuseum.org/soldiers-of-the-queens-own/stevenson-lawrence-n/#:~:text=Honorary%20Colonel%20Stevenson%20graduated%20from,Platoon%20Commander%20from%201978%2D80.)

185. Royal Military College Saint-Jean Welcomes Honorary Colonel, News Release, Dec 12 2014 (https://www.canada.ca/en/news/archive/2014/12/royal-military-college-saint-jean-welcomes-honorary-colonel.html)

186. Order of Canada for former RMR Honorary Colonel Andrew Molson, RMR Foundation, Dec 30 2020 (https://royalmontrealregiment.com/order-of-canada-for-former-rmr-honorary-colonel-andrew-molson/#:~:text=Andrew%20Molson%20was%20first%20appointed,regiment%20totalling%20a%20dozen%20years.)

187. Sonja Bata was a guiding force of the Bata shoe enterprise, Feb 21 2018 (https://www.theglobeandmail.com/news/national/sonja-bata-was-the-guiding-force-of-the-bata-shoe-enterprise/article38053718/)

188. Shoemaker to the World Thomas John Bata September 17, 1914 — September 1, 2008 (https://www.bata.cz/data/files/cs_CZ/smutecni-oznameni-rodiny-en.pdf)

189. Honorary Colonel Stanley A Milner (https://www.gg.ca/en/honours/recipients/139-661) ; Bob Brawn (https://south.abhf.ca/laureates/inductees/bob-brawn.html)

190. Roy MacLaren (politician) (https://en.wikipedia.org/wiki/Roy_MacLaren_(politician))

191. Les Voltigeurs de Québec (https://www.powercorporationcommunity.com/en/projects/community-development/les-voltigeurs-de-quebec/)

192. Anciens grands amis internationaux (https://www.voltigeursdequebec.com/copie-de-nos-grands-amis-internatio)

193. News release, Hotelier Mandy Farmer Welcomed as Honorary Navy Captain, Douglas magazine, Sept 29 2016 (https://www.douglasmagazine.com/hotelier-mandy-farmer-welcomed-as-honorary-navy-captain/)

194. Tim Hogarth (https://burlingtonfoundation.org/team/tim-hogarth/)

195. Saving the Canadian Army Reserve: A review of Relentless Struggle (https://reserves2000.ca/saving-the-canadian-army-reserve-a-review-of-relentless-struggle/)

196. Sir John Morison Gibson (http://www.biographi.ca/en/bio/gibson_john_morison_15E.html)

197. Donald Smith, 1st Baron Strathcona and Mount Royal (https://en.wikipedia.org/wiki/Donald_Smith,_1st_Baron_Strathcona_and_Mount_Royal)

198. George Stephen, 1st Baron Mount Stephen (https://en.wikipedia.org/wiki/George_Stephen,_1st_Baron_Mount_Stephen)

199. Honorary Colonel and Lieutenant-Colonel (https://pwor.ca/wp-content/uploads/2021/01/210105_U_PWOR-HLCol_Regt_SOs_Honoraries.pdf)

200. Carman Miller, The Montreal Militia as a Social Institution Before World War I, Urban History Review, 1990

201. Steven Fouchard, Connecting the unit: Meet Honorary Lieutenant-Colonel Cheryl Robertson, Sept 26 2017 (http://espritdecorps.ca/army-articles/connecting-the-unit-meet-honorary-lieutenant-colonel-cheryl-robertson)

202. Carman Miller, The Montreal Militia as a Social Institution Before World War I, Urban History Review, 1990

203. Honorary Appointments (www.army-armee.forces.gc.ca/en/honoraries/honorary-appointment.page)

204. Marc Milner, Establishing The Naval Reserve: Navy, Part 12, Nov 1 2005 (https://legionmagazine.com/en/2005/11/establishing-the-naval-reserve/)

205. Marc Milner, Canada's Navy: the first century, 62

206. Richard H Gimblett and Michael L Hadley, Citizen Sailors: Chronicles of Canada's Naval Reserve, 1910-2010, 45

Chapter 19

1. Caroline Phillips, Overhauling defence lobby group just the start for Ottawa's Christyn Cianfarani, Apr 3 2019 (https://obj.ca/article/overhauling-defence-lobby-group-just-start-ottawas-christyn-cianfarani)

2. Yves Engler, Ottawa's mercenary world of pro-military lobbying, Oct 11 2018 (https://rabble.ca/blogs/bloggers/yves-englers-blog/2018/10/ottawas-mercenary-world-pro-military-lobbying)

3. 2015 CADSI Domestic Events (https://www.defenceandsecurity.ca/UserFiles/File/EVENTS2015/2015eventsbrochureV3.pdf) ; Cyber Security Consultation, Sept 29 2016 (https://www.defenceandsecurity.ca/events/details&evtID=321)

4. Minister of Public Safety emphasizes need for collaboration, preparedness at security conference, Oct 25 2011 (https://www.publicsafety.gc.ca/cnt/nws/nws-rlss/2011/20111025-en.aspx?wbdisable=true ; Minister of Public Safety and Emergency Preparedness, Steven Blaney, to speak at SecureTech 2013, Oct 29 2013 (https://www.publicsafety.gc.ca/cnt/nws/md-dvsrs/2013/20131028-en.aspx) ; David Pugliese, Deputy Minister of Public Safety to speak at SecureTech 2014, Ottawa Citizen, Oct 19 2014 (http://ottawacitizen.com/news/national/defence-watch/u-s-special-forces-iron-man-suit-to-be-highlighted-at-securetech-2014)

5. David Pugliese, Large Government Contingent to Be at CANSEC 2017, Vol 24, issue 5, Esprit De Corps ; Canadian Commercial Corporation, CCC Congratulates CADSI on Successful CANSEC 2014, May 29 2014 (https://www.newswire.ca/news-releases/ccc-congratulates-cadsi-on-successful-cansec-2014-514382851.html)

6. Events CANSEC 2019 (https://www.

defenceandsecurity.ca/events/details&evtID=343)
7. Lee Berthiaume, Feds embed trade staff in defence, oil groups, Regina Leader-Post Jan 18 2014
8. Peter Langille, Changing the Guard, 94
9. Mitchell Thompson, Inside Canada's defence lobby, Sept 14 2015 (https://canadiandimension.com/articles/view/inside-canadas-defence-lobby)
10. Morning Brief: Alpha dogs and political theatre, Jul 20 2018 (https://ipolitics.ca/2018/07/20/morning-brief-alpha-dogs-and-political-theatre/)
11. Yves Engler, Arms firms swarm decision makers, Mar 2 2020 (https://yvesengler.com/2020/03/02/arms-firms-swarm-decision-makers/)
12. Mitchell Thompson, Inside Canada's defence lobby, Sept 14 2015 (https://canadiandimension.com/articles/view/inside-canadas-defence-lobby)
13. Amanda Connolly, Lockheed Martin hires former RCAF commander and F-35 ally as lobbyist, Oct 16 2017 (https://ipolitics.ca/2017/10/16/lockheed-martin-hires-former-rcaf-commander-and-f-35-ally-as-lobbyist/) ; Beatrice Britneff, Lobby wrap: Advocacy group registers to lobby for tax-free medical pot, Dec 11 2017 (https://ipolitics.ca/2017/12/11/lobby-wrap-advocacy-group-registers-lobby-tax-free-medical-pot/)
14. Ann Denholm Crosby, Dilemmas in Defence Decision-Making: constructing Canada's role in NORAD, 1958-96, 133
15. Ibid
16. Stevie Cameron, Ottawa Inside Out: power, prestige and scandal in the nation's capital, 186
17. Ibid
18. Mitchell Thompson, Inside Canada's defence lobby, Sept 14 2015 (https://canadiandimension.com/articles/view/inside-canadas-defence-lobby)
19. CFN Consultants (https://www.cfnconsultants.com/)
20. Charles Bouchard To Lead Lockheed Martin Canada, PR Newswire, Sept 24 2013 (https://news.lockheedmartin.com/2013-09-24-Charles-Bouchard-To-Lead-Lockheed-Martin-Canada)
21. Industry Watch: Who's who and what's what in the defence sector, May 19 2017 (espritdecorps.ca/industry-watch/industry-watch-whos-who-and-whats-what-in-the-defence-sector-4)
22. David Pugliese, Retired Maj.-Gen. David Fraser Joins INKAS Armored Vehicle Manufacturing As A Director, Apr 4 2014 (https://ottawacitizen.com/news/national/defence-watch/retired-maj-gen-david-fraser-joins-inkas-armored-vehicle-manufacturing-as-a-director)
23. David Fraser, Cancelling Canada's contract to sell LAVs to Saudis could be an Avro Arrow-sized disaster, Dec 28 2018 (https://www.theglobeandmail.com/opinion/article-cancelling-canadas-contract-to-sell-lavs-to-saudis-could-be-an-avro/)
24. Peter Desbarats, Somalia Cover-up: a commissioners journal, 175
25. Walter Niemy (https://www.legacy.com/obituaries/timescolonist/obituary.aspx?n=walter-niemy&pid=186159622&fhid=15193)
26. Larry Milberry and Ronald Arthur, Canadair: the first 50 years, 331
27. Ann Denholm Crosby, Dilemmas in Defence Decision-Making: constructing Canada's role in NORAD, 1958-96, 133
28. Stevie Cameron, Ottawa Inside Out: power, prestige and scandal in the nation's capital, 188
29. Don Martin, Lobbyists look to calendar as new rules come into play, Truro Daily News, May 24 2008
30. David Pugliese, Industry Watch: Who's who and what's what in the defence sector, May 19 2017 (http://espritdecorps.ca/industry-watch/industry-watch-whos-who-and-whats-what-in-the-defence-sector-4)
31. Press release, CGI appoints IT security leader Ken Taylor to head national cybersecurity practice, Oct 4 2011 (https://www.cgi.com/en/CGI-appoints-IT-security-leader-Ken-Taylor-head-national-cybersecurity-practice)
32. Bulletin Newsletter of the Centre for Security and Defence Studies, Nov 25 2011 (https://www3.carleton.ca/csds/csds_bulletin/CSDS%20Bulletin-25-Nov-11.html)
33. Beatrice Britneff, Lobby wrap: Advocacy group registers to lobby for tax-free medical pot, Dec 11 2017 (https://ipolitics.ca/2017/12/11/lobby-wrap-advocacy-group-registers-lobby-tax-free-medical-pot/)
34. Ann Denholm Crosby, Dilemmas in Defence Decision-Making: constructing Canada's role in NORAD, 1958-96, 134
35. News Release, Minister Finley Announces the Establishment of an Interim Defence Analytics Institute, Public Works and Government Services Canada, Feb 19 2014 (https://www.canada.ca/en/news/archive/2014/02/minister-finley-announces-establishment-an-interim-defence-analytics-institute.html)
36. Meet MDA's David Emerson, March 2006, Issue 58, Press for Conversion! (http://coat.ncf.ca/our_magazine/links/58/Articles/46-47.pdf)
37. Selling Off the Rights to RADARSAT and its Data, March 2006, Issue 58, Press for Conversion! (http://coat.ncf.ca/our_magazine/links/58/Articles/30-32.pdf)
38. Richard Sanders, "Missle Defense" Alive and Well in Canada, Sept 8 2006 (https://canadiandimension.com/articles/view/missle-defense-alive-and-well-in-canada-richard-sanders)
39. Bruce Campion-Smith, Military contract raises issue of O'Connor lobbying, Apr 12 2007 (https://www.thestar.com/news/2007/04/12/military_contract_raises_issue_of_oconnor_lobbying.html)
40. Richard J Brennan, Wright's business ties make him wrong man for PMO, critics say, Oct 4 2010 (https://www.thestar.com/news/canada/2010/10/04/wrights_business_ties_make_him_wrong_man_for_pmo_critics_say.html)
41. The Sea Bound Coast: The official history of The Royal Canadian Navy, 1867-1939, Vol 1, 192
42. Marc Milner, Canada's Navy: the first century, 24
43. James A Boutilier, The RCN in Retrospect, 1910-1968, 109
44. Marc Milner, Canada's Navy, 166
45. Gideon Rosenbluth, The Canadian Economy and Disarmament, 88
46. Marc Milner, Canada's Navy, 277
47. Tony German, The Sea Is at Our Gates: the History of the Canadian Navy, 300
48. David Pugliese, Cost of Canadian navy warship project increases to $70 billion, according to new PBO estimate Ottawa Citizen, Jun 21 2019 (https://www.thechronicleherald.ca/news/canada/cost-of-canadian-navy-warship-project-increases-to-70-billion-according-to-new-pbo-estimate-325331/)
49. Shipbuilding deals will stabilize industry, Harper says, Jan 12 2012 (http://www.cbc.ca/news/canada/nova-scotia/shipbuilding-deals-will-stabilize-industry-harper-says-1.1163199)
50. Unprecedented Procurement, Mar 1 2012 (https://vanguardcanada.com/2012/03/page/2/)
51. Irving Shipbuilding invests $4.5 million in Centre for Ocean Ventures and Entrepreneurship (COVE) (http://shipsforcanada.ca/our-stories/irving-shipbuilding-invests-4-5-million-in-centre-for-ocean-ventures-and-

entrepreneurship-cove)
52. Ibid
53. Terry Milewski, Davie shipyard boss calls Canada's national shipbuilding strategy 'bizarre', Mar 17 2016 (https://www.cbc.ca/news/politics/davie-shipyard-boss-canada-shipbuilding-plan-bizarre-1.3494460)
54. Marc Milner, Canada's Navy: the first century, 182
55. Ibid, 290
56. Janet Thorsteinson, The Seeds of Success: Naval Shipbuilding and Global Communities
57. Canadian Press, Canadian subsidiary of French defence giant gets $5.2 billion contract, Aug 17 2017 (https://www.thestar.com/business/2017/08/17/canadian-subsidiary-of-french-defence-giant-gets-52-billion-contract.html)
58. Lindsay Kines, $704-million upgrade for navy's 'R2-D2' rapid-fire war ship guns, Times Colonist Jan 26 2018 (https://www.timescolonist.com/business/704-million-upgrade-for-navy-s-r2-d2-rapid-fire-war-ship-guns-1.23156732)
59. Public Services and Procurement Canada, Government of Canada awards contract for disposal of navy ships, Aug 4 2017 (http://www.newswire.ca/news-releases/government-of-canada-awards-contract-for-disposal-of-navy-ships-638527333.html)
60. Marine Recycling Corp. awarded $5.7-million contract to dispose of HMCS Athabaskan, Jan 19 2018 (https://www.capebretonpost.com/opinion/marine-recycling-corp-awarded-57-million-contract-to-dispose-of-hmcs-athabaskan-178733/)
61. Aerospace and Defense (https://www.trade.gov/knowledge-product/canada-civil-aviation)
62. Canada's Military-Industrial Complex, The Empire Club of Canada Addresses, Nov 11 1982 (http://speeches.empireclub.org/61457/data?n=9) ; François Shalom, Pratt & Whitney gets $300-million R&D boost from Ottawa, Montreal Gazette, Dec 8 2014 (https://montrealgazette.com/business/local-business/aerospace/pratt-whitney-gets-300-million-from-ottawa-for-rd)
63. Canada's Military-Industrial Complex, The Empire Club of Canada Addresses, Nov 11 1982 (http://speeches.empireclub.org/61457/data?n=9)
64. Ron Pickler and Larry Milberry, Canadair: The First 50 Years, 14
65. Ernie Regehr, Making a Killing: Canada's arms industry, 15
66. W A March, Combat If Necessary, But Not Necessarily Combat, Sic Itur Ad Astra: Canadian Aerospace Power Studies, Vol 3 13
67. Ibid
68. The British Commonwealth Air Training Plan (https://www.veterans.gc.ca/eng/remembrance/classroom/fact-sheets/britcom)
69. Ibid
70. Democracy at War - Aircraft Production (https://www.warmuseum.ca/cwm/exhibitions/newspapers/canadawar/aircraft_e.html)
71. Randall Wakelam, Cold War Fighters: Canadian aircraft procurement, 1945-54, 25
72. D J Godspeed, A History of the Defence Research Board of Canada, 96
73. Bertram C Frandsen, The Rise and Fall of Canada's Cold War Air Force, 1948-1968, Wilfrid Laurier University (http://scholars.wlu.ca/cgi/viewcontent.cgi?article=2857&context=etd)
74. Randall Wakelam, Cold War Fighters: Canadian aircraft procurement, 1945-54, 53
75. Christopher Richard Kilford, The Other Cold War: Canadian Military Assistance in the Developing World, Queen's University thesis, 2009, 120
76. Robert Bothwell, War, business and world military-industrial complexes, 114
77. Canadair (https://en.wikipedia.org/wiki/Canadair)
78. Gideon Rosenbluth, The Canadian Economy and Disarmament, 88
79. Alistair D Edgar and David G Haglund, the Canadian Defence Industry in the New Global Environment, 111
80. Jean Charest, Charting a New Course: Canada as a Global Aerospace Champion (https://aiac.ca/wp-content/uploads/2019/06/Vision2025_EN.pdf)
81. Mr. Trudeau, Ms. Freeland, don't let an industry that has collectively taken us nearly a century to build, weaken (https://www.aeromontreal.ca/help-us-emerge-stronger-from-crisis.html)
82. Stephanie Findlay, F-35 jet still popular with aerospace industry, Apr 6 2012 (https://www.thestar.com/news/canada/2012/04/06/f35_jet_still_popular_with_aerospace_industry.html)
83. Ibid
84. Peter Hadekel, Silent Partners: Taxpayers and the Bankrolling of Bombardier, 166
85. Ibid, 161
86. Ibid, 166
87. Ibid, 165 ; H Sullivan and Larry Milberry, Power: The Pratt and Whitney Canada Story, 99 ; Mark Milke, Bombardier and Canada's corporate welfare trap (https://www.fraserinstitute.org/article/bombardier-and-canadas-corporate-welfare-trap)
88. Peter Hadekel, Silent Partners: Taxpayers and the Bankrolling of Bombardier, 163 ; Andrew Coyne, Bombardier nabbed $3.7B in subsidies, yet the mob demands we punish its executives Apr 3 2017 (https://nationalpost.com/opinion/andrew-coyne-bombardier-executives-nabbed-3-7b-in-subsidies-yet-the-mob-demands-we-punish-them)
89. Innovation, Science and Economic Development Canada, Government of Canada and Bombardier announce significant investment to strengthen leadership in aerospace, Feb 7 2017 (https://www.newswire.ca/news-releases/government-of-canada-and-bombardier-announce-significant-investment-to-strengthen-leadership-in-aerospace-613092913.html)
90. Peter Rakobowchuk, Feds invest $250M in Montreal-based flight simulator company CAE, Feb 27 2014 (https://globalnews.ca/news/1177142/feds-invest-250m-in-montreal-based-flight-simulator-company-cae/)
91. Richard Sanders, Canadian Military Components used in Israel's War Against Lebanon, Press for Conversion! (https://coat.ncf.ca/lebanon2006.html)
92. Peter Langille, Changing the Guard, 95
93. Andrew MacDonald, Canadian Defence Industry Overview, Janes' 360, May 28 2015 (https://www.janes.com/article/51769/canadian-defence-industry-overview-can2015d2)
94. Project Ploughshares, What's the DIPP in Canada's Military Production?, Peace Magazine, Oct 1986 (http://peacemagazine.org/archive/v02n5p37.htm) ; Kenneth Epps, DIPP and its Successor: New Welfare to Arms?, Ploughshares Monitor, Vol 16, Issue 4, Dec 1995, (https://ploughshares.ca/pl_publications/dipp-and-its-successor-new-welfare-to-arms/)
95. What's the DIPP in Canada's Military Production?, Peace Magazine, Oct 1986 (peacemagazine.org/archive/v02n5p37.htm)
96. The Strategic Aerospace and Defence Initiative (SADI) (https://www.ic.gc.ca/eic/site/ito-oti.nsf/

eng/h_00093.html)
97. Funding Opportunities for the Aerospace and Defence Sectors: The Strategic Aerospace and Defence Initiative (https://inacservices.com/funding-opportunities-for-the-aerospace-and-defence-sectors-the-strategic-aerospace-and-defence-initiative/)
98. Understanding IDEaS (https://www.canada.ca/en/department-national-defence/programs/defence-ideas/understanding-ideas.html)
99. Ibid
100. General Dynamics Land Systems-Canada, General Dynamics Land Systems-Canada: A Partner in Canada's Advanced Manufacturing Supercluster, PR News, Feb 20 2018 (https://www.newswire.ca/news-releases/general-dynamics-land-systems-canada-a-partner-in-canadas-advanced-manufacturing-supercluster-674616943.html)
101. Yves Bélanger and Pierre Fournier, Le Québec militaire: les dessous de l'industrie militaire Québécoise, 63
102. Andrew Godefroy, Defence and Discovery: Canada's military space program, 1945–74, 192
103. John N Vardalas, The Computer Revolution in Canada: Building National Technological Competence, 15
104. Ibid, 50
105. Ibid, 51
106. Ibid, 51
107. D J Godspeed, A History of the Defence Research Board of Canada, 242
108. Ernie Regehr, Making a Killing: Canada's arms industry, 83
109. John N Vardalas, The Computer Revolution in Canada, 52
110. D J Godspeed, A History of the Defence Research Board of Canada, 203
111. Andrew Godefroy, Defence and Discovery: Canada's military space program, 1945–74, 169
112. D J Godspeed, A History of the Defence Research Board of Canada, 103
113. Ibid, 246
114. Ibid, 78
115. Jonathan Turner, The Defence Research Board of Canada, 1947 to 1977, Institute for the History and Philosophy of Science and Technology University of Toronto, 308 (https://tspace.library.utoronto.ca/bitstream/1807/71816/1/turner_jonathan_r_201211_PhD_thesis.pdf)
116. Defence Research and Development Canada | Recherche et développement pour la défense Canada (https://ca.linkedin.com/company/drdc) ; CSPC 2017 (https://cspc2017.sched.com/speaker/dr.marcfortin)
117. Jonathan Turner, The Defence Research Board of Canada, 1947 to 1977, Institute for the History and Philosophy of Science and Technology University of Toronto, 308 (https://tspace.library.utoronto.ca/bitstream/1807/71816/1/turner_jonathan_r_201211_PhD_thesis.pdf)
118. Chief Executive Officer and Assistant Deputy Minister (Science and Technology), Dr. Marc Fortin (http://www.drdc-rddc.gc.ca/en/about/ceo-adm.page)
119. Chief Executive Officer and Assistant Deputy Minister (Science and Technology), Dr. Marc Fortin (http://www.drdc-rddc.gc.ca/en/about/ceo-adm.page) ; Department of National Defence Research Initiative (http://www.sshrc-crsh.gc.ca/funding-financement/programs-programmes/dnd-eng.aspx)
120. Defence Research and Development Canada (DRDC) collaborative activities with academic institutions to date encompass the following (http://www.drdc-rddc.gc.ca/en/partnerships-partenariats/academia.page)
121. Partnerships and opportunities: government (https://www.canada.ca/en/defence-research-development/services/partnerships-opportunities/government.html)
122. Ibid
123. Ibid
124. Event Time 2013-12-10, Ottawa Convention Centre (http://www.lobbymonitor.ca/node/2465)
125. John N Vardalas, The Computer Revolution in Canada, 280
126. Ibid, 276
127. Gideon Rosenbluth, The Canadian Economy and Disarmament, 88
128. John N Vardalas, The Computer Revolution in Canada: building national technological competence, 42
129. Ibid, 41
130. Ibid, 46
131. Ibid, 77
132. Ibid, 143
133. Ibid, 80
134. Ibid, 99
135. Ibid, 92
136. Ibid, 93
137. Ibid, 278
138. Andrew B Godefroy, The Canadian Space Program: From Black Brant to the International Space Station, 32
139. C A Franklin, Alouette/ISIS: How it all Began, Ottawa, May 13 1993 (https://www.ieee.ca/millennium/alouette/alouette_franklin.html)
140. Ibid
141. Andrew Godefroy, Defence and Discovery: Canada's military space program, 1945–74, 179
142. James Fergusson, Shall we dance? The missile defence decision, Norad renewal, and the future of Canada-US defence relations, Canadian Military Journal, Summer 2005 (http://www.journal.forces.gc.ca/vo6/no2/inter-01-eng.asp)
143. Bern Horn, The Canadian Way of War: serving the national interest, 328/336
144. Andrew B Godefroy, Defence and Discovery: Canada's Military Space Program, 1945-74 (https://www.ubcpress.ca/asset/9092/1/9780774819596.pdf)
145. The Outer Space Treaty at a Glance (https://www.armscontrol.org/factsheets/outerspace)
146. Steve Buchta, Space Weaponization and Canada-U.S. Relations: Lessons from Australia (https://jpia.princeton.edu/sites/jpia/files/2008-10.pdf)
147. News Release, Department of National Defence Awards Contracts for the Mercury Global Project (https://www.canada.ca/en/news/archive/2014/11/department-national-defence-awards-contracts-mercury-global-project.html)
148. Ibid
149. Medium Earth Orbit Search and Rescue (dgpaapp.forces.gc.ca/en/defence-capabilities-blueprint/project-details.asp?id=996)
150. GPS World Staff, Canada to Supply MEOSAR Search and Rescue Repeaters to GPS III, Aug 13 2015 (https://www.gpsworld.com/canada-to-supply-meosar-search-and-rescue-repeaters-to-gps-iii/)
151. Advanced Extremely High Frequency (AEHF) Satellite System (https://www.airforce-technology.com/projects/advanced-extremely-high-frequency-aehf/)
152. C E Kabatoff, Analysis of Department of National Defence Space Policy (https://www.cfc.forces.gc.ca/259/290/301/305/kabatoff.pdf)
153. Steve Buchta, Space Weaponization and Canada-U.S. Relations: Lessons from Australia (https://jpia.princeton.edu/sites/jpia/files/2008-10.pdf)

154. Bernd Horn, The Canadian Way of War: Serving the National Interest, 347
155. Ann Denholm Crosby, Dilemmas in Defence Decision-Making: constructing Canada's role in NORAD, 1958-96, 84
156. Richard Sanders, October 2006: We Didn't Really Say "No" to Missile Defence Canadian complicity and participation in BMD continues, Oct 1 2006 (https://www.policyalternatives.ca/publications/monitor/october-2006-we-didnt-really-say-no-missile-defence)
157. James Fergusson, Shall we dance? The missile defence decision, norad renewal, and the future of Canada-US defence relations, Canadian Military Journal, Summer 2005 (http://www.journal.forces.gc.ca/vo6/no2/inter-01-eng.asp)
158. Ann Denholm Crosby, Dilemmas in Defence Decision-Making: constructing Canada's role in NORAD, 1958-96, 84
159. Richard Sanders, October 2006: We Didn't Really Say "No" to Missile Defence Canadian complicity and participation in BMD continues, Oct 1 2006 (https://www.policyalternatives.ca/publications/monitor/october-2006-we-didnt-really-say-no-missile-defence)
160. John N Vardalas, The Computer Revolution in Canada, 278
161. Michael Byers, Don't Sell Off This Satellite! Why Canada must hang onto Radarsat-2 7 Mar 2008 (https://thetyee.ca/Views/2008/03/07/Radarsat-2/)
162. Ibid
163. Our new satellite surveillance capability, Jan 12 2008 (toyoufromfailinghands.blogspot.com/2008/01/our-new-satellite-surveillance.html)
164. David Pugliese, Defining The Future Battlefield, Mar 9 2017 (Volume 24-01) (espritdecorps.ca/feature/space-defining-the-future-battlefield)
165. Richard Sanders, We Didn't Really Say "No" to Missile Defence, Oct 1 2006 (https://www.policyalternatives.ca/publications/monitor/october-2006-we-didnt-really-say-no-missile-defence)
166. Ann Denholm Crosby, Dilemmas in Defence Decision-Making, 139
167. NASA once thought Canada's famed Alouette-1 satellite was too ambitious: space engineer, Canadian Press Sep 28 2012 (https://nationalpost.com/news/canada/nasa-once-thought-canadas-famed-alouette-1-satellite-was-too-ambitious-space-engineer)
168. Le Canada s'associe à la NASA pour le retour sur la Lune, Feb 28 2019 (https://www.lapresse.ca/sciences/astronomie-et-espace/201902/28/01-5216488-le-canada-sassocie-a-la-nasa-pour-le-retour-sur-la-lune.php)
169. Aaron Saltzman, Companies look to cash in on out-of-this-world profits in new space economy, Jul 17 2019 (https://www.cbc.ca/news/business/space-business-satellites-spacex-virgingalactic-blueorigin-1.5211974)
170. Canadian space milestones (https://www.asc-csa.gc.ca/eng/about/milestones.asp)
171. A bird, a plane? It's the Alouette!, Moments That Matter: Canadian History Since 1867 (https://blogs.mcgill.ca/hist203momentsthatmatter/2018/02/28/a-bird-a-plane-its-the-alouette/)
172. Anass Gouyez Ben Allal, Vers l'abandon de la politique de developpement industriel dans le domaine militaire: consequences pour l'industrie Quebecoise, 4
173. Chris Thatcher, Diversity, gender to factor into future defence value propositions Avatar, June 3 2018 (https://skiesmag.com/news/diversity-gender-factor-future-defence-value-propositions/)
174. Brief from the Canadian Association of Defence and Security Industries (CADSI) (https://www.ourcommons.ca/Content/Committee/411/FINA/WebDoc/WD5138047/411_FINA_PBC2011_Briefs/Canadian%20Association%20of%20Defence%20and%20Security%20Industries%20E.html)
175. Canada's Defence Industry: A Vital Partner Supporting Canada's Economic and National Interests, CADSI (https://www.defenceandsecurity.ca/UserFiles/File/IE/Military_Procurement_Main_Report_March_09_2010.pdf)
176. Gideon Rosenbluth, The Canadian Economy and Disarmament, 44
177. Ibid, 45
178. Barton preaches defence spending, but Sajjan says Ottawa spent $2.3B too little Canadian Press, May 30 2018 (https://www.canadianbusiness.com/business-news/barton-preaches-defence-spending-but-sajjan-says-ottawa-spent-2-3b-too-little/) ; Martin Lukacs, The Trudeau Formula: seduction and betrayal in an age of discontent, 18
179. David Collins, Government Procurement with Strings Attached: The Uneven Control of Offsets by the World Trade Organization and Regional Trade Agreements, Asian Journal of International Law, Dec 2016
180. Kim Richard Nossal, Charlie Foxtrot: fixing defense procurement in Canada, 97
181. Carole Giangrande, The Nuclear North, 21
182. Tanya Neima and Christopher Stoney, The Maritime Helicopter Project: The Costly Politics of Military Procurement Chapter
183. Elaine Della-Mattia, EDC gets funds to help businesses compete for defence industry contracts, Jul 29 2019 (https://www.saultstar.com/news/local-news/edc-gets-funds-to-help-businesses-compete-for-defence-industry-contracts)
184. Matt Gurney, Stop pretending Canada cares about a meaningful role on the world stage, Jun 21 2020 (https://nationalpost.com/opinion/matt-gurney-stop-pretending-canada-cares-about-having-a-meaningful-role-on-the-world-stage/wcm/7ee5c44a-e7ae-448f-ace6-06ea98542c75/) ; Jeffrey Simpson, Damn it, it's still the wrong helicopter!, July 24 2004 (https://www.theglobeandmail.com/news/politics/damn-it-its-still-the-wrong-helicopter/article1332815/)
185. Carole Giangrande, The Nuclear North, 24
186. Report on Exports of Military Goods from Canada — 2017 (https://www.international.gc.ca/controls-controles/report-rapports/mil-2017.aspx?lang=eng)
187. Gideon Rosenbluth, The Canadian Economy and Disarmament, 46
188. Ernie Regehr, Making a Killing: Canada's arms industry, 41
189. Peter Langille, Changing the Guard: Canada's defence in a world in transition, 26
190. Ann Denholm Crosby, Dilemmas in Defence Decision-Making, 112
191. Peter Langille, Changing the Guard, 98
192. ABOUT CADSI Securing alliances. Defending our future. (https://www.defenceandsecurity.ca/cms4/Association-Information)
193. Richard J Walton, Canada and the U.S.A.: A Background Book about Internal Conflict and the New Nationalism, 162
194. Ron Pickler and Larry Milberry, Canadair: The First 50 Years, 13
195. Canadian Vickers (https://en.wikipedia.org/wiki/Canadian_Vickers)
196. John Vardalas, The Computer Revolution in Canada: Building National Technological Competence, 182

197. General Dynamics Mission Systems - Canada (https://en.wikipedia.org/wiki/General_Dynamics_Mission_Systems_-_Canada#cite_note-1)
198. Frank Maas, The Success of the Light Armoured Vehicle, Canadian Military History, Vol 20, Issue 2, 2011
199. Canada First: Leveraging Defence Procurement Through Key Industrial Capabilities, Report of the Special Adviser to the Minister of Public Works and Government Services, Feb 2013 (https://www.tpsgc-pwgsc.gc.ca/app-acq/documents/eam-lmp-eng.pdf)
200. L3 WESCAM to Open Authorized Service Center in Saudi Arabia, Feb 2017 (https://www.militarysystems-tech.com/articles/l3-wescam-open-authorized-service-center-saudi-arabia)
201. Wescam (https://en.wikipedia.org/wiki/Wescam)
202. Jon Horler, Unmasking Canada's role in the drone wars, Sep 15 2020 (https://ricochet.media/en/3282/unmasking-canadas-role-in-the-drone-wars)
203. L-3 to Supply Electro-Optical and Infrared Designating Systems Under a U.S. Foreign Military Sales, Aug 30 2016 (https://www.businesswire.com/news/home/20160830006298/en/L-3-Supply-Electro-Optical-Infrared-Designating-Systems-U.S.)
204. Pratt & Whitney Canada (https://en.wikipedia.org/wiki/Pratt_%26_Whitney_Canada)
205. Ibid ; Stefan Labbé, Seven human rights violators buying Canadian military goods, Aug 18 2016 (https://opencanada.org/seven-human-rights-violators-buying-canadian-military-goods/)
206. Soaring to New Horizons: Ramping Up Presence and Support in Africa (https://www.pwc.ca/en/airtime-blog/articles/expert-talk/soaring-to-new-horizons---ramping-up-presence-and-support-in-africa) ; Romain Guillot, Pratt & Whitney Canada add five new authorized centers, including two in Europe, Jun 18 2020 (https://www.journal-aviation.com/en/news/44661-mroen2)
207. CAE INC. (https://aiac.ca/members/cae-inc/)
208. CAE USA wins U.S. Air Force contract to train aircrews of the Predator and Reaper remotely piloted aircraft, Aug 8 2013 (https://www.cae.com/news-events/press-releases/cae-usa-wins-us-air-force-contract-to-train-aircrews-of-the-predator-and-/)
209. Christopher Reynolds, Le patron de CAE veut profiter de la hausse des budgets de l'armée américaine, Aug 14 2018 (https://www.lapresse.ca/affaires/economie/transports/201808/14/01-5192967-le-patron-de-cae-veut-profiter-de-la-hausse-des-budgets-de-larmee-americaine.php)
210. CAE Inc. (https://coat.ncf.ca/P4C/66/CAE.htm)
211. Oct 14 2018 (https://twitter.com/anthonyfenton/status/1051538953076015104)
212. Murray Brewster, Global Affairs sole-source deal with Streit Group under scrutiny, Sep 15 2016 (https://www.cbc.ca/news/politics/streit-government-sales-1.3762385)
213. Canadian Forces New Sniper Rifle (https://www.m4carbine.net/archive/index.php/t-10366.html)
214. Investigation underway after Canadian rifles end up in Yemen rebel hands, Feb 23 2016 (https://www.cbc.ca/news/canada/manitoba/winnipeg-made-sniper-rifles-fall-into-yemen-rebel-hands-1.3459551)
215. Héroux-Devtek Awarded Life-Cycle Contract for the New Dassault Aviation Falcon 10X, May 6 2021 (https://www.newswire.ca/news-releases/heroux-devtek-awarded-life-cycle-contract-for-the-new-dassault-aviation-falcon-10x-808605642.html)
216. Canada's Top 10 Military Producers, The Ploughshares Monitor, Vol 24, Issue 4, Winter 2003 (https://ploughshares.ca/pl_publications/canadas-top-10-military-producers/)
217. Ellesmere Island Operations & Maintenance (https://www.atco.com/en-ca/projects/frontec-ellesmere-island-operations-maintenance.html)
218. Fire Crash Rescue Services (https://www.atco.com/en-ca/for-business/operational-support-services/support-services/fire-crash-rescue-services.html)
219. Elke Krahmann, NATO contracting in Afghanistan: the problem of principal–agent networks, Nov 4 2016 (https://doi.org/10.1111/1468-2346.12753)
220. Airfield Services (https://www.atco.com/en-ca/for-business/operational-support-services/support-services/airfield-services.html)
221. SNC-Lavalin's legal woes are putting a $500M federal defence contract at risk, Mar 28 2019 (https://www.cbc.ca/news/politics/snc-lavalin-contract-defence-bribery-1.5073996)
222. SNC-Lavalin PAE Inc. to support Canadian military through CANCAP contract, Aug 08 2013 (https://www.newswire.ca/news-releases/snc-lavalin-pae-inc-to-support-canadian-military-through-cancap-contract-512784641.html)
223. Murray Brewster, SNC-Lavalin's legal woes are putting a $500M federal defence contract at risk, Mar 28 2019 (https://www.cbc.ca/news/politics/snc-lavalin-contract-defence-bribery-1.5073996)
224. Robert Frank, Discovery Air contract could top $1.4 billion, The Suburban, Nov 22, 2017 (https://www.thesuburban.com/news/discovery-air-contract-could-top-billion/article_1470afca-4696-5a92-b740-50649ee062e0.html)
225. Sandro Frenguelli, A Former Special Forces Soldier Is Setting Up a Massive Private Military Facility in Ontario, Dec 2 2016 (https://www.vice.com/en/article/xd73e7/a-former-special-forces-soldier-is-setting-up-a-massive-private-military-facility-in-ontario)
226. Ronald Zajac, Gun range limits relaxed Ministry decision on Reticle Ventures, Aug 31 2018 (https://www.recorder.ca/news/local-news/gun-range-limits-relaxed)
227. Christopher Spearin, Canada and contracted war: Afghanistan and beyond International Journal Vol 69, No 4, Dec 2014 ; David A Borys and Joshua Matthewman, Corporate Allies: Canadian Armed Forces and the use of Private Military, Security and Logistic Companies (http://publications.gc.ca/collections/collection_2016/mdn-dnd/D12-11-16-2-eng.pdf)
228. Christopher Spearin, Canada and contracted war: Afghanistan and beyond International Journal Vol 69, No 4, Dec
229. Ben Makuch, Trudeau government spends millions on the mercenary firm formerly known as 'Blackwater', Feb 27 2018 (https://www.vice.com/en/article/xw5dzj/trudeau-government-spends-millions-on-the-mercenary-firm-formerly-known-as-blackwater)
230. The Role of the Global SOF Network in a Resource Constrained Environment (https://www.socom.mil/JSOU/JSOUPublications/Global%20SOF%20Network%20Resource%20Constrained%20Environment_FINAL.pdf)
231. Gloria Galloway, Canada spending millions on private security in Afghanistan, Nov 17 2009 (https://www.theglobeandmail.com/news/politics/canada-spending-millions-on-private-security-in-afghanistan/article4292821/)
232. Jessica McDiarmid, Canada spent $10 million for security at Afghan dam project, Mar 13 2013 (https://www.thestar.com/news/canada/2013/03/13/afghanistan_dam_project_9_million_set_aside_for_security_contractors_

including_those_in_armed_standoff.html)
233. David Perry, The Privatization of the Canadian Military: Afghanistan, Canada First and Beyond, International Journal, Vol 64, no. 3 2009
234. David A Borys and Joshua Matthewman, Corporate Allies: Canadian Armed Forces and the use of Private Military, Security and Logistic Companies (http://publications.gc.ca/collections/collection_2016/mdn-dnd/D12-11-16-2-eng.pdf)
235. Phil Miller, British security firm Saladin tries to distance itself from police war crimes investigation, Sept 18 2020 (https://www.dailymaverick.co.za/article/2020-09-18-british-security-firm-saladin-tries-to-distance-itself-from-police-war-crimes-investigation/)
236. Graham Thomson, Canadian soldier killed in shootout, Ottawa Citizen, Aug 10 2008
237. Scott Deveau, Insurgent fire killed Sask. soldier: report, Star Phoenix, Sept 15 2008
238. Christopher Spearin, SOF for Sale: The Canadian Forces and the Challenge of Privatized Security, Canadian Military Journal, Spring 2007 (http://www.journal.forces.gc.ca/vo8/no1/spearin-eng.asp#n15)
239. David Pugliese, Special forces get pay raise, Ottawa Citizen, Aug 26 2006
240. Annelle Tayao-Juego, Vulnerable firms seek ex-Green Beret for protection, Oct 23 2017 (http://business.inquirer.net/239052/vulnerable-firms-seek-ex-green-beret-protection#ixzz4wRXvcYKL)
241. Hire Our Security Guards in Muskoka (https://www.executivesecurity.ca/security-services/land-location-security)
242. ABOUT US (www.tundragroup.ca/about/)
243. Stewart Bell & Andrew Russell, The Consultant: Ex-intelligence official reveals covert operation to free Boyle family from militants, Dec 5 2017 (https://globalnews.ca/news/3892115/joshua-boyle-rescue-covert-operation/)
244. James R. Davis, Fortune's Warriors: Private Armies and the New World Order, 137
245. Saul Chernos, One gem of a mission Feds' push for mining investors in Afghanistan muddles military presence, Mar 20 2008 (https://nowtoronto.com/news/one-gem-of-a-mission/)
246. Marina Jimenez, Canadians seek fortune in land of anarchy, violence Ex-soldiers go unarmed, National Post, Aug 23 1999
247. Ibid
248. Matthew McClearn, Why is Montreal's GardaWorld on the outs in both Afghanistan and Iraq?, Mar 17 2014 (https://www.canadianbusiness.com/companies-and-industries/the-enemy-unseen-6/)
249. True Patriot Love and GardaWorld join forces to help Quebec women, Nov 1 2018 (https://www.newswire.ca/news-releases/true-patriot-love-and-gardaworld-join-forces-to-help-quebec-women-veterans-699280171.html)
250. Ibid
251. Translate your military skills into a GardaWorld career Feb 21 2018 (https://www.garda.com/blog/translate-your-military-skills-into-a-gardaworld-career)
252. Daniel Menard, former Canadian general, still in Afghan jail, Feb 13 2014 (https://www.cbc.ca/news/politics/daniel-menard-former-canadian-general-still-in-afghan-jail-1.2535691)
253. Ibid
254. Yves Engler, Private security firm GardaWorld, Canada's Blackwater, is a danger to democracy, Apr 6 2016
255. Sarah A Topol, As War Winds Down in Libya, Enter the Consultants Security firms looking for a post-Iraq market flock to Tripoli, Sep 22 2011 (https://www.bloomberg.com/news/articles/2011-09-21/as-war-winds-down-in-libya-enter-the-consultants)
256. Security Council Approves 'No-Fly Zone' over Libya, Authorizing 'All Necessary Measures' to Protect Civilians, by Vote of 10 in Favour with 5 Abstentions, Security Council SC/10200, Mar 17 2011 (https://www.un.org/press/en/2011/sc10200.doc.htm)
257. Hin-Yan Liu, Mercenaries in Libya: Ramifications of the Treatment of 'Armed Mercenary Personnel' under the Arms Embargo for Private Military Company Contractors, Journal of Conflict & Security Law, Vol 16, No 2, 2011
258. Yves Engler, Private security firm GardaWorld, Canada's Blackwater, is a danger to democracy, Apr 6 2016 (https://rabble.ca/blogs/bloggers/yves-engler/2016/04/private-security-firm-gardaworld-canadas-blackwater-danger-to-dem)
259. Argus and Garda face off, Issue No 714 June 18 2014 (https://www.intelligenceonline.com/corporate-intelligence/2014/06/18/argus-and-garda-face-off,108027339-ART)
260. Morning Joe sits down with Fred Burton and Samuel M. Katz, authors of "Under Fire", Apr 9 2013 (http://www.msnbc.com/morning-joe/morning-joe-sits-down-fred-burton-and)
261. Ibid
262. David Antonyshyn, Jan Grofe and Don Hubert, Beyond the Law? The Regulation of Canadian Private Military and Security Companies Operating Abroad, PRIV-WAR Report, Canada National Reports Series, Mar 2009 (http://psm.du.edu/media/documents/reports_and_stats/think_tanks/privwar_nationalreport_antonyshyn.pdf)
263. Ibid
264. Brett Wilkins, Jimmy Carter: US 'Most Warlike Nation in History of the World' Former president says peaceful China 'ahead of us in almost every way', Apr 18 2019 (https://www.commondreams.org/views/2019/04/18/jimmy-carter-us-most-warlike-nation-history-world)
265. Richard Sanders, Canada-US trade rules promote Canadian military exports, May 18 2009 (https://canadians.org/fr/node/4816)
266. Automatic Firearms Country Control List (https://laws-lois.justice.gc.ca/eng/regulations/SOR-91-575/page-2.html#h-1)
267. Paul Esau, Customers or allies? The dilemma of Canada's AFCCL, Ploughshares Monitor, Vol 39, Issue 3, Autumn 2018 (https://ploughshares.ca/pl_publications/customers-or-allies-the-dilemma-of-canadas-afccl/)
268. 122 countries adopt 'historic' UN treaty to ban nuclear weapons, Associated Press Jul 7 2017 (https://www.cbc.ca/news/world/un-treaty-ban-nuclear-weapons-1.4192761)
269. UN General Assembly votes on uranium weapons with a large majority in favour of the resolution, Jan 18 2021 (https://www.icbuw.eu/un-general-assembly-votes-on-uranium-weapons-with-a-large-majority-in-favour-of-the-resolution/)
270. Ibid
271. Chris Cobb, Six years later, Canada joins international treaty to ban deadly cluster bombs deadly Mar 17 2015 (https://ottawacitizen.com/news/politics/six-years-later-canada-joins-international-treaty-to-ban-deadly-cluster-bombs)
272. CMC urges Canada not to buckle to U.S. pressure and to re-draft dangerous cluster bomb law, May 18 2012 (https://reliefweb.int/report/canada/cmc-urges-canada-not-buckle-us-pressure-and-re-draft-dangerous-cluster-bomb-law)
273. Mike Blanchfield, Report links four Canadian

companies to cluster munitions investments, June 17 2016 (https://www.ctvnews.ca/business/report-links-four-canadian-companies-to-cluster-munitions-investments-1.2949721)
274. Ibid
275. Dave Coles, The Conservatives' double standards tell us who they truly support DC, July 12 2012 (https://www.thestar.com/opinion/editorial_cartoon/2012/07/12/the_conservatives_double_standards_tell_us_who_they_truly_support.html)
276. Amnesty International Stages New York City "Bananafesto" Action in Times Square June 27, Ahead of Historic Arms Treaty Talks at United Nations, June 20 2012 (https://www.amnestyusa.org/press-releases/amnesty-international-stages-new-york-city-bananafesto-action-in-times-square-june-27-ahead-of-historic-arms-treaty-talks-at-united-nations/)
277. Cesar Jaramillo and Kenneth Epps, Canada joins the Arms Trade Treaty — but will it cancel the Saudi deal?, Oct 1 2019 (https://www.opencanada.org/features/canada-joins-the-arms-trade-treaty-but-will-it-cancel-the-saudi-deal/) ; Lucas Powers, Canadian arms trade much larger than data suggests, expert says, Feb 23 2016 (https://www.cbc.ca/news/business/canada-arms-technology-trade-1.3458608)
278. Canada's ATT legislation: A loophole you could drive a tank through (https://ploughshares.ca/pl_publications/canadas-att-legislation-a-loophole-you-could-drive-a-tank-through/)
279. Murray Brewster, Global Affairs sole-source deal with Streit Group under scrutiny, Sep 15 2016 (https://www.cbc.ca/news/politics/streit-government-sales-1.3762385)
280. Ibid ; Murray Brewster, Canadian firm shipped armoured cars to lawless Libya despite UN warning, Aug 11 2016 (https://www.cbc.ca/news/politics/streit-libya-un-1.3711776)
281. Murray Brewster, Global Affairs sole-source deal with Streit Group under scrutiny, Sep 15 2016 (https://www.cbc.ca/news/politics/streit-government-sales-1.3762385)
282. Murray Brewster, Global Affairs sole-source deal with Streit Group under scrutiny, Sep 15 2016 (https://www.cbc.ca/news/politics/streit-government-sales-1.3762385)
283. Libya UN Resolution 1973: Text analysed, Mar 18 2011 (https://www.bbc.com/news/world-africa-12782972)
284. Courtney Symons, Drone delivery: Why one Ottawa man brought a robot to the rebels in the midst of the Libyan civil war, May 23 2013 (https://obj.ca/article/drone-delivery-why-one-ottawa-man-brought-robot-rebels-midst-libyan-civil-war)
285. Mr. Charles Barlow (President, Zariba Security Corporation) at the National Defence Committee, Dec 2 2014 (https://openparliament.ca/committees/national-defence/41-2/41/charles-barlow-1/only/)
286. Jameson Berkow, Libyan rebels using Canadian-made reconnaissance drone, Aug 23 2011 (https://business.financialpost.com/technology/libyan-rebels-using-canadian-made-reconnaissance-drone) ; Staff Writers, Canadian drone helped rebels in Libya, AFP Aug 24 2011 (https://www.spacedaily.com/reports/Canadian_drone_helped_rebels_in_Libya_999.html)
287. Linda Freeman, The Ambiguous Champion: Canada and South Africa in the Trudeau and Mulroney years, 119
288. Kole Kilibarda, Canadian and Israeli Defense -- Industrial and Homeland Security Ties: An Analysis (https://www.sscqueens.org/sites/sscqueens.org/files/Canadian%20and%20Israeli%20Defense%20Industrial%20and%20Homeland%20Security%20Ties.pdf)
289. Ernie Regehr, Making a Killing: Canada's arms industry, 38 ; Ernie Regehr and Simon Rosenblum, Canada and the Nuclear Arms Race, 112
290. Ernie Regehr, Arms Canada: The Deadly Business of Military Exports, 102
291. Ahmad Faroughy, Repression in Iran, Mar 16 1975 (https://www.nytimes.com/1975/03/16/archives/repression-in-iran.html)
292. Doing business with foreign defence markets, Nov 7 2018 (https://www.canada.ca/en/department-national-defence/services/doing-business-with-foreign-defence-markets.html)
293. Support for Canadian defence and security exporters (https://www.canada.ca/en/department-national-defence/services/doing-business-with-foreign-defence-markets/support-canadian-defence-security-exporters.html)
294. Sharon Scharfe, Complicity: Human Rights and Canadian Foreign Policy, 203/205
295. Lee Berthiaume, Feds embed trade staff in defence, oil groups, Regina Leader-Post Jan 18 2014
296. CADSI receives funding to promote Western Canadian companies at international security and defence events, July 24 2015 (https://www.defenceandsecurity.ca/media/article&id=277&t=c)
297. Kenneth Epps, Canada's push into new arms markets, Ploughshares Monitor, Vol 34, Iss 3, Autumn 2013 (https://ploughshares.ca/pl_publications/canadas-push-into-new-arms-markets/)
298. The Department of National Defence contributes to the Defence Security and Equipment International (DSEi) exhibition in London, U.K. Canada Pavilion, Sept 5 2013 (http://www.forces.gc.ca/en/news/article.page?doc=the-department-of-national-defence-contributes-to-the-defence-security-and-equipment-international-dsei-exhibition-in-london-u-k/hl7pec3o)
299. Richard Howard Gimblett, Peter T Haydon and Ann L Griffiths, Canadian Gunboat Diplomacy: the Canadian Navy and foreign-policy, 142
300. Sean Maloney, War with Iraq: Canada's strategy in the Persian Gulf 1990-2002, 35
301. Peter T Haydon and Ann L Griffiths, Canada's Pacific naval presence: Purposeful or Peripheral, 141
302. Jonathan Douglas, Beyond counterterrorism, Vol 10, N 2, 1014 (https://www.navalreview.ca/wp-content/uploads/CNR_pdf_full/cnr_vol10_2.pdf)
303. Anthony Fenton, Feb 19 (https://twitter.com/anthonyfenton/status/1097994150123692032)
304. Ibid
305. Brett Boudreau, Representing Canada in the UAE IDEX, FrontLine, Vol 16, No 1 2019 (https://defence.frontline.online/article/2019/1/11186-Representing-Canada-in-the-UAE)
306. Josh Lalonde, Canada & the Arms Trade: Fuelling war in Yemen & beyond, Oct 31 2020 (https://leveller.ca/2020/10/canada-the-arms-trade-military-exports-fuelling-war-in-yemen-beyond/)
307. Ibid
308. Growing Canadian Export Business, 2016–2017 Annual Report (https://www.ccc.ca/wp-content/uploads/2019/05/annual-report-2016-2017-1.pdf)
309. Dimitrios Roussopoulos, Our Generation Against Nuclear War, 166
310. Marc Whittingham, Canadian equipment can satisfy foreign military requirements, May 31 2010 (https://www.hilltimes.com/2010/05/31/canadian-equipment-can-satisfy-foreign-military-requirements/13951)
311. James Winter, Common Cents: Media Portrayal of the Gulf War and Other Events, 49
312. Victor Levant, Quiet complicity: Canadian

involvement in the Vietnam War, 59
313. Growing and Diversifying Canadian Exports, Annual Report 2019–2020 (https://www.ccc.ca/wp-content/uploads/2020/12/CCC-Annual-Report-Finaldh-EN.pdf)
314. Jerome Klassen, Joining Empire: The Political Economy of the New Canadian Foreign Policy, 279
315. Yves Engler, Why aren't dominant media questioning the use of taxpayer dollars to promote Canadian arms exports?, Oct 6 2020 (https://rabble.ca/blogs/bloggers/views-expressed/2020/10/why-arent-dominant-media-questioning-use-taxpayer-dollars)
316. Jeffrey Monaghan, Security Aid: Canada and the Development Regime of Security, 135
317. James Cudmore, General Dynamics Canada wins $10B deal with Saudi Arabia, Feb 14 2014 (https://www.cbc.ca/news/politics/general-dynamics-canada-wins-10b-deal-with-saudi-arabia-1.2537934)
318. Jeffrey Monaghan, Security Aid: Canada and the Development Regime of Security, 131
319. Kelsey Gallagher, Analyzing Canada's 2019 Exports of Military Goods report, The Ploughshares Monitor, Vol 41, Issue 3 Autumn 2020 (https://ploughshares.ca/pl_publications/analyzing-canadas-2019-exports-of-military-goods-report/#:~:text=In%202019%2C%20Canada%20reported%20the,-billion%20to%20%243.75-billion.)
320. Robert A Hackett, Richard S Gruneau and Donald Gutstein, The Missing News: Filters and Blind Spots in Canada's Press, 157 (https://www.sfu.ca/cmns/research/newswatch/pcc/95-8.html)
321. Lucas Powers, Canadian arms trade much larger than data suggests, expert says, Feb 23 2016 (https://www.cbc.ca/news/business/canada-arms-technology-trade-1.3458608)
322. State of Canada's Defence Industry 2018 (https://www.ic.gc.ca/eic/site/ad-ad.nsf/eng/h_ad03978.htm)
323. David J Bercuson and Jack Granatstein, Dictionary of Canadian Military History, 218
324. Charles Taylor, Snow Job: Canada, the United States and Vietnam (1954 to 1973), 121
325. Barry Bristman, In the Strategic Interests of Canada: Canadian Arms Sales to Israel and Other Middle East States, 1949-1956
326. Ibid
327. Richard Sanders, Canadian Military Exports to Israel: Aiding and Abetting War Crimes in Gaza (2008-2009), Coalition to Oppose the Arms Trade (https://coat.ncf.ca/ARMX/cansec/Tables.htm)
328. Transfer of Military Equipment to Colombia Exposes Loopholes in Export Controls, Briefing 01-3 (https://ploughshares.ca/pl_publications/transfer-of-military-equipment-to-colombia-exposes-loopholes-in-export-controls/)
329. Stephen Hume, Its role as arms supplier makes Canada a villain on world stage, Vancouver Sun, Jan 10 1998
330. Daniel Freeman-Maloy, Bullets over Bay Street, May 12 2005 (https://nowtoronto.com/bullets-over-bay-street)
331. Anthony Fenton, Oct 14 2018 (https://twitter.com/anthonyfenton/status/1051538953076015104)
332. Anthony Fenton, Oct 26 2018 (https://twitter.com/anthonyfenton/status/1055869018521853952)
333. Ibid
334. Anthony Fenton, Feb 21 2019 (https://twitter.com/anthonyfenton/status/1098458319377690624)

Conclusion

1. Ann Denholm Crosby, Dilemmas in Defence Decision-Making, 188
2. Gary Marcuse and Reginald Whitaker, Cold War Canada, 375
3. Stockholm Appeal (https://en.wikipedia.org/wiki/Stockholm_Appeal)
4. John Clearwater, Canadian Nuclear Weapons: The Untold Story of Canada's Cold War Arsenal, 73
5. Renee Bernard, 30 years ago, 100,000 took part in peace walk in Vancouver, Apr 29 2016 (https://www.citynews1130.com/2016/04/29/30-years-ago-100000-took-part-in-peace-walk-in-vancouver/)
6. Ann Denholm Crosby, Dilemmas in Defence Decision-Making, 187
7. Peter Langille, Changing the Guard: Canada's Defence in a World in Transition (https://s3.amazonaws.com/piquant/Langille/Canada%27s+Military-Industrial+Complex+and+Long+War+Policy.pdf)
8. Ernie Regehr and Simon Rosenblum, Canada and the Nuclear Arms Race, 207
9. Tamara Lorincz, With nuclear risks on rise, Canadians must fight for disarmament, Aug 9 2019 (https://www.thechronicleherald.ca/opinion/national-perspectives/tamara-lorincz-with-nuclear-risks-on-rise-canadians-must-fight-for-disarmament-339730/)
10. Nuclear-free zone (https://en.wikipedia.org/wiki/Nuclear-free_zone)
11. Ottawa Councillors Outlawed all future Arms Trade Shows from City Facilities in 1989 (http://coat.ncf.ca/ARMX/bylaw.htm)
12. Bob Bergen, Scattering Chaff: Canadian Air Power and Censorship during the Kosovo War (https://prism.ucalgary.ca/bitstream/handle/1880/109501/9781773850313_web.pdf?sequence=1&isAllowed=y)
13. Janice Stein and Eugene Lang, Unexpected War, 60
14. Daniel Freeman-Maloy, Bullets over Bay Street, May 12 2005 (https://nowtoronto.com/news/bullets-over-bay-street/) ; General Dynamics to Acquire Ammunition Producer SNC Technologies Inc., Feb 23 2006 (http://www.defense-aerospace.com/article-view/release/66923/gd-buys-canadian-ammunition-maker-(feb-24).html)
15. Murray Brewster, Military is off the radar of most Canadians: DND poll, Jul 20 2018 (https://www.cbc.ca/news/politics/dnd-canadians-military-poll-1.4754083)
16. John Clearwater, Canadian Nuclear Weapons: The Untold Story of Canada's Cold War Arsenal, 84
17. Secret Cold War plan included mass detentions, Oct 14 2010 (https://www.cbc.ca/news/canada/montreal/secret-cold-war-plan-included-mass-detentions-1.962421)
18. Yves Engler, Oh Canada Our home and Wire-tapped Land, Jan 10 2011 (https://canadiandimension.com/articles/view/oh-canada-our-home-and-wire-tapped-land)
19. Military Spies Then Denies Secret Surveillance of Peace Work, July 27 2007 (https://www.ceasefire.ca/military-spies-then-denies-secret-surveillance-of-peace-work/)
20. National Post Staff, Canadian Forces spent virtually all of 2013 watching Idle No More protesters, Jun 1 2014 (https://nationalpost.com/news/canada/canadian-forces-spent-virtually-all-of-2013-watching-idle-no-more-protesters)
21. Stephanie A H Belanger and Daniel Legace Roy, military operations and the mind: war ethics and soldiers well-being, 36
22. Sean Maloney, Canada and UN Peacekeeping: Cold War by other means, 1945-1970, 180

23. List of countries without armed forces (https://en.wikipedia.org/wiki/List_of_countries_without_armed_forces)
24. Yves Engler, Despite favourable polls, campaign against war plane purchase won't be easy, Nov 24 2020 (https://rabble.ca/blogs/bloggers/views-expressed/2020/11/despite-favourable-polls-campaign-against-war-plane-purchase)
25. Ibid
26. Murray Brewster, Military is off the radar of most Canadians: DND poll, Jul 20 2018 (https://www.cbc.ca/news/politics/dnd-canadians-military-poll-1.4754083)
27. Ernie Regehr and Simon Rosenblum, Canada and the Nuclear Arms Race, 77

Also from Black Rose Books

Paperback: 978-1-55164-306-9
Cloth: 978-1-55164-307-6

Also from Black Rose Books

Lies the Media tell Us

James Winter

Paperback: 978-1-55164-252-9
Cloth: 978-1-55164-253-6

Also from Black Rose Books

Militarism and Anti-Militarism

~

Karl Liebknecht

Paperback: 978-1-55164-340-3
Cloth: 978-1-55164-341-0
eBook: 978-1-55164-365-6

Also from Black Rose Books

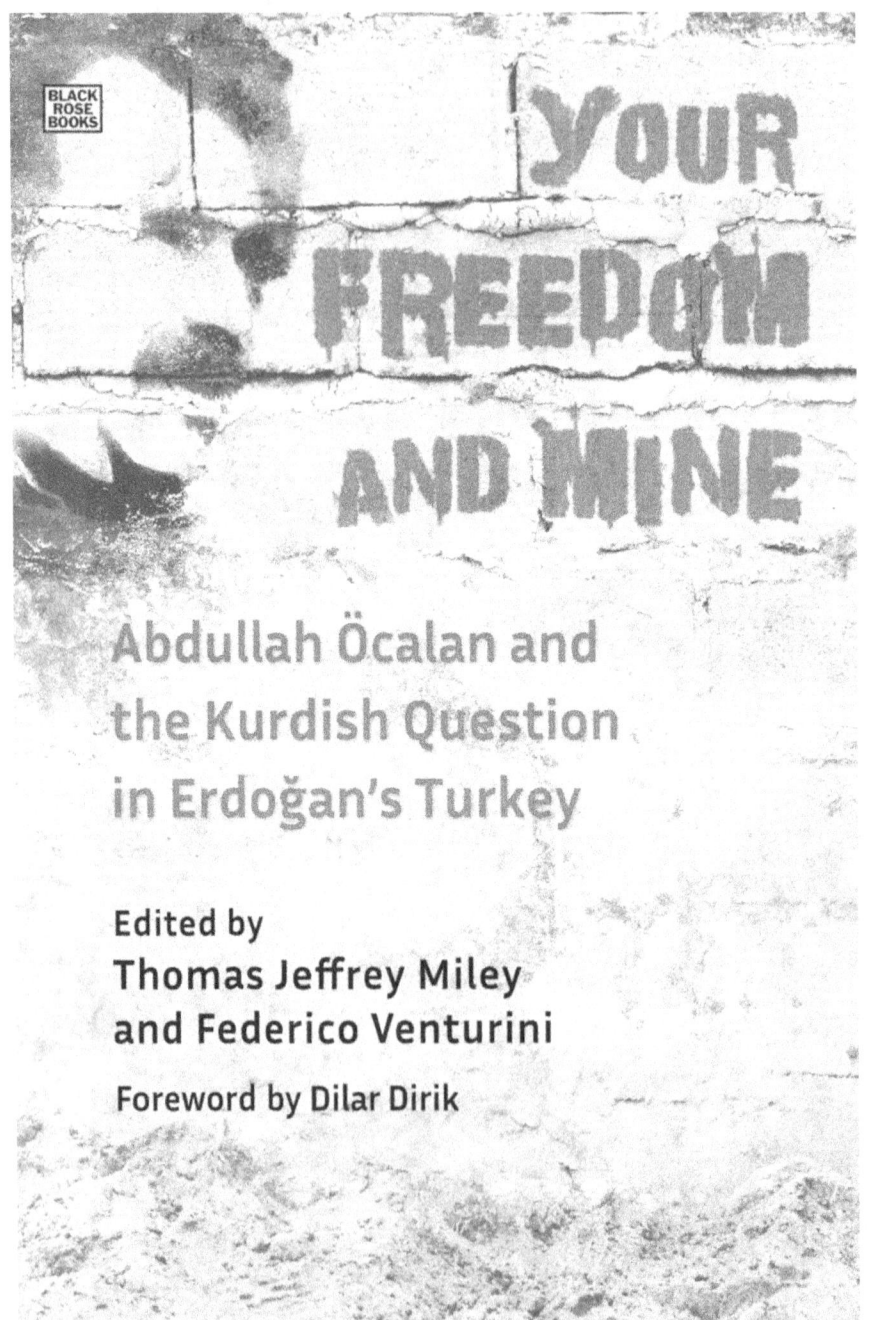

Your Freedom and Mine

Abdullah Öcalan and the Kurdish Question in Erdoğan's Turkey

Edited by
Thomas Jeffrey Miley
and Federico Venturini

Foreword by Dilar Dirik

Paperback: 978-1-55164-668-8
Cloth: 978-1-55164-670-1
eBook: 978-1-55164-672-5

Also from Black Rose Books

Paperback: 978-1-55164-294-9
Cloth: 978-1-55164-295-6
eBook: 978-1-55164-347-2

Also from Black Rose Books

Paperback: 978-1-55164-329-8
Cloth: 978-1-55164-328-1
eBook: 978-1-55164-349-6

Also from Yves Engler & Black Rose Books

Marching to the Beat of Imperial Canada

BY YVES ENGLER

Paperback: 978-1-55164-663-3
Cloth: 978-1-55164-665-7
eBook: 978-1-55164-667-1

Also from Yves Engler & Black Rose Books

Paperback: 978-1-55164-749-4
Cloth: 978-1-55164-751-7
eBook: 978-1-55164-753-1

Canadian Foreign Policy Institute

The Canadian Foreign Policy Institute informs people living in Canada about the country's diplomatic, aid, intelligence, trade and military policies abroad. The CFPI opposes the racism embedded in foreign policy. The non-partisan organization also monitors corporate Canada's international activities.

While Canadians generally believe their country is a benevolent force internationally, the facts often suggest otherwise. CFPI seeks to bridge the gap between government policy and public perception.

www.foreignpolicy.ca

About the Author

Yves Engler is a fellow of the Canadian Foreign Policy Institute (www.foreignpolicy.ca) as well as a Montréal-based journalist and author. He has published 11 previous books, all but two about Canada's role in the world. His journalism is read widely in newspapers, magazines and websites in many countries. His website is: www.yvesengler.com

Yves was born in Vancouver to union activist parents who were also involved in international solidarity, feminist, anti-racist, peace and other progressive movements. In addition to marching in demonstrations and on picket lines, he grew up playing hockey, including in the B.C. Junior League. Even back then he was a leftwinger.

Other Black Rose Books by Yves

House of Mirrors — Justin Trudeau's Foreign Policy
With heavily documented analysis, this book offers insight into the Liberals' rhetorical skills that whitewash their pro-corporate and conservative policies with progressive slogans.

Left, Right — Marching to the Beat of Imperial Canada
The left is supposed to be opposed to colonialism and at least skeptical of nationalism. However, for decades, this hasn't been the case in Canada.

www.ingramcontent.com/pod-product-compliance
Lightning Source LLC
Chambersburg PA
CBHW050158240426
43671CB00013B/2173